NetWare: The Professional Reference

Second Edition

Karanjit Siyan

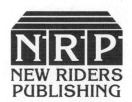

NRP
NEW RIDERS PUBLISHING

New Riders Publishing
Indianapolis, Indiana

NetWare: The Professional Reference, 2nd Edition

By Karanjit Siyan

Published by:
New Riders Publishing
201 West 103rd Street
Indianapolis, IN 46290

Printed in the United States of America   3 4 5 6 7 8 9

Library of Congress Cataloging-in-Publication Data

Siyan, Karanjit, 1954-
NetWare Professional Reference / Karanjit Siyan. -- 2nd ed.

      p.   cm.

Includes index.
ISBN 1-56205-158-x: $42.95
1. Operating systems (Computers) 2. NetWare (Computer file)
I. Title.
QA76.76.063S58 1993   93-17137
005.7'1369—dc20   CIP

Publisher
Lloyd J. Short

Associate Publisher
Tim Huddleston

Acquisitions Editor
John Pont

Marketing Manager
Brad Koch

Product Director
Drew Heywood

Production Editor
Rob Lawson

Editors
Patrice Hartmann, Steve Weiss, Lisa Wilson

Editorial Secretary
Karen Opal

Publishing Assistant
Melissa Keegan

Book Design and Production
*Matthew Morrill, Amy Peppler-Adams, Christine Cook,
Lisa Daugherty, Dennis Clay Hager, Juli Pavey, Michelle Self,
Mary Beth Wakefield, Barbara Webster*

Proofreaders
*George Bloom, Mitzi Gianakos, Howard Jones, John Kane,
Sean Medlock, Angie Trzepacz, Suzanne Tully, Phil Worthington*

Indexer
John Sleeva

Composed in Courier and Palatino

About the Author

Karanjit Siyan is president of Siyan Consulting Services, Inc. He has authored international seminars on Novell networks, TCP/IP networks, Windows NT, and Solaris SunOS and PC network integration. He also teaches advanced technology courses in the United States, Canada, and Europe. He has published articles in *Dr. Dobbs Journal*, *The C Users Journal*, and *Databased Advisor*. Mr. Siyan has been involved with installing, configuring, and designing Novell-based networks since 1985 and is an Enterprise CNE. He is also a Microsoft Certified Professional for Windows NT. Before he became an independent consultant, Mr. Siyan worked as a senior member of the technical staff at ROLM Corporation. He originally trained as an electronics engineer at the Indian Institute of Technology, Kharagpur, India, where he graduated with a Bachelor of Technology degree in Electronics and Electrical Communication Engineering. He later completed his Master of Technology degree in Computer Science from Indian Institute of Technology, Madras, India, and received an MS in Engineering from the EECS department, University of California, Berkeley. Mr. Siyan is based in Montana where he lives with his wife and two cats. He is currently working on his Ph.D in the area of fuzzy logic and neural networks for computer network management.

Acknowledgments

One of the most pleasurable tasks of being an author is to thank the people responsible for the success of a book. My heartfelt thanks to my wife Dei for her love and support. I wish to thank my father, Ahal Singh, and my mother, Tejinder; my brothers, Harjit and Jagjit; and my sisters, Kookie and Dolly. Special thanks to Mother. Without her spiritual support, this book would not have been possible. And thanks to Bali, Moti, and Kalpana who kept the author amused during some of the more intense moments.

I wish to thank Learning Group International for permission to use the material from my seminars. The contents of this book were inspired from that work. Readers interested in additional information about these seminars (Courses 255 and 261) may call 1-800-421-8166 (US), 1-800-267-1696 (Canada), or 0800282353 (U.K.). Also, thanks to John Moriarty and Rick

Adamson of Learning Group International for "getting on my case" and teasing me about errors in the first edition of *NetWare: The Professional Reference*. What are friends for, right?

I would like to thank the Institute of Electrical and Electronics Engineers, Inc. for permission to use some of their illustrations. These illustations are reprinted from IEEE Std 802-1990, IEEE Standard for Local and Metropolitan Area Networks: Overview and Architecture, copyright © 1990 by the Institute of Electrical and Electronics Engineers, Inc.

Many thanks to the staff of Paramount Publishing. In particular, I want to thank Drew Heywood for his insightful comments; Rob Lawson for his attention to this book's details; Patrice Hartmann, Steve Weiss, and Lisa Wilson for their editorial skills; and the rest of the staff of New Riders Publishing.

Trademark Acknowledgments

New Riders Publishing has made every effort to supply trademark information about company names, products, and services mentioned in this book. Trademarks indicated below were derived from various sources. New Riders Publishing cannot attest to the accuracy of this information.

ARCnet is a registered trademark of Datapoint Corporation.

AT&T is a registered trademark of AT&T.

CHECKIT is a registered trademark of TouchStone Software Corporation.

CP/M, DR DOS, and FlexOS are registered trademarks of Digital Research, Inc.

CRAY is a registered trademark of Cray Research, Inc.

IBM and Micro Channel are registered trademarks, and NETBIOS is a trademark of International Business Machines Corporation.

NetWare, NetWare Name Services, and Novell are registered trademarks, and LAN Workplace is a trademark of Novell, Inc.

LaserJet is a registered trademark of Hewlett-Packard Co.

Microsoft Windows for DOS is a registered trademark of Microsoft Corporation.

UNIX is a registered trademark of AT&T.

WaveLAN is a trademark of NCR Corporation.

Trademarks and other products mentioned in this book are held by the companies producing them.

Warning and Disclaimer

This book is designed to provide information about the Novell NetWare program. Every effort has been made to make this book as complete and as accurate as possible, but no warranty or fitness is implied.

The information is provided on an as is basis. The author and New Riders Publishing shall have neither liability nor responsibility to any person or entity with respect to any loss or damages arising from the information contained in this book.

Contents at a Glance

Contents

Introduction

Your interest in *NetWare: The Professional Reference, 2nd Edition,* indicates that you have more than a casual acquaintance with local area networks. You may be the manager of a network or a consultant whose business revolves around LANs. It seems safe to assume that the LANs you support have grown to a size that makes more basic books insufficient to meet your needs. The School of Hard Knocks has probably convinced you that LANs are far more complex than advertisers would have us believe. They can be so demanding of your knowledge and skills, in fact, that you probably have examined many books for information that expands on the basic and intermediate NetWare products that are commonly available.

The author and publisher of this book are confident that you will find this to be such a book. *NetWare: The Professional Reference, 2nd Edition* is more than a guide to managing Novell NetWare; it is a book about the whys as well as the hows of managing a LAN.

This additional depth should be apparent in the second chapter, which presents complete rules for configuring Ethernets, Token Rings, and ARCnets. Similar depth is found in the discussions about the architecture of NetWare, wide area networking, NetWare bridges, server maintenance, and so forth. As your networks grow in scale and complexity, you will appreciate this added information.

This is the second edition of *NetWare: The Professional Reference,* which has been expanded and updated to cover new NetWare features and products. Also new is a thorough command reference. The goal in designing the second edition was to make this book your one-stop reference to NetWare 2.2 and 3.11.

Although you are probably not a newcomer to local area networks, you should review the landscape by briefly scanning some terms and concepts.

Some Thoughts about LANs

Although, depending on the definition, local area networks have been around for at least two decades, they have become a popular technology only fairly recently. The following are reasons for the newfound popularity of LANs:

- The availability of low-cost, high-performance microcomputers

- The development of inexpensive network components

- The introduction of cost-effective, powerful networking software

The use of microcomputers in a LAN environment led to the concept of client/server computing, as opposed to the traditional terminal/host computing architecture used in mini- and mainframe computers. The NOS became the centerpiece of the LAN and enabled applications stored on the server to run on LAN workstations. This book is devoted to the most popular LAN NOS: NetWare, developed by Novell, Inc.

LANs provide efficient, optimized communications over a moderately sized geographic area (such as an office building, warehouse, campus, or factory). A *LAN* can be defined as a communications vehicle for interconnecting computing elements by means of well-defined interface mechanisms. The *computing elements* can be microcomputers, minicomputers, or mainframe computers. The *interface mechanisms* can be cables, network cards, software, and so on. Of the several interesting characteristics of LANs, the most important are short distances and high data rate.

The first characteristic, short distances, reflects the letter L in LAN, which stands for Local. Studies have shown that 80 percent of an organization's communications needs are within a small geographical area. (Most LANs do not exceed distances of 10 km.) There are important exceptions to this, such as the *FDDI (Fiber Distributed Data Interface)*, which is a ring-based LAN that can span distances of 200 km.

The second characteristic of a LAN is its high-speed data rate over channels that are relatively error free. Although most LANs operate over speeds between 1 Mbs to 100 Mbs, a few LANs operate at lower or faster speeds. The words *high speed* are relative: LANs utilize high speeds compared to modems and typical wide area networks. Because applications and data are stored centrally (on servers), but are used on workstations (clients), this extra speed is essential for supporting high-volume data transfers.

Nodes on a LAN

A LAN consists of a number of nodes that are connected through a shared transmission medium. The term *node*, in a network context, refers to any intelligent device that can be addressed by another intelligent device on the network. These intelligent devices are the computers on the network.

The computers on a LAN can be classified as servers or clients (work-stations). *Servers* may be general- or special-purpose microcomputers that provide a service to other nodes. A few examples of server types are the following:

- File server
- Database server
- Communication server
- Gateway server
- Management server

Servers provide services to *client workstations* on the LAN. These work-stations are general-purpose computers (such as IBM PCs, Macintoshes, and UNIX workstations) that have been equipped with network-interface hard-ware and software. The network interface enables the workstation to per-form local computer functions or to take advantage of network services, as required.

Novell NetWare comprises a family of products that provides LAN services and that enables workstations to become clients on the network. The NetWare network operating system (NOS) is sufficient for configuring a network server to provide file and printing services to clients. Additional products from the NetWare product family and from third-party vendors greatly expand the capability of the LAN to provide database services, elec-tronic mail, communication services, and much more.

The basic NetWare NOS is the focus of this book. NetWare is available in two versions: 2.2 and 3.11; version 3.11 is the more flexible and advanced product. In the course of reading this book, you will gain an understanding of the features of these two products and how they are installed and managed.

Beyond an understanding of the NetWare software, however, you will be exposed to detailed information about the environment in which NetWare operates. The NetWare NOS runs on more than 180 different variations of network hardware technologies. Network administrators find that a knowledge of these technologies is essential whenever their LANs grow to more than a trivial size. Knowing how to expand networks and how to fix them when they break requires a great deal of technical expertise.

Besides supporting communications, LANs enable users to share resources, which is a sophisticated capability of the operating system. The network administrator needs to understand the complexities so that users can share applications and data effortlessly and safely. To enable you to properly configure multiuser applications, this book demonstrates the ways that NetWare enables applications to implement special concurrency-control mechanisms, such as record and file locking.

In addition to demonstrating techniques for sharing application and data files, *NetWare: The Professional Reference, 2nd Edition* examines techniques for sharing peripheral devices, such as printers, modems, and large-capacity disks. LANs are economical, in part because they promote the sharing of expensive resources.

The Trend toward Downsizing

The cost efficiency of local area networks has inspired an industry trend to move appropriate applications to smaller, more affordable platforms. Increasing numbers of corporations are considering downsizing alternatives, and LANs appear prominently in the strategies that are being considered.

This downsizing trend means that LANs are increasingly being used to support mission-critical computing services. More than ever, it is necessary for managers of LANs to ensure that their networks are efficient and reliable. This book is intended to provide the kind of detailed information you require as the manager of a NetWare LAN to ensure that your network meets the highest expectations of your users.

How This Book Is Organized

This book starts with background information and extends through the details of installing and managing NetWare LAN components. The chapters are organized as follows:

Part 1: Network Technologies

Chapters 1 through 5 introduce the various pieces of local and wide area networks. Taken together, the chapters in this section give you a solid technical foundation for understanding how NetWare and LANs work.

Chapter 1, "NetWare Protocols," describes the most common protocols that are associated with NetWare. Protocols such as IPX/SPX, TCP/IP, NCP, and AppleTalk are discussed within the context of the Open Systems Interconnnect (OSI) seven-layered networking model.

Chapter 2, "LAN Standards for the Physical and Data Link Layers," discusses Ethernet, Token Ring, and ARCnet in the perspective of the OSI networking model. You learn the components of these network standards and the rules for extending networks as they must grow in size.

Chapter 3, "Bridging and Routing," explores devices that are used to enable networks to grow beyond a limited number of devices and beyond a limited geographic area.

Chapter 4, "WANs and MANs," considers the issues raised when networks grow to several servers and span metropolitan or larger geographic areas.

Chapter 5, "Hardware for NetWare Servers," gives you the information you need to configure high-performance servers for use with NetWare.

Part 2: NetWare 2.2 and 3.11

This part focuses on the NetWare product on the server. You will examine the fine points of installing and configuring the NetWare operating system. Most readers of this book will have performed at least one NetWare installation. Chapters 7–10 give you a little more perspective on how the NetWare products are designed and configured.

Chapter 6, "Features of NetWare 2.2 and 3.11," introduces general concepts of network operating systems and examines how NetWare is designed for performance, reliability, and richness of features. Issues of interoperability and management are also addressed.

Chapter 7, "Installing NetWare v2.2 Servers," discusses the architecture of NetWare version v2.2 and examines installation and reconfiguration issues.

Chapter 8, "Installing NetWare v3.11 Servers," performs that same service for Novell's most popular product.

Chapter 9, "Managing NetWare Servers," examines NetWare server management in general along with the specifics of managing both NetWare 2.2 and 3.11.

Chapter 10, "Managing Users," addresses the task of configuring and maintaining user network accounts.

Chapter 11, "Security," analyzes the need for security on a network and presents techniques for ensuring that your network will not be threatened by security problems.

Part 3: The NetWare Network Environment

As mentioned earlier in the introduction, NetWare employs a client/server architecture. Because the server is only half of the total architecture, this part turns its attention to the client side. You will examine various workstation operating systems and how they are used with NetWare. You also will examine the tools available for configuring a user's NetWare environment, such as login scripts, menus, and print job management. You also will look at the big picture of internetworking, viruses, and network management. These are all features that must be dealt with as your NetWare LANs grow in scope.

Chapter 12, "Supporting DOS Workstations," describes the process of configuring DOS workstations for NetWare. DOS remains the most popular PC operating system; however, system administrators will find that a lot needs to be done to optimize the setup of a DOS workstation.

Chapter 13, "Supporting Non-DOS Workstations," examines the growing nontraditional workstation. Although DOS remains the operating system of most PC users, more powerful operating systems are currently attracting more attention. Common examples are Apple System 7, OS/2 2, and UnixWare, all of which integrate nicely into NetWare LANs. Each of these operating systems is discussed in this chapter.

Chapter 14, "Managing Sessions," examines login scripts, menus, and other tools that determine the user's environment when using resources on a NetWare LAN.

Chapter 15, "The NetWare File System," is concerned with the server-disk subsystems and with the volumes, directories, and file systems that are used to store applications and data on the server.

Chapter 16, "Printing," presents options for configuring printers as server-attached or workstation-attached network devices. Techniques for managing print servers, remote printers, print queues, and print jobs are examined.

Chapter 17, "Internetworking," describes how NetWare connects to other types of networks, such as TCP/IP, X.25, Appletalk, and SNA. LANs no longer exist in isolation, and NetWare has products to solve many internetworking problems.

Chapter 18, "Viruses and Networks," examines a threat that concerns all network administrators. You will learn how viruses infect networks and examine techniques for protecting your networked resources.

Chapter 19, "Network Management," looks at the tools with which you can monitor your network and ensure that it offers top performance.

Chapter 20," Network Applications," discusses some of the issues that are encountered when installing network and non-network applications on a LAN server.

Other NetWare Titles from New Riders

New Riders Publishing offers an expanding line of books about Novell NetWare. These books are addressed at various levels of user requirements and experience.

Novell NetWare on Command is both an introduction to NetWare and a task-oriented guide to managing a NetWare network. New administrators will find that this book enables them to set up a NetWare server properly, with a minimum of fuss. Experienced administrators will find that the task-oriented approach makes this an effective reference guide to NetWare management procedures.

Inside Novell NetWare, Special Edition is New Riders' general-purpose tutorial and reference for Novell NetWare. This is an excellent first book for new systems administrators; it also covers the subject in sufficient depth that it is sure to find a permanent place among your NetWare documents.

Maximizing Novell NetWare is an intermediate book between *Inside Novell NetWare* and *NetWare: Professional Reference, 2nd Edition*. If your NetWare skills or your network have grown beyond the beginning level, you will want to examine *Maximizing Novell NetWare*.

Downsizing to NetWare is a manual of tools and techniques for downsizing large applications for local area networks. Many corporations are reducing computing costs through downsizing, and this book will tell you what you need to know to plan and implement a downsizing strategy.

The *NetWare Training Guide* consists of two volumes that assist in preparing NetWare administrators for Certified NetWare Engineer testing. The first volume, *Managing NetWare Systems*, covers the System Manager and Advanced System Manager tests. The second volume, *Networking Technologies*, covers DOS and Microcomputer Concepts, NetWare Service and Support, and Networking Technologies. This volume will be available during the summer of 1993.

New Riders Publishing

The staff of New Riders Publishing is committed to bringing you the very best in computer reference material. Each New Riders book is the result of months of work by authors and staff, who research and refine the information contained within its covers.

As part of this commitment to you, the NRP reader, New Riders invites your input. Please let us know if you enjoy this book, if you have trouble with the information and examples presented, or if you have a suggestion for the next edition.

Please note, however, that the New Riders staff cannot serve as a technical resource for DOS or DOS application-related questions, including hardware- or software-related problems. Refer to the documentation that accompanies your DOS or DOS application package for help with specific problems.

If you have a question or comment about any New Riders book, please write to NRP at the following address. We will respond to as many readers as we can. Your name, address, and phone number will never become part of a mailing list or be used for any other purpose than to help us continue to bring you the best books possible.

New Riders Publishing
Paramount Publishing
Attn: Associate Publisher
11711 N. College Avenue
Carmel, IN 46032

If you prefer, you can FAX New Riders Publishing at the following number:

(317) 571-3484

We welcome your electronic mail to our CompuServe ID:

70031,2231

Thank you for selecting *NetWare: The Professional Reference, 2nd Edition*!

Network Technologies

PART ONE

NetWare Protocols

Knowledge of *protocols*, which represent the mechanisms that enable the systems on a network to talk to each other, is important for configuring, for troubleshooting networks, and for obtaining a better understanding of the network. Protocol knowledge also is very useful in understanding the reasons that networking software from different vendors (and some times the same vendor!) do not interoperate.

Before you can understand networking protocols, you must understand the terminology used to define and understand them. The preeminent model for comparing protocols is the *Open Systems Interconnection* (OSI) Reference Model. Today, all vendors compare their proprietary, industry-standard, or international standard protocol implementations against the OSI Reference Model.

The OSI model

The OSI Reference Model was developed in 1978 by the *International Organization of Standards* (ISO) to specify a standard that could be used for the development of open systems and as a yardstick to compare different communication systems. Network systems designed according to OSI framework and specifications speak the same language; that is, they use similar or compatible methods of communication. This type of network system allows systems from different vendors to interoperate.

In the early days of computer networks (prior to the OSI model), the proprietary computer network architecture reigned supreme. In those days, an organization that was interested in installing a computer network examined the choices available, including IBM, DEC, HP, Honeywell, and Sperry and Burroughs (now Unisys). Each of those choices had its own proprietary architecture; the capability to interconnect networks from different vendors was almost nonexistent.

Once committed to buying equipment from a specific vendor, the organization was virtually "locked in." Updates or modifications to the system were provided by the vendor, and because the vendor had a closed proprietary architecture, no one could compete with that vendor in supplying equivalent services. Prices were determined based on what the customer could bear without complaining too much!

Today's users probably realize that in many areas of the computer industry, this picture has not changed much. Proprietary architecture history is still around, but the good news is that OSI can change the way it works. In fact, the big debate in computer circles today centers on the amount of time it will take to have the ISO-recommended protocols for the OSI layers to become the dominant standard in the networking industry.

For now, the OSI model can, at the very least, provide you with a clearer picture of how the different components of a network relate to each other.

Layers of the OSI Model

The OSI model has seven layers, as shown in figure 1.1. The layers, working from the bottom up, include:

Physical

Data Link

Network

Transport

Session

Presentation

Application

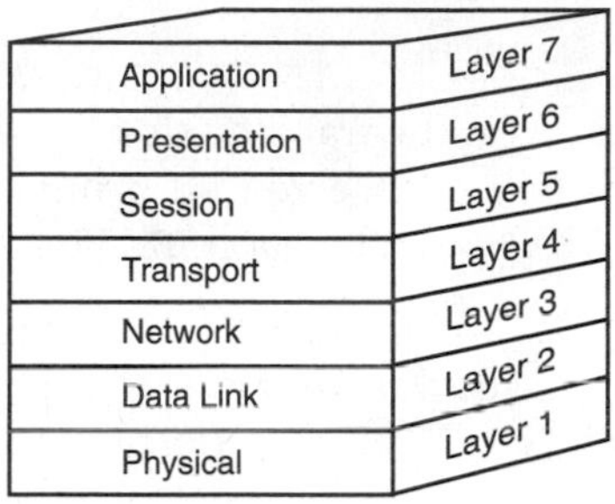

Figure 1.1:
The OSI Reference Model.

Five principles were applied when arriving at the layers:

1. A layer should be created only when a different level of abstraction is needed.

2. Each layer should provide a well-defined function.

3. The function of each layer should be chosen so that it defines internationally standardized protocols.

4. The layer boundaries should be chosen to minimize the information flow across layer interfaces.

5. Distinct functions should be defined in separate layers, but the number of layers should be small enough that the architecture does not become unwieldy.

The following is a summary of the functions of the seven layers.

Physical Layer

The *physical layer* transmits bits over a communication channel. The bits may represent database records or file transfers; the physical layer is oblivious to what those bits represent. The bits can be encoded as digital 1s and 0s or in analog form. The physical layer deals with the mechanical, electrical, and procedural interfaces over the physical medium.

Data Link Layer

The *data link layer* builds on the transmission capability of the physical layer. The bits that are transmitted/received are grouped in logical units called a *frame*. In the context of LANs, a frame could be a Token Ring or Ethernet frame.

The bits in a frame have special meanings. The beginning and ending of a frame may be marked by special bit patterns. Additionally, the bits in a frame are divided into an address field, control field, data field, and error control field. Figure 1.2 shows a typical data link frame. You see more specific examples of the data link frame in the discussion of Ethernet and Token Ring LANs.

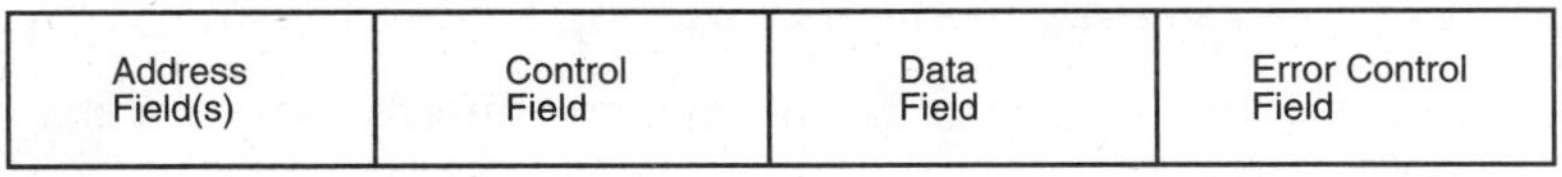

Address Field(s)	Control Field	Data Field	Error Control Field

Figure 1.2:
A typical data link layer frame.

The *address* field(s) contains the sender and receiving node address. The *control* field is used to indicate the different types of data link frames, which include data frames and frames used for managing the data link channel. The *data* field contains the actual data being transmitted by the frame. The error control field usually detects errors in the data link frame. The *data link* layer also is the first layer in which you see error control concerns. The error control field is usually a hardware-generated *checksum* that is used to detect errors in the data link frame.

Network Layer

The *network layer* builds on the node-to-node connection provided by the data link layer. The node-to-node data link services are extended across a network by this layer. An additional service provided by the data link layer is how to route *packets* (units of information at the network layer) between nodes connected through an arbitrarily complex network.

Besides routing, the network layer helps eliminate congestion as well as regulate flow of data. The network layer also makes it possible for two networks to be interconnected by implementing a uniform addressing mechanism. Token Ring or Ethernet LANs, for instance, have different types of data link addresses. To interconnect these two networks, you need a uniform addressing mechanism that can be understood by both Token Ring and Ethernet. For NetWare-based networks, this capability is provided by the *Internet Packet Exchange* (IPX), a network layer protocol.

Transport Layer

The *transport layer* provides enhancements to the services of the network layer. This layer helps ensure reliable data delivery and end-to-end data integrity. To ensure reliable delivery, the transport layer builds on the error control mechanisms provided by the lower layers. If the lower layers do not do a good enough job, the transport layer has to work harder. This layer is the last chance for error recovery. In fact, when it comes to providing error free delivery, you could say, "The buck stops here" at the transport layer.

The transport layer also may be responsible for creating several logical connections over the same network connection, a process called *multiplexing*. Multiplexing (or time sharing) occurs when a number of transport connections share the same network connection.

The transport layer is the middle layer of the OSI model. The three lower layers constitute the *subnet* (portion of the network model), and the three upper layers are usually implemented by networking software on the node. The transport layer is usually implemented on the node also; its job is to convert an unreliable subnet into a more reliable network.

Because of multiplexing, several software elements (OSI terminology uses the term *protocol entity*) share the same network layer address. To uniquely identify the software elements within the transport layer, a more general form of addressing is necessary. These addresses, called *transport addresses*, usually are a combination of the network layer address and a transport *Service Access Point* (SAP) number. Sometimes the names *sockets* or *port numbers* are used to identify transport addresses.

Examples of transport protocols used by NetWare are *Sequenced Exchange Protocol* (SXP) and *Packet Exchange Protocol* (PXP).

Session Layer

The *session layer* makes use of the transport layer to provide enhanced session services. Examples of a session include a user being logged in to a host across a network or a session being established for the purpose of transferring files.

The session layer may provide some of the following enhancements:

Dialog control

Token management

Activity management

A session, in general, allows two-way communications (*full duplex*) across a connection. Some applications may require alternate one-way communications (*half duplex*). The session layer has the option of providing two-way or one-way communications, an option called *dialog control*.

For some protocols, it is essential that only one side attempt a critical operation at a time. To prevent both sides from attempting the same operation, a control mechanism, such as the use of *tokens*, must be implemented. When using the token method, only the side holding a token is permitted to perform the operation. Determining which side has the token and how it is transferred between the two sides is known as *token management*.

The use of the word "token" here should not be confused with Token Ring operation. Token management is a much higher level concept at layer five of the OSI model. IBM's Token Ring operation belongs to layers two and one of the OSI model.

If you are performing a one-hour file transfer between two machines, and network crashes occur approximately every 30 minutes, you may never be able to complete the file transfer. After each transfer aborts, you have to start all over again. To avoid this problem, you can treat the entire file transfer as a single activity with checkpoints inserted into the datastream. That way, if a crash occurs the session layer can synchronize to a previous checkpoint. This operation of managing an entire activity is called *activity management*.

Presentation Layer

The *presentation layer* manages the way data is represented. Many ways of representing data exist, such as ASCII and EBCDIC for text files, and 1s or 2s for numbers. If the two sides involved in communication use different data representations, they will not be able to understand each other. The presentation layer represents data with a common syntax and semantics. If all the nodes used and understood this common language, misunderstanding in data representation could be eliminated. An example of this common language is *Abstract Syntax Representation, Rev 1* (ASN.1), an OSI recommendation.

Application Layer

The application layer contains the protocols and functions needed by user applications to perform communication tasks. Examples of common functions include:

- Protocols for providing remote file services, such as open, close, read, write, and shared access to files

- File transfer services and remote database access

- Message handling services for electronic mail applications

- Global directory services to locate resources on a network

- A uniform way of handling a variety of system monitors and devices

- Remote job execution

Many of these services are called *Application Programming Interfaces* (APIs). APIs are programming libraries that an application writer can use to write network applications.

In NetWare, *NetWare Control Protocol* (NCP) is an example of an application layer protocol.

ODI Protocol Layering and the OSI Model

NetWare protocol stacks are implemented using the *Open Data Link Interface* (ODI) mechanism. The ODI protocol layering provides a mechanism for systematically using the protocol components to build the protocol stack.

Strictly speaking, the ODI mechanism, the NetWare protocols, and protocols from most vendors are not in complete compliance with the OSI Reference Model. The only protocols that comply closely with the OSI Reference Model are the ISO recommendations for each of the OSI layers.

ODI Architecture

The ODI specification allows a large number of network adapters to support different protocol stacks, such as TCP/IP, OSI, SPX/IPX, and AppleTalk.

Prior to ODI and similar mechanisms (NDIS Packet Driver now called Crynwr drivers), a separate driver had to be written for each protocol stack. It also was difficult to get these separate drivers to coexist on a workstation, making it difficult to support more than one protocol stack.

The key components of ODI layers are the *Link Support Layer* (LSL) and the *Multiple Link Interface Driver* (MLID), as shown in figure 1.3.

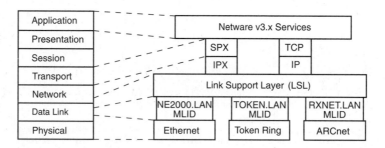

Figure 1.3:
ODI components versus OSI Model.

In figure 1.3, the Ethernet, Token Ring, and ARCnet networking technologies correspond to the first and second layers of the OSI model. The NE2000.LAN, TOKEN.LAN, and RXNET.LAN are the names of the MLID drivers. Other types of network boards can have different names. These drivers correspond to a portion of the data link layer. The drivers are written to interface with the link support layer (LSL). The LSL, which does not map well onto the OSI model, represents the boundary between the data link and the network layers. Because the LSL provides the interface between MLID drivers and the upper layer protocols, the LSL can be thought of as covering a portion of the data link layer and the lower portion of the network layer of the OSI model.

The link support layer is a key element in the ODI specification. It *virtualizes* the network adapter by providing a logical view of the network adapter. The network layer software does not have to be rewritten to understand the low-level mechanics and operational details of a new network adapter. The network layer software "sees" a well-defined virtual interface to any network adapter. The well-defined virtual interface means that protocol stacks can be written to interface with the network adapter in a standard way.

The practical significance of this is that the network layer protocol needs to be written just once to this virtual interface. When a new type of network adapter is built, the manufacturer writes an MLID driver for it that can hook into the LSL layer. The LSL provides the same virtual interface to this board, and the protocol software does not need to be rewritten for the new network adapter.

The same MLID driver can support new types of protocol software, as long as the protocols are written to the virtual interface provided by LSL. The MLID driver is able to handle packets from different protocol stacks delivered to it by the LSL.

On receiving the different protocol packets from the network, MLID forwards the packet to the LSL without interpreting the packet contents. The LSL is responsible for sending the packets to the correct protocol stack.

The LSL acts as a software switch through which multiple protocol packet types travel and are delivered to the correct MLID or the correct protocol stack. To provide this routing, the LSL contains information about the MLIDs and the protocol stacks it supports. When MLID drivers or protocol stacks are loaded, they register information about themselves with the LSL. The LSL keeps track of this information in a *data segment* (OSdata). This segment includes items such as network adapter information, protocol stack information, and binding information.

When the MLID loads, the LSL assigns a logical number to each network adapter. When a protocol stack loads and registers with the LSL, it also is assigned a logical protocol stack number. Up to 16 such protocol stacks can be supported.

The LSL also keeps information on the send-and-receive event control blocks (ECBs). *Event control blocks* are data structures that are used for transmitting and receiving packets, and contain packet ID information. LSL uses the packet ID information in ECBs, and information on network adapters and protocol stacks registered with it, to route packets.

The LSL has a set of routines for the LAN adapters below it and the protocol stacks above it. The LSL calls these routines to move data packets (fig. 1.4). Each network adapter registers a send routine and a control routine, for example. Also associated with each network adapter is a packet buffer area. The *packet buffer area* makes it possible for multiple adapters of the same type to have only one MLID that is loaded re-entrantly. In this case, even though the adapters have the same send and control routines, those adapters have a different data area. The protocol stacks above the LSL also register a similar set of support routines with the LSL.

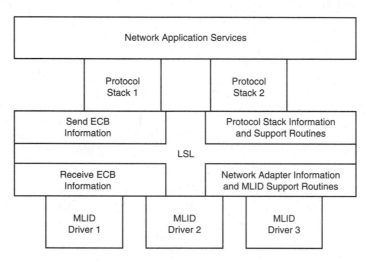

Figure 1.4:
Information stored in LSL.

The LSL module is specific to an operating system platform. That means that the actual LSL module cannot be interchanged between operating systems even though LSL is available for DOS, OS/2, NetWare v3.x, and NetWare external routers. In DOS, for example, LSL is loaded as a TSR, and in OS/2 it is loaded as a device driver called LSL.SYS.

Every packet on a network has a *Media Access Control* (MAC) frame that encapsulates the communications protocol packet (IPX, AppleTalk, TCP/IP). The MAC is the lower sublayer of the data link layer. For LANs, it represents the mechanisms by which a node on the LAN acquires access to the physical LAN. Within the ODI-based node, a protocol ID consisting of one to six bytes is prepended to the frame. This PID identifies the MAC frame and the communications protocol contained in the MAC frame. A code of 8137 (hexadecimal), for instance, is used to indicate an Ethernet II MAC frame that has IPX data inside it. The LSL uses the PID value to route the packet to the appropriate protocol stack. More information about MAC frames is available in Chapter 2.

Streams Interface and ODI

In the NetWare v3.x server, the Streams interface can be used to encapsulate the communications protocols and to provide a uniform transport interface. *Streams*, an interface developed by AT&T in UNIX System V and originally proposed by Dennis Ritchie—creator of the popular C language—defines a stream head that can be used as a common interface by applications, and a stream tail that interfaces with the drivers. Because the preferred driver in NetWare is ODI-based, the stream tail interfaces with the LSL. Between the stream head and the stream tail, a number of protocol modules can be *pushed* (fig. 1.5).

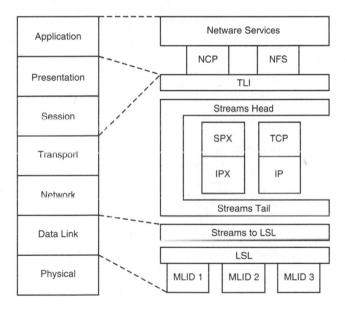

Figure 1.5:
Streams and ODI.

Think of the streams interface as providing a common *software wrapper* around the transport modules. This simplifies the writing of applications. Since Streams is a very low-level interface, an alternate *Transport Layer Interface* (TLI) that makes use of Streams is often used.

NetWare Native Protocols

The NetWare native protocols are NCP/SPX/IPX. Of these, SPX/IPX are based on Xerox's XNS protocol suite. The Sequenced Packet Exchange (SPX) protocol is based on the Sequenced Packet Protocol (XNS SPP). Internet Exchange Protocol (IPX) is based on the Internet Datagram Protocol (XNS IDP). IPX corresponds to layer three of the OSI model and is a connectionless datagram protocol. SPX, a connections-oriented protocol, corresponds to the fourth layer of the OSI model.

NetWare Core Protocol (NCP) was developed by Novell to support NetWare services. The Service Advertising Protocol (SAP) is used by NetWare to advertise NetWare services on a NetWare-based network.

In addition, Novell uses a modified form of XNS RIP as its routing protocol.

Internet Packet Exchange (IPX)

The IPX protocol is a network layer protocol that provides connectionless datagram services on top of the data link protocols such as Ethernet, Token Ring, ARCnet, and PPP (Point-to-Point) protocols. The IPX protocol can be made to work on virtually all existing data link protocols. The use of the term "connectionless" implies that prior to data transmission, no control packets are sent to establish a connection. Therefore, once the data is transmitted, no teardown or breakdown of the connection is required.

Messages are sent by breaking them into packets and sending complete source address and destination information per packet. No guarantees are made about the successful arrival of the packet (called a *datagram* when a packet for a connectionless protocol). If guarantees are to be made, an upper-layer protocol such as SPX or NCP must provide this capability. The datagram-oriented nature of IPX makes it easier to implement the underlying network technology. Datagrams work well with network services that require a broadcast capability.

A unique network address also is available from the IPX layer, per NetWare node. The IPX network address consists of a 32-bit network number and a 48-bit node address pair, making a total of 10 bytes of network address. When configuring NetWare servers, the 32-bit network number must be supplied by the installer and kept unique per physical network. There is no central registration authority to apply for a unique network number. Later chapters suggest procedures on ways to manage this network number without creating duplicate network number conflicts.

Because of IPX's origin in the XNS IDP protocol, a 48-bit node address is used (IDP originally ran on Ethernet, which has a 48-bit address). A NetWare node can have several software processes running, such as NCP, SAP, and RIP services. To uniquely identify packets to each of these processes, a *socket number* is used. The socket number is a 16-bit number assigned to each process that wants to communicate using IPX services. Internally, the socket number is used to access data structures that are used to communicate with the IPX protocol. A few of the well-known socket numbers are 451 hex for NCP, 452 hex for SAP, 453 hex for RIP, 455 hex for NetBIOS, and 456 hex for diagnostics. A complete address description of a process on a NetWare node consists of the following 3-tuple:

<Network number, Node address, Socket number>

Figure 1.6 shows the IPX packet structure. The Checksum field is usually set to FFFFF hex to indicate that checksums are disabled. IPX expects the data link layer to inform it about packet errors, because the data link protocols, such as Ethernet and Token Ring, have a hardware Cyclic Redundancy Checksum (CRC).

The *length field* is the length of the IPX packet in bytes. This includes the IPX header length of 30 bytes plus the data field. IPX originally inherited a 576-byte limit from the XNS IDP packet structure. New IPX drivers can handle larger size packets, even though most of Novell's documentation still refers to the 576 byte limit.

The Transport control field is used as a hop count field to count the number of routers traveled by the IPX packet. This field is used by IPX routers and incremented each time the IPX packet goes through a router. When the hop count reaches 16, the IPX packet is dropped. The 16 hop count limit is inherited from XNS RIP, which was used as the basis for Novell's RIP.

The Packet Type field is used for protocol multiplexing and de-multiplexing between the IPX layer and upper-layer protocols. The Packet Type identifies which upper-layer protocol must receive the data portion of the IPX packet. Some of the packet type codes are 4 for Packet Exchange Protocol (PXP), 5 for SPX, and 17 for NCP. A packet type code of 0 is reserved for an unknown packet type.

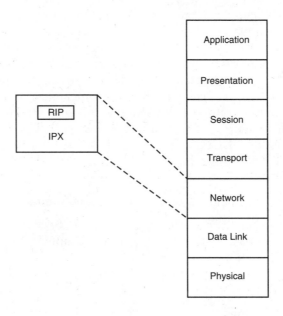

2 bytes	2 bytes	1 byte	1 byte	4 bytes	6 bytes	2 bytes	4 bytes	6 bytes	2 bytes	
Checksum	Length	Transport Control (heps)	Packet Type	Destination Network	Destination Node	Destination Socket	Source Network	Source Node	Source Socket	Data

Figure 1.6:
IPX packet structure.

The Destination Network, Destination Node, and Destination Socket uniquely identifies a process in the destination node; and the Source Network, Source Node, and Source Socket identifies a process in the source node.

The destination network number of an IPX packet is used to decide if an IPX packet should be sent locally on an IPX network or to a local router. All nodes on the same physical network must have the same network number. A node discovers its IPX network number from an IPX router on that network. Typically, the IPX router also is the NetWare file server, because all NetWare file servers contain an IPX router software module.

If the destination network number is the same as the local network number, the IPX packet is sent directly to the node on the local network. If the destination network number is different from the local network number, and this is the first time an IPX packet is being sent to the destination network, a Route Request Packet is sent via the Routing Information Protocol (RIP) to determine the fastest route.

The reply contains the address of a local router capable of forwarding the packet. The IPX packet is then forwarded to this router. IPX routers hold *routing tables* that contain routing information on all networks reachable by that router. These routing tables are kept updated by sending routing information using the RIP protocol every 60 seconds.

Sequenced Packet Exchange (SPX)

The SPX protocol is a transport layer protocol that provides connection-oriented services on top of the connectionless IPX protocol. SPX is used when a reliable virtual-circuit connection is needed between two stations. The SPX protocol takes care of flow control and sequencing issues to ensure that packets arrive in the right order. SPX also ensures that destination node buffers are not overrun with data that arrives too rapidly.

Prior to data transmission, SPX control packets are sent to establish a connection, and a connection ID is associated for that virtual circuit. This connection ID is used in all data transmissions. At the end of data transmission, an explicit control packet is sent to break down the connection. SPX makes use of an acknowledgment scheme to make sure that messages arrive at the destination. Lost packets are re-sent and sequencing is used to keep track of packets so that they arrive in the proper order and are not duplicated.

SPX uses a timeout algorithm to decide when a packet needs to be retransmitted. The timeout is dynamically adjusted based on the delay experienced in packet transmission. If a packet times out too early, its value is increased by 50 percent. This process can continue until a maximum timeout value is reached or the timeout value stabilizes. To verify that a session is still active when there is no data activity, SPX sends probe packets to verify the connection. The frequency of these probe packets can be controlled by settings in the NET.CFG file discussed in later chapters.

An interesting aspect of SPX is that many SPX connections can use the same IPX socket (fig. 1.7). This allows multiple connection IDs to be multiplexed and demultiplexed across the same IPX socket.

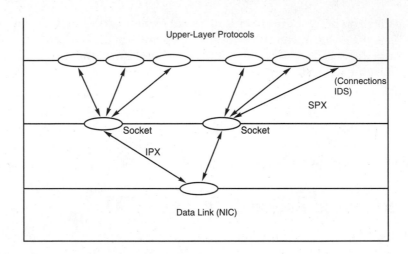

Figure 1.7:
SPX Connection IDs and Sockets

Figure 1.8 shows the SPX packet structure. The Connection Control field is used for regulating flow of data across the connection. The bit sequence 0001000, for example, is used as an end-of-message signal and the bit sequence 01000000 indicates that an acknowledgment is requested.

1 byte	1 byte	2 bytes	2 bytes	2 bytes	2 bytes	2 bytes	
Connection Control	Data Stream Type	Source Connection ID	Destination Connection ID	Sequence Number	Acknowl-edgement Number	Allocation Number	Data

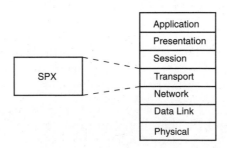

Figure 1.8:
SPX packet structure.

The Datastream Type is used to indicate the nature of the data contained in the SPX data field. It is used to identify the upper-layer Protocol to which the SPX data must be delivered. It serves a similar role to the Packet Type field in the IPX packet.

The Source Connection ID and the Destination Connection IDs are the virtual circuit numbers used to identify a session. These IDs are used to demultiplex separate virtual circuits on a single socket.

The Sequence Number field is used to number every packet that is sent. This is used by SPX to detect lost and out-of-sequence packets.

The Acknowledgment Number field is used to indicate the next packet the receiver expects. It means that all packets prior to the Acknowledgment value have been received correctly.

The Allocation Number is used to indicate how many free buffers the receiver has available on a connection. This value is used by the sender to pace the sending of data. The use of the Allocation Number helps avoid overwhelming the receiver with packets that do not have a corresponding buffer available to hold them.

The NetWare workstation does not usually make use of the SPX protocol; it uses the IPX protocol directly. Reliability of transmission is maintained by the NCP protocol. SPX is used to establish remote connections between the Print Server and remote printers. SPX also is used in NetWare SQL and remote connections to the NetWare file server through RCONSOLE (discussed in Chapter 8).

The Packet Exchange Protocol

The PXP (Packet eXchange Protocol) protocol is derived from the XNS PEP (Packet Exchange Protocol) and is a Transport Layer protocol. PXP provides a lower reliability of service than SPX but is more reliable than IPX. It is used to transmit a request and to receive a response. The request/response sequence is called a *transaction*. PXP does not keep track of duplicate requests and therefore is suitable for idempotent transactions, or upper-layer protocols that can handle duplicate requests. An *idempotent* transaction is one that causes no undue side effects even if the transaction is duplicated by mistake. An example of this is the reading of a data block from a file. If this request is mistakenly duplicated, no harm is done.

An example of an application that makes use of PXP is the NetBIOS emulation software that can run on NetWare workstations.

Figure 1.9 illustrates the structure of the PXP packet. The ID field is a 32-bit field that identifies the requesting packet. This field serves as a transaction ID that is used to match the PXP packet request and its reply.

The Client Type is used to identify the user of the PXP protocol. The user of the PXP protocol is called the Client Protocol.

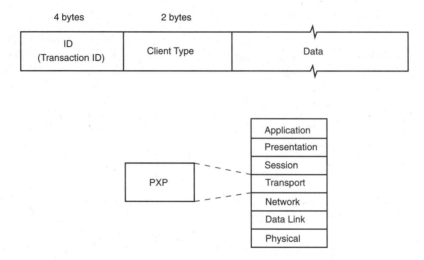

Figure 1.9:
PXP packet structure.

NetWare Core Protocol

The *NetWare Core Protocol* (NCP) is used to implement NetWare's file services, print services, name management services, file locking, synchronization, and bindery operations. A *bindery* refers to the internal database of network objects kept on the NetWare server.

NCP is implemented at the workstation and the NetWare server. On the workstation side, NCP is implemented in the NetWare shell and is limited to making requests for services to a NCP server. The NetWare server (NCP server) contains a full implementation of NCP that can execute or process requests for NCP services. NCP provides transparent remote file and print services to a NetWare client. These remote services have the appearance of being local to the client.

NCP directly uses the IPX protocol, avoiding the use of SPX or PXP. This enables NCP to be more efficient because it avoids the protocol overhead of the SPX and PXP protocols. NCP provides its own mechanism for session control, error detection, and retransmission. Figure 1.10 shows an NCP packet structure.

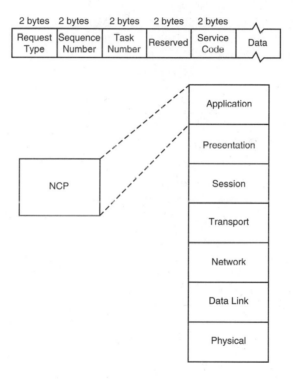

Figure 1.10:
NCP Packet Structure.

In figure 1.10, the Request Type field indicates the type of NCP request. Examples of NCP request types are Create Service Connection, Negotiate Buffer Size, Logout, Get Server Date and Time, Get Station Number, and End of Job. The *sequence number* is used as a transaction ID field and identifies an NCP request and its corresponding response. The *service code* further identifies the service requested by the workstation.

Packet Burst Mode

The NCP Protocol numbers each request and reply packet with a sequence number. This *sequence number* is used as a transaction ID field to identify an NCP request and its corresponding response for a particular session. The session is identified by the connection number and is placed in every NCP transaction.

The NCP transaction models the client/server interaction between a workstation and a NetWare server quite well. This transaction, however, introduces a new set of problems when NetWare servers are used in wide area networks. Typically, WAN link capacities today are in the range of tens of kilobits per second. This is quite small in relationship to the megabits-per-second speed used in LANs, causing WANs to run at slower speeds than LANs. In addition, WANs have longer delays because they span longer distances. Using a single request and single response model as shown in figure 1.11 means that the effective throughput of the transaction is:

$$E = (Q + N*Pn)/(N*Td) \qquad (1)$$

E = effective throughput of the NCP transaction
Q = size of the request packet
Pn = size of the *N*th single reply packet
Td = round-trip delay
N = number of reply packets

As can be seen in figure 1.11, if the reply is larger than a single packet, it has to be sent in a series of successive transactions, each of which takes additional time equal to the round-trip delay. Many earlier NetWare routers have a limit of 512 bytes per packet, which means that if a 64K file had to be transferred, 128 of the 512 bytes would have to be sent.

To get an idea of what the throughputs are like, substitute numerical values in the preceding equation. For instance, assume that a NCP request packet is 128 bytes and the reply is a 1,000-byte packet. Also, assume that the round-trip delay on the link is 1 second and the reply consists of 4 packets. Plugging in these values into the equation, you get:

$$E = (128 + 4*1000)/(4*1) = 1032 \text{ bytes/sec} = 8,256 \text{ bits/sec}$$

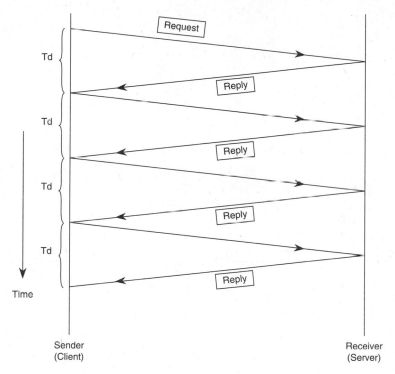

Figure 1.11:
Single request/reply transactions.

In packet burst mode, a single read reply can be sent as a series of successive packets that do not have to wait for an NCP acknowledgment of every message that is sent. Also, an NCP request can consist of a series of requests that do not have to wait to be acknowledged by a reply. Figure 1.12 shows a request and a 3-packet reply using packet burst. The effective throughput is now computed by the equation:

$$Ep = (Q + N*Pn)/Td \qquad (2)$$

Ep = effective throughput of the NCP transaction using packet burst
Q = size of the request packet
Pn = size of the Nth single reply packet
Td = round-trip delay
N = number of reply packets

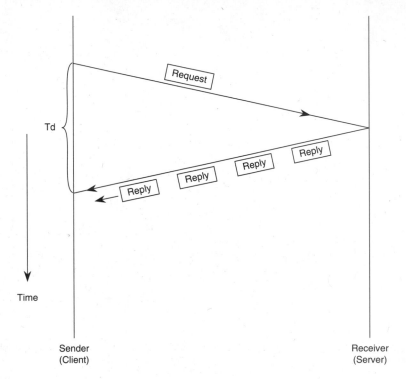

Figure 1.12:
Single request/multiple reply.

Using the preceding numerical example, you can calculate the effective throughput using packet burst as:

$$Ep = (128 + 4*1000)/1 = 4128 \text{ bytes/sec} = 33{,}024 \text{ bits/sec}$$

You can see that the effective throughput for packet burst, in this example, is 4 times that of the normal throughput. This is not surprising because dividing equation (2) by equation (1) reveals that:

$$Ep/E = N \qquad (3)$$

or that:

$$Ep = N*E \qquad (4)$$

Therefore, effective throughput of packet burst is N times that of a normal NCP. Tests done by Novell reveal that performance improvements of up to 300 percent can be achieved on a WAN. Packet burst also can improve performance in a LAN by up to 50 percent. Burst mode also can be used in situations in which a transaction consists of a multiple request/single reply sequence (figure 1.13).

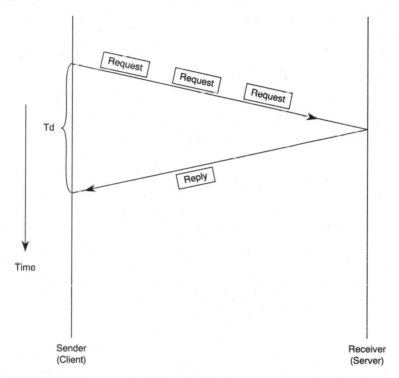

Figure 1.13:
Multiple request/single reply.

Burst mode implements a dynamic window size algorithm and dynamic timeout mechanism. The dynamic window size allows burst mode to adjust the number of frames that can be sent in burst mode. The *dynamic timeout* (also called transmission metering) adjusts itself to line quality, line bandwidth, and line delay.

To set up packet burst, you need the PBURST NLM to run on the NetWare server and the special burst shell called BNETX.COM to run at the DOS workstation. You can get the latest copies of these through the NetWire forum on CompuServe. To configure packet burst, perform the following steps:

1. Load PBURST NLM on the NetWare Server.

2. As an optional step, to observe the statistics screen on PBURST, perform the following command on the NetWare server console:

   SET ENABLE PACKET BURST STATISTICS SCREEN=ON

   This is a new command that is added when the PBURST NLM loads.

3. At the workstation, configure the following in NET.CFG:

   PB BUFFERS = N

   in which N is from 2 to 10.

   If the NIC driver can handle larger size packets, configure it using the command:

   IPX PACKET SIZE LENGTH=N

   in which N is the packet size.

4. Load BNETX.COM at the workstation.

5. The statistics screen should show the Packet Burst activity.

BNETX uses about 7 to 8K more RAM compared to the conventional NETX shell, but the enhanced performance should offset the additional memory requirement. The actual amount of memory taken by BNETX also is dependent on the PB BUFFERS parameter set in NET.CFG. To estimate the memory due to additional PB BUFFERS parameters, use the following formula:

Buffer Memory Requirement = PB BUFFERS * (102 + Packet Size)

The 102 bytes is the combined protocol overhead of IPX, NCP burst, and ECB headers. ECB stands for event control block and is a data structure in memory used to manage packet sending and receiving.

Other NetWare Protocols

This section on native NetWare protocols has focused on the major NetWare protocols and their packet structure. Other protocols such as RIP, SAP, Watchdog, Echo, Serial, and Error are discussed in other sections of this book where their discussion is more appropriate. To fully understand IPX and its relationship to RIP and SAP, for instance, you need to understand the intricacies of routing techniques and routing protocols. These protocols are discussed in detail in Chapter 3. In this chapter, some of the fundamental protocols, such as IPX, also are revisited, but in greater detail.

TCP/IP

Today, most people agree that the TCP/IP protocols have become the de facto mechanism by which interoperability can be achieved. When people talk about TCP/IP, they usually refer to a variety of communication protocols such as TCP, IP, ICMP, ARP, FTP, TELNET, and NFS. The list is quite long and impressive, as new protocols and services are continually added.

The TCP/IP protocols have evolved from the former ARPANET and from Internet. *Internet* is the largest network in the world, connecting thousands of nodes. TCP/IP is used as the primary transport and network protocol on the Internet.

The initial Internet protocols were developed at Stanford University and Bolt, Beranek, and Newman (BBN) in the 1970s. The impetus for this development came from DOD (Department of Defense) Advanced Research Project Agency (DARPA). DARPA funded the development of the Advanced Research Project Agency NETwork (ARPANET). ARPANET was one of the earliest packet-switched networks.

The TCP/IP protocol was integrated in the kernel of a very popular and seminal version of UNIX called the Berkeley Software Distribution (BSD) UNIX. BSD UNIX was a very popular version of UNIX used in many university computer science departments. Many of the commercial versions of UNIX based their TCP/IP implementation on BSD UNIX. In the mid 1980s, vendor interest in TCP/IP became very high, and it became the de facto standard for interoperability.

TCP/IP is important for the NetWare system manager, because NetWare v3.x comes with a TCP/IP stack that allows the NetWare server to function as an IP router. If you want TCP/IP application services such as File Transfer Protocol (FTP) and Network File System (NFS), you can use a product like NetWare NFS to run on the NetWare server. The relationship of TCP/IP to the OSI model is shown in figure 1.14.

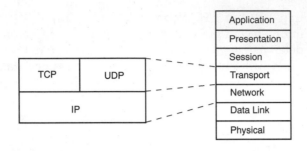

TCP = Transmission Control Protocol

UDP = User Datagram Protocol

IP = Internet Protocol

Figure 1.14:
TCP/IP and the OSI model.

Transmission Control Protocol (TCP) is a transport layer protocol, and IP (Internet Protocol) is a network layer protocol. A partial list of the TCP/IP protocols is shown in figure 1.15. As you can see from this list, TCP/IP protocols are numerous and a detailed discussion of these is beyond the scope of this book. Only a few of these protocols, such as IP and TCP, are discussed.

The IP Protocol

The IP protocol is a network layer protocol that provides connectionless datagram services on top of many data link protocols (fig. 1.15).

IP does not guarantee delivery of datagrams; it makes the best effort it can to deliver data. Upper-layer protocols, such as TCP, can be used to build guaranteed delivery services on top of IP. IP provides a number of interesting services that have become the basis of design of other protocols.

IP provides the notion of a *logical network address* that is independent of the underlying network. It makes use of an Address Resolution Protocol (ARP) to provide the binding between this logical address (called the IP address) and the physical node address of a node.

IP datagrams may get fragmented into smaller units to accommodate the *Maximum Transmission Unit* (MTU) of the underlying network. If fragmentation takes place, the fragments are created with sufficient information so that they can be reassembled. Reassembly of fragments to make up the original datagram is done at the destination node. Problems with IP, such as unreachable destinations and reassembly timeouts, are reported to the sender by the *Internet Control Message Protocol* (ICMP).

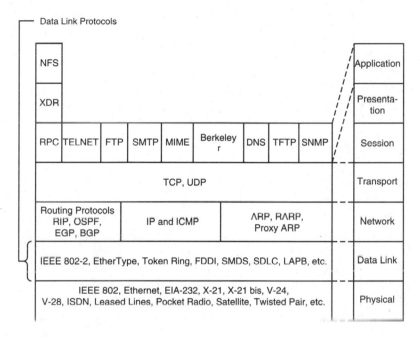

Figure 1.15:
A few TCP/IP protocols.

IP addresses are represented by a 32-bit number. Each network interface in a node that supports an IP stack must have an IP address assigned to it. The IP address is a two-part address consisting of a network ID and a host ID, as shown in figure 1.16. The most significant bits are used to determine how many bits are used for netid and the hostid. Five address classes are currently defined: Class A, B, C, D, and E. Of these, class A, B, and C addresses are assignable. Class D is reserved for multicasting and is used by special protocols to transmit messages to a select group of nodes. Class E is reserved for future use.

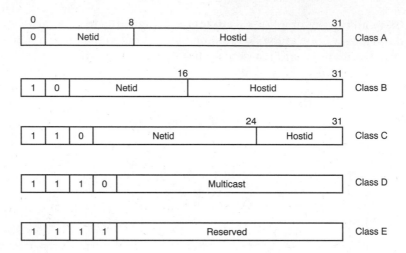

Figure 1.16:
IP address classes.

The netid portion of the IP address is similar to the network number used in IPX protocols. It identifies the network uniquely. Interconnected networks must have unique netids. If your network is going to be connected to other networks such as the Internet, you must apply to a central authority to obtain a unique netid (network number) that is not in use by anyone else. The central Internet Address Network Authority (IANA) is:

> **DDN Network Information Center**
> **14200 Park Meadow Drive, Suite 200**
> **Chantilly, VA 22021, USA**
> electronic mail address: **HOSTMASTER@NIC.DDN.MIL**

Older reference works on TCP/IP may list the *Stanford Research Institute* (SRI) as the *Network Information Center* (NIC). This no longer is true; but you can still obtain *Request For Comments* (RFCs) from SRI. Request For Comments are documents that define the Internet protocol standards and other information pertaining to the Internet. The standards that define IP and TCP protocols are RFC 791 and RFC 793, for example. RFC documents are in the public domain and their distribution is unlimited.

The different types of IP address classes are defined to address the needs of networks of different sizes. Table 1.1 shows the number of networks and nodes that are possible with each address class.

Table 1.1
Reasons for Using Specific Address Class

Address Class	Number of Networks	Number of Nodes
A	127	16,777,214
B	16,383	65,534
C	2,097,151	254

A class A network is suited for very large networks, but because their netid field (see fig. 1.16) is only 7 bits, there can be only 127 such networks. The original ARPANET is an example of a class A network. Class B networks are medium-size networks and are suited for medium to large organizations. Class C networks are suited for small organizations, in which each network can have no more than 254 nodes.

The 32-bit number is represented for convenience sake as four decimal numbers corresponding to the decimal value of the four bytes that make up the 32-bit IP address. The decimal numbers are separated by periods (.). This shorthand notation for IP addresses is called *dotted decimal notation*. Figure 1.17 shows the format of an IP packet. The following shows an IP address in its binary form and also as a dotted decimal notation.

IP Address = 10010000 0001011 01001010 1001010

IP Address = 144.19.74.202

In figure 1.17, the version number field is four bits long, and indicates the format of the IP header. This allows future IP packet structures to be defined. The current version number is four. Table 1.2 shows the other possible values of the version number field. IP Version seven may be the next possible IP format that allows for longer IP addresses; however, this is still the subject of considerable debate.

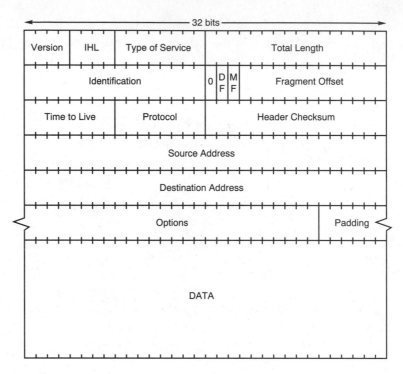

Figure 1.17:
IP packet structure.

Table 1.2
IP Version Number Values

IP Version	Meaning
0	Reserved
1–3	Unassigned
4	IP
5	Stream IP (Experimental IP)
6–14	Unassigned
15	Reserved

The *Internet Header Length* (IHL) is the length of the header in 32-bit words. This field is required because the IP header contains a variable-length option field.

The *Type Of Service* (TOS) field informs the networks of the *Quality Of Service* (QOS) desired, such as precedence, delay, throughput, and reliability. The meaning of this 8-bit field is shown in figure 1.18.

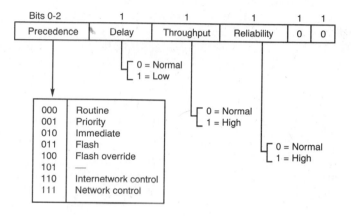

Figure 1.18:
Type Of Service field for IP packets.

The Precedence field reflects the military origin of IP networks. The following are the meanings of some of the precedence values:

- **Flash**   ASAP (As Soon As Possible). Max priority on all circuits.

- **Immediate**   Within four hours.

- **Priority**   Same day.

- **Routine**   Within one day.

Most IP implementations and routing protocols (RIP, HELLO, etc.) ignore the Type of Service field.

The Precedence field is intended for Department of Defense applications of the Internet protocols. The use of nonzero values in this field is outside the scope of the IP standard specification. Vendors should consult the Defense Communication Agency (DCA) for guidance on the IP Precedence field and its implications for other protocol layers.

Vendors should note that the use of precedence most likely will require that its value be passed between protocol layers in much the same way as the TOS field is passed. The IP layer must provide a means for the transport layer to set the TOS field of every datagram that is sent; the default is all zero bits. The IP layer should pass received TOS values up to the transport layer.

Although the TOS field has been little used in the past, it is expected to play an increasing role in the near future with routing protocols such as OSPF that could make use of the TOS field. The TOS field is expected to be used to control two aspects of router operations: routing and queuing algorithms. The TOS field also may be mapped into link-layer effective sharing of serial lines by different classes of TCP traffic.

The Total Length field contains the length of the IP header and data in bytes. The maximum size of the datagram is 65,535 bytes. All IP nodes must be prepared to receive a minimum size of 576 bytes (512 bytes of data plus 64 bytes of protocol overhead).

The Identification field is set uniquely for each datagram, and is the datagram number. It is used in conjunction with the fragment flags DF (Don't Fragment), MF (More Fragments), and Fragment Offset fields to re-assemble the datagram. If the DF flag is set to 1, that means that the data-gram should not be fragmented. If the MF flag is set to 1, that indicates to the receiver that there are more fragments to come. An MF set to 0 indicates that it is the last fragment.

The Fragment Offset field indicates the position of the fragment's data rela-tive to the start of the original datagram. This is a 13-bit field and is mea-sured in 8-byte groups. This means that the Fragment Offset value must be multiplied by 8 to get the byte offset.

The *Time To Live* (TTL) is measured in seconds and represents the maximum time an IP datagram can live on the network. It should be decremented at each router by the amount of time taken to process the packet. The intent is that TTL expiration will cause a datagram to be discarded by a router, but not by the destination host. Hosts that act as routers by forwarding data-grams (such as NetWare v3.x) must follow the router rules for TTL. The TTL field has two functions: limit the lifetime of TCP segments and terminate Internet routing loops. Although TTL is time in seconds, it also has some attributes of a hop-count, because each gateway is required to reduce the TTL field by at least one. This is why some implementers mistakenly set it to 16, because 16 is infinity for RIP. But TTL is independent of RIP metrics.

Other considerations for TTL fields are the following:

- A host must not send a datagram with a TTL value of zero, and a host must not discard a datagram just because it was received with TTL less than 2.

- A higher-layer protocol may want to set the TTL to implement an expanding scope search for some Internet resource. This is used by some diagnostic tools and is expected to be useful for locating the "nearest" server of a given class using IP multicasting, for example. A particular transport protocol also may want to specify its own TTL boundary on maximum datagram lifetime.

- A fixed value must be at least big enough for the Internet *diameter*— the longest possible path. A reasonable value is about twice the diameter, which allows for continued Internet growth.

- The IP layer must provide a means for the transport layer to set the TTL field of every datagram that is sent. When a fixed TTL value is used, that value must be configurable. Unfortunately, most implementations do not allow the initial TTL value to be set. A default value of 32 or 64 is very common.

The Protocol field is used to indicate the Upper Layer Protocol that is to receive the IP data. It is similar in function to the Packet Type field for IPX packets. The "Assigned Numbers" RFC 1060 contains the defined values for this field; for example, TCP has a protocol field value of 6, UDP has a value of 17, and ICMP has a value of 1.

The Header Checksum is used for the IP header only. The 1's complement of each 16-bit value making up the header is added (excluding the Header Checksum field). Then the 1's complement of the sum is taken. This field is recomputed at each router since the TTL field is decremented, and the header modified.

The Source Address and Destination Address are the 32-bit IP addresses of the source and destination nodes.

The IP Options are security, loose source routing, strict source routing, record route, and Internet time stamp.

The TCP Protocol

TCP is the primary Transport Protocol used to provide reliable, full-duplex, virtual-circuit connections. The connections are made between port numbers of the sender and the receiver nodes. TCP has an octet-stream orientation. An octet is a group of 8 bits. Therefore, an *octet stream* is an 8-bit stream. There is no inherent notion of a block of data. TCP can be used to provide multiple virtual-circuit connections between two TCP hosts.

Figure 1.19 shows the TCP packet structure. The Source Port and Destination Port numbers are used to identify the end-point processes in the TCP virtual circuit. Some port numbers are well-known port numbers, whereas others are dynamically assigned. RFC 1066 contains a description of some of the well-known port numbers. A few of these are shown in table 1.3

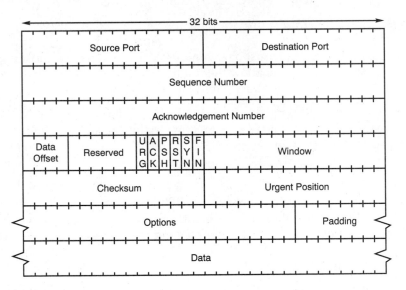

Figure 1.19:
TCP packet structure.

Table 1.3
Some Well-Known TCP Port Numbers

Port Number	Description
0	Reserved
5	Remote Job Entry
7	Echo
9	Discard
11	Systat
13	Daytime
15	Netstat
17	Quotd (Quote of the day)
20	ftp_data
21	ftp (Control)
23	telnet
25	smtp
37	time
53	name server
102	ISO-TSAP
103	X.400
104	X.400 sending service
111	Sun RPC
139	NetBIOS session source
160–223	Reserved

The 32-bit sequence number is the number of the first byte of data in the current message. If the SYN flag is set to 1, this field defines the initial sequence number to be used for that session. A 32-bit value is used to avoid using old sequence numbers that already may have been assigned to data that is in transit on the network.

The Acknowledgment Number is used to indicate the sequence number of the next byte expected by the receiver. TCP Acknowledgments are cumulative. That is, a single acknowledgment can be used to acknowledge a number of prior TCP message segments.

The Data Offset field is the number of 32-bit words in the TCP header. This field is needed because the TCP options field could be variable in length.

The Flags that follow have the following meanings:

The URG flag is used to send out-of-band data, without waiting for the receiver to process octets already in the stream. When the URG flag is set, the Urgent Pointer field is valid. RFC 1122 states that the urgent pointer points to the sequence number of the LAST octet (not LAST+1) in a sequence of urgent data, and that RFC 793 describes it incorrectly as LAST + 1. A TCP implementation must support a sequence of urgent data of any length. A TCP layer must inform the application layer asynchronously whenever the TCP layer receives an Urgent pointer with no previous pending urgent data, or whenever the Urgent pointer advances in the data stream.

There must be a way for the application to learn how much urgent data remains to be read from the connection, or at least to determine whether more urgent data remains to be read. Although the Urgent mechanism may be used for any application, it is normally used to send interrupt-type commands to a Telnet program. The asynchronous, or "out-of-band," notification allows the application to go into urgent mode, reading data from the TCP connection. This allows control commands to be sent to an application whose normal input buffers are full of unprocessed data.

When the ACK flag is set, it indicates that the Acknowledgment Number field is valid.

When the PSH flag is set, it tells TCP to immediately deliver data for this message to the upper-layer process. When an application issues a series of send calls without setting the PSH flag, the TCP may aggregate the data internally without sending it. Similarly, when a series of segments is received without the PSH bit, a TCP may queue the data internally without passing it to the receiving application.

The PSH bit is not a record marker and is independent of segment boundaries. Some implementations incorrectly think of the PSH as a record marker, however. The transmitter should collapse successive PSH bits when it packetizes data, to send the largest possible segment.

A TCP may implement PSH flags on send calls. If PSH flags are not implemented, then the sending TCP

1. Must not buffer data indefinitely

2. Must set the PSH bit in the last buffered segment (for example, when there is no more queued data to be sent)

RFC-793 erroneously implies that a received PSH flag must be passed to the application layer. Passing a received PSH flag to the application layer is now optional.

An application program is logically required to set the PSH flag in a send call whenever it needs to force delivery of the data to avoid a communication deadlock. A TCP should send a maximum-size segment whenever possible to improve performance, however. This means that on the sender side, a PSH may not result in the segment being immediately transmitted.

When the PSH flag is not implemented on send TCP calls (or when the application/TCP interface uses a pure streaming model), responsibility for aggregating any tiny data fragments to form reasonable-size segments is partially borne by the application layer. Generally, an interactive application protocol must set the PSH flag at least in the last send call in each command or response sequence. A bulk transfer protocol like FTP should set the PSH flag on the last segment of a file, or when necessary to prevent buffer deadlock.

At the receiver, the PSH bit forces buffered data to be delivered to the application (even if less than a full buffer has been received). Conversely, the lack of a PSH can be used to avoid unnecessary wake-up calls to the application process; this can be an important performance optimization for large time-sharing hosts.

The RST bit is used to reset the virtual circuit due to unrecoverable errors. The reason could be a host crash or delayed duplicate SYN packets.

The SYN flag is used to indicate the opening of a virtual-circuit connection. TCP connections are opened using the "three-way-handshake" procedure. The SYN and the ACK flags are used to indicate the following packets:

- SYN = 1 and ACK = 0   Open Connection Packet
- SYN = 1 and ACK = 1   Open Connection Acknowledgment
- SUN = 0 and ACK = 1   Data packet or ACK packet

The FIN flag is used to terminate the connection. Connection termination in TCP is accomplished by using a graceful close mechanism. Both sides must agree to terminate by sending a FIN = 1 flag, before connection termination can occur; doing this ensures that data is not unexpectedly lost by either side by an abrupt connection termination.

The Window field is used to implement flow control and is used by the receiver to advertise the number of additional bytes of data it is willing to accept.

The Checksum field is 1's complement of the 1's complement sum of all the 16-bit words in the TCP packet. A 96-bit pseudo header (fig. 1.20) is prepended to the TCP header for checksum computation. The pseudoheader is used to identify if the packet has arrived at the right destination. The pseudoheader has the protocol ID (6 for TCP), source, and destination IP address. Because the TCP header contains the source and destination port number, this describes the connection between the endpoints.

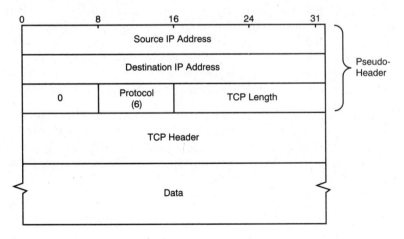

Figure 1.20:
Pseudoheader in TCP checksum.

The Options field currently defines only the Maximum Segment Size (MSS) option, which is negotiated during connection establishment.

AppleTalk

AppleTalk is a set of proprietary protocols used by Apple Computers to network their Macintosh desktop computers. AppleTalk protocols are important to NetWare users and administrators, because the Macintosh computer can be found in many organizations, and Macintosh users and other NetWare users often need to share information. You learn in later chapters of this book that Novell supports Macintosh users in NetWare-based networks by running the AppleTalk protocols directly on the NetWare server, enabling the NetWare user to emulate an AppleShare server to Macintosh clients.

Macintosh users can use their familiar graphical user interface to access the NetWare/AppleShare server. The AppleShare emulation solution also is used to connect Macintosh users to other network architectures, such as DEC VAX computers, UNIX computers, and Windows NT Advanced servers. This section helps you understand the background and protocol architecture of AppleTalk.

Development of AppleTalk protocols began in 1983 and became available in 1984. What is unusual about Apple's approach is that the AppleTalk protocols were implemented in the Macintosh OS; it was not a separate piece of client networking software that had to be loaded onto the Macintosh OS.

Also, no additional networking hardware had to be added to provide the equivalent of a Network Adapter interface. The networking hardware was built into the Macintosh system board in the form of the LocalTalk interface. LocalTalk is RS-449/RS-422 based at the physical layer, and can operate at up to 230.4 Kbps. Whereas this speed is much less than that of Ethernet and Token Ring, it is adequate for small networks and applications that do not have high network bandwidth requirements.

The first set of AppleTalk protocols had a limitation of 254 nodes per physical network and ran on LocalTalk hardware. This was called AppleTalk Phase I. In 1989, Apple released an updated set of protocols called AppleTalk Phase II. AppleTalk Phase II overcomes the 254 node/network limit by allowing a range of network numbers to be associated with a physical network. A node is identified by a pair of numbers: the network number and the node number. When a specific network number is used up to form the network number/node number pair, another network number from the network range can be used.

AppleTalk Phase II, besides providing support for LocalTalk, also supports other Data Link access protocols such as Ethernet, IEEE 802.3, and the IEEE 802.5 Token Ring. These hardware technologies are discussed in greater detail in the next chapter. The Ethernet and Token Ring network boards used in Macintosh networks are called EtherTalk and TokenTalk respectively. Figure 1.21 shows the link access technologies used in AppleTalk in relationship with the OSI model.

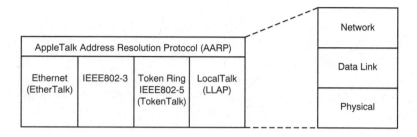

Figure 1.21:
AppleTalk link access technologies.

AppleTalk Data Link Layer

The AppleTalk Address Resolution Protocol (AARP) is modeled after TCP/IP's ARP protocol and provides a binding between upper-layer network addresses and data link layer addresses. AARP makes it possible to run AppleTalk protocols on different data link layer technologies with the data link layer address of a destination node being determined dynamically.

Figure 1.22 shows examples of how AARP can be used. AARP can be used in a situation in which a sender station knows the destination's upper-layer protocol address, but does not know the data link layer address. The data link layer address is needed by the AppleTalk drivers to send the AppleTalk frame over the physical link. In this case, an AARP broadcast request is sent that contains the destination's upper-protocol address.

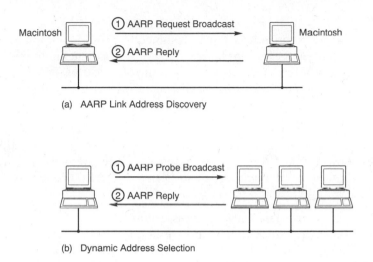

(a)   AARP Link Address Discovery

(b)   Dynamic Address Selection

Figure 1.22:
AppleTalk AARP examples.

All nodes receive the broadcast, but only the node that has the same upper-protocol address as in the AARP request packet responds with its data link address. The protocol address and data link address mappings are kept in a local cache in memory and are called the *Address Mapping Table* (AMT). Before sending a data transmission, the AMT is consulted to discover the data link address of the destination. If there is no entry in the AMT, AARP is used to discover the mapping. Old AMT entries are automatically timed-out and purged from the AMT table.

Another situation in which AARP can be used is in Dynamic Address Selection. When a Macintosh computer is booted on a network, it picks a node address randomly and sends an AARP request broadcast with the same node address. If a reply is received, it implies that the node address is in use. In this case, the station must pick another address and repeat the process until a unique node address is determined. Figure 1.23 shows the AARP packet structure.

The meanings of the fields in figure 1.23 are described as follows:

■   The Hardware Type and Protocol Type fields together define the data link and protocol address type used by AARP. The Hardware Type could be EtherTalk, TokenTalk, or LocalTalk and the Protocol Type is AppleTalk.

■ The Hardware Address Length and Protocol Address Lengths are needed because AARP was designed to provide mappings between a number of different hardware and protocol technologies. Since the length of the hardware address (data link address) and protocol address could be different, their length values are placed in the AARP packet.

■ The Function Code determines the type of AARP packet. Currently, three codes are defined for the three AARP packets. Function Code 1 indicates an AARP request; Function Code 2 indicates an AARP Reply and Function Code 3 indicates an AARP Probe used for Dynamic Address Selection.

■ The Source Hardware Address, Source Protocol Address, Destination Hardware Address, and Destination Protocol Address have lengths specified by the Hardware Address Length and Protocol Address Length fields. These fields contain the hardware address and protocol address of the nodes involved in the AARP exchange.

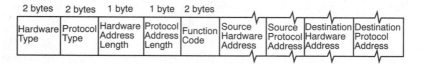

Figure 1.23:
AARP Packet Structure.

AppleTalk Network Layer

Figure 1.24 shows the network layer used in AppleTalk that is related to the OSI model. The Datagram Delivery Protocol (DDP) is the major protocol used by the network layer. Other protocols such as RTMP (Routing Table Maintenance Protocol), ZIP (Zone Information Protocol), and NBP (Name Binding Protocol) also help support the operation of the network layer.

The DDP is a connectionless protocol between two processes running on separate nodes on the network. Because it is connectionless, DDP by itself cannot be used to guarantee delivery of the datagram. Upper-layer protocols at the transport layer must be used to guarantee delivery.

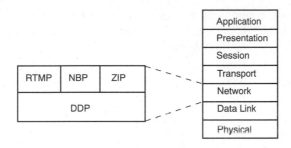

Figure 1.24:
AppleTalk network layer.

The DDP processes by which it delivers data must attach to sockets. *Sockets* are used to define the boundary points between DDP and the upper layers through which data exchange takes place. DDP sockets are similar in concept to IPX sockets and TCP/IP port numbers discussed earlier. The sockets are described by numbers ranging from 1 to 255. Numbers 1 to 127 have well-defined meanings and are *Statically Assigned Sockets* (SASs). Socket numbers from 128 to 254 are assigned dynamically on demand and are called *Dynamically Assigned Sockets* (DASs).

DDP contains a provision for assigning unique network addresses for each node by using a combination of a 16-bit network number and an 8-bit node number. To further distinguish Upper Layer Processes (ULP) running on a node, the socket number can be used. Thus a complete process address consists of the following 3-tuple:

<network number, node number, socket number>

Older networks such as LocalTalk were limited to a single network number and 8-bit node number associated with that network number. Each node number of these *nonextended networks* is unique. In AppleTalk Phase II, data link layer technologies can support more nodes than the 8-bit value of Phase I. To support these networks the concept of extended networks was introduced. Extended networks can have a range of network numbers assigned to them. This allows for more nodes than can be accommodated by an 8-bit value.

Figure 1.25 shows an example of a short header DDP packet. The short header DDP packet is designed for nonextended networks. The extended header packets have additional fields for the network number, node numbers, hop count, and checksum. The network numbers are used by routers to distinguish between the different networks. The hop count is also used by routers to determine the distance a packet has to traverse.

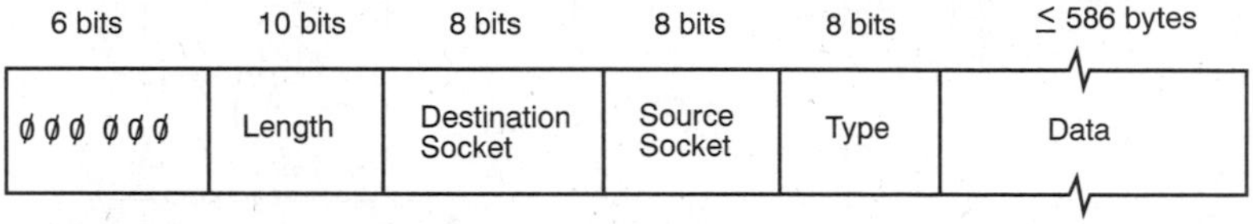

6 bits	10 bits	8 bits	8 bits	8 bits	≤ 586 bytes
0̸ 0̸ 0̸ 0̸ 0̸ 0̸	Length	Destination Socket	Source Socket	Type	Data

Figure 1.25:
Short header DDP packet structure.

The first 6 bits are unused and set to zero. The next 10 bits represent the length of the datagram which cannot exceed 586 bytes. The destination and source socket numbers follow next and identify the processes on the nodes. The Type field is used to indicate which Upper Layer Process the DDP packet data should be sent to.

In an AppleTalk Internet, several physical AppleTalk networks are connected by routers. The routers are responsible for directing the packet to the correct destination network. The source node must determine if the packet is to be sent to a router or the local network. It does this by examining the destination network number. If this number is in the range assigned to the local network, the destination node is in the local network.

If the number is not in the range assigned for the local network, it is sent to one of the AppleTalk routers. The routers exchange information using the RTMP protocol. The RTMP protocol was derived from the XNS RIP protocol and is an example of a Distance-Vector routing protocol. These classes of protocols are discussed in Chapter 3.

The *Name Binding Protocol* (NBP) is used to provide a logical association between AppleTalk names and network addresses. It is similar in concept to the *Domain Name System* (DNS) protocol used in TCP/IP networks. AppleTalk names are symbolic names used to designate services on the network and are therefore easier for users to deal with than network addresses which are numeric quantities. AppleTalk services are called *Network Visible Entities* (NVEs). Examples of NVEs are sockets and mailboxes. NVEs have names called entity names and attributes that specify the characteristics of the NVE. NBP is used to build an association (called name binding) between the NVE name and its network address. The name and address associations are kept in name tables.

All the name tables on the AppleTalk Internet make up the *name directory*. When an application wants to use a name, it consults its local name table. If it cannot find the name, it issues an NBP lookup packet to find the name's address. The address is returned by NBP. Because DDP does not perform Internet broadcasts, NBP lookups across the entire Internet are not possible. To make it possible to look up names on an Internet, the concept of a zone was created. NBP looks can be done on a zone basis.

A *zone* represents a group of logically related AppleTalk nodes. They are a means of categorizing how nodes are typically used on the Internetwork. They can span multiple networks. A zone can include a few nodes from one network, some nodes from another network, and so on. Or, a zone can include all the nodes in one physical network or only few of the nodes on that network. When a node is powered up, the zone it belongs to is selected from a list of zones for that network. All nodes in a nonextended network must belong to the same zone.

A zone-wide NBP lookup is sent to the local router that is responsible for broadcasting the NBP lookup request to all networks in the specified zone. Only nodes in the selected zone can reply to the NBP lookup packet.

When the concept of zone was created to solve the NBP broadcast problem, a mechanism was needed to maintain the mapping between a network numbers and zones. The *Zone Information Protocol* (ZIP) was created to maintain this mapping. This mapping is maintained in tables called *Zone Information Tables* (ZITs). ZITs are maintained in AppleTalk routers. When a node starts up, it uses a ZIP request packet to discover the zone it belongs to. When a router discovers new networks via the RTMP protocol, that router sends a ZIP request for obtaining the Zone List for the new network.

AppleTalk Transport Layer

Figure 1.26 shows the transport layer used in AppleTalk that is related to the OSI model. AppleTalk uses two transport protocols: AppleTalk Transaction Protocol (ATP) and AppleTalk Data Stream Protocol (ADSP).

The ATP protocol is based on the concept of completing a transaction reliably. A *transaction* is defined as a request/response sequence between a client and a server. Each transaction is numbered by a transaction ID, which enables the client to associate a transaction response with the correct transaction request. Because either a transaction request or response can get lost in transmission, it is important for the client to know which transactions must be *executed once* (XO) only, and which must be done *at-least-once* (ALO).

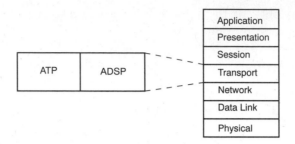

Figure 1.26:
AppleTalk transport layer.

The ALO transactions can be repeated without any harm; an example of this is a read request for a block of data in a file. ALO transactions also are called *idempotent transactions*. The XO transactions must not be repeated because they could have undesirable consequences. An example of an XO transaction is a request by a client to append a data block to the end of a file. If this command were to be repeated, an additional data block would be added to the end of the file. XO transactions also are called *non-idempotent transactions*.

If the data to be transmitted is larger than can be transmitted by the underlying network, ATP can fragment and reassemble data with the limitation that the original message must be limited to eight fragments. Because of varying delays and errors in transmission, a packet could get out of sequence or lost. A bitmap/sequence number field is used in the ATP header to keep track of packets. For a transaction request, this field represents a bitmap; for a transaction reply, it represents a sequence number. The *bitmap* refers to the number of responses expected by the client. The client allocates a buffer to hold each response.

Figure 1.27 shows an initial transaction request with a bitmap of 00000111. Each bit position that is a 1 corresponds to an expected response. The responses contain sequence numbers. In the example in the figure, responses 0 and 2 are received correctly, but response 1 is lost. The client makes a request with a bitmap of 00000010, which indicates to the server that packet 1 is outstanding and needs to be sent again. If the number of responses is less than the expected number, an end-of-message packet is sent.

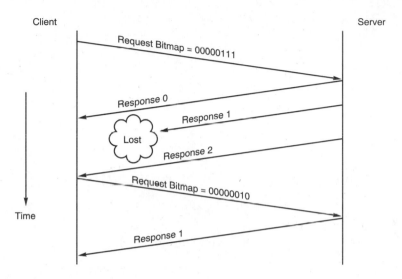

Figure 1.27:
An ATP transaction example.

The Control Information field in an ATP packet (see fig. 1.28) is used to indicate the type of ATP packet such as request, response, XO, or ALO. The Bitmap/Sequence number field is used to indicate the expected response and the sequence number of the response packet. The Transaction ID field is used to match a response with a request.

Another AppleTalk transport layer protocol is the ADSP. The ADSP protocol provides full duplex virtual circuit capability between two sockets. The data flow is stream-oriented in a manner similar to TCP. Each byte in the stream has a sequence number. Flow control is achieved by a sliding-window mechanism. The window size is adjusted based on the amount of data the other side is willing to accept and has a maximum size of 64K.

Two types of ASDP packets are defined: control and data packets. ADSP control packets are defined so that they can be used for virtual circuit operation, such as creation and teardown. The ADSP protocol, unlike ATP, does not have any inherent client/server orientation. Any side can initiate the virtual circuit connection.

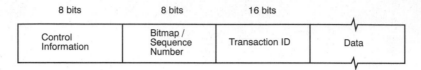

Figure 1.28:
AppleTalk transaction protocol.

AppleTalk Session Layer Protocol

Figure 1.29 shows the session layer used in AppleTalk in relationship with the OSI model. AppleTalk uses two session protocols: AppleTalk Session Protocol (ASP) and Printer Access Protocol (PAP).

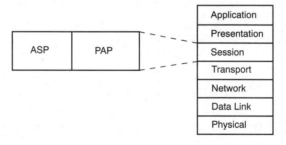

Figure 1.29:
AppleTalk session layer.

ASP is used to create, maintain, and destroy sessions that make use of the underlying transport mechanism provided by the ATP layer. ASP builds on the concept of the transaction to provide a *session* consisting of series of transactions. The ASP user, such as a workstation, does not have to deal in terms of transactions; the workstation can open an ASP session with the server, over which it can send commands and not have to worry about commands being sent out of order, lost, or duplicated.

ASP can be used by a client to obtain status information on the server. The server also can send an ASP attention command to workstations informing them of a change in server status.

The PAP session protocol is used to create, maintain, and destroy connections to remote printer services. Though designed to be used with printers, PAP is quite general and can be used to provide connections to other services as well. PAP uses the NBP protocol to obtain the address of the server and establishes a connection by building on the services provided by ATP. All transactions are sent using the XO mode of ATP. PAP can be used to read data from the server or write data to it.

AppleTalk Application Layer

AppleTalk does not have an explicit presentation layer. Its most common application layer protocols are the Apple Filing Protocol (AFP) and AppleTalk Print Services (APS) (see fig. 1.30). The APS is used to provide remote printer services to a client; it makes use of the PAP protocol to provide printer services.

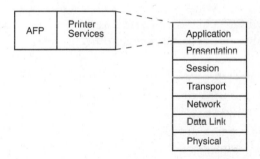

Figure 1.30:
AppleTalk application layer.

The AFP protocol makes use of ASP to provide remote file services. It is similar in concept to NetWare's NCP and the NFS protocols used in TCP/IP networks.

File access requests from application programs are processed by AFP to determine if they are for local or remote file access (fig. 1.31). AFP sends local file requests to the local file system. If the file request is remote, AFP makes use of the AppleTalk Filing Interface (AFI) to transmit the file request across the network. The AFI makes use of the AppleTalk protocols (ASP, ATP, DDP) to send the request to the server. The request is processed by the AppleTalk Protocols on the server and communicated to the File Server Control Program.

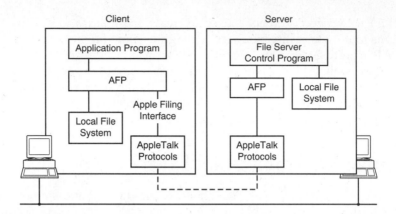

Figure 1.31:
AppleTalk filing protocol.

AFP includes security mechanisms through a user/password authentication mechanism, volume passwords, and directory access control. Directory access control consists of Search, Read, and Write privileges.

Summary

This chapter laid the foundation for a better understanding of network protocols. The OSI Reference Model was discussed as a means to compare different protocol architectures. The ODI protocol architecture was compared with respect to the OSI Reference Model.

The protocol structure of some of the major protocols such as NCP/SPX/IPX, TCP/IP, and AppleTalk was discussed. These protocols are commonly found in a NetWare environment.

LAN Standards for the Physical and Data Link Layers

You must understand LAN wiring schemes to install the LAN media and identify the locations of the servers, workstations, hosts, routers, gateways, and bridges in a LAN. You can use a variety of wiring schemes used by LANs such as coaxial cable, twisted pair wiring, and fiber optics. Even for the same media such as twisted pair wiring, the rules are different for Ethernet, Token Ring, and ARCnet. This chapter explores wiring schemes for common LANs.

A working knowledge of LAN wiring schemes is important for the LAN manager who needs to know when distance limitations for a LAN have been exceeded. Many LAN problems can be attributed to poorly designed LAN wiring schemes or wiring schemes that do not follow the wiring design rules.

Wiring schemes are just one LAN component. Other components include:

- *Network Interface Cards* (NICs)
- Network drivers
- Protocols

- *Network operating systems (NOSs)*
- Network shells and redirectors

The relationship of these components to each other is not always clear. The OSI model helps to keep a global vision of the components and how they interrelate.

The IEEE Local Area Network Standards

As you work with NetWare, you will encounter references to the *Institute of Electrical and Electronic Engineers* (IEEE) 802 standards. The first two OSI layers are most closely related to the network components of Ethernet, Token Ring, or ARCnet. The IEEE defines Ethernet as an 802.3 standard and Token Ring as an 802.5 standard. These standards constitute the majority of networks that run Novell NetWare.

The IEEE undertook Project 802 in February of 1980 to identify and formalize LAN standards for data rates not exceeding 20 megabits per second (Mbps). Standardization efforts resulted in the IEEE 802 LAN standards. The number 802 was chosen to mark the calendar date when IEEE undertook the LAN standardization efforts (80 for 1980, 2 for February).

Figure 2.1 shows the IEEE LAN standards in relationship to the OSI model. You can see that the primary emphasis of the IEEE committee was to standardize the hardware technologies used at the physical and data link layer. This is not surprising considering that networking hardware such as network interface cards and LAN wiring can be modeled completely by the two lower OSI layers.

The IEEE standards divide the OSI data link layer into two sublayers: the *Media Access Control* (MAC) and the *Logical Link Control* (LLC). The MAC layer deals with media access techniques utilized to control access to a shared physical medium. Token Ring and Ethernet have different implementations of the MAC layer because they use different methods to share the physical media.

All IEEE LANs have the same LLC layer as defined by standard 802.2. The advantage of a common sublayer such as the LLC is that upper-layer mechanisms can be the same regardless of what kind of networking hardware you use.

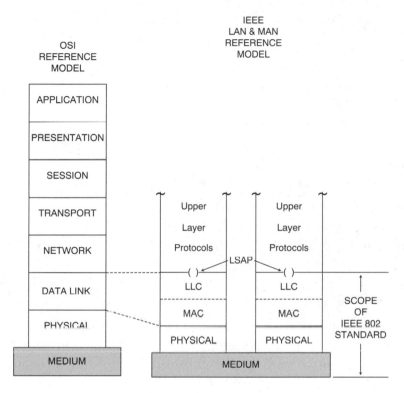

Figure 2.1:
Relationship of the IEEE 802 Standard to the OSI model. (Courtesy IEEE Standard 802-1990)

Figure 2.1 shows the interface between Upper Layer Protocols and the LLC layer defined by *Link Service Access Points* (LSAPs). LSAPs are logical data link addresses. A single MAC address, such as an Ethernet address, can have multiple LSAP addresses. These multiple addresses allow multiple end-point connections between two nodes on a LAN.

The LLC layer also provides the options of virtual circuit (connections-oriented) or datagram (connectionless) services or a combination of these two.

Unacknowledged, datagram services are modeled after postal services. In the datagram approach, every packet contains complete addressing information such as destination and source addresses. No special effort is made to ensure packets arrive intact or in the correct order. Unacknowledged, data-gram services are called Type 1 service.

In a *virtual-circuit*, a special effort is made to ensure that packets arrive error-free in the order they were sent. Virtual circuits are modeled after the telephone system and require that a connection be established between two nodes before data can be exchanged between them. When data transfer is complete, this virtual circuit needs to be closed or terminated. Virtual-circuit services are called Type 2 service.

Acknowledged, datagram services, a combination of datagram and virtual circuits, are called Type 3 services in which an effort is made to correct data errors by retransmitting packets that have data errors.

In summary, the types of services provided by LLC are as follows:

- **Type 1.** Unacknowledged, datagram service. Supports point-to-point, multi-point, and broadcast transmission.

- **Type 2.** Virtual-circuit service. Provides sequenced, flow controlled, error-free services between LSAPs.

- **Type 3.** Acknowledged, datagram service. Provides datagram point-to-point service with acknowledgments.

Figure 2.2 shows how the IEEE committee has identified the choices at the different layers. Each of the choices represents a standard protocol or specification. Their IEEE numbers and meaning are described in table 2.1.

Table 2.1
IEEE Standards

IEEE Standard	Meaning
IEEE 802.1	LAN bridging
IEEE 802.2	Logical Link Control (LLC)
IEEE 802.3	Standardization of Ethernet Technology
IEEE 802.4	Token Bus standard
IEEE 802.5	Token Ring standard
IEEE 802.6	Metropolitan Area Network (MAN)
IEEE 802.7	Broadband technical advisory
IEEE 802.8	Fiber optic technical advisory

IEEE Standard	Meaning
IEEE 802.9	Integrated Voice/Data (IVD)
IEEE 802.10	LAN security
IEEE 802.11	Wireless LANs

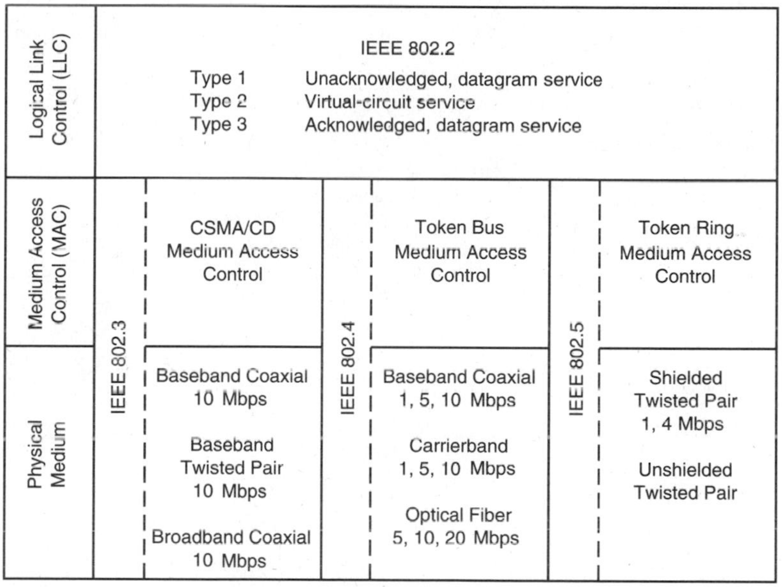

Logical Link Control (LLC)	**IEEE 802.2** Type 1 Unacknowledged, datagram service Type 2 Virtual-circuit service Type 3 Acknowledged, datagram service		
Medium Access Control (MAC)	CSMA/CD Medium Access Control	Token Bus Medium Access Control	Token Ring Medium Access Control
Physical Medium	IEEE 802.3 — Baseband Coaxial 10 Mbps Baseband Twisted Pair 10 Mbps Broadband Coaxial 10 Mbps	IEEE 802.4 — Baseband Coaxial 1, 5, 10 Mbps Carrierband 1, 5, 10 Mbps Optical Fiber 5, 10, 20 Mbps	IEEE 802.5 — Shielded Twisted Pair 1, 4 Mbps Unshielded Twisted Pair

Figure 2.2:
Services defined by various IEEE 802 standards.

LAN Wiring Topologies

Each LAN standard has its own rules for LAN wiring. These rules define the connecting media, the hardware requirements, and the way the various components are arranged. Two primary concerns exist in regard to media: the media type (usually some type of cable) and the way the various cables in the network are laid out.

The geometrical arrangement of the wiring scheme is called the *topology*. The topologies that are common in LANs are the star, bus, and ring. These are shown in figure 2.3.

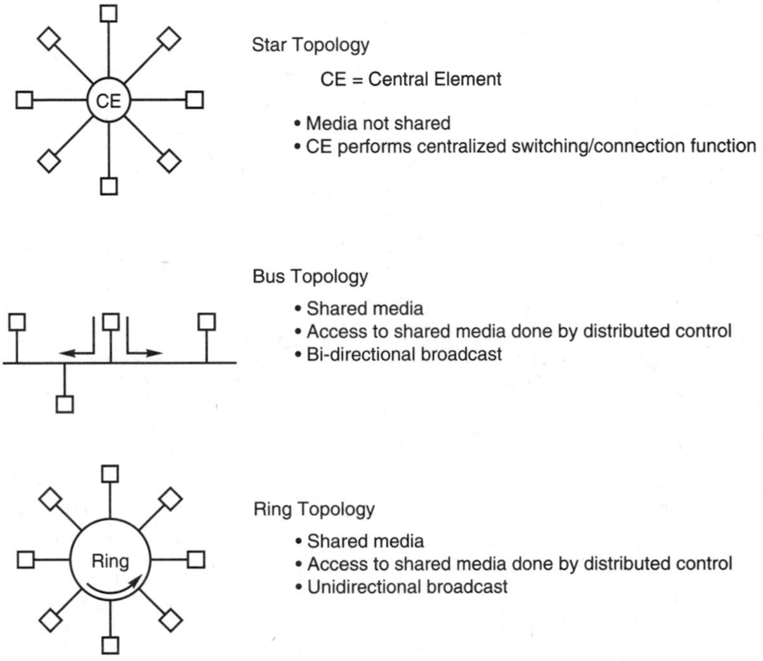

Star Topology

    CE = Central Element

- Media not shared
- CE performs centralized switching/connection function

Bus Topology

- Shared media
- Access to shared media done by distributed control
- Bi-directional broadcast

Ring Topology

- Shared media
- Access to shared media done by distributed control
- Unidirectional broadcast

Figure 2.3:
LAN topologies.

In the *star* topology, communication between any two nodes must go through a central device or switching element. The devices that connect to the central switch tend to be simple, with all of the complexity residing in the central switch. The central switching element should be reliable and provide signal isolation between ports so that failures at any one port are not propagated to other ports.

Classic examples of star topology are mainframe and minicomputer architectures in which the host is the central switch. If the host breaks down, it is time to take a coffee break! This points out the vulnerability of the star wiring topology: it is vulnerable to a single point of failure.

If, on the other hand, the central switching element is both reliable and provides signal isolation between the ports, the star topology is one of the best topologies. This explains the reason why it is used in ARCnet, Token Ring, FDDI, and 10BASE-T LANs. Another advantage is that it is easy to connect or remove stations from a central location. In many LANs, these central elements (hubs) come with advanced network management features like *Simple Network Management Protocol* (SNMP).

The *bus* topology consists of a linear cable to which stations are attached. Signals sent by a station on the bus propagate in both directions. Every transmission is available to every station on the network more or less simultaneously. A classic example of a bus topology is *Ethernet*.

The *ring* topology consists of a cable in the form of a loop with stations attached to it. Signals are sent in only one direction, and the ring can be implemented by point-to-point simplex (one direction flow) links. Stations see only the transmissions that happen to pass by them in the ring. An example of a network that uses the ring topology is a *Token Ring LAN*.

An important distinction should be noted between physical and logical network topologies. The *physical* topology of a network describes the way in which the actual cables are routed. The *logical* topology describes the way that the network behaves.

Token Ring is described as a ring topology because data is passed from station to station until it returns to the starting point. Data behaves as though it travels around a ring. Token Ring networks always are wired with an individual cable that extends from a central wiring hub to each workstation. Because the wiring system looks like a star, Token Ring has a star logical topology. Similarly, Ethernet always has a logical bus topology even when it is wired in a star using the new and popular 10BASE-T system.

You can see and touch the physical topology of the network. The person who installs the cable and hardware sees the physical topology. You cannot see the logical topology; it is the network from the perspective of how data is sent through the network.

Media Choices

This section briefly reviews common LAN media choices, such as coaxial, twisted pair, and fiber optic, as seen in figure 2.4.

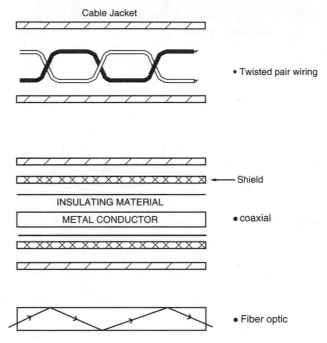

Figure 2.4:
Twisted pair, coaxial, and fiber optic cables.

Coaxial Cable

Coaxial cable consists of an inner conductor (usually made of a copper alloy) that is used for sending a signal. The return signal flows through the shield that is separated from the central conductor by a *dielectric* (electrically insulating material). The shield provides good bandwidth capabilities and electrical noise immunity. This cable type is the "granddaddy" of LAN media because some of the earliest LANs were built using it. Coax cables are typically found in bus LAN topologies.

Twisted Pair Wiring

Twisted pair (TP) wiring consists of a pair of wires wrapped around each other. These wires are twisted to minimize radiation and electrical interference. Twisted pair wiring can have a shield around it to improve its data transmission quality. Both *shielded twisted pair* (STP) and *unshielded twisted pair* (UTP) wiring are available for LANs. One wire is used for sending the signal, and the other wire acts as a signal return. Twisted pair wiring is cheap and easy to install. Many buildings are already pre-wired with data-grade twisted pair wiring.

Shielded Cables

Shielded cables surround the center conductors with a jacket of fine, braided wires. The shield helps prevent outside electrical interference from affecting the conductors and also reduces the risk of broadcasting signals that can interfere with nearby electronic devices. Although shielded cables once were required for nearly all local area network installations, recent developments permit more use of unshielded twisted pair wire, which is similar to that used for telephone communications. Networks can often use telephone wire that is already installed.

Fiber Optic Cable

Fiber optic cables consist of a strand of fiber material, usually glass, inside a protective jacket. Signals are transmitted in the form of reflected light pulses. Signals can propagate over long distances before they need amplification (provided by repeaters). Fiber optic has the best noise immunity characteristics compared to other wiring, is secure because it cannot be tapped easily, and has the best bandwidth characteristics. Today's high-speed LANs use fiber optic media. The end-component costs for fiber optic cables and the required connecting equipment, however, are higher than twisted pair and coaxial cables. Fiber optic cables, therefore, are most commonly used for high-speed connections or in situations requiring long cables or better immunity to electrical interference.

Ethernet LANs

Robert Metcalfe, along with David Boggs and others who worked for Xerox Corporation, developed a LAN based on carrier sensing mechanisms. This LAN spanned a distance of one kilometer, supported 100 personal stations, and achieved data rates of 2.94 Mbps. This system was called Ethernet in honor of that elusive substance called ether through which electromagnetic radiation was once thought to propagate.

Ethernet was proposed as a standard by Digital Equipment Corporation, Intel, and Xerox. The first Ethernet standard was published in September 1981 and was called the DIX 1.0. DIX, stood for **D**igital (DEC), **I**ntel, and **X**erox. DIX 1.0 was followed by DIX 2.0 published in November 1982.

Meanwhile, Project 802 from the IEEE had undertaken LAN standardization efforts. Not surprisingly, Digital, Intel, and Xerox proposed the adoption of Ethernet as a standard. IBM, based on prototypes built at IBM's Zurich Lab, proposed the Token Ring as a standard. The Ethernet proposal became known as the IEEE 802.3 and the Token Ring proposal became the IEEE 802.5.

True to the nature of committee design, the IEEE 802.3 standard is not quite the same as the Ethernet standard; there are important differences. Although 802.3 and Ethernet are incompatible standards, the term *Ethernet* is used in NetWare LANs to designate 802.3-compliant networks. This book bows to common usage and uses the term Ethernet for both standards, making distinctions as required when a specific standard is discussed.

Ethernet Operation

Before an Ethernet station transmits, it listens for activity on the transmission channel (see fig. 2.5). Ethernet frequently is described as a "listen before talking" protocol. *Activity* is any transmission caused by other Ethernet stations. The presence of a transmission is called a *carrier*. The station electronics can sense the presence of a carrier.

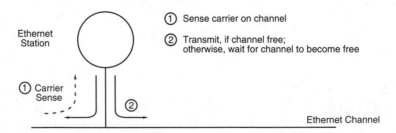

Figure 2.5:
Carrier-sense mechanism in Ethernet.

If a station detects a busy channel, the station refrains from transmission. After the last bit of the passing frame, the Ethernet data link layer continues to wait for a minimum of 9.6 microseconds to provide proper interframe spacing. At the end of this time, if a data frame is waiting for transmission, and the channel is free, transmission is initiated. If the station has no data to transmit, it resumes the carrier sense (listening for a carrier) operation. The interframe gap provides recovery time for other Ethernet stations.

If a station tried to transmit when the channel is busy, a garbled transmission would result. Garbled transmissions are called *collisions*.

If the channel is free (no carrier detected), the station is free to transmit. Because multiple stations attached to the Ethernet channel use the carrier-sense mechanism, it is called a *Carrier Sense with Multiple Access* (CSMA).

What if two stations decide to transmit at the same time and there was no activity on the channel? A collision would occur. Collisions occur during the normal operation of Ethernet LANs because stations transmit based only on one fact: the presence of a carrier on the channel. They do not know if packets are queued for transmission on other stations. Furthermore, the CSMA operation is complicated by the fact of propagation delay in LANs. In Ethernet, for example, signals propagate at 0.77 times the speed of light for standard (thick) cables and 0.65 times the speed of light on thin Ethernet cables. A delay occurs before a transmission is heard by all stations, and a station may transmit because it has yet to hear another station's transmission.

Collisions are a fact of life in Ethernet LANs. Ethernet stations minimize the effects of collision by detecting the collisions as they occur. Hence the name CSMA/CD to describe the Ethernet media access mechanism (CD stands for *Collision Detect*). The stations involved in the collision abort their transmissions. The first station to detect the collision sends out a special jamming pulse to alert all stations that a collision has taken place. After a collision occurs, all stations set up a random interval timer. Transmission takes place only after this interval timer expires. Introducing a delay before transmission can reduce the probability of collisions.

What happens when successive collisions occur? The average random time out value is doubled. This doubling takes place up to 10 consecutive collisions. Beyond that, doubling the average random time out value does not improve the performance of the network significantly. This mechanism is called the truncated binary exponential back-off algorithm.

How long does a station have to wait under heavy load conditions to transmit a frame? A station may experience a string of bad luck during which every time it transmits some other station has the bus. When collisions occur, stations introduce a delay using the random timer. But what if a station has the misfortune of timing out after the other stations have already timed out? Under the worst-case scenario, a station may have to wait indefinitely. This is not acceptable for real time applications. Hence Ethernet is not suited for real-time applications.

The next section examines different Ethernet options.

Ethernet Cable Options

Coaxial cable serves as the medium for two variations of Ethernet: the Standard Ethernet and the Thin Ethernet. A newer Ethernet version (called the 10BASE-T standard) also can run on UTP wiring. These options are shown in figure 2.6.

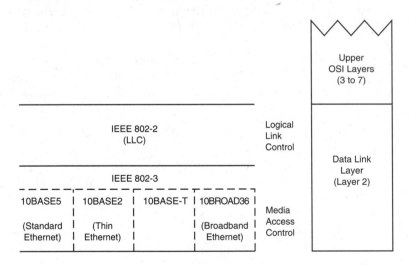

Figure 2.6:
IEEE options for 802.3 Ethernet.

Although the packet structure for Ethernet and IEEE 802.3 differ, many vendors now manufacture cards that can operate in both modes by changing the network driver setting. In NetWare, for example, you can configure the workstation and server software to operate an NE2000 or SMC (previously Western Digital) network card with the Ethernet packet structure or IEEE 802.3 packet structure.

Under most circumstances, standard Ethernet devices can coexist on a network with devices using the 802.3 standard. The two devices, however, cannot exchange data.

Standard Ethernet Wiring Rules

Another name for Standard Ethernet is Thick Wire Ethernet because the co-axial cable it uses is much thicker than that used for Thin Wire Ethernet. The IEEE version of standard Ethernet is called 10BASE5. The 10 stands for 10 Mbps operation; the BASE stands for baseband operation; and the 5 stands for 500 meters per segment.

Figure 2.7 shows some standard Ethernet components. The network board or NIC shown in this figure has a DIX connector socket and a coaxial connection. The coaxial connection is used to connect to Thin Wire Ethernet. This particular card can be used with both Thick/Thin Wire Ethernet.

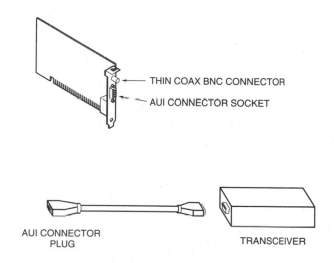

Figure 2.7:
Thick Ethernet network cable and hardware.

Stations on Thick Ethernet communicate to the external network through external transceivers attached to the shared media. The shared media is called the *trunk segment cable* or just segment. Because of signal attenuation, a segment cannot be longer than 500 meters.

The external transceiver and the NIC are connected by a transceiver cable. The DIX connector plug mates with the DIX connector socket on the NIC. A slide lock is used to secure this connection. The other end of the transceiver fits into a connector on the external transceiver.

Figure 2.8 shows the Thick Ethernet cable used to make up the trunk segments. Thick Ethernet cable is a 0.4-inch diameter, 50-ohm cable and is available in various precut lengths with an N-series connector plug attached to each end. You also can purchase Thick Ethernet cable in spools or bulk quantities. These come without the N-series connectors attached at the ends.

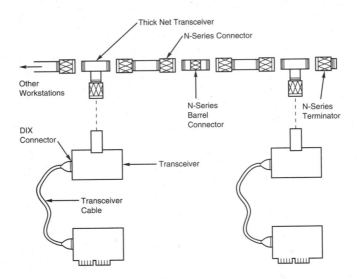

Figure 2.8:
Thick Ethernet Coaxial Cable Connectors.

Figure 2.8 also shows the N-series *barrel connector* that can be used to join two lengths of Ethernet cable. A trunk segment must be terminated with an N-series *terminator*. The N-series terminator is a 50-ohm resistor that blocks electrical interference on the segment. Additionally, it cancels out any signal reflections caused by signals reaching the end of the cable. The N-series terminator is attached to the male N-series terminator on the end of the segment. N-series terminators come with a grounding wire. One end of the cable must be grounded; the other end must remain ungrounded to avoid *ground-loop* currents.

Figure 2.9 shows an example of a Thick Ethernet network. Two trunk segments are joined together by a device called a repeater in Thick Ethernet networks. A *repeater* is an active device that allows an Ethernet LAN to expand beyond a single segment by linking two segments together. The repeater amplifies and regenerates the signal so the signal can be transmitted over longer distances. A multi-port repeater such as a DEMPR (Digital Equipment's multi-port repeater) can link a number of Ethernet segments together.

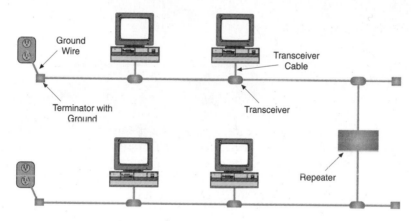

Figure 2.9:
Example of a Thick Ethernet network.

Table 2.2 describes the rules you must follow with Thick Ethernet wiring.

Table 2.2
Thick Ethernet Parameters and Wiring Rules

Thick Ethernet Parameters	Value
Max data rate	10 Mbps
Max repeaters without IRLs	2
Max repeaters with IRLs	4
Max coaxial segment length	500 meters

continues

Table 2.2
Continued

Thick Ethernet Parameters	Value
Max transceiver cable length	50 meters
Max number of link segments	2
Max combined link segment length	1000 meters
Max stations per segment	100
Max number of stations	1024
Distance between stations	Multiples of 2.5M

To travel from one station to another station on an Ethernet LAN that consists of coaxial trunk segments only (see fig. 2.10), a signal cannot travel through more than two full repeaters. A full repeater joins two coaxial segments together directly. A coaxial segment is distinct from a link segment. A link segment made of fiber optic or twisted pair cable can be used to join two coaxial segments over a longer distance. The purpose of a link segment is to extend the range of an Ethernet LAN. You can have a maximum of two link segments on an Ethernet LAN. Link segments do not have stations attached to them and are connected to coaxial segments by repeaters. Another name for them is *Inter-Repeater Link-segment* (IRL).

A half-repeater joins a coaxial segment to a link segment. Another name for a half-repeater is a remote repeater. The trunk coaxial segment length cannot exceed 500 meters. The combined lengths of the two link segments cannot exceed 1000 meters. Using these wiring parameters, you can deduce the maximum length of an Ethernet LAN.

Figure 2.11 illustrates the longest possible Ethernet. T1 through T6 represent transceivers. Using this diagram, you can calculate the length of this network:

Coax Segment 1 length	500 M
Coax Segment 2 length	500 M
Coax Segment 3 length	500 M
Combined Link Segment 1 and 2 length	1000 M
Total Ethernet Length	2500 M

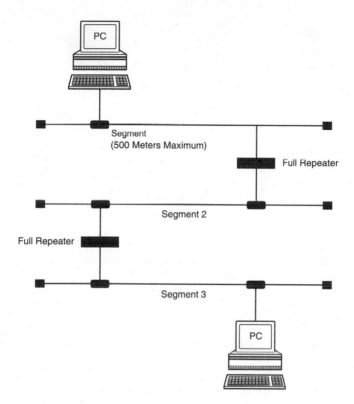

Figure 2.10:
The longest possible Thick Ethernet.

Some people cheat and add the transceiver cable lengths to transceivers T1, T2, T3, T4, T5, and T6 in figure 2.11. Because the maximum transceiver cable length is 50 meters, this gives a combined transceiver length of 300 meters. The calculations below show how to arrive at this number:

Transceiver cable length of transceiver T1	50 M
Transceiver cable length of transceiver T2	50 M
Transceiver cable length of transceiver T3	50 M
Transceiver cable length of transceiver T4	50 M
Transceiver cable length of transceiver T5	50 M
Transceiver cable length of transceiver T6	50 M
Combined transceiver cable length	300 M

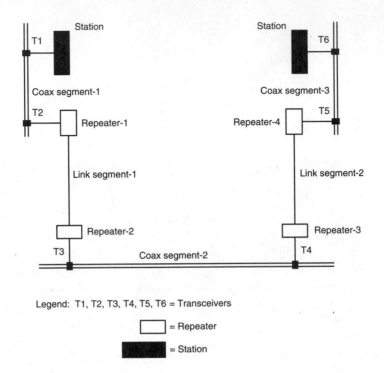

Legend: T1, T2, T3, T4, T5, T6 = Transceivers

☐ = Repeater

■ = Station

Figure 2.11:
Longest Ethernet possible.

By cheating a little, the maximum Ethernet length is 2500 meters plus 300 meters, which is 2800 meters.

The maximum number of stations that you can attach to a Thick Ethernet segment is 100, and the total number of stations cannot exceed 1024. The repeater attachment to a segment counts as one station. The minimum distance between any two stations is 2.5 meters. It is recommended that you separate stations at distances of multiples of 2.5 meters to minimize interference caused by standing waves on an Ethernet segment. *Standing waves* are formed by the presence of electrical signals on the segment.

Thin Wire Ethernet Wiring Design Rules

Other names for Thin Wire Ethernet are *Thinnet* and also *Cheapernet* (because it is cheaper than Standard Ethernet). The coaxial cable it uses is much thinner than that used for Thick Wire Ethernet. The IEEE version of Thin Wire Ethernet is called *10BASE2*. The 10 stands for 10 Mbps operation; the BASE stands for baseband operation; and the 2 stands for approximately 200 meters (actually, 185 meters) per segment.

Figure 2.12 shows some of the Thin Wire Ethernet components. The network board or NIC, in this figure, has a coaxial connection.

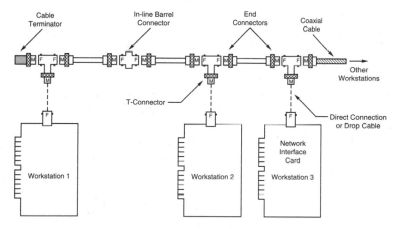

Figure 2.12:
Thin Ethernet components.

The transceiver functions for a Thin Wire Ethernet are performed by the on-board NIC electronics. No external transceiver connections are made to the NIC. BNC T-connectors are used to connect the NIC with the cable. The two opposing jacks of the T-connector are used to join two lengths of Thin Wire Ethernet cable. The remaining plug is attached to the BNC connector jack on the NIC.

The shared media is called the trunk segment cable or just segment. Due to signal attenuation, a thin wire segment cannot be longer than 185 meters. Thin Ethernet cable has a 0.2-inch diameter and RG-58 A/U 50-ohm cable, and is available in various precut lengths with a standard BNC plug attached to each end. Thin Ethernet cable also can be purchased in spools or bulk quantities that come without the BNC connectors attached at the ends.

You also can use the BNC barrel connector to join two lengths of Ethernet cable. A trunk segment must be terminated with a BNC terminator. The BNC terminator is a 50-ohm resistor that blocks electrical interference on the segment. Additionally, it cancels out any signal reflections caused by signals bouncing off the end of the cable. The BNC terminator is attached to one of the two jacks on a T-connector to which no cable is attached. There is a grounded BNC terminator that has a grounding wire. One end of the cable must be grounded; the other end must remain ungrounded to avoid ground loop current.

Figure 2.13 shows an example of a Thin Ethernet network. In this network, there are two trunk segments that are joined together by a repeater. The repeater in figure 2.13 has two ports to attach a maximum of two segments.

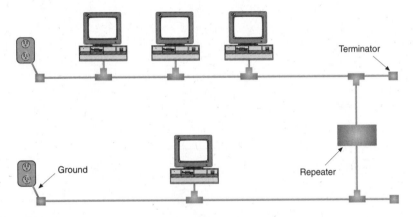

Figure 2.13:
Example of a Thin Ethernet network.

There are a number of rules related to Thin Ethernet wiring. These are summarized in table 2.3.

Table 2.3
Thin Ethernet Parameters and Wiring Rules

Thin Ethernet Parameters	Value
Max data rate	10 Mbps
Max repeaters without IRLs	2

Thin Ethernet Parameters	Value
Max repeaters with IRLs	4
Max coaxial segment length	185 meters
Max number of link segments	2
Max stations per segment	30
Max number of stations	1024
Min distance between stations	0.5 M

The repeater rules for Thin Ethernet are the same as for Thick Ethernet.

The trunk coaxial segment length for Thin Ethernet cannot exceed 185 meters. The maximum number of stations that can be attached to a Thin Ethernet segment is 30, and the total number of stations cannot exceed 1024. The repeater attachment to a segment counts as one station. The minimum distance between any two stations is 0.5 meters.

10BASE-T Wiring Design Rules

An increase in interest for 10BASE-T began in 1990 due to the lower cost components and ease of configuring networks based in UTP wiring. The 10 stands for 10 Mbps operation; the BASE stands for baseband operation; and the T stands for twisted pair wiring.

In figure 2.14, the NIC has a telephone-type RJ-45 port, which is officially called a *Media Dependent Interface* (MDI) port. The NIC shown in the figure also has a DIX connector. The DIX connector is used to connect by means of a transceiver to Thick Wire Ethernet. This particular card can be used with both 10BASE-T and Thick Ethernet. Many NICs require a switch setting to enable either the 10BASE-T or DIX port, whereas others like the SMC Elite16T card have an auto-sense mechanism.

The transceiver functions for a 10BASE-T are performed by the onboard NIC electronics.

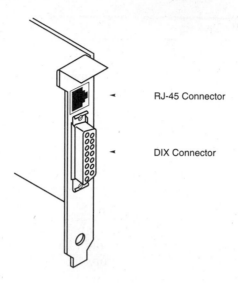

RJ-45 Connector

DIX Connector

Figure 2.14:
Connectors on a 10BASE-T network adapter card.

The 10BASE-T uses a physical star topology with the 10BASE-T concentrator serving as the central switching element. The 10BASE-T plug and connector are shown in figure 2.15. Each concentrator accepts cables to several workstations, usually twelve. UTP wiring is used to connect a 10BASE-T concentrator to the workstation. This wiring normally consists of 0.4 to 0.6 mm diameter (26 to 22 AWG) unshielded wire in a multipair cable. The performance specifications are generally met by 100 meters of 0.5 mm telephone twisted pair.

There are two twisted pairs (four wires) between each NIC and the concentrator, as shown in figure 2.16. Each two-wire path forms a simplex link segment. One simplex segment is used for transmitting and the other for receiving. Table 2.4 shows the pin assignments for a 4-pair twisted pair wiring. Only two pairs, one for transmission (TD) and another for receiving (RD), are used.

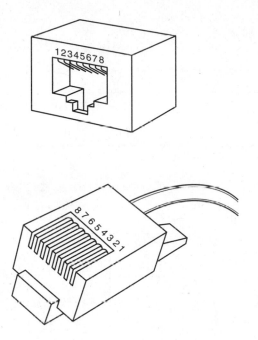

Figure 2.15:
10BASE-T plug and connector. (Source: IEEE Standard 802.3i-1990)

Table 2.4
Pin Assignments for the MDI Connector

Contact	MDI signal
1	TD+
2	TD−
3	RD+
4	Not used by 10BASE-T
5	Not used by 10BASE-T
6	RD−

continues

Table 2.4
Continued

Contact	MDI signal
7	Not used by 10BASE-T
8	Not used by 10BASE-T

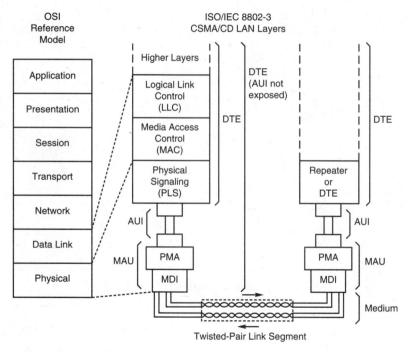

PMA = Physical Media Attachment
MDI = Media Dependent Interface

Figure 2.16:
Simplex segments used in 10BASE-T. (Source: IEEE Standard 802.3i-1990)

A crossover function is implemented in every twisted pair link so that the transmitter at one end will be connected to the receiver at the other. Figure 2.17 shows the two ways of implementing crossover functions. One way to do this is to use an external crossover UTP cable that reverses the transmit and receive pairs at the RJ-45 connector at one end of the UTP cable. A second way is an internal crossover function in which the crossover is designed as part of the internal circuitry in the 10BASE-T device. An MDI port with this function is marked with the symbol "X."

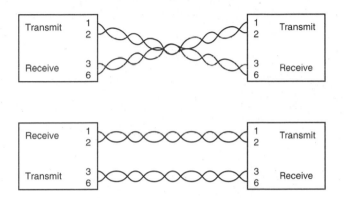

Figure 2.17:
10BASE-T crossover wiring.

Figure 2.18 shows a single concentrator 10BASE-T network. The concentrator has 12 RJ-45 ports. If the station's NIC has a 10BASE-T (RJ-45) connector, the connections can be made directly through UTP cable. For stations with 10BASE5 network boards, a 10BASE-T MAU (10BASE-T transceiver) is needed to connect the AUI cable to the station.

The 10BASE-T concentrator serves the role of a repeater. It performs the following functions:

■ Data packet retiming (IEEE 802.3 standard)

■ Per-port Link Integrity Test ("Good Link Test")

■ Per-port autopartitioning, which disconnects the port in the event of 30 consecutive collisions, an excessively long single collision, or jabber input

The proper operation of the CSMA/CD 10BASE-T network requires network size to be limited to control round-trip propagation delays (the time it takes a signal to reach extremity of network and come back). The configuration rules for more than one concentrator are as follows:

■ Maximum of four concentrators in the data path between any two stations

■ UTP segments should be no longer than 100 meters

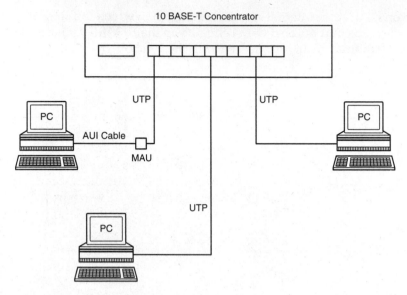

Figure 2.18:
A single concentrator 10BASE-T network.

UTP Wiring Considerations

Use of UTP wiring for data communications has come a long way from its initial use of transmitting analog voice signals to its use in 10BASE-T and *CDDI* (Copper Distributed Data Interface), which is a variation of the FDDI LAN that runs at 100 Mbps. More recently there has been a rise of interest in the use of UTP for a 100 Mbps version of Ethernet called 100BASE-T.

Although using UTP for LAN wiring needs can simplify installation and reduce wiring costs, it can, if not done properly, do just the opposite: complicate installations and increase maintenance costs. The factors to consider for an effective UTP installation are discussed next.

The lack of a shield in UTP makes it cheaper than other types of wiring and also easier to install because it is more flexible than the shielded twisted pair wiring. However, because it is unshielded, UTP can become a good antenna and susceptible to *Electro-Magnetic Interference* (EMI) and *Radio-Frequency Interference* (RFI). At such frequencies as 10 to 100 Mbps, UTP wiring results in loss of signal due to attenuation. Inductance and capacitance effects also become dominant at these high frequencies. The inductance is caused by the electromagnetic field that surrounds the UTP wire when the high-frequency signals pass through it. It can be likened to the transformer effect that induces a voltage on the secondary of the transformer due to electromagnetic coupling. The capacitance effect is caused because the conductors that make up the twisted pair wire are separated by an insulating material. These effects reduce the quality of the signal and limit the distance that can be used between devices connected by UTP. The twists that are used in twisted pair wiring help reduce inductance by creating a magnetic field that essentially cancels out inductance. For this reason, an important parameter in measuring the quality of a cable is the twists per inch of the wire. This can reduce the amount of *cross-talk,* which is the inductive coupling to other pairs of wires or noise sources. Cross-talk can lead to signal distortion (often called *jitter*) and, in the case of Ethernet networks, can be mistaken for collisions, which could degrade the network performance. In Token Ring networks, cross-talk can generate hard errors that can cause the Token Ring networks to go through reconfigurations. Reconfigurations are time-consuming and result in slow networks.

Flat silver satin wire, which works just fine in low-speed data networks such as 19.2 Kbps, has zero twists per inch. This type of cabling is common in telephone networks; however, if voice telephone cable is used in data networks that operate in the Mbps range, it can result in disaster. Besides causing the network to fail, it can create a great deal of EMI noise that can cause other devices to fail also.

The signal that is used in both Ethernet and Token Ring networks is a baseband signal. *Baseband signals* are digital signals that have sharp edges. The capacitance effect in a wire causes the signal to lose some of its sharpness so that it becomes rounded. The resistance effect causes the signal to lose its strength (attenuation). The inductance and capacitance effect can make the signal vulnerable to external noise sources to the point that the signal can be completely distorted. Figure 2.19 illustrates these effects.

Another factor to consider is that signals with sharp edges or rapidly changing signals result in high-frequency harmonics. Mathematically speaking, the *ds/dt*—the rate at which the signal changes—is high for the edges of the baseband signal. If the signal is periodic, it can be expressed as the sum of sine wave harmonics of the fundamental frequency of the signal, in which the sine wave may have different phase (starting point) differences. This means that a 20 Mbps signal is really not just a 20 Mbps signal, but a sine wave with 20 MHz fundamental frequency and harmonic components of 40 MHz, 60 MHz, 80 MHz, 100 MHz, 120 MHz, and so on. The higher harmonics are smaller in magnitude. What this means in practical terms is that the cable must be able to carry the higher harmonic components of the data signal. If it does not do this well, the signal can become distorted.

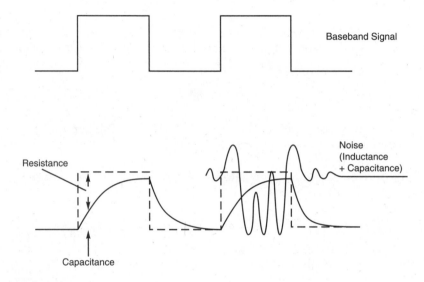

Figure 2.19:
Signal distortion and noise in cables.

Some of these factors can be mitigated by using high-quality twisted pair wiring. The characteristics of cables can be defined in terms of attenuation which is measured in decibels per 100 feet. Decibels is a logarithmic scale (to the base 10) for comparing power levels. It is defined as:

log (P2/P1)

P2 = Power at output

P1 = Power applied at input

LAN designers specify maximum distance lengths for cable segments based on attenuation characteristics of the cable medium for the frequency of data transmission. For this reason, 10BASE-T networks have a limit of 100 meters between station and wiring concentrator.

The following examples of twisted pair wiring meet the requirements for Token Ring and Ethernet installations:

- AT&T DIW 24/4
- AT&T PDS Systimax 2061
- EIA/TIA 568 Type 3, Level 3, Category 3
- Bell System 48007
- NT BDN 24 AWG

The type of sheath used to enclose the twisted pair wire affects its plenum rating. *Plenum rating* determines whether or not the cable must be encased in a conduit for fire resistance as required by some building codes. PVC (polyvinyl chloride) is the most common coating used and is not fire resistant. Another type of cable coating called *TFEP* (teflon fluorinated ethylene propylene) is rated as fire resistant. It also has a lower dielectric constant. The lower the dielectric constant, the lower the capacitance, and, therefore, the lower the signal distortion. Because of these characteristics, TFEP-coated wire can transmit the signal over longer distances with less signal distortion compared to PVC-coated wires.

In telephone networks, it is common to use a punch-down block called the 66 Block. Whereas this type of punch-down block works fine for telephone networks, it is not designed to carry data. For data networks that need to carry data in the Mbps range, you must use punch-down blocks specifically designed for data. These include punch-down blocks known as the 110s, 3m 7000D, and Krone. Data grade punch-down blocks include gold-plated or silver-plated contact points, labeling, and so forth. Data-grade patch panels also are available. Some of their features are cross-connect circuits etched on the wafer board itself. These patch panels can carry high-frequency signals in a manner similar to printed circuit boards.

Mixed Media Ethernet Networks

You can combine the different media (coaxial, twisted pair, and fiber) into one Ethernet LAN. If you combine mixed media networks, use a fiber optic, twisted pair, or coaxial cable to implement the link segment. Figures 2.20 and 2.21 show examples of mixed media networks.

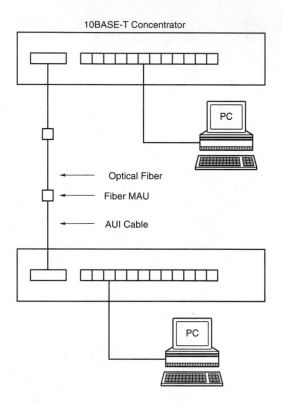

Figure 2.20:
An 802.3 network using fiber optic cable.

Table 2.5 summarizes the maximum delays of the various media segments. This table is important for the LAN manager because Ethernet segments can be built by combining cables from different vendors, each of which may differ from the specifications by small amounts. Test equipment like *Time Domain Reflectometers* (TDRs) can be used to see that the delays are within the specifications.

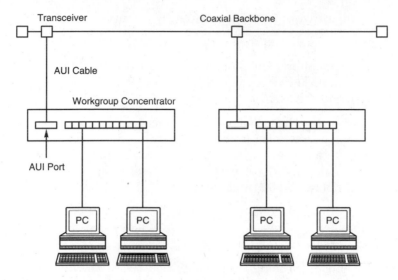

Figure 2.21:
An 802.3 network incorporating a coaxial backbone.

Table 2.5
Maximum Delays for Ethernet Media

Media Segment Type	Max MAUs per Segment	Max Segment Length (meters)	Min Propagation Velocity (ns)	Max Delay per Segment
Coaxial Segment				
10BASE5	100	500	0.77c	2165
10BASE2	30	185	0.65c	950
Link Segment				
FOIRL	2	1000	0.66c	5000
10BASE-T	2	100	0.59c	1000
AUI (Transceiver Cable)				
AUI	DTE/1 MAU	50	0.65c	257

c = 300,000,000 meters/sec (Velocity of light in vacuum)
FOIRL = Fiber Optic Inter Repeater Link

The following network topology rules apply for mixed media networks:

1. Repeater sets are required for all segment interconnections.

2. The maximum transmission path between any two stations may consist of up to five segments, four repeater sets (including optional AUIs), and two MAUs.

3. If a network path consists of five segments and four repeaters sets, up to three segments may be coaxial trunks and the remainder must be link segments. If five segments are present and *Fiber Optic Inter-Repeater Link* (FOIRL) is used as the link segment, the link segment should not exceed 500 meters.

4. If a network path consists of four segments and three repeater sets, the maximum allowable length of the FOIRL segments is 1000 meters each.

Rule two is illustrated in figure 2.22. Notice that this rule does not tell us how many segments are coaxial trunks with multiple station attachments and how many are link segments with no station attachments. Rule 3 clarifies this problem.

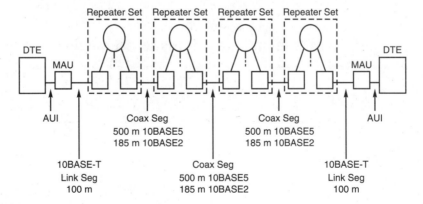

Figure 2.22:
Maximum Ethernet transmission path with three coaxial segments. (Source: IEEE Std 802.3i-1990)

Rule three is illustrated in figure 2.23. This figure shows a multimedia Ethernet network. The media used in this network is a combination of coaxial, fiber, and twisted pair. Notice in figure 2.23 that there are 5 repeater sets. This may at first glance seem to contradict the rule of a maximum of 4 repeater sets, but between any two stations, there are no more than 4 repeaters in the transmission path. There is a total of 10 segments: 7 twisted pair, 2 fiber optic, and 1 coaxial. However, there are no more than 5 segments between any two stations. Also, there is a maximum of 1 coaxial segment, which is within the maximum 3 coaxial segment rule. When the coaxial segment is included in the transmission path, the remaining 4 segments are link segments: 3 twisted pair and 1 fiber optic link segment. Because there are a maximum of 5 segments and 4 repeaters in the transmission path, the maximum FOIRL length is 500 meters. This follows from Rule three. The maximum span of this network is 1300 meters, not including AUI drops.

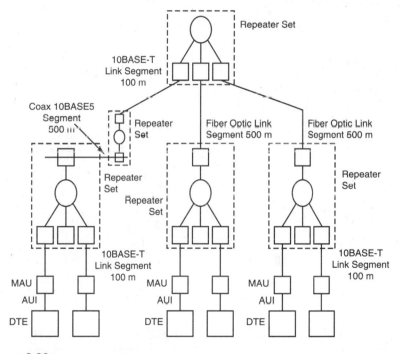

Figure 2.23:
Maximum transmission path using 802.3 coaxial segments, 10BASE-T link segments, and fiber optic link segments. (Source: IEEE Standard 802.3i-1990)

Rule four is illustrated in figure 2.24. There are 3 repeater sets and 6 segments: 4 twisted pair and 2 fiber optic. There are no coaxial segments in this figure. Between any two stations, there is a maximum of 4 segments and 3 repeaters. The 4 segments consist of 2 fiber optic and 2 twisted pair cables. Each of the FOIRL links has a maximum length of 1000 meters. The maximum span of this network is 2200 meters, not including AUI drops.

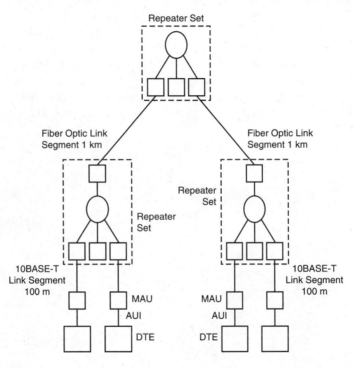

Figure 2.24:
Maximum transmission path with three repeater sets and four link segments. (Source: IEEE Standard 802.3i-1990)

Combining Thin/Thick Cable in a Segment

You can combine thin and thick Ethernet cable in a single segment by using as much thin cable as possible. Thin cable is cheaper and easier to install than thick cable. Figure 2.25 illustrates a network layout using segments made up of a combination of thin and thick cable.

Combined thin/thick cable are between 185 meters and 500 meters long. The minimum length is 185 meters because coaxial segments shorter than 185 meters can be built with thin cable exclusively. The maximum of 500 meters is the limit for a segment made out of thick coaxial exclusively.

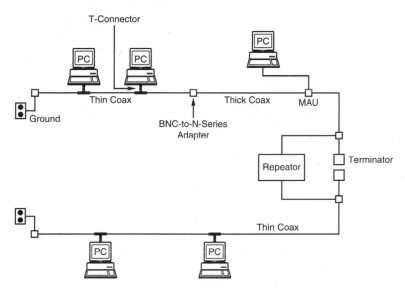

Figure 2.25:
Combining Thick and Thin coaxial Ethernet.

To compute the maximum amount of thin cable you can use in one combination trunk segment, use the following equation:

thinLen = (500-trunkLen)/3.28 meters

trunkLen = Length of trunk segment you want to build and thinLen = Maximum length of thin length cable you can use.

If you want to build a trunk segment of 400 meters, for example, the maximum length of thin coaxial cable you can use is

thinLen = (500–400)/3.28 = 30.48 meters

You can use 30.48 meters of thin coaxial with 400–30.48 = 369.52 meters of thick cable. Thin and thick coaxial cable must be connected by means of an N-series to a BNC jack.

IEEE 802.3 versus Ethernet-II (DIX 2.0)

Both Ethernet-II and IEEE 802.3 have a minimum frame size of 64 bytes and a maximum frame size of 1518 bytes. The next section examines their respective frame structures.

Ethernet-II

The Ethernet frame (see fig. 2.26) begins with a preamble of eight octets (one octet = eight bits) consisting of an alternating pattern 1010 that ends in 101011. At 10 Mbps, this preamble is of 6.4 microsecond duration and is sufficient time for the receiving station to synchronize and get ready to receive the frame.

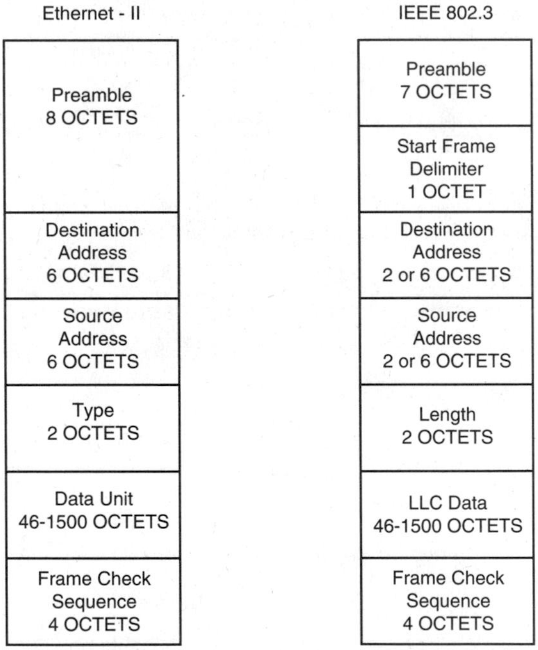

```
        Ethernet - II                         IEEE 802.3

     ┌──────────────────┐              ┌──────────────────┐
     │                  │              │     Preamble     │
     │                  │              │     7 OCTETS     │
     │    Preamble      │              ├──────────────────┤
     │    8 OCTETS      │              │   Start Frame    │
     │                  │              │    Delimiter     │
     │                  │              │     1 OCTET      │
     ├──────────────────┤              ├──────────────────┤
     │   Destination    │              │   Destination    │
     │    Address       │              │    Address       │
     │   6 OCTETS       │              │  2 or 6 OCTETS   │
     ├──────────────────┤              ├──────────────────┤
     │     Source       │              │     Source       │
     │    Address       │              │    Address       │
     │   6 OCTETS       │              │  2 or 6 OCTETS   │
     ├──────────────────┤              ├──────────────────┤
     │      Type        │              │     Length       │
     │    2 OCTETS      │              │    2 OCTETS      │
     ├──────────────────┤              ├──────────────────┤
     │    Data Unit     │              │    LLC Data      │
     │ 46-1500 OCTETS   │              │ 46-1500 OCTETS   │
     ├──────────────────┤              ├──────────────────┤
     │  Frame Check     │              │  Frame Check     │
     │   Sequence       │              │   Sequence       │
     │   4 OCTETS       │              │   4 OCTETS       │
     └──────────────────┘              └──────────────────┘
```

Figure 2.26:
Comparison of Ethernet II and 802.3 frame structures.

The *Destination Address* (DA) and the *Source Address* (SA) field follow this preamble. Each address field is six octets long. The first three octets represent a manufacturer's code and the remaining three octets are assigned by the manufacturer. This assignation is made so that an Ethernet card will have a unique six-octet address. This address is usually burned into a ROM chip on the Ethernet card. The *least significant bit* (LSB) of the first octet is the Physical/Multicast bit. It is 0 for an Ethernet address. A value of 1 for this LSB indicates a multi-cast address. For instance, a hex value of FFFFFFFFFFFF, all 1s, for the DA field represents a broadcast. The manufacturer's code was formerly assigned by Xerox; it is now assigned by IEEE.

The Type field, also referred to as Ethertype, is a two-octet field used to indicate the type of data in the data field. Thus, if the Ethernet frame is used to carry NetWare data, the Ethertype value will be 8137 hex. If it is used to carry DoD *Internet Packet* (IP) data, it will have the value 0800 hex. XNS packets used in 3COM networks will have the value 0600hex. This field is used by network drivers or the network layer to demultiplex data packets to the appropriate protocol stack. It allows multiple protocol stacks to run on a single Ethernet card.

The Data Unit field is a variable length field that can range from 46 to 1500 octets. The remaining fixed length fields add up to 18 bytes.

The FCS field is generated by the Ethernet hardware at the end of the data field and is a 32-bit *Cyclic Redundancy Checksum* (CRC) over the address, type, and data fields. It is used to detect errors in transmission. Bad frames are retransmitted.

IEEE 802.3

The IEEE frame shown in figure 2.26 begins with a preamble of seven octets (one octet = eight bits) consisting of an alternating pattern 1010. At 10 Mbps, this preamble is of 5.6 microseconds' duration, and this is sufficient time for the receiving station to synchronize and get ready to receive the frame.

The *Start Frame Delimiter* (SFD) follows after the preamble and is defined by the pattern 10101011. Note that

> IEEE 802.3 preamble + SFD = Ethernet preamble

The IEEE 802.3 preamble and the SFD field combined are identical to the eight octet Ethernet preamble.

The DA and the SA fields follow the SFD. Each address field can be six octets or two octets long. The six-octet addressing is the most common. The first three octets represent a manufacturer's code and the remaining octets are assigned by the manufacturer. This assignation is made so that any two Ethernet and IEEE cards will have a unique six-octet address. This address is usually burned into a ROM chip on the IEEE 802.3 card. The LSB of the first octet represents the Individual/Group field and is similar to the Physical/Multicast field in Ethernet. The next bit is the *Universe/Local* (U/L) field and indicates if the addressing is global or local.

The Length field follows the address fields and is two octets long. It indicates the data size of the LLC layer. A minimum of 46 octets of LLC is required to make up the minimum size of 64 octets. The maximum value of this field is 1500 to make a maximum frame size of 1518 octets.

The Data Unit field is a variable length field containing 46 to 1500 octets of LLC data.

The FCS field is generated by the IEEE 802.3 hardware at the end of the Data field and is a 32-bit *Cyclic Redundancy Checksum* (CRC) over the Address, Type, and Data fields. It is used to detect errors in transmission. Bad frames are retransmitted.

Differences between Ethernet-II and IEEE 802.3

There are differences between Ethernet-II and IEEE 802.3. You can see that Ethernet-II uses a two-byte Type field to indicate the type of data. The Type field values were at one time assigned by Xerox; they are now assigned by IEEE. Instead of the Type field, IEEE 802.3 has a two-byte Length field. The Length field for Ethernet Packets is supplied by a higher layer. In some cases, the NIC can determine the length of the frame based on signal duration and passes this information to upper layers. For IEEE 802.3 frames, the type information is supplied by the IEEE 802.2 (Logical Control Layer) frame that is part of the Data Unit field. The LLC frame type format is illustrated in figure 2.27.

For example, a hex code of E0 indicates a NetWare packet. A hex code of A0 is reserved to transmit upper layer packets that were generated by non-IEEE LANs. This is referred to as the *Sub Net Access Protocol* (SNAP) mechanism. A complete description of SNAP can be found in RFC-1042 obtainable from Stanford Research Institute, Network Information Systems Center, 333 Ravenswood Ave., Menlo Park, CA 94025, (415) 859-6387. This discussion is beyond the scope of this book.

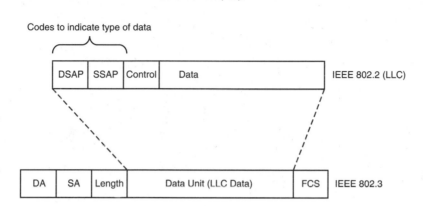

Figure 2.27:
"Type" information in IEEE 802.3.

Ethernet has no provision to pad the data to make a minimum Ethernet frame of 64 bytes. IEEE 802.3 frames have a Length field to encode the pad information. In Ethernet, the padding has to be performed by upper layers.

Incompatibility between LattisNet UTP and 10BASE-T

Before 10BASE-T became an official standard, a number of vendors jumped the gun and announced the 10BASE-T-compliant network cards and concentrators. These older cards are not compliant with the 10BASE-T cards. These cards include the popular Western Digital 8003 EtherCard PLUS series. The reasons for incompatibility follow:

■ Voltage levels for old cards are 2 V peak-to-peak. The new cards have 5 V peak-to-peak.

■ Low DC current was used in old cards to indicate link integrity. The new cards use a "good link beat" message.

■ Jabber detection was done at the concentrator for old cards. The new cards perform this at the concentrator and the transceiver.

- Equalization of signal timing was done after packet reception in new cards. The new cards do this after packet transmission.

- The noise squelch is done differently in the two cards.

One way of integrating the older cards with 10BASE-T is to use the Intellicom Model 312M concentrator. The Intellicom Model 312M has an RS-232 management port that can be used to connect to a terminal or a PC running terminal emulation software (such as PROCOMM+). Using the terminal, you can program each of the 12 individual ports in the Intellicom 312M to be compatible with the older UTP cards or 10BASE-T cards.

Token Ring LANs

Ring-based networks have been around for many years. Ring LANs are a concatenation of point-to-point links, and as such are not really a broadcast LAN like Ethernet. They may be considered to be sequential broadcast LANs with the point-to-point links forming a circle. The technology of ring LANs is digital unlike that of Ethernet LANs where the carrier sense mechanism may be analog. Another attractive feature of ring-based LANs is its deterministic response time even under heavy load conditions.

The Token Ring LAN you encounter most often is the IEEE 802.5. This LAN is often referred to as the IBM Token Ring because IBM was the prime mover behind the IEEE 802.5 standard.

Token Ring Operation

Figure 2.28 illustrates Token Ring operation. The Token Ring LAN can be seen as a concatenation of point-to-point links. Each station acts like a repeater providing the necessary amplification and correcting for signal jitter. The links can be made up of any medium such as coaxial, twisted pair, and fiber optic. For the IBM Token Ring, twisted pair is the medium of choice. Fiber optic links can be used to extend Token Ring operation over longer distances.

For proper operation of the ring, the token must circulate continuously even if there is no activity on the ring. There are 24 bits (three octets) in the token, and the ring must have enough latency or delay to hold 24 bits. If the bit rate on the ring is 4 Mbps, the ring must have a latency of 24/4 Mbps = 6 microseconds. Six microseconds may seem like a very short delay, but consider a twisted pair medium where the propagation velocity is 0.59 times the speed of light. To compute the size of the ring that will have a latency of 6 microseconds, use this formula:

Size of Ring = Latency × Propagation speed of media

= 0.0000006 × 0.59 × 3 × 100,000,000 meters

= 1062 meters

= 1.062 km

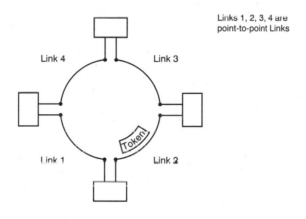

Links 1, 2, 3, 4 are point-to-point Links

Link 4   Link 3

Link 1   Link 2

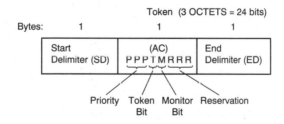

Token (3 OCTETS = 24 bits)

Bytes:	1	1	1
	Start Delimiter (SD)	(AC) P P P T M R R R	End Delimiter (ED)

Priority Token Monitor Reservation
          Bit   Bit

Figure 2.28:
Token Ring operation.

Thus the minimum size of the ring would be 1 km! This size is enormous, considering that you may want to install a few stations in a single room. For this reason, a special station designated as the Active Monitor adds a 24-bit delay buffer to the ring. This buffer also compensates for any accumulated phase jitter on the ring. The Active Monitor is important for maintaining normal operation of the ring.

Under normal operation of the ring, stations may be powered down. What happens to the bits that need to go across an inactive station? Token Ring networks are wired as star networks with a hub or wiring center. Each station's connection is controlled by a relay in the hub. In figure 2.29 the relays are held open by power from the station. When a station is powered down, the relay closes, bypassing the inactive station.

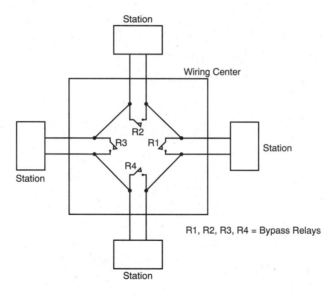

Figure 2.29:
Token Ring relay bypass mechanism.

As illustrated by figure 2.30, a token ring station operates in one of four modes:

> Transmit mode
>
> Listen mode
>
> Bypass mode
>
> Receive mode

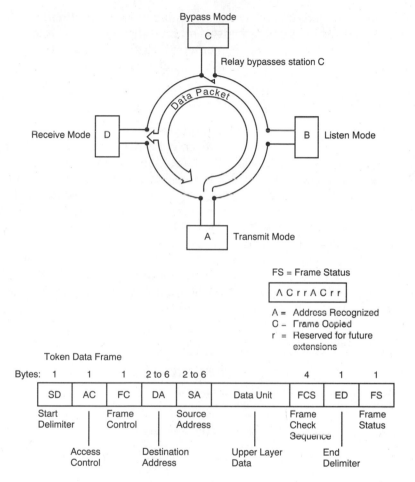

Figure 2.30:
Token Ring station modes.

Figure 2.30 shows four stations operating in these modes. Station A is in the transmit mode. To enter this mode, it seizes a free token. The token has a token bit called the *T bit*. This T bit has the value of one in a free token. The transmitting station changes this T bit to a 0, indicating a busy token and transmits the data frame. Station A is sending this data frame to station D, and the destination address field will hold station D's address, and the source address field will hold A's address.

Station B is operating in the listen mode. It checks the destination address field of the frame to see if it holds its address (B's address). Because the frame is addressed to station D, it enters the listen mode. In the listen mode, a station copies the incoming bits to the output link.

Station C has been powered down and is therefore in the bypass mode. The bits flow through the bypass relay.

Station D examines the destination address field. It discovers that it is indeed the addressed station and, therefore, enters the receive mode. In the receive mode, the data frame is copied into the station's memory and also sent along the ring. A number of flags called Frame Status flags are modified to indicate proper reception of the data frame. Station A receives the data frame that it sent and examines the Frame Status flags. The Frame Status flags serve the purpose of a hardware-based acknowledgment. The sending station can determine these flags and determine if the frame was received correctly. The Frame Status flags are the Address-recognized (A) flag, Frame-copied (C) flag, and the Error (E) flag. The E flag is computed and set by every station. The A and C flags are set by the destination station only. Table 2.6 defines these flags.

Table 2.6
Frame Status Flags

Frame Flags	Value	Meaning
A	1	Address recognized
A	0	Address not recognized
C	1	Frame copied successfully
C	0	Frame not copied
E	1	Bad Frame (CRC error)
E	0	Good Frame

The legal combinations of these flags are as follows:

- AC = 00 implies that the address was not recognized and, therefore, the copy operation did not take place.

- AC = 10 implies that the station exists, but the frame was not copied. If E = 1, a bad frame was received. If the E flag is 0, then the frame was not copied for unknown reasons.

- AC = 11 implies that the station exists and the frame was copied to the station. If E = 1 and AC = 11, this indicates that the error was produced after the frame was copied.

The only illegal combination is AC = 01, which indicates that the station was not recognized, but a user still copied the frame! In other words, some station illegally copied the data frame! This is clearly an improper condition.

As the bits that were sent by station A come back to it, they are removed from the ring.

What if station A was powered down before the frame that it sent came back? Because it is the responsibility of the sending station to remove the frame that it sent, this frame would circulate endlessly! There are many similar scenarios that could disrupt the normal ring operation. What if the token was destroyed by noise on the ring? Would stations wait for the token indefinitely? The Token Ring operation contains self-healing mechanisms to correct for these and many other possibilities. These situations are detected and handled by special control frames called MAC frames and is one of the reasons why the IEEE 802.5 operation is more complex than IEEE 802.3. The following discussion describes just a few of these self-healing mechanisms.

Although all stations seem equal, some stations are more equal than others. One such station is called the *Active Monitor*. There is a *monitor bit* (M-bit) in the token that is set to 0 by the transmitting station. The Active Monitor examines this M-bit and changes it to a 1, if it is a 0. If the Active Monitor bit sees an M-bit value of 1, it concludes that this data frame has been circulating around once too often! This could be because of a crash of the transmitting station, which failed to remove the data frame from the ring.

If the token is lost because it got mangled by noise on the ring, the Active Monitor timesout and generates a new token. The Active Monitor keeps track of this *Token Rotation Time* (TRT) and timesout if it exceeds a threshold value. For small token ring networks, the typical value of TRT is eight microseconds. Under heavy load conditions this value may rise.

The Active Monitor is not a station with special networking hardware. Any station on the Token Ring can become an Active Monitor. All other stations act as Standby Monitors. The choice of which station becomes an Active Monitor is realized through a ring-initialization procedure. You may ask, what if the Active Monitor fails? In this case, one of the Standby Monitors becomes the Active Monitor.

When no data frames are circulating around the ring, the Active Monitor issues an *Active Monitor Present* (AMP) MAC frame. This frame is sent at regular intervals of usually seven seconds. Other stations in the role of Standby Monitors send *Standby Monitor Present* (SMP) MAC frames. Standby monitors detect the AMP frame and conclude that the Active Monitor is doing its job. If the Active monitor skips a beat—if it does not send out the AMP frame when it should—one of the Standby Monitors takes over the role of the Active Monitor. The Standby Monitor that detects the failure of the Active Monitor sends its claim on the Token Ring in the form of *Claim Token* (CL_TK) MAC frames. The Standby Monitor stops sending these frames if one of the following conditions occurs:

- Another CL_TK frame is received and the sender's address is greater than this station's address. If two or more stations send out CL_TK, the station with the higher address becomes the Active Monitor.

- A *Beacon* (BCN) MAC frame is received. This frame is sent as a result of a major ring failure such as a ring break. The BCN frame is used to locate and isolate the fault. In this case, the ring needs to be healed before deciding the winner of this contest.

- A *Purge* (PRG) MAC frame is received. This frame is sent out at the end of the Claim Token procedure by the station that has become the new Active Monitor. This means that the race has already been won by another station, and so there is no point in continuing.

In any of the preceding cases, the Standby Monitor backs off. If a station receives the CL_TK frame it generated, it becomes the Active Monitor (new king of the hill!) and issues an RG MAC frame to inform other stations that there is a new Active Monitor. At this point, the new Active Monitor adds the 24-bit latency buffer to the ring and commences monitoring the network.

Before joining a ring, a new station sends out the *Duplicate Address Test* (DAT) MAC frame as part of the ring initialization procedure. The DAT frame is sent with its own address in the DA field. If another station responds with the AC bits set to 11, then another station has the same address. The new station returns an appropriate status code. Network monitoring software can detect this code and process it with an appropriate error message.

Another feature of the IEEE 802.5 is the priority access mechanism. The token has two fields called the Priority field and the Reservation field that each consist of three bits. A total of eight priorities values can be defined (0 to 7). The Reservation field is set to 0 by the transmitting station. If a station wants priority access, it can place its priority value in the Reservation field. After the transmitting station receives the frame it sent, it copies the Reservation field value in the Priority field of the new token that it generates. The token now has the requested Priority value. Only stations with higher or equal priority can access this token.

Token Ring Options

The IEEE 802.5 specifies Token Ring options (see fig. 2.31) at data rates of 1 Mbps, 4 Mbps, and 16 Mbps. The 1 Mbps uses UTP wiring. Initially the 4 Mbps and 16 Mbps used STP wiring. A demand within the industry is to have the 4 Mbps and 16 Mbps run on UTP wiring. Several products are available to support UTP wiring for 4 and 16 Mbps Token Rings. For a long time, a 16 Mbps UTP version was not available from IBM. IBM has teamed with Synoptics Communications to propose a 16 Mbps UTP standard to the IEEE 802.5 committee.

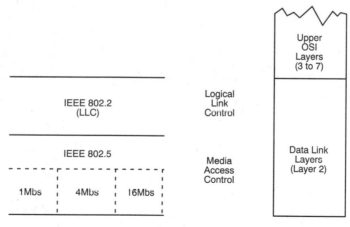

Figure 2.31:
IEEE 802.5 options for Token Ring.

The 16 Mbps stations do not wait for the return of the data frame to place the token on the network, which is called the *early token release mechanism*. This mechanism allows up to two data frames to be transmitted on a Token Ring LAN at a time.

Token Ring LAN Components

For standard-bus (ISA) stations, the following adapter cards are available from IBM:

> IBM Token Ring PC Adapter
>
> IBM Token Ring 16/4 Adapter
>
> IBM Token Ring PC Adapter II

For microchannel architecture stations, the following cards are available from IBM:

> IBM Token Ring PC Adapter/A
>
> IBM Token Ring 16/4 Adapter/A
>
> IBM Token Ring 16/4 Busmaster Server Adapter

The Token Ring network board (NIC) has a 9-pin socket that is used to connect the network adapter cables. Various manufacturers provide network adapter cards. Some manufacturers' cards are equipped with RJ-45 connectors, which makes them ready to connect directly to UTP (Type 3) wiring.

The IBM 8228 Multistation Access Unit, also called MAU but not to be confused with the Media Attached Unit (MAU) in IEEE 802.3, is a wiring center that allows up to eight stations to be connected to it. The two end ports, called *Ring In* (RT) and *Ring Out* (RO), are not used to connect Token Ring stations. These are used to connect multiple MAUs together. Four port wiring centers (also called hubs) also are available. MAUs also are available that contain a number of network management features. These are called smart or intelligent MAUs.

The IBM 8228 Setup Aid is used to test each port in the IBM 8228 before it is installed. It is used to check the operation of the bypass relay mechanism for each port.

The IBM Token Ring network adapter cable is made of eight feet of IBM Type 1 cable. Type 6 cable also can be used, although these are recommended as patch cables between wiring centers. One end of this cable connects to the Token Ring adapter and the other end is a dual-gender connector that plugs into one of the station ports in the IBM 8228 MAU.

The method of interconnecting 8228 MAUs and workstations is illustrated in figure 2.32.

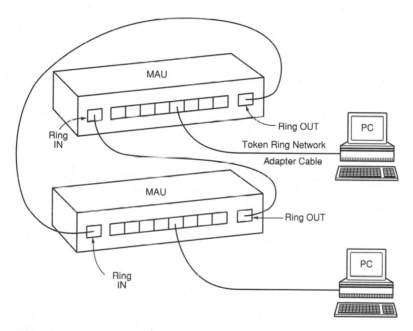

Figure 2.32:
Token Ring network cabling components.

IEEE 802.5 Design Rules

The following table summarizes the rules for Token Ring wiring:

Table 2.7
Token Ring Wiring Rules

Token Ring Parameters	Type 1, 2	Type 3
Max Devices per ring	260	96
Tested Data Rates	16 Mps	4 Mps
Station to single MAU LAN	300 M	100 M
Station to multiple MAU LAN	100 M	45 M
Max MAUs per LAN	12	2
MAU to MAU distance	200 M	120 M

Type 1, 2 Cabling

Although a maximum of 260 stations can be used with Types 1 and 2 cables, a more reasonable number is 100. The limit on the maximum stations is due to accumulated clock jitter. Interestingly enough, if you use the IBM 8228 MAU, which has a maximum of eight ports, you only use 12 MAVs (see table 2.7); you have a maximum of 8 x 12 = 96 stations on the Token Ring.

For Type 1 and 2 cables, the maximum distance between workstation to MAU is 300 meters for a single MAU LAN, but this distance drops to 100 meters for multiple MAU LANs. As a practical measure, it is better to work with the tighter constraint of 100 meters, even for a single MAU LAN, because LANs have a tendency to grow and, as you add more stations, you eventually need a multiple MAU LAN.

The maximum MAU to MAU distance for a Token Ring LAN is 200 meters for Type 1 and 2 cables.

Type 3 Cabling

For Type 3 cabling, the maximum distance between workstation to MAU is 100 meters for a single MAU LAN, but this distance drops to 45 meters for multiple MAU LANs. As a practical measure, it is better to work with the tighter constraint of 45 meters even for a single MAU LAN. The reason for this is that LANs have a tendency to grow, and as we add more stations, we would eventually need a multiple MAU LAN.

The maximum MAU to MAU distance for a Token Ring LAN is 120 meters for Type 3 cabling.

Guidelines for Token Ring Cabling

There are general guidelines for Token Ring cabling. These rules are as follows:

1. Stations located within eight feet of the MAU can be connected by using eight-foot adapter cable.

2. Stations farther than eight feet from the MAU can be connected by using extension cords (or you can build longer adapter cables).

3. To form a ring by using multiple MAUs, connect a patch cable from the RO of the first MAU to the RI of the second MAU. Continue doing this for all the MAUs until you reach the last MAU. Connect the RO of the last MAU to the RI of the first MAU.

4. You cannot connect stations to the RI and the RO ports. The RI and RO ports are only used for interconnecting multiple MAUs.

5. Patch cables (IBM Type 6) should not be spliced.

6. Patch cables (IBM Type 6) should not be used in any duct, plenum, or other space used for air handling. IBM Type 9, which is a plenum-rated cable, can be used instead.

Token Ring Troubleshooting Considerations

For the Token Ring to work correctly, the physical token loop must be maintained. Any problem that would disrupt the flow of data on the physical wire will cause the token ring to malfunction. Also, because the data flows through each workstation (each station acts as a repeater), a malfunctioning workstation can cause the entire ring to fail. For these reasons, troubleshooting token ring networks is challenging.

The Size of the Ring

Token Ring networks using STP cabling such as the IBM Type 1 and Type 2 cables have a limit as to the maximum number of stations that can be placed in a single physical ring. This limit is 260 stations for the IBM Token Ring using STP cables. Adding workstations above this limit causes clock jitter problems that make the ring fail. To have a useful ring, the minimum number of physical stations is 2. The actual number of stations on a ring is a number between these two limits: 2 and 260.

An important consideration when determining the number of stations is to keep a physical ring large enough to provide useful work but small enough to make troubleshooting easier. In a smaller ring, it is much easier to physically isolate the offending station or isolate the problem in the ring.

One way to keep a ring to a reasonable size to facilitate troubleshooting is to use Token Ring bridges as illustrated in figure 2.33. *Bridges* are devices that allow physical rings to be separate in terms of MAC Layer operation. For instance, in figure 2.33, two rings are joined by a bridge. Each ring has its own token, which is used to implement the MAC mechanism. The token is restricted to the physical ring on which it operates. Using this approach, it is possible to construct complex ring networks, in which each ring operates independently of others but can still communicate to other stations in other rings through the bridges. The bridges participate in the MAC mechanism of the rings they are connected to.

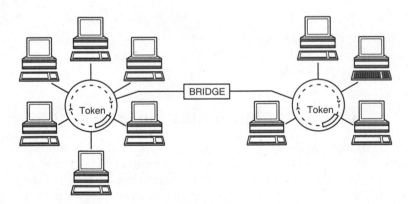

Figure 2.33:
Separate token mechanism of rings connected with a bridge.

Built-In Diagnostics

The IEEE 802.5 specification for the Token Ring specifies built-in diagnostics that are used by workstations to isolate problems with the Token Ring. Many of these diagnostics refer to the concept of a fault domain or failure domain.

The *fault domain* is a section of the ring (fig. 2.34) that consists of the following three components:

- The station transmitting the BCN Frame
- The beaconing station's *Nearest Active Upstream Neighbor*
- The cable between the beaconing station and its NAUN

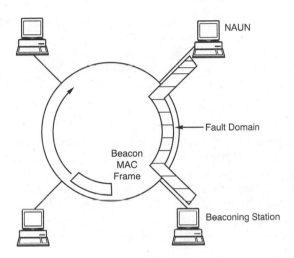

Figure 2.34:
Fault domain.

Because the data flow in a ring is unidirectional, every station has a neighbor that is upstream with respect to its position in the ring. This *upstream neighbor* is the station from which the data frame is received and is called the NAUN. The use of the word *Active* implies that the NAUN may not be the nearest physical upstream neighbor because the physically closest neighbor may not be participating in the ring. The NAUN for each station is set in the Neighbor Notification process activated by the Active Monitor.

When a station discovers a hard error, it sends a beacon MAC frame that contains its NIC address, the NAUN, and the beacon type. The contents of the beacon frame essentially define the fault domain. The beacon type is helpful in diagnosing the cause of the error. An example of a beacon type is a cable fault. The beacon frame is broadcast to all stations. All other stations enter the Beacon Repeat mode in which they copy and repeat the frame around the ring. The beacon frame is generated repeatedly by the station that detects the hard error. After the NAUN copies the beacon frame eight times, it removes itself from the ring and conducts a series of self-tests such as the DAT and the Lobe Media Test. In the Lobe Media test, the NIC transmits a Lobe Test MAC frame to the MAU port to test if it receives the frame correctly. If it receives the frame incorrectly, the lobe (cable between the NIC and the MAU port) is suspect.

If the NAUN station fails, it removes itself from the ring. Because the NAUN, which was the cause of the problem, is off the ring, the beaconing station will receive the BCN frames it sends. At this point, the station stops beaconing and retransmits the token frame onto the ring. The ring has now auto-recovered.

If the NAUN station passes its self-test, it reinserts itself in the ring. After a certain time, the beaconing station assumes that the NAUN has passed the self-test. The problem could then be with the beaconing station. Therefore, the beaconing station goes through the same series of self-tests. If the beaconing station fails its tests, it will remove itself from the ring. The Active Monitor will then initiate a Ring Recovery by issuing a Ring PRG followed by a Claim Token MAC frame. If the beaconing station passes its test, it will reinsert itself in the ring. If the beaconing condition persists, the problem requires manual troubleshooting. The problem is most likely caused by the cabling media (including the MAU) between the beaconing station and its NAUN.

Token Ring Cable Problems

One of the areas of great vulnerability in Token Ring operation is the failure of the physical cable. When the physical cable fails, the token cannot flow, and, therefore, the ring cannot function. Consult *Token Ring Troubleshooting* (New Riders Publishing) for an excellent guide to troubleshooting many of the common cable and operational problems in Token Ring networks. The discussion that follows is based on this material.

Cabling problems can be repeatable or intermittent. Repeatable problems are the easiest because they indicate a recurring condition on the network, and you can use standard divide-and-conquer troubleshooting techniques to isolate the problem. These problems are often called hard faults or solid problems. Intermittent problems, by their very definition, exist only under certain conditions. Because these conditions are often unknown or hard to reproduce, isolating these problems can be particularly difficult. If it is possible to convert an intermittent problem to a repeatable problem by simulating the conditions under which the problem occurs, troubleshooting is much easier.

The following are some of the more common problems with Token Ring cables:

- Open cables
- Shorted cables
- Crossed conductors
- Bad connectors
- Bad cable terminations
- Improper cable placement

Open cables are caused by a physical break in the cable conductor. This prevents the signal from flowing. These cables can be the result of faulty manufacture, damage to the cable during installation such as excessive crimping pressure, or physical tension. Open cables also can result from careless construction work near the proximity of the cable.

Shorted cables result from the internal conductors touching each other. Like open cables, this problem can be the result of bad manufacture, excessive force during installation, and so on.

Open and shorted cables caused by improper installation usually occur at the ends of the cables because this is where the end connectors are installed. Carelessness in installing connectors at the end can damage the cable. Besides causing physical breaks in the cable, open and shorted faults can cause signal reflection. Open and shorted cables can be detected using *Time Domain Reflectometer* (TDR) instruments. It also is possible for a damaged cable, even though there is no short nor open present, to generate enough signal reflection to bring down the network.

Crossed conductors are caused by cable conductors improperly connected to their end connectors. The Token Ring cable uses a color code standard—red (Pin 1 Receive Plus), green (Pin 6 Receive Minus), orange (Pin 9 Transmit Plus), and black (Pin 5 Transmit minus). If this standard is not adhered to while attaching the connectors, improper signaling on the Token Ring can occur. The problem may appear as failure at the station or MAU.

Bad connectors are problems in the physical connector itself, such as shorted connectors.

Bad cable terminations result from improper connections between the internal conductors and the physical connector. This can be caused by loose or disconnected conductors or crossed conductors.

Improper cable placement also can cause problems. Placing the cable near high voltage or current sources, such as High Voltage lines, can induce sufficient noise into the internal conductor to override the data signals. Improperly shielded cables can cause similar problems. This problem is even more pronounced when UTP cables are used.

To solve complex problems when troubleshooting Token Rings, a common approach is to divide and conquer. Because the Token Ring is wired in a physical star topology, the best way to solve Token Ring cable-related problems is to isolate the lobe cables from the main ring path cable and test the ring with and without the lobe cable. A *lobe cable* is the workstation to MAU cable. The main ring path cable consists of the MAU and the patch cables used to interconnect the MAUs. Removing the patch cables can isolate the MAUs, which can then be individually tested.

Sometimes a problem may be due to a port on the MAU or the failure of the NIC to generate a sufficiently strong phantom DC current to insert itself into the ring.

Token Ring NIC Failures

If an NIC encounters a solid internal fault, it generates a hard error such as a BCN MAC frame onto the ring. A protocol analyzer such as LANalyzer or Sniffer can be used to discover the station that causes the hard error. Hard errors result in the Token Ring stations entering the beaconing fault/domain process for ring recovery. At the conclusion of this process the offending node is removed from the ring.

Sometimes the cause of an NIC failure may not be an internal hardware problem at all, but an improperly configured NIC. There may be an improper hardware setting such as the I/O Base Address, *Interrupt Request* (IRQ) line, *Direct Memory Access* (DMA) line, slot setting, or NIC microcode level. Other things to check are speed settings and possible incompatibility between the NIC, lobe cable, MAU, or cabling terminator.

Another type of NIC error is a soft error. *Soft errors* can result from improper configuration of ring speed settings or NIC firmware microcode versions. When an NIC detects a soft error, it may be detecting a marginal internal failure. Soft errors are reported in a special Report Soft Error MAC frame that is addressed to the *Ring Error Monitor* (REM) that has the functional address of C00000000008. This functional address can be seen through a protocol analyzer and represents the REM that has the special task of gathering ring errors and forwarding them to the Token Ring LAN Manager station at the functional address of C00000002000.

The NIC actually waits for a period of time defined by the parameter T (Soft_Error_Report)—about 2 seconds—to acquire software-error information. When a software error is encountered, the NIC increments the count of software errors, which is then transmitted to the REM functional address. Along with the number of software errors, the Report Soft Error MAC frame also includes the transmitting station address, its NAUN, and the type of software error. The software error counter is reset after transmission of the Report Soft Error MAC frame.

A high occurrence of soft errors can cause ring performance degradation and initiate a Ring Recovery process. This includes the Claim Token process to determine the Active Monitor and the Neighbor Notification process so each station can determine its NAUN. This Ring Recovery process can consume a great deal of time and degrade the Token Ring's performance. The *soft error counter* is a 12-byte field, with each byte reserved for a special type of software error. Currently there are 10 error types defined with the remaining two bytes being reserved for future use.

ARCnet LANs

In 1976, four engineers from Datapoint Corporation built a LAN that evolved into a widely used, but relatively unknown, LAN in the industry—*ARCnet (Attached Resource Computer Network).* The goal of the design team was to develop network links between Datapoint's computer systems so that customers could share resources while still retaining the benefits of stand-alone processing.

A data rate of 2.5 Mbps was selected, primarily because that was the transfer rate of the disks that Datapoint was using at the time. A small frame size of a maximum of 508 bytes was chosen, because a study done by ARCnet's designers revealed that more than 90 percent of all messages transmitted on a network were small. The designers wanted to make the network reliable so that failures in stations and cables had a minimum impact on the rest of the network. Another requirement was to make ARCnet work with a variety of media such as coaxial, twisted pair, and fiber optic. Today, products exist that support these media.

By 1977, the project was complete. It did not make a big splash in the industry, however, primarily because ARCnet was not a separate product; it was embedded in Datapoint's computing machines.

ARCnet technology predates Ethernet technology, even though many people think that Ethernet technology was the first. The reasons for ARCnet being relatively unknown are many. As mentioned, Datapoint kept the technology proprietary. It was not until 1982 that Datapoint enabled SMC (Standard Microsystems Corporation) to market an ARCnet chip set to other OEMs. Ethernet had already become popular by this time.

Datapoint—unlike Digital, Intel, and Xerox—did not propose ARCnet to the IEEE committee, and it had less market influence compared to other companies behind Ethernet and the Token Ring standard. The SMC chip set, developed in 1982, started a grass-roots movement. More than a dozen vendors have used this chip set to manufacture ARCnet network cards.

ARCnet uses the RG/62 93-ohm coaxial cable used with IBM 3270 terminals. There are many stories about whether this was done as part of the design or it was an accident. This coaxial cable is cheaper than the 50-ohm coaxial cable used in Ethernet. Additionally, many older office buildings and airport complexes are wired with this type of cabling, making the transition to ARCnet easy.

ARCnet uses the token passing bus mechanism, which makes ARCnet deterministic. There is a fixed upper bound on the amount of time a station has to wait before it can transmit.

Despite its many advantages, ARCnet has the disadvantage of a low data rate (2.5 Mbps). A number of ARCnet vendors have banded together to form the ARCnet Trader's Association (ATA), which disseminates information to users about ARCnet technology. Membership in ATA is open to vendors, system integrators, and users. ATA is located at: 3365 N. Arlington Heights Rd., Arlington Heights, IL 60004, (708) 255-3003. Under its auspices, a new ARCnet standard (ARCnet Plus) is being developed, which has a designed data rate of 20 Mbps.

Figure 2.35 shows an ARCnet LAN. Station transmission is broadcast in the same manner as for a bus LAN, but access to the bus is determined by a token, hence the name Token Passing Bus.

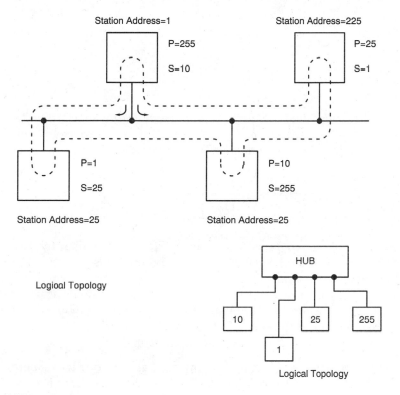

Figure 2.35:
ARCnet LAN operation.

Fig 2.35 shows stations, with node addresses of 1, 10, 25, and 255 on a bus. At startup time, a logical ordering is made, so that these stations form a logical ring. Each station keeps track of two pieces of information: who is its successor and who is its predecessor. This information is shown by the letters S (successor) and P (predecessor) for each station. A *successor* for a station is defined as the station on the ring with the next highest address. A *predecessor* for a station is defined as the station with the next lowest address.

A maximum of 255 stations is allowed in ARCnet, with the lowest station address being 1. Station address 0 is used for broadcast. The successor for station 255 is 1 and the predecessor for station 1 is 255. The predecessor and successor information for the stations in figure 2.35 is as follows:

Station	Predecessor(P)	Successor (S)
1	255	10
10	1	25
25	10	255
255	25	1

A special frame, called the *token frame*, is passed from a station to its successor. The passing of this frame from station to station forms a logical ring. The token frame is called the *Invitation To Transmit* (ITT) frame. Its structure is as follows:

ITT = | ALERT | EOT | DID | DID |

All ARCnet frames are preceded by an ALERT burst, similar to the preamble for Ethernet. An *ALERT burst* consists of 6-bit intervals of mark (1). A *mark (1)* is represented by a dipulse pulse, which consists of a positive pulse followed by a negative pulse. A space (0) is represented by the absence of a pulse. The EOT is the ASCII EOT (04 hex) and is followed by two bytes. Each of the bytes contains the successor information called the *Destination ID* (DID) number. The DID field is repeated for reliability.

A station that has the ITT frame can transmit at most one frame before passing the frame to its successor (next DID). Before a data frame is sent to a destination node, it must be queried to see if it has enough buffer space to accept the frame. A special frame called the *Free Buffer Enquiry* (FBE) performs this function.

FBE = | ALERT | ENQ | DID | DID |

The *ENQ (ENQUERY)* is the ASCII ENQ (05 hex), and is followed by two bytes. Each of the bytes contains the DID of the station whose free buffer status is desired. The DID field is repeated for reliability. If the destination node sends a positive response, known as an *Acknowledgement* (ACK) frame, the sending node can send the data frame.

A positive ACK frame consists of two bytes, as follows:

ACK = | ALERT | ACK |

The ACK is the ASCII ACK (06 hex). When sent in response to an FBE frame, it indicates availability of buffer spaces at the receiver. There is no DID field because it is sent as a broadcast frame.

A *Negative Acknowledgment* (NAK) is the ASCII ACK (15 hex). It indicates nonavailability of buffer space at the receiver. It is not sent to indicate improper data frame reception. There is no DID field because it is sent as a broadcast frame.

A NAK frame consists of two bytes, as follows:

NAK = | ALERT | NAK |

Once an ACK frame is received in response to an FBE frame, a data frame can be sent. Data frames are transmitted by the PAC (packet) frame.

PAC = | ALERT | SOH | SID | DID | DID | CP | DATA | CRC | CRC |

The *Start of Header* (SOH) is the ASCII SOH (01 hex). The source and destination address are indicated by the *Source ID* (SID) and DID fields. Again, the DID field is repeated for reliability. The *Continuation Pointer* (CP) field indicates where in its memory the station finds the beginning of the transmitted data. The data field DATA is of variable length between 1 to 508 bytes. A two-byte CRC, determined by the DATA field, is appended by the sender for error-checking purposes.

If a fault occurs to disrupt the proper passing of the token, the network must be reconfigured. Reconfiguration or resequencing also takes place when a station is added or removed from the token passing ring.

If an active node fails to receive an ITT token frame after 840 milliseconds (or if it is powered up), a RECON pattern, consisting of eight mark intervals followed by one space, is sent 765 times. This pattern is illustrated by figure 2.36.

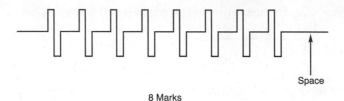

Space

8 Marks

Figure 2.36:
A RECON pattern.

This RECON burst lasts for 2754 microseconds, which is long enough to disrupt any token frame transmission that is under way. The result is that the token frame is lost. The stations wait for another 78 microseconds, and if there is no activity, it is safe to assume that a reconfiguration is in progress. Each station then sets its successor (NID) to its own address (ID) plus one, and it sets a time out value according to the following equation:

$$\text{Time out} = 146 \times (255\text{-}ID) \text{ microseconds}$$

The node with the highest address has the first time out and issues an ITT to its successor (NID). A station with address 255 has a time out value of 0. If no activity occurs after 74 microseconds (less than 78 microseconds), the highest address station assumes that the node with the successor address of NID does not exist. It increments the NID value and sends another ITT with the DID field set to the new NID value. This procedure is repeated until the highest address station discovers its successor. At this time, the token is transferred to the successor, and the successor repeats this process.

Once all active nodes are found, the normal token-passing operation is resumed. Reconfiguration can take between 24 to 61 milliseconds, depending on the number of active nodes and the value of their node addresses. To minimize the initial time out value to 0 and to reduce the reconfiguration time, set at least one ARCnet node to address 255. This should be a node such as a server, which is likely to be up all the time.

Deleting a node is a simpler process under ARCnet and does not invoke the full reconfiguration mechanism. If, in our example, station 10 drops from the ring and does not respond to the ITT sent from station 1 for a period of 74 microseconds, station 1 assumes that station 10 is no longer active. Node 1 then increments its NID value (new value 11) and sends an ITT to station 11. If there is no response, the process repeats in another 74 microseconds. Because the next station address is 25, within (25–10) x 74 microseconds = 1.1 milliseconds, station 1 figures out that its successor is station 25.

If station 10 wants to reenter the network, it waits for a period of 840 milliseconds for the token. If it has not been invited to transmit through an ITT frame sent to it, it invokes the full reconfiguration mechanism.

ARCnet Components

Figure 2.37 shows some typical ARCnet components. An RG-62/U 93-ohm cable is used to connect the components of an ARCnet LAN. BNC twist-lock connector plugs are attached to both ends of the cable. BNC connector jacks mate with the BNC connector plugs and are located on several pieces of ARCnet hardware such as active and passive hubs, network cards, and active links.

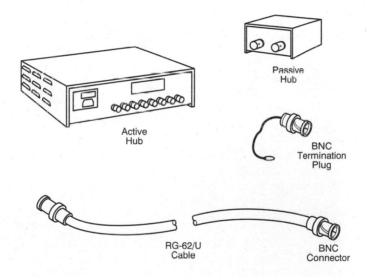

Figure 2.37:
ARCnet hardware components.

Active hubs serve as repeaters in other LANs. An active hub amplifies and reconditions the signal. They usually have eight ports, although active hubs with more ports are available. Terminating unused ports on an active hub is recommended, but not necessary because of the isolation circuitry used in most ARCnet active hubs.

Passive hubs usually come with four ports to which network cables such as the RG-62/U can be attached. Unused ports in passive hubs must be terminated. Unlike the active hubs, they do not have special isolation circuits.

ARCnet Star Wiring Design Rules

Figure 2.38 illustrates the design rules for an ARCnet LAN using distributed star topology. These rules are summarized in table 2.8. All distances in the figure are maximum distances.

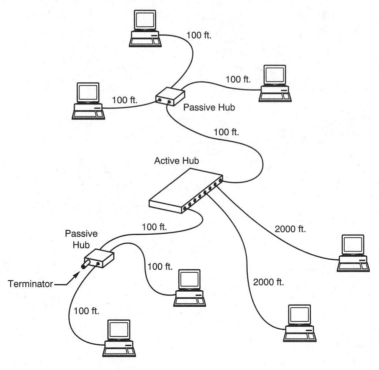

Figure 2.38:
ARCnet using star-wiring rules.

Table 2.8
Cable Distance Limitations

From	To	Max Distance (feet)
One network end	The other end	20,000
Network station	Active hub	2000
Network station	Passive hub	100
Active hub	Active hub	2000
Active hub	Passive hub	100
Passive hub	Passive hub	Does not work

Thus, the maximum span of an ARCnet network is 20,000 feet (3.8 miles). ARCnet LANs are quite resilient to out-of-spec installations for distances between active components. They can span distances of 4.5 miles, even though this is outside the ARCnet specification. When passive hubs are employed, the distances cannot exceed 100 feet. Also, a passive hub cannot be connected in a series with another passive hub—the signal attenuation is too great for this to work.

The following are general rules for ARCnet networks:

1. Active hubs can connect to other hubs (active and passive) and ARCnet stations.

2. Passive hubs can connect to active hubs and ARCnet stations. They cannot connect to other passive hubs directly.

3. Do not create loops in an ARCnet LAN. A *loop* is created when a cable coming from a hub goes through other hubs and then connects back into the original hub.

4. Always terminate unused ports in a passive hub.

5. Keep a log of station addresses. Two stations cannot have duplicate addresses. No automatic mechanism exists to prevent this from occurring, as is the case in IEEE 802.5.

6. To minimize reconfiguration time, set the most reliable station that is active most of the time to station address 255, which can be your file server.

7. Many ARCnet NICs enable you to set the token rotation time threshold before reconfiguration ensues. For Pure Data cards token rotation times can be set to 74.7, 283.4, 561.8, and 1118.6 microseconds. All cards that participate in the token mechanism—that is, belonging to the same ARCnet LAN—need to have the same setting. Usually, the 74.7 microsecond setting is large enough for a 20,000-foot ARCnet LAN. For an unusually large number of active and passive hubs, this value may need to be increased. In general such large configurations should be avoided. It is better to use routers or bridges, discussed in Chapter 3, for connecting many small LANs.

ARCnet Coaxial Bus Design Rules

ARCnet can be used in a bus topology in which up to eight stations can be daisy-chained with RG-62/U cables over a maximum distance of 1000 feet (see fig. 2.39). In the bus topology, a T-connector is used to connect the workstations; a single bus segment must be terminated with a 93-ohm impedance at both ends.

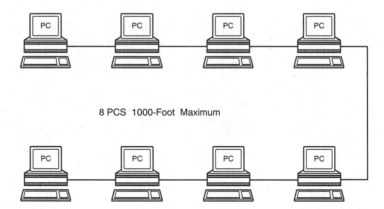

Figure 2.39:
ARCnet bus topology.

ARCnet coaxial bus topology can be mixed with the distributed star topology provided by an active hub. One end of the bus can be connected to an active hub. The total number of workstations that can be connected to a single eight-port active hub in this manner is $8 \times 8 = 64$. If two active hubs are to be connected, one port in each active hub is used up for connecting the active hubs. Therefore, each active hub supports 56 stations; the two active hubs support a total of 112 stations. Table 2.9 summarizes the configuration rules for the coaxial bus.

Table 2.9
Configuration Rules for ARCnet Coaxial Bus

Parameters	Value
Max stations per bus	8
Max length of bus	1000 feet
Max stations on single 8-port active hub	64

ARCnet Twisted Pair Wiring Design Rules

Twisted pair wiring can be used for ARCnet LANs (see fig. 2.40). With ARCnet, twisted pair bus topology is functionally and logically equivalent to the coaxial bus topology. Only one pair of twisted pair wiring is needed. The twisted pair ARCnet board has two six-pin modular jacks that can be used to daisy-chain the ARCnet board, unless the board is at the beginning or end of the daisy-chain segment. Terminators must be placed on unused plugs. A maximum of 10 stations can be used in the twisted pair daisy-chain, whose length cannot exceed 400 feet. The minimum spacing between stations in the daisy chain is 6 feet.

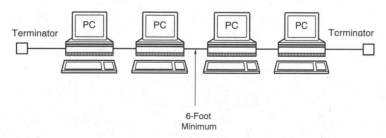

Figure 2.40:
ARCnet with twisted pair wiring.

Twisted pair bus topologies can be mixed with the distributed star topology provided by an active hub. One end of the bus can be connected to an active hub. Table 2.10 summarizes the configuration rules for the twisted pair bus.

Table 2.10
Configuration Rules for ARCnet Twisted Pair Bus

Parameters	Value
Max stations per TP bus	10
Max length of TP bus	400 feet
Min distance between nodes	6 feet
Max stations on single 8-port active hub	80

Large ARCnet Networks

The total number of stations in a single ARCnet LAN cannot exceed 255, and its maximum span is 20,000 feet. Within these limitations any combination of distributed star, coaxial bus, or twisted pair bus can be used. Figure 2.41 shows an ARCnet LAN using XINET components and a mix of cabling technologies.

20 Mbps ARCnet Plus

One of the most amazing features of the 20 Mbps ARCnet Plus is that it improves the performance of ARCnet by a factor of 8; yet it retains downward compatibility with the 2.5 Mbps ARCnet. Figure 2.42 shows the differences between ARCnet Plus and ARCnet.

Nodes on the standard ARCnet signal a logical one by a single cycle of a 5 MHz sine wave, followed by a silence of equal length. A logical 0 consists of two intervals of silence. (The interval is 1/5MHz = 200 nanoseconds' duration.) Two such intervals are necessary to send one bit (0 or 1) of information, which works out to a duration of 400 nanoseconds (a maximum data rate for ARCnet of 1/400 nanoseconds = 2.5 Mbps).

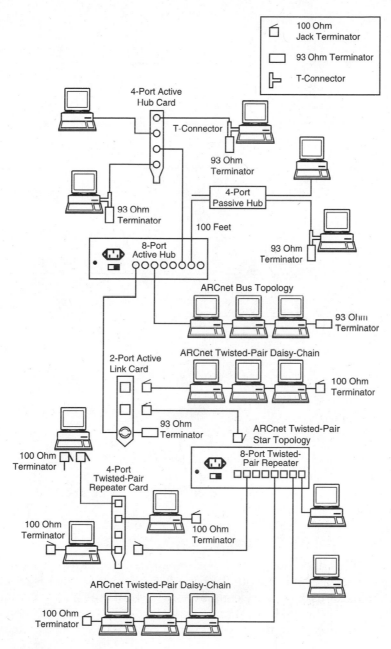

Figure 2.41:
A large, mixed media ARCnet. (Source: XINET)

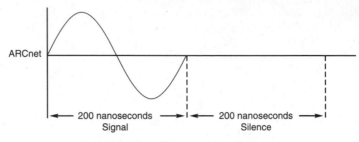

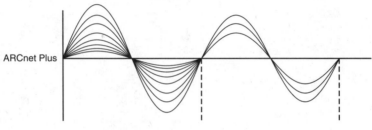

Figure 2.42:
ARCnet and ARCnet Plus signals.

ARCnet sends data in integral multiples of bytes. Each byte is preceded by a three-bit calibration pattern (110) to keep the receiver in pace with the transmitter. There is an overhead of three bits for every eight bits of data. Therefore, the effective data rate for ARCnet is 8/11 x 2.5 Mbps = 1.82 Mbps, which is a lot of wasted bandwidth. The periods of silence are wasteful and the calibration overhead takes up 27 percent of the bandwidth.

ARCnet Plus uses the bandwidth more effectively. One way of achieving higher data rates is to cut out the periods of silence. Another is to send calibration patterns once every eight bytes. The most ingenious technique it uses is to use Amplitude Modulation to squeeze four bits of information into every 200-nanosecond interval. A pulse can be either a positive or negative sine wave with eight possible amplitudes from 0 to 12 volts. This gives a total of 2 x 8 = 16 combinations of pulses, enough to represent four bits of data.

Hence, the total ARCnet Plus data rate = 4 bits × 5 million pulses per second = 20 Mbps, excluding overhead. When you take into account the calibration overhead, this yields an effective data rate of 16.84 Mbps, which is faster than Ethernet and the 16 Mbps Token Ring.

During initialization, the ARCnet Plus node sends a special signal that informs others that it can operate at higher speeds. This signal also is sent when an ARCnet Plus node passes the token. An ARCnet Plus node communicates to another ARCnet Plus node at 20 Mbps, but steps down gracefully to 2.5 Mbps to communicate with a 2.5 Mbps ARCnet node.

The new standard enables packet lengths of up to 4096 bytes and a maximum of 2047 nodes. IEEE 802.2 or DoD IP addressing mechanisms can be used for easier integration with Ethernet, Token Ring, and TCP/IP networks.

To upgrade to ARCnet Plus, follow these steps:

1. To mix the two types of cards together, the cabling can remain the same but the active hubs have to be replaced with ARCnet Plus active hubs. If older active hubs are used, the high-speed ARCnet Plus signals are filtered out.

2. Another way to solve this problem is to use older ARCnet active hubs, but to make sure that you do not put two ARCnet Plus nodes on opposite sides of the older active hub.

LocalTalk

LocalTalk is Apple Computer's proprietary physical LAN used to connect Macintosh computers. LocalTalk corresponds to layers 2 and 1 of the OSI model (see fig. 2.43). As the layer 2 (Data Link) protocol, it is known as the LocalTalk Link Access Protocol (LLAP). LocalTalk was initially conceived in 1983 but formally announced in 1984. It is unusual, in the sense that the LocalTalk protocols are built into the motherboard of every Macintosh computer. All that is required are the physical connector cables and the AppleTalk protocols.

LocalTalk makes use of STP wiring. The physical interface is RS 449 with the RS-422 balanced option. The balanced option allows LocalTalk to reject common mode noise. This principle is illustrated in figure 2.44. Signals are split into positive- and negative-going signals. The receiver electronics takes the difference of these two signals. Legitimate signals are doubled in strength, and noise signals, which appear as a common signal (common mode noise), are canceled. The encoding method used in LocalTalk is a bi-phase encoding scheme referred to as FM-0, also sometimes called bi-phase space. Bi-phase encoding requires at least one transition per bit time and is self-clocking. That is, clocking information is encoded in the same signal used to represent data. The Manchester encoding scheme used in Ethernet and the Differential Manchester encoding scheme used in Token Ring (IEEE 802.5) are examples of bi-phase encoding.

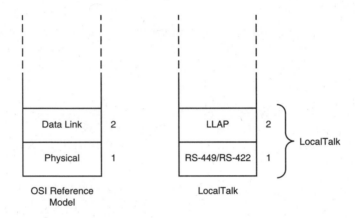

Figure 2.43:
LocalTalk and the OSI model.

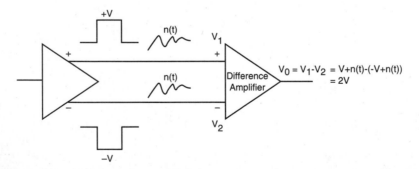

Figure 2.44:
RS-222 balanced signals in LocalTalk.

LocalTalk networks are limited to speeds of 230.4 Kbps and distances of 300 meters. Each LocalTalk segment can support a maximum of 32 devices.

LocalTalk uses an unusual scheme for determining physical addresses of LocalTalk stations. Physical addresses are not preassigned—they are determined dynamically using a dynamic address assignment process. When a LocalTalk station (Macintosh computer) boots, it picks an address at random and broadcasts it in an AARP (AppleTalk Address Resolution Protocol) request (see fig. 2.45). The AARP request essentially asks the question "Is there anyone out there with the address listed in this packet?". If a reply is heard, it means that the address is in use or there is a duplicate address, and the LocalTalk station picks another address and repeats the process until a unique address is discovered.

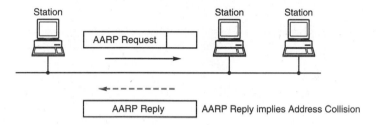

Figure 2.45:
Dynamic Address Assignment in LocalTalk.

LocalTalk addresses can range from 1 to 255 and are divided into two groups for user and server addresses. Addresses ranging from 1 to 127 are assigned to the user, and addresses from 128 to 254 are assigned to servers. The address 255 is a special address used for broadcasts. This address division allows LocalTalk to quickly determine clients from servers. This is useful in situations when clients and servers must be treated differently. Servers, for instance, are usually more overworked than clients and can therefore be given more time to respond to Duplicate Address AARP queries.

LocalTalk Access Mechanism

LocalTalk defines its own vocabulary to distinguish between ordinary and broadcast transmissions. Ordinary transmissions consist of a sequence of frames called a transmission dialog. The frames in a transmission dialog must be separated by a minimum time called the *Inter Frame Gap* (IGP), which is 200 microseconds. The minimum gap between transmission dialogs is called the *Inter-Dialog Gap* (IDG) and is 400 microseconds. These concepts are illustrated in figure 2.46.

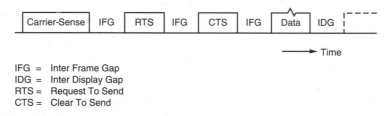

IFG = Inter Frame Gap
IDG = Inter Display Gap
RTS = Request To Send
CTS = Clear To Send

Figure 2.46:
LocalTalk transmission.

The mechanism used to arbitrate access to the common LocalTalk bus is *Carrier-Sense with Multiple Access/Collision Avoidance* (CSMA/CA). Unlike Ethernet, which uses collision detection, LocalTalk does not detect collisions. It attempts to avoid collisions by prefacing each transmission dialog with a *Request To Send* (RTS) and *Clear To Send* (CTS) signal sequence. The RTS/CTS sequence warns all other nodes of an impending transmission. Also, because this exchange is relatively small compared to an actual data transmission, it is better to have collisions in the smaller time period used in this exchange. If a collision does take place, LocalTalk does nothing to handle it. It leaves it to the upper layer protocols to timeout if the data transmission is delayed. All data transmissions in LocalTalk have a 2-byte *Frame Check Sequence* (FCS). The receiving node accepts the data transmission only if the FCS it calculates matches that in the transmitted frame. If the FCS does not match, the data transmission is assumed to be in error, and the data frame is discarded without informing upper layer software of the incident.

LocalTalk uses the carrier sense mechanism to determine if the LocalTalk bus is busy. The carrier sense period lasts for at least the minimum IDG, which is 400 microseconds. Because dialog transmissions are separated by the IDG, this gives a fairly reasonable assurance that the collision interval will be within the carrier sense interval. Before transmitting, LocalTalk nodes sense the channel for the carrier.

If the channel is busy, the LocalTalk node waits and defers from transmitting. The waiting period is a function of the deferral history and a random time out element. Under heavy network loads, many deferrals could take place. The waiting period is adjusted to become longer. This effectively causes the stations to perform a back-off, similar to Ethernet operation.

If the channel is free, the transmitting node sends an RTS frame. It then waits for the IFG of 200 microseconds for the receiving node to respond with a CTS frame. If a proper CTS frame is not received, the transmitting node assumes that a collision has taken place, and the transmitting node goes into the deferral mode. If the CTS frame is received correctly, the transmitting node must send a data frame within the IDG time period.

Broadcast transmission dialogs in LocalTalk occur in a manner similar to directed transmissions. The difference is that the RTS is broadcast with a destination address of 255. This RTS broadcast informs the nodes on the network of an impending transmission. The transmitting node does not expect a CTS in response. If the channel remains free, the broadcast message is sent.

LocalTalk Frame Format

LocalTalk uses control frames and data frames. The control frame is used by the MAC layer operation of LocalTalk, and the data frame is used for actual data transmission.

The packets are preceded by a 2-byte preamble, followed by a 1-byte destination and a 1-byte source address. The structure of the LocalTalk frame is shown in figure 2.47.

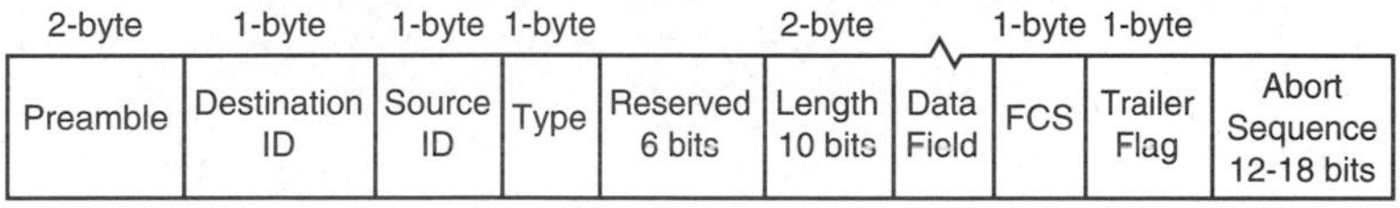

2-byte	1-byte	1-byte	1-byte		2-byte		1-byte	1-byte
Preamble	Destination ID	Source ID	Type	Reserved 6 bits	Length 10 bits	Data Field	FCS	Trailer Flag	Abort Sequence 12-18 bits

Figure 2.47:
LocalTalk frame structure.

The *preamble* consists of the bit pattern 01111110 repeated twice. Its purpose is to inform the receiver of an impending frame, so that the receiver can synchronize itself to receive the frame.

The *destination and source IDs* are each 1-byte and describe an address from 0 to 255.

The *type* field is 1-byte and specifies if this is a control or data frame. Values of 1–127 are used for control frame and 128–255 are used for data frames. If the type field indicates a control frame, the data field is absent. For data frames, the value classifies the content of the data field, so it can be delivered to the correct upper-layer protocol software. This value is used by upper-layer protocol software for multiplexing and de-multiplexing purposes.

If the type field indicates a data frame, a data length field is present and indicates the length of the data field. This is a 2-byte field, with the lower 10 bits used to indicate the length in bytes of the data field. The upper 6 bits are reserved for use by upper-layer protocol software.

The *Data* field contains the actual data delivered to upper-layer protocols. It can consist of from 0 to 600 bytes.

The FCS is a 16-bit CRC value. It is calculated on the destination address, source address, data length, and data fields.

A *Trailer Flag* consisting of the bit sequence 01111110 is used to mark the end of the frame.

The *Abort Sequence* consists of a run of 12 to 18 "1" bits. This run forces nodes to lose synchronization with respect to the bi-phase encoding scheme. It is used to confirm that the transmitting node has finished using the LocalTalk bus.

Understanding Network Adapters

This section focuses on the network adapters inside LAN nodes. These devices go by the following names:

- Network Adapter Unit/Board/Cards
- Network Controllers
- Network Interface Cards (NICs)
- Network Cards
- Network Adapters
- Intelligent Network Interface Cards (INICs)

These terms all refer to the network electronics that fit inside a node on a LAN and implement layers 2 and 1 of the OSI model. You can use any of the names for a network adapter.

Functional Description of a Network Adapter

There are a number of modules on the network adapter that perform specialized processing, which include the following:

- Transmit/Receive Module
- Encode/Decode Module
- Frame Buffers Area
- MAC Layer Processing Module
- Host-Bus Interface Module

These modules and their functions are described in the next sections. A functional description of a network adapter is shown in figure 2.48.

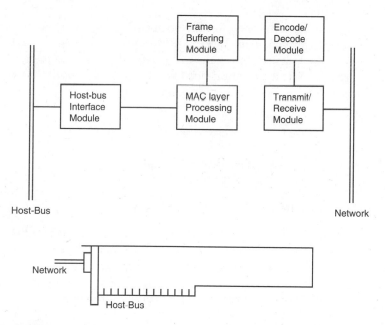

Figure 2.48:
Block diagram of a network adapter.

Transmit/Receive Module

The *Transmit/Receive Module* contains the interface electronics to drive the signal on to the network media and receive the signal from the network. As signals propagate through the network media, they are reduced in strength. The transmitting station must send the signal with sufficient power to be understood by the furthest node that needs to hear the signal.

For example, in the case of 10BASE5, the signal must be sent with sufficient power to span a distance of 500 meters. The Transmit/Receive Module contains the amplifier electronics to perform this function. This module corresponds roughly to the *Physical Layer Signaling* (PLS) and the *Media Attachment Unit* (MAU) in the IEEE standards.

Encode/Decode Module

Before a signal is transmitted, it may be encoded to put clock information as part of the data stream. The clocking information is necessary for the receiving station to keep its clock synchronized to the transmitter clock. When a signal is received by a station, it needs to decode the signal; that is, to recover the data bits. The *Encode/Decode Module* performs these functions.

There are a variety of encoding techniques used by different LANs. Ethernet and IEEE 802.3 use Manchester Encoding, IEEE 802.5 uses Differential Manchester Encoding, and FDDI uses a combination of NRZI (Non Return to Zero Inverted) and 4B/5B encoding.

Frame Buffer Area

When a frame is to be transmitted to the network or it has just been received from the network, it is kept in a special area of memory on the adapter card for processing. In many network adapters, this *frame buffer area* is implemented by RAM chips on the network adapter. The amount of memory reserved for frame buffering can vary from a few kilobytes to a megabyte.

Many network adapters implement intelligent buffer management algorithms in firmware. Some use scatter algorithms that can keep the header separate from the data portion of the frame, which eliminates the need to move header and data into a contiguous block of memory prior to transmission.

MAC Layer Processing Module

The MAC Layer Processing Module is perhaps the most important module in the Network Adapter. It performs the following important functions:

- Encapsulation/decapsulation functions. The *encapsulation* function is performed by the transmitting station and includes generation of the correct address, control, and frame check sequence fields. The *decapsulation* function is performed by the receiving station and includes processing of the address, control, and frame check sequence fields. Error detection also is performed by the decapsulation function.

- Implementation of the MAC algorithms (the CSMA/CD access mechanism for Ethernet and the token access mechanism for Token Ring).

These functions require processing power. Earlier network cards borrowed this processing power from the station's CPU. Needless to say, these network cards were very slow. Today, all network adapters have their own processing functions. These are special microprocessors that have their own ROM or microcode containing the MAC algorithms. These network controller chips have their own RAM for processing the MAC algorithms.

Host-Bus Interface Module

The exchange of control and data information between the network adapter and the station is performed through the host-bus interface. The host-bus interface module must have a built-in understanding of the protocol used for data transfer on the host bus. There are many bus standards; network cards are classified by whether they work for an ISA bus, EISA bus, or a Micro Channel bus. Apple's Macintosh machines use Nu-Bus and these must have their own network cards.

The width of a bus is defined by the number of data bits it can transmit in parallel. The wider the data bus, the more efficient the network adapter. For IBM PCs, eight-bit network cards are very common. 16-bit cards provide better performance, and 32-bit network cards for EISA and Micro Channel give the best performance.

Hardware Elements of a Network Adapter

When installing a network adapter and setting up networking software, such as NetWare, you may have to set several hardware parameters such as IRQ, DMA, Base Address, I/O address, and so on. This section discusses these hardware elements.

Interrupt Lines

When a packet arrives at a station, how does the network adapter inform the station's CPU of this event? The station is busy performing other tasks for the user and it needs to be informed that a packet has arrived so it can process it. The mechanism to perform this task is called an *interrupt*.

When an interrupt occurs, the CPU stops (after making a careful record of the last thing it is doing) and examines on which line the interrupt occurred. The CPU uses the interrupt line number to consult a table that it keeps in the lower memory. This table, called the *interrupt vector table*, is organized like an address book and contains the address of the program (interrupt service routine) that knows how to handle this packet. The CPU transfers control to this program. When it finishes processing the packet, the program transfers control back to the CPU, which resumes the task it was performing prior to the interrupt.

Interrupts also are used by peripheral devices, such as the keyboard, disk, or printer, to communicate with a CPU. The Intel processors used in IBM PCs have a number of IRQ lines. Some of these lines are dedicated for special functions. Table 2.11 shows some common IRQ assignments. (This table shows only the common devices used in an XT and AT.)

Table 2.11
IRQ Assignments

IRQ	XT	AT
2	EGA/VGA	EGA/VGA
3	COM2	COM2
4	COM1	COM1
5	Hard Disk	LPT2

IRQ	XT	AT
6	Floppy Controller	Floppy Controller
7	LPT1	LPT1
10	N/A	Unused
11	N/A	Unused
15	N/A	Unused

To install a network adapter, you must set its IRQ to an unused interrupt. For example, the hard disk inside an XT is likely to use IRQ 5, and the LPT2 port in an AT is likely to use IRQ 5. Avoid using IRQ 5 for these components.

Sometimes conflicts are acceptable if you are not using a specific device. Many network cards use a default configuration of IRQ 3, which means that serial port COM2 cannot be used. Many common station configurations do not use COM2, so this conflict is acceptable.

Some IRQ levels may be usable, even though there may be a conflict. For example, IRQ 2 is a default setting for many ARCnet cards. Although this may conflict with EGA/VGA cards, many stations work fine with such a configuration. The reason for this is that not many applications make use of the interrupt mechanism in EGA/VGA cards. Likewise, you may not have any conflict using IRQ 7, even though a printer is installed at LPT1, because many applications do not use LPT1 with interrupts.

DMA Lines

How is a packet transferred from the network adapter's buffers to the station's memory? One mechanism for doing this is through *Direct Memory Access* (DMA). Using DMA, the network card is able to transfer the packet to the station's memory without involving the station's CPU. This is desirable because the CPU can continue processing without interruption. When the CPU is not accessing its memory, the DMA mechanism steals memory cycles and transfers data to the station's memory.

DMA channel 0 is used to refresh Dynamic RAM chips. No two devices should share a DMA channel.

Shared or Base Memory

Many network adapters do not use DMA to transfer data. Instead, they use a technique called *Direct Memory Mapping* or *Shared Memory*.

The network adapter's buffers are mapped to an area of memory above 640K. The area of memory between 640K to 1M is used by devices such as video adapters, network adapters, and the PC's BIOS (Basic Input/Output System).

By sharing a common address space for applications and the network adapter's buffers, programs can be written to access the network adapter's buffers as easily as accessing any other area of memory. There is no need to move packets in RAM because the packets can be processed while they reside on the network adapters.

When installing network adapters that make use of shared memory, you need to specify the base address. The base address is the start of the area above 640K, where the network adapter's buffer memory is to be mapped. There may be switch settings to specify the size of buffer memory that will be used. Typical values of buffer memory size range from 4K to 64K. Care must be exercised to ensure that RAM addresses for various devices do not overlap. Figure 2.49 shows RAM above 640K (A0000 hex) used by some common devices.

I/O Port Addresses

Network adapters contain status and control registers. Networking software such as network drivers make use of these registers to control the operation of the adapter and find its status.

The control and status registers are accessed through Input/Output (I/O) ports. I/O ports form an address space that can be accessed by the PC's IN and OUT instructions. I/O ports have been defined for some common devices. These are shown in table 2.12. I/O port addresses must be selected to avoid conflicts with other devices.

Device	Memory Range
MONO	B0000 – B1000
CGA	B8000 – C0000
EGA	A0000 – C0000
VGA	A0000 – C4000
EXP. MEM	D0000 – E0000
XT BIOS	F4000 – 10000
IBM AT BIOS	E0000 – 10000
CLONE AT BIOS	F0000 – 10000

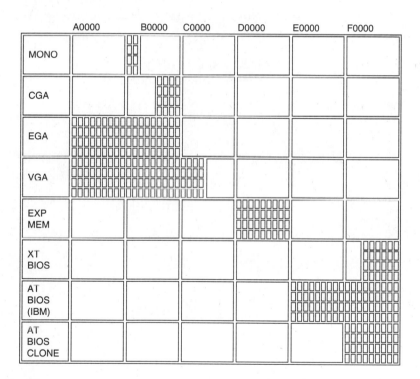

Figure 2.49:
RAM usage between 640K and 1M.

Table 2.12
Input/Output Ports for Common Devices

Possible I/O Base Address (hex)	Devices and Their Typical I/O Addresses
200	Game controller/Joystick (200–20F) Expansion Unit (210–217)
220	Novell NetWare Key Card (older NetWare)
260	LPT2: (278–27F)
280	LCD display on Wyse 2108 PC Western Digital EtherCard factory setting
2E0	COM4: (2E8–2EF) GPIB-Adapter 0 (2E1) COM2: (2F8–2FF) Data Acquisition (2E2–2E3)
300	Prototype Card (300–31F) 3COM EtherLink factory setting (300–31F)
320	XT Hard Disk Interface (320–32F)
360	LPT1: (378–37F)
380	SDLC/Secondary Bi-Sync Interface (380–38C)
3A0	Primary Bi-Sync Interface (3A0–3A9) Monochrome Display (3B0–3BB)
3C0	EGA Display (3C0–3CF) CGA Display (3D0–3DF)
3E0	COM3: (3E8–3EF) Floppy Disk Controller (3F0–3F7) COM1: (3F8–3FF)

Performance Considerations for Network Adapters

Many LAN administrators ask which network adapter is faster—Token Ring, Ethernet, or ARCnet. The answers are not always obvious because studies can be biased or skewed in favor of one adapter. The studies all conclude that 10-Mbps Ethernet and 16-Mbps Token Ring are faster than

ARCnet at 2.5 Mbps. These results are not so surprising considering their data rates. The ARCnet Plus at 20 Mbps can be expected to be faster than both Ethernet and ARCnet. FDDI at 100-Mbps will be the fastest among these. Thomas-Conrad has a 100 Mbps fiber optic proprietary LAN that is a combination of ARCnet and FDDI.

In designing a network interface card, a vendor makes several design choices that affect the price/performance trade-off. The four major characteristics that contribute to NIC performance are the following:

- Media Access Scheme
- Raw Bit Rate
- Onboard Processor
- NIC to Host Transfer

Media Access Scheme

The *media access scheme* such as CSMA/CD or Token Access is an important parameter in NIC performance. Token Access gives a deterministic performance; CSMA/CD does not. On the other hand, CSMA/CD is simpler and faster under light loads compared to Token Access.

Raw Bit Rate

The *raw bit rate* is the maximum bit rate possible on a given media. The actual effective bit rate is much less, taking into account protocol overhead and timing delays. Nevertheless, the raw bit rate represents an upper limit for the given media.

Fiber optic media can be used for data rates in the hundreds of Mbps range. FDDI at 100 Mbps is only the beginning—you can expect higher-speed LANs based on fiber optic cables.

Coaxial cable can generally accommodate data rates up to 50 Mbps and STP wiring around 20 Mbps.

ARCnet Plus uses a 5-MHz sine wave but by using special encoding techniques can pack 4 bits of information in every cycle, yielding a maximum of 20 Mbps.

Onboard Processor

Effective use of an onboard processor can speed up an NIC. If the firmware for the NIC is poorly written, however, it can have just the opposite effect. Some vendors implement upper layer protocol processing on the NIC card itself for better overall throughput. An example of such an NIC is the Federal Technologies EXOS series board that has onboard TCP/IP processing.

When NetBIOS was created by IBM for the IBM PC Broadband LAN, it was implemented in firmware on the NIC itself. However, because of an inefficient implementation, it ran slower than NetBIOS implemented in software.

NIC to Host Transfer

The NIC to host channel can be implemented in several ways: shared memory, DMA, or I/O ports. NICs can use any of these methods or a combination of them. Observations have shown that shared memory is the fastest, I/O ports are next, and DMA is the slowest.

The data width of the bus interface has a dramatic effect on NIC to Host transfer speeds. This width can be 8, 16, or 32 bits. The wider the data width, the faster the data transfer.

The type of host bus also affects the transfer rate. EISA and Micro Channel NICs are faster than ISA NICs.

Summary

The physical network is a complex combination of tangibles and intangibles. The tangibles include cables, connectors, hubs, and a wide variety of other devices. The intangibles include electrical signals and protocols that organize the electrical signals into meaningful communications. NetWare professionals will frequently find the need for a thorough understanding of these network characteristics.

NetWare has a long history of supporting a wide variety of network cabling systems, and a book might be required to describe them all. However, the tendency in the LAN industry has been toward support of a relatively small number of standards that offer reliability, low or moderate cost, high performance, and broad industry support. This chapter has examined the most prominent physical layer standards that are used to implement NetWare LANs.

IEEE 802.3 Ethernet and IEEE 802.5 Token Ring are used to implement the majority of local area networks. Therefore, these standards have received extensive treatment. ARCnet and LocalTalk have become well established in certain niches, and most NetWare technicians will encounter them from time to time. A thorough understanding of the control mechanisms and cabling systems employed with these standards will enable you to plan reliable networks and troubleshoot them effectively when problems arise.

Discussion in this chapter has frequently assumed fairly simple LANs. At a certain point, however, it may become necessary to subdivide your network. You may, for example, have too much traffic on your Ethernet or too many stations for a single Token Ring. In the next chapter you will see how bridges and routers are used to expand networks to support large numbers of devices, large physical areas, or to control data traffic.

Bridging and Routing

I f the network manager must go beyond the capabilities of a single LAN and access network or computing resources on other networks, he must determine which devices to use to extend the range of a LAN. Bridges, repeaters, and routers are often the choices to extend the range of a single LAN or to combine a number of LANs in a single internetwork.

In this chapter, you learn to connect NetWare LANs. This chapter first lays the foundation for understanding bridges, repeaters, and routers, and then discusses the way to configure and install NetWare routers. The latter part of this chapter examines NetWare v2.x routing problems and the way NetWare v3.x overcomes these problems. You also learn about performance issues for internal/external and dedicated/nondedicated routers.

Understanding Repeaters, Bridges, and Routers

Repeaters, bridges, and routers are devices that extend the range of a LAN. Most LANs such as Ethernet, ARCnet, and Token Ring have distance limitations. The maximum span of an Ethernet LAN, for example, is 2500 meters using multiple segments and repeaters. Although you can use repeaters to go beyond a single coaxial segment, you cannot use more than four repeaters. If you use bridges and routers, you can go beyond the 2500-meter Ethernet limitation.

Each Ethernet LAN still has the 2500-meter and four repeater rule, but once a packet crosses a bridge it is on another logical LAN and subject to the restrictions of that LAN only.

Bridges and routers do more than extend the range of a LAN. You can use them to connect dissimilar LANs and to alleviate traffic bottleneck problems. The IBM 8209 bridge, for example, can be used to connect an Ethernet and a Token Ring LAN together. Conceptually these devices *bridge* the gap between dissimilar LANs. They also can connect to LANs of the same type, such as two Ethernet LANs.

Although bridges and routers are described as devices, you may wonder exactly what that means. They consist of a computer that runs algorithms to perform bridging or routing functions. If high performance is desired, these devices are special dedicated computers that can perform bridging and routing functions efficiently. For bridges, the algorithms are usually encoded in EPROM (firmware) for rapid execution. Routers, as you learn shortly, are more complicated than bridges and may require frequent fixes by the vendor to correct problems. It is easier to implement the routing algorithms in software so that they can be changed more easily.

Many vendors allow incremental expanding of their bridges and routers. Hardware modules that consist of one or more network boards can be used to connect to different types of networks. These hardware modules fit into a slot in the bridge or router and connect to a high-speed backplane bus that is used for data transfer between the modules.

Vendors who make routers and bridges include Cisco, DEC, Vitalink, Wellfleet, New Bridge, 3COM, Timeplex, BBN, Novell, and many others. Novell does not make a specialized router product like the other vendors. Routers from Novell are workstations or servers that run routing software. Up to four NICs (16 in NetWare v3.x) can be added to a server or a workstation so that it can perform routing among the network boards.

In earlier Novell literature, the routing function provided by NetWare was called a *bridge*. To be compatible with the rest of the industry, Novell now calls it a *router*.

What Is a Repeater?

A *repeater* operates at the physical layer of the OSI model. It takes a signal from one LAN, reconditions and re-times it, and sends it to another LAN.

The reconditioning usually amplifies and boosts the power level of the signal. The repeater has no knowledge of the meaning of the individual bits in the packet. A repeater cannot be addressed individually; no address field exists in the packet for a repeater.

The repeater's job is simple. Detect the signal, amplify and retime it, and send it through all the ports except the one on which the signal was seen. In the case of Ethernet, the signals that are transmitted include data packets and even collisions. The segments of the LAN that are connected participate in the media access mechanism such as CSMA/CD or Token Access (see Chapter 2). For Token Ring LANs, each station performs the repeater function so that usually no separate repeater device is needed. Some fiber optic media extensions to the Token Ring may use special repeater devices to boost the signal over long distances.

What Is a Bridge?

Bridges connect two separate networks to form a logical network. An example of a bridge between an IEEE 802.3 and IEEE 802.5 LAN is shown in figure 3.1. This bridge has two network cards: a Token Ring card and an Ethernet card. The Token Ring card is used to connect the bridge to the Token Ring LAN and the Ethernet card is used to connect to the Ethernet LAN.

One way of looking at this concept is that a bridge has a split personality. It behaves as a Token Ring station and also as an Ethernet station, and herein lies the key to understanding its function. In figure 3.1, a packet sent from station A to station B does not cross the bridge in its normal mode of operation. The bridge detects that stations A and B are on the same LAN and a bridging function is not required.

If, however, station A sends a packet to station C, the bridge realizes that station C is on another LAN (Token Ring) and places the packet on the Token Ring LAN. It cannot place the Ethernet packet directly to the Token Ring LAN because the Ethernet frame cannot be understood by the Token Ring LAN. The bridge must remove the Ethernet header and replace it with a Token Ring header containing C's address. The bridge also must wait for a free token before placing the packet on the Token Ring LAN. As it waits, other packets may be sent to it for transmission to the Token Ring LAN. These packets must be queued for processing. A bridge, therefore, must have storage capacity to store frames and acts as a store-and-forward device.

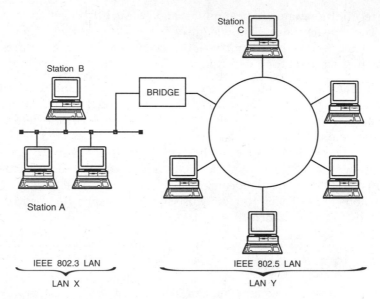

Figure 3.1:
Bridge between IEEE 802.3 and IEEE 802.5 LAN.

In figure 3.1, most of the stations on LAN X communicate among themselves. Occasionally, stations in LAN X may need to communicate with stations in LAN Y. Another way of saying this is that most of the traffic is intra-LAN (within a LAN), and a small fraction is inter-LAN (between two LANs). A good rule of thumb is the 80/20 rule. About 80 percent or more of traffic should be intra-LAN traffic and 20 percent or less should be inter-LAN traffic.

If the 80/20 rule is violated frequently, the stations generating excessive inter-LAN traffic should be detected and relocated to another LAN so that they do not cause excessive inter-LAN traffic. Stations generating excessive traffic can be detected by using protocol analyzers, such as LANalyzer, or SNMP managers, such as LANtern Services Manager. Novell makes both of these products.

A bridge operates at the data link layer of the OSI model. A bridge performs most of its work at layer 2. Bridges examine the *Media Access Control* (MAC) header of a data packet. The MAC address corresponds to the layer 2 address and represents the physical station address or the hardware address of the network board. MAC addresses are unique for every station. Bridges rely on MAC addresses for their operation.

Unlike a repeater, a bridge actually sees the data packet. Bridge ports have unique MAC addresses. A bridge has an understanding of the data packet up to the data link layer and can decode it up to this level. Bridges isolate the media access mechanisms of the LANs to which they are connected. Thus, collisions in a CSMA/CD LAN do not propagate across a bridge. In the case of Token Ring LANs joined by a bridge, the token does not cross a bridge. Because bridges are selective about which data packets can be transferred, they help solve traffic bottleneck problems.

Bridges are effective for a small number of LANs, but as the number of LANs grow, the number of possible paths between the sender and receiving station become very large. Not all the possible paths are optimal—some paths involve roundabout ways of getting to the destination, and this can create unnecessary traffic. If a bridge is to be effective for large LANs, it must have knowledge about the optimal path. But a bridge only operates at the data link layer, and the routing information is part of layer 3 (network layer) operation. By definition, therefore, bridges cannot make decisions about routes through the network because information on routes is encoded in the network address. And the network address is accessible only by the network layer.

Although a bridge can seem limited, it is a simple and an inexpensive way to interconnect two LANs. To perform intelligent routing decisions, you need a router.

What Is a Router?

A *router* operates at the network layer of the OSI model. A router performs most of its work at layer 3. Bridges are limited to examining the MAC address of a data packet, but routers can examine the network address. Because the network address usually has routing information encoded in it, routers can make use of this capability to make intelligent decisions. Thus, a *route* in a network consists of network addresses and paths. Routers are aware of many possible paths to get to a destination and also are aware of which path is the most optimal. The optimum path can be determined by various cost metrics. A *cost metric* is a formula that can be based on the following parameters:

- Is the destination reachable?

- How many hops does it take to reach the destination? The link between two store-and-forward devices is one hop.

- What is the time delay to reach the destination?
- What is the cost of transmission for the paths along the route?
- What is the data transfer capacity (bandwidth) of various paths?
- What is the status of links along the path?

The cost metric for determining the best route can become complex. Routers can be distinguished on the basis of the criteria they use to determine the optimal path.

Because routers have a lot more information to work with, they can do more things with a packet than a bridge, and they also are more complex. Because they are more difficult and costly to develop, routers cost more. They do more processing of the packets than a bridge; therefore, they tend to be slower than bridges.

Routers are the devices of choice to use to interconnect large LANs. You also can use routers to connect LANs over long distances. In figure 3.2, a gateway device is shown operating at layer 7. In general, a *gateway* is a device that can operate at any layer of the OSI model and provides translation between two incompatible protocols. A gateway operating at layer 7 is an application layer gateway. Examples of this concept are X.400 gateways. Devices that connect to IBM's SNA networks are usually called gateways because SNA protocols are proprietary and wholesale translation must be done to connect to IBM's SNA networks.

Repeaters, Bridges, Routers, and the OSI Model

The best way to understand the difference between repeaters, bridges, and routers is in reference to the OSI model. If you are not familiar with the OSI model, you may want to review the discussion in Chapter 1.

Figure 3.2 shows a model for several interconnection devices in relationship to the OSI model. The model shown in this figure is for a repeater, bridge, and router.

Local versus Remote Connections

Bridges and routers also can be classified on the basis of whether they are local or remote (wide area network). The difference depends on their network interfaces or ports.

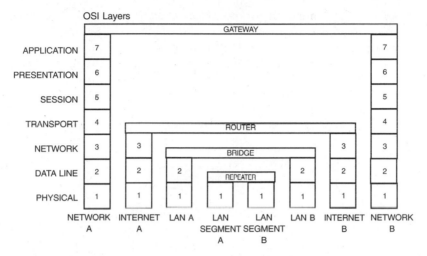

Figure 3.2:
OSI model for repeaters, bridges, and routers.

Local bridges and routers have ports that connect them to local transmission media over relatively short distances. An example of this setup is the transceiver cable used in Ethernet LANs. You can choose from a variety of choices such as coaxial, twisted pair, and fiber optic media to connect local devices to a network. The actual media choice often is dictated by the LAN that is being connected.

Remote bridges and routers require ports that can connect them to long-haul transmission media. You have fewer interface choices for long transmission media. Some popular choices include RS-232 ports and V.35 ports. Many remote devices have two or more remote connections and at least one local connection. LANs separated by large distances, therefore, can be connected by two remote devices as shown in figure 3.3. Router A has two local ports and one remote port. Router B has one remote port and one local port. The remote ports are connected by a point-to-point link. You can run a number of protocols on these point-to-point links. Some of the choices include X.25, Frame Relay, T1, SONET, and SMDS (see Chapter 4).

Besides point-to-point links, you also can use *cloud* technologies to connect LANs. *Point-to-point* links are telephone circuits, or T1 circuits, that you can lease from telephone companies or other vendors. Because these lines are dedicated for the communications from the sender point to a destination point, they are named point-to-point. *Cloud* technologies, such as the type shown in figure 3.4, are based on switching systems. The router, acting as the Customer Premise Equipment (CPE) is used to connect to the cloud. The details of the cloud are not known to the LAN. It may use an X.25/X.75 protocol, Frame Relay, SMDS switches, or a proprietary technology. The cloud or wide area network (WAN) is managed by the organization that provides the long-haul service.

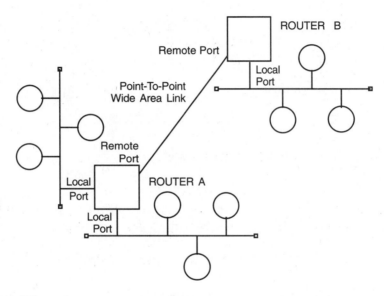

Figure 3.3:
Remote routers.

A difference between local and remote bridges and routers is the cost of the connection. Because local connections are managed entirely by the organization that owns the LAN, no additional cost is incurred. For remote connections, you must pay for the services provided by the long-haul vendor. Typical costs of such services are $2000 per month or higher. This amount is beyond the budget of small organizations. With advances in technology, it is hoped that these costs will come down.

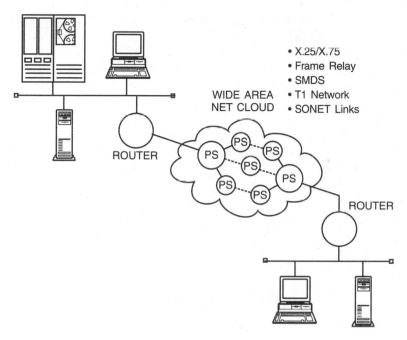

Figure 3.4:
Routers connected by means of WAN cloud technologies.

Transparent Bridges versus Source-Routing Bridges

The two predominant methods of bridging are the *Transparent Bridge* (TB) and the *Source-Routing* (SR) bridge. In transparent bridging (also called *spanning tree bridges*), the decision to relay packets is performed by the bridge and is transparent to workstations.

Figure 3.5 shows a transparent bridge network. Each bridge maintains a table that keeps track of station addresses. Transparent bridges examine the source address of every packet they see and record this source address in the bridge table along with the number of the port on which the packet was seen. Transparent bridges also maintain a timeout field for each table entry so that old entries can be periodically purged.

Consider what happens if station A transmits a packet to station Z. Bridge 1 sees the packet and consults its table to see whether or not it has an entry for station Z. If it does not, it forwards the packet through all of its out ports, excluding the port on which the packet was observed. Bridge 1 also checks the source address field of the packet and records it in its table that station A can be reached at its port 2. When Bridge 2 sees the packet, it repeats the algorithm just described. If there is no entry for station Z, it forwards the packet through all its outgoing ports (flooding). It also records the fact that station A can be reached through its port 3. When station Z acknowledges the message from A, it sends a packet with source address Z and destination address A. After Bridge 2 consults its table, it notes that A can be reached through port 3, and forwards the packet only through port 3. It also records that station Z can be reached through its port 2.

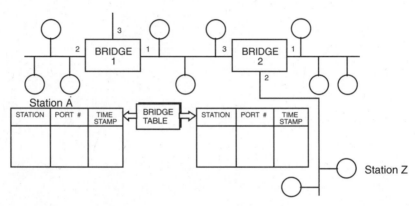

Figure 3.5:
Transparent bridge network.

To prevent endless circulation of packets, transparent bridge networks cannot have loops. The transmission path forms a spanning tree that covers all the stations on the network. If there are bridges that could form a loop, as shown in figure 3.6, these bridges must remain inactive. The inactive bridges act like redundant bridges. Redundant bridges are activated after the spanning tree topology changes. Topology changes are transmitted by *Bridge Protocol Data Units* (BPDUs). This special protocol is used to maintain the overall spanning tree topology. The process of arriving at the spanning tree is called the *spanning tree algorithm*. One bridge in the spanning tree becomes the *root* and all other bridges transmit frames in the direction of the root by using a least-cost metric.

The spanning tree bridge is the preferred method for Ethernet and IEEE 802.3 networks and is supported by vendors that manufacture bridges for these LANs.

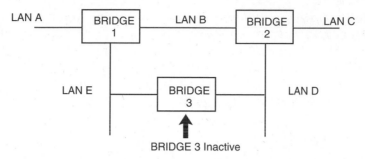

Figure 3.6:
Avoiding loops on transparent bridge networks.

Source routing, a different method sponsored by IBM, connects bridges to its Token Ring networks. In Source Routing, the source (sender) must determine the best path to get to a destination. After this path is discovered, the source station maintains this path in its routing table and includes this path in the *Routing Information* (RI) field for every packet that is sent. The RI field is shown in figure 3.7 along with its relationship to the Token Ring packet. The RI field is present whenever the I/G bit of the source address is set to 1. This I/G bit also is referred to as the *Routing Information Indicator* (RII) bit. The Token Ring frame structure is discussed in Chapter 2. The *Routing Designator* (RD) fields contain the path the packet must follow to arrive at the destination. RD fields consist of a ring number and a bridge number pair. SR bridges simply follow the directions in the routing information field. A total of 14 RD fields are possible, which limits the largest transmission path to 13 bridges or hops. IBM's implementation currently limits total RD fields to eight, which corresponds to seven bridges or hops.

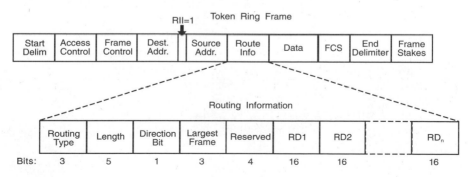

Figure 3.7:
Routing information field.

Figure 3.8 shows the path from station A to Z using source routing. The details of the routing field also are shown.

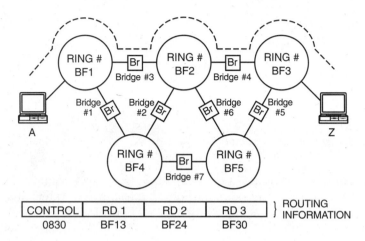

CONTROL	RD 1	RD 2	RD 3	} ROUTING INFORMATION
0830	BF13	BF24	BF30	

Figure 3.8:
Transmission using source routing.

The key to the operation of source routing is discovering the initial route. This is done by sending a *discovery frame* that is broadcast by the source node when it wants to discover the best path to a destination. The discovery frame circulates on the network and arrives at the destination with a record of the path taken. The discovery frames are returned to the sender, who then selects the best possible path.

IEEE 802.5 networks prefer the source routing method. How do you connect IEEE 802.3 networks that use Transparent Bridges with IEEE 802.5 networks that use source routing? One method is to have a bridge, such as the IBM 8209 bridge, that provides translation of routing information between the two separate bridge mechanisms. Another method is to use a bridge that is a combination of source routing and transparent bridges. These bridges are called *Source Routing Transparent* (SRT) bridges. In SRT, transparent bridging is used when there is no RI field; otherwise, source routing is used. The model for SRT bridges is shown in figure 3.9. The MAC layer entity consists of SR and TB algorithms. These algorithms are invoked depending on the setting of the RII bit.

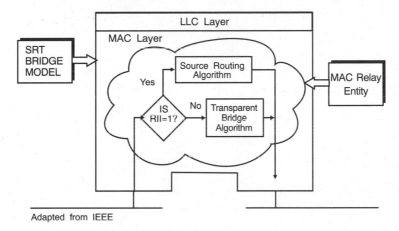

Adapted from IEEE

Figure 3.9:
Source Routing Transparent (SRT) bridges.

How Does Routing Work?

An internetwork based on routers consists of many distinct logical networks (see fig. 3.10). A logical network is characterized by having its own unique network address. This network address is common to all the nodes in the logical network. The individual nodes in a logical network are distinguished by their own unique addresses. For LANs, this is the MAC layer or physical address, such as an Ethernet address or Token Ring address. Therefore, to address a node on a different logical network, the sending station must know the network address and the node address of the destination node. This information is then encoded in the packet that is sent. Routers that connect these two networks rely on the network address information in the packet to forward the packet to its correct destination.

The logical networks in the internetwork can be managed by potentially independent organizations and can be viewed as separate administrative domains. These separate administrative domains make their own decisions about which kind of networking software to run. Because different networking software use different protocols, the internetwork runs a variety of protocols. Any router used to connect the logical networks must understand all these different protocols. Most routers that are made today, therefore, are multiprotocol routers. Some of the common protocols that are supported by multiprotocol routers are as follows:

- IPX/SPX
- XNS Protocols
- TCP/IP
- SLIP (Serial Line Internet Protocol)
- PPP (Point-to-Point Protocol)
- SNAP (Sub-Net Access Protocol)
- DECnet
- SNA (Systems Network Architecture)
- X.25
- CLNP (Connectionless Network Protocol)
- IS-IS (Intermediate System to Intermediate System)
- ES-IS (End System to Intermediate System)

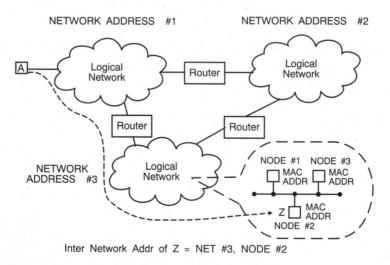

Figure 3.10:
Internetworking addressing.

Novell routers are designed to connect Novell networks and to understand IPX protocols only. NetWare v3.x-based routers can be extended to provide IP routing.

Not all protocols are routable. Examples of nonroutable protocols are *Local Area Transport* (LAT) from DEC, LU 6.2, and NetBIOS protocols from IBM. These protocols do not have an explicit network layer. Routers depend on the network layer for their operation. Protocols that do not have a network layer are unroutable. Unroutable protocols must be bridged.

Routers examine the network layer source and destination address in the packet to determine where a packet came from and where it needs to be delivered. The packets may not tell the router how it should accomplish this task. Routers are expected to figure out the best possible path. A number of criteria, such as cost and distance, help determine the best possible path. The information related to determining the best possible path is kept in an internal database called the *routing table*. A fundamental requirement of a router is to initialize and maintain its routing table. Based on the routing table information, it should determine the next hop in the journey of the packet.

Routing tables can be global or local. Global routing tables have a table entry for every node on the network and can therefore use global optimization techniques to determine the best possible path. For large networks, the cost of maintaining a very large routing table with the most recent information can become prohibitive. Most modern routers use local routing information, where routers know information about the "local" portion of the internetwork they connect to. The routing tables for such routers tend to be smaller and more manageable.

Another distinction between routers is the manner in which the information in routing tables is updated. There are two approaches: static and dynamic. In static routing, the administrators manually must set each entry in the routing table. Although this approach may be advantageous for total security and control, it also is inflexible and does not automatically adapt to network changes. In dynamic routing, the routing tables are set automatically by each router. Special packets that contain routing information are exchanged by routers. These packets contain updates on path information and are used by routers to update their routing tables. The manner in which these special packets exchange information constitutes a routing protocol. Many types of routing protocols exist. The routing protocol used in NetWare routers is based on Xerox's XNS protocols. Dynamic routing always involves the use of some routing protocol and is more flexible than static routing. Dynamic routing is the preferred approach in most modern routers.

To make the most current information available to the network, a router broadcasts information whenever it detects a change in the network. If a certain link goes down or a new link is available to form an additional path, the information concerning it is broadcast by using a routing protocol. The amount of information that is sent can vary from an incremental update to an entire routing table. The number of routers to which this information is sent and the actual amount of information that is sent depends on the routing protocol that is used.

After a router sees a packet, it examines its routing table for the destination address to send the packet along the best possible path. The determination of the best possible path depends on these factors:

- The routing metric
- The routing algorithm
- Available information in the routing table
- The topology of the network, and the locations of the routers in the network

If the routing metric is based on distance, the best possible path is the shortest path. Most routers use a simplifying metric, which is called the *hop metric*, to measure distances. A hop is a path between two store-and-forward devices such as a router or a station. The number of hops, therefore, is a measure of the number of times a packet has to be processed by a router.

The shortest path can turn out to be the most expensive path. A metric is needed that can factor other variables such as economic cost, line speed, and transmission delay. The routing algorithms that make use of these metrics can be classified into two broad categories: *Distance Vector Algorithms* (DVAs) and *Link State Algorithms* (LSAs).

A knowledge of these classifications is important. LSA-based networks, for example, adapt more quickly to network changes and are more robust than their DVA counterparts. Because of their quick response time, LSA-based networks make better use of communications facilities and have better performance figures.

The major distinction between DVA and LSA is the manner in which they compute the cost for each path. In DVA, the model of the network is computed by each router telling its neighboring routers information about the rest of the network. This process is much like the party game in which a message is whispered to one individual who whispers it to another and so on, until everyone has heard the information. The last person to hear the information, often hears an entirely different message. Although routers tend to transmit information more reliably than people, this example points out the weakness of the DVA algorithm. As information is propagated from router to router, not all routers have the same view of the network. Also, it takes a while for the information to propagate. During this period of time, the routing tables will be inconsistent with the network topology, and this may lead to transient anomalies such as packets being lost or delivered by inefficient routes. NetWare routers handle this problem by providing a RESET ROUTER command that can cause routing tables to be updated immediately.

LSAs compute the model of the network based on each router telling the rest of the network about its connections. Because each router knows exactly who its neighbors are and the type of connections it has, other nodes on the network have a more complete picture. LSA-based routers contribute to more router traffic on the network and more work for the router. An advantage of LSA is that the topological map of the network can be more easily constructed from LSA information. Topological maps are a great help in routing hierarchical networks.

Hierarchical networks are useful in the construction of large networks (see fig. 3.11). To make routing more manageable, the network is divided into regions or areas. Each area has its own routers. The routers within an area only perform routing for nodes in that area. These intra-area routers are called level 1 routers. Areas are joined together by inter-area routers called level 2 routers. The level 2 routers form a logical router backbone, which is used for transmitting inter-area traffic. An example of a hierarchical network is DECnet or the DoD internet.

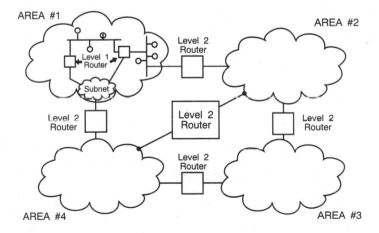

Figure 3.11:
Hierarchical networks.

The other type of network is a flat network, which consists of only one level. This network contains no hierarchy of areas and routers. All routers are on the same logical level with no distinction between parts of the network. Flat area networks are suited for small networks. An example of a flat network is NetWare LANs connected by NetWare routers.

Both DVA- and LSA-routing algorithms can be used for either flat or hierarchical networks. LSA works better, however, with hierarchical networks because the network topology can be derived more easily from it.

Until recently, most routing protocols have been DVA-based and implemented on flat networks. The XNS routing protocol on which Novell's routing protocol is based is DVA-based. The XNS routing protocol is called the *Routing Information Protocol* (RIP). Do not confuse it with the protocol of the same name, RIP, that is used for TCP/IP-based networks. The TCP/IP RIP and XNS RIP are different. TCP/IP RIP also is DVA-based.

Newer protocols, such as *Open Shortest Path First* (OSPF) for TCP/IP networks and *Intermediate System to Intermediate System* (IS-IS) for OSI-based networks, use LSA techniques.

DVA- and LSA-based routing techniques have been used for flat and hierarchical networks. The LSA algorithm, because it deals with topological maps of the network, can be used more easily to partition networks into areas. This is exactly what is required for hierarchical networks that are divided into special areas. Therefore, LSA techniques adapt better to hierarchical networks.

As networks grow in size, DVA-based routers do not perform very efficiently. They transmit their entire routing tables, which can get very large as networks grow in size. Networks that make use of LSA-based routers scale much better as networks grow.

Initially, most of the networks started using DVA-based routers. The problems with DVA did not surface until the networks began growing in size. A classic example of this is the TCP/IP-based internet, in which networks that connect to the backbone still make use of DVA-based RIP. Many of the DVA-based protocols were derived from XNS routing protocol, also called RIP, which also stands for Routing Information Protocol. This includes the TCP/IP RIP and Novell's RIP. All three RIPs (XNS, TCP/IP, and Novell) are different, and unfortunately, they all use the same acronym. If you are dealing with a multivendor network, you are likely to see all three on the internet, and this can cause some confusion.

The two LVA-based routing protocols that you should be aware of are OSPF for TCP/IP networks and IS-IS for OSI-based networks. Both protocols use LSA techniques. As networks evolve to more open standards, vendors may be forced to adopt these routing protocols.

A discussion of these protocols is beyond the scope of this book. This book focuses on Novell's RIP.

Bridges versus Routers

Bridges and routers can both be used to consolidate networks. They provide a wide range of functionality and features that can be helpful in simplifying the task of network administration. Bridges and routers have their own unique advantages and disadvantages. Table 3.1 summarizes the pros and cons of bridges, and table 3.2 examines the advantages and disadvantages of routers.

Table 3.1
Bridging: Pros and Cons

Pros	Cons
Simple to install and load configure	Cannot perform effective balancing
Perform automatic reconfiguration	Can cause traffic overload problems
Can be used with protocols that cannot be routed	Ineffective in preventing broadcast storms
Can be moved easily with bridge networks	Certain applications may not run on bridge networks
Have good cost/performance ratio	

Table 3.2
Routing: Pros and Cons

Pros	Cons
More flexible than bridges	More difficult to set up
Can perform load balancing/sharing	Moving stations can be difficult
Are effective in controlling broadcast storms	Routers based on static routing can cause problems
More effective for large networks with arbitrary topologies	Some protocols cannot be routed
Can accommodate growth more easily	

Bridges do not require complex configurations. You can power them on and connect them to networks without any problem. This makes them easy to install. Some of the more advanced bridges may require some configuration if you want to manually enter routing information in the bridges' tables, but the interface is easy to use.

Because bridges do not have a network address (they operate below the network layer), the networking software on the nodes does not need to be configured to recognize newly installed bridges. In other words, under typical circumstances, bridges are transparent to the network software. The only time you may have to do any configuring at the nodes is if you are dealing with IBM bridges that use source routing.

Because bridges operate below the network layer of the OSI model, they need to know about protocol details of upper layers. There are numerous upper-layer protocols, and the complexity of dealing with them is hidden from bridges. A consequence of this is that bridges do not have to be configured for upper-layer protocols, as long as they can understand the data link protocols, such as Ethernet, Token Ring, and so on. Certain upper-layer protocols, such as NetBIOS (PC networks), LU6.2 (IBM SNA networks), and LAT (DECnet), cannot be routed effectively, but they can be used with bridges because bridges do not need to know the details of upper-layer protocols.

Bridges form a single logical network that has the same network address. The stations and bridge ports in a bridge internetwork have their own unique node address, but because they share the same network address, they can be moved around in the same logical network without having to configure them for new network addresses.

Bridges provide very rapid packet transfer at relatively low cost. In many situations, there is a negligible penalty paid (1 to 5 percent drop in data rate) when transferring data between two networks.

Because bridges are not aware of redundant paths on the network, they cannot perform load sharing across these paths. A single path can get heavily congested by internet traffic even though alternative paths can be used to reduce the congestion.

Bridges can flood the network unexpectedly. This results in very slow networks.

Large networks connected by bridges may experience what are called *broadcast storms*. As the name suggests, there is a sudden rise in the number of broadcast packets. Broadcast packets are used by the upper-layer protocols (layers 3 and above) to communicate general information about themselves to the rest of the network. An example of this is the SAP and RIP protocols used by NetWare (discussed later in this chapter). Bridges use BPDUs that are broadcast to all other bridges. All of this extra traffic can cause significant load. Most of these broadcast protocols use a 60-second (or a multiple) interval, and if they get synchronized, very high-peak loads can occur at 60-second intervals.

Bridges can prevent certain types of applications from running on the networks. Some applications need unique network names based on the network address. Because there is one network address for a bridged network, multiple copies of the application cannot run on the same network.

Routers have more options for partitioning networks in different ways. For instance, they can perform load sharing if alternate paths of equal cost are available. They can associate a cost metric called the *Route Path Cost* (RPC) for each route and select the optimum route. The route-path cost can be determined as a function of economic cost, data rate, path delays, security cost, and priorities.

Routers can be configured to prevent broadcast storms. They can be used to selectively filter out certain types of traffic for networks. For example, there is no sense in broadcasting a NetWare SAP packet to an interconnected

AppleTalk network if there are no NetWare servers on that network. Routers can be used to contain broadcast traffic within a single network because they have knowledge of the broadcast protocols.

Routers are more effective than bridges for maintaining and configuring large networks. They can support arbitrary topologies and can more easily accommodate network growth.

Setting up routers may require specialized training. Many router vendors offer week-long training classes. Each individual protocol that will be routed needs to be set up independently. The information on protocols in this book will help you understand a router's configuration parameters.

Moving end systems (ES-OSI terminology for user stations) between network segments is more difficult because their network addresses have to be changed to the network address of the relocated end system.

Some routers make use of static routing. This means that routing information has to be entered manually into the router's table by the network manager. This can be a very laborious and tedious process. Also, manual entry is always prone to errors and can easily get out of date when network changes are made. Many networking problems on large networks can be traced to incorrect entries in static routing tables.

Some protocols, such as NetBIOS, LU6.2, and LAT, cannot be routed. Many of these protocols do not follow the OSI model in terms of having an explicit network layer. The router needs an explicit network header from which a network address can be extracted. If the protocol cannot provide a router with this information, it cannot perform routing. For this reason, some vendors provide a product which is a combination of a bridge and a router (*Brouter*=Bridge + Router). A brouter will try to route a protocol. If it cannot do so, it will try to bridge it.

Examining NetWare Routers

This section discusses NetWare-based routers. The actual routing mechanism that is used is discussed followed by a discussion about the IPX, RIP, and SAP mechanisms that are essential to routing. This section also discusses limitations of NetWare-based routers and how to manage the network number assignment for routers.

Understanding NetWare Routing

All NetWare servers can act as internetwork routers. Additionally, you can configure ordinary PC workstations to act as routers. Because servers perform the dual role of router and server, such configurations are called *internal routers*. If a PC workstation is set up to perform DOS and routing functions, it also is a nondedicated router; if it is set up to perform routing functions only, it is called a dedicated router. And because the routing is done on a separate external device, such routers are called external routers.

Figure 3.12 shows the routing processes running on a router. This routing process is an integral part of a NetWare server. The routing software also can be generated and configured for external routers by using Novell's ROUTEGEN utility. The use of this utility is discussed later in this chapter.

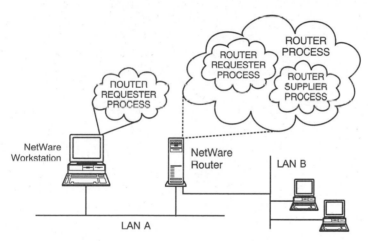

Figure 3.12:
NetWare router processes.

All stations on a NetWare LAN are somewhat aware of routing. They all have a *router requester process* that is used for requesting routing information from other routers. NetWare routers additionally have a *router supplier process* that is used to supply routing information to the router requester process. In short, all stations, including routers, have a router requester process. Only NetWare routers have the router supplier process (see fig. 3.12). The request for routing information and the reply to it are transmitted by using the routing information protocol.

When a packet is sent to a router (see fig. 3.13), the NIC card in the router observes the packet and reports it to the network driver by using the hardware interrupt mechanism. The network driver performs data link layer processing (layer 2 of OSI model) on the packet. This process strips the data link layer header and passes the data to the next higher layer, which is the network layer. The network layer in NetWare routers implements the IPX protocol. If the destination network address of the IPX packet differs from the network address of the network on which the IPX packet was seen, the IPX packet is sent to the routing process. The routing process determines which of its NIC ports should be used to forward the packet.

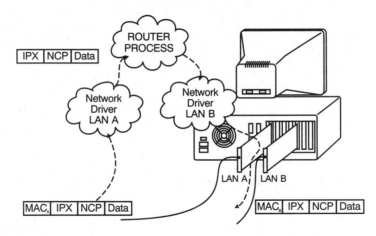

Figure 3.13:
NetWare router packet processing.

Figure 3.14 shows two LANs that are connected by a NetWare router. Each network to which the router connects has a unique logical network address. In a pure NetWare-based network that only uses NetWare routers, stations on the same cabling plant or logical network have the same unique network address (also called the network number). If stations have the same network address, no routing is necessary to transfer packets between them. Destinations on the same logical network are reached using the broadcast mechanism inherent in LANs. If the destination has a different network address, a router is needed to route the packet to the appropriate destination LAN. If a packet is sent from station A to station B, no routing is necessary because both stations are on the same LAN and have the same network number. If a packet is sent from station A to station C, routing is necessary because station C has a different network number from station A.

The full destination address of a packet is encoded in the IPX header and consists of the network number, the node address, and the socket number. The node address is the data link layer address of a station and is the address of the NIC card in a station. This address is fixed (burned in ROM on NIC) or set by switch settings on the NIC. The socket number uniquely identifies the software process that is running on the station.

In figure 3.14, the internet IPX address of a packet sent from station A to station C is shown. The routing requester process at station A realizes that the network destination is different than LAN X. Station A knows of router R on the network. During data link encapsulation, the destination data link address is set to that of the router. The router receives the packet that was addressed to it and decapsulates the data link header. This process recovers the original IPX packet that was sent from station A. The IPX packet's destination address is examined by the routing process in the router. The routing process consults its routing table and determines that the destination network is connected to one of its ports. It then sends the packet to the appropriate NIC port for encapsulation and transmission. Finally, destination C receives the packet and decapsulates it. On further examination of the IPX destination address, station C determines that it is indeed the correct recipient of the packet.

If the router had determined after examining its routing table that the destination LAN was not directly attached to one of its ports, then the router would forward the packet on one of its ports. The decision on which port to send the packet would be based on the hops and delays it would take to reach the destination.

In general, there are three possibilities for forwarding a packet:

- If the router is an internal router and the destination is the internal router, the packet is passed directly to the *File Service Process* (FSP).

- If the destination number of the IPX packet is the same as that of the network number to which the router is directly connected, the router forwards the packet to the directly-connected network. Before sending this packet, it properly encapsulates it by using the MAC header (data link layer header). This situation is essentially the same as that discussed in figure 3.14.

- If the destination number of the IPX packet is different than that of the directly connected networks, the router must determine the next router responsible for transmission of the packet. This determination is based on the entry for the destination network in its routing table, which contains the fastest path to get to the destination network.

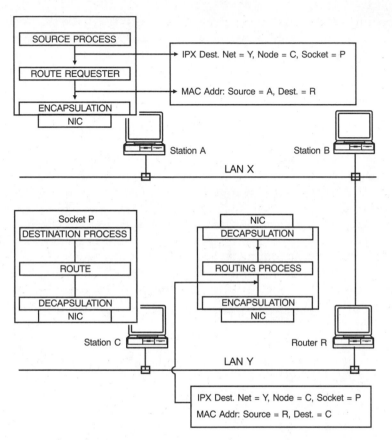

Figure 3.14:
NetWare routing model.

As the packet passes through the routers, the IPX source and destination addresses do not change. Only the MAC header changes by the encapsulation and decapsulation process. The MAC header contains the immediate source and immediate destination address to forward the packet on its next hop. The IPX header essentially remains the same so that all routers can follow the same algorithm to reach the destination. The only modification is that the transport control field (discussed in the next section) is incremented to count the number of routers the packet has passed through.

Internet Packet Exchange (IPX)

To understand NetWare routing, you should understand the manner in which stations are addressed in a NetWare LAN. This address is encoded in the IPX packet and is used by routers. RIP and the algorithms associated with it are based on the semantics of the IPX packet structure. This section introduces the fundamentals of IPX semantics. Some of the information in this section may seem a little too detailed, but if as a LAN manager, you are involved in managing your LAN with a protocol analyzer, this information is invaluable.

Figure 3.15 shows an IPX packet encapsulated by an Ethernet packet. The IPX packet encapsulates upper-layer protocols such as SPX and NCP. The meaning of the fields in the IPX packet are summarized in table 3.3. The diagram is shown for descriptive purposes. In actual practice, Novell avoids the use of the SPX protocol to minimize protocol overhead.

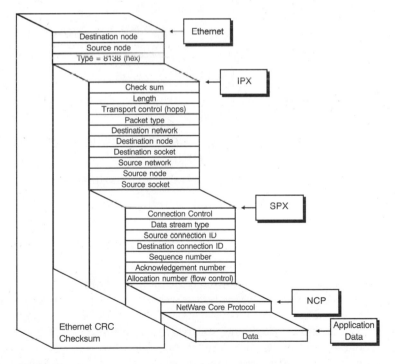

Figure 3.15:
IPX packet. (Drawing courtesy of Learning Group International)

The *checksum* field is a ones complement add-and-left-cycle (rotate) of all the 16-bit words in the IPX packet. The checksum does not include the checksum word itself and is designed to be easily computable. Another characteristic of the checksum is that it can be incrementally computed if only a few words change, such as a change in the network address fields. The checksum is inherited from the XNS *Internet Datagram Protocol* (IDP) packet from which IPX is derived. It is in addition to any hardware-generated checksums used at the data link layer of the OSI model.

Table 3.3
IPX Packet Structure

Field	Meaning
Checksum	Optional 1s complement checksum
Length	Byte length of IPX packet
Transport Control	Used by routers as a "hop count" field
Packet Type	Identifies type of data encoded in the data portion of IPX packet
Destination Network	Uniquely identifies destination network from a number of interconnected networks
Number Destination Node Address	Uniquely identifies the node address of the destination station
Destination Socket	Software address in destination node
Source Network Number	Uniquely identifies source network from a number of interconnected networks
Source Node Address	Uniquely identifies the source node of the sending station
Source Socket	Software address in sending node

At the time XNS was designed, hardware and memory systems were not very reliable. One of the functions of this checksum is to verify the data path between the NIC and memory in the station. IPX ignores the checksum field and places all 1s (FFFF hex) in this field to indicate that the field is not used.

NetWare-based networks rely on the data link control and other upper-layer mechanisms for error control. This avoids the processing overhead of computing the checksum.

The *length* field contains the complete maximum length of the IPX packet measured in bytes. This figure includes the IPX header length of 30 bytes plus the data. If the packet contains an odd number of bytes in the data portion of the packet, an extra "garbage" byte is added to make the packet an integral number of 16-bit words. The garbage byte is not included in the length field. Originally, IPX packets had a nominal maximum length of 576 bytes. Allowing for 30 bytes of IPX header, this allowed a maximum of 576 − 30 = 546 bytes of data. This maximum length was inherited from the specification of the XNS IDP packets. Many LANs can accommodate larger packet sizes (1514 bytes for Ethernet), and the 576 byte maximum length restriction has been removed by Novell. IPX packets that use a longer packet length than 576 bytes do not interoperate with pure XNS routers that use smaller packet sizes. But because there are few installed examples of the original XNS routers, this is not a serious problem.

The *transport control* field is used for transporting internet packets across routers. This field is utilized only by routers. Workstations set this field to zero when sending a packet. The transport control field is an eight-bit field, but only four bits are used:

Transport Control

Bit: 7 6 5 4 3 2 1 0

         X X X X H H H H

Bits marked X X X X are unused and set to zero. Bits marked H H H H represent the hop count field. The hop count field is increased by one each time it is processed by a router. A router can determine the number of routers encountered by the packet. The four-bit hop count field limits the maximum number of routers in any path. A maximum of 15 routers are permissible on any transmission path. After the hop count field reaches a value of 16 (that is, when it reaches the sixteenth router), it is discarded. The XNS Error protocol is used to transmit this fact to the source. But because a datagram protocol (IPX) is used for this, there is no guarantee that the message will be seen by the source. Applications that need greater reliability must use the SPX protocol or some other internal mechanism.

The maximum hop count field ensures that IPX packets are not routed indefinitely in a loop. With a maximum value of 15 for the hop count field, you can have a maximum of 16 networks in any transmission path.

The *packet type* field is used to identify the data contents of the data portion of the IPX packet. This field is used for protocol multiplexing. It allows a number of client protocols to reside on top of IPX and allows the IPX module to determine which of the client protocols, SPX, PXP, NCP, Echo, Error, Serial (copy protection), Watch Dog, RIP, or SAP to send the packet to (see fig. 3.16). Some of the more common packet types are shown in table 3.4. Developers interested in a new packet type assignment must contact Xerox.

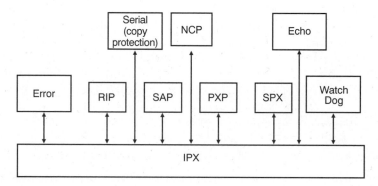

Figure 3.16:
IPX clients.

Table 3.4
Common Packet Type Assignments for IPX

Packet Type	Protocol
1	Routing Information Protocol (RIP)
2	Echo
3	Error
4	Packet Exchange Protocol (PXP)
5	Sequenced Packet Exchange (SPX)
17	NetWare Core Protocol (NCP)
20-37	Experimental

Network numbers identify uniquely the logical network to which a station is attached. Network numbers are primarily used for routing. The router routes the packet to the LAN that has the same destination number as the destination number in the IPX packet. This network number field in the IPX packet is four bytes. This field can, therefore, accommodate a network number size of eight hexadecimal digits. If the routing is to work correctly, all logical networks in an internetwork must have a unique network number. The network number must be different than the internal network number for NetWare v3.x servers. The network number is assigned at the time of installation for each logical network connected to the router. A value of zero for the destination network number means that the packet is not to be processed by an internetwork router.

From an administrative point of view, you must exercise control in keeping these network numbers unique within an organization. This administrative control is essential if LAN operations within an organization are decentralized. The *node address* uniquely identifies the station NIC within a logical network. After a packet is routed to the correct destination LAN, it must be sent to the correct station. The node address uniquely identifies the station to receive the packet. The IPX packet has a six-byte field for the node address and can accommodate a 12-digit hexadecimal number. XNS networks were originally designed for Ethernet, which has a six-byte address field. Fortunately, the six-byte address field is the same size used for IEEE LANs and FDDI. For LANs that use a smaller address size for stations, such as ARCnet or Proteon-10, the address field can be padded with zeros in the most significant digits. A node address of all 1s (hexadecimal FF FF FF FF FF FF) indicates a broadcast packet.

The *socket number* identifies the software or client process that is running at a station. A station can have a number of client processes running (see fig. 3.17). Because they run on the same station, they each have the same network number and node address. If a packet is to be sent to a specific client process, a means should exist to identify it uniquely. The socket number is used to identify the client process uniquely. Socket numbers are analogous to mail boxes. A client process is notified when a packet is delivered to its mail box. Sockets are implemented as data structures that can be used to send and receive packets at a unique software address within a station. They are inherently bidirectional in their nature.

Certain protocols make use of a standard socket number. These standard socket numbers are called *well-known socket numbers*. Table 3.5 lists some well-known socket numbers. You can obtain well-known socket numbers by contacting Xerox or Novell. Socket numbers above 8000 (hex) are assigned by Novell.

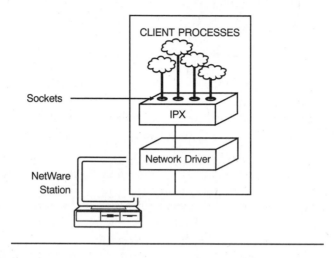

Figure 3.17:
IPX socket numbers.

Table 3.5
Well-Known Socket Numbers for IPX

Socket Number (hex)	Meaning
1	XNS Routing Information Protocol (RIP)
2	Echo Protocol Packet
3	Error Handler Packet
20 – 03F	Experimental
1 – BB8	Registered with Xerox
BB9 –	Dynamically Assignable
451	NetWare File Service Packet
452	NetWare Service Advertising Packet (SAP)
453	NetWare Routing Information Protocol (RIP)

Socket Number (hex)	Meaning
455	NetBIOS Packet
456	NetWare Diagnostic Packet
4001	NetWare Watchdog Packet
4003	NetWare Shell Socket
8000 –	Well-Known Socket Numbers Assigned by Novell

Using RIP and SAP

Routers use the RIP protocol to maintain a cache containing routing information (routing table). The routing algorithms used by routers serve the following purposes:

- Quickly initializes the routing table after the router starts
- Ensures that the routing table adapts quickly to changes in network topologies
- Ensures that if routers come up or go down, other routers learn about this change as quickly as possible

Every routing table contains at least the following information for every network that can be reached by the router:

- Timing delay to reach the network
- Number of hops to network
- A list of networks directly connected to the router
- Node address of a router on the directly connected network by which packets will reach the specified network for the amount of time delay and hops in the table entry
- A timer used for routing table maintenance to age out old entries

Figure 3.18 illustrates the routing table in a router.

During initialization, the router initializes the routing table to contain network numbers for directly connected networks. In figure 3.18, the directly connected networks LAN A, LAN B, LAN C, and LAN D have network numbers 1001, 1002, 1003, and 1004. This information is built into the router during installation time, and the routing process simply reads this information and initializes its routing table.

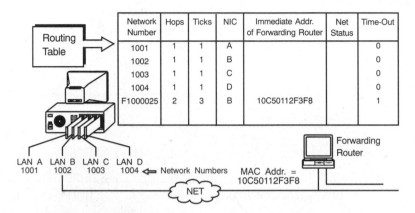

Network Number	Hops	Ticks	NIC	Immediate Addr. of Forwarding Router	Net Status	Time-Out
1001	1	1	A			0
1002	1	1	B			0
1003	1	1	C			0
1004	1	1	D			0
F1000025	2	3	B	10C50112F3F8		1

Figure 3.18:
Routing table in a NetWare router.

Requests for routing information and their corresponding replies are encoded in a RIP packet. Because transmission on the LAN is through a broadcast mechanism, routers see all RIP responses. Some responses answer RIP requests originated by the router and others are gratuitous information in reply to RIP requests from other routers. The router updates its tables if any of the following conditions is true:

- The RIP reply originated from an internetwork router connected to the directly connected network

- The existing entry in the routing table has not been updated for 90 seconds

- A better route was discovered to the specified network

Every time the router entry is updated, its timeout value is reset to 90 seconds. If a table entry has not been updated for three minutes (twice 90 seconds), it is assumed to be suspect. The number of hop fields is set to infinity (actually set to 16) to indicate that the network is no longer reachable. These entries are kept for another 60 seconds before being purged so that other routers know that the network cannot be reached.

Routers also broadcast a copy of their routing table in the RIP packet to other routers on all the networks to which it is connected. This response packet is sent at intervals of 60 seconds. In addition, whenever a router modifies its routing table entry, the change is broadcast to all routers on its directly connected networks. As the recipients of this information modify their routing table entries, they too, send RIP response packets to routers on their directly connected networks. This ripple effect quickly transmits the changes throughout the network.

When routers broadcast information they follow the "best information algorithm." The first rule is that the router will not broadcast routing information about networks to a directly connected network that was obtained from the same directly connected network. In figure 3.19, when router ROUTER_BC sends information on segment B, it should not include any information that it received from ROUTER_AB about segment A. If it did, a user might think that segment A could be reached directly through ROUTER_AB and ROUTER_BC. The second rule is similar to the first rule. It states that a router should not include information about a directly connected network to which they are sending routing information broadcasts. In the example in figure 3.19, ROUTER_BC cannot broadcast information about segment B on segment B. It can broadcast only on segment B information on segments C and D.

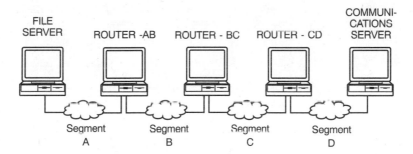

Figure 3.19:
Multiple LAN segments joined by NetWare routers.

Figures 3.20 to 3.23 provide an illustration of the router operations. When the router ROUTER_BC is first brought up, it initializes its routing tables with information on its directly connected networks. Next, the router sends an initial RIP response (see fig. 3.20) to inform routers on its directly connected segments (ROUTER_AB and ROUTER_CD) of the segments it will now make available (segments B and C).

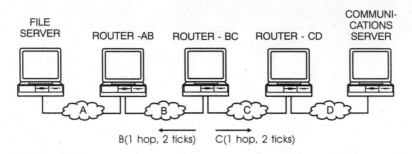

Figure 3.20:
Initial router broadcast.

Next, the router broadcasts a general RIP request on its directly connected networks for information on all network segments that exist on the internetwork (see fig. 3.21). All routers on its directly connected segment (ROUTER_AB and ROUTER_CD) send a RIP response to this request by using the best information algorithm. The router then initializes its routing table with this information. At periodic intervals the router is the recipient of routing information from other routers (see fig. 3.22).

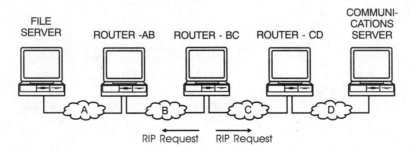

Figure 3.21:
Initial router request.

After the router is up, it broadcasts its routing information in a RIP response packet at 60-second intervals (see fig 3.23).

When routers are shut down gracefully by using the DOWN command (the power plug is not pulled suddenly), they broadcast a RIP response packet, which sets the delay for all networks it can reach to infinity. This response packet informs other routers that the router has been shut down and that it cannot be used.

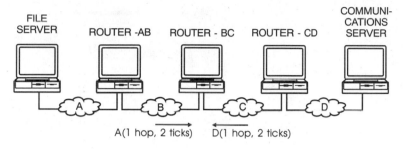

Figure 3.22:
Response from router.

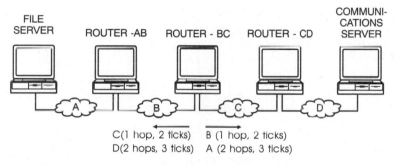

Figure 3.23:
RIP broadcasts at 60-second intervals.

This mechanism is illustrated in figure 3.24. When ROUTER_BC is shut down, it sends a RIP response to other routers, such as ROUTER_AB and ROUTER_CD, that it are no longer available. These routers then update their tables.

If you do not use the DOWN command to shut down a router or you have an unexpected power failure or hardware glitch, the neighboring routers are not immediately aware that a change has occurred. Unexpected shutdown can cause transient routing problems until the timeout mechanism for routing table entries goes into effect. It takes a delay of three minutes before other routers remove the entries in their routing table for the failed router.

When a router receives a request for information, it supplies the information in a RIP response packet. If it does not have the information, it returns a delay of infinity for the requested network to indicate that the network cannot be reached.

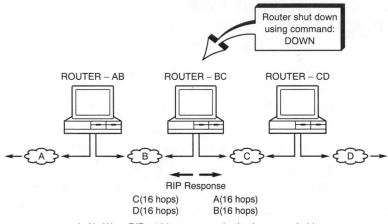

In NetWare RIP—16 hops means destination unreachable.

Figure 3.24:
RIP events when shutting down a server.

The RIP protocol is crucial so that routers can keep their routing tables up-to-date. Figure 3.25 shows the structure of the RIP packet, and figure 3.26 shows a RIP packet captured and decoded through Novell's LANalyzer. Figure 3.27 shows the RIP packet structure defined by Xerox. The only difference between the Novell RIP and the Xerox RIP is the addition of the Time Delay measured in ticks, with each tick being approximately 1/18 second. (There are 18.21 ticks in a second.) This change improves NetWare router's capability to select the fastest route to a destination. It also prohibits a straight integration between Novell's RIP and pure XNS implementations.

The *operation* field of the RIP packet indicates whether the packet is a request or response. The following codes are used for the operation field:

Operation	Description
1	Request
2	Response

After the operations field comes the contents field, which describes one or more sets, or *tuples,* of routing information. Each tuple describes an object network's network number and the number of hops and time ticks it takes to get to that network number.

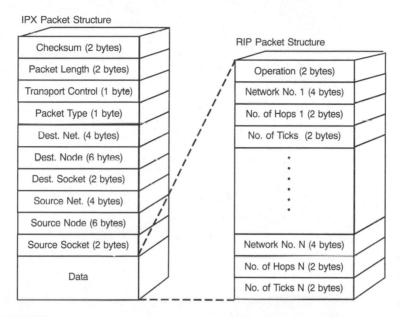

Figure 3.25:
Novell RIP packet structure.

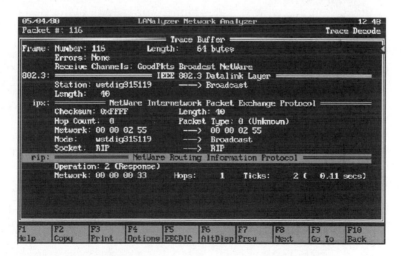

Figure 3.26:
RIP packet captured and decoded by LANalyzer.

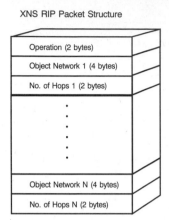

XNS RIP Packet Structure

Operation (2 bytes)

Object Network 1 (4 bytes)

No. of Hops 1 (2 bytes)

•
•
•
•
•

Object Network N (4 bytes)

No. of Hops N (2 bytes)

Figure 3.27:
XNS RIP.

A hop is counted every time a packet goes through a router. The maximum number of permissible hops is 15. A value of 16 is synonymous to infinity and means that the destination is unreachable.

The time delay field measures (in clock ticks) how much time it takes to get to the network number. Novell added the time field to better determine the fastest path. The time delay also permits better integration with IBM SNA or T1 networks that are more time-sensitive.

If the operation specified in the RIP packet is a request (1), then each tuple represents the object network for which the requester wants routing information. If the requester wants information on all object networks, only one tuple is included whose network number field is set to all 1s. If the operation specified in the RIP packet is a response (2), then each tuple represents routing information for the object network in the form of number of hops and clock ticks to reach the network number. If the number of hops field is set to infinity (16), it indicates that the destination is unreachable.

NetWare routers also act as repositories of other information. They contain a database of services provided by servers on the network. They obtain this information through *Service Advertising Protocol* (SAP). The SAP follows the spirit of the Xerox Clearinghouse Protocol, but differs from it in detail and implementation.

The Service Advertising Protocol permits servers such as file servers, print servers, and gateway servers to advertise their services and addresses. These services are dutifully recorded by Novell routers in a table called the *Server Information Table* (SIT). The Server Address field includes the full internetwork address, the network number, node address, and socket number of the server. The Server Type holds the type of service being performed. Examples of some server type designations are as follows:

Type of Service (Server Type)	Object Type Code (Hex)
File Server	4
Job Server	5
Gateway	6
Print Server	7
Archive Server	9
Administration	B
NAS SNA Gateway	21
Remote Bridge Server	24
Bridge Server	26
TCP/IP Gateway	27
Time Synchronization Server	2D
Advertising Print Server	47
TES - NetWare for VMS	7A
NetWare Access Server	98
Portable NetWare	9E
NNS Domain	133

The Time Since Changed or Time-Out field is used to age and retire entries for servers that unexpectedly go down. Currently, the SIT information is not organized for quick database-type queries. To rapidly access SIT information, this information is copied to the file server's bindery, which is an internal database used to keep track of certain resources on the server. SAP agents in the file server periodically update the file server's bindery so that any client attached to a server can obtain information on other services on the internetwork. If a client needs to determine which services are available on the network, it can query a nearby router or server.

The SAP packet makes use of the IPX packet for its transport. Figure 3.28 details the SAP packet.

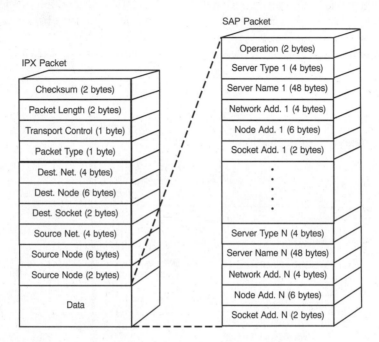

Figure 3.28:
Service Advertising Protocol (SAP).

The *operation* field in the SAP packet defines the type of operation being performed. The four possible values for this operation code are as follows:

- A request by a client for the name and address of a server of a certain type (such as file server, print server, and communications server). If the client loads the NetWare shell, it issues this SAP request.

- A response to the nearest server query.

- A general request for information on all servers of a certain type.

- A response to the general request.

Figures 3.29 to 3.31 illustrate these SAP packets obtained by using Novell's LANalyzer.

The Server Information Table in a router is updated in a manner similar to the RIP table, except that the request/response packets are SAP packets. SAP request/responses also follow the best information algorithm for RIP packets. After a server is brought up for the first time, it broadcasts information about itself to all routers. At every 60-second interval, the router process broadcasts SAP packets that contain information about all servers of which they are aware. After a server is shut down, it broadcasts a SAP packet to indicate that its services are no longer available.

Figure 3.29:
SAP request packet.

Tracking Network Numbers

You must keep network numbers unique within an organization. If you do not keep network numbers unique, you encounter problems. The NetWare router detects duplicate routing number assignments.

When network numbers are not kept unique, the NetWare router detects that there is a conflict in the routing number assignment. You see the following displayed:

```
1/11/93 7:18am: 1.1.112 Router configuration error detected
Router at node C0DC3F19 claims network 00000333 should be 00000255
1/11/93 7:18am: 1.1.112 Router configuration error detected
Router at node C0DC3F19 claims network 00000333 should be 00000255
```

```
1/11/93 7:18am: 1.1.112 Router configuration error detected
Router at node C0DC3F19 claims network 00000333 should be 00000255
1/11/93 7:18am: 1.1.112 Router configuration error detected
Router at node C0DC3F19 claims network 00000333 should be 00000255
```

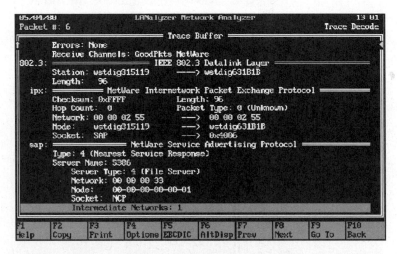

Figure 3.30:
SAP response packet.

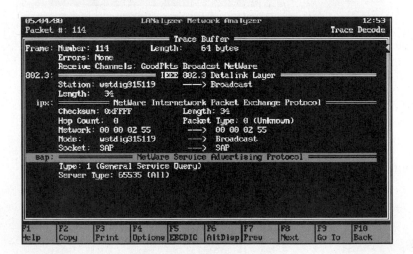

Figure 3.31:
SAP general request packet.

The router error message is saying that another node claims that the network number is incorrect. In this case network number 00000333 should be 00000255 because the other node (router) has this number in its configuration. Set the same network number in the configuration for both routers to solve this problem.

In many large organizations, LAN operations are decentralized. As a result, different installers may select the same network numbers, with the default network number of 1 being the most common. When it is time to internetwork the separate departmental LANs, the network number conflicts become painfully apparent. You can avoid these conflicts by using a universal network number assignment scheme. This scheme is not something that is mandated by Novell; it is a recommendation to simplify network administration.

The network number field in IPX packets is four bytes long, which means that the network number can be eight hexadecimal digits. These eight hexadecimal digits can be assigned the following meaning:

Byte 3	Byte 2	Byte 1	Byte 0
I D	D N	N N	N N
I =	1-digit hexadecimal code for network number or internal network number (NetWare v3.x). A value of 0 (hex) indicates a network number. A value of F (hex) indicates an internal network number.		
D D =	2-digit hexadecimal number for department code.		
N N N N N =	5-digit hexadecimal number for each logical network or internal network number.		

Consider the example of an organization with the following departments: Corporate, Engineering, Manufacturing, Marketing, Accounting, and Field Services. Each of these departments has its own LAN. Department codes can be assigned as indicated in table 3.6. This table also illustrates examples of some network numbers and internal assignments.

Table 3.6
Network Number Assignments

Department	Code (D D) Hex
Corporate	10
Engineering	11
Manufacturing	12
Marketing	13
Accounting	14
Field Services	15

Network Number or Internal Number	Comments
0 1 0 0 0 0 0 1	Network number (0) for department Corporate (10) and logical network 00001
F 1 0 0 0 0 0 2	Internal network number (F) for department Corporate (10) and NetWare v3.x server 00002 (second file server)
0 1 5 0 0 0 0 7	Network number (0) for department Field Services (15) and logical network 00007
F 1 3 0 0 0 0 9	Internal network number (F) for department Marketing (13) and NetWare v3.x server 00009 (ninth file server)

You can tell at a glance whether the network number assignment is for a cable segment or NetWare v3.x internal number by examining the first hexadecimal digit. The next two digits tell you the department that is responsible for administering the network number. Within the department, they can keep track of their network number assignments. Using this scheme greatly simplifies the problem of network number assignments.

Limitations of NetWare Routers

NetWare routers understand only IPX. Multiple protocol routers tend to be protocol-independent. Because pure NetWare routers do not have an understanding of other protocols such as DECnet and SNA, they cannot be used to connect networks that use multiple protocols.

NetWare routers are limited by the performance of the PCs and the type of NICs installed in them. Despite these limitations, NetWare routers are extremely useful for pure NetWare environments. One big advantage they have is low cost. The routing software is bundled with NetWare, which enables you to install a NetWare router for the cost of the PC and NICs.

Configuring an Internal Router

Instructions for configuring an internal router are described in the installation of the server in Chapter 8. Figure 3.32 shows two drivers selected for NetWare v2.2 during the installation process. If the NetWare v2.2 is generated with the configuration shown, it acts as an internal router that performs routing between two LANs.

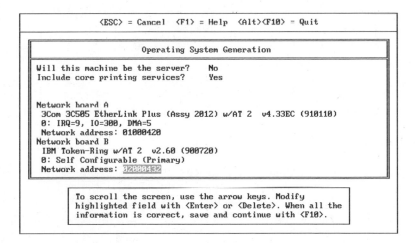

Figure 3.32:
NetWare v2.2 internal router configuration.

Figure 3.33 shows the AUTOEXEC.NCF file for NetWare v.3x. Notice that two drivers (WDPLUSSV and NE2000) are loaded. To bind the two loaded drivers to the IPX protocol stack, two BIND commands were used. Each BIND command specifies a different network number. With this configuration, NetWare v3.x acts as an internal router that performs routing between two LANs.

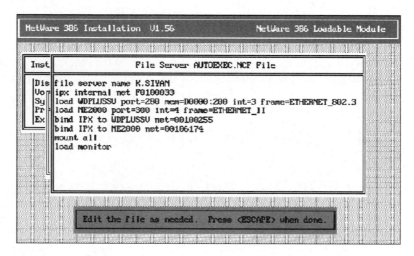

Figure 3.33:
NetWare v3.x internal router configuration.

Installing and Managing External NetWare Routers

This section discusses installation procedures for NetWare routers. You learn to configure NetWare routers through a guided tour. You can configure NetWare routers in several ways: dedicated/nondedicated and protected/real mode. You learn about the differences between these configurations in the following sections.

Dedicated and Nondedicated Mode Routers

A *dedicated router* is a computer that performs only routing functions. It cannot be used as a DOS workstation. Because all of the computer resources are set aside for routing functions, dedicated routers have better performance. Another advantage of the dedicated router approach is greater reliability and security. No applications are running on the computer that could cause it to hang, and because users cannot use it as a workstation, it also is more secure from inadvertent reboot of the router computer.

A *nondedicated router* is a computer that performs both routing and workstation functions. It can be used as a DOS workstation to run applications while the routing function is performed in the background. Because computer resources are shared between routing functions and applications running on the router, nondedicated routers have poorer performance. The advantage of the nondedicated router approach is that it saves the cost of an extra workstation. Because nondedicated routers are exposed to applications and users, they are less reliable and secure compared to dedicated routers.

Dedicated router configuration should be selected if possible because of potential problems with the nondedicated approach. Choose the nondedicated router approach only if severe budgetary constraints do not permit the purchase of an additional computer.

The dedicated mode router can be set up in the protected mode or real mode depending on the microprocessor inside the workstation. If an Intel 8086 microprocessor is being used, the router can operate only in real mode. Real-mode routers can use memory up to 1M (see fig. 3.34). If the workstation has an Intel 80286, 80386, or higher microprocessor, and if it has sufficient extended memory, it can run in protected mode (see fig. 3.35).

In protected mode, only 12M of RAM is used for external routers. This 12M is currently a NetWare router limitation. Nondedicated routers can operate only in protected mode.

Router Hardware and Software Requirements

Each PC that must act as a router must be installed with two or more NICs. The limit is four NICs for external routers. The NICs should have no hardware conflicts with each other or with other hardware inside the PC.

Hardware parameters such as interrupt request line, DMA channels, I/O ports, and base memory addresses must be set uniquely. If a protected-mode router is to be configured, you must allow at least 500K of extended memory for the router process. You can have up to 12M of RAM in the protected-mode router. Extra memory can be used for router buffers to improve the performance.

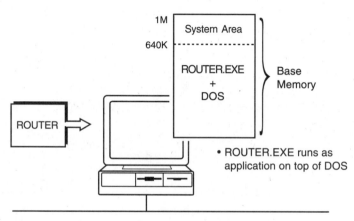

Figure 3.34:
Real-mode router.

The software requirements are as follows:

- ROUTEGEN disk

- Network driver disks such as LAN_DRV_XXX

- DOSUTIL-1 disk containing CONSOLE.COM if nondedicated router is to be set up

Installing a NetWare Router

Figure 3.36 shows the process of generating the routing software. The utility to generate the routing software is ROUTEGEN, and this utility can be found in the ROUTEGEN disk that comes with NetWare (v2.x and v3.x). The ROUTEGEN utility is the same for NetWare v2.x and NetWare v3.x.

The end result of the ROUTEGEN.EXE is a ROUTER.EXE program that implements the router. This ROUTER.EXE program file must be copied to the router boot disk. The router must then be configured to boot correctly. The boot process is slightly different between dedicated and nondedicated routers and is discussed after a guided tour of the router installation.

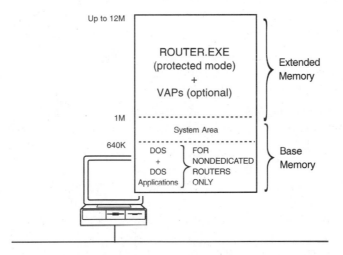

Figure 3.35:
Protected-mode router.

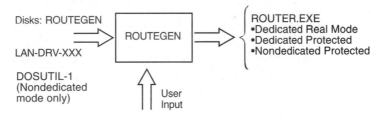

Figure 3.36:
Router generation.

Router Generation

To install a router, follow these steps:

1. Install the NICs into the workstation to be used as a router. You can install up to four NICs. Base address must not conflict with any other hardware in the router. Only two IBM Token Ring network boards can be used in a router.

2. Boot the workstation to be used as a router with DOS 3.x or higher.

3. Insert the ROUTEGEN disk in drive A and enter **ROUTEGEN**. After a `Please Wait` message, a screen appears.

4. Press Enter to continue. The Router Generation screen appears with the following fields:

Operating system mode—You have a choice between two modes of configuration: dedicated and nondedicated. If you select nondedicated mode, you must assign a process address.

Nondedicated process address—This address is a unique hexadecimal. It identifies the workstation DOS environment to the router process.

Number of communication buffers—Communication buffers are temporary areas in the router's RAM to hold incoming/outgoing packets. The default number is 150, which is adequate for most router configurations. If you anticipate heavy router traffic, the number of communication buffers should be increased. The maximum number of communication buffers is 1000.

Network board—This field shows information on the router's NICs. The first NIC is called Network board A, the second Network board B, and so on.

Driver—For a given network board, the driver to be used is shown. To deselect a driver, press Del. To see a list of available drivers, press Enter. If the driver you want is not listed, press Ins and follow the instructions to select another driver.

Configuration option—A driver can have a number of combinations of its parameter settings. You must select the setting that corresponds to the NIC's settings. Some NICs and drivers are software-configurable.

Network address—Every cabling segment attached to the Network boards A, B, C, and D must have a unique address. This address is expressed as an eight-digit hexadecimal number and is used by the IPX packets to uniquely identify the different networks. It is part of the internetwork address, which consists of network address, node address, and socket number.

5. Select either the dedicated or nondedicated router operating mode.

6. Increase the number of communication buffers to 200.

7. Highlight the Driver field under Network board A and press Enter.

   A list of drivers for network board A is displayed. If the driver you want is not listed, you must press Ins and follow the instructions to add it to the list.

   ROUTEGEN contains a bug; therefore, if you are adding a driver to the list, and it does not work, copy the drivers to the ROUTEGEN disk and repeat the preceding steps.

8. After you select the driver, highlight Configuration option and press Enter. A list of configuration options is displayed.

9. Highlight the configuration option that matches the NIC's setting and press Enter.

10. Assign a unique network address for the LAN connected to the NIC. This address is an eight-digit hexadecimal number. You do not need to enter leading zeros.

11. Repeat steps 7 to 10 for as many NICs as are in the router. These steps must be done for network boards B, C, and D.

12. Review the information. Make any corrections. If satisfied, press F10 to continue. A series of messages appears to inform you that the router is being linked.

Creating the Router Boot Disk

The ROUTER.EXE file created in the preceding section must be copied to the router boot disk. The router can be booted from either the hard disk or a floppy disk.

Both of these disks must be DOS-bootable and run DOS 3.x or higher. To make the DOS disk bootable, use the FORMAT command with the /S parameter.

Installing a Dedicated Router

After you create the DOS boot disk, perform the following steps:

1. Copy the ROUTER.EXE file from the ROUTEGEN disk to a DOS bootable disk.

2. Create an AUTOEXEC.BAT file with the ROUTER command.

3. Boot the router machine. ROUTER.EXE loads and activates the router.

Installing a Nondedicated Router

To install a nondedicated router, follow these steps:

1. Copy the ROUTER.EXE file from the ROUTEGEN disk to a DOS bootable disk.

2. Create an AUTOEXEC.BAT file with the following commands:

   ```
   ROUTER
   NETx
   F:
   LOGIN
   ```

   After the ROUTER program loads, it activates the router. NETx (x can be 3, 4, 5, or X for generic shell) loads the shell, which permits the router to be used as a workstation. IPX.COM is not needed because the IPX protocols are implemented by ROUTER.EXE.

3. Create a CONFIG.SYS file on the boot device with the FILES= and BUFFERS= parameters set to 20 each.

4. Boot the router machine. ROUTER.EXE loads and activates the router and NETx.COM activates the workstation.

   Note that if you forget that you are on the router and reboot the workstation, you reboot the router!

5. To switch to the router console from the DOS mode, type **CONSOLE**. To switch to the DOS mode from the console mode, type **DOS**.

Running VAPs at the Router

If the router is running in protected mode (dedicated or nondedicated), VAP applications also can run at the router. The VAP files can be copied to the boot disk that is used for the router. If the router detects a VAP file during the boot process, it asks you the following:

```
Value added processes have been defined. Do you wish to
load them?
```

Press Y to load or press N to ignore VAPs.

You may want to have VAPs load automatically. You can create the ROUTER.CFG file in the same directory as the ROUTER.EXE file. In the ROUTER.CFG file, you include the following command:

```
VAP WAIT number
```

In the preceding syntax, *number* is the number of seconds the router should wait before loading the VAPs automatically. A waiting period of 10 to 360 seconds can be specified. If the *number* is omitted, the default is 10 seconds.

If the VAPs cannot fit in the same directory as the ROUTER.EXE file, you can specify the path to locate the files in the ROUTER.CFG file. The general syntax of this command is the following:

```
VAP DISK path
```

If *path* is omitted, a default of drive A is assumed.

If the VAP files are kept on drive C under the directory VAP_APPS, the ROUTER.CFG file may look like the following:

```
VAP DISK C.\VAP_APPS
VAP WAIT 15
```

Using the Router Commands

You must type all router commands at the router console. The RESET ROUTER command initializes the router table if you suspect that this table is inaccurate or corrupted.

If you use the DOWN command to shut down routers, they broadcast a RIP response to indicate that the networks connected to it can no longer be reached. All other routers that see this broadcast update their tables. But if a router goes down unexpectedly, the RIP response is not sent, and it may take up to three minutes before other routers discover that the router is down. During this time, the router tables are inaccurate. Routing decisions made using inaccurate information may result in undeliverable packets or inefficient routing paths.

If you issue the RESET ROUTER command at a router, it sends a RIP request to nearby routers and rebuilds an accurate routing table.

The TRACK ON command provides three types of information:

- Routing information (RIP packets)
- Server information (SAP broadcast packets)
- Workstation connection requests (SAP request/response)

Figure 3.37 shows the TRACK screen for a NetWare v3.x internal router. Use the Alt-Esc and Ctrl-Esc key combinations to switch between the track screen and the console screen for NetWare v3.x.

```
Router Tracking Screen
OUT [00000033:FFFFFFFFFFFF]  6:59:44am   S386         1   S386         2
OUT [00000255:FFFFFFFFFFFF]  6:59:44am   S386         1   S386         2
IN  [00000033:000000000001]  6:59:51am   S386         1
OUT [00000033:FFFFFFFFFFFF]  7:00:14am   00000255   1/2
OUT [00000255:FFFFFFFFFFFF]  7:00:14am   00000033   1/2
IN  [00000033:000000000001]  7:00:19am   S386         1
OUT [00000033:FFFFFFFFFFFF]  7:00:43am   S386         1   S386         2
OUT [00000255:FFFFFFFFFFFF]  7:00:43am   S386         1   S386         2
IN  [00000033:000000000001]  7:00:46am   S386         1
OUT [00000033:FFFFFFFFFFFF]  7:01:13am   00000255   1/2
OUT [00000255:FFFFFFFFFFFF]  7:01:13am   00000033   1/2
IN  [00000033:000000000001]  7:01:14am   S386         1
IN  [00000033:000000000001]  7:01:41am   S386         1
OUT [00000033:FFFFFFFFFFFF]  7:01:42am   S386         1   S386         2
OUT [00000255:FFFFFFFFFFFF]  7:01:42am   S386         1   S386         2
IN  [00000033:000000000001]  7:02:08am   S386         1
OUT [00000033:FFFFFFFFFFFF]  7:02:12am   00000255   1/2
OUT [00000255:FFFFFFFFFFFF]  7:02:12am   00000033   1/2
IN  [00000033:000000000001]  7:02:36am   S386         1
OUT [00000033:FFFFFFFFFFFF]  7:02:42am   S386         1   S386         2
OUT [00000255:FFFFFFFFFFFF]  7:02:42am   S386         1   S386         2
IN  [00000033:000000000001]  7:03:03am   S386         1
<Use ALT-ESC or CTRL-ESC to switch screens, or any other key to pause>
```

Figure 3.37:
NetWare 3.x internal router track screen.

The Route information for NetWare v3.x has the following syntax:

InOut **[*LAN:NodeAddr*]** *Time NetNum Hops/Ticks NetNum Hops/Ticks ...*

The NetWare v2.x route information differs slightly by not having the Time field and has the following general syntax:

InOut **[*LAN:NodeAddr*]** *NetNum Hops/Ticks NetNum Hops/Ticks ...*

InOut specifies whether the information is being received from the network (IN) or the router is transmitting the information (OUT).

LAN specifies which LAN card (NIC) received/transmitted the routing information. The LAN cards are labeled A, B, C, and D.

NodeAddr specifies a six-byte (12 hex digits) node address of the NIC. In figure 3.37, node address FFFFFFFFFFFF indicates a broadcast to all nodes on the local network.

Time is displayed in hours, minutes, and seconds and is the time that the information was transmitted/received.

NetNum is the network number of the logical network or the internal number of a NetWare v3.x server.

Hops is the number of routers that a packet would traverse to reach the indicated network number.

Ticks is the time delay to reach the specified network number and is measured in 1/18-second increments. For low-speed asynchronous lines, this number can be as high as 999. For asynchronous and X.25 routers, *Ticks* is computed as the following:

Ticks = 4 × One-way transport time in 1/18th second increments + 10

For LANs such as ARCnet, Ethernet, and Token Ring one hop represents one tick, even if the actual transmission takes less time.

The server information is broadcast by using SAP packets, and these also are reported by means of the TRACK screen. The server information for NetWare v3.x has the following syntax:

```
InOut [LAN:NodeAddr] Time NetNum ServName Hops  ServName Hops ...
```

The NetWare v2.x server information differs slightly by not having the Time field and has the following general syntax:

```
InOut [LAN:NodeAddr] NetNum ServName Hops  ServName Hops ...
```

ServName is the name of the server on the network for which information is being propagated, and *Hops* indicates the number of routers a packet must traverse to get to the server. VAPs and NLMs that advertise services also are reported on the TRACK screen.

To turn off the TRACK screen enter **TRACK OFF**.

You can use the TRACK command to help solve Unknown File Server errors. If network numbers are set incorrectly, a server may not be seen through the SLIST command. Workstations attempting to log in see Unknown file server errors. Turning the TRACK screen on may cause the WARNING!! MULTIPLE ROUTER WITH SAME INTERNET ADDRESS! or ROUTER CONFIGURATION ERROR!!! ROUTER xxxxxxxxxxxx claims LAN A is yyyyy! errors to occur. To fix these problems, follow the guidelines in this chapter's earlier section "Tracking Network Numbers."

Using NetWare v3.x as an IP Router

Novell is striving to integrate their proprietary architecture with non-Novell networks. One such trend is with UNIX-based networks. Novell is a major shareholder of USL (Unix Systems Lab), which manages the UNIX product line for AT&T. NetWare integration with UNIX-based networks is currently available only through NetWare v3.x.

NetWare v3.x allows the integration of NetWare with TCP/IP- and IPX-based networks.

Understanding TCP/IP-Based Networks

Before you can understand how TCP/IP and NetWare integration works, you must understand TCP/IP and how it differs from Novell's native SPX/IPX protocols.

What Is TCP/IP?

TCP/IP is two protocols: TCP and IP. TCP is a transport protocol that fits into layer four of the OSI model. IP is a network protocol that fits into the layer three of the OSI model. The relationship between TCP/IP and the OSI model is illustrated in figure 3.38. The *User Datagram Protocol* (UDP) is a cousin of TCP but is simpler and not as reliable as TCP.

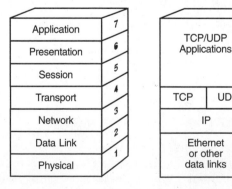

Figure 3.38:
TCP/IP comparison with OSI model.

Note that the OSI model is commonly used as a means of describing the functionality of a protocol such as TCP/IP; it is not meant to imply that TCP/IP is an International Organization of Standards recommendation. The transport layer's job is to ensure end-system to end-system data integrity.

Over the years, TCP has acquired a reputation for robustness and reliability. TCP has had its trial by fire and has had to undergo changes to fix problems dealing with data transmission integrity. In addition to reliability, TCP allows software processes within a node to be referred to by unique addresses. This address is called the TCP port number. This port number is similar in concept to the IPX/SPX sockets discussed earlier.

Whereas the TCP protocol runs on an end-system, such as a user system or a host/server, the IP protocol can run on intermediate systems used to connect the end-system together (see fig. 3.39). Examples of these intermediate systems are IP routers. The job of the IP layer is to prepare the messages from the TCP layer. The IP layer must know the address of the destination IP layer. This address is a 32-bit address called the IP address (or the internet address). In general, the destination node can be on a different network, so a portion of this IP address is used to refer to the network number of the destination network. The remaining portion is used to refer to the host number within that network.

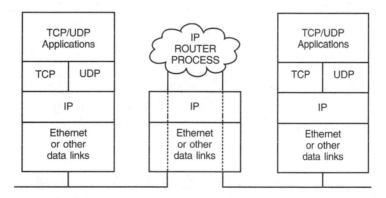

Figure 3.39:
IP router connecting end-systems.

The IP layer must send the message by the best route it can. If the message is too large, it may be broken down into smaller pieces (fragmented or segmented) by the sender or at any point along the path to the destination. At the destination, the fragments must be put back together in the correct order. The IP layer adds enough information to each piece of message to accomplish this task.

The IP layer provides a means of connecting a large number of networks. An IP packet can go across 255 routers. NetWare LANs are limited to 15 routers along a transmission path. One benefit of integration with IP networks is that a NetWare packet can be routed across larger networks using the more flexible IP mechanism.

NetWare TCP/IP Architecture

The BSD 4.3 socket interface and the AT&T *Transport Layer Interface* (TLI) are *Application Programming Interfaces* (APIs) that come with the Network C Language Compiler (see fig. 3.40). The *Network File System* (NFS) server comes with NetWare for NFS an implementation of SUN's NFS. The *Open Datalink Interface* (ODI) is a flexible mechanism to write network card drivers so that multiple protocol stacks can be associated with an NIC.

Simple Network Management Protocol (SNMP) is a popular network management protocol for TCP/IP-based networks. SNMP agents can run on NetWare servers and report information on configuration and status of nodes. The information that is available is a set of managed objects that is referred to as a *Management Information Base* (MIB). SNMP clients such as TCPCON.NLM can access TCP/IP protocol stack managed objects.

The SNMPLOG.NLM processes SNMP trap messages and logs them in to a file in SYS:ETC/SNMP$LOG.BIN.

The TCPLOG.NLM presents a menu-driven interface that enables you to use SNMP to access TCP/IP MIB locally or from a remote node. It also allows access to the SNMP log file.

Configuring NetWare v3.x as an IP Router

Novell has added a mechanism for adding new protocol support in the NetWare 3.x network operating system. This mechanism is the NetWare *Loadable Module architecture* (NLM). NLMs are software engines or tasks that can be dynamically loaded and unloaded from the server console. The TCP/IP protocols are implemented as an NLM (TCPIP.NLM) in NetWare 3.11 and beyond.

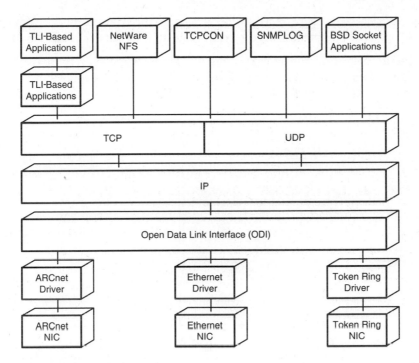

Figure 3.40:
The NetWare TCP/IP architecture.

To load TCP/IP on the NetWare 3.11 server, enter the following command at the server console:

```
LOAD TCPIP
```

Protocol dependencies are built into TCPIP.NLM so that any NLM that it requires that is not loaded in server memory is automatically loaded. The TCPIP.NLM requires that STREAMS, CLIB, and SNMP.NLMs be loaded first. If these NLMs are not loaded, loading TCPIP.NLM results in an automatic load of these NLMs.

The LOAD TCPIP command has a number of interesting options. The general syntax is the following:

```
LOAD TCPIP [FORWARD = {YES/NO}] [RIP={YES/NO}]
[TRAP=IP_ADDR]
```

The FORWARD parameter is used to turn the NetWare 3.11 server into an IP router. Use this parameter to connect two or more IP networks. The default value is NO.

The RIP parameter is used to enable or disable the IP routing information protocol. This RIP protocol is different than that used by Novell.

When the RIP protocol is enabled, the RIP traffic is monitored and updates are made to an internal routing table. If FORWARD is set to YES, it broadcasts RIP updates to other IP routers. If disabled, it does not monitor RIP traffic. The default RIP value is YES.

The TRAP parameter is used to specify the IP address to which the server will send SNMP trap messages.

After the TCP/IP protocol is loaded, it must be bound or associated with a network card driver that will be used to access the TCP/IP network.

The BIND command is used to build the logical association between the TCP/IP stack and the driver. The following is an example list of commands necessary to complete this binding:

```
LOAD NE2000 INT=3 PORT=2E0 NAME=ENG_NIC FRAME=ETHERNET_II
LOAD TCPIP
BIND TCPIP TO ENG_NIC ADDR=10.1.1.5
```

The ADDR= parameter represents an IP address. IP addresses are 32 bits or four bytes long. The conventional way of representing IP addresses is to use the dotted decimal notation in which each number represents one of the four bytes that make up the IP address. These numbers are separated by the period (.) symbol.

The BIND command for IP has the following general syntax:

```
BIND IP TO boardName
[ADDR=ipAddress] [MASK=maskAddress]
[BCAST=bcastAddress] [GATE=gateAddress]
[DEFROUTE={YES|NO}] [ARP={YES|NO}]
[COST=numberOfHops] [POISON={YES|NO}]
```

The parameter values are described in table 3.7.

Table 3.7
BIND Parameters for IP Routing

Parameter	Description
ADDR	IP address assigned to NIC connected to this interface.
MASK	Subnet mask assigned to IP network.

Parameter	Description
BCAST	Default IP address to be used for broadcasting. If not specified, it is FF FF FF FF.
GATE	Default gateway on IP network. When not specified, routing is performed by using RIP.
DEFROUTE	If TCPIP was loaded with FORWARD=Yes, the node is to be used as a default gateway through RIP. Default value is No.
ARP	Should the Address Resolution Protocol to map IP addresses to hardware addresses be used? Default value is Yes.
COST	Number of hops of cost assigned to this interface. Default cost is 1. Maximum is 15.
POISON	Used to control poisoned reverse for routing updates sent to this interface. The default value of No reduces IP traffic at a small cost to stability.

Integrating IPX and IP Networks

In this section, you examine different scenarios that show how IPX and IP networks can be integrated.

Scenario 1

Suppose that you have a single Ethernet network that contains the following setup:

■ Several NetWare and UNIX clients

■ NetWare v3.x server

■ UNIX server

Figure 3.41 shows how these network elements can be integrated. Notice that because this network is an IP network and an IPX network, it must have a unique IP and IPX network numbers. The IPX network number is 01700022, and the IP network number is 130.1.0.0. Each IP node must have a unique IP address. The NetWare server has a single Ethernet NIC interface that is shared by IPX and IP stacks. The NetWare v3.x's AUTOEXEC.NCF file would contain commands similar to the following:

```
LOAD NE2000 PORT=300 INT=3 NAME=IPX_NETWORK
LOAD NE2000 PORT=300 INT=3 NAME=IP_NETWORK
FRAME=ETHERNET_II
LOAD TCPIP
BIND IPX TO IPX_NETWORK NET=01700022
BIND TCPIP TO IP_NETWORK ADDR=130.1.0.13
```

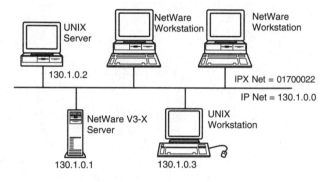

Figure 3.41:
Single network with IPX and IP nodes.

Scenario 2

Suppose, for example, that you have an IPX Token Ring network connected to an IP Ethernet with a NetWare v3.x server having the following elements:

- Several NetWare and UNIX clients

- NetWare v3.x server used to connect the two networks

- UNIX server

Figure 3.42 shows how these network elements can be integrated. Notice that the separate IP and IPX networks have a unique IP network and an IPX network number. The IPX network number is 01700022, and the IP network number is 130.1.0.0. Each IP node must have a unique IP address. The NetWare server has an Ethernet NIC interface and a Token Ring NIC. The

NetWare v3.x's AUTOEXEC.NCF file would contain commands similar to the following:

```
LOAD TOKEN NAME=IPX_NETWORK
BIND IPX TO IPX_NETWORK NET=01700022
LOAD NE2000 PORT=300 INT=3 NAME=IP_NETWORK
FRAME=ETHERNET_II
LOAD TCPIP
BIND TCPIP TO IP_NETWORK ADDR=130.1.0.1
```

Note that NetWare v3.x acts as an IPX node and an IP node. It can be used to provide file services to both IPX and IP networks.

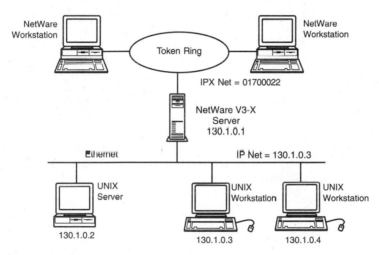

Figure 3.42:
Separate IPX and IP networks.

Scenario 3

An IPX Token Ring network connected to an IP Ethernet with a NetWare IP router:

- Several NetWare and UNIX clients
- NetWare v3.x server used as a router
- UNIX servers

Figure 3.43 shows how these network elements can be integrated.

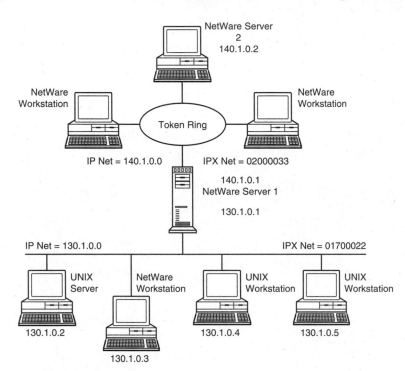

Figure 3.43:
IPX Token Ring network connected to IP Ethernet with NetWare IP router.

Notice the two separate IP and IPX networks. Each of these networks must have unique IP network and IPX network numbers. The IPX network numbers are 01700022 and 0200033, and the IP network numbers are 130.1.0.0 and 140.1.0.0. The NetWare server has an Ethernet NIC interface and a Token Ring NIC. Each NIC is shared by IPX and IP protocol stacks. The two NetWare v3.x servers' AUTOEXEC.NCF files would contain commands similar to the following:

```
NetWare v3.x server 1

LOAD TOKEN NAME=IPX_TOKEN
LOAD TOKEN NAME=IP_TOKEN FRAME=TOKEN_RING_SNAP
LOAD NE2000 PORT=3000 INT=3 NAME=IPX_ETHER
LOAD NE2000 PORT=300 INT=3 NAME=IP_ETHER FRAME=ETHERNET_II
```

```
BIND IPX TO IPX_TOKEN NET=02000033
BIND IPX TO IPX_ETHER NET=01700022
LOAD TCPIP FORWARD=YES
BIND IP TO IP_TOKEN ADDR=140.1.0.1
BIND IP TO IP_ETHER ADDR=130.1.0.1

NetWare v3.x server 2

LOAD TOKEN NAME=IPX_TOKEN
LOAD TOKEN NAME=IP_TOKEN FRAME=TOKEN_RING_SNAP
BIND IPX TO IPX_TOKEN NET=02000033
LOAD TCPIP
BIND IP TO IP_TOKEN ADDR=140.1.0.2
```

IP Tunneling

The IP tunnel LAN driver (IPTUNNEL NLM) can be run on a NetWare v3.x server that allows IPX packets to be encapsulated by UDP/IP packets for transmission across a potentially large IP network. IP tunneling allows IPX nodes to communicate with other IPX nodes by using an IP cloud (see fig. 3.44). The IP tunnel driver converts the IP cloud into a logical network interface so that IPX protocols can communicate with it as if it were another NIC driver.

The IPX packet is encapsulated by a user datagram protocol packet and transported across the IP network. At the destination, the UDP header is stripped to recover the IPX packet. The UDP checksum is used to ensure data integrity of the IPX packet.

The NetWare v3.x IP tunnel driver can be used with SK-IPX/IP gateway from Schneider & Koch to connect NetWare v3.x nodes to NetWare v2.x nodes. It also works with IP tunnel client driver from LAN WorkPlace for DOS or the Schneider & Koch DOS end-node product.

To configure the NetWare v3.x server to use the IP tunnel, you must load it as a LAN driver. The TCPIP.NLM must be loaded prior to loading IPTUNNEL.NLM.

The LOAD IPTUNNEL command line has the following syntax:

```
LOAD IPTUNNEL [PEER=remoteIpAddr]
[CHKSUM={Yes/NO}] [LOCAL=localIpAddr]
[PORT=udpPortNumber] [SHOW={YES/NO}]
```

The parameters are summarized in table 3.8.

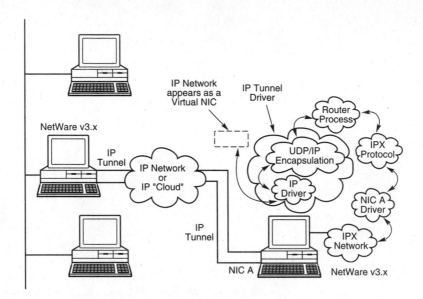

Figure 3.44:
IP tunneling.

Table 3.8
IPTUNNEL Parameters

Parameter	Description
PEER	Adds IP address to peer list. Peers are IPX routers to which NetWare RIP broadcast messages should be sent. IP networks have limited broadcast capabilities and, to avoid excessive traffic over a large IP network, the peer list is used.
CHKSUM	Enables UDP checksums. The default is to enable checksums.
LOCAL	Specifies a local IP address for the tunnel.
PORT	Specifies the UDP port number for the tunnel. Default value is 213, the officially assigned UDP port number for IPX packets.
SHOW	Requests a configuration report on the tunnel driver.

Avoiding Routing Problems

Novell reports that NetWare v2.x-based internal routers have some unique routing problems. You learn about some of these problems and how to avoid them in the following sections. You also learn about how NetWare v3.x-based routers avoid these problems by introducing the concept of the internal network number.

NetWare v2.x Routing Problems

Redundant paths often are used to improve the reliability of the network. In NetWare v2.x-based networks these redundant paths can lead to inefficient routing.

Figure 3.45 shows a NetWare v2.x-based network on which the file servers FS_1 and FS_2 act as internal routers. The network contains a redundant path between the two servers. Consider what happens when workstation WS_B4 tries to attach to server FS_1. The shortest path to FS_1 is through segment B. But there is a good chance that the packets may go through router FS_2 onto segment A and reach FS_1 through NIC A on FS_1.

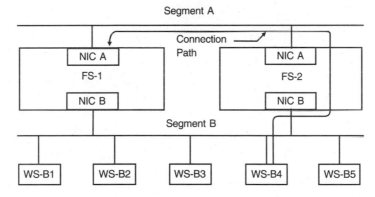

Figure 3.45:
NetWare v2.x routing problem.

When the server advertises itself through service advertising protocol, the SAP packet must be encapsulated in an IPX packet for transmission. The network number and node address used in this IPX packet constitutes the internetwork address of the file service process. NetWare v2.x uses the internetwork address of NIC A in the file server for the file service process. The logical representation of this file service addressing is shown in figure 3.46. When the workstation on segment B seeks to connect to a file server FS_1, it wants to connect to the file service process whose internet work address is the same as NIC A. The file service process is logically on segment A. Figure 3.47 shows this logical positioning of the file service processes for FS_1 and FS_2.

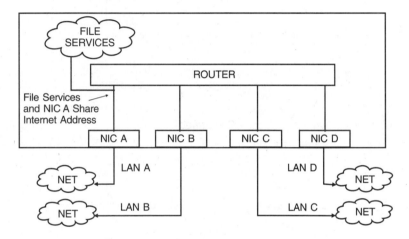

Figure 3.46:
NetWare v2.x file services addressing.

When WS_B4 tries to make a connection to FS_1, it sends a RIP request for the fastest route to file service process FS_1. Two routers will respond to this request: router FS_1 and router FS_2. Because they both report the same distance, as far as the workstation is concerned, they are both equally good paths. If FS_2 responds to the RIP request before FS_1, the workstation sends a create connection NCP request through FS_2. After a connection path is established by a workstation, it remains for the duration of the connection.

Solving NetWare v2.x Routing Problems

One way to solve the problem described in the preceding section is shown in figure 3.48. The workstations are connected to the same segment as the file server's NIC A, if there are redundant paths.

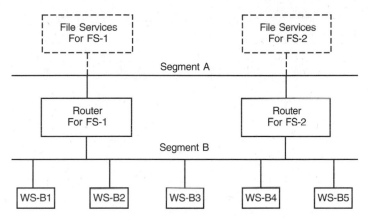

File 3.47:
Logical positioning of file services.

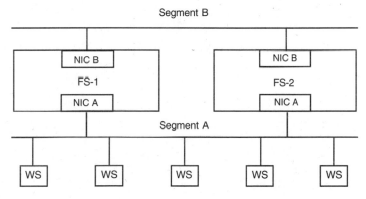

Figure 3.48:
NetWare v2.x routing solution with stations connected to one segment.

The logical positioning of the file service processes for FS_1 and FS_2 are on the same segment as the workstations, and there is no need to go through a router to get to the file service process.

If workstations are connected to both segments, the solution in figure 3.49 can be used. Workstations that connect most often to FS_1 are on the same segment as FS_1s NIC A. Workstations that connect most often to FS_2 are on the same segment as FS_2s NIC A.

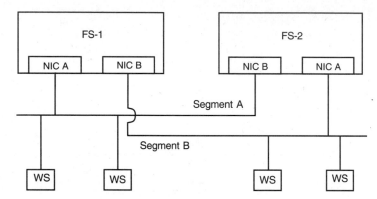

Figure 3.49:
NetWare v2.x routing solution with stations connected to both segments.

Solving NetWare v3.x Routing Problems

NetWare v3.x avoids the NetWare v2.x routing problem by having a separate internetwork address for the file service process that is not tied to the internet address of LAN A or any other NIC in the server. Figure 3.50 shows the addressing for NetWare v3.x.

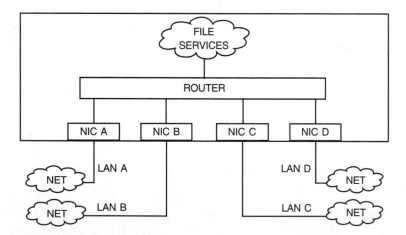

Figure 3.50:
NetWare v3.x file services addressing.

The internetwork address of the file service process is referred to as the *internal network number* and is assigned during NetWare v3.x installation. This internal network number must be distinct from all other internal network numbers and network numbers on the internet.

Router Efficiency

Novell has performed a number of studies measuring performance of internal and external routers. These studies are a great help in designing optimal router configurations. The tests were done with NE2000 and NE1000 NICs on AT 286 and Compaq 386 25 MHz machines. Although the tests were done for SFT NetWare v2.15 and NetWare 386 v3.0 and are, therefore, somewhat dated, the trend they represent can be extrapolated for NetWare 2.x and NetWare v3.x.

Throughput of Internal Routers

Figure 3.51 shows throughput for internal routers set up in the following configurations:

- No router

- Busy and non-busy SFT NetWare 2.15

- Busy and non-busy NetWare 3.0

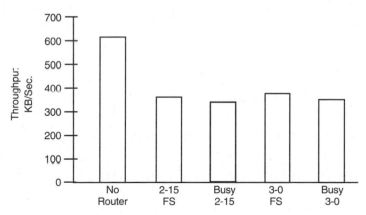

Figure 3.51:
Internal router performance.

The tests show that there is a substantial performance drop when a packet goes through a router. This drop can be as much as 41 percent compared to the no router test. Another interesting point is that SFT NetWare v2.15 and NetWare v3.0 routers have comparable performance.

Throughput of External Dedicated Routers

The test that was performed consisted of adding from one to six routers in series and testing the throughput of the system as each router was added. The performance degradation curve that was measured is shown in figure 3.52.

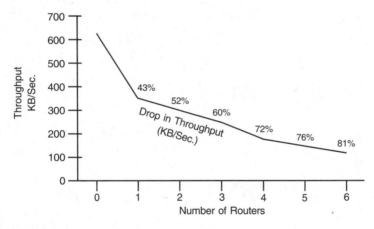

Figure 3.52:
Multiple router performance.

The performance drop after going through one router was 43 percent. After that, there was a four- to eight-percent drop for every router that was added. With six routers in series, the performance drop was 81 percent. The effective bandwidth of the network was only 19 percent of the bandwidth available on a network without routers.

Throughput of External Nondedicated Routers

The test for external dedicated routers was repeated for nondedicated routers. The nondedicated routers performed some background processing to simulate their typical use. After going through only one router, the performance dropped by 60 percent. And after two routers, it dropped to 67 percent (see fig. 3.53).

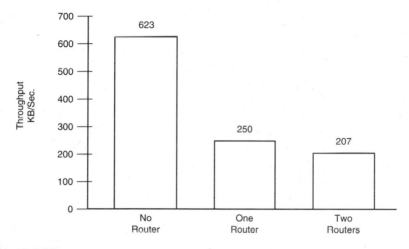

Figure 3.53:
Throughput drop of external nondedicated routers.

These results point out that the nondedicated router configuration is the slowest of the router configurations. Figure 3.54 compares the performance of dedicated and nondedicated external routers. These results underscore the author's opinion that nondedicated router configurations should be avoided.

NetWare Multiprotocol Router

For those who want support for routing of protocols other than IPX, there is the multiprotocol router. This NLM runs on a NetWare server and performs routing for OSI, AppleTalk, NetBIOS, IPX, and TCP/IP. When used in conjunction with WAN Links, it can provide routing over wide-area links. Routers from vendors such as Cisco perform similar functionality but at a higher performance and cost. The NetWare Multiprotocol router, on the other hand, can provide routing for small networks at a much lower cost.

In addition to routing, the Multiprotocol router provides Telnet, X-Windows, SNMP, and *Point-to-Point Protocol* (PPP) support. The Telnet service is particularly valuable because it allows stations running a Telnet client session to log in remotely to the router and perform basic administration functions. X-Windows support allows the router to be managed by UNIX workstations running X-Windows and TCP/IP protocols. The PPP capability permits point-to-point connection with other routers, such as Cisco routers, that support this protocol.

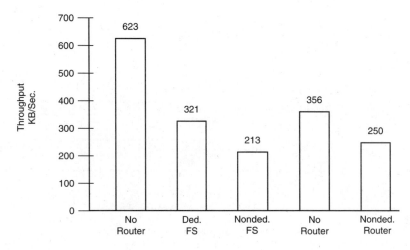

Figure 3.54:
Performance of dedicated and nondedicated external routers.

The network management station can be Novell's Network Services Manager for Windows and for third-party network management stations such as SUN's SunNet Manager, Hewlett-Packard's OpenView, and IBM's NetView 6000.

The router runs a SAP filter that can be used to limit the number of times SAP broadcasts are made on a wide-area link. Without this filter, the frequent SAP broadcasts that are done to advertise networks consume the already limited bandwidth of many wide-area links.

WAN Links can be run with multiport serial boards, and a WANIS interface is defined that can enable third-party manufacturers to support WAN Links. WANIS extends Novell's ODI to the WAN environment.

The Multi-Protocol router includes NetWare Hub Services. This is a monitoring and management system for hubs that can run on a NetWare platform. These hubs, installed in PC workstations, allow the PC to be controlled by the NetWare hub services.

Hardware-Based Routers

Although internal routers based on NetWare and the NetWare multi-protocol router can be used for most networks, they are not designed to handle heavy traffic loads. For handling heavy traffic loads, special computers designed for routing functions are used. Besides handling heavy loads, these computers can be used for routing almost any industry-standard protocol. These hardware-based routers are made by a number of companies such as Cisco, Wellfleet, Proteon, Digital, Timeplex, and Advanced Computer Communications.

The hardware-based routers use a multiprocess architecture and proprietary high-speed buses to facilitate high-speed routing. A diagram that models the general architecture for most hardware-based routers is shown in figure 3.55.

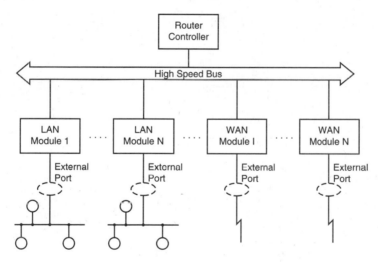

Figure 3.55:
Model for high-speed routers.

The router architecture is modular and allows for network hardware modules to be installed in bus slots. Addition of each of these modules gives the router the ability to connect to a specific type of network. These network modules can be designed for LANs and WANs. Each network module is designed for a specific type of network. To connect to an Ethernet network, for example, an Ethernet network module needs to be installed. To connect the Ethernet network to an FDDI network, an Ethernet and an FDDI module needs to be installed. The router controller in figure 3.55 is usually implemented on the router's motherboard.

Routers can be purchased with standard network module configurations. Popular choices are Ethernet and Token Ring for LAN modules, and T1, leased-line, or dial-up lines for WAN modules. These routers permit multiple links to a network. The secondary links can be used as a backup and, in some routers, also can be used for *load balancing*—when traffic is diverted equally among the links to achieve a higher sustained throughput. This feature is particularly valuable for point-to-point wide-area links, as shown in figure 3.56.

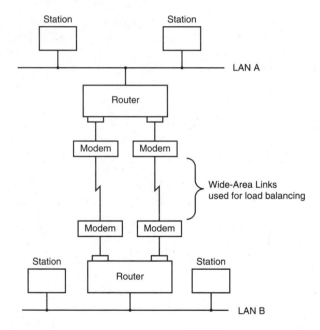

Figure 3.56:
Load balancing on wide-area links.

Some hardware-based routers can be booted from a special floppy disk that contains the routing software. The advantage of this is that the routing logic can be easily updated when bug fixes and new features need to be released. An example of this kind of router is ACS 4200 from Advanced Computer Communications. Many of the routers available today also can be configured to act as bridges. As mentioned earlier in this chapter, these routers are called brouters. The bridge operation is particularly useful for protocols such as *NetBIOS Extended User Interface* (NetBEUI) and LAT that are not routable because they do not have a network layer.

Routers can be configured through a local terminal attached to an RS-232 port on the router box. If a dumb terminal is not available, a computer running terminal emulation software such as PROCOMM or SmartCom can be used. Some of the high-end routers also provide TELNET server services. This means that any computer running TELNET client services can log in remotely to the router and configure the router. The variety of configuration options is shown in figure 3.57.

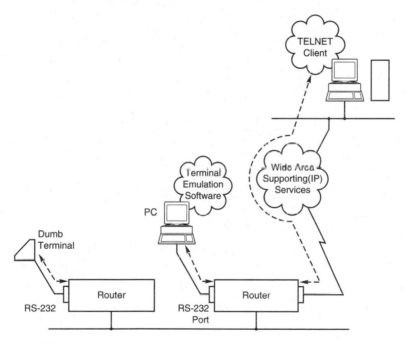

Figure 3.57:
Router configuration options.

The router configuration is typically done through a command-line or menu-driven interface. The TimeLan 100 router, for instance, has a menu-driven interface. Many of the Wellfleet and ACC routers have a command-line interface.

The router must be configured for each protocol it needs to route. An example of the configuration commands needed for the IP network routing in figure 3.58 is shown next. The example commands are shown for the ACS 4200 router connecting two LANs over a wide-area link. Other routers have similar commands. The syntax details are different, but the semantics are very similar.

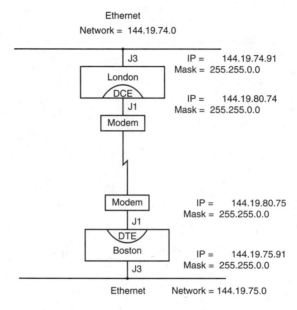

Figure 3.58:
Simple IP routing example.

Configuration for the London router:

```
login netman              # Login to the router
set prompt to london      # For descriptive purpose only
add ip network entry 144.19.74.91 255.255.255.0 j3
add ip network entry 144.19.80.74 255.255.255.0 j1
# The above commands assign IP address and subnet masks
# to the router's J3 and J1 ports.

set rip protocol on
# This activates the IP RIP protocol. Other choices
# are OSPF etc.
```

```
delete ip route entry 144.19.75.0
# This command deletes any routing table entry for the
# network 14.19.75.0

add ip route entry 144.19.75.0 255.255.255.0 144.19.80.75 1
# This command adds an entry to the routing table that
# says that network 144.19.75.0 can be reached by sending
# IP traffic to port 144.19.80.75. The network is 1 hop
# away.

reset                    # This makes the change permanent
```

Configuration for the Boston router:

```
login netman            # Login to the router
set prompt to london    # For descriptive purpose only
add ip network entry 144.19.75.91 255.255.255.0 j3
add ip network entry 144.19.80.75 255.255.255.0 j1
# The above commands assign IP address and subnet masks
# to the router's J3 and J1 ports.

set rip protocol on
# This activates the IP RIP protocol. Other choices
# are OSPF otc.

delete ip route entry 144.19.74.0
# This command deletes any routing table entry for the
# network 14.19.74.0

add ip route entry 144.19.74.0 255.255.255.0 144.19.80.74 1
# This command adds an entry to the routing table that
# says that network 144.19.74.0 can be reached by sending
# IP traffic to port 144.19.80.74. The network is 1 hop
# away.

reset                    # This makes the change permanent
```

Summary

In this chapter you learned the differences between bridges and routers and the advantages and disadvantages of using them. The operation of two types of bridges—the spanning tree and source routing—were examined.

The operation of routers was discussed in some detail, both from a general point of view and a Novell-specific point of view. Guidelines for installing NetWare routers were discussed. Also discussed were integration techniques for NetWare v3.x and UNIX networks.

You also learned about performance issues for internal/external and dedicated/nondedicated routers and routing problems with NetWare v2.x networks.

WANs and MANs

A s networks expand, you must connect islands of LANs to provide an integrated network computing platform. This chapter discusses the technologies you use to create large LANs.

You may want to interconnect LANs for the following reasons:

- Integrating existing LANs
- Extending the capabilities of existing LANs
- Increasing performance by providing access to faster networks or networks with more powerful servers and hosts
- Improving network availability by providing redundant network links, hosts, and servers

Wide Area Networks

Local Area Network (LAN) technologies offer high performance, but they are suited for use only in limited geographic areas, usually within a building or campus setting. If you must connect LANs for longer distances, you must use other technologies. Networks that span long distances frequently are referred to as *Wide Area Networks* (WANs). This section introduces the methods you can use to interconnect LANs over large geographic areas. Each method has advantages and disadvantages based on cost, availability, and performance.

FDDI

Fiber Distributed Data Interface (FDDI) is regarded by many as a high speed LAN (100 Mbps). Because it can span a distance of 100 kilometers, however, it can be used as a WAN to interconnect LANs or serve as a backbone to LANs. FDDI spans layers two and one of the OSI model and can be used to provide IEEE 802.2 or LLC services to upper layers (see fig. 4.1). FDDI can be used to run client/server applications that rely on IEEE 802.2 services, including NetWare, which provides IEEE 802.2 encapsulation. The FDDI physical station address follows the IEEE 48-bit (6 octet) addressing convention.

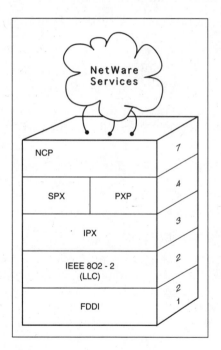

Figure 4.1:
FDDI spans layers 1 and 2 of the OSI model.

A full FDDI configuration consists of two fiber rings. The primary ring is used for data transfer, and the secondary ring serves as a backup ring, in case the primary ring fails. If the primary ring fails, an auto-sense mechanism causes a ring wrap so that traffic is diverted to the secondary ring (see fig. 4.2). Only stations that have a dual-attachment (connected to primary and secondary rings) tolerate this failure.

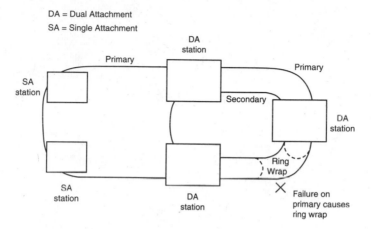

Figure 4.2:

FDDI ring with dual and single attachments.

FDDI is based on the Token Ring access method that runs at 100 Mbps. A token is used to control access to the ring, but the details of token management are different from IEEE 802.5 LANs (see discussion in Chapter 2). The maximum length of FDDI is 200 kilometers (100 kilometers for dual rings), and the distance between two nodes on a FDDI LAN cannot exceed two kilometers. Distance parameters are based on a maximum latency (delay) of 1.617 milliseconds. Maximum FDDI frame size is 4500 bytes. This size makes it suited for high speed file transfers, such as graphic, image, and other data files. Because the frame size is larger, more data can be packed into the frame and fewer packets are needed to send the file. The total number of connections to an FDDI ring cannot exceed 2000 (1000 for dual-attached stations).

The FDDI networks expect that PC workstations will not be attached directly to it, but attached by means of an FDDI concentrator or router (see fig. 4.3). PC workstations are turned on and off often in normal usage. If workstations are connected directly to the FDDI ring, their powering on and off causes frequent ring reconfigurations that may become costly in a large FDDI network. PC workstations connected directly to FDDI networks also may not keep up with the high data rates in FDDI. The newer AT computers, based on Intel 80386, 80486, or 80586 chips, may keep pace with the FDDI data rates, but they are hampered by slow I/O buses.

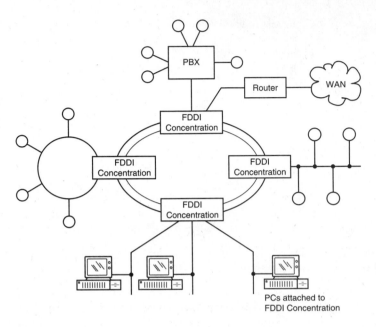

Figure 4.3:
FDDI network with router.

The FDDI concentrators, or *Multi Access Station Units* (MAUs), also serve as a fan-out box so that multiple stations can be connected. Several FDDI concentrators can be cascaded to increase the fan-out. Although the FDDI concentrator has a dual attachment, the stations attached to the concentrator have a single attachment to save on FDDI NIC costs. FDDI concentrators should be powered on all the time to reduce ring reconfigurations.

FDDI token management enables several FDDI frames to be resident on the ring at a time, which better utilizes the data bandwidth on the ring.

The FDDI ring operates in two modes: synchronous and asynchronous. In *synchronous mode*, stations are guaranteed a percentage of total bandwidth available on the ring. This bandwidth allocation is calculated in terms of percentage of *Target Token Rotation Time* (TTRT). The TTRT is the expected token rotation time for the expected traffic on the network and is negotiated during ring initialization. A station with synchronous bandwidth allocation can transmit data for a period of time not to exceed the percentage of TTRT allocated to it. Any remaining time that is left after all stations finish synchronous transmission is allocated to the remaining nodes. Thus, if the actual

Token Rotation Time (TRT) is less than TTRT, the leftover time (TTRT–TRT) is used for asynchronous transfer.

In *asynchronous mode*, transfer can take place in two modes: restricted and nonrestricted. A station can perform an extended transfer in restricted asynchronous mode. The *Station Management* (SMT) negotiates a maximum restricted time. Stations running in restricted asynchronous mode should not take up the entire ring for a period of time greater than TTRT.

In nonrestricted mode, leftover time is divided between any node that wants to send data. This mode of operation is the default. The division of time can be based on priority schemes in which stations have a threshold TRT. Stations with lower threshold TRT are cut off earlier.

FDDI uses multimode fiber. Extensions to FDDI that use single-mode fiber currently are in development. Although multimode can use a mix of light frequencies, a single-mode fiber uses laser and a smaller-core diameter fiber. Single-mode fiber has less signal attenuation and can be used over longer distances. With these FDDI extensions, two stations can be up to 60 kilometers apart. FDDI-II permits circuit switching in the synchronous mode with up to 16 synchronous channels of 6.144 Mbps each.

Many vendors are interested in running the FDDI protocols over a copper medium. Some vendors propose *Unshielded Twisted Pair* (UTP) wire, whereas other vendors favor *Shielded Twisted Pair* (STP) wire. ANSI's goal is to have one unifying protocol, rather than separate protocols for STP and UTP wiring. Using copper-based FDDI wiring is cheaper than using the fiber-based products. One problem of using twisted pair wiring is compliance with FCC regulations and signal attenuation that limits the distance between a workstation and the FDDI concentrator. It is the goal of copper-based FDDI to have at least distances of 100 meters between workstations and FDDI concentrators.

Some vendors, such as Crescendo Communications, Inc. of Sunnyvale, California, have copper-based FDDI products. Crescendo Communications' CDDI (Copper Distributed Data Interface) runs on UTP wiring. Crescendo currently offers an eight-station MAU (1000 Workgroup Concentrator) that connects workstations at distances of 50 meters. An SBus CDDI adapter can be used as the FDDI interface for the Sun Microsystems, Inc. Sparcstation. IBM offers a version of FDDI on STP wiring.

HIPPI

The *High Performance Parallel Interface* (HIPPI) is a LAN standard that the ANSI X3T9.3 committees currently are investigating to provide data rates between 800 Mbps to 1600 Mbps.

HIPPI transfers 32 bits of data in parallel across distances of about 25 meters. The parallel transmission runs over a 50-pair twisted pair wire cable—32 pairs are used for data lines and the remaining lines are used for control.

HIPPI evolved from the proprietary HSX I/O bus that CRAY supercomputers use. Graphic workstations require high I/O data rates to perform real-time modeling and display.

Figure 4.4 shows how you can adapt HIPPI for LAN usage. The HIPPI standard proposes a HIPPI Framing Protocol Layer that allows IEEE 802.2 protocol to run on top of it. Any protocol stack that uses IEEE 802.2, such as NetWare, can make use of HIPPI.

Because of distance limitations and cabling costs, the current HIPPI will probably not be used for the backbone or WAN connectivity. Nevertheless, it represents an interesting development for those applications that require very high speed LANs.

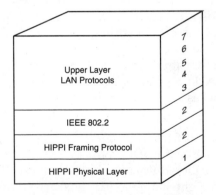

Figure 4.4:
Adapting HIPPI for LAN usage.

Metropolitan Area Network

Metropolitan Area Networks (MANs) are an interesting development in computer network standards. The MAN standard originally was intended for local area networking, but its size and scope mandate that it be managed by a central body, such as the telephone company or other commercial organizations. In this regard, it is similar to WANs.

You can implement city-wide MANs that can carry data rates as high as 155 Mbps. The IEEE 802.6 committee is trying to standardize MANs. The MAN standard has a checkered past. MAN structure originally was based on co-axial technology with a slotted ring approach, but that standard was superseded by growth in fiber optic technology.

The following list summarizes the differences between LANs and MANs:

- City and suburban areas employ MANs, whereas areas that cover smaller geographical distances employ LANs.

- Public operation of MANs through a telephone company raises issues of security, reliability, cost, and central billing that do not arise in LAN setups.

- MANs can serve as high speed backbones that are faster than FDDI.

- MANs can carry a mix of voice, video, and data traffic more effectively than LANs.

- MANs cross public rights of way. Service utilities such as telephone companies have these permissions; LAN owners typically do not.

MANs can transmit a mix of voice and data traffic. Another possible use of MAN technology is to provide LAN connectivity. The media access technology used by MAN, Dual Queue Dual Bus (DQDB), unlike FDDI, scales very well across longer distances and higher data rates than the current MAN specification. It is for this reason, perhaps, that Bell Communications Research (Bellcore) is interested in using DQDB as one of the techniques for its *Switched Multi-Megabit Data Stream* (SMDS) services.

MAN services can be supplied city-wide by phone companies or by commercial organizations. You can use routers with a MAN connection to interconnect LANs at data speeds up to 100 Mbps. Or the MAN can be used as a backbone for LANs.

MAN networks are of two types: private and public. These types are similar to private and public X.25 networks. For organizations that have stringent security or large data transfer requirements, a private MAN, such as that depicted in figure 4.5, can be used. Private MANs use dedicated cables; because only the organization's data is on the MAN, this simplifies security and billing issues. This type of MAN is like a very large LAN. Not all organizations, however, can justify the expense of a private MAN. Most organizations use shared cables that have traffic from a variety of sources, including city and state governments, and private organizations.

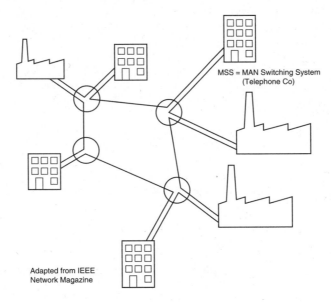

MSS = MAN Switching System
(Telephone Co)

Adapted from IEEE
Network Magazine

Figure 4.5:
A MAN configuration.

DQDB is the media access protocol used in MAN and is based on a proposal by Telecom Australia and its subsidiary QPSX. Originally, this protocol was known as the QPSX (Queued Packet and Synchronous Exchange) protocol, but was later changed to DQDB to avoid confusion with the QPSX company. It consists of two loops of fiber in the form of a bus (see fig. 4.6). DQDB is arranged in the form of a ring so that a central station can provide clocking and synchronization information for transmission of frames. Data frames are sent on both buses but in opposite directions. Fault isolation mechanisms can bypass malfunctioning nodes or breaks in the cable. The dual bus architecture permits the use of a clever MAC protocol that enables requests for transmission from stations to be placed in a distributed queue. This distributed queue mechanism provides access characteristics independent of network size and speeds.

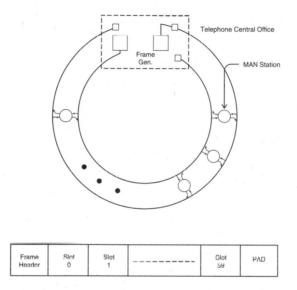

Figure 4.6:
DQDB architecture and frame format for MANs.

The MAN data frame is shown in figures 4.6 and 4.7. Each slot contains two control bits, BUSY and REQ. A BUSY bit indicates that a slot is busy and REQ is used by a station to request an empty slot. A station that wants to send data on a bus makes its request on the reverse bus by setting the REQ bit flag. The REQ bit informs the upstream neighbors that a station downstream wants access to a slot. Each node keeps track of requests downstream from it by counting the REQ bits as they pass on the reverse bus (see fig. 4.7). The REQ counter is incremented for requests on the reverse bus. The REQ counter contents are transferred to the *Count Down* (CD) counter (see fig. 4.8). The CD counter is decremented for each free slot on the forward bus because a free slot will be used by a station downstream that previously made its request through the REQ bit. A station can use the first free slot after its CD counter reaches zero. Using these counters, a first-in-first-out queue is formed. The queue position is indicated by the value of CD in each station. It is truly a distributed queue that is 100 percent fair.

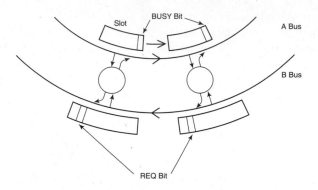

Figure 4.7:
Distributed Queue formation on a bus for MAN.

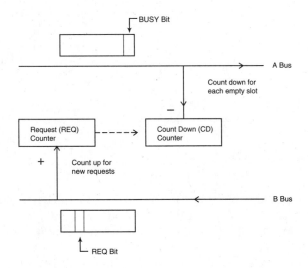

Figure 4.8:
DQDB operation used in MAN.

X.25

Figure 4.9 shows the elements of an X.25 network, and figure 4.10 shows how these elements can be used to connect LANs. An X.25 network contains a number of packet switches that switch and route packets transmitted between two nodes, such as a terminal and host machine. Although data transfer takes place using packets, the appearance to higher layers of software is that a single continuous logical channel (or virtual circuit) exists between two nodes. Typical packet sizes of X.25 networks are 128 bytes, although other sizes are possible and can be negotiated at connection time.

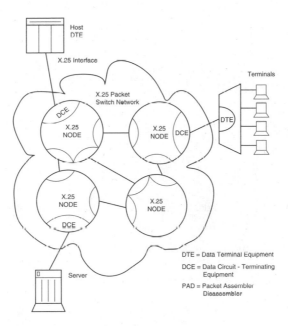

Figure 4.9:
Elements of an X.25 network.

Although terminals are attached to the X.25 network through a *Packet Assembler Disassembler* (PAD), host machines can be attached directly or through synchronous modems. The X.25 network uses the X.25 protocols, which actually are three protocols. These protocols include the X.21 or X.21bis at the physical level, *Link Access Procedure Balanced* (LAPB) at the data link level, and X.25 *Packet Level Protocol* (PLP) at the network level. This relationship is shown in figure 4.11.

The X.25 protocol enables a maximum of 4095 virtual circuits to be time-multiplexed across a physical link between the node and an X.25 network. In actual practice, fewer virtual circuits are used because most physical links cannot support the aggregate data rate for 4095 virtual circuits.

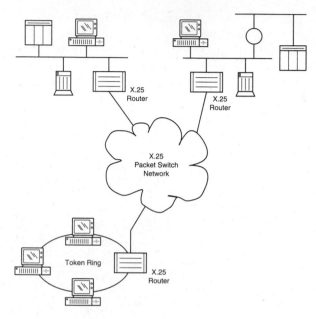

Figure 4.10:
Connecting LANs through the X.25 network.

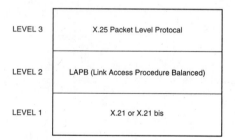

Figure 4.11:
X.25 protocols.

Typical transmission speeds of X.25 networks are 64 Kbps, but higher speeds are available. If two LANs are connected through an X.25 network, data transfer between the LANs is limited to this speed. This setup limits the kind of applications that you can run across X.25 networks. Many LAN applications require data-transfer rates of at least 1 Mbps to run efficiently. File transfers and terminal emulation applications run efficiently across an X.25 network, but workstation applications run slowly.

Frame Relay

Frame Relay technology was developed for *Broadband Integrated Services Digital Network* (B-ISDN). It can provide higher transfer-data rates by eliminating much of the overhead inherent in an X.25 network. Multiplexing and switching are provided at the lower data link layer rather than the network layer. The flow control and error control that exists between packet switch nodes for X.25 does not exist in Frame Relay. Frame Relay relies on higher-level software mechanisms to provide this service if necessary. Frame Relay assumes that the media used for data transmission is inherently reliable and much of the error checking can be eliminated.

Interest in Frame Relay is rising. Frame Relay overcomes the limitations of X.25 networks by enabling you to connect LANs at speeds up to 2 Mbps. These speeds, which rival LAN speeds, allow workstation applications to run well. As the need for LAN interconnectivity over wide area networks increases, so will the interest in Frame Relay technology.

T1

The *T1 circuit* is a point-to-point full-duplex digital circuit that originally was meant for carrying digitized voice. You can connect several point-to-point circuits to form a T1 network. The T1 circuit can use a variety of media besides copper, such as coaxial cables, fiber optics, infra red, 18- and 23-Gigahertz microwave radio or satellite links.

T1 networks provide a physical level connection with a data rate of 1.544 Mbps. This rate is in the range that can run workstation applications efficiently across T1 networks. The basis for T1 networks is the T1 circuit. Figure 4.12 shows two LANs connected by a T1 circuit.

Broadband ISDN

X.25, Frame Relay, and T1 networks can be used to interconnect LANs at 2 Mbps or less. One technology under development to interconnect LANs at higher data rates is based on B-ISDN. B-ISDN was developed to respond to the need to improve the basic and primary rates provided by ISDN (Narrowband ISDN). Voice, video, data, image, and multimedia are examples of applications that require high bandwidth.

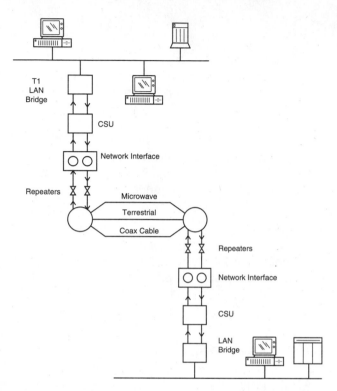

Figure 4.12:
LANs connected by means of T1 circuit.

Initial B-ISDN interfaces provide data-rate transmission of 51 Mbps, 155 Mbps, or 622 Mbps over fiber optic media. Figure 4.13 shows that the physical-layer support for B-ISDN is provided by ATM and SONET, which are described in the following sections. With appropriate adaptation layers, SONET and ATM can be used for LAN interconnectivity. A client layer in figure 4.13 can be frame relay, SMDS, or IEEE 802.2, for example.

SONET

The *Synchronous Optical Network* (SONET) was first proposed as a standard by Bellcore for a family of interfaces to be used in optical networks. The lack of standards for high-speed digital transport to be used for single-mode fiber led to a number of proprietary standards. SONET is now an international standard accepted by ANSI and CCITT.

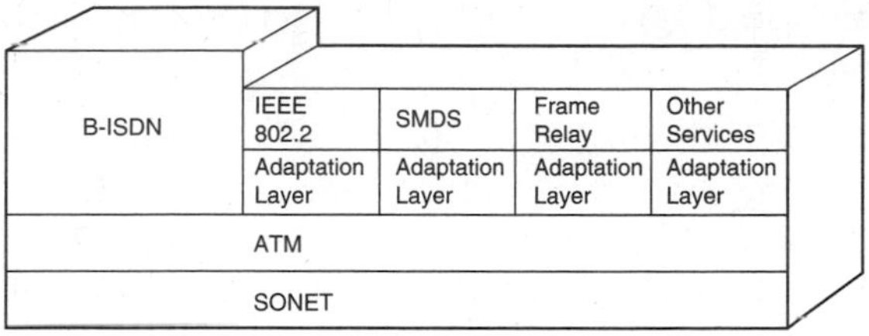

Figure 4.13:
B-ISDN support infrastructure.

The SONET standard provides a point-to-point link over fiber optic media. It provides the physical layer connection for B-ISDN and is defined in terms of a hierarchy of data rates. This hierarchy is defined in terms of the Optical Carrier (OC) speeds and the corresponding electrical signals (Synchronous Transport Signals) used to interface with electrical components. Table 4.1 shows this hierarchy.

Table 4.1
SONET Data Rates

OC Hierarchy	STS Hierarchy	Data rate
OC-1	STS-1	51.84
OC-3	STS-3	155.52
OC-9	STS-9	466.56
OC-12	STS-12	622.08
OC-18	STS-18	933.12
OC-24	STS-24	1244.16
OC-36	STS-36	1866.24
OC-48	STS-48	2488.32

The OC and STS rates are multiples of 51.84 Mbps. The basic building block is the 51.84 Mbps line rate. Thus OC-8 is 48 x 51.84 Mbps = 2488.32 Mbps. The standard defines up to OC-240; that is, 240 x 51.48 = 12.4416 Gbps rate.

STS-1 rates are roughly equivalent to the T3 (45 Mbps) data rates that are available today.

Design goals of SONET included providing a way to accommodate T3 data rates and resolving the incompatibility between the North American and European digital hierarchies, as expressed in the T1, T2, and T3 signals. The North American standard is based on a T1 rate of 1.544 Mbps, whereas the European standard is based on 2.048 Mbps. As a result of this incompatibility, T1-based routers for NetWare LANs operate differently in North America than they do in Europe.

STS data streams can be combined to yield higher STS rates. Three STS-1 rates multiplexed together, therefore, can yield a data rate of STS-3.

The STS-1 frame is 810 bytes and is made up of a 90 column-by-9-row matrix with each cell of this matrix being one byte long. This data matrix is transmitted in one STS-1 frame, as seen in figure 4.14. The first three bytes of each row contain overhead information. The first three rows contain nine bytes of section overhead, and the remaining six rows contain 18 bytes of line overhead. The combined section and line overhead of each frame is 27 bytes. The remaining 87 columns contain the payload or data. This frame payload is called the *synchronous payload envelope* (SPE) and works out to be 783 bytes (9 x 87). Not all of the SPE contains data; the first nine bytes contain path information.

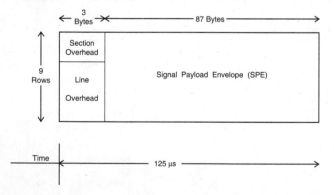

Figure 4.14:
STS-1 frame in SONET.

The STS-1 frame is sent once every 125 microseconds or at the rate of 8000 frames every second. Because each byte in the frame is eight bits, the data for each byte of data in a frame corresponds to an 8000 x 8 = 64,000 bps channel. You can use this data rate to transport digitized speech or data.

Of the 783 bytes that make up the SPE nine bytes are used for transport overhead for every row. This transport overhead contains a pointer to the location in the SPE that the actual data begins, thus allowing data to float.

Detailed consideration of section, line, and path overhead are beyond the scope of this book. A table of their definitions is included, however, to show the reader the rich functionality and robustness of SONET, as well as the reasoning for an interest in it for WAN/LAN communications.

Asynchronous Transfer Mode (ATM)

ATM provides a flexible and fast packet-switching service on top of SONET. The packets are called cells and are 48 bytes in size. These cells are the fundamental units for data transport. Data traffic from multiple channels are multiplexed at the cell level. ATM can support a broad spectrum of traffic types, including LAN traffic. In the case of LAN traffic, the longer packet sizes are broken down to small cells by LAN Terminal Adapters that implement the Adaptation Layer. The packet switch services provided by ATM also can be used by other transport services, such as Frame Relay (see fig. 4.14).

The cell multiplexing in ATM provides better bandwidth utilization. Cells are allocated on demand during times of high traffic, which is typical of many LAN applications. If there is no traffic to send, no new cells are generated.

Cell size has been the subject of much controversy. The voice people wanted small cell sizes of 32 bytes to increase the likelihood of cells being available when they are needed on short notice. The data people felt that small cells introduced greater overhead in packet splitting and recombination because data packet sizes in LAN applications tend to be large. They were willing to settle for a cell size of 64 bytes. A compromise of 48 bytes-per-cell was adopted by both factions.

Each cell is preceded by a five-byte header, making the total cell size 53 bytes. The header contains the cell destination. Before two ATM nodes exchange cells, they go through a *call establishment phase* in which a *virtual circuit identifier* is assigned. This virtual circuit identifier must be used in the data transfer phase. Each data cell contains this virtual circuit identifier.

ATM nodes can generate a mixture of data traffic types such as voice, data, and video. The cells that contain this data traffic are multiplexed across the same physical link between two ATM nodes. To identify this common physical link, an identifier called a *virtual path identifier* is included in each cell. An ATM switch can use the virtual circuit identifier and the virtual path identifier to determine where the cell should go.

Some vendors are considering using ATM to provide the media access control mechanism for LANs. LANs traditionally use datagram services at the MAC layer, which does not guarantee reliable delivery. Reliable services are provided by upper-layer mechanisms, such as the transport layer. In some applications, such as real-time modeling, it makes sense to provide a guaranteed service between a supercomputer and a graphic workstation so that image transfers can be performed at high rates.

Switched Multi-Megabit Data Service (SMDS)

Switched Multi-Megabit Data Service (SMDS), developed by Bellcore, interfaces with WAN/LAN by using a three-layer approach. These layers are shown in figure 4.15. The top layer, the SMDS Interface Protocol level 3 (SIP 3), provides a datagram service of up to 9188 bytes. At level 2 (SIP 2), this datagram is broken down to 53-byte ATM cells. The ATM cells are transported over the MAN network, discussed earlier in this chapter.

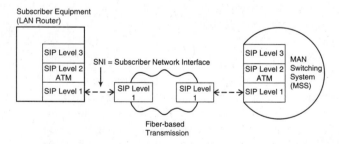

Adapted from IEEE Network Magazine

Figure 4.15:
SMDS protocol stack.

SMDS is compatible with B-ISDN in its use of ATM. ATM cells in turn use the MAN standard, which is the subject of standardization by IEEE (IEEE 802.6). Figure 4.16 shows an SMDS network based on MAN. The router to the 10BASE5 LAN serves the role of *Customer Premise Equipment* (CPE) and *Channel Service Unit* (CSU). The OSI stack shown next to this router provides translation between Ethernet protocols and SMDS protocols. Since SMDS in its current version uses MAN, the router uses the DQDB to communicate with the *Metropolitan Switching System* (MSS). This link is the *Subscriber Network Interface* (SNI) used to connect the LAN subscriber to the MSS. The MSS switches are provided to the subscriber by the telephone company or other commercial organization.

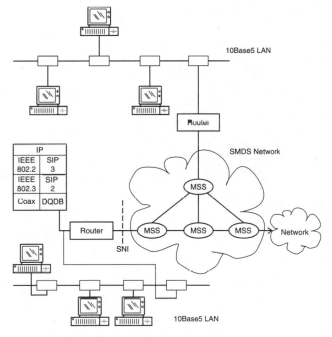

Figure 4.16:
SMDS network used to interconnect LANs.

Summary

In this chapter, you learned some of the reasons why you need to expand the range of a LAN to include WANs. Technologies discussed included X.25, Frame Relay, MANs, SONET, SMDS, and FDDI. You learned the principles behind MANs, SONET, SMDS, and FDDI.

Hardware for NetWare Servers

System Managers generally want to optimize the throughput they can obtain from a given hardware configuration. Many factors determine the ideal hardware for a NetWare server. This chapter explores some of the components that affect server performance and examines some of the choices that are available in designing the optimal hardware platform. Many different server-platform possibilities are currently available. To fully exploit your options, you should be familiar with the following hardware features that can influence the performance and reliability of servers:

- CPU power
- BUS configuration
- Network I/O
- Disk I/O

CPU Power

CPU Power or bandwidth refers to the processing speed of the server. In general, a faster CPU gives better performance, all other factors being equal. Sometimes running NetWare on a faster CPU may not give expected performances if the bottleneck in system throughput is due to other factors such as bus speed, network I/O or disk I/O.

Because of historical reasons and the success of the Intel processors in providing low-cost computing solutions, the dominant server platform for NetWare is Intel-based. NetWare v3.x and v4.x can run on Intel 80386 or higher microprocessors, such as the 80486, the P5 (Pentium), and chips that are upward-compatible to the 80386 architecture.

Compaq and other computer vendors have developed multiprocessor-based machines that can run NetWare. Multiprocessor servers fall into two general categories: Symmetrical Multiprocessing (SMP) and Asymmetrical Multiprocessing (AMP). Figure 5.1 demonstrates some of the differences between these two approaches.

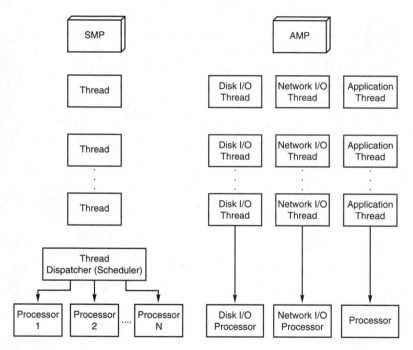

Figure 5.1:
SMP versus AMP.

In Symmetrical Multiprocessing, the threads of a server process can run on whichever CPU is available. That is, execution can take place on any of the available processors. (A *thread* is a sequence of instructions that is executed. A NetWare *process* or *task* can have many threads, which allows parallelism in computation.)

In Asymmetrical Multiprocessing, certain threads are dedicated to run on special processors. A processor, for example, could be dedicated for disk I/O, another could be dedicated for network I/O, and another for application computation.

It is generally agreed that SMP is a more flexible architecture than AMP because SMP keeps all the processors busy. In AMP, it is quite possible for some processors to be very busy while others are idle, waiting for a specific type of job. To use SMP servers effectively, software in the operating system must be aware of the multiple-processor architecture so that it can schedule threads on the processors.

The NetWare architecture is currently being modified to take advantage of multiprocessor computers, though this feature is not available at the time of this writing.

An exciting area of development is a *processor-independent* version of NetWare that allows NetWare to be ported on other processor architectures, such as RISC-based platforms. NetWare for HP's RISC Precision Architecture is one example of this new technology. More recently, a joint venture has been formed between SUN Microsystems and Novell to port NetWare to the SPARC Architecture. The SPARC architecture is one of the earlier RISC architectures and still commands a market lead over other RISC platforms. NetWare may well become the first non-SunOS operating system to run on SPARC stations. SPARC stations come in scalable platforms ranging from the low-end SPARC Classic to the mainframe-performance SPARC-Center 2000 that is multiprocessor-based. The SPARC Classic has a higher price/performance ratio than the 80486-based systems and is in the same price range.

Figure 5.2 shows the architecture of a processor-independent version of NetWare. The basic NetWare services comprising the NetWare OS, NLMs, and CLIB are separated out and interact with the hardware-specific platform through a well-defined interface called NSI (NetWare System Interface). Existing application NLMs that use CLIB for system services and do not use undocumented hooks to the operating system can be recompiled to work under the new platform.

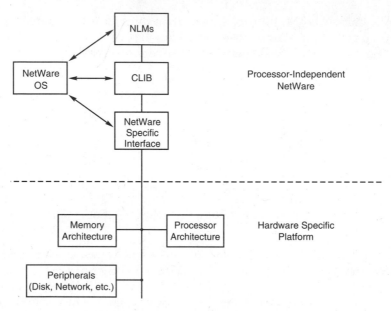

Figure 5.2:
Architecture of processor-independent NetWare.

The hardware-specific platform details are below the NSI layer (see fig. 5.2) and consist of the peripheral devices and software specific tools, such as compilers, linkers, and libraries, for the new platform.

NetWare services have been hosted on other operating system platforms, such as UNIX, VMS, and Stratus VOS. These were at one time referred to as *Portable NetWare*. More recent names are NetWare for UNIX, NetWare for VMS, and so on. NetWare SunLink is a product from SUN Connect that provides NetWare services on SunOS 4.1.x and Solaris. Whereas other operating systems and the underlying hardware they support can be used as a server platform for NetWare, there is a performance penalty for interfacing through another operating system. If the underlying hardware is fast, as in the case of Stratus XA 2000 and XA/R Continuous Processing minicomputers and mainframes, then there are gains in performance over the Intel platforms.

Also available are super-server hardware platforms that are Intel-based (from Compaq Computer Corp. and NetFrame Systems, Inc.). Both of these support NetWare v3.x.

The Compaq SystemPro LAN Server is built around the high-end Intel processor family and consists of a number of system processor modules that have a microprocessor, a numeric coprocessor, separate cache memory, and a cache memory controller. The system processor modules communicate through a 32-bit processor/memory bus. A shared system memory module also is connected to the processor/memory bus. The shared system memory module cannot only hold programs that are executing on the system processor modules but also synchronize processing between the system processor modules. I/O peripherals are supported by an EISA bus. The EISA bus controller connects to both the processor/memory bus and the EISA bus.

The NetFrame Systems super-servers, although based on Intel processors, represent a radical departure in terms of I/O bus design. When compared to minicomputers and mainframes, PC-based servers have a slow I/O bus. EISA and MCA buses do not measure up to the I/O bandwidths of minicomputers and mainframes. To overcome the PC bus limitations, NetFrame has designed a proprietary I/O bus that borrows from the architecture used in mainframes.

NetFrame uses a hierarchical bus design. These buses are arranged in a hierarchical tree, with the lower speed buses represented by the leaf nodes of the tree. The lower-speed buses actually are 32-bit 25 megabytes/sec buses, and they funnel data to higher-speed buses as they travel up toward the root of the tree. The root of the tree represents multiple Intel-based processor modules that receive data through a 64-bit 64 megabyte/sec bus. A shared memory module with a 64M or higher capacity also is attached to this bus. A dedicated diagnostic processor module called the Server Activated Maintenance (SAM) module is used for detecting and correcting errors. The SAM module can interrogate other system modules and record status information for recovery and repair.

SAM also has some other interesting capabilities such as remote diagnostics. It can be configured to dial predefined telephone numbers, to leave voice-synthesized messages, or to dial pagers (beepers). The system manager then can dial into SAM and perform a certain amount of remote diagnostics over any touch-tone telephone.

Devices such as I/O servers and application servers connect to the 32-bit 25 megabyte/sec bus. The I/O server boards contain support for a variety of disk and network technologies. A single I/O server can contain Ethernet or Token Ring network connections, and ports for RS-232, LocalTalk, and SCSI-II. An Intel processor runs on each I/O server and executes the drivers for the various peripheral devices.

Host-Bus Interface and Bus Mastering

The exchange of control and data information between the network adapter and the server's CPU is performed by means of the host-bus interface. The host-bus interface module must have a built-in understanding of the nature of the host bus. A network card is designed to interface with a very specific I/O bus such as the ISA (Industry Standard Architecture) bus, EISA (Extended Industry Standard Architecture) bus, or a MCA (Micro Channel Architecture) bus. Apple's Macintosh machines use Nu-Bus, and SUN's Sparcstations use S-Bus; these must have their own network cards.

The *width of a bus* is defined by the number of data bits it can transmit in parallel. The wider the data bus, the more efficient the network adapter will be. For the IBM PCs, 8-bit network cards are very common. 16-bit cards provide better performance but also cost a little more. 32-bit network cards for EISA and Micro Channel are available. Another important consideration is the speed of the bus measured in MHz (megahertz) and the data transferred per cycle of the bus.

The EISA and Micro Channel buses have a *bus-mastering capability*. This means that network adapters designed for these buses can transfer data to the computer at high data rates with minimal interaction from the CPU. ISA bus network adapters can be placed on an EISA bus, but these will not benefit from the bus-mastering capability of the EISA bus. In other words, EISA buses are downward-compatible with ISA buses. ISA network adapters, on the other hand, cannot interoperate with Micro Channel buses. Micro Channel buses require specially designed network adapters.

The data transfer rate of a bus can be characterized by the following formula:

$$B = S * (D/C)$$

In this formula, B = bus transfer rate (bus throughput), S = speed of bus (MHz), D = width of data transferred, and C = cycles to transfer D bits.

For ISA buses, the bus speed is 8.33 MHz, and 16-bits are transferred in 2 cycles. Therefore, the ISA bus throughput is:

$$B \text{ (ISA)} = 8.33 \text{ MHz} * (2 \text{ bytes}/2 \text{ cycles}) = 8.33 \text{ Megabytes/sec}$$

For EISA buses, the bus speed is 8.33 MHz, and 32-bits are transferred per cycle. Therefore, the EISA bus throughput is:

$$B \text{ (EISA)} = 8.33 \text{ MHz} * (4 \text{ bytes}/1 \text{ cycle}) = 33.32 \text{ Megabytes/sec}$$

For MCA bus, the bus speed is 10 MHz, and 32-bits are transferred in per cycle. Therefore, the MCA bus throughput is:

$$B (MCA) = 10 \text{ MHz} * (4 \text{ bytes}/1 \text{ cycles}) = 40 \text{ Megabytes/sec}$$

A new type of bus called the *Local Bus* has become popular to bypass the ISA, EISA, or MCA bus for video traffic between the CPU and the video adapter. This bypass is useful for avoiding the bus bottleneck. The local bus on many systems operates at 33 MHz and transfers 32-bits per cycle. Using the preceding formula, the throughput of the local bus works out to be:

$$B (Local \ Bus) = 33 * (4 \text{ bytes}/1 \text{ cycle}) = 132 \text{ Megabytes/sec}$$

For the S-bus used in SUN Microsystem's SPARC station, the bus speed is 50 MHz, and 32-bits are transferred in per cycle. Therefore, the S-bus throughput is:

$$B (S-Bus) = 50 \text{ MHz} * (4 \text{ bytes}/1 \text{ cycles}) = 200 \text{ Megabytes/sec}$$

This is one of the reasons running native NetWare on SPARC stations yields higher performance than Intel platforms.

Network I/O

Network Input/Output determines the overall performance of a file server. *Network I/O* is a measure of how rapidly data can be transferred between a server and a workstation. Because the server acts as a repository of data files on a remote file system, it is important to understand what the factors are that affect it.

A few of the more important factors that make up a server configuration and that have a direct impact on network I/O are:

- Network interface cards (NIC)
- Network drivers
- Protocols
- Network operating system
- Bus speeds at the server

These elements can conspire with each other to either improve or worsen network performance. The discussion that follows addresses some of these issues.

Understanding Network Adapters

Network adapters provide the physical connection between a node (workstation or server) on a LAN and the LAN cable.

These devices go by several names:

Network Adapter Unit/Board/Cards

Network Controllers

Network Interface Card (NIC)

Network Cards

Network Adapters

Network Interface Module (NIM)

Intelligent Network Interface Cards (INIC)

They all refer to the network electronics that fit inside a node on a LAN and implement layers 2 and 1 of the OSI model.

A functional description of a network adapter is shown in figure 5.3.

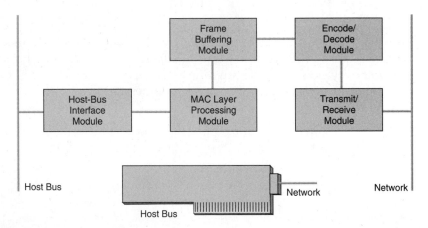

Figure 5.3:
Block diagram of a network adapter.

A number of modules on the network adapter perform specialized processing. These are:

Transmit/Receive module

Encode/Decode module

MAC layer processing

Frame buffers

Host-Bus interface

The discussion that follows explains how these modules interact with each other. It is important to understand this interaction because it can help pinpoint potential adapter-related network I/O bottlenecks.

The transmit/receive module contains the interface electronics to drive the signal to the network media and to receive the signal from the network. As signals propagate through the network media, they are reduced in strength. The transmitting station must send the signal with sufficient power to be understood by the furthest node that needs to hear the signal.

Before a signal is transmitted, it may be encoded to add clock information to the data stream. The clocking information is necessary for the receiving station to keep its clock synchronized to the transmitter's clock. When a signal is received by a station, it needs to decode the signal; that is, recover the data bits. The Encode/Decode module performs these functions. A variety of encoding techniques are used by different LANs. Ethernet and IEEE 802.3 use Manchester Encoding, IEEE 802.5 uses Differential Manchester Encoding, and FDDI uses a combination of NRZI (Non Return to Zero Inverted) and 4B/5B encoding.

When a frame is to be transmitted to the network or has just been received from the network, it is kept in a special area of memory on the adapter card for processing. In many network adapters, this frame buffer area is implemented by RAM chips on the network adapter. The amount of memory reserved for frame buffering can vary from a few kilobytes to a megabyte. Many network adapters implement, in firmware, intelligent buffer management algorithms to efficiently process packets received from the network. Some use scatter algorithms that can keep the header separate from the data portion of the frame. This eliminates the need for moving header and data into a contiguous block of memory prior to transmission.

The MAC layer processing module is perhaps the most important module in the Network Adapter. It performs several important functions:

1. **Encapsulation/decapsulation functions.** The encapsulation function is performed by the transmitting station and includes the generation of correct address, control, and frame check sequence (CRC) fields. The decapsulation function is performed by the receiving station and includes processing of the address, control, and frame check sequence fields. Error detection is also performed by the decapsulation function.

2. **Implementation of the MAC algorithms.** This would be the CSMA/CD access mechanism for Ethernet and the Token Access mechanism for Token Ring.

These preceding functions require processing power. Earlier network cards borrowed this processing power from the station's CPU. Needless to say, these network cards were very slow. Today, all network adapters have their own processing functions. These are special microprocessors that have their own ROM or microcode containing the MAC algorithms. These network controller chips also have their own RAM to process the MAC algorithms.

Performance Considerations for Server Network Adapters

Many LAN administrators would like to know which network adapter is faster—Token Ring, Ethernet, or ARCnet? This is an important question because the network adapter can become a bottleneck, and it is useful to know which one of the networking alternatives can eliminate the problem. Studies all conclude that 10 Mbps Ethernet and 16 Mbps Token Ring are faster than ARCnet at 2.5 Mbps. These results are not so surprising considering the data rates. The ARCnet Plus at 20 Mbps can be expected to be faster than both Ethernet and standard ARCnet. FDDI at 100 Mbps is the fastest of these. Thomas-Conrad has a 100 Mbps fiber optic proprietary LAN that is a combination of ARCnet and FDDI.

In designing a network interface card, a vendor makes several design choices that affect the price/performance tradeoff. The four major characteristics that contribute to NIC performance are:

1) Media Access Scheme

2) Raw Bit Rate

3) Onboard Processor

4) NIC to Host Transfer

These characteristics are considered next.

Media Access Scheme

The media access schemes such as CSMA/CD and Token Access are important factors to consider in determining NIC performance. Token Access gives a deterministic performance whereas CSMA/CD does not. On the other hand, CSMA/CD is simpler and faster under light loads compared to Token Access.

Raw Bit Rate

This is the maximum bit rate that is possible on a given media. The actual effective bit rate, taking into account protocol overhead and timing delays, is much less. Nevertheless, the raw bit rate represents an upper limit for the given media.

Fiber-optic media can be used for data rates in the 100s of Mbps range. FDDI at 100 Mbps is only the beginning. We can expect higher speed LANs based on fiber-optic cables.

Coax cable can generally accommodate data rates up to 50 Mbps and shielded twisted pair wiring around 20 Mbps.

ARCnet Plus uses a 5 MHz sine wave but by using special encoding techniques it can pack 4 bits of information in every cycle, yielding a maximum of 20 Mbps.

Onboard Processor

Effective use of an onboard processor can speed up a NIC. If the firmware for the NIC is poorly written, however, it can have just the opposite effect. When NetBIOS was created by IBM for the IBM PC Broadband LAN, it was implemented in firmware on the NIC itself. However, because of an inefficient implementation, it ran slower than NetBIOS implemented in software.

Some vendors implement upper-layer protocol processing on the NIC card for better overall throughput. An example of such a NIC is Federal Technologies EXOS series board that has onboard TCP/IP processing. (The EXOS product line was sold by Excelan to Federal Technologies, after the merger of Excelan with Novell.)

NIC to Host Transfer

The NIC to host channel can be implemented in several ways: shared memory, DMA, or I/O ports. NICs may use any of these methods or a combination of them. Observations have shown that shared memory is the fastest, I/O ports are next, and DMA is the slowest.

The data width of the bus interface has a dramatic effect on NIC-to-Host transfer speeds. This width can be 8, 16, or 32 bits. The wider the data width, the faster will be the data transfer.

The type of host bus also affects the transfer rate. EISA and Micro Channel NICs are faster than ISA NICs.

Disk I/O

Disk mirroring/duplexing is an option that can be used with NetWare to improve the fault tolerance of the server disk subsystem should the server disk fail. This fault tolerance is obtained at the expense of purchasing twice as much storage as would normally be required, since each disk holding programs and data has a secondary backup disk. The performance of a mirrored disk subsystem is approximately the same for disks that are not mirrored. Actually, reads are sightly faster and writes to the disk are slightly slower, but these are not significant changes.

Another solution to the mirrored disk approach was proposed in a paper by David A. Patterson, Garth Gibson, and Randy Katz of the University of California, Berkeley (Report no. UCB/CSD 87/39, December 1987). The report titled "A Case for Redundant Array of Inexpensive Disks or RAID" discusses the concept of using an array of disks to distribute data that can provide reliability and improve disk performance. Because disk performance continues to be a bottleneck on PC server-based solutions, there has been a great deal of interest in RAID technology.

The key concept behind RAID is a technique called striping. *Striping* allows data blocks to be interleaved across several drives that have the same performance and storage characteristics, instead of storing them on the same drive. Each drive operates independently of the others, and this allows data to be transferred in parallel from each drive. This means that if an array of n disks are operating in parallel, the data will be transferred in $1/n$ the time compared to data transferred using a single disk, resulting in an n-fold improvement in disk transfer rate. Figure 5.4 shows data being read in a RAID subsystem using 3 drives. The numbers in the figure represent data blocks and show that they are interleaved across the 3 disks.

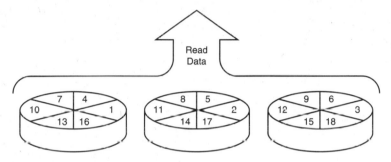

Figure 5.4:
Disk striping.

Reliability in RAID is achieved by using one of the disks for storing a *check byte*. The check byte is constructed in such a way that should one of the drives fail, the data in that drive can be reconstructed from the remaining data drives (including the check byte drive). A popular algorithm to construct the check byte is the exclusive OR (XOR) operation. Figure 5.5 shows how the XOR checksum byte can be used to reconstruct the data in a 3-disk RAID drive. Two of the drives are used to hold the data, and the third drive is the "check" drive. The first data drive in this example has a bit pattern of 11100011, and the second drive has the data pattern 11101101. The check byte using the XOR operation is 11010111. If drive 2 fails, its data can be recovered by an exclusive OR (XOR) operation of the bytes in the remaining drives (see fig. 5.5).

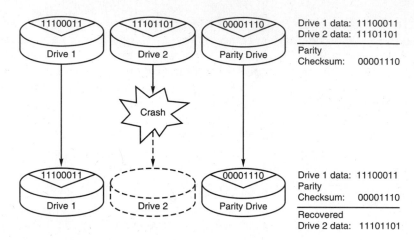

Figure 5.5:
Reconstructing data for a failed drive.

Table 5.1
Exclusive OR Operation for Computing Check Byte

Drive	Drive Status	Bit Pattern
Data drive 1	Running	11100011
Data drive 2	Running	11101101 XOR
Check Byte drive	Running	00001110

If data drive 2 fails, table 5.2 shows how data can be reconstructed.

Table 5.2
Recovering Data from a Failed Drive

Drive	Drive Status	Bit pattern
Data drive 1	Running	11100011
Check Byte drive	Running	00001110 XOR
Data drive 2	Failed	11101101

The check byte is recomputed if a byte location is changed and if the changed check byte has to be written to the check disk. If the check byte is maintained on a single drive, it could result in a bottleneck that would negate the speed improvements of the interleaved drives. For this reason, the check byte is distributed across the disks for improving performance.

The check byte disk represents a storage overhead, but for an n-array RAID system, it is $1/n$ of the total storage. For a value of n larger than 2, it represents a smaller overhead than a mirrored/duplexed system.

Disk arrays that use RAID technology are classified in terms of RAID levels 0 to 5.

RAID level 0 only makes use of the striping feature of RAID but has no provision for redundancy. Striping improves the performance of the disk array, but because no check bytes are used, there is no improvement in fault-tolerance compared to a single-disk system.

RAID level 1 provides disk mirroring along with striping. Every disk has a mirror that has an exact data copy of the primary disk. For best performance, the disks should be designed so that the reads and writes can be performed independently. This will result in speed improvements because the read request will be completed by the first drive that returns the result.

RAID level 2 has a provision for data recovery with one disk reserved for data recovery. The striping function is performed at the bit level. This means that the bits are scattered consecutively across the disks. The first bit, for example, is written on the first disk in the array, and the second bit on the second disk, and so on. RAID 2 is not commonly implemented for microcomputers.

RAID level 3 provides striping at the byte level, with one disk reserved for the check byte. The check-byte disk is called the parity drive and, as already explained, can be used to recover information on the failed drive. It is common to design the spindle rotation of disks so that parallel reads can be done efficiently.

RAID level 4 provides striping at the block level. A block is the amount of data transferred in a single read/write operation. Like RAID level 3, a disk is reserved for a parity drive.

RAID level 5, like RAID level 4, provides striping at the block level. Unlike RAID level 4, however, it spreads the error-correcting block data evenly across the disks. This avoids the bottleneck of writing error-correcting data to a single disk.

RAID disk drivers are available from the manufacturers of the drives for NetWare and other operating system platforms such as OS/2, UNIX, and Windows NT.

Regardless of whether one chooses the disk mirroring/duplexing approach or the RAID approach, the disk subsystem should be fast and reliable. You can build server disk subsystems using IDE, ESDI, or SCSI. The best choice is SCSI because of its flexibility for both disk mirroring/duplexing approaches and RAID.

Summary

This chapter discussed some of the factors that determine the ideal hardware for a NetWare server. System managers should consider such hardware features as CPU speed, server bus type, network I/O characteristics of NICs, and the speed and reliability of disk subsytems.

These factors have to be balanced against the amount of money one is willing to spend on the server platform. An exciting area of development for NetWare servers is native NetWare running on powerful RISC-based workstations. RISC platforms offer greater speeds and freedom from the PC-based bus approaches such as EISA and MCA which do not rival the performance of mainframe and minicomputer-based bus architectures. An important development in disk subsystem performance is the availability of cost-effective RAID solutions to improve disk speed and reliability.

NetWare 2.2 and 3.11

PART TWO

Features of NetWare 2.2 and 3.11

This chapter examines some of the capabilities of a network operating system (NOS). This includes an examination of the functions of a NOS and examines its relationship to the OSI model. Other issues that are examined include security, management, and interoperability issues for a NOS.

Understanding Network Operating Systems

Before understanding what a network operating system is, you must understand what an operating system is. An *operating system* (see fig. 6.1) is a program that manages resources of a single computer. The following are some of the resources that an operating system manages:

- Local file system

- Memory in a computer

- Loading and execution of application programs that run in the computer memory

- Input/output to peripheral devices attached to a computer

- CPU scheduling among application programs

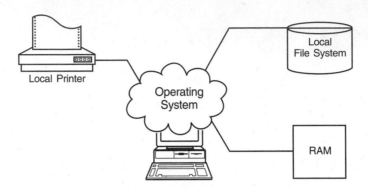

Figure 6.1:
Resources managed by an operating system.

A network consists of resources, such as stations and printers, and communication devices, such as bridges, routers, and gateways. The job of a network operating system is similar to that of an operating system except that it has to manage resources on a much larger scale. A *network operating system* (see fig. 6.2) is a program that manages resources across an entire network. The following is a list of some of the resources a network operating system manages:

- Remote file systems that are accessible by other workstations

- Memory on the computer that a NOS runs on

- Loading and execution of shared application programs

- Input/output to shared network devices

- CPU scheduling among NOS processes

Examining the Features of a Network Operating System

The NOS software can be distributed equally among all nodes, or a major portion of the NOS can reside in a central node. A NOS that is distributed equally among all nodes is called a *peer-to-peer NOS*. An example of this is NetWare Lite. A NOS whose major portion runs on a central node is a *centralized NOS*. The central node is called the *server*. Applications that make use of resources managed by the central node NOS are called *clients*. This architecture generally is referred to as the *client/server architecture*.

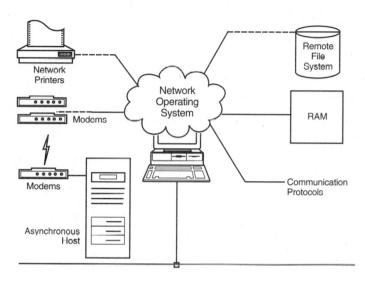

Figure 6.2:
Resources managed by a network operation system.

Because the client software runs on workstations, the workstations are sometimes referred to as *clients*. Only applications that make use of services, however, should be called *clients*. Applications or system software that provide services to other applications are called *servers*.

When a client communicates with the server, it must have a small portion of the NOS running on it. In NetWare terminology, the NOS running on the client is called the *shell*. Examples of the centralized NOS are NetWare v2.x and NetWare v3.x

When a NOS runs on a user node (workstation), it must communicate and interact with the native operating system on the user node. The native operating system that runs on the workstation is called a *workstation operating system* (WOS). Examples of WOSs are DOS, OS/2, UNIX, and Macintosh's System 7.

NOS and the OSI Model

Figure 6.3 shows the NOS in relationship with the OSI model. You can see in this figure that the NOS spans layers 3 to 7 of the OSI model. The NOS has three major aspects:

- Network driver

- Subnet protocols

- Application layer protocols (APIs)

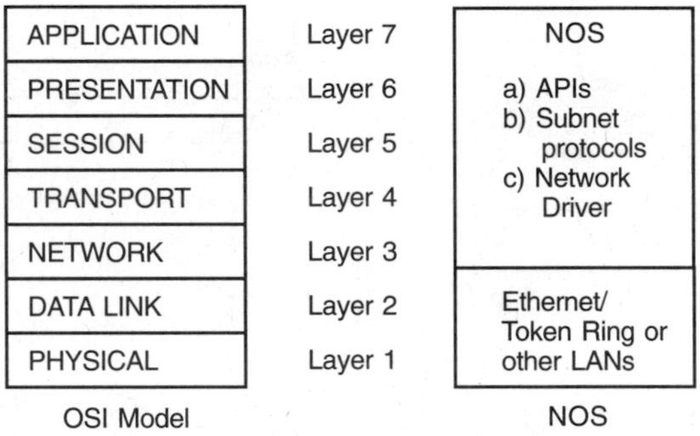

OSI Model		NOS
APPLICATION	Layer 7	**NOS**
PRESENTATION	Layer 6	a) APIs
SESSION	Layer 5	b) Subnet protocols
TRANSPORT	Layer 4	c) Network Driver
NETWORK	Layer 3	
DATA LINK	Layer 2	Ethernet/ Token Ring or other LANs
PHYSICAL	Layer 1	
OSI Model		NOS

Figure 6.3:
The relationship between the NOS and OSI.

The NOS communicates with the LAN hardware by means of a network driver. The network driver acts as a liaison between the NIC and the subnet protocols. The subnet protocols are communication protocols needed to send application and system messages across the network. The application layer protocols implement the NOS services and communicate with the subnet protocols. Each of these major aspects of a NOS are discussed in the next few sections.

Network Drivers

A *network driver* is a program that spans portions of layers 2 and 3 of the OSI model. It provides an interface between the NIC and the upper-layer protocols.

The network driver masks the complexities of the way a NIC must be controlled for transmitting and receiving packets from upper layers. The network driver has an intimate understanding of the hardware operation of the NIC, such as the various control/status registers, DMA, and I/O ports. Vendors producing NICs according to LAN standards, such as the IEEE 802.5, implement the details of the NIC differently. This means that two IEEE 802.5 nodes may be able to communicate across a LAN despite differences in implementation, such as IRQ lines, DMA, and I/O port mechanisms. Because the implementations are different, each NIC must have a different network driver even though NICs can communicate with each other by using the same IEEE 802.5 protocol.

Network installers select the correct network driver for the card and integrate this network driver with the NOS. As you will see later in this chapter, in NetWare v2.x this process is done by generating NetWare. NetWare v3.x uses a more flexible dynamic binding mechanism to accomplish this task.

NetWare comes with drivers for some popular cards. Drivers not included with the NetWare disks must be obtained from the manufacturer of the card. Usually, an NIC comes with a floppy disk containing drivers for operating systems such as NetWare, LANMAN, VINES, and UNIX. Many NIC vendors maintain their own bulletin boards, and you can download network drivers for them. Some vendors supply drivers through the NetWire forum on CompuServe.

Subnet Protocols

Subnet protocols span layers 3 to 5 of the OSI model. These layers provide the network services that are essential for sending data across a LAN. The functions of layers 3 to 5 were discussed in Chapter 1. Review the discussion in that chapter for a better understanding of the subnet protocols.

Subnet protocols play an important role in the performance and functionality of a NOS. Fast subnet protocols result in a fast NOS. On the other hand, slow subnet protocols make for a sluggish NOS. Also, a subnet protocol that is fast on a LAN may be slow on a wide area network (WAN).

The native subnet protocols used by NetWare are IPX for layer 3 and either SPX or PXP for layer 4.

In most situations, a layer 5 protocol is not necessary for NetWare. If an application is written to make use of the NetBIOS protocol, an optional layer 5 can be provided that implements the NetBIOS protocol. The NetBIOS software emulator implements its services by making use of the SPX protocols.

The subnet protocols and their relationship to the OSI model are shown in figure 6.4.

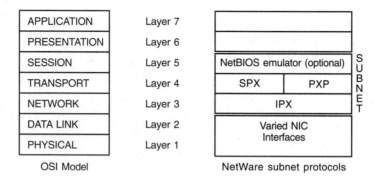

Figure 6.4:
The relationship between OSI and the NetWare subnet protocols.

The native NetWare protocols were derived from Xerox's XNS (Xerox Network Standard) protocols. The relationship between XNS and NetWare protocols is shown in table 6.1.

Table 6.1
XNS and NetWare Protocols

XNS Protocol	NetWare Protocol
IDP (Internet Datagram Protocol)	IPX (Internet Packet Exchange)
PEP (Packet Exchange Protocol)	PXP (Packet Exchange Protocol)
SPP (Sequence Packet Protocol)	SPX (Sequence Packet Exchange)

Novell based its subnet protocols on XNS because these protocols had the reputation of working efficiently in a LAN environment. XNS protocols were not designed to be used for wide area networks, which have larger time delays. Because of this, Novell's IPX, PXP, and SPX protocols suffer from the same limitations as XNS protocols for WAN applications. Novell offers a streamlined version of its protocols for WANs to overcome some of these limitations. This streamlined version—the *packet burst* NLM—is available for only NetWare v3.x and higher.

In retrospect, Novell could have avoided some of these problems and gained an early lead in WANs had they chosen the Internet UDP/TCP/IP protocols. UDP (User Datagram Protocol) works efficiently across LANs, and TCP (Transmission Control Protocol) works efficiently across WANs. The Internet protocols and others are available for NetWare v3.x.

The IPX protocol provides the capability to send data across different interconnected LANs. IPX is a datagram (connectionless) service. SPX provides a virtual circuit (connections-oriented) service for those applications that need it. SPX has a larger overhead in terms of processing time and additional packets, so NetWare avoids this for its internal operation. PXP is a transport protocol that is connectionless. It is patterned after Xerox's PEP protocol.

Application Layer Protocols (APIs)

The single most important application layer protocol that NetWare provides is NetWare Core Protocol (NCP). Without NCP, none of the file services offered by NetWare would be possible. A number of reference materials mistakenly show the NCP protocol as belonging to layer 5 or layer 6. NCP provides remote file services to client nodes and rightfully belongs in layer 7 of the OSI model.

Some of the misunderstanding about NCP protocol functions probably arises because the definition of the NCP protocols is not publicly available. Novell is extremely reluctant to reveal details about the NCP protocol. Developers can, for a lot of money, obtain details of NCP protocols after they sign appropriate nondisclosure agreements.

The following are some of the functions that NCP provides:

- Opens files under different modes

- Closes open files

- Reads data blocks from open files

- Writes data blocks to open files

- Gets a list of directory entries

- Manipulates the server database (bindery)
- Provides high-level connection services
- Provides synchronization operations

Multitasking versus Single Tasking NOS

Operating systems like DOS are single tasking. This means that DOS can perform only one thing at a time. For the environment and applications for which DOS was originally conceived, this was not a problem. The operating system needed to manage only one user and one application at a time.

Some of the earlier NOSs, such as MS-NET from Microsoft and its derivatives, provided NOS services on top of DOS. A big performance penalty was paid by these earlier NOSs. Consider, for example, what would happen if several packet requests came to a server that was running MS-NET on top of DOS. MS-NET would have to make use of DOS to provide access to the hard disks on the server. If a second packet request was allowed to be processed while the first one was in progress, the MS-NET server would crash. Why? Because DOS is nonre-entrant.

Nonre-entrant means that a piece of program code can be entered or executed only once at any given time. *Re-entrant* code can be entered or executed by a number of processes at any time. 3+SHARE from 3COM, an earlier NOS based on MS-NET, also was based on DOS. It avoided the DOS bottleneck by providing a re-entrant piece of code that could access the server's resources. 3COM called this piece of re-entrant code CIOSYS (Concurrent I/O System). Earlier MS-NET versions queued packet requests and allowed only one packet to be processed at a time.

Microsoft solved the MS-NET problem in LAN Manager because LANMAN runs on top of OS/2. OS/2 is a multitasking operating system and is re-entrant; it can process several packet requests at a time.

Another popular NOS, Virtual Network System (VINES) from Banyan, runs on top of a modified UNIX System V. UNIX is multitasking and re-entrant and can process multiple packet requests.

A NOS must be multitasking and re-entrant. If a NOS runs on top of another operating system, that operating system must, in turn, be multitasking and re-entrant.

NetWare is multitasking and re-entrant, but it is not based on a general purpose operating system like OS/2 or UNIX. (Novell does have a version of NetWare that runs on UNIX called NetWare for UNIX, but it is another product line.) NetWare is built from the ground up as a multitasking operating system.

In a general purpose operating system, issues of fairness are more important than throughput and efficiency. Consider a general purpose multitasking operating system (such as UNIX) that is running several user applications. Although some applications (foreground tasks) may be more important than others (background tasks), it is important that no applications are starved for CPU time. To achieve this goal, a process is given a certain amount of time, and then the CPU turns its attention to another process, regardless of what it may be doing at the time. Although this procedure may be more democratic and fair, it has an adverse effect on the system throughput, especially when critical processes are interrupted.

NetWare adopts the philosophy that a process can monopolize the CPU for as long as it needs to complete critical tasks. Processes need to yield the CPU to others when done performing critical tasks. This *nonpremptive scheduling* mechanism is used in the design of many real-time operating systems.

The NetWare Network Operating System

NetWare was first developed in 1983 as a NOS that ran on a proprietary Motorola 68000 microcomputer that acted as the central element in a star topology. This network was called the S-Net. Novell abandoned the proprietary hardware approach and developed NetWare for the IBM XT platform, calling it NetWare 86. NetWare 86 was followed by the Advanced NetWare 286 and SFT NetWare 286 products. Macintosh support was added to SFT NetWare 286 v2.15. Novell then announced ELS NetWare, which was developed to compete with entry-level LANs. ELS NetWare was not very successful and has given way to NetWare Lite.

When the Intel 80386-based AT personal computer was designed, Novell released a completely revamped version of NetWare to run on 386-based ATs. This NetWare version was rewritten by using Watcoms 32-bit C compiler and became NetWare 386. The NetWare 386 product line now is called NetWare v3.x, and the NetWare 286 product line merged into a unified NetWare v2.2. The rewrite of NetWare in C led to the development of Portable NetWare, which consists of NetWare services ported to different operating system platforms. Portable NetWare has since been retitled NetWare for UNIX. Novell continues to form strategic alliances with major networking vendors, such as IBM, DEC, HP, and AT&T, to make NetWare available on as wide a range of platforms as possible.

NetWare has pioneered features such as System Fault Tolerant (SFT) servers, security services, and performance improvement mechanisms. Many of the other network operating systems now support these features. Novell did not invent these features because similar features existed and exist on minicomputer and mainframe-based systems. Novell, however, was the first to use these features on PC-based networks.

Other NOS Choices

Several excellent NOS choices are available in the NOS market place, including LAN Manager from Microsoft, VINES from Banyan, and IBM LAN Server from IBM. The history of these products is shown in figure 6.5.

Today, NetWare's main competitor is LANMAN. LANMAN was first marketed through 3COM and other OEMs. For many years, the most advanced version of LANMAN was available from 3COM and was called 3+OPEN. Microsoft made the decision to market LANMAN through 3COM because 3COM was then the well-known archrival of Novell. 3COM added many improved features to LANMAN, such as sophisticated network administration, Demand Protocol Architecture (DPA), and Macintosh support. 3COM, however, quit the NOS business by early 1991.

LANMAN now is supported and marketed by Microsoft. Many of the 3+OPEN features are being integrated into LANMAN. LANMAN runs on the OS/2 platform. Microsoft has announced that future versions of LANMAN will run on its New Technology (NT) operating system platform. LANMAN also is available on UNIX platforms through a port made by AT&T. Initially, HP and AT&T worked on this port, but HP eventually dropped out. Micro-Tempus has a LANMAN version for the IBM MVS mainframe platform. Many other licenses of LANMAN exist.

IBM's first NOS offering was the IBM PC LAN Program (PCLP). PCLP was based on MS-NET and suffered from all the performance problems of running on DOS. PCLP still is available from IBM and is an example of a peer-to-peer NOS. When Microsoft released LANMAN as part of OS/2, IBM, through a license agreement with Microsoft, developed a NOS based on LANMAN. This NOS from IBM is the IBM LAN Server. It is based on

OS/2 EE (Extended Edition). OS/2 EE has the additional components of a Communications Manager to interface with IBM SNA networks and a Database Manager that supports the IBM mainframe database (DB2). Although IBM has its own NOS offering, it became a reseller of Novell's NetWare in early 1991.

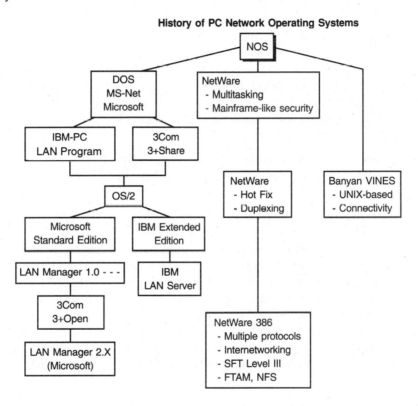

Figure 6.5:
The history of network operating systems. (Graphic courtesy of Learning Group International)

VINES from Banyan is based on a modified UNIX System V. It is a robust NOS with features comparable to NetWare and LANMAN. Because UNIX comes with protocols like TCP/IP that work well with WANs, it is not surprising that VINES has very good support for wide area networking. Banyan went one step further and designed a powerful distributed naming service that enables network resources to be accessed by a symbolic name, regardless of their location anywhere on the network. This naming service is called StreetTalk and is one of the reasons VINES enjoys an edge in LAN/WAN integration. Novell plans to come up with a similar capability based on X.500 in a newer NetWare version.

Understanding NetWare's NOS Security

When NetWare came out in 1984, it quickly acquired a reputation of being a secure NOS. Other NOSs that were based on MS-NET, such as MS-NET, IBM PCLP, and 10NET, had very poor security. In contrast to these NOSs, NetWare provided security features that rivaled those of minicomputer and mainframe operating systems.

The next few sections briefly examine some of the security features of NetWare.

User Account Security

All versions of NetWare have a username/password security feature. To use NetWare, a user must have an account and a valid password on the system. In earlier versions of NetWare, passwords were sent over the LAN in unencrypted form. When protocol analyzers became quite common, unencrypted passwords became an obvious security deficiency. Protocol analyzers examine packets on a LAN and easily see the password that is sent by a user workstation during the log-in sequence. Now, all versions of NetWare encrypt the password at the station before sending it across the LAN.

Time Restrictions

By using the system administration utility SYSCON, a NetWare administrator can impose time restrictions on when a user can log in. The time restrictions can be imposed in terms of half-hour intervals and can be set for any of the weekdays.

The time restriction feature is designed for network sites that have strict security measures in which access to the network needs to be denied to users.

Station Restrictions

NetWare administrators can use the system administration utility SYSCON to impose station restrictions on where a user can log in. The station restriction enables a user to log in from only stations that have a specified station address.

The station restriction feature is designed for network sites that have strict security measures in which access to the network is possible through certain physical areas only. Station restrictions prevent users from wandering to other areas of the building and using workstations that do not belong to them.

Space Restrictions

One of the questions a network administrator has to ask is: How much server disk space should a user be allowed? If a user does not have any restrictions, the user can, by design or accident, use up all the space on the server disk.

Suppose, for example, that a user runs an application that creates a temporary file on the server disk. If a bug is in the application, the application can keep on entering data in the temporary file until it expands and fills all available disk space on the server. This situation is not too uncommon and when it occurs, all the users on that server are affected.

You can safeguard available disk space by limiting disk space on an individual user basis, based on the applications a user runs. Typical values allocated per user on the server range from 1M to 20M.

Diskless Workstations

When LANs began to become popular and became a legitimate platform for running business applications in corporations, some MIS managers had misgivings about the LAN client/server technology. One reason for this misgiving was that user workstations had removable media, such as disks. It would be possible for an unscrupulous user to download sensitive information to a floppy disk or hard disk and walk away with the disk. With the traditional terminal/host architecture, the user can view this information on-screen but cannot walk away with a disk containing sensitive information.

One way to keep users from copying sensitive information onto floppy disks is to install diskless workstations. Diskless workstations do not have any storage media, such as floppy disk drives or hard disks. They boot their native operating system, such as DOS, from a copy of the operating system boot image that is stored on the server. The NIC cards on diskless workstations have a special boot Programmable Read Only Memory (PROM) that enables the NIC to fetch the boot image from a public directory on the server. In the case of NetWare, this is the SYS:LOGIN directory under volume SYS: on the server.

Media Security

In many applications, LAN media security is a big concern. The LAN cabling should be installed so that it is not possible for an unauthorized user to access the LAN cables. Coaxial cables and twisted pair cables are easy to tap and read data. They also emit electromagnetic radiation. A determined person with sufficient resources can read LAN traffic through these emanations. Some military applications install LAN cabling in a metal conduit to prevent noise emanations and bury the cable in concrete to prevent physical access to the LAN cables.

The best LAN media for security purposes is fiber optic because it is more difficult to tap. If a probe is inserted into the fiber optic conductor, it can cause additional reflections and interference to the light signals and cause the fiber optic link to crash.

Encryption

How do you secure data on the file server? One way is to make use of the security permissions provided by the NOS. The network administrator with supervisor or equivalent privileges, however, can read all files and directories on the server. This becomes a problem with sensitive information that you do not want other users, including the supervisor, to see. One way of handling this is to encrypt databases and files that contain sensitive information. Some database systems, such as Novell's Btrieve record manager, have the capability to encrypt data files. The file is decrypted when it is opened and encrypted when it is closed. As you can imagine, however, performance suffers because of the encryption and decryption operations.

A number of encryption programs are available. Some encryption programs are bundled with software tools, such as Borland's SideKick and Central Point's PC-TOOLS. Many use the DES (Data Encryption Standard) algorithms for encryption.

Encryption also can be done in hardware at the NIC level before transmitting packets across the LAN media. When encrypting LAN packets, only the data portion of the packet is encrypted. The network address and control fields in the packets usually are not encrypted so that devices such as bridges and routers can interpret the network address and control fields.

Motorola's wireless LAN uses encryption to prevent users from tapping into the microwave frequency used for transmission. Wireless LANs have sophisticated encryption algorithms in which the seed used for encryption is changed randomly every 2 milliseconds. The *seed* is a number or code that is used as the key for the encryption algorithm.

Audits

LAN audits are very helpful for performing an analysis of the threats to which a NOS has been subjected.

A hostile user, for example, might try to guess passwords by repeatedly trying password combinations. In NetWare, one way to prevent this is to lock out the user after a certain number of failed password attempts. Another way is to have an audit of all password attempts. Some audit messages are reported directly to the server console, whereas others are kept in an audit trail file.

Computer Viruses

Computer viruses are a form of networking terrorism that network managers must be aware of. A few misguided programmers spend countless hours devising techniques to terrorize innocent users by wiping out their data, or infecting the data in such a manner that the software virus can propagate itself.

It is much more difficult for virus writers to break the security of a NOS such as NetWare. A network manager can use a number of preventive measures to reduce the threat of viruses. Virus detection and correction software also are available that can be used in a network environment. Computer viruses are discussed in detail in Chapter 18.

Managing Interoperability Issues in a NOS

As networks grow in size, one of the major problems a network administrator faces is *interoperability*. When all the hardware and software components are from the same vendor, the system usually functions flawlessly. This is the reason why many users and corporations prefer a single vendor solution.

Many MIS departments are pure IBM, or pure DEC, or pure Novell. Network applications and requirements have become so broad and diverse that it is difficult for a single vendor to supply all possible needs. The larger vendors, such as IBM, DEC, and HP, come very close to supplying these needs, but many of their solutions require the purchase of a proprietary platform. The vendor then can lock the user into a particular computing architecture, which makes it difficult to purchase equipment that is not from the same vendor.

Some end users are perfectly happy to be locked into a vendor's solution because they do not have to deal with interoperability issues—the vendor does instead. Solutions from a single vendor, however, usually are not the most cost-effective. Competition and the free market system tend to drive down equipment prices and increase performance. Also, vendors have strengths in different areas. Many network managers exploit the strengths of various vendors, leading to multivendor networks.

One solution to the interoperability dilemma is the adoption of open systems in which vendors make products compliant to universally accepted standards. The development of the OSI model and standardization efforts of organizations, such as ISO, ANSI, IEEE, and ECMA, are steps in the right direction. Only time will tell the success of these efforts.

The following section discusses some of the more important aspects of interoperability as it relates to multi-vendor networks.

Defining Interoperability

Interoperability means that all the hardware and software components in a system cooperate at all levels. This is a broad, yet accurate, definition of interoperability and encompasses a wide range of issues. Although the term interoperability may be difficult to define, you begin to appreciate the *lack* of interoperability when your network stops working because of conflicting components.

As the following examples point out, interoperability usually is not discussed unless the hardware and software do not interoperate.

You can, for example, buy a telephone from a variety of sources and plug it in any telephone socket. You do not have to be a technician or electrical engineer to perform this task. As long as that telephone jack is enabled by the telephone company, you can dial any telephone in the world. This is an example of interoperability at the highest level.

Another example is Centronics parallel printer cable for IBM personal computers. You can buy it from any source, and it works just fine with any IBM PC clone. Likewise, all FAX machines can "talk" to each other because they use the same Group 3 FAX as the language used in sending facsimile data.

All of these examples have one thing in common. They all conform to the same standard. In the case of telephones, the phone jacks and the signals used for communications comply to a standard. For the Centronics parallel printer cable, the cable connectors and the wiring conform to a standard. In the FAX machine example, all FAX machines use the same Group 3 FAX code. When components operate as they should operate, interoperability usually is not a topic of discussion.

On the other hand, if you install a NetWare server on the same LAN as a VINES server and try to get the two servers to share data and applications, you begin to realize the importance of interoperability. Because NetWare and VINES use different architectures, they cannot communicate. This is an example of network software interoperability. Hardware interoperability issues also exist.

You cannot, for example, connect a Token Ring station directly to an Ethernet bus because each system uses different connectors and cables. Even if you manage to connect the Token Ring NIC to the Ethernet bus by a liberal use of a soldering iron and a wire cutter, the two stations will not be able to talk to each other. Ethernet uses a carrier-sense mechanism and Token Ring uses token access. In other words, the two stations are incompatible at the physical and data link layers of the OSI model.

On the other hand, you can connect a 10BASE5 Ethernet LAN and a 10BASE-T Ethernet LAN and expect them to interoperate. Both use different cable types; 10BASE5 uses coaxial cable and 10BASE-T uses unshielded twisted pair wiring. You can, however, join these two LANs by a 10BASE-T transceiver, enabling the stations on the two LANs to communicate as if they were part of the same network. This is possible because both 10BASE5 and 10BASE-T use the same carrier-sense access mechanism. In this example, the two LANs are compatible at the data link layer of the OSI model.

The OSI model is indispensable in analyzing problems concerning interoperability issues within networks. As you learned earlier in the chapter, interoperability problems stem from lack of standardization. If all networks followed the same standards, the term *interoperability* probably would not have been created by the networking industry. (The term does not yet exist in the English dictionary.) Read Chapter 1 for a description of the OSI model.

Interconnectivity versus Interoperability

Sometimes the term *interconnectivity* is confused with *interoperability*. You can, for example, put a Token Ring NIC in a NetWare server, an IBM LAN Server, and a VINES server, and then connect them to the same Token Ring LAN. The token in this Token Ring circulates through each of these servers. Data and control packets generated by each of these servers circulate to other servers. Compatibility exists at the data link layer of the OSI model because each of these servers uses the same token access mechanism. These servers, however, cannot share and exchange applications and data. In this example, you have *interconnectivity* among these servers but not *interoperability*. Figure 6.6 shows compatibility at the physical (layer 1) and data link (layer 2) layers of the OSI model, but no compatibility at the upper layers.

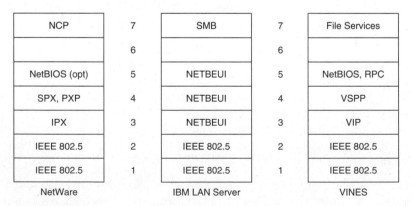

NCP	7	SMB	7	File Services
	6		6	
NetBIOS (opt)	5	NETBEUI	5	NetBIOS, RPC
SPX, PXP	4	NETBEUI	4	VSPP
IPX	3	NETBEUI	3	VIP
IEEE 802.5	2	IEEE 802.5	2	IEEE 802.5
IEEE 802.5	1	IEEE 802.5	1	IEEE 802.5
NetWare		IBM LAN Server		VINES

Figure 6.6:
Server compatibility at the physical and data link layer only.

In the preceding figure, NETBEUI is IBM's NetBIOS extended user interface, SMB is IBM's file services protocol (Server Message Block), VIP is VINES Internet protocol, VSPP is VINES sequenced packet protocol, and RPC is VINES remote procedure call.

You can compare interconnectivity and interoperability to a room full of English-speaking and French-speaking people talking at the same time. Interconnectivity exists because each person can hear the utterances of each speaker. The English and French speakers, however, cannot understand each other (unless they understand both languages). In other words, *interoperability among the people speaking in the room does not exist.*

Different Levels of Interoperability

Interoperability should be considered in terms of the applications used by users. Can these applications run on different platforms? Can data files and information be exchanged between them? If a user can perform these general tasks, you will not hear much about interoperability problems.

In terms of the OSI model, interoperability exists when you have compatibility at the application layer (layer 7). How does layer 7 interoperability affect the other layers 1 to 7 of the OSI model? In the OSI model, a layer depends on the services provided by the layer below it. Layer 7 of the OSI model, therefore, uses the services provided by layer 6, which in turn uses the services provided by layer 5 and so on all the way down to layer 1. In order to have interoperability at layer 7, or the application layer, you must have interoperability at layers 1 to 6. The sole purpose of layers 1 to 6 is to provide interconnection between the application layers of two stations that are sharing information.

File transfer protocols, such as Kermit, XMODEM, and File Transfer Protocol (FTP), are examples of interoperability. Kermit and XMODEM can be found on many different systems, and yet you can exchange files by using asynchronous dial-up lines (telephone lines) between these systems. FTP implementations exist on DOS machines, NetWare v3.x servers, and UNIX machines. You can use FTP to transfer files between these systems.

In the preceding discussion, *interconnectivity* is compatibility at layers 1 to 6 of the OSI model. *True interoperability* is compatibility at layer 7 (the application layer) of the OSI model and the application software that makes use of it. True interoperability cannot exist without the interconnectivity support of layers 1 through 6 of the OSI model.

Examining Levels of Interoperability

The preceding section discussed interpretability issues at the different layers of the OSI model. The OSI model is used as a yard stick only because not many commercial implementations make use of ISO recommendations for the protocols at the OSI layers. Even among the OSI recommendations, several options are available from which to choose. Some of the layers have incompatible options. Two implementations, therefore, can both claim to be OSI compatible, but because they use incompatible options at some of the layers, no interoperability exists between them.

Interoperability at the Physical Layer

If stations are attached to the same physical media, such as coaxial cable, twisted pair cable, or fiber optic, then they have interoperability at the physical media, or layer 1, of the OSI model. Examples of this are Ethernet stations that are connected by coaxial cable, or Token Ring stations connected by IBM Type 1 twisted pair wiring. Figure 6.7 shows the OSI model for two stations connected by the same media.

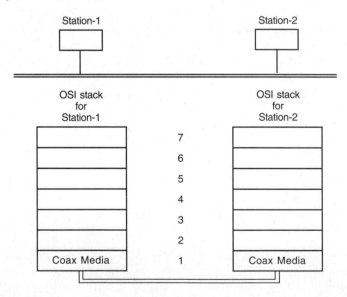

Figure 6.7:
Interoperability at the physical layer with same cable.

You also can have physical layer interoperability even when stations are connected by different media types. You can, for example, interconnect stations on a coax Ethernet LAN and on a 10BASE-T LAN. Interoperability is established between the two LANs by a *10BASE-T transceiver* that joins a 10BASE-T link to the transceiver cable and provides the signal conversion. Figure 6.8 shows the interoperability between these stations as it relates to the OSI model.

Interoperability at the Data Link Layer

Figure 6.8 also shows interoperability at the data link layer. Both stations use the same IEEE 802.3 mechanism for accessing the LAN, which assures interoperability at the data link layer.

You also can have interoperability for Ethernet and Token Ring LANs indirectly through a translating device, even though they use different data link layer mechanisms. The translating device that provides interoperability between dissimilar data link layers is called a *bridge*. The IBM 8209 bridge, for example, can be used to connect Ethernet and IBM Token Ring LANs. Figure 6.9 shows an example of a bridge.

Interoperability at the Subnet Layers

Two NetWare stations can communicate with each other because they use the same protocols at the subnet layers. Subnet layers are defined as layers 3 to 5 of the OSI model. Figure 6.10 shows two NetWare stations that are interoperable at the subnet layer. In examining their OSI representations, you can see that the NetWare stations use the same protocols at layers 3, 4, and 5. In this example, the stations are using Novell's NETBIOS implementation to communicate. Two NetWare stations can use just layer 3 (IPX) to communicate. Many applications that run on NetWare use just the IPX layer for interoperation. An important point illustrated in figure 6.9 is that to have interoperability at the subnet layers, you must have interoperability at the physical and data link layers (layers 1 to 2).

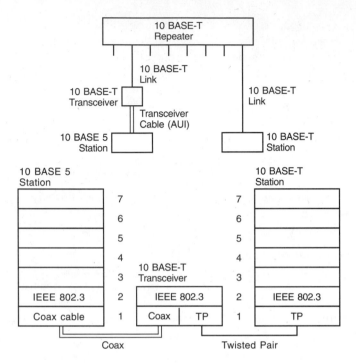

Figure 6.8:
Interoperability at the physical layer with coaxial and twisted pair cables.

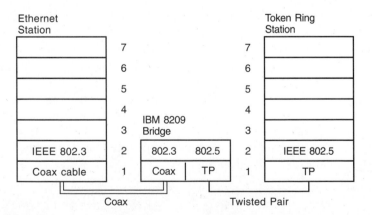

Figure 6.9:
Interoperability at the data link layer through a bridge.

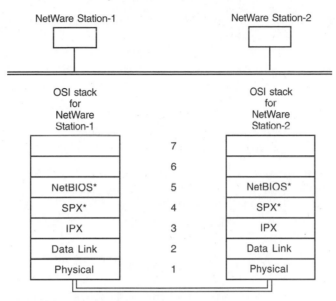

* The NetBIOS and SPX layers are optional.

Figure 6.10:
Interoperability at subnet layers for NetWare stations.

Interoperability at the Application Layer

Earlier in this chapter, you saw that transferring files is an example of interoperability at the application layer. One area of great interest to many corporations is interoperability of different electronic mail systems. For PC-based networks, a defacto standard is Novell's Message Handling System (MHS). MHS was developed by Action Technologies of Emeryville, California and now is controlled by Novell. Many electronic mail packages, like DaVinci Mail and cc:Mail (a subsidiary of Lotus Corp.), use and support MHS. You even can use MHS on CompuServe. If you do not have a need to go outside PC-based LANs, MHS provides sufficient capabilities for interoperation between electronic-mail systems. If you need to send electronic mail to an IBM mainframe or to stations on DECnet, however, MHS does not work. The bigger vendors, such as IBM and DEC, have their own electronic-mail standards.

Electronic mail is represented by an international standard called X.400. X.400 is a general standard that enables text, binary, voice, and facsimile data to be sent in an electronic-mail message. All the major vendors in the United States, such as IBM and DEC, and the network industries in Europe and Japan support X.400. Many vendors use their own proprietary systems, but to interoperate with each other, vendors use X.400 gateways. X.400 gateways translate the proprietary message format into the X.400 format and vice-versa. A related standard exists that is called the X.500 and handles network name services on a worldwide scale that is used in conjunction with X.400.

Other interoperability issues at the application layer deal with application-level interoperability. The following section discusses how to run applications on both IBM PC and Macintosh computers. You also learn how to exchange application data files between the IBM and Macintosh.

Data Interoperability for DOS

Lotus 1-2-3 and Microsoft Excel spreadsheets can run on both the IBM PC and Macintosh platforms. These applications contain conversion routines to import and export spreadsheets between these two platforms. These conversion routines are necessary because the IBM PC and Mac operating systems use different file systems and methods to represent data. Data transparency does not exist between these systems. Excel and 1-2-3, for example, have built-in support for this conversion. Not all applications provide conversion routines, but third-party support tools that provide data conversion are available. Conversion between text files from IBM PC to Macintosh is easy. More complex file structures require special utilities. The following are some utilities (and their manufacturers) that you can use to convert more complex files between IBM PCs and the Macintosh:

- AutoImport (White Crane Software)
- Catapult (Tangent Group)
- DataLens Driver (Digital Networks)
- PC/SQL-Link Database Gateway (Micro Decisionware)
- Ally (Unisys)

Data Interoperability Provided by NetWare

A network operating system such as NetWare v3.x enables Macintosh, DOS, OS/2, and UNIX workstations to store files on the server. (NetWare v2.x supports DOS, OS/2, and Macintosh file systems.) Figure 6.11 shows that each of these workstations sees its own file system on the same NetWare server. Macintosh users see folders and iconic representations of files, and DOS users see file names (eight-character file name and three-character extension) on the server. NetWare supports this file transparency by using a general representation for files on the server called the *Universal File System*.

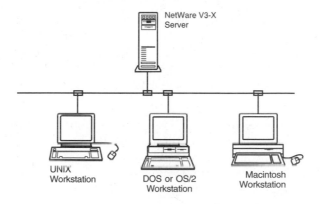

Figure 6.11:
Multi-workstation support on NetWare v3.x.

Data Interoperability under Microsoft Windows and OS/2

Applications running in the Microsoft Windows or OS/2 environments can export and import data between applications. The most primitive mechanism for doing this is the cut-and-paste operations that can copy application data into a temporary buffer. This data then can be imported into other applications that are running under Windows or OS/2. A much more powerful mechanism for providing data exchange is *Dynamic Data Exchange* (DDE). DDE enables you to set up an interprocess communications link between two applications operating in a Windows or OS/2 environment. When data changes are made in one application, the changes are automatically sent to the linked application.

The problem with DDE is that it works with only true Windows or OS/2 Presentation Manager applications. Also, DDE does not provide data transparency. The applications linked by DDE need to understand each other's message format. DDE is concerned only with getting the message across. In this sense, DDE is similar to the transport and session layer protocols in the OSI model.

Data Interoperability Using Object Linking and Embedding

To better support data transparency, vendors, such as Microsoft, have developed *object linking and embedding* (OLE). OLE provides a way to share data between different applications. OLE introduces the notion of *data ownership*. The application that first creates the data, owns the data. This association between application and data exists even when the data is exported to other applications.

If, for example, you have OLE-aware versions of AutoCAD and PageMaker, you can create an illustration under AutoCAD, and then export it to PageMaker. Because the illustration was created in AutoCAD, an ownership association exists between AutoCAD and the illustration and is retained even though the drawing now is in a PageMaker document. You can modify the illustration by using PageMaker, but each time you do this, AutoCAD is invoked to change the illustration. Pointers associated with the illustration notify the OLE-aware application as to what you are trying to accomplish and transparently take care of the operation by invoking the owner of the imported data. Although the illustration appears in the PageMaker document, it physically belongs to AutoCAD.

OLE manages data by treating it as an object. An *object* (see fig. 6.12) is a specific instance of a user-defined data class and consists of the data representation and the programs required to manipulate it. To manipulate and link (import) an object to other applications, the object is placed in a *container*. The container has simple controls for the object. In most situations, these controls are all that you need to manipulate the object. If greater control is desired, OLE can be used to call the owner of the application directly.

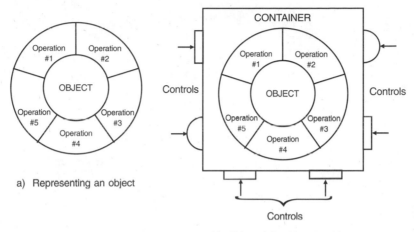

a) Representing an object

b) Object defined in a container

Figure 6.12:
Data object definitions.

The problem with the OLE approach is that currently it is not easy to transport or convert documents to non-OLE systems. In the preceding example, if the AutoCAD illustration is moved to a system that does not have AutoCAD, the illustration vanishes.

Data Interoperability Using OMF

Hewlett-Packard's NewWave is an object-oriented system that runs under Microsoft Windows. In NewWave, data export and import is controlled by a centralized Object Management Facility (OMF). NewWave's interprocess data communications capability enables it to interoperate with non-Windows systems. OMF also runs under UNIX with a distributed network version that can run on a server.

HP and SUN Microsystems have collaborated to develop a plan for a Distributed Object Management Facility (DOMF) and have submitted it to the Object Management Group (OMG). *OMG* is a consortium of vendors whose goal is to establish a network object management architecture. DOMF is ambitious; its goal is to provide data transparency on different computing platforms across mixed types of networks.

Examining NetWare's Management Tools

NetWare comes with several management tools. Most of these tools are software-based; that is, they do not require any hardware other than the server and workstations on the network. Hardware-based tools, such as the SNMP LANtern Monitor and SNMP LANtern Management Station, also are available from Novell, but they must be purchased as separate products. SNMP-based products were discussed in Chapter 4.

Some of the NetWare built-in management tools run directly on the server, whereas others run at the workstation and access management information from the server. The purpose of these management tools is to report the status of the server, such as server memory utilization, server cache statistics, and status of disk drives. By monitoring the server and network-wide parameters, the LAN manager can determine whether the network is behaving normally. If a failure occurs in any part of the network, one or more of the monitored parameters indicate an abnormal value.

The NetWare management tools are distinct from other tools, such as SYSCON. SYSCON performs server administration, such as managing user accounts, groups, and server accounting.

Monitoring the File Server Console

The TRACK console command can be used to monitor some types of server traffic. The TRACK ON command initiates a tracking display on the console monitor. You can cancel tracking by using the TRACK OFF command.

Both versions of NetWare support a console MONITOR facility, but they are similar only in name. The MONITOR NLM is the primary server monitoring utility for NetWare v3.x (see Chapter 10). The MONITOR command in NetWare v2.x displays only the file activity for active workstations. Under NetWare v2.x, FOCONSOLE is the closest equivalent to the MONITOR NLM in NetWare v3.x.

When you use the MONITOR command at a NetWare v2.x console, NetWare displays a screen that shows the server utilization and six window panels that contain information on activities of stations 1 to 6. The MONITOR command accepts the station number as a parameter. To see stations 6 to 11, however, you need to use the following command:

```
MONITOR 6
```

The server utilization is the server CPU utilization and must not be confused with the network utilization, which measures the amount of traffic on the network. Typical values for server CPU utilization are in the range of 0 to 60 percent. Execution of some server applications can bring this utilization to as high as 90 to 99 percent. Some users even reported a server utilization of over 100 percent. This usually happens when older versions of NetWare v2.x are running on a very fast AT 386 or 486 (33 MHz or more). These older versions of NetWare v2.x have a bug in the formula for computing server utilization on machines with a very fast clock rate.

Using Workstation Monitoring Tools

The workstation monitoring tools that come with NetWare run on the workstation and monitor server performance and volume utilization.

The two workstation monitoring tools are FCONSOLE. These tools run on both NetWare v2.x and NetWare v3.x. VOLINFO is a simple tool that shows the server disk volume utilization.

FCONSOLE is a much more sophisticated tool and displays information on server statistics at the workstation and works well for NetWare v2.x servers. FCONSOLE's functions have been largely replaced by the MONITOR NLM in NetWare v3.x. It is invoked by typing the command **FCONSOLE** at the workstation.

Using the Remote Management Facility

A useful tool that is available only on NetWare v3.x is the Remote Management Facility (RMF). RMF enables a supervisor or remote console operator to perform console operations from a remote location, such as from another workstation. This means that you can set up a virtual server console at any workstation, and then control any server that has the appropriate RMF software loaded on it. Because server console operations can be performed at the workstation, you can keep the server in a restricted area with the keyboard locked or removed. This makes for a more secure networking environment.

Table 6.2 lists the components that make up the RMF software, and figure 6.13 shows how these components can be used to control a server through a workstation. The server can be controlled by a direct link across the network, through an asynchronous link, or by any combination of these two methods.

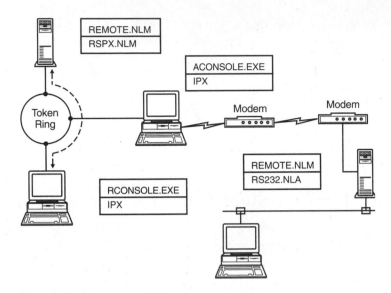

Figure 6.13:
Remote management.

Table 6.2
Remote Management Facility Components (RMF)

Utility	Description
REMOTE.NLM	Acts as the console and keyboard manager. REMOTE.NLM interfaces with communications drivers in RSPX.NLM and RS232.NLM.
RSPX.NLM	Provides SPX support for REMOTE.NLM. RSPX.NLM is an NLM communications driver.
RS232.NLM	Provides asynchronous communications support to REMOTE.NLM. RS232.NLM is an NLM communications driver.
RCONSOLE.EXE	Runs at the workstation to provide a virtual console direct link across the network.
ACONSOLE.EXE	Runs at the workstation to provide a virtual console asynchronous link through modems and dial-up lines.

Configuring the NetWare NOS

As you configure NetWare, you need to make a number of choices. Some of these features are selected at the time NetWare is configured and generated. NetWare generation is required in NetWare v2.x because the NetWare object modules need to be statically linked. These procedures are discussed in the following sections.

Setting Up Nondedicated and Dedicated Servers

In NetWare v2.x, the server can be set up in one of two modes: dedicated or nondedicated. This decision is made at the time of NetWare generation and has a big impact on server performance and the way the server is used.

Nondedicated NOS

A nondedicated NOS is a station that can be used as a server and as a workstation simultaneously. In the case of NetWare, this is possible by having two partitions on the server disk: one for NetWare and one for DOS. The NetWare partition must be the one that is active and bootable. You can set up a nondedicated server only with NetWare v2.x—not with NetWare v3.x.

The server's RAM is divided into an area for DOS and NetWare. DOS programs run in real mode, and NetWare runs in protected mode. The real mode is used in AT 286 and higher machines to maintain compatibility with DOS that was designed to run on Intel 8086 microprocessors. The 8086 has a maximum addressable memory (physical RAM) of 1M. NetWare on an AT 286 requires more RAM and makes use of the protected mode of Intel 80286 chips. This allows for a maximum addressable memory of 16M.

To run DOS and NetWare, simultaneously, the microprocessor must switch between real and protected modes rapidly. When the Intel 80286 is first powered on, it comes up in real mode. Programs can issue an instruction to switch the microprocessor to protected mode. After the microprocessor has switched to protected mode, however, it cannot switch back to real mode without resetting (rebooting) the microprocessor.

For ATs made after 1986, the BIOS was modified to distinguish between a fake and a real reboot. To switch between protected and real mode, a fake reboot is initiated by the keyboard processor. This causes the 80286 to reset, switch to real mode, and execute the BIOS reset code, but the modified BIOS recognizes this as a fake reboot and does not execute the reset code. This explains why nondedicated mode does not run on old ATs that do not have a modified BIOS. Also, some ATs display sluggish performance because they use a different design for the keyboard whose processor is used to initiate a reboot. To correct this problem, use an IBM keyboard or a true IBM-compatible keyboard.

Dedicated NOS

A dedicated NOS is one that only the NOS can run on. DOS and the NOS do not coexist on the server. The server RAM is used exclusively for their NOS.

Choosing between Dedicated and Nondedicated NOS

In the nondedicated mode, DOS is run as an application on top of NetWare. The server's CPU is shared between DOS and the NOS, thus slowing them both down. Also, if the DOS application crashes, it would crash the NOS. In the nondedicated mode, exposing the server machine to users is a security risk.

Not all DOS applications can run on the server in the nondedicated mode, such as the following types of applications:

- Applications that require extended and expanded memory drivers. NetWare takes over all memory above 640K for its own purpose. Extended and expanded memory drivers conflict with NetWare memory usage.

- Applications that try to directly manipulate interrupt vectors, I/O ports, and other hardware in the PC. NetWare controls the hardware. DOS and application software run as applications on top of NetWare. Direct control of hardware conflicts with NetWare usage of the server machine.

For all these reasons, nondedicated mode is no longer as attractive as it was once thought to be. The real reason behind a nondedicated NOS is to save the cost of an extra machine. With the AT prices under a thousand dollars, the problems of nondedicated NOS are not worth it.

Understanding SFT Levels

Novell has defined three System Fault Tolerant (SFT) levels for its NetWare NOS to improve its reliability:

- SFT Level I
  Hot fix

- SFT Level II
  Disk mirroring
  Disk duplexing

- SFT Level III
  Server duplexing

SFT Level I, or the hot fix level, is defined as read-after-write verify (see fig. 6.14). In all versions of NetWare, whenever a block is written, it is immediately read to verify that what was read is the same as what was written. If the two blocks are different, the area on the disk is bad, and the block is re-written into a special area called the *redirection area*. About 2 percent of the disk is reserved as the redirection area. The bad spot on the disk is recorded in a bad-block table. That area of the disk is never written into until the disk is formatted and prepared again for server installation by using a utility called *Comprehensive Surface Analysis* (COMPSURF).

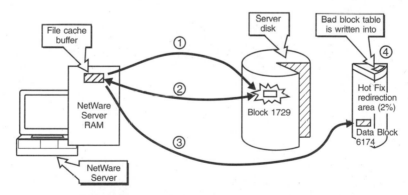

① File cache buffer is written to disk block 1729
② Read-after-write verify check
③ Disk block 1729 was bad: file cache buffer rewritten to
   Hot Fix redirection area
④ Location of bad block 1729 is recorded in bad block table

Figure 6.14:
SFT Level I (hot fix). (Graphic courtesy of Learning Group International)

SFT Level II has two options. The first option is disk mirroring. Most ISA disk controllers support two disk channels. Two disks of the same size are attached to the disk controller. One of the disks is designated as the primary controller, and the other disk is designated as the secondary disk (see fig. 6.15). The secondary disk acts as a mirror image of the primary. When a block is written, it is written to both disks. When a block is read, the read command is issued to both disks. The fastest disk read response is the one that is used.

If the primary disk fails, the secondary disk takes over. When the primary disk is repaired, the secondary disk information is transferred to the primary disk. If the disk controller fails, a secondary disk attached to the same controller is not useful. Disk duplexing (see fig. 6.16) enables the primary and secondary disks to be attached to separate disk controllers. This makes the server fault-tolerant toward disk controller failures. SFT Level II includes SFT Level I.

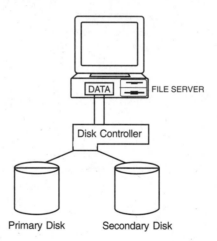

Figure 6.15:
SFT level II (disk mirroring).

SFT Level III enables a second server to act as a backup for a primary server. The two servers are connected by a high speed bus. If the primary server fails, the secondary server takes over. SFT Level III includes SFT Level II.

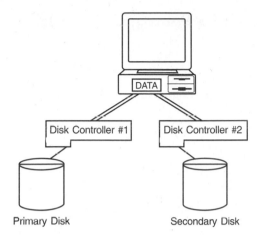

Figure 6.16:
SFT level II (disk duplexing).

Examining Peer-to-Peer Network Operating Systems

Peer-to-peer NOS offers an attractive low-cost alternative to the more expensive centralized servers. For small networks, a peer-to-peer NOS can be adequate for most networking needs. This section briefly examines peer-to-peer network operating systems.

A peer-to-peer NOS, such as NetWare Lite, enables any DOS machine to become a server. A DOS station can be a server, a workstation, or both.

Many small businesses are intimidated by the complexity involved in setting up a NOS like NetWare, IBM LAN Server, LANMAN, or VINES. All they would like to do is be able to share files, printers, and a few applications. Many such organizations already have stand-alone PCs. All they really need is networking hardware and a simple and cheap NOS. The easiest small-business solution is a peer-to-peer NOS, also called an entry-level NOS.

Advantages of a Peer-to-Peer NOS

The following are the advantages of the peer-to-peer NOS over the central-server approach:

■ Peer-to-peer NOSs are cheaper and easier to install and administer for a small number of users compared to most central-server NOSs like NetWare, LANMAN, IBM LAN Server, and VINES.

■ Any DOS machine (usually with a hard disk) can be converted into a server for a peer-to-peer NOS. This is useful for quick sharing of files between users. Most central-server NOSs require special preparation of hard disks. Also, in the dedicated mode, servers on central-server NOSs cannot be used as a DOS station. Even in the nondedicated mode, central-server NOSs may have limitations as to the amount of memory available for applications, and you may not be able to use special memory management drivers, such as expanded and extended memory management drivers.

■ You do not need to dedicate a special machine as a server on peer-to-peer NOSs. This results in reduced costs for LANs.

Limitations of a Peer-to-Peer NOS

Compared to the central server approach to LANs, the peer-to-peer NOS does have disadvantages. For a larger number of nodes (over 25 or 50), the peer-to-peer NOS may quickly become unmanageable. Because users can set their workstation as a server, they can spend an inordinate amount of work time playing with and administering their server. Network administration can become an absorbing and interesting task. Consider an organization of 50 users of a peer-to-peer LAN who spend several hours a day putting special files, such as games, on their server and administering and fine-tuning their server. You can imagine what would happen to the productivity of the organization. For a large number of servers and nodes, central control still is one of the most effective ways of administering the network.

In stark contrast to this model of centralized control is the network administration on Internet, which can be best described as near anarchy! Luckily, there is no shortage of Internet experts and hackers (in the good sense of the word) who fix problems as they arise.

Because DOS is used as a server, the performance of peer-to-peer NOSs are limited by the DOS file system and DOS memory limitations. A DOS-based server can support fewer nodes effectively compared to the central-server. This may not be a big disadvantage because peer-to-peer NOS-based LANs generally have fewer nodes to support.

Another disadvantage of peer-to-peer NOSs is that organizations tend to grow in size, and when companies grow, networks must grow. When the number of nodes becomes very large, the networks may become difficult to manage. Also, for a larger number of nodes, the peer-to-peer LANs may become more expensive. If this happens, consider switching to NetWare v2.x, which costs approximately $30 per user node. NetWare Lite, a peer-to-peer NOS, costs $50 per node. For a 60-node LAN, the cost of NetWare Lite is $3000. For a larger number of nodes, the cost actually gets more expensive than NetWare v2.x. Although these costs are not fixed and will probably change by the time you read this, you can apply the same reasoning to decide when NetWare Lite becomes too expensive.

Examining Multipurpose NOSs

The earliest NOSs that were introduced in the networking industry were disk servers. *Disk server technology* provided remote disks to users on a LAN, but the users could not share files easily. Disk server technology was replaced by *file server technology*, in which files could be shared among users. File server technology gave LAN users a remote file system that could be accessed by the workstation operating system (WOS) commands and software interfaces. Generally speaking, file server technology gave birth to the client/server model for PC networks.

Depending on the application that is run on a server, the file server can be treated as a special application server. A file server that has gateway software to networks, such as IBM's SNA network, can be called a *gateway server*. A file server that supports a pool of modems that can be used to dial out or dial in is called an *asynchronous communications server*. A file server can be treated as a general purpose computing platform and not just a provider of file services. Today, these computing platforms are called *servers*.

Servers are multifaceted and can provide a number of dedicated services. The following describes some of these services.

Internal Routers

A number of NIC cards can be placed in a server, and a LAN can be connected to each NIC. The server software performs routing functions between the different LANs. In NetWare v2.x, up to four NIC cards can be placed in a server. In NetWare v3.x, this number is 16.

To perform this routing function, each LAN needs to have a unique network address. A *network address* is used in the IPX packet to send data packets across an Internet LAN. This network address, or network number, can be considered to be associated with the cabling system used to interconnect the LAN. The first NIC in the server is called LAN A, the second LAN B, the third LAN C, and the fourth LAN C.

Because NetWare supports over 180 different NIC cards, the server can perform routing functions between over 180 different LANs for IPX packet traffic.

External Routers

A routing function can be performed by a dedicated workstation, rather than by a server. The same number of NICs can be placed in a workstation, and routing software generated by the ROUTEGEN utility can be run at the dedicated workstation. A router built in this manner is called an *external router*. The rules for a unique network address for the different LANs are the same for internal routers.

Internal Routers versus External Routers

The advantage of internal routers is that the server machine does double duty as a server and as a router. An extra machine is not needed to perform routing functions. The disadvantage of this approach is the performance penalty for sharing a single machine. When router traffic is heavy, the file server performance suffers, and when the file server is busy, the router performance suffers.

External routers, because they are dedicated machines, have a better performance than internal routers. They are recommended over internal routers for networks with heavy Internet traffic. The disadvantage is the price of an extra machine for the external router.

Summary

In this chapter, you learned about some of the capabilities of network operating systems and the types of services they provide. You learned how to analyze a NOS in relationship to the OSI model and how the NOS functions map to the OSI model.

You also learned about the different types of interoperability and interconnectivity issues in a network environment.

Installing NetWare 2.2 Servers

In this chapter, you examine installation issues relating to NetWare v2.2. Before you learn about installation issues, however, you need to cover some background material that will help you better understand the installation process.

NetWare v2.x is designed to run on IBM PC ATs that have an Intel 80286 microprocessor or higher (Intel 80386, 80486, or 80586). NetWare v2.x runs in the *protected mode* of the Intel chip. In this area, the entire address space of the Intel 80286 is available. The Intel 80286 has 24 address lines, creating an address space (RAM size) of 2 to the 24th power, or 16M. This address space enables the NetWare operating system to implement many of its performance improvement features directly in RAM, improving the LAN's performance.

The attraction of NetWare v2.x is its lower price compared to NetWare v3.x. NetWare v2.x also is a high-performance network operating system (NOS). In fact, much of Novell's dominance in the LAN market was established by the NetWare v2.x product line. NetWare v2.x still has a larger installed base compared to NetWare v3.x, although this may change in the future with installations converting over to NetWare v3.x.

NetWare v2.x represents the culmination of the NetWare product for the Intel 80286 processor. All future enhancements to the NetWare product line will be made to the 3.x series.

Understanding Versions of NetWare v2.x

This section examines the history of NetWare v2.2 and its previous versions. Prior to the NetWare v2.x product line, Novell NetWare ran on a Motorola 68000 (M68000) microprocessor and even on a PC/XT platform under 640K of RAM. The M68000-based server was called NetWare 68, or NetWare/S, and used a proprietary S-Net (Star) topology. Up to 24 PCs could be attached to the server by using modified RS-422 connections running at 232 Kbps. The server used MUX boards made by Gateway Communications, which acted as a multiplexor for the six RS-422 ports on the MUX board. You could install up to four MUX boards in the server, giving a maximum of 24 ports. Later, support for ARCnet boards in the NetWare 68 server was added, which gave it higher speeds (2.5 Mbps).

The birth of NetWare began with a project for developing a disk server operating system by a group of graduate students from Brigham Young University. They called themselves the Superset team, and had a six-week contract with Novell Data Systems (NDS)—as Novell was known in those days—to develop server software to support CP/M and UNIX workstations. DOS had not yet been developed at that time. The six-week contract was renewed several times as the project grew in size. File sharing, as opposed to disk sharing, was incorporated as the NOS matured. When DOS became available on IBM PCs, the Superset team wrote shells to enable a DOS or CP/M-86 machine to access the server.

NDS went bankrupt in the early 1980s and was bailed out by Safeguard Scientifics. After the reorganization in 1983, a new company called Novell, Inc. arose out of the ashes, under the stewardship of its new president and CEO, Ray Noorda. The M68000-based server was named ShareNet. DOS machines were supported by a proprietary NIC connected to the central ShareNet server.

When IBM released its PC/XT, ShareNet was renamed NetWare/S-Net and Novell began porting the server software to run on the PC/XT under 640K RAM and a 10M hard disk. This product was known as NetWare/86.

On the workstation side, Novell supported CP/M and DOS machines, and even had special S-Net NIC cards for machines such as the Victor 9000 and TI Professional. Support for CP/M was dropped in 1986 when MS-DOS had clearly won the PC workstation operating system wars.

The last release of NetWare/S-Net was 2.1 and the last release of Advanced NetWare/86 was v2.0a.

Advanced NetWare

When the IBM PC AT became available, Novell began working on a version of NetWare to exploit the capabilities of the Intel 80286 microprocessor, which the AT was built around. Advanced NetWare v1.0 was released in 1985 followed by version 2.0 in 1986. This NOS supported PC/XTs and PC/ATs. As can be expected, Advanced NetWare/286 was rewritten to use the Intel 80286 microprocessor's protected mode and more powerful instruction set.

Advanced NetWare (ANW) supported up to 100 simultaneous connections to the server. The server software could be configured in either the *dedicated* or *nondedicated* mode. Accounting features were introduced in ANW, along with features such as hot fix. *Hot fix* (later called SFT Level I) performed read-after-write verify checks for every block of data written to the server's hard disk. Router support at the server was added in ANW. This enables up to four NICs to be added to a server with ANW working double duty as a router and a server. ANW also enables external disk subsystems to be added to the server, for a total of 2G of disk storage.

With Advanced NetWare, NetWare began to gain recognition for performance and reliability.

SFT NetWare

SFT NetWare was released in 1987, with the idea of adding greater reliability at the server. NetWare was making inroads into corporate-wide computing, and a need arose to have the reliability that MIS managers had come to expect from mainframe- and minicomputer-based systems.

Novell named the hot fix feature introduced in Advanced NetWare as SFT Level I. SFT stands for *System Fault Tolerance*. Plans were announced to introduce SFT Level II and SFT Level III.

SFT Level II includes the hot fix feature and provides greater reliability at the server disk subsystem by using disk mirroring or disk duplexing. In *disk mirroring*, a second hard disk acts as a mirror image of the primary disk. In *disk duplexing*, a second controller card with a disk duplicates the primary disk controller and disk.

SFT Level III includes SFT Level II support. In addition, SFT Level III adds a second file server connected to the primary server to act as a backup, if the primary server crashes (server duplexing). SFT Level I and SFT Level II support became available for SFT NetWare, but not SFT Level III. SFT Level III support probably will be available only in NetWare v3.x

SFT also includes transaction tracking features called TTS (Transaction Tracking System). TTS enables database and file operations at the server to be backed out in the event of a crash. This capability exists because of the technology obtained from the Btrieve product that was incorporated in NetWare after the purchase of Softcraft by Novell in 1987. Data files in SFT NetWare can be flagged with a transactional attribute (by using the FLAG command), to protect them against incomplete operations. TTS is similar to the checkpointing capability in larger DBMS systems.

The TTS and SFT Level I and II options require more processor resources (such as CPU time, RAM, and disk space) and can be selected during server installation time. You always should keep the hot fix (SFT Level I) feature enabled.

SFT NetWare always runs in the dedicated mode. If you run under a nondedicated mode, the reliability of the server is suspect when DOS applications running on the server machine could easily crash the server. Also, SFT NetWare does place an additional processing burden on the servers CPU.

Consolidated NetWare v2.2x

With NetWare v2.2, Novell has decided to consolidate its NetWare 286 line. NetWare v2.2 replaces ELS, ANW, and SFT NetWare. NetWare v2.2 is available in 5-, 10-, 50-, or 100-user versions. These versions have all the same features, such as disk mirroring, disk duplexing, and TTS support—they are distinguished only by the number of users they support.

NetWare v2.2 is the next level after SFT NetWare. You can configure NetWare v2.2 in dedicated or nondedicated mode. A large number of NICs are supported by NetWare v2.2, as can be seen in the following list. Also, drivers for NICs not listed are available through the NetWire forum on CompuServe.

NICs with Drivers on NetWare v2.2 Disks

Novell NE-1000	IBM PC Network II (PC)	3COM 3C501
Novell NE-2000	IBM PC Network II (PS/2)	3COM 3C503
Novell NE/2 (PS/2)	IBM PC Token Ring/A	3COM 3C505
Novell RX-Net	IBM PC Token Ring/A (PS/2)	3COM 3C523
Novell RX-Net/2 (PS/2)		

Determining NetWare v2.x Server Requirements

Before you begin installing NetWare v2.x, you should plan the server requirements, such as the amount of memory to be used at the server and the amount of server disk space needed.

In this section, you review some guidelines for estimating server memory and disk space for NetWare v2.2. The end of the section shows you an example that will help you estimate the server memory and disk space requirements for your LAN.

Estimating Server Memory Requirements

Table 7.1 and figure 7.1 summarize the memory utilization of the server components. The table and figure show that a number of parameters are necessary in determining server memory utilization.

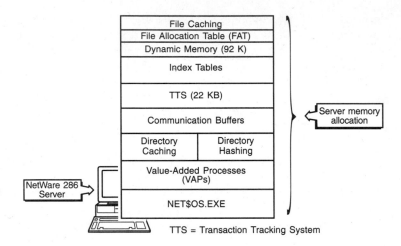

Figure 7.1:
Server memory requirements for NetWare v2.2. (Graphic courtesy of Learning Group International)

Table 7.1
Memory Utilization of Server Components for NetWare v2.2

NetWare Operating System Component	Memory Usage	Units
Operations system program (NetWare v2.x)	506K	Total
File allocation table	1K	Per M of disk
Directory caching table	32 bytes	Per table entry
Directory hashing table	4 bytes	Per table entry
Communication (routing) buffers	630 bytes	Per buffer
Transaction Tracking System (TTS)	22K	Total
Indexed file	1K	Per file index
Value-added processes (VAP)	Any size	Per VAP
Dynamic memory	92K	Total
File caching	Remaining	Total memory

File caching (see fig. 7.2) is used by the server to increase the server disk performance. When a request to read a disk block is made, the server looks for it in its cache file in RAM. If the disk block is not found in the file cache, the disk block is read from the server disk and delivered to the server. At the same time, a copy of the disk block is kept in the file cache. Subsequent reads of the same disk block will find the disk block in the file cache. Because applications spend most of the time working in a localized area of a file, the disk blocks for that area of the file end up in the file cache. When a disk block is written, it is written to the file cache. A background file cache process is responsible for writing it back to the disk.

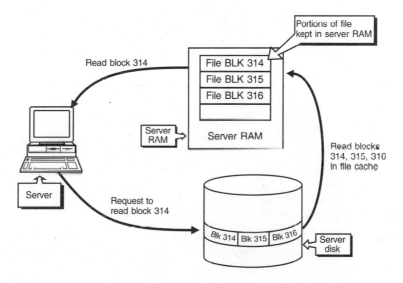

Figure 7.2:
File caching as a server memory component. (Graphic courtesy of Learning Group International)

Because RAM speeds are 1000 times faster than today's disk speeds, file caching can dramatically improve the server performance, especially for slow server disks. One of the limitations with the ISA bus architecture (and even other PC-based bus architectures) is its lower data transfer rate compared to minicomputers and mainframe buses. File caching overcomes some of these limitations by providing a fast intermediate storage for server files. One file-caching problem is that if the server crashes, the disk blocks in the file cache are lost, and this may leave the server disk out of synchronization with the file cache. This problem is more serious for file allocation tables (FATs) that are kept in RAM. These problems usually are corrected by using NetWare's VREPAIR utility.

Figure 7.3 shows a copy of the file allocation table on the server disk. The FAT is used to store information on the disk block locations for a file. NetWare reads the disk volume FAT into RAM to speed requests for file access.

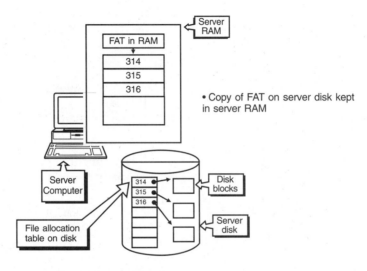

Figure 7.3:
The file allocation table (FAT) on the server disk. (Graphic courtesy of Learning Group International)

Figure 7.4 shows dynamic memory usage in the server. *Dynamic memory* is divided into three pools and is used for the server's internal tables and stack area for File Service Processes (FSPs). The dynamic memory organization has been greatly improved in NetWare v2.2, enabling a larger number of FSPs to run. Some of the other parameters stored in the dynamic memory area are drive mapping tables, buffers, core print services information, open files, file locks, semaphores, and routing information.

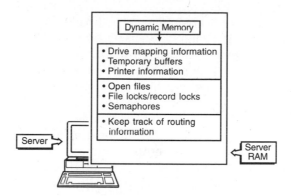

Figure 7.4:
Dynamic memory usage in the server. (Graphic courtesy of Learning Group International)

The TTS feature (see fig. 7.5) enables incomplete file operations to be backed out in the event of a crash. TTS can be implemented on a file by flagging the file with a transaction attribute by using the FLAG command. You also can use TTS when you are using Novell's Btrieve database engine. Application writers can use this to encapsulate transactions by the begin transaction and end transaction operations. If the operations defined in the transaction cannot be completed, the entire transaction can be rolled back to the begin transaction point. The TTS feature takes up approximately 27K for programs and 5K for data.

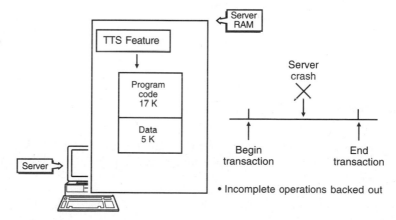

Figure 7.5:
Transaction tracking system memory requirements and operation. (Graphic courtesy of Learning Group International)

Figure 7.6 shows NetWare v2.2's use of directory caching, hashing, and index tables. Directory hashing speeds up finding a directory entry in the table. The term *directory entry* refers to directories and files. To implement directory hashing, a hashing table is kept in RAM (see fig. 7.6). The name of the directory entry being searched, X for example, is used as an argument for a mathematical hashing function H(X) to find the probable locations of the directory entry in the directory (also cached in RAM). Because the directory table can be very large, directory hashing greatly speeds up access to a directory entry. After the directory entry is found, a pointer in the directory entry is used to access the FAT. The FAT then can be used to locate the file block in the file cache or on the server disk. If the directory entry for a file indicates that it is indexed, an index table (turbo FAT) is used instead of the regular FAT. Index tables can be used to significantly speed access to files that are 2M or larger.

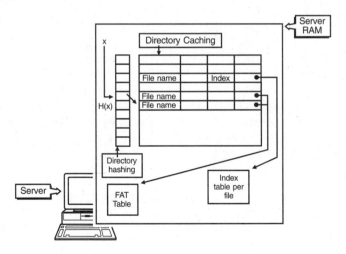

Figure 7.6:
Directory caching, hashing, and index tables in the server memory. (Graphic courtesy of Learning Group International)

Figure 7.7 shows that applications can be written that run directly on the server. These are called *value added processes* (VAPs) and take up server RAM space.

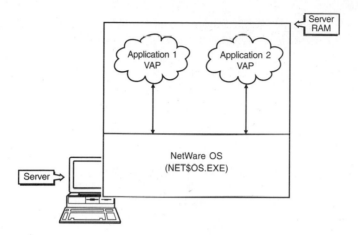

Figure 7.7:
Value added processes in the server memory. (Graphic courtesy of Learning Group International)

You can use the preceding table and figures to estimate server memory requirements. Many experienced installers use a rule of thumb to estimate server memory. For NetWare v2.2, start with 2M of RAM and, for every 100M of disk, add 1M of RAM. This rule of thumb usually results in a larger value of server memory, but as you will see in the following example, extra RAM is used for file caching.

Estimating Server Disk Requirements

The server disk space is utilized by the following resources:

- NetWare operating system and system files

- Application programs and data

- User's disk space

- The hot fix redirecton area (defaults of 2 percent of volume)

The NetWare v2.2 NOS and associated system files take up approximately 6M. The disk space taken by application programs and data varies from application to application. Refer to the application documentation to get this information.

In NetWare, a disk quota can be implemented that limits the amount of disk space per user. If you want to limit the disk space per user, you need to enable the feature during server installation. You can allocate disk space per user by using the SYSCON utility. The amount of disk space per user can range from 1M to several megabytes, depending on how the server is used.

Also, 2 percent of the disk is dedicated for the hot fix redirection area. Hot fix is discussed in Chapter 6. It dynamically detects and compensates for disk errors.

When estimating disk space, you should plan for future growth. Most network managers are familiar with the law *Files expand to fill all available disk space*. For this reason, you should keep the disk space usage to less than 75 percent of the total disk space.

Estimating NetWare v2.2 Server Memory and Disk Space

Suppose, for example, that you need to estimate the amount of server memory and disk space needed for a NetWare v2.2 server that is to be installed. The following are the server requirements:

- A minimum of 24 users will be connected to the server at any one time and each user will have no more than 100 files and directories.

- Each user is allocated a maximum of 1M of data (this value in many situations may be much larger).

- The NetWare NOS takes up 200 directory entries and 6M of disk space for its programs and data.

- The following two major applications need to be installed on the server:

    A marketing database with 970 directory entries and 40M of data

    An accounting package that takes up 2000 directory entries and 75M of programs and data

- For future growth, you need to allow for an additional 2000 directory entries.

- The number of communication buffers for NetWare v2.2 is 150. (*Communication buffers*, which are temporary areas in RAM used to hold packets, are discussed later in this chapter.)

- A management VAP-application, which takes up 500K of memory, needs to run on the server.

- The applications require the TTS feature for data integrity.

- Ten large data files need to be indexed so that all of the users can have quick access to them.

- The server has two disks, each with a capacity of 117M.

The following can be used as a worksheet to estimate server memory requirements. The parameters used in this worksheet are the same as the ones shown in table 7.1.

You can calculate the server RAM by using the following steps:

1. Number of users connected to server: 24
2. Maximum directory entries per user: 100
3. Total directory entries used by users ([1][2]):   2400
4. Total directory entries used by NetWare OS: 200
5. Determine the total application directory entries, as follows:

Application	Directory Entries
Marketing DB	970
Accounting package	2000
Future growth	2000
Total application directory entries:	4970

6. Total directory entries([3]+[4]+[5]):   7570
7. Corrected directory entries (multiples of 128):   7680
8. Memory for directory caching ([7]32 bytes):   245760 bytes
9. Memory for directory hashing ([7]4 bytes):   30720 bytes
10. Memory for NetWare NOS: 506K
11. Memory for File Allocation Table (1K per M):   234M

    Two disks are on the server, each of which have 117M, for a total disk space of 234M (2117 = 234M).

12. Number of communication buffers: 150

13. Memory for communication buffers ([11]630 bytes): 94500

14. Memory for TTS feature (22K): 22K

15. Number of indexed files: 10

16. Memory for indexed files (1K per index file): 10K

17. Memory for Value Added Processes: 500K

18. Dynamic Memory (92K): 92K

19. Sum of server memory components (8-11, 13-14, 16-18): 1768K

20. Actual physical memory: 4096K

    (You have a choice of 2M or more. Because memory is inexpensive, use 4M in this example. If, however, memory cost becomes an issue, you can use 2M.)

21. Memory used for file caching ([20] - [19]): 2328

The following can be used as a worksheet to estimate server disk requirements. The parameters used in this worksheet are taken from the preceding example.

1. Number of users connected to server: 24

2. Maximum disk space per user: 1M

3. Total disk space used by users ([1] × [2]): 24M

4. Disk space used by NetWare operating system: 6M

5. Determine the total disk space used by applications, as follows:

Application	Disk Space
Marketing DB:	40M
Accounting package:	75M
Total disk space used by applications:	115M

6. Total disk space used on server ([3]+[4]+[5]): 145M

7. Server disk types used on server:

   Default hot fix usage is 2 percent of disk space.

Disk Type	Capacity	Hot Fix Usage	Available
Disk-1	117M	2.34M	114.66M
Disk-2	117M	2.34M	114.66M

8. Allocation of programs and data across server disks:

Disk Type	Available	Program Allocation		% Utilization
Disk-1	114.66M	Users	(24M)	61.1
		NetWare	(6M)	
		Market DB	(40M)	
		Total	70M	
Disk-2	114.66M	Acct. appl.	(75M)	65.4

Installing NetWare v2.2

This section examines the NetWare v2.2 installation process. You need to make a number of important decisions during the installation. These decisions are made by the proper selection of installation parameters.

The information on NetWare v2.2 installation is contained in the following Novell manuals:

NetWare Version 2.2, Installing and Maintaining the Network

NetWare Version 2.2, Using the Network

NetWare Version 2.2, Concepts

The information in these manuals is complete, but the manual is written for advanced and novice users. Some users find these manuals difficult to follow. One of the problems with the manuals is that, because of the number of different parameters that can be selected, a number of installation paths a user can select are shown. The manuals are written to accommodate all possible installation paths. Although the information is complete, it is scattered throughout the manuals. Additional manuals for installing print servers and Macintosh support using NetWare for Macintosh also are available.

NetWare v2.2 is much easier to install than the previous versions of NetWare that v2.2 is designed to replace. In these earlier versions, you had to walk through a maze of menus to select the correct parameters. In NetWare v2.2, the menu choices are considerably simplified. You choose the parameters on a forms-oriented user interface, rather than through excessive menus and lists of choices.

As is true for any major installation, NetWare v2.2 installation must be done with care and planning. You might have the tendency to jump right into the installation. Although this sometimes can save time, it also can lead to unforeseen situations in which the installation has to be abandoned because of unavailability of the right drivers or equipment. Even if the installation proceeds without a problem, the result is a server installation with no documentation or record of why the server parameters were selected a certain way.

After a discussion on selecting server parameters, this chapter shows you how to install NetWare v2.2. As you install the network, you should have a notebook that can be used as a log book for installation and maintenance. Whenever a key decision is made, such as selecting a parameter, you should write it in the installation log. You can model your worksheets after the ones in the Novell manuals.

Understanding the INSTALL Program

NetWare v2.2 installation is done by a program called INSTALL that is on the SYSTEM-1 disk. This INSTALL program replaces the NETGEN program used in NetWare v2.15. If you are familiar with earlier versions of NetWare, table 7.2 gives you a list of installation programs used with older versions of NetWare.

Table 7.2
Installation Programs for NetWare 286 Product Line

Program Name	Description
INSTALL	Generates and installs NetWare v2.2
NETGEN	Generates and installs NetWare 286 v2.1x
ELSGEN	Generates and installs ELS NetWare v2.1x
GENOS	Generates and installs Advanced NetWare v2.0x

In table 7.2, you can see that the installation programs have to generate and install NetWare. If you have installed applications on machines, you may be familiar with the installation part, but why do you have to generate NetWare?

You need to generate NetWare because of the large number of configuration choices available for NetWare. NetWare supports over 180 network cards and a large number of disk subsystems. If a single version of NetWare contained the drivers for this large variety of hardware, it would be very large and inefficient. It probably would not even fit in 16M of RAM. Based on the server machine's physical configuration, such as NIC type and disk controller type, you need to select the correct drivers and "bind" them to the NetWare NOS.

Binding is performed in the same way that application writers develop programs. Applications developed in languages such as C or Assembly are written in different *modules*. These modules then are compiled separately to produce object modules (machine code). Next, the application writer selects the object modules that he needs to link into one *executable* (or binary image) *file*. (The executable file is the program that gets installed on computers and implements the applications.) The NetWare generation performs the exact same steps, except that the NetWare disks already contain the object modules or code pieces that make up the NOS.

The NetWare object modules then need to be linked with the driver object modules that are selected by the installer. Figure 7.8 shows the process of linking the object modules. The network drivers are on the floppy disks labeled LAN_DRV_*nnn*, and the disk drivers are on the floppy disks labeled DSK_DRV_*nnn*. The *nnn* value is a number ranging from 001 to 999. Disks labeled LAN_DRV_001 and DSK_DRV_001 come with the NetWare disks and contain the drivers that are directly supported by Novell. Third-party drivers available from vendors or bulletin boards are on disks labeled LAN_DRV_200 and so on (other values of *nnn*). In the installation process, NetWare gives you an option to add third-party drivers to the list of driver choices, and then they can be used to generate NetWare.

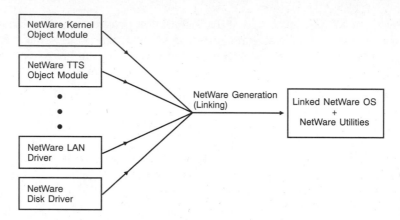

Figure 7.8:
Linking of NetWare object modules.

Using the INSTALL Program

You need to perform four major steps when you use the INSTALL program. Depending on the type of installation (new or reinstallation), you might perform some or all of steps. The complete INSTALL process consists of the following steps:

1. Entering the operating system parameters

2. Generating the NetWare operating system and utilities (see fig. 7.9)

3. Performing complete or partial disk preparation

4. Entering the file server parameters and installing the operating system on the server (see fig. 7.10)

Steps 1 and 2 can be performed at a workstation or at the server. Steps 3 and 4 must be performed on the NetWare server.

All of these procedures should be performed by using copies of the distribution NetWare disks. NetWare backups are needed for several reasons. The obvious one is that you want to preserve the originals from accidental damage. Another reason is that the generation and installation process actually writes files onto the installation disks. You can see in figure 7.9 that a number of files are produced by the NetWare generation process. The NetWare NOS is contained in a file called NET$OS.EXE. In earlier versions of

NetWare when the NetWare disks also were released on 5 1/4-inch 360K floppy disks, the NetWare NOS was spread across two disks (OSEXE-1 and OSEXE-2) in files NET$OS.EXE, NET$OS.EX1, and NET$OS.EX2. NetWare v2.2 is released on high-density floppy disks and the generated NOS can fit on a single disk (disk OSEXE), meaning that only one image file is needed.

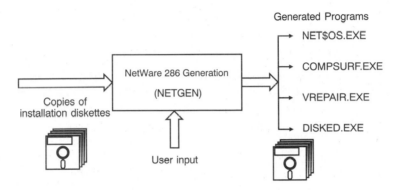

Figure 7.9:
NetWare generation flow diagram. (Graphic courtesy of Learning Group International)

Step 2 of the installation process creates the NET$OS.EXE file and several utilities that must be customized for each server. NET$OS.EXE is the NetWare operating system program. When NET$OS.EXE is installed on the server, it can be booted up by using the cold boot loaders on the server disk. Alternatively, it can be started from a floppy disk containing the NET$OS.EXE program. In the latter case, the server machine first must be booted under DOS and then NET$OS.EXE executed from the command line or a DOS batch file, such as AUTOEXEC.BAT. The capability to start NetWare from a DOS floppy disk may seem unimportant, but if the boot loaders or the NET$OS.EXE file on the server hard disk is corrupted, you can boot from the NET$OS.EXE file on the floppy disk.

The COMPSURF.EXE, VREPAIR.EXE, and DISKED.EXE utilities are generated on the UTILEXE disk and are used for server disk maintenance. These utilities are linked with the drivers selected in the installation process and are unique for the server being installed. For future server maintenance, you should make a copy of these utilities from the UTILEXE disk.

VREPAIR is used for performing minor volume repairs and correcting problems that occur with server crashes or the server being powered down unexpectedly. These events can cause the file allocation table and the directory entry table (DET) in the server RAM to be out of synchronization with the copy on the server disk. VREPAIR can check the data integrity of these tables, and where possible, recover data. It cannot recover data that was in the server memory at the time of the crash. VREPAIR changes are nondestructive—that is, they do not wipe out data. VREPAIR can be run only with the server down. The server must be booted under DOS, and then VREPAIR must be run. The user interface is a simple character-driven menu interface and is fairly straightforward. Its use is documented in the *NetWare v2.2, Using the Network* manual in the Utilities reference section.

DISKED is a low-level disk editor used for modifying the disk subsystem at the byte level. It is similar in function to the DOS DEBUG utility that can be used to modify DOS disks. DOS DEBUG does not work with NetWare disks because NetWare uses a different file system. DISKED must be run with the server down. The server machine must be booted under DOS, and then DISKED can be run. The menu interface to DISKED is simple. The list of commands can be obtained by using the one-letter command H for help. DISKED must be used with great care because the changes it makes are destructive, and you could end up damaging the file system.

COMPSURF is discussed later in this chapter.

Figure 7.10 shows the NetWare installation after the generation is complete. The INSTALL program gives you the option of completing the installation as a separate task or as the next step immediately after NetWare generation.

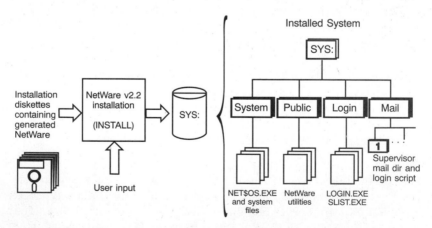

Figure 7.10:
NetWare v2.2 installation flow diagram. (Graphic courtesy of Learning Group International)

In the installation process, the NetWare operating system, the cold boot loader, and the system and public files are copied on the server disk. These files are copied to a well-defined directory structure. The directory structure (shown in figure 7.10) is discussed in greater detail in Chapter 15.

After the installation, the server can be booted from the hard disk by using the NetWare cold boot loaders. The server also can be booted from DOS by running the program NET$OS.EXE contained in the OSEXE disk.

Running INSTALL from a Network or Hard Drive

To run INSTALL from a hard disk drive or a network drive, you must upload the NetWare v2.2 installation disks to that drive. To perform the upload process, run the UPLOAD program on the SYSTEM-1 disk from a floppy drive. UPLOAD prompts you to install the hard disks. UPLOAD creates a directory named NETWARE, which contains a subdirectory for the contents of each of the INSTALL disks. After running INSTALL, the generated NetWare can be downloaded by running DOWNLOAD from the NETWARE directory.

Examining the INSTALL Options

When INSTALL is run without any parameters, the menu shown in figure 7.11 appears. The Basic installation option is used when the network has the following characteristics:

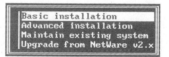

Figure 7.11:
The Basic installation option.

- One file server
- One internal hard disk
- One network card in the server

- One parallel port

- No routers or external hard disks

For all other situations, the Advanced installation option must be used. The Advanced installation option provides the maximum flexibility and can be used to overcome the limitations of the Basic installation option.

The Maintain existing system option enables you to reconfigure a system after it already has been installed. You can use this to change any of the server parameters, including regenerating the NetWare operating system with new drivers.

The Upgrade from NetWare v2.x option enables you to upgrade your system from an earlier version of NetWare.

Help can be obtained at any time in the INSTALL process by pressing F1. To quit installation at any time, press Alt-F10.

The different INSTALL options enable you to begin and end at various points in the installation process. The installation process consists of a number of modules (see fig. 7.12) that are executed in a certain sequence.

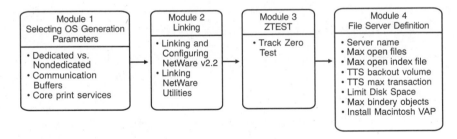

Figure 7.12:
NetWare v2.2 INSTALL modules.

The track zero test in Module 3 is optional because it wipes out data on the server disk. INSTALL command-line flags can be used to control where INSTALL starts and ends. In the next few sections, you are shown how to use the INSTALL command-line flags.

Using INSTALL -E and INSTALL -L

You can use the INSTALL -E command to control the module execution in one of two ways. You can perform operating system generation (Module 1) and linking (Module 2) (see fig. 7.13). Or, you can use the INSTALL -E command to perform all the steps, including operating system generation (Module 1), linking (Module 2), track zero test (Module 3), and file server definition (Module 4) (see fig. 7.14).

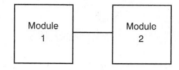

Figure 7.13:
Using the INSTALL -E command to perform modules 1 and 2 only.

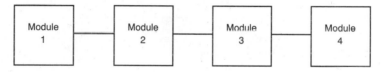

Figure 7.14:
Using the INSTALL -E command to perform all installation modules.

Use the latter choice for the INSTALL -E command if the generation and installation are done on the machine that is used as the server.

The first choice of the INSTALL -E command gives you more flexibility of generating and linking the operating system on any machine. After this is done, the generated NetWare can be taken to the server machine on which the installation of the server software can continue. During the INSTALL -E process, the INSTALL program asks, "Will this machine be the server?" If you reply No, you have selected the first choice of the INSTALL -E command.

To continue with the server installation, you can use the INSTALL -L command. This command completes the installation by performing the track zero test (Module 3) and file server definition (Module 4).

Using INSTALL -N and INSTALL -C

The INSTALL -N command executes only Module 1 (operating system generation). During the INSTALL -N process, you are asked "Is this the file server?" If you answer No, NetWare does not enable you to proceed with Module 2 (linking).

When you use Module 1, the operating system generation parameters are stored in CFG (configuration) and LNK (link) files on the SYSTEM-2 disk. This enables you to save the operating system generation parameters and mail the SYSTEM-2 disk to another location that can continue with linking and the rest of the installation. Third-party developers also use this option to change the CFG and LNK files.

To proceed with linking after you use the INSTALL -N command, you must use the INSTALL -C command, which performs linking (Module 2), track zero test (Module 3), and file server definition (Module 4) as illustrated by figure 7.15.

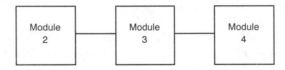

Figure 7.15:
Using the INSTALL -C command to complete installation begun with INSTALL -N.

Using INSTALL -M and INSTALL -M -L

The INSTALL -M command can be used for maintenance installation of an already installed NetWare v2.2 server. It controls module execution in two ways. You can use it to perform operating system generation (Module 1) and linking (Module 2) (see fig. 7.16). This option stops before performing the track zero test.

You also can use the INSTALL -M command to perform all the steps, including operating system generation (Module 1), linking (Module 2), track zero test (Module 3), and file server definition (Module 4) (see fig. 7.17).

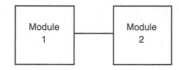

Figure 7.16:
Using the INSTALL -M command to perform modules 1 and 2 only.

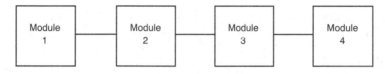

Figure 7.17:
Using the INSTALL -M command to perform all installation modules.

Use the latter choice of the INSTALL -M command when you are changing operating system generation options and maintenance on the machine that is to be used as the server.

The first choice of the INSTALL -M gives you more flexibility in performing maintenance functions, such as operating system generation and linking on any machine. After this is done, the reconfigured NetWare can be taken to the server machine on which the maintenance can be completed. During the INSTALL -M process, the INSTALL program asks you, "Will this machine be the server?" If you reply No, you select the first choice of the INSTALL -M command.

To continue with the server maintenance after you select the first choice of the INSTALL -M command, you must use the INSTALL -M -L command.

INSTALL -E and INSTALL -M, may seem very similar. They are. The difference is that when you use INSTALL -M, the previously configured parameters are not erased. They are displayed in the operating system generation (Module 1) screen so that you can change them.

With INSTALL -E, any previously configured parameters are forgotten because NetWare considers this action to be a new installation.

Using INSTALL -F

The INSTALL -F command executes only the file server definition module (Module 4). This option enables the user to make changes in any of the information recorded in this module. These changes include the following:

- Server name
- Maximum number of open files
- Maximum number of open index files
- TTS backout volume
- Maximum number of TTS transactions
- Limit disk space
- Maximum number of bindery objects
- Install Macintosh VAPs

The INSTALL -F command is a big improvement over earlier releases of NetWare. In earlier versions of NetWare, you had to perform lengthy configuration processes to change any of the preceding information.

Using INSTALL -U and INSTALL -U -L

The INSTALL -U command is used for upgrading an existing v2.x server to NetWare v2.2. It controls module execution in one of two ways. It performs operating system generation (Module 1) and linking (Module 2). Or, you can use the INSTALL -U command to perform all of the steps of installation, including operating system generation (Module 1), linking (Module 2), track zero test (Module 3), and file server definition (Module 4).

You use the latter choice of the INSTALL -U command if you are changing operating system generation options and upgrading on the machine that is used as the server.

The first option of the INSTALL -U command gives you more flexibility in performing upgrade functions, such as operating system generation and linking on any machine. After this is done, the upgraded NetWare can be taken to the server machine on which the upgrade can be completed. During the INSTALL -U process, the INSTALL program asks you, "Will this machine be the server?" If you reply No, you select the first option of the INSTALL -U command.

To continue with the server upgrade when you use the first option of the INSTALL -U command, use the INSTALL -U -L command.

Managing NetWare v2.2 Server Configuration Parameters

When you execute the NetWare v2.2 INSTALL program, you must make the following decisions about the server parameters:

- Dedicated versus nondedicated mode
- Number of communication buffers
- Whether to install core print services
- Network board drivers
- Disk drivers
- Whether to run ZTEST and COMPSURF
- Maximum number of open and index files
- TTS backout volume and maximum number of TTS transactions
- Limit disk space
- Maximum number of bindery objects
- Install Macintosh VAPs

These parameters are discussed in the next few sections.

Dedicated versus Nondedicated Mode

Figure 7.18 shows a dedicated server and a nondedicated server. In the nondedicated mode, DOS is run as an application on top of NetWare. This saves the cost of an extra workstation. The server's CPU is shared between DOS and NOS. This slows both the server and the DOS application. If the DOS application crashes, it crashes NetWare. Also, the server needs to be in an exposed location for users to run DOS applications on it.

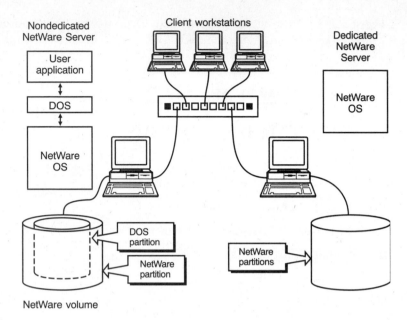

Figure 7.18:
Dedicated and nondedicated servers. (Graphic courtesy of Learning Group International)

Not all DOS applications can run on the server in the nondedicated mode, such as the following:

■ Applications that require extended and expanded memory drivers. NetWare takes over all memory above 640K for its own purpose. Extended and expanded memory drivers would conflict with NetWare memory usage.

■ Applications that try to manipulate the hardware directly, such as interrupt vectors and I/O ports. NetWare controls the hardware, and DOS and application software run as applications on top of NetWare. When applications attempt to directly control hardware, they will conflict with NetWare.

In the dedicated mode, only NetWare runs on the server. Because the server resources are dedicated for NetWare, there is no contention with DOS applications, and NetWare runs faster and more efficiently. Also, you eliminate the reliability and security problems of the nondedicated mode.

Number of Communication Buffers

Communication buffers are temporary storage areas in the server's memory that are used for holding packets being transmitted or received from the NIC. The use of communication buffers is illustrated in figure 7.19.

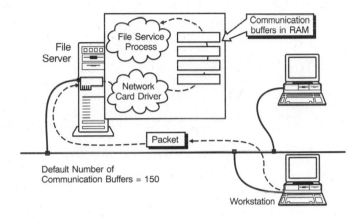

Figure 7.19:
Communication buffers. (Graphic courtesy of Learning Group International)

Data packets sent by a user application to the server first must pass through the NIC driver. The NIC driver processes these data packets and performs link layer decapsulation. The IPX protocols perform the network layer decapsulation and the data packet then ends up in the communication buffers. A communication buffer is needed for every data packet waiting to be processed.

The server defines a number of tasks called *file server processes* (FSPs) for the purposes of processing file service requests. The FSPs process the requests contained in the data packets. When you have insufficient FSPs or insufficient communication buffers, server performance suffers.

Earlier NetWare versions had many ways to help you determine the number of communication buffers. In NetWare v2.15, the Novell manuals recommended using $n + 40$ for the number of communication buffers, in which n was the number of connections to the server. NetWare v2.2 does not have a similar formula in its installation manual. NetWare v2.2, however, does use a default value of 150. Because you can have a maximum of 100 users on

NetWare v2.2, you can use the formula $n + 50$ to determine the number of communication buffers. The minimum amount of communication buffers in NetWare v2.2 is 40 and the maximum is 1000. You should increase the number of communication buffers when your server acts as a router and you have a large amount of router traffic.

After you select the number of communication buffers, you cannot change them without bringing down the server.

Core Print Services

Core print services are NetWare print services that are linked to NetWare v2.2 NOS during the execution of Module 2 (operating system linking). In earlier releases of NetWare, this was the only way in which networking printing was available from Novell. In NetWare v2.2, you can select core print services or a general form of print service called Print Server that can be defined external to the server (see Chapter 16 for more information on NetWare print servers).

Core print services are selected from the NetWare Operating System Generation screen (Module 1) of INSTALL. After installing print core services, they can be configured by using the SPOOL, QUEUE, and PRINTER console commands. These are discussed in Chapter 16.

The console commands enable you to configure the core print services without bringing down the server. In earlier releases of NetWare, the server had to be brought down and the installation program run to configure network printers.

Network Board Drivers

You must select the correct NIC drivers for the networking hardware in the server. NetWare v2.2 comes with a limited number of drivers on the disks. Additional drivers on LAN_DRV_*nnn* disks must be obtained from the NIC vendor or the NetWire forum on CompuServe.

The current release of INSTALL has a bug in adding new drivers. If you encounter a problem adding additional drivers, copy the driver files on to the LAN_DRV_001 disk and proceed with the installation.

After you select the NIC driver, you must configure it by selecting NIC parameters, such as I/O port address, interrupt request line, and DMA address. These configuration options are coded into the driver and you must set your NIC to match the selected configuration. Sometimes, the NIC settings you want may not be available from the list of configuration choices. In these cases, you need to contact the NIC vendor for a driver that has the configuration option you want. Some vendors, such as Western Digital (now SMC), provide you with a patch utility to change the driver configuration options.

You can configure up to four NICs on the server. Each NIC has to be assigned a unique network address consisting of up to eight hexadecimal digits. This network address refers to the cabling segment attached to the NIC. These NICs are referred to by INSTALL as Network boards A, B, C, and D. By placing more than one NIC in a NetWare server, you enable the server to act as a router. Because the routing function is internal to the NetWare NOS, this configuration is called an *internal router*. A router configuration is shown in figure 7.20. This figure shows an Ethernet and Token Ring LAN connected by a NetWare server acting as an internal router. Routers are discussed in greater detail in Chapter 3.

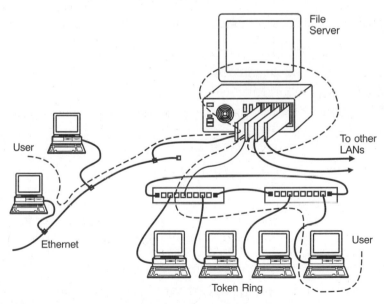

Figure 7.20:
Multiple network cards in the server. (Graphic courtesy of Learning Group International)

Disk Drivers

NetWare v2.2 comes with drivers for the following internal hard disk controller types:

- ISA
- PS/2 MFM
- PS/2 ESDI
- PS/2 SCSI

Additional drivers on DSK_DRV_*nnn* disks must be obtained from the disk vendor or the NetWire forum on CompuServe.

The current release of INSTALL has a bug in adding new drivers. If you encounter a problem adding additional drivers, copy the disk driver files onto the DSK_DRV_001 disk and proceed with the installation.

In NetWare v2.2, channel 0 drives are internal disk drives, and channels 1 to 4 are external disk drives. You must select a disk driver for the channel on which the disk has been installed. After you select the disk driver, you must configure it by selecting disk parameters, such as I/O port address and interrupt request lines. The I/O port address of most ISA disk controllers is set to 1F0 (hex), and the interrupt line is set for E (hex). For IDE or ISA ESDI drives, select the ISA disk driver.

NetWare v2.2 allows up to 2G (gigabytes) of total hard disk storage space or up to 32 hard disks.

ZTEST and COMPSURF

In earlier versions of NetWare, you had to run a program called COMPSURF to check the reliability of the server disk. COMPSURF stands for *comprehensive surface analysis*. It is one of the utilities generated on the UTILEXE disk during NetWare generation. COMPSURF is linked in with the disk driver selected for NetWare generation.

Figure 7.21 shows you the way COMPSURF can be used to improve the reliability of the server disk. COMPSURF improves the reliability of a disk by performing a number of rigorous tests to find all the bad blocks. It also performs a low-level formatting of the disk. It does a special test for track zero. Track zero is particularly important because it is used to hold the boot sector and the bad block table used in a hot fix.

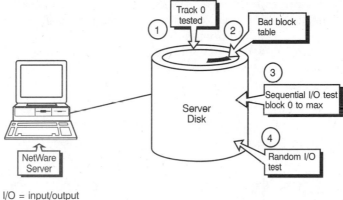

I/O = input/output

Figure 7.21:
Using COMPSURF to improve reliability. (Graphic courtesy of Learning Group International)

COMPSURF then performs a sequential I/O test in which it does a read-after-write verify on every block on the disk. The default number of sequential passes on the disk is three. The minimum number of sequential passes is zero and the maximum is five. The sequential test can take several hours. After the sequential I/O test, the random I/O test is performed.

Random I/O is designed to simulate normal server operation. Like sequential I/O, random I/O performs a read-after-write verify. Any bad blocks that are discovered are recorded in the bad block table.

After the random I/O is performed, the interleave factor needs to be entered. The interleave factor is selected to match the disk speed with the disk controller and server CPU speed. The correct interleave factor is important for optimum data transfer speeds between the server CPU and the disk. For ISA disks, the interleave factor typically is 2:1. For ESDI drives it is 1:1.

To save time, you can purchase disks that already have been exposed to the COMPSURF utility. These disks are called *NetWare-ready disks*. Ontrack's Disk Manager-N utility also can be used to cut down on COMPSURF time. Disks that are specially formatted have warnings from the manufacturer telling you not to use COMPSURF on them. If you use COMPSURF on NetWare-ready disks, you will ruin them and will have to send them back to the manufacturer for reformatting.

To save time installing NetWare v2.2, the COMPSURF test is replaced with a test to check for only track zero. This test is called the ZTEST. For NetWare-ready disks, you should bypass the ZTEST. ZTEST is very simple and takes very little time (less than one minute), but can save you a great deal of frustration and grief in the long run. It is worth doing. ZTEST wipes out data on the server disk because track zero contains DOS FATs and directories.

You must run the DISKSET utility on external disks. DISKSET records the disk drive configuration information on the system, enabling communication with the disk drive.

Maximum Number of Open and Index Files

Any workstation connected to the NetWare v2.2 server can make requests to open a file on the server. The files that are opened are kept in a table on the server RAM. Each entry in the open file table takes up 100 bytes. At NetWare generation time, the INSTALL program needs to know the maximum number of files that can be opened at the server so that it can determine the size of the maximum open file table it can keep in RAM. The default value of maximum open files is 240. You can specify as few as 40 and as many as 1000 open files.

Any file on the server can be flagged with an index attribute by using the FLAG command. The index attribute significantly speeds up random reads and writes to files with sizes of 2M or larger. This means that you can quickly access large database files by using indexing. The increased speed is done by creating special index tables called *turbo FATS* for the indexed file. During NetWare generation, you need to tell the INSTALL program the maximum number of index files that can be opened at the server. This enables the INSTALL program to determine the size of the index file table. The default value of the maximum open index files is 0. The minimum value of open index files is 0 and the maximum is 1000. Each index file takes up 1034 bytes (approximately 1K).

The maximum number of open and index files are set in the file server definition (Module 4) module of the INSTALL program.

TTS Backout Volume and Maximum Number of TTS Transactions

Any file on the server can be flagged with a transaction attribute by using the FLAG command. The transaction attribute activates the TTS (transaction tracking system) mechanism. TTS prevents data corruption by ensuring that all or no changes are made to files being modified that have the transaction attribute.

The transaction attribute feature is valuable for database files in which data can be corrupted easily, especially in the case of a server or workstation crash. Until the transaction is complete, the information needed to backout a transaction is kept on a designated *transaction backout volume*. This volume must have sufficient free space to maintain a copy of the transactions that your application program defines.

The default transaction backout volume is SYS. If another volume is available, you should keep the transaction backout volume on a separate disk with a separate disk controller from the volume that has the database files. If a volume is damaged, TTS data on another volume can be used to back out the damaged records. Also, you should keep at least 1M of free space available. At least 20M of free space is recommended for serious database applications.

The transaction attribute must be used with care for large database files. Depending on the way the application modifies the database file, a large amount of free space can be consumed on the transaction backout volume.

At any given time, you have a limit on the maximum TTS transactions occurring at the server. A conservative estimate is to have maximum TTS transactions be twice the number of active user applications making use of the TTS feature. A user application can have one transaction in progress and one or more previous transactions being finalized. The default maximum TTS transactions is 100. You can specify as few as 20 and as many as 200 TTS transactions.

The TTS backout volume and maximum TTS transactions are set in the file server definition (Module 4) module of INSTALL.

Limit Disk Space

NetWare v2.2 enables you to limit the amount of server disk space each user can utilize. The default is not to limit disk space. For a large network, you should enable this option. This option makes management of user disk space much easier. The actual disk space assignment per user is done by using the system configuration utility SYSCON. To use SYSCON to limit disk space, however, the limit disk space option must be enabled during installation.

The limit disk space option is changed in the file server definition module (Module 4) of INSTALL.

Maximum Number of Bindery Objects

If you specified Yes for the limit disk space option, you must specify the number of bindery objects that can be defined on the server.

The *bindery* is a server database used to keep track of users, groups, workgroups, and other objects. Each entry in the bindery is called a *bindery object*. A bindery object can be a user, group, server name, or a print server name. It represents a logical entity that the server needs to keep track of. The bindery object has an association with a property and a property data set.

Properties are attributes of the bindery object, such as passwords, account restrictions and balances, group members, lists of authorized clients, and workgroups. Actual values for the properties are kept in property data sets.

The bindery can be recognized as hidden files kept on the SYS:SYSTEM directory with the names NET$BIND.SYS and NET$BVAL.SYS. NET$BIND.SYS holds the bindery object and properties, and NET$BVAL.SYS holds the property data sets.

The default number of 1500 is adequate for most server configurations. The minimum value is 500 and the maximum is 5000.

The limit disk space option is changed in the file server definition module (Module 4) of INSTALL.

Install Macintosh VAPs

If you plan to support Macintosh workstations, you can select the Install Macintosh VAPs option. This option installs the Macintosh VAPs that run at the server. The Install Macintosh VAPs option implements the AppleTalk Phase 2 protocol stack on the server machine. This enables Macintosh stations to see the NetWare v2.2 as an AppleShare server.

Details of Macintosh VAP installation can be found in the NetWare services section of your Macintosh documentation.

The Install Macintosh VAPs option is set in the file server definition module (Module 4) of INSTALL.

Installing NetWare v2.2

This section shows you how to generate and install NetWare v2.2 by using the Advanced Generation method. This method gives you the maximum flexibility in installing your network. The following are the requirements to perform the steps in this section:

- Server AT that has an Intel 80286 processor or higher

- Server PC must have networking hardware installed (must be connected to the network to test the installation)

- NetWare v2.2

- DOS disk with version 3.x or higher

You now need to prepare your system for the NetWare v2.2 Advanced Generation. Complete the following steps:

1. Boot up the machine to be used as a server with a DOS boot disk (DOS v3.x or higher).

2. Place the disk labeled SYSTEM-1 in drive A. Start the generation process by entering the following command:

   ```
   INSTALL -E
   ```

   You now should see a screen such as the one shown in figure 7.22.

3. To continue, press Enter.

   You now should see the Operating System Generation box (see fig. 7.23).

   You now need to select the operating system generation parameters by using the following steps.

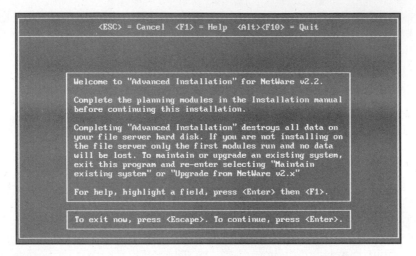

Figure 7.22:
The welcome screen to the Advanced Installation of NetWare v2.2.

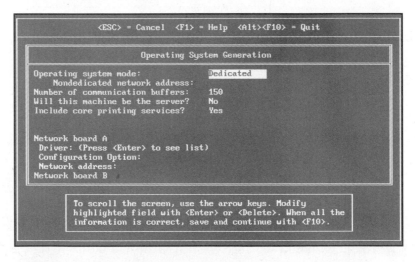

Figure 7.23:
The Operating System Generation box.

4. Select the following operating system generation parameters:

```
Operating system mode: Dedicated
Number of communication buffers: 150
Will this machine be the server? Yes
Include core printing services? Yes
```

This chapter and Chapter 2 discuss the reasons for configuring the server in the dedicated mode. The value of 150 is the default number of communication buffers and each buffer is about 0.5K. If the machine that you are working on is not being used as the server, enter No at the `Will this machine be the server?` prompt. If you enter No, the NetWare installation stops after the generation, and the system software is not installed on this machine (to continue installation on another machine, enter **INSTALL -E -L**). If you select Yes, NetWare continues installing the system software on the machine that you are working on.

5. Highlight the Network board A option and press Enter. A list of drivers similar to the one in figure 7.24 displays.

   The Network board A option refers to the first NIC in the server machine. Up to four NICs (Network boards A, B, C, and D) can coexist in the server machine, enabling the server to provide routing functions between the four NICs.

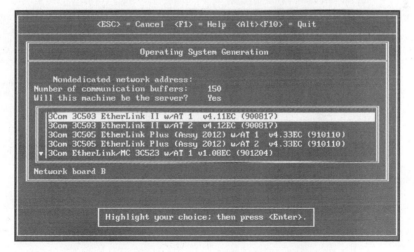

Figure 7.24:
Choosing a network driver.

6. Highlight the driver that matches your network board. If the driver you want is not listed, press Ins and follow the instructions to enter disk containing the driver.

7. Highlight `Configuration Option` on the Operating System Generation box (see fig. 7.18) and press Enter. You are prompted to select one of the configuration choices for the network board. Select the one that matches your NIC's hardware settings.

8. Highlight the Network address option and enter the network address of board A. The network address in this example is an eight-digit hexadecimal number that identifies the network cabling scheme to which the network board is connected.

9. If you have other Network boards, repeat steps 5 through 8 for each board.

10. Scroll through the list of network drivers until you come to the entries for channel 0. Highlight the Driver option for channel 0 and press Enter. A list of disk drivers appears on-screen (see fig. 7.25).

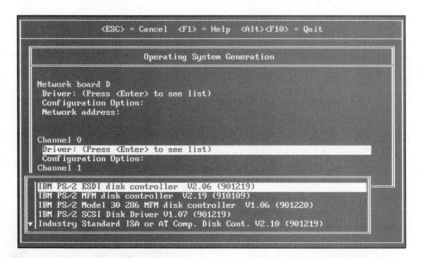

Figure 7.25:
Selecting disk drivers.

11. Highlight the disk driver for your server configuration and press Enter.

12. Highlight `Configuration Option` for channel 0 and press Enter. Select the configuration that matches channel 0.

13. Repeat steps 10 through 12 for any other disk channels in your server.

14. Examine the parameters for the operating system generation to make sure that they are correct and press F10 to save these parameters and continue.

    You now need to link file server-specific utilities by using the following steps.

15. When you are prompted, insert disk SYSTEM-2. The following message displays:

    ```
    Creating file server specific utilities:
    Novell Linker, Version 2.x
    Linking SYSTEM-2:ZTEST.EXE
    Novell Linker, Version 2.x
    Linking SYSTEM-2:INSTOVL.EXE
    Insert disk SYSTEM-1 in any drive.
    Strike a key when ready . . .
    ```

16. Insert the SYSTEM-1 and SYSTEM-2 disks when you are prompted for them. A message similar to the following one displays:

    ```
    Novell Linker, Version 2.x
    Linking SYSTEM-2:COMPSURF.EXE
    Novell Linker, Version 2.x
    Linking SYSTEM-2:VREPAIR.EXE
    Configuring file server specific utilities.
    Insert disk SYSTEM-1 in any drive.
    Strike a key when ready . . .
    ```

17. Insert the SYSTEM-1 and SYSTEM-2 disks when you are prompted to do so. A message similar to the following displays:

    ```
    Creating NetWare v2.2 operating system:
    Novell Linker, Version 2.x
    Linking OSEXE:NET$OS.EXE
    Insert disk OSOBJ in any drive.
    Strike a key when ready . . .
    ```

18. Insert the following disks in the order shown when prompted to do so:

> OSOBJ
>
> LAN_DRV_001
>
> SYSTEM-2
>
> OSOBJ
>
> OSEXE
>
> OSOBJ
>
> OSEXE

A message similar to the following appears on-screen:

```
Configuring NetWare v2.2 operating system.
Insert disk SYSTEM-2 in any drive.
Strike a key when ready . . .
```

19. Insert the following disks in the order shown when prompted to do so:

> SYSTEM-2
>
> OSEXE
>
> SYSTEM-2

You now need to perform the track zero test, as shown in the following steps. The track zero test message box appears on-screen (see fig. 7.26).

20. If your drive is NetWare ready, press Esc to bypass this test. Otherwise, press Enter to test the hard disk.

21. Highlight the hard disk to be selected and press Enter. Verify that you want to test and destroy all data on this hard drive by selecting Yes to the verification query.

When you start the track zero test, a box similar to the one shown in figure 7.27 appears.

If hard disk passed the test, the Pass message appears next to the drive description.

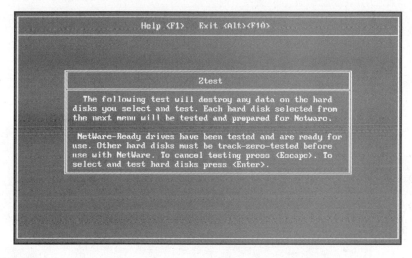

Figure 7.26:
The Ztest message box.

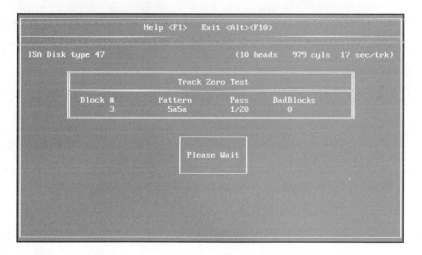

Figure 7.27:
The Track Zero Test box.

22.   Press F10 when the track zero test stops.

You now need to define the file server, as shown in the following steps.

23. When the following message appears, insert the SYSTEM-1 disk and press any key:

```
Insert disk SYSTEM-1 in any drive.
Strike a key when ready . . .
```

The File Server Definition box appears (see fig. 7.28).

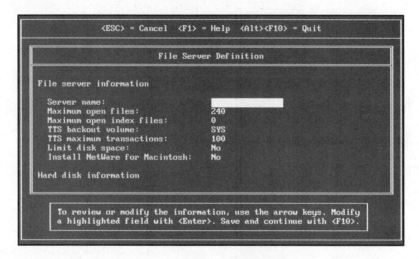

Figure 7.28:
The File Server Definition box.

24. Enter information in the following fields of the File Server Definition box; the parameter values will vary depending on your installation requirements:

    Server name:

    Maximum open files:

    Maximum open index files:

    TTS backout volume:

    TTS maximum transaction:

    Limit disk space: **Yes**

    Install NetWare for Macintosh:

You can press F1 to find out additional information on the fields in the File Server Definition box.

If the disk space is limited, you must specify the maximum number of bindery objects. As you learned earlier, the *bindery* is an internal database that the server uses to keep records of users, groups, and rights information. The bindery consists of a fixed number of bindery objects, which are similar to records in a database.

The default value of the number of bindery objects is 1500. This is adequate for most purposes. The actual usage can be monitored by using FCONSOLE. The bindery object limits are shown in table 7.3.

Table 7.3
Bindery Object Limits

Bindery Objects	Value
Minimum	500
Maximum	5000
Default	1500

Set the Install NetWare for Macintosh option to Yes when you need to install the Macintosh utilities and VAP on the server. For this example, this option is set to No.

25. Press F10 to save the configuration and continue.

    You now need to install the cold boot loaders and the operating system, as shown in the following steps.

26. Insert the SYSTEM-1 disk and press any key. The following messages appear on-screen:

    ```
    Installing NetWare v2.2 Operating System files:
    Installing the cold boot loader on track 0 of hard
    disk 0.
    The cold boot loaders have been successfully
    installed.
    Insert disk OSEXE in any drive.
    Strike a key when ready . . .
    ```

27. Insert the OSEXE disk and press any key. The following screen displays:

```
Copying NET$OS.EXE to SYS:SYSTEM
Insert disk DOSUTIL-1 in any drive.
Strike a key when ready . . .
```

Use the following steps to install the system and public files.

28. Insert the following disks in the order shown when prompted to do so:

DOSUTIL-1

DOSUTIL-2

DOSUTIL-3

DOSUTIL-4

PRINT-1

PRINT-2

HELP-1

HELP-2

SYSTEM-2

SYSTEM-1

The following messages appear on-screen:

```
Installation of NetWare v2.2 is now complete.
For instructions on booting your file server see
the appropriate manual:

    Basic Installation - Getting started

Advanced Installation, Upgrade, or Maintenance -
Using the Network.
```

You now have completed the Advanced Installation.

29. If a floppy disk is in drive A, remove it and reboot the server machine. Messages similar to the following ones appear on-screen:

```
Novell File Server Cold Boot Loader
(C) Copyright 1988 Novell, Inc., All Rights Reserved.
Mounting Volume SYS
```

```
Initializing Transaction Tracking System
Checking Bindery
Checking Queues
Initializing LAN A
Novell Dedicated NetWare V2.2(100) Rev. A 02/11/91
(C) Copyright 1983-1991 Novell Inc.
All Rights Reserved.
OCTOBER 16, 1991    12:55:00 pm
   :
```

You now have linked, installed, and booted your NetWare v2.2 server by using the Advanced Installation method. You now need to examine the CONFIG.DAT file.

The CONFIG.DAT file on the SYSTEM-1 disk is created during the NetWare generation process and contains configuration information for the NetWare operating system that was generated. You should remember the contents of this file and its location for future reference.

30. Put a DOS boot disk in drive A and reboot your machine. If you are using the server machine to do this, you first must shut down the server by typing **DOWN** at the console. Next, replace the DOS boot disk in drive A with the SYSTEM-1 disk and type the following command:

    `TYPE CONFIG.DAT`

You should see a screen similar to the following one:

```
 NetWare v2.2 Configuration Information
Operating system type: Dedicated NetWare v2.2
Core printing services included: Yes
Communication buffers: 150
LAN A:
        IBM Token-Ring w/AT 2 v2.60 (900720)
           0: Self Configurable (Primary)
           Network address: A1
    Disk channel 0:
           Industry Standard ISA or AT Comp. Disk Cont.
           V2.10 (901219)
           0: ISADIS RIMARY  Verify=OFF I/O=1F0h IRQ=14
```

Examining NetWare v2.2 MAINTENANCE:

You can change a number of NetWare v2.2 parameters by using INSTALL with the -M option. The following example helps to illustrate how to use the -M option. In this example, you are shown how to perform some maintenance chores on a NetWare v2.2 server. The server in the example was set up with default parameters and, because the network has grown, you need to increase these default values. You also are shown how to change the server name.

The new parameters for the server are shown in the following list:

Parameter to change	Value
Server name	SAGAR
Communication buffers	200
Maximum number of open files	500
Maximum number of index files	12
Maximum number of transactions	170
Maximum number of directory entries	8320

To make these changes, complete the following steps:

1. Boot the server with a DOS boot disk.

2. Place the disk labeled SYSTEM-1 in drive A. Start the generation process by entering the following command:

   ```
   INSTALL -M
   ```

   The Operating System Generation screen appears on the screen.

3. From the Operating System Generation screen, change the values to those specified in the preceding list.

4. Save the changes by pressing F10. The Actions to be performed box appears (see fig. 7.29).

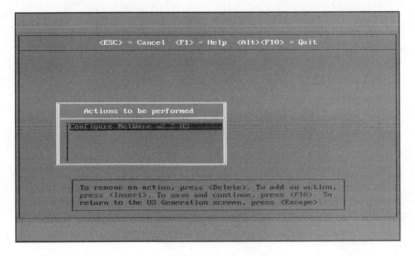

Figure 7.29:
Actions to be performed box.

5. Although the file server already has been linked and configured under the basic installation mode, you need to configure the server again because you have changed the network address of LAN A. You do not need to link the NetWare operating system if no drivers have been added or changed. If choices other than Configure NetWare v2.2 OS are listed in the Actions to be performed box, you need to delete them. Do this by highlighting each option except Configure NetWare v2.2 OS and pressing Del.

6. Press F10 to save the selected actions and continue. The following messages appear:

```
Insert disk SYSTEM-2 in any drive.
Strike a key when ready . . .
```

7. Insert the following disks as requested:

    SYSTEM-2

    OSEXE

    SYSTEM-1

    The File Server Definition box (see fig. 7.30) appears.

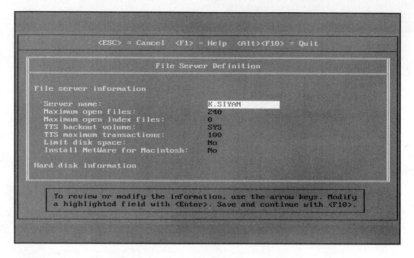

```
           <ESC> = Cancel  <F1> = Help  <Alt><F10> = Quit

                         File Server Definition

 File server information
    Server name:                        K.SIYAN
    Maximum open files:                 240
    Maximum open index files:           0
    TTS backout volume:                 SYS
    TTS maximum transactions:           100
    Limit disk space:                   No
    Install NetWare for Macintosh:      No

 Hard disk information

       To review or modify the information, use the arrow keys. Modify
       a highlighted field with <Enter>. Save and continue with <F10>.
```

Figure 7.30:
File Server Definition box.

8. Change the values on this screen as specified in the previous list. When you finish making changes to the File Server Definition box, press F10 to save your changes and to continue. The Actions to be performed box appears (see fig. 7.29).

   By loading the operating system and replacing track zero information, you save the configuration changes and the new file server definition information on the server disk.

9. Press Ins to examine other choices. If you already understand these options, you can bypass the next step.

   You also can select the install Macintosh VAPs and load system and public files options. You need to load the NetWare operating system and system and public files if you alter the partition size.

10. Press Esc because no other actions are required.

11. Press F10 to continue with the installation. The following messages appear:

        Installing NetWare v2.2 Operating System files:
        Installing the cold boot loader on track 0 of
        hard disk 0.
        The cold boot loaders have been successfully
        installed.

```
Insert disk OSEXE in any drive.
Strike a key when ready . . .
```

12. Insert disk OSEXE and press any key. The following messages appear:

```
Copying NET$OS.EXE to SYS:SYSTEM
Insert disk SYSTEM-1 in any drive.
Strike a key when ready . . .
Installation of NetWare v2.2 is now complete.
```

13. You have reconfigured the operating system. Remove the floppy disk from drive A and reboot the server machine to restart NetWare.

Using the DCONFIG Utility

A relatively unknown but extremely useful utility is the driver configuration utility (DCONFIG) that comes on the WSGEN disk. DCONFIG can be used to change the configuration options for network and disk drivers in the NetWare NOS and the NetWare shell (used at a DOS workstation). It also is used to change the number of communication buffers.

DCONFIG can be used for a quick fix configuration. It can be run from DOS on a stand-alone machine or on a workstation logged in to the server.

Examining DCONFIG Flags

You can view the syntax of the DCONFIG utility by typing **DCONFIG** without any options on the DOS command line, as follows:

```
DCONFIG

Usage: dconfig [volume:]file [parameter list]
   or
   dconfig -i[volume:]file (Take input from specified
file.)

Where [parameter list] is zero or more of:
 A-E: [net address], [node address], [configuration #];
 C0-7: [driver type], [configuration #];
 OTHER: [signature], [Configuration #];
 SHELL: [node address], [configuration #];
 BUFFERS: [number of buffers];
```

You can see that the DCONFIG utility can be used to configure NICs for the server (A-E:), disk drivers (C0-7), workstation shells (SHELL:), communication buffers (BUFFERS:), and the BACKUP and RESTORE utilities (OTHER:).

The following examines some examples of how DCONFIG can be used for configuring the server operating system.

Using DCONFIG

To see the current driver configuration in NET$OS.EXE, type the following command. You must be in the directory that has NET$OS.EXE (OSEXE disk or the SYSTEM directory on the server), and DCONFIG must be in your DOS search path. The response to the command also is shown.

```
DCONFIG NET$OS.EXE

Buffers: 150
LAN A Configuration:
 Network Address: 00000255
 Node address is determined automatically.
 Hardware Type: Western Digital Star/EtherCard PLUS V3.06
EC (900330)
 0: IRQ=3, I/O Base=280h, RAM at CA00:0 for 8k
 1: IRQ=5, I/O Base=240h, RAM at CE00:0 for 8k
 2: IRQ=2, I/O Base=220h, RAM at D000:0 for 8k
 3: IRQ=7, I/O Base=300h, RAM at D400:0 for 8k
 4: IRQ=5, I/O Base=260h, RAM at CC00:0 for 16k
 5: IRQ=10, I/O Base=340h, RAM at D000:0 for 16k, 16 Bit
Only
 6: IRQ=11, I/O Base=240h, RAM at D800:0 for 16k, 16 Bit
Only
 7: IRQ=15, I/O Base=200h, RAM at DC00:0 for 16k, 16 Bit
Only
 8: IRQ=7, I/O Base=380h, RAM at C400:0 for 16k
 9: IRQ=4, I/O Base=2C0h, RAM at C800:0 for 16k
*10: IRQ=3, I/O Base=280h, RAM at D000:0 for 32k
11: IRQ=5, I/O Base=300h, RAM at C800:0 for 32k
12: IRQ=2, I/O Base=220h, RAM at C000:0 for 32k
13: IRQ=7, I/O Base=2A0h, RAM at D800:0 for 32k
14: First Software Configured Adapter
15: Second Software Configured Adapter
```

```
16: Third Software Configured Adapter
17: Fourth Software Configured Adapter
18: First Micro Channel Adapter
19: Second Micro Channel Adapter
20: Third Micro Channel Adapter
21: Fourth Micro Channel Adapter
Disk Driver: Industry Standard ISA or AT Comp. Disk Cont.
V2.10 (901219)
Channel 0 Configuration:
* 0: ISADISK PRIMARY  Verify=OFF I/O=1F0h IRQ=14
1: ISADISK PRIMARY  Verify=ON  I/O=1F0h IRQ=14
2: ISADISK SECONDARY Verify=ON  I/O=170h IRQ=11
3: ISADISK SECONDARY Verify=ON  I/O=170h IRQ=12
4: ISADISK SECONDARY Verify=ON  I/O=170h IRQ=14
5: ISADISK SECONDARY Verify=ON  I/O=170h IRQ=15
6: ISADISK SECONDARY Verify=OFF I/O=170h IRQ=11
7: ISADISK SECONDARY Verify=OFF I/O=170h IRQ=12
8: ISADISK SECONDARY Verify=OFF I/O=170h IRQ=14
9: ISADISK SECONDARY Verify=OFF I/O=170h IRQ=15
Channel 1 unused.
0: ISADISK PRIMARY  Verify=OFF I/O=1F0h IRQ=14
1: ISADISK PRIMARY  Verify=ON  I/O=1F0h IRQ=14
2: ISADISK SECONDARY Verify=ON  I/O=170h IRQ=11
3: ISADISK SECONDARY Verify=ON  I/O=170h IRQ=12
4: ISADISK SECONDARY Verify=ON  I/O=170h IRQ=14
5: ISADISK SECONDARY Verify=ON  I/O=170h IRQ=15
6: ISADISK SECONDARY Verify=OFF I/O=170h IRQ=11
7: ISADISK SECONDARY Verify=OFF I/O=170h IRQ=12
8: ISADISK SECONDARY Verify=OFF I/O=170h IRQ=14
9: ISADISK SECONDARY Verify=OFF I/O=170h IRQ=15
Channel 2 unused.
0: ISADISK PRIMARY  Verify=OFF I/O=1F0h IRQ=14
1: ISADISK PRIMARY  Verify=ON  I/O=1F0h IRQ=14
2: ISADISK SECONDARY Verify=ON  I/O=170h IRQ=11
3: ISADISK SECONDARY Verify=ON  I/O=170h IRQ=12
4: ISADISK SECONDARY Verify=ON  I/O=170h IRQ=14
5: ISADISK SECONDARY Verify=ON  I/O=170h IRQ=15
6: ISADISK SECONDARY Verify=OFF I/O=170h IRQ=11
7: ISADISK SECONDARY Verify=OFF I/O=170h IRQ=12
8: ISADISK SECONDARY Verify=OFF I/O=170h IRQ=14
9: ISADISK SECONDARY Verify=OFF I/O=170h IRQ=15
Channel 3 unused.
```

```
0: ISADISK PRIMARY   Verify=OFF I/O=1F0h IRQ=14
1: ISADISK PRIMARY   Verify=ON  I/O=1F0h IRQ=14
2: ISADISK SECONDARY Verify=ON  I/O=170h IRQ=11
3: ISADISK SECONDARY Verify=ON  I/O=170h IRQ=12
4: ISADISK SECONDARY Verify=ON  I/O=170h IRQ=14
5: ISADISK SECONDARY Verify=ON  I/O=170h IRQ=15
6: ISADISK SECONDARY Verify=OFF I/O=170h IRQ=11
7: ISADISK SECONDARY Verify=OFF I/O=170h IRQ=12
8: ISADISK SECONDARY Verify=OFF I/O=170h IRQ=14
9: ISADISK SECONDARY Verify=OFF I/O=170h IRQ=15
Channel 4 unused.
0: ISADISK PRIMARY   Verify=OFF I/O=1F0h IRQ=14
1: ISADISK PRIMARY   Verify=ON  I/O=1F0h IRQ=14
2: ISADISK SECONDARY Verify=ON  I/O=170h IRQ=11
3: ISADISK SECONDARY Verify=ON  I/O=170h IRQ=12
4: ISADISK SECONDARY Verify=ON  I/O=170h IRQ=14
5: ISADISK SECONDARY Verify=ON  I/O=170h IRQ=15
6: ISADISK SECONDARY Verify=OFF I/O=170h IRQ=11
7: ISADISK SECONDARY Verify=OFF I/O=170h IRQ=12
8: ISADISK SECONDARY Verify=OFF I/O=170h IRQ=14
9: ISADISK SECONDARY Verify=OFF I/O=170h IRQ=15
```

In the preceding screen display, the first line indicates that the number of communication buffers has been set for 150. The lines under LAN A Configuration show the driver configuration choices for the driver for Network board A. The network address for LAN A is 00000255. This is an eight-digit hexadecimal number and is unique for all cabling segments attached to the server. The node address is the NIC address and is determined automatically.

The hardware type is a Western Digital Star/EtherCard PLUS V3.06 EC (900330). Twenty-one configuration options are available for the Western Digital Star/EtherCard and the current configuration is indicated by the asterisk (*) symbol. The following is the configuration number 10:

```
*10: IRQ=3, I/O Base=280h, RAM at D000:0 for 32k
```

The disk driver type is Industry Standard ISA or AT Comp. Disk Cont. V2.10 (901219). The screen display also shows that only Channel 0 Configuration (internal disk) is used. The current configuration is indicated by the asterisk (*) symbol. The following is configuration number 0:

```
* 0: ISADISK PRIMARY  Verify=OFF I/O=1F0h IRQ=14
```

Channels 1 to 4, which are used for external drives, are not used in the preceding example.

Aside from viewing the current configuration, you can change the number of communication buffers. To change the number of communication buffers to 240, for example, use the following command:

DCONFIG NET$OS.EXE BUFFERS:240

```
Buffers: 240
LAN A Configuration:
 Network Address: 00000255
 Node address is determined automatically.
 Hardware Type: Western Digital Star/EtherCard PLUS V3.06
EC (900330)
 0: IRQ=3, I/O Base=280h, RAM at CA00:0 for 8k
 * 1: IRQ=5, I/O Base=240h, RAM at CE00:0 for 8k
```

The rest of the list is similar to the previous example.

You also can change the network driver configuration by using the DCONFIG utility. To change the network driver configuration option for LAN A to 0, for example, use the following command:

DCONFIG NET$OS.EXE A:,,0

```
Buffers: 240
LAN A Configuration:
 Network Address: 00000255
 Node address is determined automatically.
 Hardware Type: Western Digital Star/EtherCard PLUS V3.06
EC (900330)
 * 0: IRQ=3, I/O Base=280h, RAM at CA00:0 for 8k
 1: IRQ=5, I/O Base-240h, RAM at CE00:0 for 8k
```

The rest of the list is similar to the previous example.

You can use the DCONFIG utility to change the network driver configuration and network address. To change the network driver configuration option to 1 and the network address to 108, for example, use the following command:

DCONFIG NET$OS.EXE A:108,,1

```
Buffers: 240
LAN A Configuration:
Network Address: 00000108
Node address is determined automatically.
 Hardware Type: Western Digital Star/EtherCard PLUS V3.06
EC (900330)
 0: IRQ=3, I/O Base=280h, RAM at CA00:0 for 8k
 * 1: IRQ=5, I/O Base=240h, RAM at CE00:0 for 8k
```

The rest of the list is similar to the previous example.

The DCONFIG utility enables you to change the network driver configuration, network address, and communication buffers. To change the network driver configuration option to 2, the network address to 99, and the number of communication buffers to 200, use the following command:

DCONFIG NET$OS.EXE A:99,,2; BUFFERS:200

```
Buffers: 200
LAN A Configuration:
 Network Address: 00000099
 Node address is determined automatically.
 Hardware Type: Western Digital Star/EtherCard PLUS V3.06
EC (900330)
 0: IRQ=3, I/O Base=280h, RAM at CA00:0 for 8k
 1: IRQ=5, I/O Base=240h, RAM at CE00:0 for 8k
 * 2: IRQ=2, I/O Base=220h, RAM at D000:0 for 8k
```

The rest of the list is similar to the previous example.

Summary

This chapter examined the architecture of the NetWare v2.x family of network operating systems with an emphasis on the most recent version, NetWare 2.2. You examined the features of NetWare 2.2 and the factors that must be taken into account when configuring a NetWare 2.2 server. The process of configuring and installing NetWare 2.2 by using the INSTALL program was presented in considerable depth. Finally, you saw how DCONFIG can be used to change some server characteristics without reconfiguring with INSTALL.

Installing NetWare v3.11 Servers

NetWare v3.x is Novell's flagship product. It is the successor to NetWare v2.x and has implemented a number of novel and unique features. NetWare v3.x is a complete rewrite of NetWare for the Intel 80386 architecture. NetWare v2.x is written for the Intel 80286 architecture in assembly language. NetWare v3.x is written in the portable C language.

This chapter discusses the evolution of NetWare v3.x and examines its features and architecture. The chapter outlines the installation requirements and steps for NetWare 3.x, showing you the server parameters you need to select at installation time. This chapter concludes with a guided tour of the installation steps, and how and when to upgrade from NetWare v2.x to NetWare v3.x.

Examining NetWare v3.x

Before you understand the NetWare v3.x installation process, you should understand the need that NetWare v3.x is designed to fulfill. Some of these topics include the following:

- The evolution of NetWare v3.x to its current form
- Features and functionality of NetWare v3.x

History of NetWare v3.x

NetWare 386 v3.0 was released in 1989 and provided an evolutionary upgrade path from earlier releases of NetWare, such as NetWare v2.x. The release of NetWare 386 v3.0 also marked a change in Novell's open approach to network computing.

NetWare 386 v3.0 provided an open architecture and support for a rich variety of *Application Programming Interfaces* (APIs), which enabled third-party vendors to provide extensions and functionality to the NOS. Figure 8.1 shows NetWare's open-computing platform approach. This figure shows that the software architecture (called the NLM software bus) enables you to easily add application and network services, such as additional transport protocols and database services, to the platform.

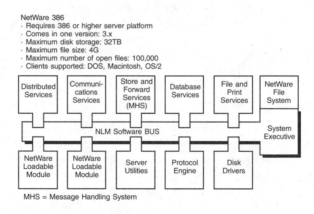

Figure 8.1:
NetWare 386 v3.0's open computing platform approach. (Graphic courtesy of Learning Group International)

The initial release of NetWare 386 v3.0 had support for only one transport protocol: SPX/IPX. NetWare 386 v3.0 did not support AppleTalk protocols or the popular TCP/IP protocol. In practical terms, this meant that Macintosh workstations, which need AppleTalk, and UNIX workstations, which need TCP/IP, could not communicate with the NetWare 386 v3.0 server. Subsequent releases of NetWare remedied many of these problems and added other features and capabilities.

NetWare 386 v3.0 was followed by NetWare 386 v3.1 and NetWare v3.11. With the release of NetWare v3.11, the "386" was dropped from the product name. The NetWare 386 product line was named NetWare v3.x, and, at the same time, the NetWare 286 product line was named NetWare v2.x. The release of NetWare after NetWare v3.x is called NetWare v4.x.

Because NetWare v3.x was written in the portable C language, NetWare services were better separated from the operating system functions, such as the tasking model, memory management, and transport protocols. The portable NetWare services enabled users to run NetWare on other operating system platforms, such as UNIX. This version of NetWare is called *Portable NetWare* (now renamed NetWare for UNIX) and is discussed later in the book. Also, projects are under way to do a native port of NetWare to non-Intel architectures. One such attempt is the port of NetWare to HP's *Precision Architecture* (PA) RISC machines.

Features and Functionality of NetWare v3.x

NetWare v3.11 implements the following features:

- Multiple transport protocol support

- Promise of support of SFT Level III

- Multiple name space support

- Support for *Network File System* (NFS)

- Support for OSI's *File Transfer Access Management* (FTAM)

- A server-based backup architecture around SBACKUP.NLM

- Common transport interface, such as STREAMS and TLI, and support for BSD sockets

- Enhanced management capabilities: SNMP support, IBM's NetView support, and third-party management NLMs

- *Remote Management Facility* (RMF)

These features are discussed in greater detail in the following sections.

Multiple Transport Protocol Support

Multiple transport protocol support includes transport protocol support for SPX/IPX, TCP/IP, AppleTalk, LU6.2, and FTAM. Support for other transport protocols, such as the DECnet transport XNS, can easily be added in the future because of the flexibility of the NOS architecture. The transport protocols are implemented in the form of *NetWare Loadable Modules* (NLMs). As you will see later, this enables the network manager to dynamically configure support for multiple protocols. The practical benefit of multiple transport protocols is that the NetWare v3.x server can exist and operate in non-Novell environments. This means that interoperability exists at the transport layers, which is a key step in achieving interoperability in a multivendor environment.

TCP/IP support includes *IP routing*, which enables the NetWare v3.x server to be used as an IP router, in addition to being used as an IPX router. NetWare also supports IP tunneling. *IP tunneling* means that the IPX packets can be encapsulated in an IP packet and routed ("tunneled") by an Internet subnet consisting of IP routers. This enables you to connect two NetWare LANs over the large distances spanned by Internet.

SFT Level III

SFT Level III support has been in beta testing for a long time and has been demonstrated at various network shows. SFT Level III is planned only for NetWare v3.x. *SFT Level III support* means that you have file-server duplexing. (See Chapter 6 for more information about SFT levels.) The primary file server has a backup file server that performs the same operations. If the primary server crashes, the backup server takes over the server responsibilities, giving uninterrupted service to the users.

Multiple Name Space Support

One of the problems in achieving data-level interoperability is that different client workstations use different file systems because their operating systems are different. The Macintosh operating system uses two files—a *data fork* and a *resource fork*—to represent a file folder. OS/2 and UNIX enable you to use longer file names than does DOS. OS/2 implements a High Performance File System that has improved performance and security, compared to DOS.

NetWare v3.x enables support for multiple file systems by implementing a general, or *universal*, file system at the server. The universal file system enables you to map a client's file system to the NetWare v3.x file system. You can store Macintosh, UNIX, and DOS workstations files on the NetWare v3.x server and perform operations on the files.

Multiple name space support is implemented by running the appropriate name space NLM at the server.

Support for Network File System

NFS is a popular server architecture on UNIX networks. It was developed by Sun Microsystems and is licensed to a large number of vendors. The NFS protocols support remote file systems that can be accessed across a LAN by clients that may be running different operating systems. NFS traditionally has been implemented on UNIX; therefore, NFS servers usually are UNIX-based. NFS implementations also exist on many non-UNIX platforms.

NetWare for NFS is a Novell product that can run as an NLM on the NetWare v3.x server. It is not included as part of NetWare v3.x and must be purchased separately.

Support for OSI's File Transfer Access Management

FTAM is similar to NFS in that it provides a virtual file system at a machine that can be accessed by other FTAM clients (called *initiators*). FTAM is part of GOSIP 1.0 and 2.0 recommendations. *Government Open Systems Interconnection Profile* (GOSIP) is a procurement guideline for federal agencies to buy OSI-compliant products. FTAM is a layer 7 protocol and is included in the GOSIP document.

NetWare for FTAM is a Novell product that can run as an NLM on the NetWare v3.x server. It is not included as part of NetWare v3.x and must be purchased separately.

Server-Based Backup Architecture

NetWare v3.x comes with a backup NLM utility called SBACKUP.NLM that enables you to back up files directly at the server. In previous versions of

NetWare, backups typically were performed at client stations across the network. If the network was down, backups could not be performed. Using SBACKUP, backups can be performed even if the network is down. SBACKUP can be used to back up all files, including Macintosh files.

Common Transport Interface

NetWare v3.x supports common transport interfaces, such as STREAMS, TLI, and BSD sockets.

STREAMS is a general-purpose transport protocol interface developed by AT&T that enables you to build protocol stacks dynamically. The head of the STREAMS protocol is the STREAMS interface, and the tail usually is the network card driver. Between the head and the tail, you can connect any number of protocol elements as if they were part of a string or stream. These protocol elements can be the transport and network protocols, such as SPX/IPX or TCP/IP.

The *Transport Layer Interface* (TLI), also developed by AT&T, is functionally similar to STREAMS. Like STREAMS, TLI provides a uniform transport interface to upper-layer protocols. This enables applications to be written to a common programming interface, making them portable across different environments implementing the same TLI interface. It differs from STREAMS in the details of the mechanism and the actual interface to upper-layer protocols. The NetWare v3.x TLI implementation follows the spirit of the AT&T definition but differs from it. Also, TLI currently supports only SPX/IPX and TCP/IP.

The *Berkeley Software Distribution* (BSD) socket interface was developed as part of BSD UNIX at University of California, Berkeley. BSD is a popular and simple interface to the TCP/IP protocols. Many programmers are fond of the BSD socket interface and prefer it over the more general (and also more complicated) STREAMS and TLI interfaces.

Management Support

NetWare v3.x comes with support for a *Simple Network Management Protocol* (SNMP) agent that can run on the server. SNMP is covered in detail in Chapter 4. The SNMP.NLM acts as an agent for remote clients. It has an understanding of *Management Information Base* (MIB) objects relating to TCP/IP and can generate trap messages, as required by the TCP/IP protocol stack. NetWare v3.x does not support a full-blown SNMP manager NLM as yet.

Instead, a primitive SNMP manager, called the TCPCON.NLM, enables you to poll SNMP agents. Also, an NLM called SNMPLOG is provided that can be used for logging trap events generated by SNMP agents. The SNMPLOG can be considered to be a client of the SNMP.NLM agent that runs on the server.

In addition to support for SNMP, NetWare v3.x supports IBM's NetView. This support consists of a group of NLMs that allow a Token Ring adapter installed in a NetWare v3.x server to forward NetView alerts to a NetView host. The NetWare Management Agent for NetView NLM (NVINSTAL.NLM) also responds to statistics requests from an IBM host.

A number of management NLMs, such as Frye Utilities and Monitrix, provide proprietary management capabilities. The number of management tools is likely to grow as NetWare v3.x evolves and matures. Some of these management tools will come directly from Novell.

Remote Management Facility

RMF is a boon to many network managers. It enables network managers to administer servers from a remote location, such as any workstation on the network. RMF enables users with console-level privileges to execute server console commands at remote workstations, as if they were actually using the keyboard and monitor on the server.

To support RMF, two NLMs, REMOTE.NLM and RSPX.NLM, must be run on the server. The workstation that runs as a remote console must execute a program called RCONSOLE.EXE. RCONSOLE.EXE establishes connections with REMOTE.NLM running on the server using the SPX protocol. This connection enables keyboard strokes at the workstation to be sent to the server and screen image changes at the server to be sent to the remote workstation. This enables the workstation to "take over" the server console.

When REMOTE.NLM is run on the server, it uses the *Server Advertising Protocol* (SAP) to advertise its existence. Servers and routers record the SAP broadcast in an internal temporary database. When RCONSOLE is run at a workstation, it can query any server for servers that are available for remote management. The list of remote servers available for remote management is shown on a list. The user can select a server to be managed remotely from this list. After the user provides the correct password that is set when REMOTE.NLM is loaded on the server, the user can take over the remote server console. Any command that can be run at the server then can be run at the workstation. This includes the capability to run console utilities, such as MONITOR, INSTALL, and VREPAIR, as well as the LOAD and UNLOAD commands to load and unload NLMs.

You also can perform remote management by using the serial port. This is handy when the network is down. You can connect a modem to the serial port on the server and a user can use a modem and telephone line to dial in and perform remote management. For performing remote management over dial up lines, the RS232.NLM must be run on the server.

Understanding the Internal Architecture of NetWare v3.x

NetWare v3.x represents a radical departure from NetWare v2.x in terms of its internal architecture. One of the key differences is the dynamic manner in which NetWare v3.x can be configured. The server parameters in NetWare v3.x are not fixed when you install v3.x. They can be changed any time without bringing down the server. No longer do you need to determine the number of communication buffers or maximum open and indexed files; these values can now be changed dynamically. In many situations, the server is capable of monitoring its own parameter usage and fine-tuning them based on its history of parameter usage. This section examines some of the elements of the NetWare v3.x internal architecture that make it dynamically configurable. The following are the architectural elements that are discussed:

- NetWare Loadable Module
- Memory architecture
- NetWare kernel
- Application services

NetWare Loadable Module Environment

In the Chapter 7 discussion about NetWare v2.x, you learned that object modules selected during the installation process need to be "bound" together. The mechanism used is called *static linking* or the *NetWare generation process*.

In NetWare v3.x, NetWare generation is not needed because object modules can be linked at "run" time or at the time they are loaded in memory. This linking at run time is called *dynamic linking*. Readers familiar with OS/2 or Microsoft Windows might have heard of *Dynamic Link Libraries* (DLLs). The dynamic link libraries in NetWare v3.x are called NLMs. NLMs are more than DLLs. They actually are processes or tasks that run under NetWare. If you combine DLLs and processes, you have NLMs. You can think of NLMs as a group of cooperating software tasks or engines.

NLMs are activated by using the LOAD command with the name of the NetWare Loadable Module, as follows:

```
LOAD nameofNLM
```

NLMs that come with NetWare are installed on the SYS:SYSTEM directory on the server. The only exception to this is BTRIEVE.NLM. The LOAD command, therefore, searches the SYS:SYSTEM directory for NLMs. If NLMs are installed in another location, their full path names need to be specified or their locations made known by using the SEARCH command at the console. To add SYS:MANAGE to the search path, for example, issue the following command:

```
SEARCH ADD SYS:MANAGE
```

This adds the search path SYS:MANAGE at the end of the search path list. To make SYS:MANAGE the first path to be searched, use the following command:

```
SEARCH ADD 1 SYS:MANAGE
```

NLMs can be deactivated by unloading them. Use the UNLOAD command followed by the name of the NetWare Loadable Module, as follows:

```
UNLOAD nameofNLM
```

When an NLM is loaded, it takes up a certain portion of the server RAM and competes with other processes for CPU time. The amount of memory taken by an NLM can vary, depending on the task being performed. The actual amount of memory used can be monitored by using the MONITOR NLM. Some NLMs make system calls to allocate additional memory for the tasks they are performing. Also, this requested memory can be released during execution, so the actual size of the NLM can vary during execution. When an NLM is unloaded, all allocated resources are returned to the NetWare NOS.

NLMs are written by Novell or third-party developers. NLMs can be written to establish a loading sequence. This means that RSPX.NLM cannot be loaded until REMOTE.NLM is loaded first. Also, when an NLM is loaded, it expects to have all of its needed external interfaces already in memory. If it cannot find the necessary external interface, an error message is reported, and the NLM will not load. Certain NLMs, such as network cards or disk drivers, can accept command-line parameters to modify its behavior. If these are not specified, you are prompted for the parameter values. The WDPLUSSV.NLM, a driver for Western Digital Star/EtherCard PLUS, for example, can be loaded in the following two ways:

```
LOAD WDPLUSSV port=280 mem=D0000:200 int=3
frame=ETHERNET_802.3
```

or

```
LOAD WDPLUSSV
```

In the first example, all the parameters are specified on the command line in the *parameter=value* syntax. In the second example, the parameters are not specified. On loading, the WDPLUSSV.NLM prompts the user for these parameter values.

Network card driver NLMs also can be bound to the protocol stack with which they will be communicating. This protocol stack also is written in the form of an NLM, except in the case of SPX/IPX. SPX/IPX protocols are implemented in the operating system kernel.

TCP/IP protocols are implemented in the form of the TCPIP.NLM. SNMP agent support is implemented as SNMP.NLM. Any extensions to the server operating environment by third-party vendors are provided by NLMs. NLMs permeate the entire NetWare v3.x architecture.

NLM utilities can be loaded whenever they are needed. After they are used, they can be unloaded. Other NLMs, especially drivers, need to be loaded every time the server is booted. The commands to load them are stored in files with a *NetWare Command File* (NCF) extension. The NCF files are similar to DOS batch files, and contain commands for loading the driver NLMs. Configuration commands to establish the server operating environment, such as loading and binding of drivers, are stored in AUTOEXEC.NCF.

NLM names have an extension. You can tell the nature of the NLM by examining the extension portion of its name. These conventions are described in table 8.1.

Table 8.1
Common Extensions Used for NLM Names

NLM extension	Meaning
DSK	Disk driver
LAN	NIC driver
NLM	Management utilities and server applications
NCF	NetWare command file
NAM	Name space modules

Table 8.2 lists some common NLMs that come with NetWare v3.x.

Table 8.2
NLMs Distributed with NetWare v3.x

NLM name	Description
CLIB	Provides access to the standard C library function calls with extensions to include calls to the STREAMS interface and many low-level APIs.
EDIT	Modifies and creates text files that are smaller than 8K at the server console on DOS and NetWare partitions. Particularly useful for modifying NCF batch files.
ETHERRPL	Implements Ethernet protocol stack to enable remote booting of Ethernet stations. Must be bound with Ethernet driver on server by using ETHERNET_802.2 frames.

continues

Table 8.2
Continued

NLM name	Description
INSTALL	Performs install functions, such as server disk maintenance, loading NetWare v3.x floppy disks on server, server configuration, and installing and configuring products on the server.
IPCONFIG	Configuration utility for the IP protocol when TCPIP.NLM is loaded.
IPXS	Implements IPX protocol for STREAMS services. Automatically binds to the TLI.NLM, which must be loaded before IPXS.
MAC	Implements support for Macintosh file names on server. This is the Macintosh name space module.
MATHLIB	Interfaces with the math coprocessor on the server. Makes use of CLIB, which must be loaded before MATHLIBC.
MATHLIBC	Emulates the math-coprocessor functions in software. Used on a server (Intel 80386) that does not have a math coprocessor. Makes use of CLIB, which must be loaded before MATHLIBC.
MONITOR	Performs file server monitoring.
NMAGENT	Registers NIC drivers and passes network management parameters. Must be loaded prior to the NIC driver. If not loaded, the NOS tries to automatically loads NMAGENT.
NVINSTAL	Provides IBM NetView Management Agent support at server.
PSERVER	Supports a server-based print server.

NLM name	Description
PCN2RPL	Enables remote boot for IBM PCN2 NIC.
REMOTE	Implements RMF at server.
RS232	Provides asynchronous communications support. Used for remote management support.
RSPX	Sends keystrokes and screen information across the LAN. The RSPX utility is a SPX/IPX protocol used for RMF.
SNMP	Provides SNMP Agent support on server.
SNMPLOG	Logs SNMP trap messages.
SPXCONFG	Configures SPX parameters.
SPXS	Implements SPX protocol for STREAMS services. Automatically binds to the TLI.NLM, which must be loaded before SPXS.
STREAMS	Implements STREAMS protocol. Must be loaded before CLIB.
TCPIP	Implements TCP/IP protocols.
TCPCON	TCP console utility that can be used to poll SNMP agents and display SNMP traps recorded by the server.
TCPCONFG	Enables you to configure TCP/IP.
TOKENRPL	Enables remote boot for IBM Token Ring network boards.
UPS	Implements the software link between server and *Uninterrupted Power Supply* (UPS) device.
VREPAIR	Repairs minor volume problems.

THE CLIB.NLM is the major programming interface for application writers. It provides access to the standard C library as well as many low-level functions exported by the NetWare kernel. It has knowledge about the internal data structures used by NetWare v3.x and exports this knowledge by means of functions. NLMs such as CLIB usually export functions to other NLMs. They also may, in turn, import functions from other NLMs. Other NLMs that want to gain access to the NetWare NOS must do so by functions exported by CLIB. The advantage of this is that although the internal data structures of the NOS might change in future releases, the function interface will remain the same. This is the data-hiding concept used in well-designed programming interfaces.

Memory Architecture

NetWare v3.x manages its memory by using a dynamic approach. A maximum of 4G of RAM is available. This 4G limit is available because of the Intel 80386 microprocessor's 32 address lines. (The maximum RAM for this kind of machine is 2^{32}, which is 4G.) The Intel 80386 architecture can support a virtual address space up to 48 terabytes, but NetWare v3.x does not make use of virtual memory. NetWare v3.x uses the flat memory model and uses only one segment. (A segment is 4G on the Intel 80386.) This currently is enough for NetWare because a PC has not been built that can handle 4G of RAM.

Virtual memory actually would slow down the NOS. Virtual memory works well at the desktop because it gives applications more memory, and a slight slowing down of applications usually is not noticed by the user.

A controversial aspect of NetWare's memory usage is that all programs—the kernel and applications—run in ring 0 of the Intel 80386 architecture. The Intel 80386 architecture defines four rings—rings 0 to 3 (see fig. 8.2). The operating system kernel runs at ring 0 and the other programs run at one of the outer rings. Programs running at ring 3, for example, can access the RAM used by programs running in ring 3 but cannot directly access RAM for programs running at rings 2, 1, and 0. If the operating system kernel is running in ring 0, a program at ring 3 needs to make an inter-ring gate call to make service requests from the operating system kernel. When a program crashes, it cannot affect the operating system kernel. This architecture makes the system more reliable at the cost of reduced speed because of the inter-ring call overhead. An example of an operating system that uses the ring architecture is OS/2.

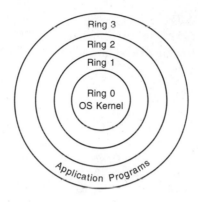

Figure 8.2:
Intel 80386 processor ring architecture.

NetWare v3.x does not use the ring architecture. The NetWare OS, NLMs, and all server-based programs run in ring 0. What NetWare loses in reliability, it gains in simplicity and speed. Moreover, Novell has an NLM certification program to check the reliability of third-party NLMs. Also, development tools, such as those from Nu-Mega, are available that developers can use to detect badly behaved NLMs.

For some systems, NetWare v3.x does not recognize more than 16M of RAM. In these situations, you must use the REGISTER MEMORY command at the console. This command uses the following syntax:

```
REGISTER MEMORY memorystartinhex memorylengthinhex
```

Thus, to add 4M of memory above 16M (for a total of 20M RAM), you need to enter the following:

```
REGISTER MEMORY 1000000 250000
```

This command can be added to the AUTOEXEC.NCF file for automatic registration of memory when the server is booted.

For EISA-based machines, the SET command must be used for registering memory above 16M.

NetWare v3.x uses memory for a variety of functions. 2M of RAM is required, but at least 4M is recommended, to run a useful number of NLMs. Figure 8.3 shows memory utilization at the server. DOS, which is necessary to initially boot the server, uses up to 640K of RAM in low memory. When the NetWare v3.x NOS loads, it sets up in *extended memory*, which is memory above 1M. After NetWare v3.x is loaded, DOS can be unloaded if more memory is desired for the NOS. DOS is unloaded by using the following command:

```
REMOVE DOS
```

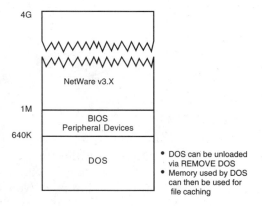

Figure 8.3:
NetWare v3.x memory map.

With DOS unloaded, NetWare v3.x can use the freed memory for file caching. When DOS is unloaded, you can do a warm reboot of the server by using the EXIT command. This is a technique that sometimes is used to reboot the server by using RMF from a remote workstation.

Memory not used by the NetWare operating system and DOS is given to three primary memory pools (see fig. 8.4), as follows:

- File cache buffer pool
- Permanent memory pool
- Alloc memory pool

Initially, NetWare v3.x allocates as little memory as possible to the permanent and alloc memory pools, enabling these pools to grow or shrink, based on actual demand. Memory not allocated to these pools and the NOS kernel is used for file caching.

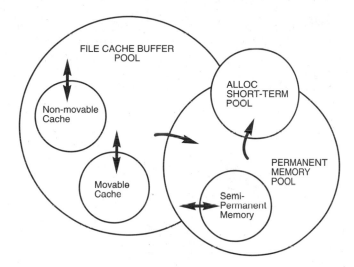

Figure 8.4:
NetWare v3.x memory pools.

The file cache buffer pool is used to store file blocks from the most frequently used files. It uses a *least recently used* (LRU) algorithm to manage file-block usage. Two secondary pools, called *movable* and *non-movable caches*, interact with the file cache buffer pool. They obtain their memory from the file cache buffer pool and, when done, return memory back to it. The movable pool is used for system tables that change size, such as FATs and hash tables. Tables and objects in the movable pool can be moved around in memory to prevent excessive memory fragmentation. If objects need to be moved, NetWare allocates relatively large objects from the movable pool so that it can reduce fragmentation. Moving memory around to get larger chunks of free memory, sometimes called *garbage collection*, is a popular technique used in many operating systems, such as OS/2 and Mac OS. The non-movable pool can be used for NetWare loadable modules by NetWare.

The permanent memory pool is used for long-term memory needs, such as directory cache buffers and packet receive buffers. Although it is called *permanent memory*, the permanent memory pool actually is quite dynamic. A portion of the pool is static and a portion of it is semidynamic. Communications buffers, for example, use permanent pool memory. When NetWare loads and initializes itself, it sets up a specific number of communication buffers. With rising network activity, NetWare allocates additional communication buffers to store the extra data packets. These buffers are allocated from permanent memory, but once allocated, they will not be released even if the network activity subsides. This allocates enough resources to handle peak loads on the network.

The alloc memory pool is used to store information about the following elements:

- Drive mappings
- Service request buffers
- SAP tables
- Open and lock files and semaphores
- User connection information
- NLM tables
- Queue manager tables
- Messages queued for broadcasting

The alloc memory is used on a temporary basis for fulfilling short-term processing needs. As NetWare executes, data objects may need to be created dynamically and destroyed after the NOS is finished using them. The following are examples of resources used in the alloc memory pool:

- SAP table entries
- Drive mappings
- User connection information

Memory used for the alloc memory pool is managed by a *linked list* of free memory blocks. By using the linked list approach, the NOS can quickly find the memory it needs. When memory is needed, it is allocated from this free list. When released, the memory returns to the free memory list where it can be reused. Another advantage of this approach is that it prevents memory fragmentation.

NetWare tries to allocate memory for NLMs from the alloc memory pool. As memory requirements for NLMs increase, the alloc memory pool is depleted. To satisfy the NLM memory requirement, NetWare borrows memory from the file cache buffer pool. Once borrowed, this memory is not returned to the file cache pool, even if the NLMs are unloaded. The worst case situation is when many NLMs are loaded and unloaded frequently. Under these circumstances, the permanent borrowing of memory from the file cache area can deplete the cache memory severely, degrading the performance of the server. This is called *memory leakage*. You can use the SET command to limit the size of the alloc pool to prevent memory leakage. The SET command normally is set to a default of 2M, but it can be set as high as 16M and as low as 50K. (SET commands are discussed in Chapter 9.)

NetWare Kernel

The NetWare kernel consists of the following components:

- System executive
- Scheduler
- Native protocols, such as SPX/IPX and NCP
- Router mechanism
- Memory management: file cache, permanent pool, and alloc pool
- File systems that can support multiple name space and file and record locking
- Semaphore management
- TTS
- ODI device driver support for multiple protocols

As can be seen from the preceding list, the NetWare kernel is kept quite busy doing a number of tasks. By means of a scheduling mechanism, it can perform these tasks simultaneously. The *NetWare scheduler* is a group of processes in the kernel that control the execution of all other tasks. It determines which task (including NLMs) should run next, but not how long a task should run. Tasks are expected to relinquish control of the CPU frequently to enable other tasks to run. This scheduling mechanism is called *non-preemptive*. The alternative to non-preemptive scheduling is *preemptive* scheduling, in which the scheduler determines how long a task should run. Preemptive scheduling is common in many desktop operating systems or operating systems that perform time sharing between user applications.

In an operating system based on preemptive scheduling, time is a resource that is shared by processes, but the scheduler determines how much time a process should have. Preemptive scheduling works well when issues of fairness are more important than system throughput. In preemptive scheduling, a process is given a certain amount of time, and at the completion of the process, the CPU turns its attention away from the process, regardless of what it may be doing at the time. Although preemptive scheduling may be more democratic and fair than non-preemptive scheduling if other processes are waiting, it has an adverse impact on the system throughput, especially when critical processes are interrupted.

NetWare enables processes to monopolize the CPU for as long as they need to complete critical tasks. For practical reasons, an upper limit is usually set to prevent an NLM from going "haywire" and hogging the CPU. Processes need to yield the CPU to other processors when finished performing critical tasks. Non-preemptive scheduling also is the preferred approach used in the design of many real-time operating systems.

Application Services

The application services include:

- Printing services
- Message services
- Accounting services
- Diagnostic services
- Security services
- Bindery services

Application services are covered in greater detail in later chapters in this book.

Estimating Server Memory Requirements for NetWare v3.x

The amount of RAM needed for a server depends on the size of DOS, NetWare, and any multiple-name space partitions. Also, a certain amount of RAM is needed for server file caching, the permanent memory pool, and the alloc memory pool.

The following section shows you how to estimate server RAM. You then can apply this knowledge to an example that uses these formulas to set up RAM in a server.

RAM Usage Formulas

The NetWare operating kernel needs about 2M of RAM. For every DOS partition and NetWare volume at the server, the amount of server RAM needed can be estimated in megabytes by using the following formula:

$$M(DOS) = 0.023 \times volumesize / blocksize$$

In the preceding formula, *volumesize* is the size of the volume in megabytes. The *blocksize* parameter is the size of the block in megabytes. The default block size is 4M.

For each volume with added name space, the amount of server RAM needed can be estimated in megabytes by the following formula:

$$M(NAME\ SPACE) = 0.032 \times volumesize / blocksize$$

The remaining memory is used for the file cache buffer pool, the permanent memory pool, and the alloc memory pool.

Estimating Server RAM

Suppose, for example, that you need to estimate the amount of RAM needed for a NetWare v3.x server that is to be installed. You need to configure the server so that it has a DOS, SYS, UNIX, and Macintosh volume on it. The volume and block sizes need to match the ones shown in table 8.3.

Table 8.3
Volume and Block Sizes

Volume	Size	Block Size
DOS	60M	4K
SYS	120M	4K
UNIX	600M	8K
MAC	100M	4K

You can calculate the server RAM by using the following steps:

1. NetWare Kernel RAM (2M): 2M

2. Use the server and name space formulas to calculate the RAM for each server volume, as follows:

M(DOS)	$= 0.023 \times 60 /4$	$= 0.345M$
M(SYS)	$= 0.023 \times 120 / 4$	$= 0.69M$
M(UNIX)	$= 0.032 \times 600 / 8$	$= 2.4M$
M(MAC)	$= 0.032 \times 100 /4$	$= 0.8M$

Total RAM for server volumes $= 4.235M$

3. Calculate the total RAM for the server by adding steps 1 and 2, as follows:

   $2M + 4.235M = 6.235M$

4. Calculate the total RAM to the nearest megabyte, in this case 7M.

5. To allow for additional memory, a final physical memory of 8M is selected.

6. You now can calculate the RAM for file caching and other memory pools by subtracting the value in step 5 from the value in step 3, as follows:

   $8M - 6.235M = 1.765M$

From the preceding example, you find that the server needs 6.235M of RAM. You used a physical size of 8M, knowing that additional RAM (1.765M) will improve performance through additional file caching.

Installing NetWare v3.3x

Some fundamental differences exist between NetWare v2.x and NetWare v3.x installation. NetWare generation is not required for NetWare v3.x. This alone cuts down on the installation time and makes for an easier and simpler installation. The other distinction is that, unlike NetWare v2.x, NetWare v3.x does not have its own cold boot loaders. To boot the server, you must boot from a DOS partition. The DOS partition can be a DOS boot floppy or a small area of the server disk. A small DOS partition on the hard disk speeds up the boot process. Some network managers prefer to boot with a floppy and then lock it for security reasons. Without this boot floppy, you cannot restart the server.

Although NetWare v3.x does not require NetWare generation, and the installation is simpler, you still need to document the decisions made for parameter values. This section discusses server parameters and shows you how to install NetWare v3.x. As you go through these instructions, you should note in an installation log book the key parameters that are selected. You can model your worksheets after those in the Novell manuals or use the worksheets from the *Hands-On Novell Networking* seminar from Learning Group International.

Figure 8.5 illustrates the various steps and decisions that you need to make when you install NetWare v3.x. The following sections detail each step in the installation process.

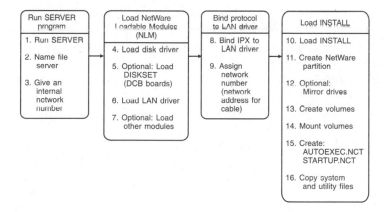

Figure 8.5:
NetWare v3.x installation steps. (Graphic courtesy of Learning Group International)

Running Program SERVER.EXE

Program SERVER.EXE must be run from a DOS partition at the file server and can run only on an Intel 80386-based AT or higher. The SERVER.EXE loads in extended memory and switches the Intel 80386 microprocessor to the protected mode, enabling it to address up to 4G of RAM.

You must run the SERVER.EXE when the server is first installed and also to start the server after it is installed. Upon loading, SERVER.EXE looks for and executes STARTUP.NCF and AUTOEXEC.NCF. The STARTUP.NCF file is similar to the CONFIG.SYS file used in DOS and must exist on the DOS partition from which the server is booted. If STARTUP.NCF does not exist (as when you install NetWare for the first time), SERVER.EXE assumes that an installation is being performed. If the SYS: volume and STARTUP.NCF have already been created in an earlier installation step, the SERVER.EXE program mounts (activates) it. It then looks for the AUTOEXEC.NCF file on the SYS:SYSTEM directory on the server. If this is a first-time install, SYS: will not exist and will not be mounted. Also, SERVER.EXE will not search for AUTOEXEC.NCF if you are performing a first-time installation.

The SERVER.EXE program can be invoked from the DOS prompt by using a number of parameters. If this is the first time that you have installed NetWare v3.x, the discussion on the SERVER.EXE parameters may not be of much interest to you. You can, however, use this discussion as reference for future problems or concerns.

The SERVER.EXE program executes the STARTUP.NCF file, if STARTUP.NCF exists on the DOS boot partition. After STARTUP.NCF executes, the AUTOEXEC.NCF file executes from the SYS:SYSTEM directory. Sometimes, however, you might want to experiment with a different boot sequence. The SERVER.EXE has a number of options to make this job easy.

Suppose, for example, that you want to use a different startup file than STARTUP.NCF. You can start the server by using the following command:

```
SERVER -S ALTSTART.NCF
```

The ALTSTART.NCF file contains an alternate set of startup commands.

To ignore the processing of STARTUP.NCF and AUTOEXEC.NCF and experiment with a different boot sequence, for example, use the following command:

```
SERVER -NS
```

If you want to stop the processing of the AUTOEXEC.NCF file but not the STARTUP.NCF file, use this command:

```
SERVER -NA
```

Selecting the File Server Name

All servers on a multiserver NetWare internetwork must have a unique name that is used to identify the server from all other servers. The name, which can comprise alphanumeric characters, hyphens (-), and underscores (_), can have between 2 and 47 characters with no spaces. The first character, however, cannot be a period.

You should make the server name descriptive of the function it will perform. Also, keep the server name to a reasonable length because it is used in many NetWare commands. Future network managers who are not fast and accurate touch typists will bless you for a reasonably short server name.

Assigning the Internal Network Number and Network Address

You must assign a unique internal number to identify the server process. This number must be different from all internal network numbers for other servers and the network addresses used to identify different cabling segments.

The *internal network number* is used to identify a logical network distinct from the physical network. Its real use is to solve some routing problems that are inherent with NetWare v2.x servers, in which the server process is identified by the network address assigned to the first NIC card (LAN A) in the server. This leads to some inefficient routing paths (discussed in Chapter 3).

A unique network address must be assigned to every cabling segment. NetWare v3.x allows up to 16 LAN cards to be connected to a server. Each of these must have a unique number. This network address must be different from all other network addresses on all servers on the internetwork. This network address is referred to as the *network number* during the installation. The network address used in this context must not be confused with the network address of the LAN card. The network address of a LAN card is referred to as the *node address*.

Figure 8.6 shows a LAN with three servers, with one server being used as a router. The internal network numbers of 33, 3A, and 3F are distinct from each other and from the network address of AA3B and BF17 used for the two cabling segments. The NICs attached to the same cabling segment have the same network address. Their node addresses (NIC card addresses) of 05, 06, 08, and 09 are distinct.

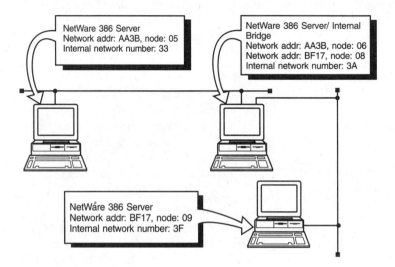

Figure 8.6:
Assigning an internal network number. (Graphic courtesy of Learning Group International)

Internal network numbers and network addresses can be eight-digit hexadecimal numbers. You can omit leading 0s when entering these values in the installation process.

Loading the Disk Driver NLMs

Disk drivers are written as NLMs and must be loaded so that the server can communicate with the disks. They are loaded by using the LOAD command. Issue the following command, for example, to load the ISADISK driver:

```
LOAD ISADISK
```

To load the PS/2 ESDI driver, for example, issue the following command:

```
LOAD PS2ESDI
```

Hardware parameters, such as port numbers and interrupt numbers, can be specified as parameters to the LOAD *diskdriverNLM* command. If you do not specify hardware parameters, the disk driver prompts you for a value.

The parameter settings for the ISADISK driver are as follows:

Parameter	Supported values (hex)	Default (hex)
INT	B, C, D, E	E
PORT	170, 1F0	1F0

If more than one ISADISK controller exists on the server, the LOAD ISADISK command can be issued a second time. When the driver is loaded a second time, it loads itself re-entrantly and accepts only an alternate set of parameters.

To specify the ISADISK parameters at the command line, you need to use the following command:

```
LOAD ISADISK INT=E PORT=1F0
```

The PS/2 SCSI driver can be loaded four times, and it loads itself re-entrantly. For Micro Channel Architecture, you must specify the SLOT parameter, such as in the following example:

```
LOAD PS2SCI SLOT=2
```

Loading NIC Driver NLMs

The network adapters (NICs) are activated by loading their NLM driver. To load the TOKEN driver for Token Ring, issue the following command:

```
LOAD TOKEN
```

To load the Novell Ethernet driver for NE2000 and define a logical name ETHER for it, you need to use the same command, but in the following way:

```
LOAD NE2000 NAME=ETHER
```

Because you can have multiple NICs in a server to form an internal router, you must issue the LOAD command for every NIC. Driver names enable NetWare to distinguish between several loaded instances of the same driver.

Hardware parameters, such as port numbers and interrupt numbers, can be specified as parameters to the LOAD *diskdriverNLM* command. If you do not specify hardware parameters, the NIC driver prompts you for a value.

The remainder of this section discusses more advanced topics on loading NIC driver NLMs that are not necessary for a first-time simple installation. You should, however, use these as references when dealing with more complex installations.

Most NIC drivers use one or more of the following parameters:

DMA = *number*

INT = *number*

MEM = *address*

PORT = *address*

NODE = *number*

RETRIES = *number*

SLOT = *number*

NAME = *board name*

FRAME = *name*

For the actual parameter values, you must consult the vendor's documentation. Table 8.4 gives a brief explanation of these parameters. Table 8.5 shows a list of parameters specifically used for Token Ring networks.

Table 8.4
Card Parameters in LOAD NIC_DRIVER Command

Parameter	Meaning
DMA	Specifies the DMA channel number of NIC.
INT	Specifies the IRQ level NIC is set to.
MEM	Refers to the base memory address of RAM on driver.
PORT	Specifies the I/O port address setting of NIC.
NODE	Overrides node address on NICs that permit it, such as NICs that use IEEE MAC-addressing schemes.
RETRIES	Denotes the number of times NIC driver retries failed packet transmissions. Default for most adapters is 5. Can be set to as high as 255.

Parameter	Meaning
SLOT	Used for Micro Channel Architecture and EISA bus computers. Tells NOS to which NIC to link driver. Hardware parameters, such as I/O port and IRQ, are set by using the reference disk.
NAME	Specifies a unique name (up to 17 characters) for an NIC. Useful for many NICs of the same type. NAME can be used in the BIND command.
FRAME	Specifies the type of MAC layer encapsulation to be used. Used for Ethernet and Token Ring.

Table 8.5
Token Ring Specific Parameters for LOAD TOKEN Command

Parameter	Meaning
LS	Specifies the number of IEEE 802.5 link stations.
SAPS	Denotes the number of Service Access Points for Token Ring driver.
TBC	Refers to the Transmit Buffer Count for Token Ring driver. The default is set to 2.
TBZ	Refers to the Transmit Buffer Size for Token Ring driver. Values range from 96 to 65,535, although not all values are supported. The default value is 0, and it implies the maximum that works for the NOS or the NIC.

Most of the preceding parameters are fairly straightforward. The one that may require a little explanation is the FRAME parameter. The FRAME parameter can be used for Ethernet and Token Ring NICs and tells the NIC driver the type of header to be used for packets. In other words, FRAME controls the MAC layer encapsulation.

In Chapter 2, you saw that many modern Ethernet NICs can generate either IEEE 802.3 encapsulation or Ethernet II (version 2.0) encapsulation.

NetWare's default Ethernet encapsulation is IEEE 802.3, as shown in figure 8.7. This corresponds to a FRAME value of ETHERNET_802.3. In practical terms, it means that the NetWare server, by default, can speak only to stations or other computers that can understand the IEEE 802.3 headers in the packets. Many non-Novell networks, such as UNIX-based networks or DECnet, use Ethernet II encapsulation. To communicate with these networks, NetWare provides the flexibility of changing the MAC layer encapsulation to Ethernet II (see fig. 8.8). This is done by setting the FRAME parameter in the LOAD NIC_DRIVER command to ETHERNET_II. Other values for the FRAME parameter for Ethernet are ETHERNET_802.2 and ETHERNET_SNAP.

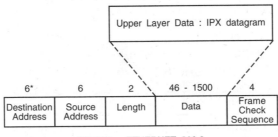

FRAME = ETHERNET_802.3

* Numbers represent byte length

Figure 8.7:
NetWare's default FRAME encapsulation for Ethernet (ETHERNET_802.3).

If ETHERNET_802.2 is used for the FRAME parameter, it implies an IEEE 802.3 MAC layer encapsulation. In addition, the data portion of the IEEE 802.3 frame contains an IEEE 802.2 frame (see fig. 8.9). IEEE 802.2 or *Logical Link Control* (LLC) was discussed in Chapter 6. By using LLC, multiple sessions are possible between *Link Service Access Points* (LSAPs). If NetWare v3.x is being used on a network that uses IEEE 802.2, you should configure the NIC driver to use IEEE 802.2 encapsulation. Experience has shown that not doing this can crash nodes that expect IEEE 802.2 encapsulation.

The *SNAP* in ETHERNET_SNAP stands for *Sub-Network Access Protocol*. SNAP, described in RFC 1042, was developed as a means to send IP datagrams and *Address Resolution Protocols* (ARPs) used in the Internet over IEEE 802.3, IEEE 802.4 (Token Bus), IEEE 802.5 (Token Ring), and FDDI networks. IP datagrams historically have been tied to Ethernet II frames; and

SNAP offers a way of transporting them across non-Ethernet II networks. The SNAP mechanism, however, is general enough to be used by other protocols, such as AppleTalk Phase 2 used for Macintosh networks. NetWare v3.x supports AppleTalk- and TCP/IP-based networks and defines a FRAME value of ETHERNET_SNAP for Ethernet and TOKEN_RING_SNAP for Token Ring networks.

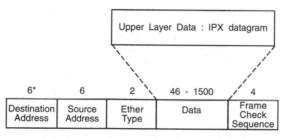

Figure 8.8:
Ethernet II frame encapsulation.

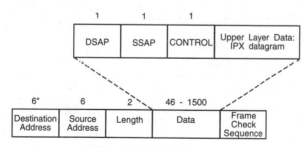

Figure 8.9:
IEEE 802.2 frame encapsulation.

The use of SNAP is illustrated in figure 8.10. The first three bytes of IEEE 802.2 and the SNAP protocol are the same; that is, the LLC headers are the same. This is not surprising because SNAP was designed to use IEEE 802.2. In SNAP, a special value of AA (hex) for the *Destination Service Access Point* (DSAP) and *Source Service Access Point* (SSAP) in the LLC header means that the next five bytes (40 bits) contain a special PROTOCOL IDENTIFIER. The first three bytes of the PROTOCOL IDENTIFIER represent the *Organizational Unit Identifier* (OUI) and, as the name suggests, is unique to an organization. Apple's OUI, for example, is 00 00 F8 (hex). The remaining two bytes contain information similar to the Ether Type field used for Ethernet. The translation of an Ethernet II frame to SNAP format is shown in figure 8.11. The OUI is assumed to be 00 00 F8. In this translation, you should notice that the size of the frame grows by 8 bytes, which represents the SNAP header length. If the original Ethernet II had a maximum size of 1500 bytes for the data size, this translates to a data frame size of 1508. This exceeds the maximum data frame size of 1500 bytes for IEEE 802.3 and potentially can cause problems for IEEE 802.3 networks.

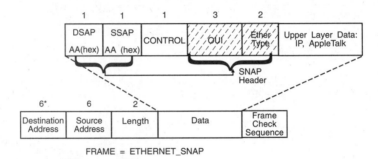

FRAME = ETHERNET_SNAP

* Numbers represent byte length

Figure 8.10:
SNAP frame encapsulation for Ethernet.

For Token Ring, the possible FRAME values are TOKEN_RING and TOKEN_RING_SNAP. TOKEN_RING uses the IEEE 802.2 header in its data portion, and TOKEN_RING_SNAP uses the SNAP header in the data portion of the Token Ring frame (see fig. 8.12).

TOKEN_RING_SNAP and ETHERNET_SNAP can be used for supporting TCP/IP applications on Token Ring and Ethernet, respectively. The different frame types are summarized in table 8.6.

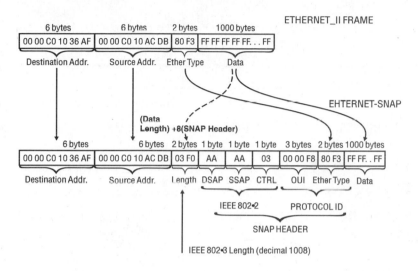

Figure 8.11:
Translation of original ETHERNET II frame to ETHERNET_SNAP in NetWare v3.x.

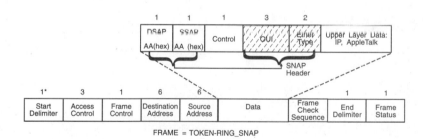

Figure 8.12:
SNAP frame encapsulation for Token Ring.

Table 8.6
FRAME Parameter Values

FRAME	Meaning
ETHERNET_802.3	Default Ethernet encapsulation.
ETHERNET_II	Ethernet II encapsulation. Uses Ether Type value of 8137 (hex) for IPX packets.
ETHENET_802.2	LLC encapsulation in Ethernet data.
ETHERNET_SNAP	SNAP encapsulation in Ethernet data.
TOKEN-RING	Default Token Ring encapsulation. IEEE 802.2 (LLC) encapsulation in Token Ring data.
TOKEN-RING_SNAP	SNAP encapsulation in Token Ring data.

Binding Protocol Stacks to NIC Drivers

Before an NIC driver can receive packets and send them to the appropriate protocol stack, you must specify with which protocol stack it must work. This is done by a process called *binding*, in which an NIC driver is logically associated with a protocol stack.

After the Token Ring driver TOKEN is loaded, it must be bound to the IPX protocol stack. Other protocol stacks, if loaded, also can be used. To use SPX/IPX, Novell's native protocol stack, you must bind it by using the BIND command, as follows:

```
BIND IPX TO TOKEN
```

The BIND command accepts a number of parameters, the most important of which is the NET parameter. The NET parameter must be set to the value of the network address (*cabling number*) of the cabling segment to which the NIC is connected. If this is not specified, the BIND command prompts you for a unique network address. To specify the NET parameter with value AA3F (hex) in the BIND command, issue the following:

```
BIND IPX TO TOKEN NET=AA3F
```

The BIND command needs to be issued for every NIC in the server. If you have more than one NIC of the same type on the server, the BIND command needs to distinguish between the different driver instances. This can be done by including that driver's parameters along with the BIND command. You do not need driver parameters if you bind a protocol to a board name. To register a board name for the driver, it must be loaded by using the NAME parameter.

Running the INSTALL NLM

After the drivers are loaded and protocol stacks are bound to their appropriate drivers, you must run the INSTALL NLM to complete the installation. You do this by issuing the following command:

```
LOAD INSTALL
```

The INSTALL NLM is a menu-driven utility and can be used for a number of tasks, including the following:

- Formatting the server and performing surface analysis
- Creating NetWare partitions
- Mirroring and duplexing server disks
- Creating and configuring server volumes
- Creating and editing STARTUP.NCF and AUTOEXEC.NCF files
- Loading NetWare v3.x disks

You are shown how to use the INSTALL command in the following section.

Installing NetWare v3.x

Suppose, for example, that you need to install a NetWare v3.x server. The name of the server is KALI_ECG. The network address of 6174 is to be used for the cabling segment the first NIC will be connected to. The server's internal network number is 108.

The following requirements must be met before you can install the server:

- The server must be equipped with an Intel 80386 processor or higher.

- The server PC must have networking hardware installed. To test the installation, you must have it connected to the network.

- Backup copies of the NetWare disks.

- DOS disks with version 3.x or higher must be available.

Use the following steps to install the KALI_ECG server:

1. Create a bootable DOS drive C partition at least 3M in size. Leave the remainder of the hard drive for NetWare. You might want to consult your DOS manual on the use of FDISK and FORMAT commands to perform these tasks.

2. Copy SYSTEM-1 and SYSTEM-2 disks into drive C. If your network drivers are not supported in NetWare v3.x disks, copy these to the DOS partition from the disk provided with your network board.

   You now need to assign the file server name and internal network number.

3. Enter SERVER at drive C to start the installation process.

   After a short delay, NetWare returns output similar to the following:

   ```
   Novell NetWare v3.XX (250 user) 2/20/91
   Processor speed: 130
   (Type SPEED at the command prompt for an explanation
   of the speed rating)
   File Server Name:
   ```

4. Enter the file server name. The following appears on-screen:

   ```
   IPX internal network number:
   ```

5. Enter the IPX internal number. A screen similar to the following should appear:

   ```
   Total server memory: 15.7 Megabytes
   Novell NetWare v3.XX (250 user) 2/20/91
   (C) Copyright 1983-1991 Novell Inc.
   All Rights Reserved.
   Thursday December 19, 1991 2:47:03 pm
   :
   ```

The server program is up and running at this point! The server machine uses an *Industry Standard Architecture* (ISA) bus. Issue the following command to load the ISADISK driver NLM so that the server program can communicate with the server disk.

6. Enter LOAD ISADISK to load the disk driver NLM. You should see a message that is similar to the following:

```
Loading module ISADISK.DSK
        NetWare 386 ISA Device Driver
        Version 3.11          February 15, 1991
    Copyright 1991 Novell, Inc. All rights reserved.
    Supported I/O port values are 1F0, 170
    I/O port: 1F0
```

The ISA disk controller board can be set at either port address of 1F0 (hex) or 170 (hex). Your NetWare 386 server has one primary disk controller that is set at port address 1F0 (hex).

7. Select the displayed port address of 1F0 by pressing Enter. The following should appear on-screen:

```
Supported interrupt number values are E, F, B, C
Interrupt number: E
```

8. Select the displayed interrupt number of E (hex) by pressing Enter.

   If your server disks were attached by *Disk Coprocessor Board* (DCB), you would need to run LOAD DISKSET after loading the disk driver. Because this is not the case for your server disks, you need to bypass this step in this example.

9. Enter the following command to load the network driver NLM:

   LOAD *networkdriver*

   In the preceding command syntax, replace *networkdriver* with the name of the driver you are using. Enter the parameters for your NIC in the server machine when prompted to do so.

   NetWare v3.x enables you to use transport protocols other than IPX/SPX to function on the network. You now can make a choice of protocols to be supported on the server. In the following step, the IPX/SPX NetWare transport protocol is used.

10. Bind the IPX/SPX protocol to the network card driver by issuing the following command:

    BIND IPX TO *networkdriver*

    The following should appear on-screen:

    ```
    Network number:
    ```

    Each network card must be assigned the network number that identifies the cabling system to which it is attached. The number is a hex number that is eight hex digits long. You do not need to enter leading zeroes.

11. Enter the network number. A message similar to the following should appear on-screen:

    ```
    IPX LAN protocol bound to networkdriver
    ```

    You now need to prepare the server disk to load the NetWare system files by using the following step.

12. Enter **LOAD INSTALL** to load the INSTALL NLM. The Installation Options menu displays, as shown in figure 8.13.

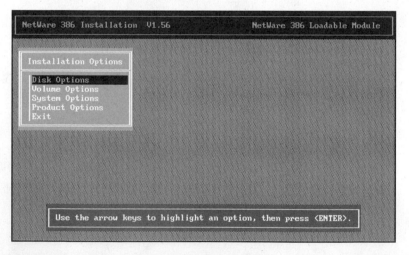

Figure 8.13:
NetWare's Installation Options menu.

The INSTALL program is an NLM and can be used to format server disks, create NetWare partitions, perform surface analyses, mirror disks, create volumes, create file server initialization files, and load operating systems on the server disk.

13. Highlight the Disk Options choice and press Enter. This displays the Available Disk Options menu (see fig. 8.14).

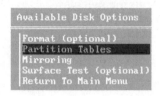

Figure 8.14:
NetWare's Available Disk Options menu.

In the Available Disk Options menu, the Format option is needed only if the drive has never been formatted on DOS or NetWare.

14. Highlight Partition Tables and press Enter to create the NetWare v3.x partition. The Partition Options menu appears, showing you the two partitions that you created.

15. If the partition to be used for NetWare v3.x shows a partition type different from NetWare 386 Partition, delete it by using the Delete Partition option.

16. Next, create a NetWare partition by using the Create NetWare Partition option. You should see a screen similar to the one shown in figure 8.15.

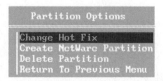

Figure 8.15:
NetWare's Partition Options menu.

The redirection area used for a hot fix is by default 2 percent of the partition space. This number can be increased or decreased, but in this example you need to leave it as is.

17. Press Esc to return to the Available Disk Options menu.

    The `Surface Test` option can be executed next, but for this example, you can bypass this step. The `Surface Test` option is functionally similar to the NetWare v2.x COMPSURF program, as discussed in Chapter 7.

    The `Mirroring` option in the Available Disk Options is used for mirroring the hard disk partition you have just created.

18. Press Esc to return to the Installation Options menu.

    You now need to create the NetWare 386 volumes.

19. Highlight the `Volume Options` choice and press Enter. The Volume Information box displays (see fig. 8.16). Press Ins to add a new volume.

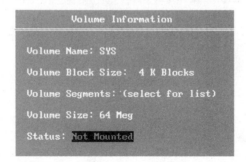

Figure 8.16:
The Volume Information box.

20. Press Esc and answer Yes to the question `Create Volume?`. Press Alt-Esc to return to the console prompt.

21. From the console prompt, enter **MOUNT ALL** to mount all the volumes that you just created. Alternatively, you can use the MOUNT command to mount individual volumes.

    NetWare displays messages that are similar to the following after you execute the MOUNT ALL command:

```
Mounting Volume SYS:
Initializing Transaction Tracking System
9/30/90 10:09pm: Bindery open requested by the SERVER
```

22. Press Alt-Esc to return to the INSTALL NLM.

23. From the Installation Options menu (see fig. 8.13), highlight the
    `System Options` choice and press Enter to create the
    AUTOEXEC.NCF and STARTUP.NCF files (see fig. 8.17).

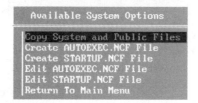

Figure 8.17:
NetWare's Available Systems Options menu.

24. Highlight the `Create AUTOEXEC.NCF File` choice and press Enter.

    The commands in AUTOEXEC.NCF are executed to complete the
    boot process after SERVER.EXE executes commands in the
    STARTUP.NCF file. Because AUTOEXEC.NCF is saved in and runs
    from SYS:SYSTEM, you should place most of the boot commands in
    SYS:SYSTEM for added protection.

25. Use the cursor movement keys and move to the end of the file and
    add the following commands:

    > **MOUNT ALL**
    > **SET ALLOW UNENCRYPTED PASSWORDS=ON**

    Press Esc and save the changes. A box similar to the one shown in
    figure 8.18 appears.

    In the preceding step, the SET ALLOW UNENCRYPTED
    PASSWORDS=ON line is optional. This line is needed only if you
    have older versions of the NetWare utilities on other NetWare
    servers on your network.

26. Press Esc to return to the Available System Options menu. Highlight
    the `Create STARTUP.NCF File` option and press Enter. The Path
    For STARTUP.NCF File menu appears on-screen.

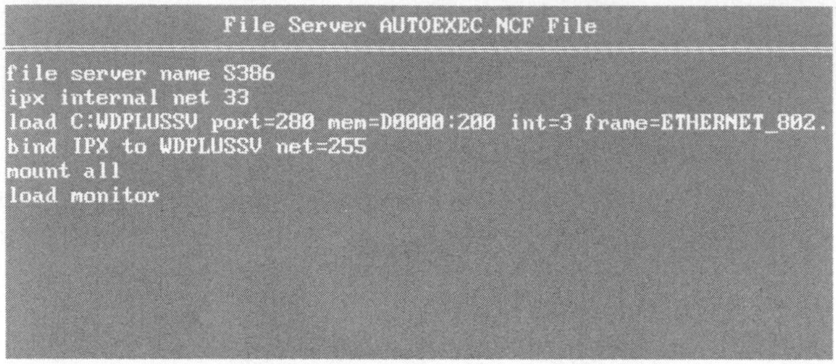

```
           File Server AUTOEXEC.NCF File

file server name S386
ipx internal net 33
load C:WDPLUSSV port=280 mem=D0000:200 int=3 frame=ETHERNET_802.
bind IPX to WDPLUSSV net=255
mount all
load monitor
```

Figure 8.18:
The File Server AUTOEXEC.NCF File box.

27. Press Enter and select the displayed file. A box similar to the one shown in figure 8.19 displays.

```
           File Server STARTUP.NCF File

load ISADISK port=1F0 int=E
```

Figure 8.19:
The File Server STARTUP.NCF File box.

The commands in STARTUP.NCF file are executed by the SERVER.EXE program. SERVER.EXE usually is stored on the same media you boot from, either a DOS partition or floppy disk. It contains the commands to load disk drivers and non-DOS name support for the server.

28. Press Esc and answer Yes to save the STARTUP.NCF file.

You now need to copy the system and public files.

29. Press Esc to return to the Available System Options menu. Highlight the `Copy System and Public Files` option and press Enter. A box appears prompting you to insert the NetWare 386 SYSTEM-2 disk.

30. Place the NetWare 386 SYSTEM-2 disk in drive A and press Esc.

    The Installing System and Public Files box displays, showing a list of files that are being installed on the server disk (see fig. 8.20).

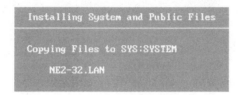

Figure 8.20:
The Installing System and Public Files box.

31. NetWare now prompts you for a number of installation disks that you need to insert in drive A. Follow the instructions as they appear on-screen.

    NetWare displays the message `File Upload Complete` when it finishes copying the floppy disks.

32. Press Esc until NetWare displays the Exit Install prompt. Answer Yes.

    You now need to bring down and reboot the server by using the following step.

33. Bring down the server by typing the following commands from the server console:

        DOWN
        EXIT

34. To bring up the server automatically every time the server machine is turned on, you can add DOS commands in your AUTOEXEC.BAT file to change to the directory containing the system files and to issue the SERVER command.

Upgrading from NetWare v2.x to NetWare v3.x

Although NetWare v2.x is adequate for small- to medium-size networks, NetWare v3.x is more suitable for large enterprise-wide networks. Advances in NetWare technology are likely to be seen in NetWare v3.x before they are seen in NetWare v2.x.

Upgrading to NetWare v3.x

Table 8.7 shows the functional differences between NetWare v2.x and NetWare v3.x. Table 8.8 shows the feature differences. From table 8.7, you can see that the parameter limits in NetWare v3.x are much higher and are unlikely to be exceeded by most systems. In practical terms, this means that NetWare v3.x-based networks can grow to large proportions without encountering any major limitation.

Table 8.7
NetWare v2.x and v3.x Functions

NetWare v2.x	NetWare v3.x
Runs value-added processes	Runs NetWare loadable modules
FSPs limited by 64K data segment	FSPs created dynamically
Maximum file size of 254K	Maximum file size of 4G
1000 files open concurrently	100,000 files open concurrently
200 concurrent TTS transactions	25,000 concurrent TTS transactions
Maximum volume size of 255M	Maximum volume size of 32 terabytes
100 concurrent users	1000 concurrent users (NetWare 1000)
4 LAN adapters per server	16 LAN adapters per server

NetWare v2.x	NetWare v3.x
Allows encrypted passwords	Can enforce encrypted passwords
Directory caching and hashing	Improved directory caching and hashing
Allows only IPX/SPX, AFP, and NetBIOS protocols	Allows the same protocols as NetWare v2.x, with the additional options of NetWare STREAMS, OSI, TCP/IP, TOPS, SMP, and TLI
No dynamic configuration	Dynamic configuration
No virtual console	Virtual console through the RCONSOLE utility
API support	Very rich API support
32,000 directory entries per volume (16-bit FAT)	2 million directory entries per volume (32-bit FAT)

Table 8.8
NetWare v2.x and v3.x Features

Feature Summary	286 NetWare ELS I	286 NetWare ELS II	286 NetWare Advanced	NetWare v2.x	NetWare v3.x
Maximum disk storage	2 internal hard disks	2 internal hard disks	2G	2G	32 terabytes
Maximum number of open files	256M	256M	256M	256M	4G
Maximum number of users	4	8	100	100	100,000
Bus support	MCA, ISA	MCA, ISA	MCA, ISA	MCA, ISA	MCA, ISA, EISA

continues

Table 8.8
Continued

Feature Summary	286 NetWare ELS I	286 NetWare ELS II	286 NetWare Advanced	NetWare v2.x	NetWare v3.x
DOS support	3.x only	2.x, 3.x, 4.x	2.x, 3.x, 4.x	2.x, 3.x, 4.x, 5.x	2.x, 3.x, 4.x, 5.x
Windows support	No	Yes	Yes	Yes	Yes
OS/2 support	No	Yes	Yes	Yes	Yes
Mac support	No	Yes	Yes	Yes	Yes
NetBIOS support	No	Yes	Yes	Yes	Yes
IPX/SPX	Yes	Yes	Yes	Yes	Yes
Dynamic configuration	No	No	No	No	Yes
Workgroup management	No	No	No	No	Yes
Password encryption	No	Yes	Yes	Yes	Yes
SFT level	I	I	I	II	III
Operation	286 Ded.	86 Ded. 286 Ded. 286 Nonded.	286 Ded. 286 Nonded.		386 Ded.
Application server processes	No	VAP	VAP	VAP	NLM
Alternative protocols	No	No	No	No	Yes
LAN drivers	1	1	4	4	16
Multiple name space	No	No	No	No	Yes

Feature Summary	286 NetWare ELS I	286 NetWare ELS II	286 NetWare Advanced	NetWare v2.x	NetWare v3.x
Trustee rights at file level	No	No	No	No	Yes
Extensible file server	No	No	No	No	Yes
Virtual console	No	No	No	No	Yes
Workgroup Manager	No	No	No	Yes	Yes

The following lists some of the reasons to switch from NetWare v2.x to NetWare v3.x.

- NetWare v2.x parameter limitations.

- NetWare v3.x is easier to install and maintain.

- NetWare v3.x enables you use larger file sizes and more directory entries than you can with NetWare v2.x.

- NetWare v3.x offers a wide variety of transport protocol support.

- NetWare v3.x offers better integration with non-Novell networks.

- Future enhancements are likely to continue on NetWare v3.x.

When NetWare v2.x networks come up against limitations described in table 8.7, you might want to migrate to NetWare v3.x. You can upgrade to NetWare v3.x by using the UPGRADE utility that comes with NetWare v3.x.

Using the UPGRADE Utility

Figure 8.21 shows a diagram of how you can use the UPGRADE utility to upgrade to NetWare v3.x. Although a number of precautionary backups are needed while you are using UPGRADE, these backups are well justified if you have any problems, such as a server crash, during the upgrade. If your server crashes during the upgrade, you need to repeat the upgrade process.

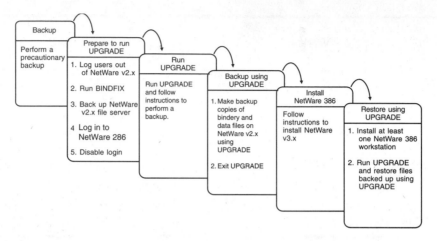

Figure 8.21:
Using the UPGRADE utility. (Graphic courtesy of Learning Group International)

Although the UPGRADE utility works quite well, a few annoying problems might occur, particularly concerning security rights. Some security rights from pre-NetWare v2.2 do not convert over to the NetWare v3.x perfectly. For this reason, many Network Managers prefer to back up all the data files on NetWare v2.x, create user accounts from scratch on NetWare v3.x, and then restore the data files to the NetWare v3.x server.

If users have been created by using the batch creation utility MAKEUSER (discussed in Chapter 10), re-creating the NetWare v3.x users is a fairly simple task. Good documentation on a user's configuration is extremely useful for re-creating the user on NetWare v3.x. Third-party utilities, such as BindView Plus, can assist in obtaining this documentation.

Summary

In this chapter, you examined the architecture and features of NetWare v3.x. You learned the type of factors that can affect the configuration of the server hardware and of the server memory. You also learned how to install NetWare v3.x on a server, how to initialize the server volumes, and how to configure the server's network interface.

Managing NetWare Servers

In the previous chapters, you learned how to install and configure a NetWare-based network. Several factors affect network performance. In this chapter you learn what these factors are and how you can improve the performance of your network. Some of the decisions that affect network performance can be made before installing a network, whereas others can be made only after installation. Decisions made prior to network installation include the choice of server machine platforms, network adapters, disk subsystems, and so on. To fine-tune the network after installation, you must monitor how well the network is performing. Some of these tools, such as MONITOR NLM for NetWare v3.x, are provided by Novell. Third-party tools such as the Frye Utilities perform similar functions and work on both NetWare v2.x and NetWare v3.x.

Future versions of NetWare are expected to improve on network management and performance monitoring functions. Protocol analyzers such as Novell's LANalyzer are powerful tools for improving network performance. The purpose of such monitoring tools is to analyze current performance, checking for bottlenecks. When you discover the bottlenecks, you can take steps toward eliminating them.

Understanding the Factors Affecting Network Performance

Because the network is made up of hardware and software components, the factors that affect network performance are hardware- and software-related.

This section enables you to have better understanding of the hardware and software performance factors. There is a strong relationship between hardware and software factors, and both must be considered together to evaluate the performance of a network. This chapter first examines the hardware performance factors, and then the software factors.

Hardware Components Affecting Server Performance

The following major hardware-related factors affect network performance:

- Disk subsystem: speed and storage capacity
- Network adapters: speed, bus width, and bus interface
- Network access technology
- Speed of server and workstation computers

The hardware-related factors are not confined to any single piece of equipment, such as the server machine, but also include the type of network adapters at the server and the workstation, and the network access speed and method (CSMA/CD, Token Access, and so on). One of the most important hardware elements is the server computer, its disk subsystem, and the type of network adapter inside the server. In NetWare LANs, the server computer plays a central role; any improvements on the server hardware directly affect network performance.

Sometimes, installing a faster computer as the server does not necessarily improve performance. Understanding this point is important because the performance of the entire network is limited by its slowest component. If the physical layer is the slowest component of the network, for example, replacing the server machine or disk subsystem with a faster component does not improve performance in general.

Some of the tools described here can help you determine which component is the cause of the bottleneck. Generally, however, no cut-and-dry formulas for determining performance bottlenecks currently exist. Most experienced network managers use a combination of knowledge of their network, knowledge of underlying technology, and good common sense and intuition to detect and isolate performance-related problems. Some promising technology exists in the area of expert systems to better solve these problems. But expert systems are only as good as the people programming them; they can help guide you to a solution to the problem but cannot necessarily solve the problem for you.

Disk Subsystem

The most important function a NetWare server performs is to provide file services. Because the server files are stored on the server disk, a fast disk subsystem results in faster file services and, from a user's perspective, a faster network.

The data-transfer rate between the CPU and the disk is determined by the disk, the disk controller, and the bus interfaces. The older PC AT disks that used MFM encoding are among the slowest hard disks. Today, most disks use a higher level of RLL encoding, allowing them to pack more data per sector, which means that the disk has to rotate smaller distances (requiring less time) to deliver the same amount of data. This translates to faster data-transfer rates.

The types of disks that give the best performance in the marketplace today are disks based on Integrated Device Electronics (IDE), Enhanced Small Devices Interface (ESDI), and Small Computers Systems Interface (SCSI).

The IDE disks replace the older AT-style disks and provide a higher performance interface between the computer and the disk, enabling them to be faster than the AT-style disks. The ESDI interface developed out of the I/O interface used in minicomputer environments and is faster than the IDE disks. The SCSI interface is the most versatile because it allows multiple devices to be connected to an external I/O bus. SCSI disk drives usually are external; they have their own power supply and therefore tend to be more reliable.

The disk manufacturers seem to have voted on the SCSI interface as the best technique for providing high-capacity, high-speed disks. The current SCSI interface, called the *SCSI-II interface,* has some performance improvements over the older SCSI interface.

SCSI devices can transfer data at rates of 32 Mbps, which is well over the speed of Ethernet (10 Mbps), Token Ring (16 Mbps), and ARCnet PLUS (20 Mbps). In actual practice, these devices achieve smaller data-transfer rates if used with the ISA-style bus because the ISA bus currently is limited to transfer rates of 4 Mbps to 8 Mbps. Therefore, for best performance, use SCSI devices with either the microchannel or EISA bus that can support higher data rates.

A new type of disk subsystem, called RAID, may become popular in the future. It has the potential of providing a high degree of reliability through a fault-tolerant architecture. *RAID* (Redundant Array of Inexpensive Disks) allows data to be distributed across multiple inexpensive disks, so that if any disk were to fail, data can be recovered based on information on the other active disks.

Network Adapters

In a networking environment, the network adapters determine the data-transfer rate through the network media. Not all adapters for a network technology are created equal. There are many manufacturers of Ethernet adapters, for example; although they all comply with the Ethernet standard of 10 Mbps, they have different effective data rates. Network adapters from 3COM are quite popular, but there are at least two types of adapters for IBM PCs: 3COM EtherLink and 3COM EtherLink Plus. The 3COM EtherLink Plus is a higher-performance card, and is therefore more expensive. It has more packet buffers and faster circuitry. Ideally, all stations on a network should have high-performance cards to obtain the maximum possible data-transfer rate. If cost is a major factor, at least the server computer and external routers should have a high-performance card. Using a high-performance network adapter for the server can dramatically improve the network performance.

The following factors affect the performance of a network adapter:

- Media access scheme
- Raw bit rate
- Onboard processor
- NIC-to-host transfer

The *media access scheme* refers to the arbitration mechanism, inherent in baseband LANs, that limits how the messages are placed on the media. Examples of this are CSMA/CD, used in Ethernet and IEEE 802.3, and Token

Access, used in IBM Token Ring (IEEE 802.5). Token Access gives a deterministic performance even under heavy network loads, whereas CSMA/CD is susceptible to reduced throughput because of collisions under heavy loads. Under light loads, on the other hand, the CSMA/CD access method is simpler and faster than Token Access.

The *raw bit rate* is the maximum bit rate possible on a given medium. The effective bit rate (taking into account protocol overhead, and queue and processing delays) is much less. The raw bit rate represents an upper limit for the medium.

Effective use of an onboard processor can speed up a network adapter. If the firmware for the NIC is poorly written, however, it can have just the opposite effect as that seen in the earlier IBM PC Broadband LAN adapters. Some vendors implement upper-layer protocol processing on the NIC card itself for better overall throughput. An example of such an NIC is Federal Technologies' EXOS series board that has onboard TCP/IP processing.

Data arriving on the network adapter needs to be transferred into the host computer's memory. The NIC connection to the host channel can be implemented using shared memory, DMA, or I/O ports. NICs may use any of these methods or a combination of them. Observations have shown that shared memory is the fastest, followed by I/O ports, with DMA the slowest. Avoid NICs that use DMA exclusively for transferring data, as these probably are slow NICs. Some cards use a combination of shared memory and DMA, which gives them a certain level of parallelism that can improve their performance.

The data width of the bus interface has a dramatic effect on NIC-to-host transfer speeds. Current data widths are 8, 16, or 32 bits. The wider the data width, the faster the data transfer. EISA and Micro Channel NICs are faster than ISA NICs. It is a good strategy to use an EISA or Micro Channel machine with an EISA or Micro Channel adapter at the server because network traffic is concentrated at this point.

Try to avoid mixing network adapters from different vendors on one LAN. Although all vendors claim to follow a standard, important implementation differences that can affect the performance of a network may exist between them. Some Ethernet vendors implement the random-time backoff algorithm differently, for example, so that in case of Ethernet bus contention and collision, they will timeout before network adapters from other vendors. In practical terms, this means that these network adapters access the LAN bus before network adapters from other vendors. Another way to look at this is to see these network adapters as "poor citizens" on the network. One way to handle these network adapters is to isolate them in their separate LAN segment, where they have minimum impact on other stations on the network.

Another property of most PC LANs, and LANs based on the IEEE standards, is that the bigger (in geographical size) they are, the smaller their network utilization is. This factor is often overlooked during the design of backbone LANs to span large distances. Network administrators are surprised by the drop in network utilization, and hence data throughput, as LAN size increases. The reason for this is a bit technical but very interesting and is explained next.

Network utilization is defined as the percentage of time spent in transferring data, not including the time spent in packet processing and transmission delays. One can estimate the maximum utilization achievable by assuming that under the best possible conditions, there will be zero processing delay and queue delay, but you cannot avoid the transmission delay due to the finite propagation speed of the signal.

The Data Transmit Time (Tx) is the time it takes to deliver data to the LAN media for a given transmission rate. The transmission delay (Td) is caused by the finite propagation speed of signals in the LAN media. Under the highest possible data-transfer rate, the messages are sent one after another with minimal delays. The message consists of a channel-use time of Tx and a propagation delay (nonuse) time of Td. The actual utilization (*U*) is the fraction of useful time spent transmitting data. You can make this determination by using the following formula:

$$U = Tx / (Tx + Td)$$

$$= 1 / (1 + Td/Tx)$$

$$U = 1 / (1 + a) \qquad (1)$$

in which a = Td/Tx.

If the LAN data rate for transmitting a packet of size *P* bits is *D* bps, then

$$Tx = P/D \text{ seconds} \qquad (2)$$

If the propagation velocity of signal in media is V meters/sec and the size of the LAN is L meters, then

$$Td = L/V \text{ seconds} \qquad (3)$$

Studies show that the average packet size for most LAN applications is small (about 128 bytes). Using this, you can compute the network utilization of the 10BASE-T LAN.

In the 10BASE-T LAN of figure 9.1, the maximum length of the LAN will be 200 meters, not including the backplane. The backplane CSMA/CD bus in the 10BASE-T concentrator has a length of about 0.5 meters. Using the formulas for 10BASE-T LAN, and assuming a signal propagation speed of 0.7 times speed of light in vacuum, you can make the following calculation:

P (Packet size) = 128×8 bits = 1024 bits

D (Data Transfer Rate) = 10 Mbps (fixed for Ethernet)

L (Length of LAN) = 200.5 meters

V (Signal Propagation speed) = $0.7 \times$ speed of light in vacuum

$$= 0.7 \times 3 \times 100{,}000{,}000$$

$$= 2.1 \times 100{,}000{,}000$$

$Tx = P/D = 1024/10$ Mbps = 102.4 microseconds

$Td = L/V = 200.5/(2.1 \times 100{,}000{,}000) = 0.95$ microseconds

$a = Td/Tx = 0.95/102.4 = 0.0093$

U (10BASE-T) = $1/(1 + a) = 1/(1 + 0.0093) = 99$ percent

Figure 9.1 also shows a larger LAN, such as an IEEE 802.3 10BASE5 LAN that has a maximum size of 2800 meters. Repeating the calculations with the 10BASE5 parameters gives the following result:

P (Packet size) = 128×8 bits = 1024 bits

D (Data Transfer Rate) = 10 Mbps (fixed for Ethernet)

L (Length of LAN) = 2800 meters

V (Signal Propagation speed) = $2.1 \times 100{,}000{,}000$ meters/sec

$Tx = P/D = 1024/10$ Mbps = 102.4 microseconds

$Td = L/V = 2800/(2.1 \times 100{,}000{,}000) = 13.3$ microseconds

$a = Td/Tx = 13.3/102.4 = 0.13$

U (10BASE5) = $1/(1 + a) = 1/(1 + 0.13) = 88.4$ percent

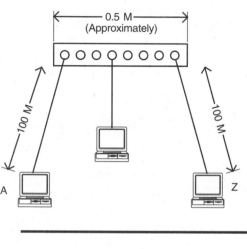

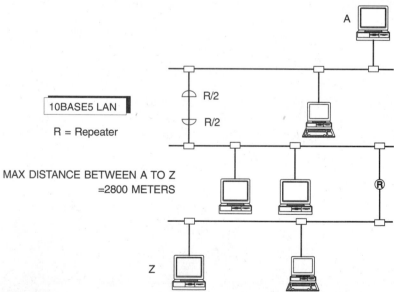

Figure 9.1:
A larger 10BASE-T LAN.

A drop in performance of about 10 percent is noted between 10BASE-T (99%) and 10BASE5 (88.4%). These calculations do not include processing and queuing delays at the network adapters. Actual network utilization is much less if these additional delays are taken into account; nevertheless, it explains why connecting a 10BASE-T LAN to a 10BASE5 by means of a repeater results in a drop in performance for the 10BASE-T stations. One solution to this problem is to connect the 10BASE-T LANs to the 10BASE5 through bridges, so that the CSMA/CD mechanism is partitioned into separate domains (see fig. 9.2).

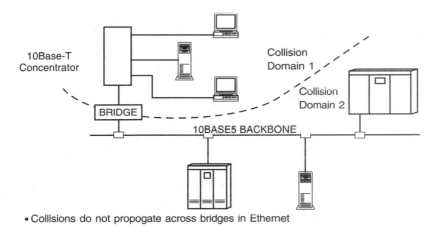

Figure 9.2:
Partitioned CSMA/CD mechanism.

CPU Speed of Server

A fast server computer executes the NetWare operating system code faster and gives better performance. Server CPU performance is often rated in MIPS (millions of instructions per second).

The overall performance of the server system speed can be measured for NetWare v3.x server's, and this number can be used as a speed index to fine-tune the server's performance.

When NetWare v3.x loads, using the SERVER.EXE program, it performs a system speed test. The purpose of this speed test is to inform the network administrator of the server's operating speed. Some Intel 80386-based machines come with selectable speeds; during system startup time they may be operating at speeds as low as 6 MHz or 8 MHz. A low speed is an indication that the server is not operating at its maximum clock speed and that server performance will be affected accordingly. Actually, the speed rating is a function of more than the CPU clock speed. It is a measure of the following factors:

- CPU type
- CPU clock speed
- Memory speed
- Memory wait states
- Speed and size of CPU cache
- Overall system design

Because of the preceding factors, the speed rating is a good indication of the server's overall performance. A higher rating indicates a faster system. Table 9.1 shows the speed ratings of different server machines. From this table, you can see that the Compaq 386S, which has a 80386SX CPU at 16 MHz, has a speed rating of 98, whereas a 80386 CPU running at the same 16 MHz clock has a speed rating of 121 because of its wider data bus. Properly designed 80486 machines can have speed ratings of over 600. The speed rating also indicates that computers requiring memory wait states should be avoided as server machines.

Table 9.1
Speed Index Rating

Computer	Chip	Clock speed	Wait state	Rating
Compaq	386S	80386SX	1	98
Novell	386AE	80386	1	121
Compaq	386/25	80386	0	242

The server speed test is a simple loop that runs for approximately 0.16 seconds and counts the number of times a given piece of code can be executed in less than 2/100ths of a second. A larger number of iterations indicates a faster machine. The flowchart in figure 9.3 shows the speed test. Before the speed test begins, the floppy drive is shut off. (Some computers automatically switch to a slower speed when the system floppy is accessed, which affects the speed rating.) The piece of code executed checks the timer to see whether three clock ticks (0.16 seconds) have elapsed. This operation involves a number of instructions that move data from CPU registers and memory. A faster CPU and faster memory increment the counter to a larger value in the same amount of time. The counter is divided by 1000; the result is displayed as the speed index. A speed rating of 242 means that the counter was incremented 242,000 times in three clock ticks.

Software Aspects Affecting Server Performance

The software factors that determine network performance focus primarily on the Network Operating System. Because the bulk of the NOS runs on the server computer, software performance usually is concerned with fine-tuning the NOS operation on the server.

Aspects that affect server performance are as follows:

- Server memory management
- Server file caching, directory caching, and hashing
- Elevator seeking
- Tuning server parameters

Server Memory: NetWare v3.x versus NetWare v2.x

Server memory is allocated in NetWare v3.x on a dynamic basis, depending on the situation at hand. NetWare v3.x does its best to allocate memory so that overall system performance is improved. It occasionally needs some help from the network administrators through use of SET parameter commands, which are examined in greater detail later.

The NetWare v2.x scheme of memory allocation is not so flexible. Most of these problems occur because of the 64K-segmented architecture of the Intel 80286 microprocessor on which NetWare v2.x is based. NetWare v2.x is written in assembly language. To keep the code efficient, it tries to avoid using segment arithmetic for data access. This means that internal data segments end up confined to memory segments of no more than 64K. This has some direct consequences in NetWare v2.x performance, such as a limit to the number of File Service Processes at the server, which limits the number of file requests that can be handled simultaneously.

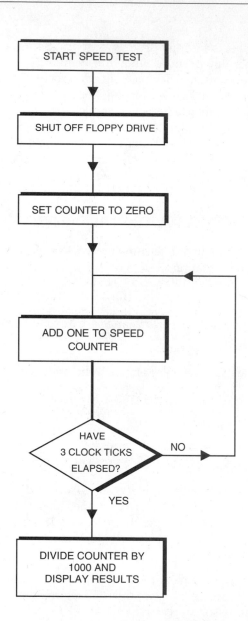

Figure 9.3:
The speed test.

Segmentation remains with NetWare v3.x and the Intel 80386 microprocessor, but the segment size is 4G (gigabytes). NetWare uses 4G segments for program code and data (called the *flat memory* model). Because the segment size is larger than the RAM available on most machines, this is not a problem.

Caching and Hashing

Memory that remains after allocating space for the NetWare operating system kernel, data tables, and NLM processes and applications is used for file caching. *File caching* is an attempt to substitute fast RAM for the slower disk memory. The difference in speed between RAM and most disks is in the order of 100 to 1. Substituting the use of RAM wherever possible can result in a file access 10 to 100 times faster than disk access. If disk speeds were the same as RAM speeds, there would be no need for file caching. As long as disks are slower than RAM, file caching can be used to improve file access.

In file caching, server RAM is used to keep the most frequently used disk blocks. Disk blocks ahead of the one currently being read may be prefetched in server RAM, in anticipation of subsequent disk-block needs. These techniques can improve server performance on server reads. For server file writes, the disk block is written out first to cache and then to the server disk by a background process controlled by the SET parameter value of DIRTY DISK CACHE DELAY TIME.

Normally, a copy of the server directory is kept on the server disk. Many file operations require the reading of the disk's directory entries. These operations can be speeded up if the directory is maintained in RAM (this is called *directory caching*). To further accelerate access to the desired directory entry, a directory hashing function can be used to localize the search for a directory entry. Both NetWare v3.x and NetWare v2.x implement file caching and directory caching and hashing, provided that enough RAM space is available to implement these features.

Elevator Seeking

NetWare uses elevator seeking to minimize excessive arm movements of the disk when satisfying multiple read/write requests from several workstations. If the I/O operations were performed in the order in which they arrive, disk requests arriving in random order could lead to excessive disk arm movements, called *disk thrashing*. One way to avoid this problem is to sort the disk operations by the track number of the disk blocks being accessed, rather than by their order of arrival. The disk arm needs to make fewer sweeps to handle the disk requests. This is called *elevator seeking*.

Elevator seeking not only results in faster I/O operations but also reduces wear and tear on the disk.

Tuning NetWare v3.x Performance

NetWare v3.x does a good job of monitoring its resources, and changes parameters automatically to try to improve server performance. For most system resources, the parameters specify minimum and maximum limits as well as a wait-time limit that specifies how rapidly a resource is allocated. The wait-time limit parameters smooth out peak load demands for system resources so that the operating system does not overreact to a transient demand situation.

These parameters also can be controlled or viewed through the SET command. When you type **SET** at the DOS prompt, NetWare v3.x lists the following configuration categories and asks which category you want to view:

1. Communications

2. Memory

3. File caching

4. Directory caching

5. File system

6. Locks

7. Transaction tracking

8. Disk

9. Miscellaneous

From a performance point of view, many of these parameters are closely associated. The SET commands for memory, file caching, and directory caching affect the server's memory performance. The SET commands for the file system, locks, and transaction tracking categories, for example, affect file system performance. Because of this interrelationship, the SET commands are grouped and discussed here as follows:

- Memory performance tuning
- File system performance tuning
- Communications performance tuning
- Operating system processes tuning
- Threshold and warning parameters

To change a SET parameter value, the general command is

```
SET parameter description=New parameter value
```

To view a parameter's current setting, use

```
SET parameter description
```

Certain parameters cannot be set at the console prompt or in the AUTOEXEC.NCF file. They can be set only in the STARTUP.NCF file. A list of these parameters follows:

```
AUTO REGISTER MEMORY ABOVE 16 MEGABYTES
AUTO TTS BACKOUT FLAG
CACHE BUFFER SIZE
MAXIMUM PHYSICAL RECEIVE PACKET SIZE
MAXIMUM SUBDIRECTORY TREE DEPTH
MINIMUM PACKET RECEIVE BUFFERS
```

Memory Performance Tuning for NetWare v3.x

NetWare v3.x manages memory in a much more flexible manner than NetWare v2.x. Generally, this memory management is transparent to the user, but you need to understand some principles that can help you take corrective action if memory becomes a bottleneck.

The server memory is divided into three NetWare NOS application areas:

1. File-cache buffer pool
2. Permanent memory pool
3. Alloc memory pool

The permanent and alloc memory pools grow or shrink according to actual demand. Memory not allocated to these pools and the NOS kernel is used for file caching.

The file-cache buffer pool is used to store file blocks from the most frequently used files. Two pools (called *movable* and *nonmovable*) interact with the file-cache buffer pool. They obtain their memory from the file-cache buffer pool and, when done, return memory to it. The movable pool is used for system tables that change size, such as FATs and hash tables. Tables and objects in the movable pool can be moved in memory to prevent excessive memory fragmentation. The nonmovable pool is used for *NetWare Loadable Modules* (NLMs).

The permanent pool is used for long-term memory needs such as directory cache buffers and packet receive buffers. Although it is called permanent memory, it is quite dynamic. A portion of it is static but the rest is semi-dynamic. Communications buffers are an example of permanent pool memory usage. When NetWare loads and initializes itself, it sets up a certain number of communication buffers. With rising network activity, NetWare allocates additional communication buffers to store the extra data packets. These buffers are allocated from permanent memory. Once allocated, they will not be released even if network activity subsides. The reasoning behind this approach is to allocate enough resources to handle peak loads on the network.

The alloc memory pool is used to store information about the following:

- Drive mappings
- Service request buffers
- SAP tables
- Open/Lock files and semaphores
- User connection information
- NLMs
- Queue manager tables
- Messages queued for broadcasting

The alloc memory is used temporarily for fulfilling short-term processing needs. During NetWare execution, data objects may need to be created dynamically and destroyed after the NOS finishes using them. Memory used for the alloc pool is managed by a linked list of free memory blocks. Using this linked list approach, the NOS can quickly find the memory it needs. When memory is needed, it is allocated from this free list. When released, it returns to the free memory list where it can be reused.

NetWare tries to allocate memory for NLMs from the alloc pool. As memory requirements for NLMs increase, the alloc pool is depleted. To satisfy the NLM memory requirement, NetWare borrows memory from the file-cache buffer pool. Once borrowed, this memory is not returned to the file-cache pool, even if the NLMs are unloaded. The worst-case situation would be that many NLMs are frequently loaded and unloaded. Under these circumstances, permanently borrowing memory from the file-cache area could deplete it severely, which would degrade the server performance. NetWare has control mechanisms to prevent this *memory leakage* from occurring. SET commands can be used to limit the size of the alloc pool. The alloc pool has a default of 2M but can be set as high as 16M and as low as 50K.

The following SET command restricts the size of the alloc pool and can be used to solve the file-cache buffer pool leakage problem:

`SET MAXIMIMUM ALLOC SHORT TERM MEMORY=n`

in which n is the maximum size (in bytes) of alloc pool memory. The valid range is from 50,000 bytes to 16,777,216 (16M). The default value is 209,712 bytes (2M).

File caching also affects server memory performance. File caching allows data blocks from files that are being read or written to be kept in RAM, thus speeding access to these files. File caching is independent of other caching techniques such as those used by disk-caching controllers. The file-caching tunable parameters deal with the number of file-cache buffers, concurrent disk writes, and disk synchronization (cache-write delays).

Other SET parameters that affect server memory performance are described next. To use the parameters with the SET command, the SET command must precede the parameter, as shown in the preceding example (for changing the maximum alloc short-term memory).

`MAXIMUM ALLOC SHORT TERM MEMORY=n`

This determines the amount of memory (n) the server allocates (when it is booted) for alloc pool. Its value can range from 50,000 to 16,777,216 bytes, with a default value of 2,097,152. Normally, you should not have to change this value, but you can decrease it if you need some additional memory, such as loading other NLMs. Increasing this value is easier to determine; if there is insufficient memory in the alloc pool, the server starts issuing warning messages that operations cannot be completed. Increment the value in units of 1K until the messages disappear.

`AUTO REGISTER MEMORY ABOVE 16 MEGABYTES=[ON|OFF]`

EISA machines can support more than 16M of RAM. Under certain circumstances, you may have to use this parameter to allow NetWare to handle extra memory correctly. Setting this parameter in the STARTUP.NCF file allows NetWare to register this memory when it first comes up. This parameter cannot be set at the console prompt or in the AUTOEXEC.NCF file. NetWare needs to know all the memory available when it first boots up. The default value is ON. If you are using a board that can address only 24 bits of RAM, you may have to set this value to OFF, or you may have corrupted lower memory because 24 bits can address only 16M. Any higher address value maps to lower memory.

CACHE BUFFER SIZE=n

Because NetWare v3.x can support variable disk block sizes, NetWare enables you to set the size of the cache buffer that can hold disk blocks. The default value of 4096 bytes also is the default size of the disk block and should be adequate in most situations. If a larger disk block size is being used, you may want to increase this value because it can improve performance. Be aware that NetWare does not mount any volume disk block size smaller than the cache size. This parameter must be set in the STARTUP.NCF file; it cannot be set in the AUTOEXEC.NCF file or at the console prompt. Legal parameter values are 4,096; 8,192; and 16,384. A convenient way to experiment with different parameter values is the cache size -c parameter that can be used with SERVER.EXE (SERVER -c cacheSize).

MINIMUM FILE CACHE BUFFERS=n

File caching can be used to improve the performance of file I/O operations. NetWare uses memory remaining after allocation of the operating system and NLMs for file caching. In NetWare v3.x, you can set aside a certain amount of memory for file caching. The file-cache memory also acts as a memory reserve. The server draws on this memory reserve for its needs. The problem with this is that the file-cache memory can be severely depleted, which can seriously affect server performance. A certain amount of memory should always be reserved for file caching (this parameter can be used to set the minimum amount reserved for file caching). If file I/O seems slow, or long delays and timeouts occur for network operations, the file cache may have fallen below the minimum value necessary for acceptable server performance. If such is the case, the value of this parameter should be increased. The default value for this parameter is 20, which also is the minimum value. The number should be increased gradually to a maximum of 1000 (the file-cache buffer's usage using MONITOR NLM). Using an extremely high value for this parameter could result in wasted memory that could impact other critical data structures that need memory. The NetWare server should give warning if the file-cache buffer reserve falls below the minimum level.

Tuning Server File System Performance for NetWare v3.x

File caching allows faster access of frequently used files by keeping the disk blocks in fast RAM for read and write operations. Write operations are performed in a delayed fashion, with the writes being done first to RAM. A background process writes these disk buffers (dirty buffers) to the disk during less critical moments but within the time specified by the Dirty Disk Cache Delay Time parameter.

File caching affects both memory and file system performance. The minimum file-cache buffers parameter, discussed in the section on memory performance tuning, affects both memory performance and file system performance.

Directory caching also plays an important role in file system performance, because it allows fast access to frequently used directories. Directory tables are kept in directory buffers in RAM, and the server uses a "least recently" algorithm to keep the directory entries in memory. When the server starts, NetWare starts with a *minimum directory cache buffers* (default is 20). When the minimum directory cache buffers is used up, the server must wait for a *directory cache allocation wait time* (default 2.2 seconds) before allocating another buffer. Under periods of sustained directory access, the number of directory entries could increase to the *maximum directory cache buffers* (default 400). As directory-cache buffers increase, the number of buffers available for file caching decreases. Hence, there is a trade-off between directory caching and file caching; they must be carefully balanced for optimum performance.

The following are SET parameters for file system performance.

MAXIMUM CONCURRENT DISK CACHE WRITES= *n*

Unlike DOS, NetWare can perform several disk writes concurrently. One reason for this is that NetWare does not rely on the single-threaded BIOS on the machine to perform I/O. The disk drivers for NetWare allow multithreaded or concurrent I/O. To speed up disk I/O operations, a number of requests can be placed on the elevator mechanism. The *elevator mechanism* allows the disk head to move in continuous sweeps across the disk, which are more efficient than the random back-and-forth movements. This mechanism can be used to set the number of write requests (n) that can be queued on the disk elevator for a single sweep across the disk surface. A high value for this parameter makes write requests more efficient; a lower number makes read requests more efficient. One way to decide how to set this parameter is to monitor the number of dirty cache buffers using MONITOR. If this number says that a majority of the buffers (70 percent or more) are dirty buffers, the writes are more predominant than reads. In this case, you can improve performance by increasing this parameter. The value ranges from 10 to 100, with a default of 50.

DIRTY DISK CACHE DELAY TIME= n

To improve disk I/O, the server performs delayed writes by writing first to RAM and then from RAM to disk during idle times. NetWare enables you to control how long this wait period should be. If there are many small requests, buffering the writes in RAM before writing them out to the disk is more efficient. This is especially true if the write requests are contiguous sectors on the disk because these can be combined as a smaller number of disk writes. A disk-cache delay time that is too small is the same as disabling the delayed write mechanism. Without delayed writes, server performance could suffer. The default value of 3.3 seconds is long enough for a typical mix of disk I/O operations that take place on the server. The value can be as small as 0.1 seconds, but not more than 10 seconds. An extremely high value can make the server file system more vulnerable in the event of a server crash because many disk I/O operations would be in RAM and not committed to the disk.

MINIMUM FILE CACHE BUFFER REPORT THRESHOLD= n

NetWare issues a warning if the number of file-cache buffers falls below a certain threshold. The first warning that the number of cache buffers is getting too low is issued when the following condition is met: Current number of cache buffers + minimum file-cache buffers <= minimum file-cache buffer report threshold. Suppose that the minimum file-cache buffers parameter is set to 20, and the minimum file-cache buffer report threshold is set to 30; when the current number of cache buffers is 50, the previously described condition is met and a warning message is issued. If the number of cache buffers continues to fall to the minimum file-cache buffers, the warning `Cache memory allocator exceeded minimum cache buffer left limit` is issued on the server console. The default value of the threshold is 20, which means that if the minimum file-cache buffer is set to its default of 20, the first warning is issued when the cache number falls to 40. The minimum value of this parameter is 0; it cannot exceed 1000.

MINIMUM FILE DELETE WAIT TIME= *n*

When a file is deleted, it is not purged immediately from the volume. This parameter controls the minimum amount of time a file should remain on the volume before being purged. Files that have been deleted will not be purged for at least this time, even if the volume is full and the user is unable to create new files. The parameter value ranges from zero to seven days, with a default of 1 minute 5.9 seconds.

FILE DELETE WAIT TIME= *n*

When a file is deleted, it is not purged immediately from the volume. This parameter controls the amount of time a file should remain on the volume before being purged. Files that have been deleted will not be purged for this time. After this time, the server is free to purge these files. The server keeps at least 1/32nd of its disk space free, and starts purging files (starting with the oldest file) to meet this criteria. The parameter value ranges from zero seconds to seven days, with a default of 5 minutes 29.6 seconds. A small value for this parameter could slow down the server if many deletions are being made. A large value could adversely impact availability of disk space if the server disks were almost full.

MINIMUM DIRECTORY CACHE BUFFERS= *n*

In NetWare, directories are cached in RAM for fast directory searches and directory updates. The directories are kept in directory cache buffers, whose minimum number is controlled by this parameter. This number must be high enough to perform most directory searches quickly. If the number is set too high, the unused portion is not available for file caching and other server operations. If the server responds slowly to directory searches, especially when it is first booted, monitor this number through the MONITOR NLM. The delay could be caused because the minimum directory cache-buffers parameter is set too low and the server spends time allocating new directory buffers. The value ranges from 10 to 2000, with a default of 20.

MAXIMUM DIRECTORY CACHE BUFFERS= *n*

As the number of directory entries and files increases, the server allocates more directory-cache buffers to hold the directories. To prevent the situation from getting out of hand with all available space being used for directory caching, the server enables you to set a limit on the maximum number of directory-cache buffers. If the file server continues to respond slowly, this parameter can be increased after consulting the MONITOR NLM on the directory-cache usage. If the MONITOR NLM reports a shortage of available RAM, and if this parameter is too high, the parameter value should be reduced. Because the server does not release memory automatically if this parameter value is reduced, it must be restarted to free up the unused memory. The parameter value ranges from 20 to 4000, with a default of 500.

DIRECTORY-CACHE BUFFER NONREFERENCED DELAY= *n*

Only a finite amount of space is in the directory-cache buffers. As new directory entries are loaded into RAM, the older ones can be overwritten. Overwriting older directories too quickly can be a waste, especially if the older directory entries are needed again. This parameter controls the amount of time a directory entry should remain in RAM in the nonreferenced state before it can be overwritten by another directory entry. A higher value indicates that the directory entry is more likely to be cached in memory when needed. This not only speeds up directory access, but also increases the number of directory-cache buffers because directory entries are held longer in the cache. A lower value can slow down directory access because they can be overwritten by new directory entries and will not be in RAM when needed. The parameter value ranges from 1 second to 5 minutes, with a default of 5.5 seconds.

DIRTY DIRECTORY-CACHE DELAY TIME= *n*

Directory entries that are modified in RAM need to be written out to disk to keep the directory on the server disk synchronized with changes in the file system. This parameter controls how long a directory entry can remain in RAM before it must be written to disk. Keeping this parameter high results in faster directory writes but also increases the chance of directory tables getting out of synch with those on disk in the event of a crash. A low value for this parameter reduces the possibility of directory tables becoming corrupt, but the more frequent writes can reduce the performance. The parameter value ranges from zero seconds to 10 seconds, with a default of 0.5 seconds. A zero setting disables the cache delay. Directory entries must be written immediately to disk, which causes slower directory writes.

MAXIMUM CONCURRENT DIRECTORY-CACHE WRITES= n

To speed up directory operations, several requests can be placed on the elevator mechanism. The elevator mechanism allows the disk head to move in continuous sweeps across the disk, which are more efficient than the random back-and-forth movements for disk I/O. This parameter controls the number of directory writes that can be queued on the elevator. A high value makes write requests more efficient; a lower number makes read requests more efficient. The parameter value ranges from 5 to 50, with a default of 10.

DIRECTORY-CACHE ALLOCATION WAIT TIME= n

NetWare does not respond immediately to a demand for new cache buffers. It waits for a period of time before satisfying this demand. This period of time, which is set by this parameter, is used to smooth out peak transient requests that may cause allocation of more directory-cache buffers than are needed. If the wait time is too low, the server will seem too eager to satisfy transient loads and may allocate more directory-cache buffers than are needed. If the server delays too long to satisfy the request, it will seem sluggish and seem to adapt slowly to user needs. The parameter value ranges from 0.5 second to 5 minutes, with a default of 2.2 seconds.

NCP FILE COMMIT=[ON|OFF]

This parameter controls the behavior of an NCP FILE COMMIT request by a client. If this parameter is set to ON, an NCP FILE COMMIT request causes all pending writes to be written immediately to disk. If the parameter is set to OFF, the cache manager flushes the pending writes to disk later. The default value for this parameter is ON. Changing this parameter to OFF can lead to small speed improvements, at the risk of a small chance of data corruption should the server crash before the disk writes are done.

TURBO FAT RE-USE WAIT TIME= n

Turbo FATs (indexed tables) are used for indexed files (files with more than 64 entries) and take time to build. If a number of indexed file operations are being performed, releasing the turbo FATs when they may be used again does not make sense. On the other hand, not releasing turbo FATs after their use consumes RAM space that could be used by NetWare. This parameter can be used to set the period of time turbo FAT buffers should remain in memory after an indexed file is closed. After the wait time value, the turbo FAT buffer can be reused for another indexed file. If applications perform random accesses and close many large files, this parameter value should be increased to avoid the overhead of rebuilding the turbo FAT index. If you want memory to be released for other operating system resources, this parameter can be increased. The parameter value ranges from 0.3 seconds to 1 hour 5 minutes 54.6 seconds, with a default of 5 minutes 29.6 seconds.

AUTO TTS BACKOUT FLAG=[ON|OFF]

In NetWare v3.x, the TTS feature is built into the operating system. In the event of a server crash, files that have been flagged transactional can be restored to a previous consistent state. Setting this parameter to ON causes the server to back out any incomplete transactions automatically at start-up time. The default value is OFF, which means that the user is prompted with the message `Incomplete transaction(s) found. Do you wish to back them out?` This parameter can be set only in the STARTUP.NCF file, not at the console prompt or AUTOEXEC.BAT file.

TTS ABORT DUMP FLAG=[ON|OFF]

The TTS feature allows incomplete writes to a transactional file to be backed out in the event of a server crash. With this parameter set to ON, NetWare creates a file called TTS$LOG.ERR on the SYS volume, to back out incomplete writes for transactional files. The default value is OFF, which means that the information to perform the backout is not saved. The result is faster writes and less reliability.

MAXIMUM TRANSACTIONS= n

Because NetWare is multitasking, the transaction operations can occur simultaneously. NetWare enables you to set the number of transactions that can be performed simultaneously on the server. Decrease this value if few transactions are used on the server. The parameter value ranges from 100 to 10,000, with a default of 10,000.

TTS UNWRITTEN CACHE WAIT TIME= *n*

Transactional data is held in RAM to be written out later. NetWare enables you to control the amount of time transactional data can be held in memory. If a transactional block is held in memory after this time, other write requests are held up until the transactional data is written. The default value of 1 minute 5.9 seconds is adequate for most purposes. Increasing this value can result in small speed improvements if the TTS feature is used extensively by applications. The parameter value ranges from 11 seconds to 10 minutes 59.1 seconds.

TTS BACKOUT FILE TRUNCATION WAIT TIME= *n*

The TTS backout file holds backout information for files, so that the files can be backed out if the server crashes. NetWare clears the backout file when the file is not in use. NetWare enables you to determine how long an allocated block remains available for the TTS backout file when these files are not being used. The parameter value ranges from 1 minute 5.1 seconds to 1 day 2 hours 21 minutes 51.3 seconds, with a default of 59 minutes 19.2 seconds. The default value works well in most situations.

ENABLE DISK READ AFTER WRITE VERIFY=[ON|OFF]

This enables and disables the hot-fix mechanism, which performs a read after a write, and compares the block read with that in memory. You should leave this parameter set to its default value of ON. If disk mirroring or duplexing is used and you are ensured of disk reliability, turning this parameter OFF can lead to faster disk writes.

MAXIMUM RECORD LOCKS PER CONNECTION= *n*

NetWare allows any station to issue record locks. Every record lock consumes server resources. NetWare enables you to limit the number of record locks any workstation can issue, to prevent any one station from consuming too many resources. The number of locks can be monitored also through the

MONITOR NLM. The parameter should be increased if an application fails while locking records. The parameter should be decreased if the workstation is consuming too many server resources. The parameter value ranges from 10 to 10,000, with a default value of 500.

MAXIMUM FILE LOCKS PER CONNECTION= n

NetWare allows any workstation to issue file locks. NetWare enables you to limit the number of file locks any workstation can issue, to prevent any one station from consuming too many resources. The number of locks can be monitored also through the MONITOR NLM. The parameter should be increased if an application fails while locking records. The parameter can be decreased if the workstation is consuming too many server resources. The parameter value ranges from 10 to 10,000, with a default value of 250.

MAXIMUM RECORD LOCKS= n

NetWare enables you to set a system-wide global parameter that sets a limit on the total number (n) of record locks NetWare can process simultaneously. The purpose of this parameter is to prevent too many record locks from consuming too many server resources. Increase this number if applications are failing and receiving messages about insufficient record locks. The parameter value ranges from 100 to 200,000, with a default value of 20,000.

MAXIMUM FILE LOCKS= n

NetWare enables you to set a system-wide global parameter that sets a limit on the total number (n) of file locks NetWare can process simultaneously. The purpose of this parameter is to prevent too many file locks from consuming too many server resources. Increase this number if applications are failing and receiving messages about insufficient file locks. The parameter value ranges from 100 to 100,000, with a default value of 10,000.

Tuning Communications Performance

The communications parameters control characteristics of communication buffers. *Communication buffers* are areas in the server RAM dedicated for holding packets. The packets remain in memory before they are processed by the File Service Processes (FSPs).

The following sections describe how these SET parameters can affect the communications performance of a server.

MAXIMUM PHYSICAL RECEIVE PACKET SIZE= *n*

The size of a packet that can be transmitted is determined by the networks physical access mechanism and driver limitations. On the server side, NetWare enables you to define the maximum size (*n*) of a packet that can be processed by the file server. When a workstation makes a connection to the server, the packet size is negotiated, based on the settings of the network driver being used at the workstation. This parameter value needs to be large enough to accommodate the maximum packet size used by a workstation. The parameter value ranges from 618 to 4,202 bytes, with a default of 1,130 bytes. Generally, a large packet size can speed communications but consumes more RAM. The parameter can be set only in the STARTUP.NCF file.

MAXIMUM PACKET RECEIVE BUFFERS= *n*

The server needs to keep a certain number of packet buffers in RAM to avoid being overrun by data. Normally, the server allocates receive buffers dynamically, based on its needs. NetWare enables you to set an upper limit on the number of packet receive buffers (*n*) the operating system can allocate. The MONITOR NLM can be used to monitor current usage of this parameter. If this parameter is close to the maximum value, increase the value until you have at least one packet receive buffer per workstation. For OS/2 and MS Windows, increase this value, based on the number of simultaneously running network applications at the workstations. Allow for at least one buffer per application. The MONITOR NLM can be used also to monitor the No ECB available count errors. If these errors are being reported, increase this parameter in increments of 10. For EISA and Micro Channel server machines, increase this parameter to allow for five to 10 packet receive buffers per EISA/Micro Channel network board. If the number of file service processes reported by MONITOR NLM is close to its maximum, you can increase the parameter maximum number of service processes to reduce the need for more packet receive buffers. The parameter value ranges from 50 to 2000, with a default of 100.

MINIMUM PACKET RECEIVE BUFFERS= *n*

NetWare enables you to set a minimum number of packet receive buffers (*n*) at the server. The MONITOR NLM can be used to monitor current packet receive buffers. The default value is 10. Too few receive buffers will cause the server to respond sluggishly when it first comes up. If No ECB available count errors are reported through the MONITOR NLM after the server boots, increase this parameter. For EISA and Micro Channel server machines, increase this parameter to allow for at least five packet receive buffers per EISA/Micro Channel network board. The parameter value ranges from 10 to 1000.

NEW PACKET RECEIVE BUFFERS= *n*

NetWare enables you to set up a waiting period before a request for a new packet receive buffer is satisfied. The reason for this wait is to smooth out peak demands for receive buffers and allocate receive buffers for sustained network loads only. Otherwise, you would end up with more receive buffers than are needed for optimal performance. If the parameter is set to a high value, the server will be slow to respond to sustained peak loads. If it is set too low, the server may respond too quickly to peak loads, and may end up allocating more receive buffers than are necessary. Novell recommends that this parameter not be changed for EISA bus master boards in the server. The parameter value ranges from 0.1 to 20 seconds, with a default of 0.1 second.

DELAY BETWEEN WATCHDOG PACKETS= *n*

This is the time interval (*n*) between watchdog packets sent from the server to the workstation after there is no response to the first watchdog packet. The watchdog packet is sent to see whether the workstation is still "alive" on the network. If this parameter is set too low, this could generate excessive network traffic because the watchdog packet is sent to every station attached to the server. The parameter value ranges from 1 second to 10 minutes 26.2 seconds, with a default of 4 minutes 56.6 seconds. Normally, the default value is adequate for most networks. For workstations and servers connected by wide area networks, the parameter value can be increased to avoid extra overhead and to account for extra delays. On a wide area network, the setting of this parameter can be critical. Setting the delay too low causes a second watchdog packet to be sent without waiting to receive a response from the first. The delay between watchdog packets must be set greater than the round-trip delay to the workstation.

DELAY BEFORE FIRST WATCHDOG PACKET= *n*

The server sends watchdog packets to a station that has been quiet for some time. NetWare enables you to set how long a server should wait before polling a station that has been inactive; then a watchdog packet is sent as a probe to see whether the station is still alive. The parameter value ranges from 15.7 seconds to 20 minutes 52.3 seconds.

NUMBER OF WATCHDOG PACKETS= *n*

The NetWare server sends repeated watchdog packets if the workstation does not respond to a poll from the first watchdog packet. In a heavily congested network, the workstation response to a watchdog packet or the server watchdog packet can get lost. The NetWare server gives the workstation a few more chances (*n*) before declaring it dead and clearing the connection. The parameter ranges from 5 to 100, with a default value of 10. Setting a low delay between watchdog packets when the number of watchdog packets is high can cause excessive network traffic and affect the network performance.

Tuning Operating System Processes

A number of parameters deal with tuning the process scheduling time in the NetWare v3.x operating system. These SET parameters for operating system processes are described in the following sections.

PSEUDO PREEMPTION TIME= *n*

NetWare uses nonpreemptive scheduling. Processes must relinquish control voluntarily. This parameter forces certain NLMs to relinquish control if they use too much CPU time. The parameter value should be set along the guidelines that come with the NLMs you run. The values range from 1000 to 10,000, with a default of 2000. Each value represents a raw CPU time of approximately 0.84 seconds.

MAXIMUM SERVICE PROCESSES= *n*

In NetWare 3.x, file service processes are created on demand. NetWare enables you to set an upper limit on the number of file service processes (*n*) it can create. This number also can be monitored by the MONITOR NLM. Increase this parameter if the server is always near its maximum. The parameter ranges from 5 to 40, with a default value of 20.

NEW SERVICE PROCESS WAIT TIME= *n*

NetWare creates file service processes on demand. Under transient peak loads, too many file service processes can be created. NetWare enables you to smooth out transient demands for file service processes by setting up a waiting period. The parameter ranges from 0.3 seconds to 20 seconds, with a default value of 2.2 seconds. This parameter prevents NetWare from reacting too quickly to peak loads and from allocating too many file service processes.

MAXIMUM OUTSTANDING NCP SEARCHES= *n*

Directory searches for existing files are common on a NetWare server because of the flexibility of NetWare's search-mode feature. Normally, only one NCP search operation is permitted per workstation connection. If your applications support it, multiple NCP searches can speed up the application. This parameter enables you to set a limit on the maximum number of *NetWare Core Protocol* (NCP) searches that can be outstanding at any time. The parameter ranges from 10 to 100, with a default value of 51.

Threshold and Warning Parameters

NetWare v3.x has many parameters that generate warning messages when their threshold values are crossed. These parameters do not affect the performance of the system directly, but are important for status alert messages and system operation. These SET threshold and warning parameters and their descriptions follow.

CONSOLE DISPLAY WATCHDOG LOGOUTS=[ON|OFF]

The watchdog process clears inactive connections with workstations. Normally it does this silently. If you want a report of when the connection is cleared on the server console, set this parameter ON. The default value is OFF.

IMMEDIATE PURGE OF DELETED FILES=[ON|OFF]

NetWare allows deleted files to be salvaged by the SALVAGE utility. When this parameter is set to ON, all files are immediately purged on deletion; that is, the salvage file feature is disabled. The default value (OFF) permits deleted files to be salvaged.

VOLUME LOW WARN ALL USERS=[ON|OFF]

NetWare allows users to be informed when a volume is almost full. The default value is ON; users are alerted when the volume is almost full.

VOLUME LOW WARNING THRESHOLD= n

NetWare enables you to set how many free disk blocks (n) remain on a volume before it issues a warning. To estimate this number, you must divide the desired free-space threshold by the disk-block size. The value for this parameter can range from 0 to 100,000 blocks, with a default value of 256.

VOLUME LOW WARNING RESET THRESHOLD= n

The VOLUME LOW WARNING THRESHOLD issues the first warning that disk space is low. NetWare enables you to set the number of disk blocks that must be freed (n) before a second warning is issued. This parameter is used to prevent repeated warning messages being sent if free space hovers around the threshold set by VOLUME LOW WARNING THRESHOLD. When the first warning VOLUME LOW WARN ALL USERS is issued, and users reduce disk space just below the threshold, having a warning message may not be desirable if disk-space utilization rises above the threshold. Actually, this process could repeat several times—dipping below the threshold and then rising again—and the repeated warning messages could be a source of great annoyance to the user. The value for this parameter can range from zero to 100,000 blocks, with a default value of 256.

MAXIMUM PERCENT OF VOLUME USED BY DIRECTORY= n

NetWare enables you to set an upper limit on the percentage (n) of a volume that may be used as directory space. This percentage value ranges from 5 to 50, with a default value of 13.

MAXIMUM PERCENT OF VOLUME SPACE
ALLOWED FOR EXTENDED ATTRIBUTES=n

NetWare v3.x supports multiple file-name spaces such as Macintosh, NFS, OS/2, and FTAM. These names spaces require extended attribute support. NetWare enables you to set and limit the percentage (n) of a volume that may be used for extended attribute storage. When the volume is being mounted, the setting becomes effective. This percentage value ranges from 5 to 50, with a default value of 10.

MAXIMUM EXTENDED ATTRIBUTES PER FILE OR PATH= n

NetWare enables you to set an upper limit on the number of extended attributes (n) that can be assigned to a file or path. This parameter setting affects all server volumes. The parameter value ranges from 4 to 512, with a default value of 32.

MAXIMUM SUBDIRECTORY TREE DEPTH= n

NetWare enables you to set the number of directory levels supported by the NetWare file system. The default value of this parameter is 25, even though some DOS applications cannot support more than 10 levels. The parameter value ranges from 10 to 100. This parameter can be set from the STARTUP.NCF file only. It cannot be set from the console prompt.

ALLOW UNENCRYPTED PASSWORDS=[ON|OFF]

When set to OFF, this parameter enables users to use encrypted passwords only. The OFF setting is used if all file servers are NetWare v3.x. If servers on the network are below NetWare v3.x, this parameter can be set to OFF to avoid log-in problems. If the servers are v2.12 and above, the NetWare v3.x utilities can be copied to these servers and password encryption can be enabled by keeping this parameter value OFF. For NetWare servers below v2.12 (such as NetWare v2.0a), this parameter should be set to ON.

DISPLAY SPURIOUS INTERRUPT ALERTS=[ON|OFF]

NetWare enables you to be alerted about spurious interrupts. *Spurious interrupts*, caused by IRQ conflicts between devices on the server, generate the message `Spurious hardware interrupt <number> detected`. The default setting is ON because spurious interrupts need to be resolved for the proper functioning of the server. A value of OFF is provided as a convenience (to turn off the messages while waiting for a resolution of the problem).

DISPLAY LOST INTERRUPT ALERTS=[ON|OFF]

NetWare enables you to be alerted about lost interrupts. This message is generated when a driver or adapter generates an interrupt request and then drops the request before the CPU can respond to it. This generates the message `Interrupt controller detected a lost hardware interrupt`. The default setting is ON because lost interrupts can degrade server performance. A value of OFF is provided as a convenience (to turn off the messages while waiting for a resolution of the problem). This usually indicates a driver or board problem.

DISPLAY DISK DEVICE ALERTS=[ON|OFF]

NetWare enables you to be alerted to disk events such as a hard disk added, activated, deactivated, mounted, or dismounted. The default setting is OFF. Setting the parameter to ON during disk testing and debugging can yield information that may be helpful.

DISPLAY RELINQUISH CONTROL ALERTS=[ON|OFF]

NetWare enables you to be alerted when an NLM uses the server CPU continuously for more than 0.4 seconds, without relinquishing control to other processes. This parameter is meant for software developers during the testing phase of their NLM product. Its default value is OFF.

DISPLAY OLD API NAMES=[ON|OFF]

Some of the API names were changed in NetWare v3.1x, and resource tracking was added for better monitoring and control of NLMs and their use of system resources. Also, resource tracking forces NLMs to release all their resources when they are unloaded. The default value of this parameter is OFF. Set this parameter to ON to monitor whether old APIs are being used. If older APIs are being used, contact the vendor of the software to get a more compatible version of the API.

Monitoring Tools

Several monitoring tools are available. Some are among the NetWare products; others, such as the Frye Utilities, must be purchased through the product vendor.

The following sections examine the console NLM, Frye Utilities, and Protocol Analyzers for network monitoring.

Console MONITOR NLM

MONITOR is one of the most useful utilities for monitoring server performance. The MONITOR utility, an NLM that can be run from the server console, can be used to view information about any of the following:

- Server CPU utilization and overall activity
- Cache memory status
- Disk drives
- Mounted volumes
- LAN drivers
- Loaded NLMs
- File lock status
- Memory usage

The most important screens are displayed and discussed in this section. Menu selections to reach a particular screen from the MONITOR NLM are described by the following convention:

> MONITOR -> Selection 1 -> Selection 2

which shows that from the MONITOR main menu, you select the `Select 1` option and then the `Select 2` option.

MONITOR Main Screen

When invoked from the console, the main screen shown in figure 9.4 is displayed. The main screen displays a wealth of information, most of which is related to server utilization and caching. The top part of the screen displays the operating system version, server name, and how long the server has been up. The *Utilization* shows the percentage of time the server is busy. This value can give an indication of server activity.

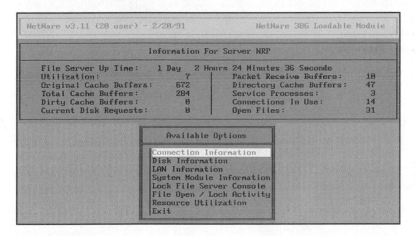

```
NetWare v3.11 (20 user) - 2/20/91              NetWare 386 Loadable Module

                        Information For Server NRP

 File Server Up Time:    1 Day   2 Hours 24 Minutes 36 Seconds
 Utilization:                 7       Packet Receive Buffers:     10
 Original Cache Buffers:    672       Directory Cache Buffers:    47
 Total Cache Buffers:       284       Service Processes:           3
 Dirty Cache Buffers:         0       Connections In Use:         14
 Current Disk Requests:       0       Open Files:                 31

                          Available Options
                    ┌──────────────────────────────┐
                    │ Connection Information        │
                    │ Disk Information              │
                    │ LAN Information               │
                    │ System Module Information     │
                    │ Lock File Server Console      │
                    │ File Open / Lock Activity     │
                    │ Resource Utilization          │
                    │ Exit                          │
                    └──────────────────────────────┘
```

Figure 9.4:
MONITOR main screen.

When the server starts, several file-cache buffers are available to it. (The number is indicated by Original Cache Buffers.) The server satisfies memory requests for new NLMs from this cache pool, and over a period of time the number of cache buffers available may decrease. The current number of file-cache buffers is indicated by Total Cache Buffers. The server writes to a disk block by first writing to a copy of the disk block in a file-cache buffer in RAM. These buffers eventually need to be written to disk by a delayed background process controlled by the SET parameter DIRTY DISK CACHE DELAY TIME. While it is waiting to be written out, these buffers are called *dirty cache buffers*.

As the I/O activity on the server disk rises, not all disk requests can be processed simultaneously, and some have to wait in queue to be serviced. The number of disk requests waiting in queue is indicated by Current Disk Requests.

A certain number of buffers (indicated by Packet Receive Buffers) must be available to handle workstation requests.

The total number of buffers allocated to speed directory access are indicated in Directory Cache Buffers. The number of processes dedicated for handling file service requests is indicated by Service Processes. This number can increase on demand, and never decreases unless the server is restarted. The total number of connections in use at the server is indicated by the Connections In Use, and the total number of files opened at the server is indicated by Open Files.

MONITOR Connection Information

The MONITOR connection information screen is shown in figure 9.5. This screen can be reached through:

> MONITOR -> Connection Information

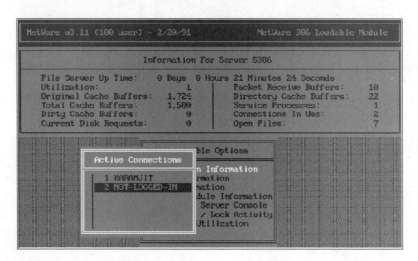

Figure 9.5:
MONITOR connection information screen.

Users who are logged out are indicated by NOT-LOGGED-IN. They show up in the connection information list because the shell at the workstation is still attached to the server.

If a displayed user is selected, information on that user is displayed as shown in figure 9.6. The top half of the screen in figure 9.6 displays statistics on the user; the bottom half indicates the files opened by the user. The statistics for the user indicate the following:

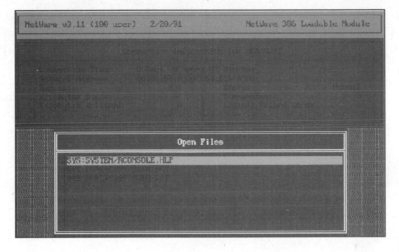

Figure 9.6:
MONITOR user information.

- **Connection time.** Measured in days, hours, and minutes.

- **Network Address.** This address consists of three parts: network number (cable segment number), node address, and socket address. The socket address for the workstation shell is 4003 (hex); this is the software address of the workstation shell process.

- **Requests.** The total number of NCP requests generated by the workstation connection are displayed.

- **Kilobytes Read.** Measure of amount of information read. If enabled through accounting services, a user can be charged for this service.

- **Kilobytes Written.** Measure of amount of information written. If enabled through accounting services, a user can be charged for this service.

- **Status.** A user status can be *Normal*, which means the user is logged in; *Waiting*, which means the station is waiting for a file to be unlocked; or *Not-logged-in*, which means the shell attached to the server by the user is not logged in.

- **Semaphores.** Displays the number of semaphores used by the station. Semaphores can be used to arbitrate access to resources (NICs, areas of RAM, bus), and also to limit the number of workstations that can use a shared application.

■ **Logical Record Locks.** Displays the number of logical locks used by a connection. A *logical lock* is implemented by assigning a logical name to a resource and locking that name. Other applications check for a lock on the name before accessing the resource. A logical record is enforced by applications. (This is different from physical locks that are enforced by the network operating system and can lock a range of bytes on a file. If another user attempts to access a range of bytes that is physically locked, the user receives an `Access Denied` error message.)

The physical locks for an open file can be displayed by selecting an open file and pressing Enter. Figure 9.7 shows the headings for the physical locks. The Start and End columns indicate the byte offset at which the lock begins and ends. The Record Lock column indicates one of the four types of record locks defined in table 9.2.

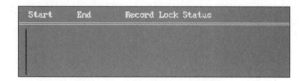

Figure 9.7:
MONITOR physical locks for user connection.

Table 9.2
Types of Physical Locks

Physical Lock	Description
Locked Exclusive	Locked so that no one else can read or write to the specified range of bytes
Locked Shareable	Locked so that reads are allowed but only one station can write
Locked	Logged for future locking
TTS Holding Lock	Unlocked by application but still locked by TTS because transactions are not complete

The Status column indicates a Not Logged status, which signifies that no lock requests are pending. A Logged status indicates that several records are being prepared for locking. The server logs each lock before performing the lock, to avoid deadly embrace or deadlock conditions.

MONITOR Disk Information

The MONITOR disk information screen is shown in figure 9.8. This screen can be reached through:

MONITOR -> Disk Information -> Select a hard disk

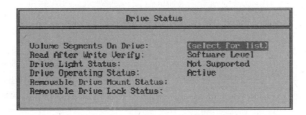

Figure 9.8:
MONITOR disk information.

Figure 9.8 displays driver information for the selected hard disk. The top part of the screen indicates information on the disk driver; the bottom half of the screen, the Drive Status. The driver information includes the following:

- **Driver.** This is the driver name.

- **Disk Size.** Size in megabytes of all partitions on the disk.

- **Partitions.** Number of partitions defined on the hard disk.

- **Mirror Status.** The values are *Mirrored*, which indicates that disk mirroring is in place; *Not Mirrored*, which indicates that disks are being used independently; and *Remirroring*, which indicates that data is being transferred between disks so that they can be mirrored.

- **Hot Fix Status.** *Normal* indicates that hot fix is enabled. *Not-hot-fix* indicates that hot fix has been disabled or has failed.

- **Partition Blocks.** Total space in disk blocks on the server disk.

- **Disk Blocks.** Number of blocks from the total partition blocks that can be used for data.

- **Redirection Blocks.** Number of blocks reserved for the Hot Fix Area.

- **Redirected Blocks.** Number of bad blocks found and redirected by hot fix.

- **Reserved Block.** Used for hot-fix tables.

Note: When Redirected Blocks + Reserved Blocks = Redirection Blocks, Hot Fix has failed, and the Hot Fix Status should be Not-hot-fixed.

The Drive Status fields are explained in the following list:

- **Volume Segments On Drive.** A volume can be made up of many disk partitions or disks; they are listed if this field is selected.

- **Read After Write Verify.** Normally set to Software Level Verify, because Hot Fix performs read-after-write verify. Some disk controllers can perform this test, in which case Hardware Level Verify may be selected. The Disable Verify disables the read-after-write verify. This option should be selected only for benchmark tests. Under normal operation, always have some form of read-after-write verify check.

- **Drive Light Status.** Can be used to physically flash the drive-light status indicator at regular intervals, so that you can identify the physical disk. This option may not be supported for some disk drivers/drive types.

- **Drive Operating Status.** Used to manually deactivate/activate disk; used primarily for testing disk drives.

- **Removable Drive Mount Status.** Used to manually mount/dismount removable media. The values can be Mounted/Dismounted.

- **Removable Drive Lock Status.** Used to lock a removable medium to prevent its physical removal. The values can be Locked/Unlocked. If the status value is Unlocked, the removable medium can be dismounted and removed.

MONITOR LAN Information

The MONITOR LAN information screen is shown in figure 9.9. This screen can be reached through:

> MONITOR -> LAN Information -> Select a LAN driver

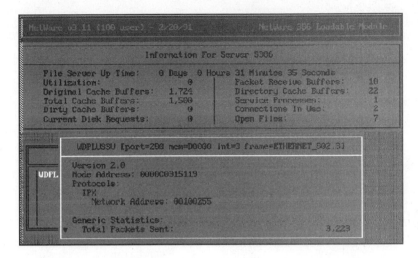

Figure 9.9:
MONITOR LAN driver information.

Figure 9.9 displays the LAN driver information for the selected LAN driver. The bottom half of the screen shows a window titled with the name of the LAN driver selected. The LAN driver information indicates the version number, node address of the NIC in the server, protocols bound to the LAN driver, and the network address of the cabling segment on which the LAN driver is working.

Figure 9.10 shows more of the Generic Statistics information. The statistical information for a LAN driver cannot fit on-screen, but you can use the cursor or PgDn keys to see the rest of the information.

Generic Statistics information, available for all LAN drivers, is described in table 9.3.

In addition to Generic Statistics, Custom Statistics specific to the NIC hardware are being used. These are reported by the driver for that NIC and are different for different network hardware. Figure 9.11 shows the custom statistics for an Ethernet NIC. Among other statistics, a variety of custom statistics deal with collision count. This is in keeping with the operation of Ethernet (see Chapter 6).

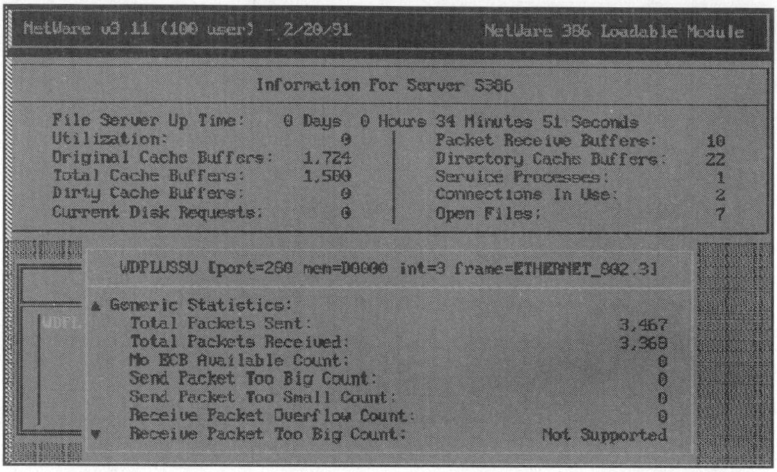

Figure 9.10:
MONITOR LAN Generic Statistics.

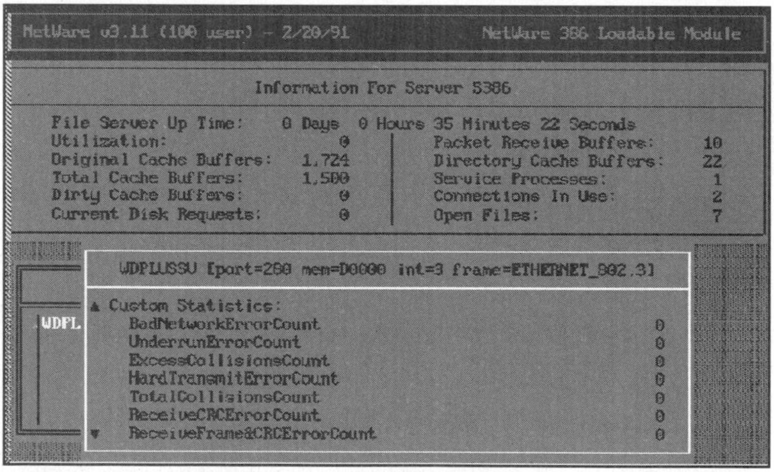

Figure 9.11:
MONITOR LAN Custom Statistics.

Table 9.3
MONITOR Generic Statistics for LAN Drivers

Parameter	Description
Total Packets Sent	Total packets sent through this LAN driver; indicates which driver is handling most of the traffic, and how much traffic.
Total Packets Received	Total packets received by this LAN driver; indicates which driver is handling most of the traffic, and how much traffic.
No ECB Available Count	A counter that increments when a packet receive buffer is not available for an incoming packet. Server allocates packet receive buffers on demand until the MAXIMUM PACKET RECEIVE BUFFERS is reached (see the earlier section in this chapter on SET parameters).
Send Packet Too Big Count	A counter that increments when server transmits a packet too big for the NIC to handle; indicates an incorrect setting of MAXIMUM PHYSICAL RECEIVE PACKET SIZE or a problem with the server software or NIC driver.
Send Packet Too Small Count	A counter that increments when server transmits a packet too small for the NIC to handle; indicates a problem with the server software or NIC driver.
Receive Packet Overflow Count	A counter that increments when server receives a packet too big to store in a cache buffer; indicates a problem with workstation software in negotiating a proper packet size; could also be a problem with NIC driver or card at sender.
Receive Packet Too Big Count	A counter that increments when server receives a packet too big for the NIC to handle; indicates an incorrect setting of MAXIMUM PHYSICAL RECEIVE PACKET SIZE or a problem with sender software or NIC driver.

continues

Table 9.3
Continued

Parameter	Description
Receive Packet Too Small Count	A counter that increments when server too small count receives a packet too small for the NIC to handle; indicates problem with sender software or NIC driver.
Send Packet Miscellaneous Errors	A catch-all error counter that increments when an error occurs during transmission of a packet that does not fit any other category. A large value could indicate problems with network hardware.
Receive Packet Miscellaneous Errors	A catch-all error counter that increments when an error occurs during reception of a packet that does not fit any other category. A large value could indicate problems with network hardware.
Send Packet Retry Count	A counter that increments when server retries sending a packet because of a hardware error; indicates a problem with cabling or NIC hardware, or a problem with long delays across a Wide Area Network. Try increasing the retry count using the LOAD driver command.
Checksum Errors	A counter that increments when a data error is detected by the CRC checksum at the end of the MAC frame (packet); indicates a problem with NIC hardware, noise, or cabling.
Hardware Receive Mismatch Count	A counter that increments when the packet length indicated by the length field in a packet does not match the size of the packet received by the NIC; indicates a problem with NIC or NIC driver.

MONITOR System Module Information

The MONITOR System Module List screen is shown in figure 9.12. This screen can be reached through:

MONITOR -> System Module Information

Figure 9.12:
MONITOR system module list.

Figure 9.13 displays the information for the selected system module. The top part of the screen indicates the module size in RAM and the file name under which the system module was loaded. The bottom half of the screen shows the resource tags for that system module. A *resource tag* is a mechanism introduced in NetWare v3.10 to keep track of system resources. It also allows NetWare to ensure that all tagged resources are released when the system module is unloaded. Because the system modules can be written by third-party vendors over whom Novell has little control, this is a useful addition to the NetWare operating system, allowing it to release resources when a module unloads.

Figure 9.13:
MONITOR system module information.

Selecting a resource (see fig. 9.14) displays the tag name (Tag), the name of the parent module this resource belongs to (Module), the type of resource (Resource), and the amount of memory used by the resource (In Use).

MONITOR File Open/Lock Activity

The MONITOR File Open/Lock Activity screen is shown in figure 9.15. This screen can be reached through:

MONITOR -> File Open/Lock Activity -> Select path name of a file

Resource Information
Tag: Directory Cache Buffers
Module: NetWare Server Operating System
Resource: Permanent Memory (Bytes)
In Use: 31,344

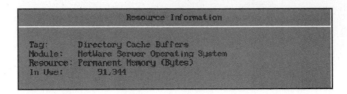

Figure 9.14:
MONITOR resource tag information.

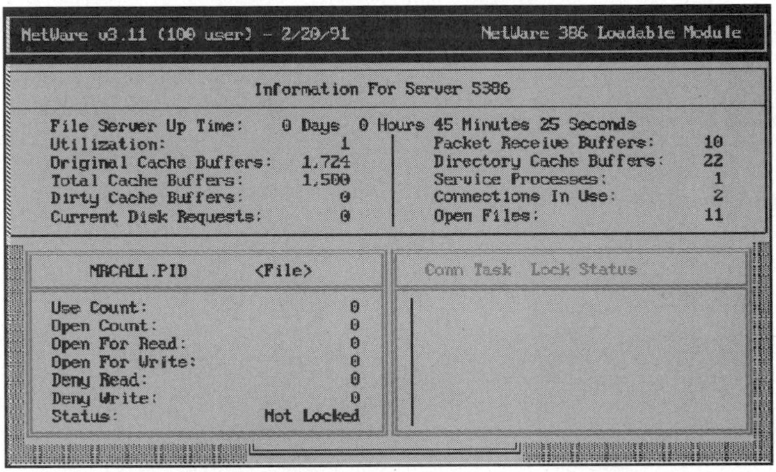

NetWare v3.11 (100 user) - 2/20/91
NetWare 386 Loadable Module
Information For Server S386
File Server Up Time: 0 Days 0 Hours 45 Minutes 25 Seconds
Utilization: 1
Original Cache Buffers: 1,724
Total Cache Buffers: 1,500
Dirty Cache Buffers: 0
Current Disk Requests: 0
Packet Receive Buffers: 10
Directory Cache Buffers: 22
Service Processes: 1
Connections In Use: 2
Open Files: 11
MRCALL.PID <File>
Use Count: 0
Open Count: 0
Open For Read: 0
Open For Write: 0
Deny Read: 0
Deny Write: 0
Status: Not Locked
Conn Task Lock Status

Figure 9.15:
MONITOR File Open/Lock activity.

Use Count is the number of connections that have the file opened or locked. Open Count defines the number of connections that currently open the file; Open Read indicates the number of connections reading from the file; and Open Write, the number of connections writing to the file. The following relationship holds true at all times:

Open Count = Open Read + Open Write

The Deny Read and Deny Write fields indicate whether the file lock for the open operation is exclusive or shared. Deny Read indicates the number of connections that have opened the file, but denies even the read operation (exclusive file lock). Deny Write indicates the number of connections that have opened the file, but denies writes to other stations (shared read).

The Status field indicates whether the file is Locked or Unlocked. The Conn column indicates a list of connections using that field. The Task is an internal number used by the NetWare shell for the application using the file. The lock status can have the values of Exclusive, Shareable, TTS Holding Lock, Logged, or Not Logged. The Exclusive lock means that no one else can read or write to the record; Shareable means that others may read but not write to the record. TTS Holding Lock means that the file was unlocked by an application, but because the transactions are not complete, the TTS has the file locked. Logged means that a set of records is being prepared for locking, to avoid a deadly-embrace situation. Not-Logged, the normal condition, indicates that no locks are pending.

MONITOR Resource Utilization

The MONITOR Resource Utilization screen is shown in figure 9.16. This screen can be reached through:

> MONITOR -> Resource Utilization -> Select a resource

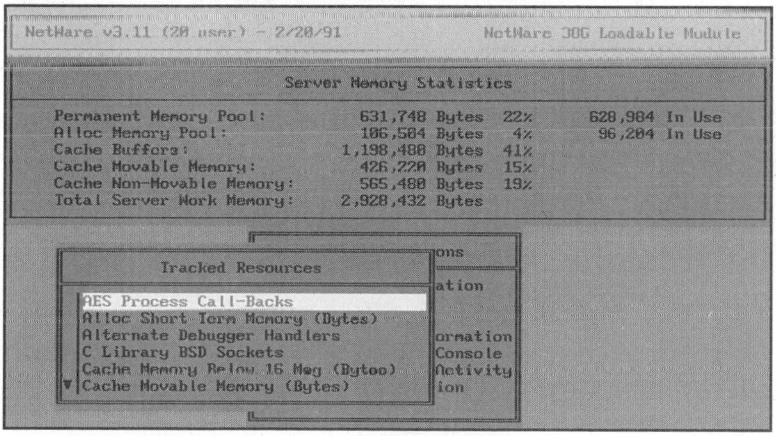

Figure 9.16:
MONITOR tracked resources.

In figure 9.16, the bottom part of the screen shows a list of resources tracked by NetWare. The server tracks resources such as the Alloc Memory Pool by forcing procedures to use a resource tag when doing an allocation. The top part of the screen contains server memory statistics. The individual fields are as follows:

- **Permanent Memory Pool.** Memory used by processes when they do not intend to return it for awhile (if ever). When more memory is needed, cache buffers are transferred to this pool; these cache buffers will never be returned to the cache buffer pool. The directory-cache buffers as well as the packet-receive buffers are contained in this pool.

- **Alloc Memory Pool.** Memory used by processes when they do not intend to use it for long periods of time. When more memory for this pool is needed, it is transferred from the Permanent Memory Pool; this memory will never be returned to the Permanent Memory Pool. This is the preferred memory pool for loadable modules to use when allocating small pieces of memory.

- **Cache Buffers.** The amount of memory in the cache buffer pool. This memory currently is being used for file caching. The amount of memory in this area should be greater than that in any other area.

- **Cache Movable Memory.** Memory allocated directly from the cache buffer pool. When freed, this memory will be returned to the cache buffer pool. It differs from Cache Non-Movable Memory in that the memory manager may move the location of these memory blocks to optimize memory usage. Volume tables and hash tables typically use this memory.

- **Cache Non-Movable Memory.** Memory allocated directly from the cache buffer pool. When freed, this memory will be returned to the cache buffer pool. Used when large pieces of memory are needed.

- **Total Server Work Memory.** This is the sum of all the memory pools.

To view the list of resource tags with a specific resource type, highlight the resource type and press Enter. You may then select a specific resource tag and view additional information associated with it.

Figure 9.17 shows resource tags for the tracked resource process. The resource tags are listed on the screen's right. Notice that the resources under the tracked resource Processes are NLMs. This is to be expected because the NLMs act as processes. Selecting a specific resource tag gives more information on that resource. Figure 9.18, for instance, shows the resource information for the process RSPX.NLM.

Figure 9.17:
MONITOR Resource Tags.

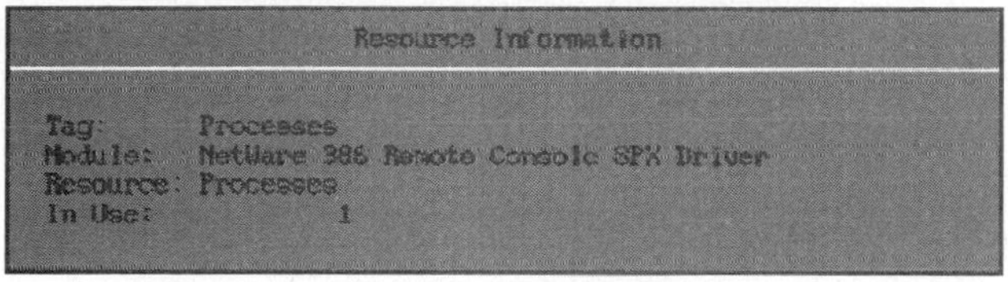

Figure 9.18:
MONITOR Resource Information.

Undocumented MONITOR OPTION: LOAD MONITOR -P

If the MONITOR utility is loaded using an undocumented option, a new option, Processor Utilization, is displayed.

```
LOAD MONITOR -P
```

Selecting Processor Utilization gives a screen similar to that shown in figure 9.19, which lists the Available Processes and Interrupts. The list includes active processes (or threads) as well as all available hardware interrupts. To select multiple processes for observation, mark them with the F5 key and press Enter.

The screen in figure 9.20, for example, shows the process activity for seven processes marked with the F5 key. The Time column indicates the amount of time the CPU spent executing the code in the context of that process. For interrupts, this is the amount of time spent in the Interrupt Service Routine (ISR) associated with that interrupt. The Count column represents the number of times the process ran during a sample period. For interrupts, this number indicates the number of interrupts serviced during a sample period. The Load column gives the percentage of time the CPU spent in this process or interrupt.

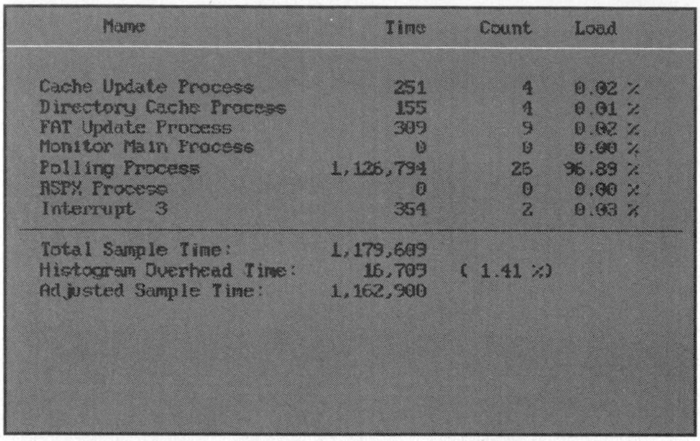

Figure 9.19:
Available processes and interrupts.

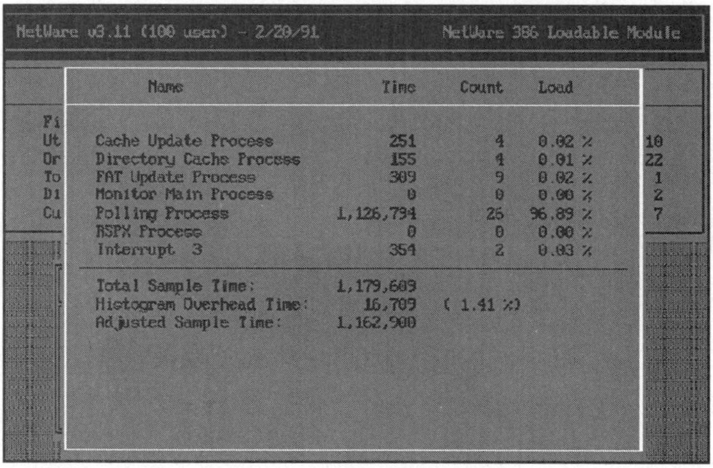

Figure 9.20:
Process activity.

At the bottom of the screen, an overhead summary displays the total sample time, the amount of time spent generating the utilization information (along with the percentage), and the adjusted sample time—the amount of time available for all the processes and interrupts to use. All the process and interrupt statistics are relative to the adjusted sample time.

Note that the utilization information is generated only when MONITOR is in this screen. When you enter this screen, MONITOR turns on the statistics-generation engine in NetWare. When you leave this screen, MONITOR turns off the statistics-generation engine, and the operating system returns to its normal mode of operation.

When the server is idle, the CPU will spend most of the time in the Polling Process and the STREAMS Q Runner Process if STREAMS is loaded. This can be used as an indication of low CPU utilization. Server Processes are used to service workstation requests. If other processes or interrupts have an unusually high percentage of the CPU's time, it may indicate bad hardware, drivers, or NLMs, or simply a busy server.

As you can see from figure 9.21, most CPU time is allocated to the Polling Process. Because there was no other activity on the system on which this measurement was taken, most of the time was spent in the polling process. The NIC setting on the server was set to Interrupt 3; as packets are processed by the NIC, Interrupt 3 shows activity. Whenever packets were transferred between workstation and server, the Interrupt 3 activity jumped up, as figure 9.21 shows.

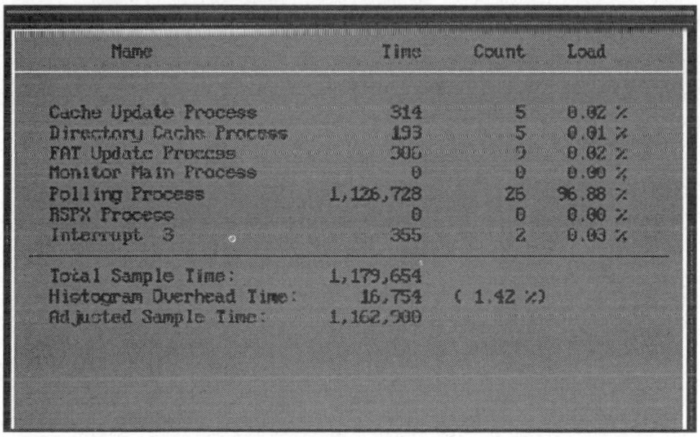

Name	Time	Count	Load
Cache Update Process	314	5	0.02 %
Directory Cache Process	193	5	0.01 %
FAT Update Process	306	9	0.02 %
Monitor Main Process	0	0	0.00 %
Polling Process	1,126,728	25	96.88 %
RSPX Process	0	0	0.00 %
Interrupt 3	355	2	0.03 %
Total Sample Time:	1,179,654		
Histogram Overhead Time:	16,754	(1.42 %)	
Adjusted Sample Time:	1,162,900		

Figure 9.21:
Polling Process time and increase in Interrupt 3 activity.

Frye Tools

Other third-party tools provide performance-related information for NetWare. One such tool—the Frye Utilities for Network Management, from

Frye Computer Systems, Inc. (617-451-5400)—can monitor performance of both NetWare v3.x and NetWare v2.x servers. In addition to performance tuning, the utilities also provide diagnostic reports, server documentation, and weekly maintenance reports. The Frye Utilities for NetWare includes an Early Warning System that indicates automatic notification of errors when certain threshold conditions are met. Figure 9.22 shows some of the parameters that can be monitored. Notification alert messages can be sent to designated users on the network through electronic mail, fax, or a pager system.

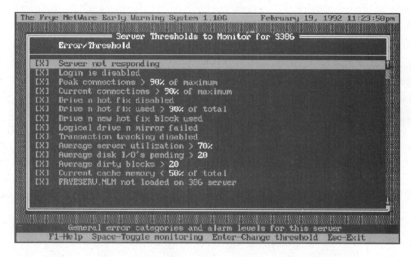

Figure 9.22:
Frye Tools: Parameter thresholds.

The performance-monitoring capability of Frye Utilities goes beyond what the MONITOR utility currently offers.

Nu-Mega Technology Tools

When a new application or system NLM is installed, it must share the CPU resources with the NetWare operating system. Depending on how NLMs are written, they can have a serious impact on server—and hence network—performance. This is particularly true if an NLM contains bugs, is poorly written, and starts monopolizing the server CPU time or starts writing to areas of memory to which it is not supposed to write.

Nu-Mega Technologies, Inc. (603-889-2386) provides Net-Check and the NLM-Profile tools, which are invaluable for detecting and monitoring ill-behaved NLMs. The NET-Check tool can be used to monitor NLMs and prevent them from writing into another NLM's code or data area. Normally, the developer should catch such behavior so users should not see the problem. But if a software bug escapes he software developer (as it often does), you have to deal with it. NET-Check is able to detect NLMs that make an out-of-bounds memory overwrite. It can be configured to prevent these overwrites from taking place, or to allow them to take place and inform you of these overwrites.

NET-Check provides this protection by running most of the NLMs and NetWare in ring 3 of the Intel 80386 microprocessor. Normally, NetWare and NLMs run in ring 0, where they have access to all the hardware resources and there is no protection. By running at ring 3 and making use of pages, NET-Check is able to use the hardware protection mechanisms of the Intel 80386 microprocessor to catch ill-behaved NLMs.

Run NET-Check whenever you install a new NLM application on your server, and when you want to monitor for any illegal actions, until you are satisfied that the installed NLMs are behaving properly. Because NET-Check monitors for illegal activities, it also can help in detecting viruses attached to NLMs. Nu-Mega claims that NET-Check can be run all the time without affecting server performance.

The NET-Profile tool gives a profile of CPU usage for the processes and NLMs running on the server. The NetWare scheduling mechanism is nonpreemptive (it is up to a process to relinquish control of the CPU). Although this makes for a very efficient scheduler, a poorly written NLM can hog CPU time to the detriment of overall server performance. NET-Profile can detect these errant NLMs. The NET-Profile tool adds a small amount of overhead to the server operation. If performance is a critical issue, NET-Profile should be run to monitor behavior of newly installed NLM applications. When you are sure that all the NLMs are behaving, NET-Profile can be unloaded from the server memory.

PERFORM3 Benchmarking

One of the most difficult aspects of improving the performance of a network is not knowing to what extent a particular network component contributes to the overall network performance. The PERFORM3 utility can help you measure the performance of various configurations. To evaluate the impact of a network component, replace the component and use PERFORM3 to observe how much impact the replacement has on network performance.

PERFORM3 is a performance-measurement utility that measures data-transfer throughput, which is dependent on several factors, such as the following:

- Server speed (type of server, bus type, and so on)
- Network hardware/topology
- LAN driver
- Server disk subsystem
- Network operating system

PERFORM3, an improved successor to the earlier PERFORM and PER-FORM2 utilities, is available through NetWire on CompuServe. The operation of PERFORM3 is independent of the type of Network Operating System used, as long as DOS workstations running on Intel microprocessors are supported. PERFORM3 can be used, for example, to measure performance of networks based on NFS, LANMAN, VINES, PATHWORKS, and NetWare.

Novell also uses PERFORM3 extensively to benchmark and test various network configurations. The benchmarks mentioned in Chapter 3 (on router performance) were made using PERFORM2.

PERFORM3 measures average and peak data throughput for single or multiple stations performing a benchmark test. The results can be displayed in graph form or printed.

Some of the many applications of PERFORM3 are mentioned here:

- Measuring performance improvements caused by a higher priced or higher throughput network card at the server. You can use this to verify vendor's claims about their network cards.
- Measuring the effect on network throughput of a faster server machine.
- Measuring the effect on system throughput of faster workstations with high-performance network cards.
- Measuring the effect on system throughput of faster server disks.

A study published by Novell in *LAN Evaluation Report 1986* is an example of the usefulness of the performance studies. The study was done using PER-FORM to measure throughput of 286A, 286B, PC AT, and PC XT file servers running on different network hardware. The partial report reproduced in table 9.4, for available maximum bandwidth, was performed using six IBM PC AT workstations running at 6 MHz. Performance of the specialized 286A server made by Novell is much higher. Although Novell has discontinued this server, the report points out an important fact—specialized server machines (Compaq SystemPro and so on) result in higher data throughput.

Table 9.4
Available Maximum Bandwidth Using PERFORM
(Numbers represent kilobytes/second)

Network Type	286A	PC AT	PC XT
SMC ARCnet	115.31	104.54	76.34
3COM EtherLink	235.15	167.40	81.61
3COM EtherLink+	410.11	278.30	125.65
IBM PC Network	34.83	33.62	26.88
IBM Token Ring/4 Mbps	241.33	226.17	130.30

To find out how to use PERFORM3, simply type **PERFORM3** at the DOS prompt. The following is displayed:

```
PERFORM3 version 1.61
Syntax is:

.PERFORM3 <graph name> <...configurable options...>
where options are:
 <test time seconds to test (12 to 65535)>    default = 12
 <start size  (1 to 65535)>                    default = 1
 <stop size   (start size to 65535)>   default = (stop-
start+1)/128
C:\PERFORM>
```

Figure 9.23 shows the results of using PLOTOUT on a test run using the command:

```
PERFORM3 WDPLUS1 12 1 2048 64
```

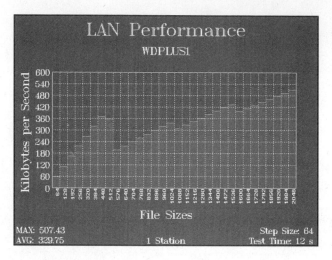

Figure 9.23:
PERFORM3 plot results for file sizes up to 2048 bytes.

The command line tells you that the plot file was WDPLUS1, test time was 12 seconds, and from 1 to 2048 bytes were transferred at increments of 64 bytes. The peak transfer rate was 507.43 Kbps and the average transfer rate was 329.75 Kbps.

Figure 9.24 shows the results of PERFORM3 done on the same network using the command **PERFORM3 WDPLUS3 12 1 8192 256**. If you compare figure 9.24 to figure 9.23, you can see that the data throughput is higher (Peak: 810.69 Kbps, Average = 613.55 Kbps) for large file transfers.

Protocol Analyzers

Protocol analyzers are another tool that can be used to monitor performance of networks. Novell has a protocol analyzer tool called LANalyzer that allows the monitoring of a variety of statistics on the network. LANalyzer is a hardware/software package that can be installed in an IBM-compatible PC with a hard drive. The hardware consists of a special Ethernet or Token Ring board that can operate in *promiscuous mode* (it can capture and store all packets, even those not directly addressed to the LANalyzer). Special digital processing techniques are used on the network boards to obtain timing and collision information that would not be possible with ordinary network boards.

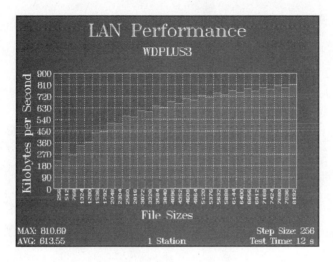

Figure 9.24:
PERFORM3 plot results for file sizes up to 8096 bytes.

For a discussion of packet trace decodes that were taken with LANalyzer, see Chapter 12.

Figure 9.25 shows LANalyzer in the process of collecting traffic on a NetWare Ethernet LAN. As it captures packets and stores them in a trace buffer, LANalyzer also reports conditions on the network such as local collisions, remote collisions, CRC/Alignment errors, and illegal packet lengths. LANalyzer uses the concept of traffic channels to classify traffic. A *channel* is a user-definable category of network traffic. If a packet satisfies the user-defined criteria, it is counted by that channel and saved into the trace buffer. A packet may satisfy more than one channel and therefore be counted more than once. Only one copy of the packet will be saved, however. The bar graph window in figure 9.25 corresponds to the *Rate* column. The musical symbol represents an alarm that sounds if the rate exceeds a certain threshold indicated by the position of the musical symbol.

In addition to capturing and decoding packets, LANalyzer comes with several preconfigured applications designed for NetWare LANs. The applications listed in figure 9.26 are for a NetWare Ethernet LAN.

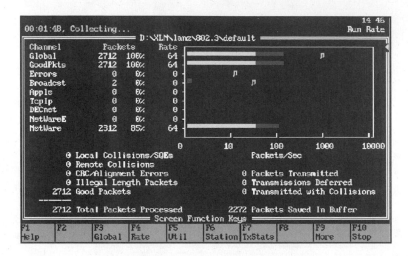

Figure 9.25:
Novell LANalyzer capturing traffic.

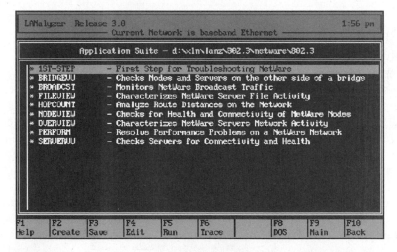

Figure 9.26:
Novell LANalyzer NetWare-specific applications.

Besides providing trace decodes of NetWare protocols, LANalyzer also can be used for decoding the following classes of protocols:

AppleTalk I & II	SMB
DECnet	SNA
NetWare	TCP/IP
NetWare Lite	Vines
NFS	XNS
OSI	

Protocol analysis tools such as LANalyzer from Novell or The Sniffer from Network General can be quite expensive. Fortunately, relatively inexpensive software-based protocol analysis tools also are available. These tools, which use the network board inside a workstation, consist of software that can capture and decode network traffic. One such tool is LANWATCH, from FTP Software (508-685-4000); another is LANdecoder, from Triticom (612-937-0772).

Figures 9.27 and 9.28 show NetWare traffic captured using LANWATCH and LANdecoder.

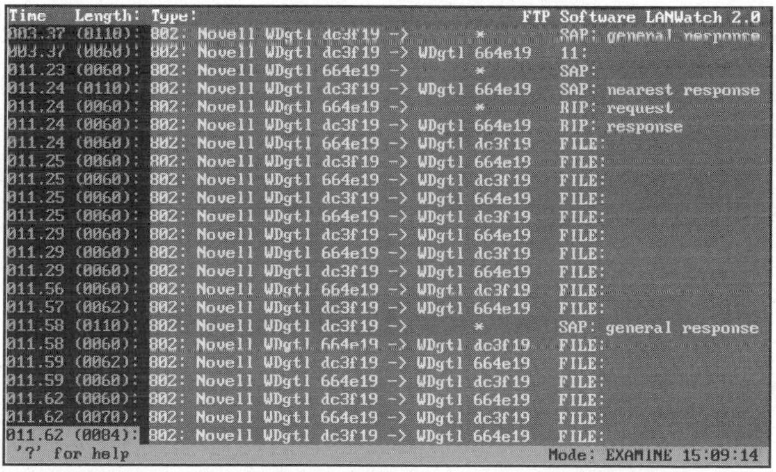

Figure 9.27:
FTP Software's LANWATCH decode.

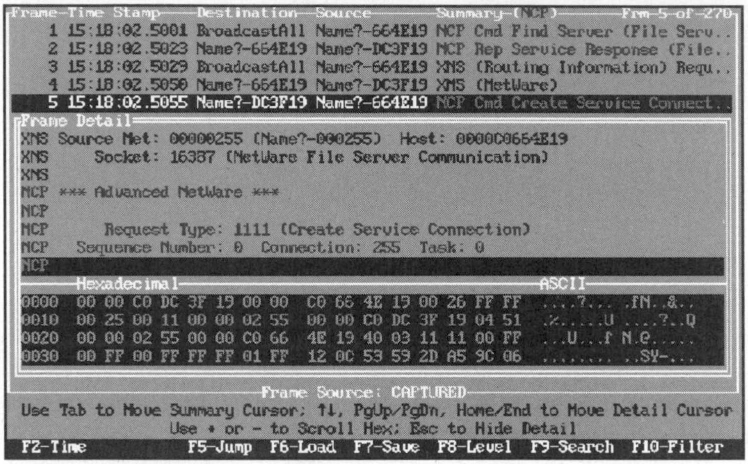

Figure 9.28:
Triticom's LANdecoder.

Understanding How FSPs Affect Server Performance

The number of File Service Processes (FSPs) is vital for good server performance. An FSP is a process that handles file service requests (NCP requests) from workstations. For optimum performance, there need to be as many FSPs as there are simultaneous file service requests.

In NetWare v3.x, the number of FSPs are increased on demand, in keeping with the flexible nature of NetWare v3.x's memory and resource-allocation architecture. In NetWare v2.2, resource allocation is not so flexible. The number of FSPs in NetWare v2.2 is fixed. This number, which is determined by the installation parameters, cannot be changed easily without reconfiguring NetWare v2.2. NetWare versions earlier than v2.2 suffer from the same problem and have fewer FSPs than NetWare v2.2. A symptom of this problem is that the server seems to slow down under heavy loads.

This section examines the NetWare v2.2 File Service Limitation problem. The information is based on application notes (*NetWare Application Notes, June, 1990*) describing the FSP problem, published by Novell.

Role of FSP in Server Performance

To understand exactly why a lower number of FSPs can cause problems, one needs to understand the role the FSP plays on the server.

When a workstation sends an NCP request to read a block of data, the FSP servicing the NCP request schedules the appropriate process to retrieve the information from the disk. The FSP then instructs this disk process to wake it up after it has completed the read operation; then it goes to sleep. If all FSPs are sleeping or otherwise occupied, no other NCP requests can be processed until an FSP becomes available. The server delays or ignores any new NCP requests that come in during this time, and as the packet receive buffers get full, additional packets that are received are dropped. When the workstations do not receive a reply from the server, they timeout and retransmit the request, further aggravating the situation and causing excessive network traffic.

Using FCONSOLE To Monitor FSP Shortage

You can use FCONSOLE statistics to determine whether your server has FSP problems. This statistic can be seen from the LAN I/O Statistics screen that can be reached through:

> FCONSOLE -> Statistics -> LAN I/O Statistics

The field File Service Used Route number indicates how many File Service Packets had to wait for an FSP. You should monitor the value of this field periodically. The difference between two readings gives you the number of NCP requests delayed because of lack of FSPs.

You can use the total File Service Packets to determine the total number of packets processed and compute the percentage of packets that experienced FSP shortage (this percentage should not exceed 10 percent). One word of caution: the field values roll over at 65,536. You may have to take this into account if a latter reading is less than the first.

Also, because of the way some drivers (such as for the Racal-Interlan NP600 NIC) are written to prefetch receive buffers, the File Service Used Route counter increments for every File Service Packet delivered to the server, and this field will be incorrect. You cannot rely on the FCONSOLE technique to make a determination on FSP shortage.

Reason for FSP Limitation

The real reason for FSP limitation is that buffers used by FSPs for incoming File Service Packets are allocated out of a 64K data segment called the *DGroup segment*. The 64K segment is a limit on the data-segment size for pre-Intel 80386 processors. Because the DGroup segment is used also for many other purposes, it limits the number of File Service Packet buffers that can be allocated. The number of buffers available for File Service Packet requests also determines the number of FSPs that can be running on the server. By improving on the scheme for allocating this space, used in NetWare v2.1x servers, NetWare v2.2 can have more FSPs.

For comparison purposes, figure 9.29 shows the memory allocation used for NetWare v2.15 and NetWare v2.2. This figure also explains how data in the DGroup segment is allocated. The Global Static Data (GSD) area is used for global variables defined in NetWare v2.2, as well as for variables defined by NIC drivers and disk controller drivers. The Process Stacks area provides stack space for all the different NetWare processes. The Volume and Monitor Tables contain information about all disk volumes mounted on the server, as well as information for the server's MONITOR screen. Dynamic Memory Pool 1 is used by virtually all NetWare processes and routines as either a temporary or semipermanent workspace.

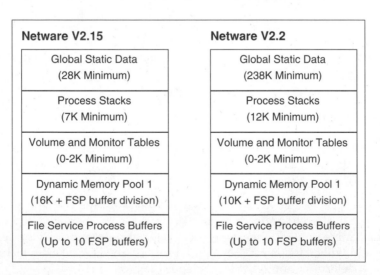

Netware V2.15	Netware V2.2
Global Static Data (28K Minimum)	Global Static Data (238K Minimum)
Process Stacks (7K Minimum)	Process Stacks (12K Minimum)
Volume and Monitor Tables (0-2K Minimum)	Volume and Monitor Tables (0-2K Minimum)
Dynamic Memory Pool 1 (16K + FSP buffer division)	Dynamic Memory Pool 1 (10K + FSP buffer division)
File Service Process Buffers (Up to 10 FSP buffers)	File Service Process Buffers (Up to 10 FSP buffers)

Figure 9.29:
DGroup data-segment map for NetWare v2.15 versus NetWare v2.2.

The major improvements in memory allocation in NetWare v2.2 are that the Global Static Data area and Dynamic Memory Pool 1 have decreased. The Global Static Data area has decreased by 5K, which is offset by a 5K increase in the Process Stacks area.

The Global Static Data area was decreased by moving some information out of the DGroup data segment and into other memory areas. Also, installers can now choose to configure the server with or without core printing services. When core printing services are not linked, an additional reduction occurs in the Global Static Data area.

Reductions in Dynamic Memory Pool 1 are achieved by removing drive mappings for workstations to a new Dynamic Memory Pool 4 area.

One of the design goals for NetWare v2.2 was to correct the problem of FSP shortages. The removal of drive mappings to a separate dynamic memory pool, and a decrease in the Global Static Data area, provide additional RAM for FSP Buffers. After upgrading to v2.2, users can expect to have two to four additional FSPs.

FSP Buffer Size

Table 9.5 shows the memory requirements for each FSP buffer.

Table 9.5
FSP Buffer Components

Buffer Component	Size (bytes)
Reply buffer	94
Workspace	106
Stack space	768
Receive buffer	512 to 4096

As you can see from this table, the total size of the FSP buffer depends on the receive buffer size. The receive buffer size is the largest packet size of any NIC driver configured into the operating system. If you have configured an Ethernet driver with a packet size of 1024 bytes and an ARCnet driver using 4096 byte packets, for example, the size of the FSP buffers for this server is

94 + 106 + 768 + 4096 = 5064 bytes

Also, the Ethernet packets use only 1992 bytes (94 + 106 + 768 + 1024 = 1992); the remaining 3072 bytes in the Ethernet packet are wasted.

This shows that configuring a server with NIC drivers that use different packet sizes can be very inefficient. Try to keep all of the NIC driver packet sizes the same to avoid wasted space. Table 9.6 shows three types of NIC drivers, their respective possible packet sizes under NetWare, and their DGroup buffer sizes.

Table 9.6
FSP Buffer Sizes

NIC Driver	Packet Size (bytes)	FSP Buffer Size (bytes)
Ethernet	1024	1192
Token Ring	1024 to 4096	1192 to 5064
ARCnet	512 to 4096	1480 to 5064

Increasing FSPs

To increase FSPs, you must increase FSP buffers. Before you do this, you should estimate how close you are to gaining another FSP for your NetWare v2.2 configuration. To do so, follow these steps:

1. Figure out the FSP buffer size, using the tables described earlier in this chapter.

2. Take the maximum RAM in Dynamic Memory Pool 1 and subtract it from the fixed size of Dynamic Memory Pool 1 (16K for 2.1x, or 10K for v2.2).

3. Subtract the number in Step 2 from the FSP buffer size. The result is the number of bytes that must be made available before you gain an additional FSP.

For example, if a NetWare v2.2 server has a 1992-byte FSP buffer size and the maximum Dynamic Pool Memory 1 of 10,660 bytes, to get an additional FSP you would have to free an additional 1572 bytes of DGroup. Here is the computation:

$$1992 - (10{,}660 - 10{,}240) = 1572$$

To free this much space, you must know which items have the biggest impact on DGroup RAM allocation. In order of importance they are as follows:

1. NIC driver packet size. The NIC driver packet size has the biggest impact on FSP allocation because it determines the divisor used to allocate FSP buffers. The larger the packet size, the larger the FSP buffer size (and hence the smaller the number of FSPs).

2. Amount of disk space mounted and directory entries allocated. Disk configurations have the second largest impact on DGroup RAM allocation. Mounting a single volume of 2G with 10,000 directory entries would require 13,584 bytes of DGroup RAM.

3. NIC and disk-driver global variables. The size of NIC and disk variables can be significant. The Async WNIM driver alone requires 9942 bytes of DGroup RAM.

4. Possible RAM lost to DMA workaround. In some PCs, the DMA hardware cannot handle receive buffers that straddle a 64K boundary; NetWare will skip memory which, depending on the size of the receive buffer, could be from 0 to 4095 bytes. By changing to a non-DMA NIC driver, this problem can be avoided.

Here is the reasoning used to define this list:

1. The NIC driver packet size has the biggest impact on FSP allocation because it determines the divisor used to allocate FSP buffers. The larger the packet size, the larger the FSP buffer size (and hence the smaller the number of FSPs).

2. Disk configurations have the second largest impact on DGroup RAM allocation. Mounting a single volume of 2G with 10,000 directory entries would require 13,584 bytes of DGroup RAM.

3. NIC and disk variables can be significant in size. The Async WNIM driver alone requires 9942 bytes of DGroup RAM.

4. The maximum DGroup RAM that can be lost to this DMA workaround is 4095 bytes.

5. The maximum DGroup RAM that can be allocated to print spooler stacks is 3340 bytes. (Because NetWare v2.2 allocates these stacks from Dynamic Memory Pool 1, this applies only to v2.1x.)

6. For NetWare v2.1x, the TTS process stack uses 250 bytes of DGroup RAM. Also, Global Static Data variables for TTS in v2.1x can run from 142 to 152 additional bytes.

Based on the preceding list, you can devise an action plan for gaining additional FSP buffer space. These steps are listed in order of increasing impact on the server.

1. For NetWare v2.1x, remove spooled printers.

2. Decrease the number of directory entries, if you have directory entries to spare. The current directory entry usage can be monitored using VOLINFO.

3. Exchange DMA NIC drivers with non-DMA ones.

4. Decrease the NIC driver packet size.

5. Remove TTS (v2.1x only).

6. Decrease disk space.

7. Use Dynamic Memory Pool 1 patch for qualified servers (v2.1x only). This can be obtained from Netwire Forum on CompuServe.

Limiting FSP Buffers

The title of this section may seem to run counter to the previous discussions because the goal all along has been to increase the number of FSP buffers, and hence the number of FSPs.

Limiting FSP buffers is useful when additional Dynamic Memory Pool 1 memory is needed. Whatever memory is not made into an FSP buffer is used for Dynamic Memory Pool 1.

To limit the FSP buffers, place the following statement in the SERVER.CFG file and restart the server. The value of *n* can range from 3 to 10.

```
FILE SERVICE PROCESSES=n
```

Managing Complex NetWare Networks

One of the main problems of managing complex NetWare-based networks is server management. NetWare servers are available in licenses of 20, 50, 100, or 1000 users. Long before a server reaches the license limit, it may become necessary to add additional servers.

You may want to add additional servers for the following reasons:

- To increase server processing power available to users

- To prevent network traffic from becoming a bottleneck at a single server

- To increase remote file system storage capacity on the network

- To split application usage across servers for better performance

The server must process file requests from workstations. In NetWare v2.x, a fixed number of task engines called *File Server Processes* (FSPs) are available (see fig. 9.30). Because each FSP processes only one request at a time, the number of simultaneous requests that can be processed are limited. NetWare v3.x has a more flexible technique for managing the number of FSPs, and uses dynamic memory management to create more FSPs if needed. As the number of users increases, the probability of file service requests waiting in a queue to be processed increases. You can increase the number of FSPs and CPU power by adding servers.

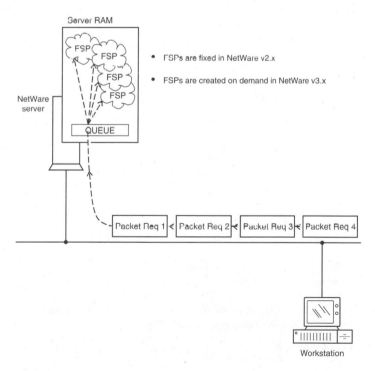

Figure 9.30:
File server processes in NetWare.

The nature of server-based computing is such that the majority of file service requests are directed to the server. If you have a single server, this server and the NIC in the server can become overloaded. Introducing a second server can reduce the amount of network traffic directed to a single server (see fig. 9.31). Cost-conscious organizations often add a second NIC card on a single server and divide the LAN into two LANs interconnected by a server (see fig. 9.32). This scheme also increases effective NIC bandwidth at the server. The second approach does not, however, add more processing power for the server.

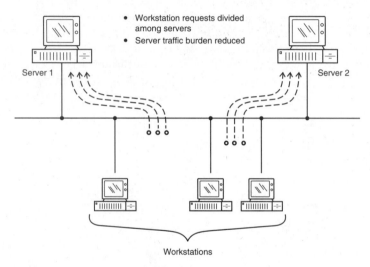

Figure 9.31:
Reducing network traffic with multiple servers.

If the disk storage on the server is not sufficient to support the users, you can add a second disk or a second server with additional storage capacity.

You can use a server to run a variety of network applications. Some applications, primarily those that are database-intensive, place great demands on processing power and server disk storage. These applications are best placed on their own server platform so that they have the dedicated resources of their own server without impacting other applications.

Figure 9.33 shows a LAN with a number of servers. This LAN contains five file servers, six database servers, and a communications server. A user can log in to a number of these file servers to access the resources. NetWare limits the number of servers to which a user can attach to no more than eight.

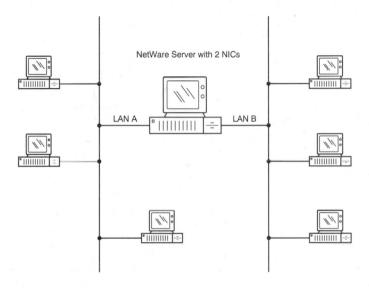

- Assumption: LAN A users seldom need to send direct messages to LAN B users

Figure 9.32:
Reducing network traffic with multiple NICs.

Managing a Multiserver Configuration

Figure 9.33 depicts a setup in which the user must have an account on each of the servers. To log in to the first server, the user must execute the LOGIN command. To log in to additional servers, you must use the NetWare AT-TACH command, and you must make a drive mapping to a directory on the server.

Figure 9.33 demonstrates that when you add an account for a new user, you must create the account on each server. If each server does not contain the accounts, the user cannot access resources on the server.

If the user profile, or login script, must be changed for a user, the login script may need to be changed on all servers. You cannot have one account for all the servers. As the internetwork grows in size, more users need access to resources on several sources. Keeping track of these resources can become difficult.

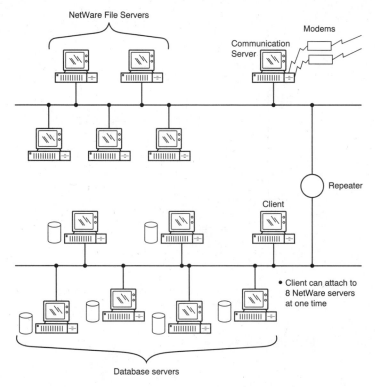

Figure 9.33:
Multiserver configuration.

The Domain Concept

The *domain concept* solves some of the problems of managing a multiserver configuration. The domain consists of a number of servers. To workstations on the network, however, the domain appears as a single logical server. The users are presented with a logical view of the server resources on the network. Note that the domain concept and NetWare name service work only on NetWare v3.x and that this package must be purchased separately.

Rather than logging in to multiple servers one by one, users can log in to the domain and access the resources on the network. One server is designated as the *domain controller*, which manages access to the domain. The domain and domain controller concepts are illustrated in figure 9.34. You need to add a user account just once to the domain, rather than adding the account to each individual server. The user accounts are distributed to the servers on the domain.

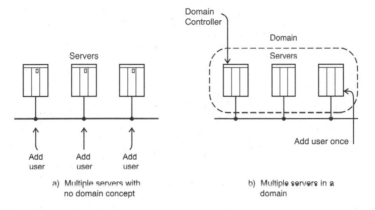

Figure 9.34:
Domain concept.

Each server has the same users, groups, and print queues as all the other servers in the domain. Each user has the same password on each server in the domain. A user can access multiple servers in the domain with a single login command and can print to any print queue in the domain. The domain is set up and maintained by the *domain administrator*.

NetWare Name Service (NNS)

To support the domain concept, Novell designed a distributed name service called the *NetWare Name Service*. NNS is an optional product, which is supported by NetWare v3.x only. The following rules apply to NNS domains:

- Domains cannot overlap. A server can be in one, and only one, domain. Not all servers on the internetwork must be in a domain.

- A domain can contain a maximum of 400 servers. A more practical limit is 10 to 30 servers per domain.

- No limit applies to the total number of domains in the internetwork.

■ Membership of a server in a domain is independent of geographical location, networking topology, or cabling. All servers must, however, be reachable through the internetwork.

Figure 9.35 shows servers for the engineering, corporate, and manufacturing departments of an organization. Using NetWare Name Service, these servers are divided into three domains. The engineers do not log in to each server separately; they log in to the engineering domain and access all three servers. The manufacturing and corporate personnel also log in once to their respective domains.

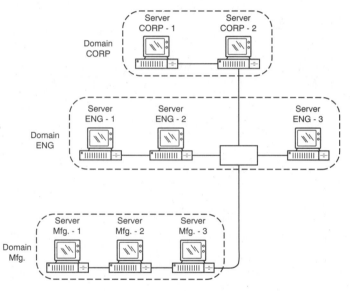

Figure 9.35:
Departmental LAN with domains.

Server access is determined by a user profile. The user profile is a group-level login script that sets up the user's network environment.

The profile has a name that distinguishes it from other profiles and a list of users or groups who are members of this profile. Users have a default profile. Unless otherwise specified, a user logs in by using the default profile. The profile can contain up to eight servers, to which the user automatically attaches after log-in. The profile also contains a profile login script that is executed after the domain login script. Then the user's login script is executed. (Login scripts are covered later in the book.) Under the NetWare work group manager feature, managers can be assigned to profiles. Profile managers can modify the profile they manage.

In the example in figure 9.36, PROFILE_A and PROFILE_B can be defined for the engineering domain. Half of the engineers are assigned to PROFILE_A and can access servers ENG_1 and ENG_2. The remaining engineers are assigned to PROFILE_B and can access all the engineering servers.

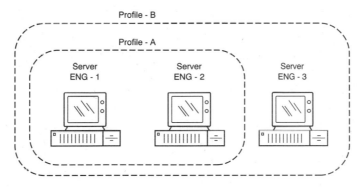

Figure 9.36:
Profiles in a single domain.

If a user or group is added, deleted, or modified on one server in the domain, the change is replicated to every server in the domain. The servers in the domain are synchronized; they have the same copy of the Name Service Database.

You use the NSINSTAL program to install NNS. You must install NNS on every server in the domain. Most NetWare utilities behave the same under NNS. Some utilities may have enhanced options to support the domain concept.

SYSCON (System Configuration), which is examined later in this book, is replaced by NETCON on the NNS database. You must use NETCON instead of SYSCON on servers that are part of a domain. An NNS-aware SYSCON ships with the NNS disks. You must install this version on servers that are not part of a domain. It is designed to protect the NNS database from accidental corruption by nondomain users.

NNS is not exactly transparent to the user. Trustee rights, users object ID, disk space restrictions, intruder lockout, grace logins, and accounting are specific to each server. More importantly, if a server in the domain is down when the Name Service database is changed, synchronization is not automatic when the server is brought up again. You must use the NETCON utility to resynchronize the domain. NetWare v4.x corrects many of these shortcomings by providing a true distributed database (based on X.500) for name services.

Summary

In this chapter, you learned about the factors that affect network performance. These factors can be hardware-based and software-based. The most important factors in each category were discussed.

Some of the monitoring and performance tools discussed in this chapter are the MONITOR NLM, Frye Utilities, Nu-Mega Utilities, PERFORM3, LANalyzers, LANWATCH, and LANDecoder. These tools can be used to fine-tune the network after installation, and to monitor how well the network is performing.

You also learned about the importance of the File Service Process and learned about key aspects of managing complex networks.

Managing Users

This chapter helps you understand the different ways that user and group accounts can be created and managed. Managing user accounts is the most common task that the network supervisor has to perform. To simplify this task, the Supervisor can delegate responsibilities and tasks to assistant Supervisors called *workgroup managers*. In this chapter, you learn how to set up workgroup managers.

NetWare delegates the responsibility for Supervisor tasks one step further by defining file-server console operators who can perform administrative tasks at the file server console.

Also, you can manage the server console remotely by means of the Remote Management Facility (RMF). The MONITOR NLM utility enables you to monitor users. You learn about remote management later in the chapter.

Understanding User Administration

User account administration can be divided into two phases: creating and establishing the user account and maintaining the user accounts.

User accounts can be created in several ways. The most popular way is by using the SYSCON utility because it is an interactive menu-driven utility that is easy to work with. Most NetWare administrators are familiar with its use.

In many environments, user accounts must be created for a large number of users with similar needs. Creating users one at a time with SYSCON can become a daunting task. In these situations, the MAKEUSER utility can be used for a batch creation of users. MAKEUSER defines its own script language, which can be used for creating or deleting users and setting up individual parameters for them.

Colleges and universities are good examples in which user accounts are created in batch. As new students enroll every semester or quarter, old accounts must be deleted and new accounts must be created. The deletion and creation of these accounts can easily be done by using the MAKEUSER utility.

In large networks, multiple servers can be organized as *domains*. Instead of creating user accounts for each server in the domain, a domain user account can be created by using the NETCON utility.

The second phase, maintaining user accounts, involves maintenance of the network. User accounts are never static because the needs of the organization (and thus the needs of the users in the organization) change and evolve with time. The SYSCON and NETCON utilities can be used for the maintenance of most of the user parameters that need to be modified.

Managing User Accounts

This section focuses on managing user accounts. You learn how to perform user-account management for accounts that use SYSCON. In a later section, you learn how to use MAKEUSER to manage a batch of user accounts.

Creating User Names

Before a user account can be created, you must decide which user name will be used to identify the account. A uniform and consistent method should be used for assigning the user names for the user accounts. The following lists some of the conventions for creating user names:

- **User's first name.** The user's first name works well in small LANs, in which everyone is on a first-name basis. Examples of user names for accounts are MARY, JOHN, DAVID, and so on. If there is more than one user with the same first name, there is a name-collision problem—use another naming scheme.

- **User's last name.** The user's last name is common in more formal organizations. If there is more than one user with the same last name, again there is a name-collision problem—again, another naming scheme can be used.

- **User's first name and last name initial.** Although the first name and last name initial usually works to avoid most name collisions, it is not foolproof. If more than one user has the same first name and last name initial, use another naming scheme.

- **User's first name initial and last name.** The user's first name initial and last name also works well to avoid most name collisions.

- **User's initials.** Although the user's initials for the user name is not very common, it can be used in organizations in which people are usually identified by their initials. To avoid name collisions, the initials of first, middle, and last names can be used. Examples of user names are KSS, DGS, JFK, and so on. Unless these names are easily recognizable, they should be avoided. (Some users may not like to be referred to by their initials.)

User names can be up to 47 characters long, but it is preferable to limit them to no more than 8 characters. It is convenient, when assigning home directories, to make the home directory name the same as the user name (see fig. 10.1). Because directory names under DOS cannot contain more than 8 characters, the user name also should contain 8 characters or fewer.

Creating Groups and Group Names

Sometimes users need the same type of access from the server, particularly if they are on the same project team, or if their jobs are similar. NetWare provides a convenient scheme to manage these users. Users with common needs are considered to be part of the same *group*, which has a group name (up to 47 characters long) associated with it. The group is assigned a set of access privileges. All users who are members of the group can then inherit the access rights assigned to the group.

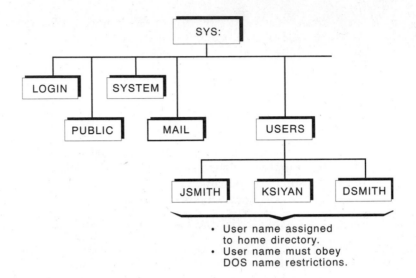

Figure 10.1:
User names assigned to home directories.

Groups simplify user account administration. Instead of assigning access privileges individually, for example, the privileges can be assigned to a group—the users then automatically inherit the privileges of the group. Other benefits of groups are the following:

- Access privileges can be revoked from all users in a group

- Access privileges can be granted to all users in a group

- If a user no longer is a part of the workgroup, he or she can be removed from the membership list for the NetWare group

- When a new user joins the workgroup, he or she can be made a member of the NetWare group

Thus, groups make user account administration easier. They do not have home directories or mail directories, as do user accounts. The concept of groups is used extensively for simplifying user-account management with SYSCON.

SYSCON (SYStem CONfiguration), a menu-driven utility that creates and modifies user accounts, is commonly used to manage user accounts. You also can use the USERDEF and MAKEUSER utilities to manage these accounts.

The following sections give you the steps to follow for the various tasks that SYSCON performs, and show you the SYSCON screens for NetWare v3.x. (SYSCON from NetWare v3.x also can be used for administering user accounts for NetWare v2.x.)

SYSCON's many options reflect the fact that almost all system administration tasks can be performed with this utility. Because choosing these tasks can be bewildering, the user administration tasks discussed in this chapter are grouped by logical functions. These tasks also are presented in a logical order, so if you are setting up users for the first time, you can follow the discussion to simplify creation and maintenance of users. (If a batch creation of users is desired, MAKEUSER/USERDEF can be used. For setting up workgroup administrators, SYSCON can be used.)

The following sections discuss in detail three important system-administration tasks:

- Setting up user accounting

- Creating and assigning group accounts

- Creating a user account

Setting Up User Accounting

Before setting up user accounts, you must plan your account setup. The NetWare manuals include planning sheets you can use for this purpose. You also can use the planning sheet designed by the author. The difference between this and other planning sheets is that user information is presented in a one-user-per-worksheet form (see table 10.1), rather than on one large sheet containing information about many users.

Table 10.1
User Information Worksheet

1. User name: _____

2. Full name: _____

3. Home directory: _____

4. Security equivalences: _____

5. Trustee Directory Assignments:

    Directory   *Trustee Assignment*

    _____   _____

    _____   _____

6. Trustee File Assignments:

    File   *Trustee Assignment*

    _____   _____

    _____   _____

7. Member of groups: _____

8. Managed by workgroup managers: _____

9. Workgroup Manager for:

    Users   *Groups*

    _____   _____

10. Password restrictions: _____

11. Account restrictions:_____

12. Station restrictions:_____

13. Time restrictions:_____

14. User ID (hexadecimal number): _____

For a large network, keeping this information up-to-date can be critical. Store your planning worksheets in a secure place in case of a server disk crash or the loss of the server bindery (internal database) that is used to keep track of user information. These worksheets can help to rebuild the system.

It also is important to keep these worksheets current because user needs evolve with time. Network administrators often are too overworked (or do not set aside the time) to maintain good user-account documentation. If the server disk crashes, it is usually the network administrator who must "rebuild" the system.

The table 10.1 worksheet can be used throughout this book to compile information about the user. Another way to manage worksheets is to utilize an application database in which the worksheet corresponds to a record in a database (or table). Some excellent database-management packages include Paradox, Btrieve, dBASE, or any SQL-based package.

Database worksheets have a disadvantage, however. If you want to share the database, you probably want to keep it on the server, and if the server disk crashes, you lose this database. For this reason, it is best to maintain a hard copy (or paper record) of all information as a backup.

Creating and Assigning Group Accounts

A worksheet similar to table 10.1 can be used to keep track of group information (see table 10.2). Again, the information is presented in the form of one worksheet per group for easy reference.

Table 10.2
Group Information Worksheet

1. Group name: _____

2. Full group name:_____

3. Member list:_____

    _____

    _____

4. Trustee Directory Assignments:

    Directory   *Trustee Assignment*

    _____   _____

    _____   _____

5. Trustee File Assignments:

    File   *Trustee Assignment*

    _____   _____

    _____   _____

After you have filled out the worksheet for groups you want to define, follow these steps to create the groups by using SYSCON:

1. Log in to the server as the Supervisor. The following instructions assume that you are logging in to a NetWare v3.x server. The procedure for NetWare v2.x servers is very similar.

2. Invoke the SYSCON program. A menu appears, showing the SYSCON options.

3. Select the `Group Information` option from the Available Topics box. The Group Names box displays the groups defined on the server, as shown in figure 10.2.

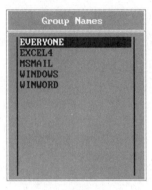

Figure 10.2:
Group Name box, showing groups defined on the server.

4. To add a new group, press Ins. The New Group Name dialog box appears, prompting you for the new group name (see fig. 10.3).

Figure 10.3:
New Group Name dialog box.

5. Enter the new group name and press Enter. The group name that you just added—in this case, DBASE—should display in the Group Names box, as shown in figure 10.4.

Figure 10.4:
New group name displays.

6. Repeat the preceding steps to add new group names.

7. From the list of groups in the Group Names box, select a newly created group and press Enter. The Group Information box for the selected group appears, as shown in figure 10.5.

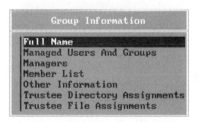

Figure 10.5:
Group Information box.

8. Select the Full Name option and enter a descriptive name for the group.

9. Both the Managed Users And Groups option and the Managers option can be used to set up other groups and users managed by this group, and to set up managers for members of this group.

10. To add new members to the group, select the Member List option from the Group Information box. The Group Members box appears, as shown in figure 10.6.

Figure 10.6:
Group Members box.

11. To add members, press Ins. To delete members, press Del. The Not Group Members box appears, as shown in figure 10.7.

Figure 10.7:
Not Group Members box.

12. From the list of user names that are not members of the group, mark the new members by pressing F5, and then Enter. (You also can highlight a new member, press Enter, and then repeat the process.) The new member names appear in the Group Members box (see fig. 10.8).

Figure 10.8:
New members listed in the Group Members box.

13. Select the Other Information option from the Group Information box. A box displays, as in figure 10.9, showing the group ID and whether the group members are file server console operators.

Figure 10.9:
File Server Console Operator and Group ID box.

14. Press Esc to return to the Group Information box, and select the Trustee Directory Assignments option. A box displays, showing a list of Trustee Directory Assignments for the group. If this is a new group, the list will initially be empty. Figure 10.10 shows this box.

15. To make other trustee directory assignments, press Ins. A dialog box appears, prompting you to enter the directory in which the trustee should be added (see fig. 10.11).

In the current release of NetWare, the default rights assigned for a directory assigned to a group are Read and File Scan. To change the trustee directory assignment, highlight the trustee directory assignment that is displayed, and then press Enter. The Trustee Rights Granted box appears.

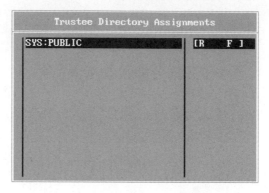

Figure 10.10:
Trustee Directory Assignments dialog box.

Figure 10.11:
Directory In Which Trustee Should Be Added dialog box.

To add to this list, press Ins; to delete from this list, highlight the entry to be deleted and press Del. If the Ins key is pressed, the Trustee Rights Not Granted box appears. Mark the trustee assignment to be made by pressing F5, and then press Enter. Press Esc a few times to return to the Trustee Directory Assignment box.

16. To make trustee file assignments, select the `Trustee File Assignments` option from the User Information box. The Trustee File Assignments box appears (see fig. 10.12).

17. To make other trustee file assignments, press Ins. A dialog box appears that asks you to enter the path name of the file for which the trustee assignment is being set, as shown in figure 10.13. To modify the trustee file assignment, follow the same steps used for modifying trustee directory assignments.

18. Press Esc several times or press Alt-F10 and answer YES to exit SYSCON.

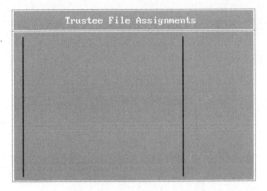

Figure 10.12:
Trustee File Assignments dialog box.

Figure 10.13:
Select the Directory To Select A File From dialog box.

Creating a User Account

In this section, you learn how to use SYSCON to create a user account. The assumption is that you have used SYSCON to create groups. (If you are not sure how to do this, consult the previous sections.)

Suppose, for example, that you are setting up an account for a single user. (Multiple-user accounts can be set up by repeating the steps for a single-user account.) Before you start, you must know the user's trustee assignments and the groups that the user belongs to (fill out the worksheets shown in tables 10.1 and 10.2). Then follow these steps:

1. Log in to the server as Supervisor. The assumption is that you are logging in to a NetWare v3.x server. The procedure for NetWare v2.x servers is very similar.

2. Invoke the SYSCON program. The SYSCON Available Topics box displays, as shown in figure 10.14.

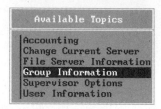

Figure 10.14:
Available Topics box.

3. Select the User Information option from the Available Topics box. The User Names box appears, showing the names of the users defined on the server (see fig. 10.15).

Figure 10.15:
User Names box.

4. Press Ins to add a new user. A dialog box appears, asking for the new user name, as shown in figure 10.16.

Figure 10.16:
User Name dialog box.

5. Enter the user name for the user to be created, and then press Enter. A screen with a default path name for the user's home directory displays.

6. Change the home directory for the user to SYS:USERS/*UserName*, and then press Enter. If asked to verify creation of the home directory, select YES. The new user that has been created—in this case, ADMIN—is highlighted in the User Names box (see fig. 10.17).

Figure 10.17:
New user highlighted in User Names box.

7. Highlight the user name from the dialog box, and then press Enter. The User Information box appears, displaying a list of user attributes, as in figure 10.18.

Figure 10.18:
User Information box, showing user attributes.

8. Select the `Full Name` option, and enter the full name when asked to do so.

9. Select the Groups Belonged To option. A box appears, with a list of groups to which the user belongs, as shown in figure 10.19. By default, the user belongs to the group EVERYONE.

Figure 10.19:
The default group EVERYONE highlighted in the Groups Belonged To box.

10. Press Ins to display a list of groups the user does not belong to. A box appears, with a list of groups the user does not belong to (see fig. 10.20).

Figure 10.20:
Groups Not Belonged To dialog box.

11. Press F5 to mark the groups you want to make the user a member of, and then press Enter. Alternatively, you can highlight a group name

and press Enter. After adding the user to new groups, the Groups Belonged To box reappears, showing the new list of groups that the user is a member of (see fig. 10.21).

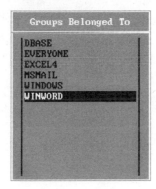

Figure 10.21:
New groups listed in the Groups Belonged To box.

12. Press Esc to return to the User Information box. (For information on creating login scripts, see Chapter 16.)

13. Select the Other Information option from the User Information box and press Enter. A dialog box appears (see fig. 10.22).

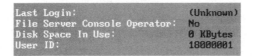

Figure 10.22:
Dialog box for Other Information.

14. Record the User ID in the worksheet in table 10.2. (The *user ID* is the internal name under which the user's information is kept in the bindery. It also is the name of the directory under SYS:MAIL, in which the user's login script is kept.)

15. To create a Trustee Directory Assignment for a user, press Esc to return to the User Information box, and then select the Trustee Directory Assignments option. A Trustee Directory Assignments box appears, as shown in figure 10.23.

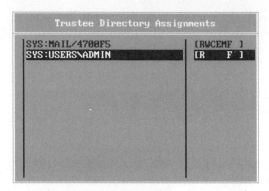

Figure 10.23:
Trustee Directory Assignments box.

16. To make other trustee directory assignments, press Ins. A dialog box displays, in which you add the trustee directory (see fig.10.24).

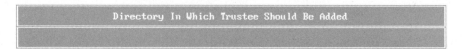

Figure 10.24:
Directory In Which Trustee Should Be Added dialog box.

In the current release of NetWare, the default rights assigned for a directory other than the home directory are Read and File Scan. To change the trustee directory assignment, highlight the trustee directory assignment that is displayed and press Enter. The Trustee Rights Granted box appears. To add to this list, press Ins; to delete from this list, press Del. When Ins is pressed, the Trustee Rights Not Granted box appears. Press F5 to mark the trustee assignment to be made, and then press Enter. Press Esc a few times to return to the Trustee Directory Assignments box.

17. To make trustee file assignments, select the `Trustee File Assignment` option from the User Information box. A dialog box showing a list of Trustee File Assignments appears, as in figure 10.25.

Figure 10.25:
Trustee File Assignments dialog box.

18. To make other trustee file assignments, press Ins. A dialog box appears (see fig. 10.26) and expects you to enter the path name of the file for which the trustee assignment is being set.

Figure 10.26:
Select the Directory To Select A File From dialog box.

To modify the trustee file assignment, follow the same steps used for modifying trustee directory assignments. (For setting security restrictions on user accounts, see Chapter 11.)

19. Press Esc several times, or press Alt-F10 and answer YES to exit SYSCON.

Creating Users with the MAKEUSER and USERDEF Utilities

NetWare comes with a powerful user batch-creation utility, MAKEUSER, that can be used to automate user creation. A script language, consisting of statements (or directives), can be used to specify the information to be entered into the system bindery.

The following is a sample list of a script file, SAMPLE.USR, that can be used to create a user in batch mode. The MAKEUSER script files have a default extension of USR. The MAKEUSER command language consists of a number of reserved words, described in table 10.3. These reserved words are preceded by the pound symbol (#). The only exception to this rule is the reserved word REM (# is optional). To continue on to the next line, the continuation symbol (+) can be used at the end of a line. The sample of the script file is as follows:

```
rem
rem * Create a batch of users. This template file is meant
rem * as a sample MAKEUSER file only.
rem
rem Establish the home directory
#home    sys:users
rem * Users will be members of group students and
engineers
#groups   students; engineers
rem * Users will use a common login script specified by
rem * the contents of the file specified below.
#login_script sys:public/scripts/eng.scr
rem * Max disk space per user=10MB=10MB/4KB=2500 blocks
rem * Note: block #'s = disk space/ block size
#max_disk_space SYS,2500
rem #create User; FullName;Password;groups;rights
#create User1; Full Name;reimman$gauss;wpusers;sys:apps
rwcemf^
#create User2; Full Name;laplace#cauchy;sysop;sys:apps
rwcemf^
```

The #HOME statement specifies that the home directory for users created by #CREATE will be the user name under the directory SYS:USERS. Statements like #HOME, #GROUPS, #LOGIN_SCRIPT, and #MAX_DISK_SPACE establish a context for user creation. This *context* means that the values defined by these statements are valid for all users created by the #CREATE statements, until explicitly cleared by the #CLEAR directive.

The #GROUPS statement specifies that users are members of the groups students and engineers.

The #LOGIN_SCRIPT statement specifies that the login script for the users is described by the contents of the file SYS:PUBLIC/SCRIPTS/ENG.SCR.

The maximum disk space allowed for users is specified by the #MAX_DISK_SPACE statement—it is 2500 blocks or 10M, assuming a disk block size of 4K.

The two #CREATE commands create two users. Their passwords are specified as REIMANN$GAUSS and LAPLACE$CAUCHY. For security reasons, the users must be forced to change these passwords because anyone with access to the MAKEUSER file can see them.

User1 and User2 have membership to groups other than what is specified in the #GROUPS statement. User1 is a member of group WPUSERS and User2 is a member of group SYSOP. Both users have an explicit trustee assignment of RWCEMF to the directory SYS:APPS.

The MAKEUSER script file can be created with a text editor or through the menu-driven front end to MAKEUSER, USERDEF. An additional benefit of MAKEUSER is that it contains the documentation about user information that can be used to re-create user accounts if the bindery becomes corrupted or if the server disk file crashes.

There are a number of commands that can be used to create or delete assign rights to users. In the sample, you saw the use of some of these commands. The first word of the command following the pound symbol (#) is the *keyword*. All commands must be preceded with this character. Comments can be placed by preceding them with the semicolon (;) or the keyword REM.

Table 10.3 lists the different statements that can make use of these keywords; it also contains a description of their meanings. At a minimum, the #CREATE or #DELETE keyword must be in every USR script file.

The NetWare manuals state that #CREATE must have a caret symbol (^) to terminate the statement (or if all the options are not used). Although the caret (^) can be omitted for the current releases of NetWare, it may become mandatory in the future. It is thus a good idea to specify it to terminate the #CREATE statement.

Table 10.3
MAKEUSER Statements

Statement	Description
#ACCOUNT_EXPIRATION *M,D,Y*	Specifies the date on which the accounts expire: *M* is the month number, *D* is the day number, and *Y* is the year number.

**Table 10.3
Continued**

Statement	Description
#ACCOUNTING *B,L*	Specifies the balance *B* to be used for users, and the lower limit value *L* for this balance.
#CLEAR or #RESET	Resets the values of keywords and the contexts they define.
#CONNECTIONS *N*	Specifies the maximum concurrent connections *N* for users.
#CREATE *U[;F][;P] [;G][;D [R]]*	Creates user *U*, whose full name is *F* and has password *P*. *G* is a list of groups the user is a member of. The directory trustee assignment and rights of the user group are specified by *D* and *R*.
#DELETE *U [;U]*	Deletes user *U*.
#GROUPS *G [;G]*	Specifies the group context so that all users created with #CREATE are members of the group *G*.
#HOME_DIRECTORY *P*	Specifies the home directory context so that all users created with #CREATE have their home directory under the directory specified by *P*.
#LOGIN_SCRIPT *P*	Specifies the path name *P* of the file that will be used for the login script file for the users that are created by #CREATE.
#MAX_DISK_SPACE *V,N*	Specifies maximum disk space allowed by created users in terms of number *N* of disk blocks for volume *V*. (The actual disk space depends on the disk block size. For NetWare v3.x, the disk block size has a default value of 4K and is set during volume creation. For NetWare v2.x, the disk block size is fixed at 4K.)

Statement	Description
#PASSWORD_LENGTH	Specifies the minimum password length for the user.
#PASSWORD_REQUIRED	Specifies that passwords are mandatory.
#PASSWORD_PERIOD D	Specifies the number of days D between password expirations.
#PURGE_USER_ DIRECTORY	Works in conjunction with #DELETE. Deletes the home directory when #DELETE is processed.
#REM or REM	Specifies comments in the script file.
#RESTRICTED_TIME D,S,E [;D,S,E]	Specifies the day D during the week, the start S, and the end E times that a user is allowed to log in to the server. The D value can be mon, tue, wed, thu, fri, sat, sun. To specify all days, use *everyday*. The S and E values are the time of the day in *hh:mm am_pm* format. Examples of S and E values are 12:00 am and 2:30 pm.
#STATIONS N,S [,S] [N,S [,S]]	Restricts a user to log in from the specified station only. N is the network address, and S is the station address of the station a user is allowed to log in from. N can be up to 8 hexadecimal digits long, and S can be up to 12 hexadecimal digits long. If all stations are to be included with any network address, the keyword "all" can be used.
#UNIQUE_PASSWORD	Specifies that the user cannot use a password that was used previously.

The following script file is an example of a more elaborate use of these statements. This script file shows that it is possible to set complex account restrictions, such as password length, and time and station restrictions through the MAKEUSER script file. The #CLEAR statement can be used for defining new user contexts in the same script file.

```
rem
rem * Create a batch of users.
rem
rem
rem * Establish the user context
rem
#home      sys:users
#groups    advgroup
#login_script sys:public/scripts/adv.scr
#max_disk_space SYS,1000
#password_length 9
#password_period 35
#password_required
#unique_password
#restricted_time mon,8:00am,6:00pm;+
   tue,7:00am,7:00pm;+
   wed,7:00am,7:00pm;+
   thu,7:00am,7:00pm;+
   fri,7:00am,7:00pm;+
   sat,7:00am,1:00pm
#stations  01200344,all;01300451,22,34,42
#create KARANJIT;KARANJIT SIYAN;$ama;;sys:apps rwcemfa^
#create DEI;DEI SIYAN;$ita;sysop;sys:apps rwcemfa^
#clear
#home      sys:users
#groups    sales;support
#login_script sys:public/scripts/sales.scr
#max_disk_space SYS,500
#password_length 12
#password_period 45
#password_required
#unique_password
#restricted_time everyday,8:00am,6:00pm
#stations    01300451,563
#create BALI;;moti;sysop^
```

To delete user accounts, the following script file can be used. The #HOME and the #PURGE_USER_DIRECTORY ensure that, when the user account is deleted, the user's home directory also is deleted (purged).

```
rem
rem * Delete a batch of users.
rem
rem
rem * Establish the user context
rem
#home     sys:users
#purge_user_directory
#delete user1;user2;user3
#delete user4
```

Using the USERDEF Utility

The USERDEF utility can be used for the following tasks:

- Creating users by using the default or previously defined template
- Setting up a customized template
- Creating users based on the template

These tasks are described in the following sections.

Creating Users by Using the Default Template

To create users by using the default or previously defined template, follow these steps:

1. Log in as a Supervisor and enter the command **USERDEF**. The Available Options box displays, as shown in figure 10.27.

Figure 10.27:
Available Options box.

2. Select the `Add Users` option from the Available Options box. A box appears showing a list of templates that can be used for creating users (see fig. 10.28). One of these templates is the DEFAULT template. The others, if displayed, are templates created by the `Edit/ View Templates` option.

Figure 10.28:
Templates box.

3. Select a template for creating a user. The Users box displays (see fig. 10.29), showing a list of those users that have been created.

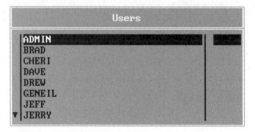

Figure 10.29:
Users box.

4. To create a new user, press Ins.

5. Enter the appropriate responses when prompted for the following information:

Full name

Login name

The new user that is created should be displayed in the Users box and should have a (new) tag next to it, as shown in figure 10.30.

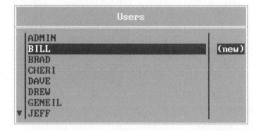

Figure 10.30:
Users box showing new user with tag.

6. Press Esc, and when prompted to Create New Users by using Template, select Yes. The MAKEUSER utility should be run to create the user. If error messages are generated, make sure that you are in a directory in which the default MAKEUSER script is accessible.

7. Press Esc several times, or press Alt-F10 and answer Yes to exit USERDEF.

Creating a Customized Template

To create a customized template, follow these steps:

1. Log in as a Supervisor and enter the command **USERDEF**. The Available Options box for USERDEF displays.

2. Select the Edit/View Templates option from the Available Options box. The Templates box that can be used for creating users displays (see fig. 10.31). One of the templates should be the DEFAULT template. The others, if displayed, are templates created by the Edit/View Templates option.

3. Press Ins to add a new template to be used for creating a user. You are prompted for the name of the new template, as shown in figure 10.32.

Figure 10.31:
Templates box showing DEFAULT template and other templates.

Figure 10.32:
Template prompt.

4. Type the new template name and press Enter. A box displays with the list of the new template options (see fig. 10.33).

Figure 10.33:
Template NEWT box showing new options.

5. Select the `Edit Login Script` option for the new template. A default login script for the new template displays, as shown in figure 10.34.

   To modify the login script, see Chapter 14 for different options. Press Esc to exit. If the login script is modified, save the changes.

6. Select the `Edit Parameters` option from the Template NEWT box for the new template. The Parameters for Template NEWT box displays (see fig. 10.35).

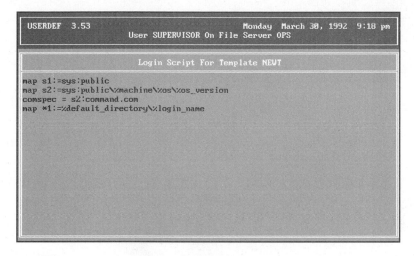

Figure 10.34:
Login Script For Template NEWT box.

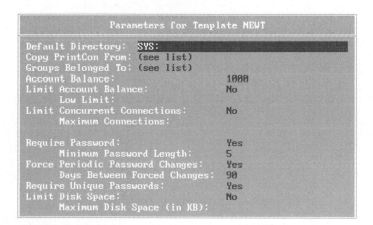

Figure 10.35:
Parameters for Template NEWT box.

To modify the parameters, see Chapter 16 for print job definitions for a user, Chapter 11 for security, and this chapter for account restrictions. At the minimum, change the default directory to the home directory of SYS:USERS. Press Esc to exit, and then save any changes. Press Esc to return to the Templates box. The newly created template should be highlighted.

7. Press Esc several times, or press Alt-F10 and answer Yes to exit USERDEF.

Restricting a User by Using USERDEF

1. Log in as a Supervisor and enter the command **USERDEF**. The Available Options box displays.

2. Select the `Restrict User` option. The Users On Server box displays, showing the users that can be restricted (see fig. 10.36).

Figure 10.36:
Users On Server box.

3. Select a user to be restricted. Select the volume to restrict for the user. The User Disk Space Limitation Information dialog box appears (see fig. 10.37), containing user disk-space restrictions.

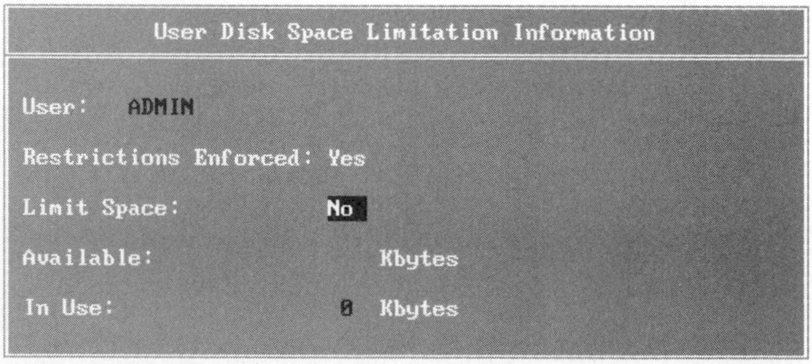

Figure 10.37:
User Disk Space Limitation Information box.

4. To restrict disk space, change the Limit Space: field to YES, and enter the amount of disk space for the user in the Available: field.

5. Press Esc several times, or press Alt-F10 and answer YES to exit USERDEF.

Using Workgroup Managers

The Supervisor can delegate responsibilities for user administration to other special users, called *workgroup managers*. Workgroup managers can administer a group of users or groups assigned to them. This section shows you how to set up a workgroup manager.

Suppose, for example, that you have at least two user accounts, called USER1 and USER2, and that you want to set up USER1 as a workgroup manager over USER2.

Setting Up the Workgroup Manager

1. Log in as a Supervisor on the S386 server. Once logged in, invoke the SYSCON utility.

2. Select the `User Information` option from the Available Topics box, and then press Enter.

3. Highlight a user name in the window titled User Names, and then press Enter. A User Information box displays, as shown in figure 10.38.

Figure 10.38:
User Information box.

4. Select the `Managed Users And Groups` option, and then press Enter. The Managed Users And Groups box displays (see fig. 10.39) and contains all users and groups managed by the user.

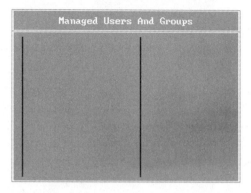

Figure 10.39:
Managed Users And Groups box.

5. Press Ins to add a user or group to be managed. The Other Users And Groups box displays, as shown in figure 10.40.

Figure 10.40:
Other Users And Groups box.

6. Highlight the user that is to be managed. Press Enter to redisplay the Managed Users And Groups box (see fig. 10.41).

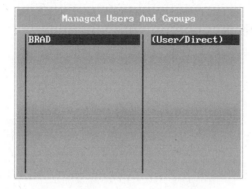

Figure 10.41:
A group highlighted in the Managed Users And Groups box.

> *Steps 7 to 9 are optional. By following these steps, you verify that the manager/managed relationship between the two users is created.*

7. Press Esc a few times to return to the User Names dialog box.

8. Highlight the user selected in step 6, and then press Enter.

9. Select the Managers option from the User Information box and press Enter. The Managers box displays the designated Manager for this user, as shown in figure 10.42.

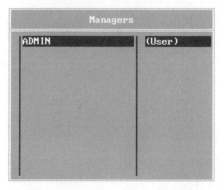

Figure 10.42:
Managers box showing designated Manager.

The list in the Managers box shows all users and groups that are managers of the user designated as USER2.

10. Select Supervisor Options from the Available Topics box in SYSCON. The Supervisor Options box appears, showing the available options (see fig. 10.43).

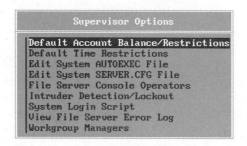

Figure 10.43:
Supervisor Options box.

11. Highlight the Workgroup Managers option and press Enter. The Workgroup Managers box appears (see fig. 10.44).

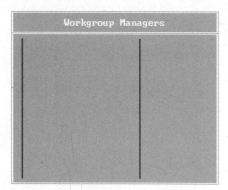

Figure 10.44:
Workgroup Managers box.

12. Press Ins to create a workgroup manager. The Other Users And Groups box appears (see fig. 10.45), showing a list of users and groups who are not workgroup managers.

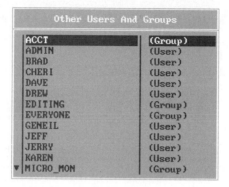

Figure 10.45:
Other Users And Groups box.

13. Highlight a user name, and press Enter. The user is added to the box of workgroup managers (see fig. 10.46).

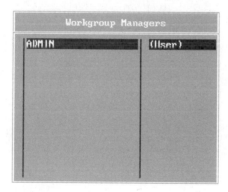

Figure 10.46:
User added to Workgroup Managers box.

14. Press Esc several times, or press Alt-F10 and answer Yes to exit SYSCON.

Managing User Accounting

With the release of NetWare v2.x, Novell provided resource accounting tracking. *Resource accounting* provides the functionality of a billing system in which users can be charged for services used at the file server. The resources that can be tracked include connection time, disk blocks read/written, service charges, and disk space utilized. For logging in to a bulletin board service (BBS), for example, there is a connect-time cost (the telephone call cost) and sometimes a surcharge for using features of the BBS. NetWare resource accounting mimics these functions.

In reality, very few installations make use of NetWare resource accounting directly to bill users for services. There are two reasons for this. First, NetWare servers are administered and used by departments that own the network, so they do not charge for services provided internally.

Second, NetWare resource accounting, by itself, is not a complete system for charging and billing users. To provide a complete system, third-party products must be used that are written with NetWare Accounting APIs (Application Programming Interfaces).

NetWare resource accounting, while not sophisticated enough to provide direct billing of users, is still valuable because it provides statistics on server usage. The accounting usage data is logged in to an internal audit file (NET$ACCT.DAT) at the server. Two utilities, ATOTAL and PAUDIT, can be used to interpret the internal audit files.

Other reasons to use resource accounting are to justify the purchase of a LAN or to compare costs of downsizing from a minicomputer or mainframe environment.

A university computer lab, for example, can use resource accounting to fix the amount of network usage for a semester. A certain quota of resource usage, for example, can be assigned to the user on the basis of the duration of the semester, the typical amount of disk space used, and so on. As the students use network resources, their resource usage is subtracted from their initial quota by the resource-accounting software. When their quota expires, they may request an additional resource quota from the network administrator. Such a system can prevent indiscriminate use of server resources.

Resource accounting also keeps track of dates and times of log-in and log-out attempts. This information is invaluable if you suspect that someone is trying to break in to the system. (In Chapter 11, you will learn other ways to thwart security breeches.)

Overview of NetWare Resource Accounting

NetWare resource accounting can be used to track the following resources:

- Disk blocks read (number of blocks)

- Disk blocks written (number of blocks)

- Disk storage (number of block-days)

- File service requests (number of services)

To install NetWare resource accounting, you, as the Supervisor, must select the Accounting option from the SYSCON main menu. When asked if you want to install resource accounting, answer YES. Resource accounting needs to be enabled just once when the server is installed.

Tracking Connect Time

Connect time is recorded in minutes; it measures the amount of time a user is logged in to the server. Connect-time costs are similar to those used in BBSs and time-share systems. Connect time can be used as the basis for billing users; it also can discourage users from leaving unattended workstations that are logged in to the server. Unattended stations can be a big security risk—imagine what could happen if an unscrupulous user has access to a station logged in with a Supervisor account.

Figure 10.47 shows the resource accounting screen for connect charges.

To get to the menu shown in the figure, log in to the server as the Supervisor and invoke SYSCON. Make the following menu selections:

Accounting

Connect Time Charge Rates

The connect-time charge is based on half-hour intervals. A charge of 1 signifies No Charge. To change a charge, highlight a half-hour interval and press Enter. When the Select Charge Rate menu appears, highlight Other Charge Rate, and then press Enter. The New Charge Rate box appears. Figure 10.48 shows this process.

```
 SYSCON  3.62                      Tuesday  March 31, 1992  8:30 am
                      User SUPERVISOR On File Server OPS

                                       Sun  Mon  Tue  Wed  Thu  Fri  Sat
        Connect Time Charge Rates   8:00am  1    1    1    1    1    1    1
                                    8:30am  1    1    1    1    1    1    1
                                    9:00am  1    1    1    1    1    1    1
 Sunday                             9:30am  1    1    1    1    1    1    1
 8:00 am To 8:29 am                10:00am  1    1    1    1    1    1    1
                                   10:30am  1    1    1    1    1    1    1
 Rate  Charge     Rate  Charge     11:00am  1    1    1    1    1    1    1
   1   No Charge   11              11:30am  1    1    1    1    1    1    1
   2               12              12:00pm  1    1    1    1    1    1    1
   3               13              12:30pm  1    1    1    1    1    1    1
   4               14               1:00pm  1    1    1    1    1    1    1
   5               15               1:30pm  1    1    1    1    1    1    1
   6               16               2:00pm  1    1    1    1    1    1    1
   7               17               2:30pm  1    1    1    1    1    1    1
   8               18               3:00pm  1    1    1    1    1    1    1
   9               19               3:30pm  1    1    1    1    1    1    1
  10               20               4:00pm  1    1    1    1    1    1    1
      (Charge is per minute)        4:30pm  1    1    1    1    1    1    1
```

Figure 10.47:
Connect Time Charge Rates screen.

```
 SYSCON  3.62                      Tuesday  March 31, 1992  8:33 am
                      User SUPERVISOR On File Server OPS

                                       Sun  Mon  Tue  Wed  Thu  Fri  Sat
        Connect Time Charge Rates   7:30am  1    1    1    1    1    1    1
                                    8:00am  1    1    1    1    1    1    1
                                    8:30am  1    1    1    1    1    1    1
 Sunday                             9:00am  1    1    1    1    1    1    1
 8:00 am To 8:29 am                 9:30am  1    1    1    1    1    1    1
                                            1    1    1    1    1
 Rate  ┌─Select Charge Rate──ge─┐  ┌─New Charge Rate────┐ 1    1    1    1
   1   N                           │                    │ 1    1    1    1
   2   │  1 No Charge          │   │Multiplier       1  │ 1    1    1    1
   3   │  Other Charge Rate    │   │Divisor          1  │ 1    1    1    1
   4   └──────────────────────┘   └────────────────────┘ 1    1    1    1
   5               15               1:00pm  1    1    1    1    1    1    1
   6               16               1:30pm  1    1    1    1    1    1    1
   7               17               2:00pm  1    1    1    1    1    1    1
   8               18               2:30pm  1    1    1    1    1    1    1
   9               19               3:00pm  1    1    1    1    1    1    1
  10               20               3:30pm  1    1    1    1    1    1    1
      (Charge is per minute)        4:00pm  1    1    1    1    1    1    1
```

Figure 10.48:
Setting connection-time charges.

The actual charge amount is computed by the following formula:

$$ChargeAmount = AmountUsed \times Multiplier/Divisor$$

AmountUsed represents the units of resources that are consumed; Multiplier and Divisor represent scale factors to convert this figure into a monetary value. Because the AmountUsed resource is a large number, the Divisor should be larger than the Multiplier to scale down resource usage to reasonable cost values. To set the charge to 0, enter **0** for the multiplier value.

Tracking the Number of Disk Blocks Read

A *block* is a unit of storage information. In NetWare v2.x, the disk-block size is fixed at 4K. NetWare v3.x gives you the option of changing the disk-block size during the time of volume definition (see Chapter 8). The default disk-block size for NetWare v3.x is 4K, which is adequate for most systems (most installations use the default disk-block size).

The actual usage depends on the type of application that is running. Database applications that do a large number of disk I/Os, for example, can have a large impact on this statistic.

NetWare accounting can be used to keep track of charges for the number of disk blocks read. It is not realistic to charge users for disk blocks read because even the execution of a program or NetWare utility at the server increases this number. (This is because the entire program is read from the server disk into the workstation memory, which contributes a large number to the number of disk blocks read.)

Figure 10.49 shows the resource accounting screen for disk blocks read charges. To get to the menu shown in the figure, do the following:

1. Log in to the server with a Supervisor account and invoke SYSCON.

2. Make the following menu selections:

   Accounting

   Blocks Read Charge Rates

The blocks read charge is based on half-hour intervals. A charge of 1 signifies No Charge. To change a charge, highlight a half-hour interval and press Enter. When the Select Charge Rate menu appears, highlight the Other Charge Rate option, and press Enter. The screen shown in figure 10.50 appears, showing the New Charge Rate box.

The actual charge amount is computed by the following formula:

ChargeAmount = AmountUsed × Multiplier/Divisor

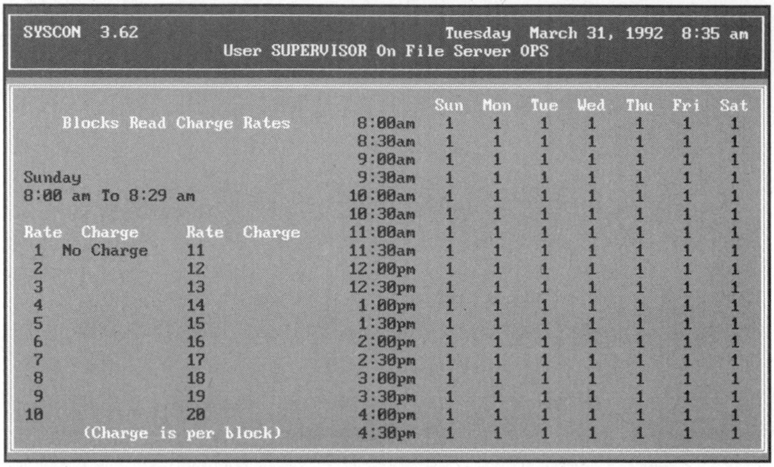

```
SYSCON  3.62                         Tuesday  March 31, 1992  8:35 am
                      User SUPERVISOR On File Server OPS

                                          Sun  Mon  Tue  Wed  Thu  Fri  Sat
         Blocks Read Charge Rates   8:00am  1    1    1    1    1    1    1
                                    8:30am  1    1    1    1    1    1    1
                                    9:00am  1    1    1    1    1    1    1
Sunday                              9:30am  1    1    1    1    1    1    1
8:00 am To 8:29 am                 10:00am  1    1    1    1    1    1    1
                                   10:30am  1    1    1    1    1    1    1
Rate  Charge     Rate  Charge      11:00am  1    1    1    1    1    1    1
  1  No Charge    11               11:30am  1    1    1    1    1    1    1
  2               12               12:00pm  1    1    1    1    1    1    1
  3               13               12:30pm  1    1    1    1    1    1    1
  4               14                1:00pm  1    1    1    1    1    1    1
  5               15                1:30pm  1    1    1    1    1    1    1
  6               16                2:00pm  1    1    1    1    1    1    1
  7               17                2:30pm  1    1    1    1    1    1    1
  8               18                3:00pm  1    1    1    1    1    1    1
  9               19                3:30pm  1    1    1    1    1    1    1
 10               20                4:00pm  1    1    1    1    1    1    1
         (Charge is per block)      4:30pm  1    1    1    1    1    1    1
```

Figure 10.49:
Blocks Read Charge Rates.

AmountUsed represents the units of resources that are consumed; Multiplier and Divisor represent scale factors to convert the number into a monetary value. Because the AmountUsed resource is a large number, the Divisor amount should be larger than the Multiplier amount to scale down resource usage to reasonable cost values. To set the charge to 0, enter **0** for the multiplier value.

Tracking the Number of Disk Blocks Written

You also can keep track of the number of disk blocks written by the user to the server disk. The actual usage depends on the type of application that is running. Database applications that do a large number of disk I/Os have a large impact on this statistic; word processing applications have relatively few disk-block writes. Word processing applications perform most of the editing functions on file buffers kept at the workstation—disk blocks are written only when the file is saved to the server disk.

Figure 10.51 shows the resource accounting screen for disk block written charges.

To get to the menu in the figure, perform the following:

1. Log in to the server with a Supervisor account and invoke SYSCON.

2. Make the following menu selections:

      Accounting

      Blocks Written Charge Rates

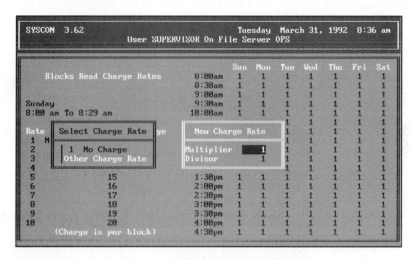

Figure 10.50:
Setting blocks read charges.

Figure 10.51:
Blocks Written Charge Rates screen.

The blocks written charge is based on half-hour intervals. A charge of 1 signifies No Charge. To change a charge, highlight a half-hour interval and press Enter. When the Select Charge Rate menu appears, highlight the Other Charge Rate option, and press Enter. The screen shown in figure 10.52 appears. The actual charge amount is computed by the following formula:

$$ChargeAmount = AmountUsed \times Multiplier/Divisor$$

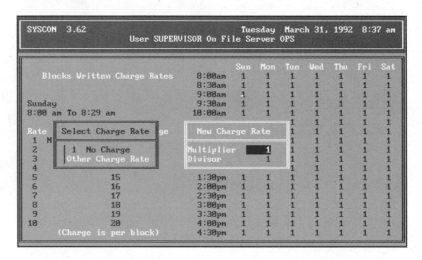

Figure 10.52:
Setting blocks written charges.

AmountUsed represents the units of resources that are consumed; the Multiplier and Divisor represent scale factors to convert the figure into a monetary value. Because the AmountUsed resource is a large number, the Divisor should be larger than the Multiplier amount to scale down resource usage to reasonable cost values. To set the charge to 0, enter **0** for the multiplier value.

Tracking Server Disk Space Charge Rates

The amount of server disk space utilized for a user can be measured in terms of *block-days*. One block-day can be interpreted as one disk block of storage kept by the user for one day; or two disk blocks, each kept for one-half day. The block-day is the product of the amount of disk space and the time over which the disk space is used.

If users are charged for disk space, they are encouraged to clean their files on the server by deleting useless files, or by removing files that are seldom used and can be backed up. The Limit Disk Space option in SYSCON also can be used to prevent users from using large amounts of disk space.

Figure 10.53 shows the resource accounting screen for disk block storage charges.

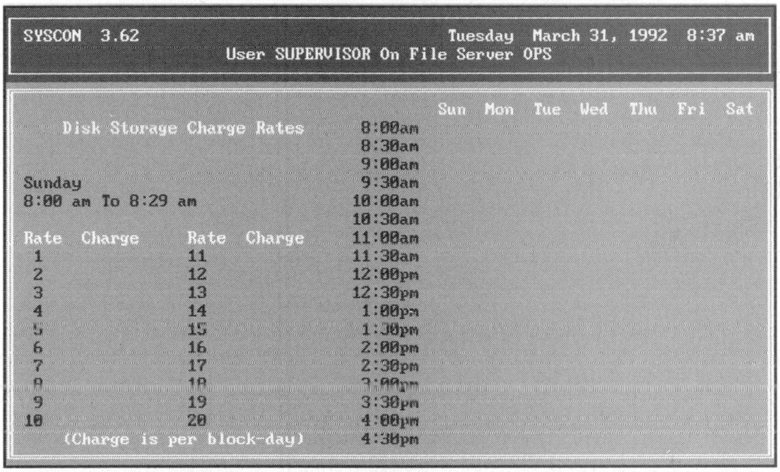

Figure 10.53:
Disk Storage Charge Rates screen.

To get to the menu shown in the figure, perform the following:

1. Log in to the server with a Supervisor account and invoke SYSCON.

2. Make the following menu selections:

> Accounting

> Disk Storage Charge Rates

The disk storage charge is based on half-hour intervals. A charge of 1 signifies No Charge. To change a charge, highlight a half-hour interval, and then press Enter. The New Charge Rate box, shown in figure 10.54, appears.

Figure 10.54:
Setting disk storage charges.

The actual charge amount is computed by the following formula:

$$ChargeAmount = AmountUsed \times Multiplier/Divisor$$

AmountUsed represents the units of resources that are consumed; the Multiplier and Divisor represent scale factors to convert the figure into a monetary value. Because the AmountUsed resource is usually a large number, the Divisor should be larger than the Multiplier amount to scale down resource usage to reasonable cost values. To set the charge to 0, enter **0** for the multiplier value.

Tracking Services Used

Figure 10.55 shows the resource accounting screen for service requests charges.

```
 SYSCON  3.62                         Tuesday  March 31, 1992  8:38 am
                        User SUPERVISOR On File Server OPS

                                          Sun  Mon  Tue  Wed  Thu  Fri  Sat
        Service Requests Charge Rates  8:00am  1    1    1    1    1    1    1
                                       8:30am  1    1    1    1    1    1    1
                                       9:00am  1    1    1    1    1    1    1
 Sunday                                9:30am  1    1    1    1    1    1    1
 8:00 am To 8:29 am                   10:00am  1    1    1    1    1    1    1
                                      10:30am  1    1    1    1    1    1    1
 Rate  Charge     Rate  Charge        11:00am  1    1    1    1    1    1    1
   1  No Charge    11                 11:30am  1    1    1    1    1    1    1
   2               12                 12:00pm  1    1    1    1    1    1    1
   3               13                 12:30pm  1    1    1    1    1    1    1
   4               14                  1:00pm  1    1    1    1    1    1    1
   5               15                  1:30pm  1    1    1    1    1    1    1
   6               16                  2:00pm  1    1    1    1    1    1    1
   7               17                  2:30pm  1    1    1    1    1    1    1
   8               18                  3:00pm  1    1    1    1    1    1    1
   9               19                  3:30pm  1    1    1    1    1    1    1
  10               20                  4:00pm  1    1    1    1    1    1    1
 (Charge is per request received)      4:30pm  1    1    1    1    1    1    1
```

Figure 10.55:
Service Requests Charge Rates screens.

To get to the menu in figure 10.55, perform the following:

1. Log in to the server with a Supervisor account and invoke SYSCON.

2. Make the following menu selections:

   Accounting

   Service Requests Charge Rates

The service requests charge is based on half-hour intervals. A charge of 1 signifies No Charge. To change a charge, highlight a half-hour interval, and press Enter. When the Select Charge Rate box appears, highlight the Other Charge Rate option, and press Enter. The screen shown in figure 10.56 appears.

```
 SYSCON  3.62                                  Tuesday  March 31, 1992  8:39 am
                        User SUPERVISOR On File Server OPS

                                               Sun  Mon  Tue  Wed  Thu  Fri  Sat
           Service Requests Charge Rates   8:00am  1    1    1    1    1    1    1
                                           8:30am  1    1    1    1    1    1    1
                                           9:00am  1    1    1    1    1    1    1
 Sunday                                     9:30am  1    1    1    1    1    1    1
 8:00 am To 8:29 am                       10:00am  1    1    1    1    1    1    1
                                                   1    1    1    1    1    1    1
 Rate    Select Charge Rate      ge        New Charge Rate    1    1    1    1    1
  1   N                                            1    1    1    1    1    1    1
  2        1  No Charge              Multiplier        1      1    1    1    1    1    1
  3        Other Charge Rate        Divisor           1      1    1    1    1    1    1
  4                                                1    1    1    1    1    1    1
  5                15               1:30pm  1    1    1    1    1    1    1
  6                16               2:00pm  1    1    1    1    1    1    1
  7                17               2:30pm  1    1    1    1    1    1    1
  8                18               3:00pm  1    1    1    1    1    1    1
  9                19               3:30pm  1    1    1    1    1    1    1
 10                20               4:00pm  1    1    1    1    1    1    1
 (Charge is per request received)  4:30pm  1    1    1    1    1    1    1
```

Figure 10.56:
Setting service requests charges.

The actual charge amount is computed by the following formula:

$$ChargeAmount = AmountUsed \times Multiplier / Divisor$$

AmountUsed represents the units of resources that are consumed; Multiplier and Divisor represent scale factors to convert this figure into a monetary value. Because the AmountUsed resource is normally a large number, the Divisor should be larger than the Multiplier amount to scale down resource usage to reasonable cost values. To set the charge to 0, enter **0** for the multiplier value.

Using the ATOTAL and PAUDIT Utilities

If accounting services have been enabled, the resource usage-per-user data is stored in records in an internal database file called NET$ACCT.DAT. The chargeOrNote field of an accounting record can hold connect-time charges, disk-storage charges, log-in/log-out times, account-lock events, or server time-modified events.

The information in the NET$ACCT.DAT file can be accessed by the ATOTAL utility, which produces a report on resource usage. This report, consisting of daily and weekly totals of accounting usage, includes connect time, blocks read and written, block-days, and server requests. If there is no charge for a resource, the corresponding entry for that charge is zero. The ATOTAL utility can be invoked from the DOS prompt after logging in to a server. Running ATOTAL produces a list similar to the following:

```
2/13/92:
    Connect time:     32    Server request: 457
    Blocks read:       0    Blocks written: 0
    Block days:       21
2/14/92:
    Connect time:     17    Server request: 2333
    Blocks read:       0    Blocks written: 0
    Block days:       46
Totals for week:
    Connect time:     49    Server request: 2790
    Blocks read:       0    Blocks written: 0
    Block days:       67
```

The PAUDIT utility also makes use of the NET$ACCT.DAT file by displaying an audit report of user activities, such as the log-in and log-out times of a server. The following is a sample list produced by running PAUDIT.

```
9/24/91 14:02:18  File Server KSS
    NOTE: about User KARANJIT during File Server services.
    Login from address 00000352:42608C3C6A93.
9/24/91 14:30:58  File Server KSS
    NOTE: about User KARANJIT during File Server services.
    Logout from address 00000352:42608C3C6A93.
9/24/91 14:31:28  File Server KSS
    NOTE: about User KARANJIT during File Server services.
    Login from address 00000352:42608C3C6A93.
```

```
9/24/91 14:33:46  File Server KSS
   NOTE: about User KARANJIT during File Server services.
   Logout from address 00000352:42608C3C6A93.
9/24/91 15:31:55  File Server KSS
   NOTE: about User KARANJIT during File Server services.
   Login from address 00000355:42608C3C6A93.
10/24/91 9:49:38  File Server KSS
   NOTE: about User SUPERVISOR during File Server
services.
   Login from address 00000255:0080C8706571.
10/24/91 10:03:14  File Server KSS
   NOTE: about User SUPERVISOR during File Server
services.
   Logout from address 00000255:0080C8706571.
```

Each entry in the report consists of three lines. The first line indicates the date and time of the audit event and the name of the server on which the event took place. In the second line, the NOTE item in the report indicates which user account and file services are involved. The third line indicates the event, such as login, logout, and so on. Intruder alerts caused by unauthorized access attempts also are reported in the PAUDIT report. Whenever the file server's time is changed, the event also is recorded in the file.

After a certain period of time (usually a month), the NET$ACCT.DAT file becomes very large, and it is necessary to reduce its size. If the file NET$ACCT.DAT is deleted, it is automatically created the next time a resource entry is made to this file. To reduce the size of the NET$ACCT file, follow these guidelines:

1. Generate hard copies of reports by using the ATOTAL and PAUDIT utilities. The following commands can be used to generate a text file containing the reports, which can then be printed and/or archived:

   ATOTAL 28MAY92.ATO (generated May 28, 1992)

   PAUDIT 28MAY92.PAU (generated May 28, 1992)

2. Archive (back up) the NET$ACCT.DAT file, and then delete it. It will be automatically created by the resource accounting administrator to have console capability at any workstation.

To set up the RMF capability, use the following programs to perform these steps:

RCONSOLE.EXE or ACONSOLE.EXE (workstation)

RSPX.NLM or RS232.NLM (server)

1. Create a customized boot disk for the remote server

2. Bring up the new file server with a remote boot disk

3. Install NetWare from a remote workstation

4. Copy the NetWare file remotely to the server

Managing User Support Remotely

A number of tools are available to enable you to take over a user's work-station remotely. These tools are designed for you to support users remotely and walk them through a problem. Although the process is similar to that described for the Remote Management Facility for the server console, a user's monitor and keyboard are now available remotely to the user. Table 10.4 lists some of the tools that are available for this purpose.

Table 10.4
User Remote Management Support Tools

Software Tool	Publisher
Close-Up/LAN	Norton Lambert
NetRemote+	Brightwork Software
Commute	Central Point Software

In NetRemote+, for example, stations that can be taken over by the network administrator must run a program called NRLISTEN. This program loads as a TSR and can be configured so that a password must be entered before the user workstation can be taken over. Typically, NRLISTEN is loaded auto-matically during the log-in process and takes up about 8K of RAM. The net-work administrator who wants to support a user remotely runs the program NRCALL.

Figure 10.57 shows the NRCALL screen. A list of users that are logged in to the network are displayed. The users that have NRLISTEN running at their workstations are highlighted. To take over the user's workstation, the user name must be highlighted and the Enter key used to select the user. At this time, the user workstation is under the control of the network administrator. To relinquish control and invoke the NetRemote menu, press F1. A useful feature of NetRemote+ is its memory map of the user workstation that can be displayed (see fig. 10.58). The memory map enables the administrator to view remotely the programs that are running at the user workstation. You also can view the version of the IPX/SPX and NetWare shell being run at another workstation.

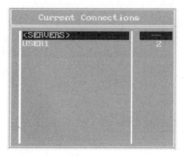

Figure 10.57:
NetRemote+ NRCALL screen.

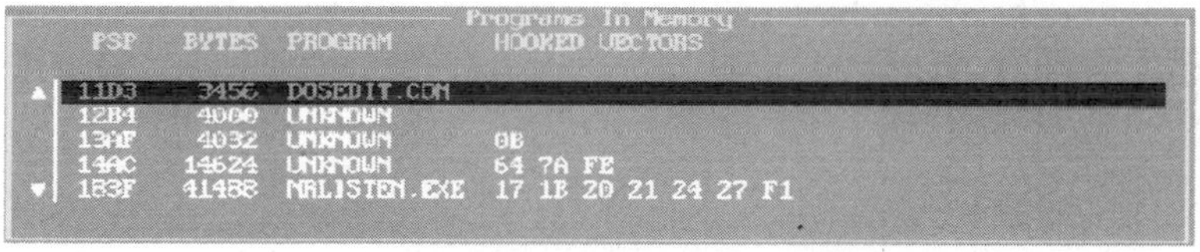

Figure 10.58:
NetRemote+ user workstation memory map.

Summary

This chapter showed you the two ways that user and group accounts can be created and managed using the SYSCON and MAKEUSER utilities.

The SYSCON utility can be used for setting up user accounts and for creating groups and user accounts. It also can be used for controlling user accounting, restricting passwords, and restricting stations and times.

Use the MAKEUSER utility when you need to create several users with similar accounts. MAKEUSER is a command-line utility that uses a text file, containing special statements, to create and delete user accounts. Several examples of using MAKEUSER—from the simple to the more complex—were presented. You also learned specifically how to do common tasks using the SYSCON utility.

The chapter discussed a special class of users, the workgroup manager, that can delegate supervisor responsibilities. The supervisor makes this assignment through SYSCON. You learned how the server can be managed remotely by using the RMF facility in NetWare v3.x. To manage users remotely, several third-party products are available.

Security

Sharing resources in a network environment has its advantages. Along with these advantages, however, come a variety of security problems. These concerns usually take the form of making sure that only the *right* amount of information is shared by users. On a network, there is a need for a mechanism that prohibits unauthorized access to the system or to certain files. For example, a user's personal files on the server should be kept private—other users should not be able to access these files. Also, system files should be accessible only by a network administrator   an ordinary user should not be able to modify or remove applications installed on the server.

NetWare provides security features rivaling those of many mainframe/minicomputer environments. Unless these security features are understood and implemented correctly, however, they do not protect the network. This chapter gives you an overview of NetWare security features and how to implement them.

Exploring NetWare Security Features

To address the rising concern of network security, Novell has published a research report, titled "NetWare Security: Configuring and Auditing a Trusted Environment." The report is lengthy and fairly involved, but it presents a global view of network security that is very relevant for today's network environment. It also discusses specific methods that NetWare uses to meet many of the security requirements published in the *Orange Book* and the *Red Book*.

The *Orange Book* and *Red Book* are U.S. Department of Defense (DoD) publications and, collectively, have become the standard for security of computer systems and networks. (The nicknames come from the color of their covers.)

The *Orange Book* is formally titled *Trusted Computer System Evaluation Criteria* (or the DoD85 standard) and was published in 1985. These standards were later applied to networks, and were then published in 1987: *Trusted Network Interpretation of the Trusted Computer System Evaluation Criteria* (known as the *Red Book*). A companion document, *Trusted Network Interpretation Environments Guideline*, was published in 1990.

For information on these publications contact:

> National Computer Security Center
> 9800 Savage Road
> Fort George G. Meade, MD 20755-6000
> (410) 859-4371

A discussion of these documents' coverage of security requirements would make a complete book in itself. Some definitions from these documents are necessary, however, as you examine NetWare security features.

Seven security classifications can be applied to computers or networks. These classifications define progressively more secure systems and are presented in table 11.1. For example, DOS is classified as a class D system because it has minimal protection.

Table 11.1
Security Classifications from DoD Orange Book

Security Class	Description
D	Minimal Protection
C1	Discretionary Security Protection
C2	Controlled Access Protection
B1	Labeled Security Protection
B2	Structured Protection

Security Class	Description
B3	Security Domains
A1	Verified Design

Source: Trusted Computer System Evaluation Criteria, U.S. Department of Defense.

Each of the classes defines a security policy that is defined in table 11.2. This table is used by the Department of Defense to determine the security classification of computer systems. Table 11.3 presents simplified versions of these classifications that can be applied to commercial systems such as NetWare.

Table 11.2
Requirements for DoD Security Ratings

Criteria	Classes						
Security Policy:	**D**	**C1**	**C2**	**B1**	**B2**	**B3**	**A1**
Discretionary Access Control	x	R	R	-	-	R	-
Object Reuse	x	x	R	-	-	-	-
Labels	x	x	x	R	R	-	-
Label Integrity	x	x	x	R	-	-	-
Exportation of Labeled Info	x	x	x	R	-	-	-
Label Human-Readable Output	x	x	x	R	-	-	-
Mandatory Access Control	x	x	x	R	R	-	-
Subject Sensitivity Labels	x	x	x	x	R	-	-
Device Labels	x	x	x	x	R	-	-

continues

Table 11.2
Continued

Criteria	Classes						
Accountability:	**D**	**C1**	**C2**	**B1**	**B2**	**B3**	**A1**
Identification/ Authentication	x	R	R	R	-	-	-
Audit	x	x	R	R	R	R	-
Trusted Path	x	x	x	x	R	R	-
Assurance:							
System Architecture	x	R	R	R	R	R	-
System Integrity	x	R	-	-	-	-	-
Security Testing	x	R	R	R	R	R	R
Design Spec/ Verification	x	x	x	R	R	R	R
Covert Channel Analysis	x	x	x	x	R	R	R
Trust Facility Management	x	x	x	x	R	R	-
Trust Recovery	x	x	x	x	x	R	-
Trusted Distribution	x	x	x	x	x	x	R
Documentation:							
Security Features User Guide	x	R	-	-	-	-	-
Trusted Facility Manual	x	R	R	R	R	R	-

Criteria	Classes						
Documentation:	**D**	**C1**	**C2**	**B1**	**B2**	**B3**	**A1**
Test Documentation	x	R	-	-	R	-	R
Design Documentation	x	R	-	R	R	R	R

x = no requirement.
- = same requirements as the next lower class
R = additional requirements over the lower classes
Source: Trusted Computer System Evaluation Criteria, U.S. Department of Defense.

Table 11.3
Commercial Interpretation of Security Classifications

Criteria	Classes			
Security:	**D**	**C**	**B**	**A**
Discretionary Access Control	x	R	R	-
Object Reuse	x	R	-	-
Labels	x	x	R	-
Label Integrity	x	x	R	-
Exportation of Labeled Information	x	x	R	-
Labeling Human-Readable Output	x	x	R	-
Mandatory Access Control	x	x	R	-
Subject Sensitivity Labels	x	x	R	-
Device Labels	x	x	R	-

continues

Table 11.3
Continued

Criteria	Classes			
Accountability:	D	C	B	A
Identification and Authentication	x	R	R	-
Audit	x	R	R	-
Trusted Path	x	x	R	-
Assurance:				
System Architecture	x	R	R	-
System Integrity	x	R	-	-
Security Testing	x	R	R	R
Design Specification/Verification	x	x	R	R
Covert Channel Analysis	x	x	R	R
Trust Facility Management	x	x	R	-
Trust Recovery	x	x	R	-
Trusted Distribution	x	x	x	R
Documentation:				
Security Features User Guide	x	R	-	-
Trusted Facility Manual	x	R	R	-
Test Documentation	x	R	R	R
Design Documentation	x	R	R	R

x = *no requirement.*
- = *same requirements as the next lower class*
R = *additional requirements over the lower classes*
Source: Trusted Computer System Evaluation Criteria, U.S. Department of Defense.

Many systems claim to satisfy a certain security classification when, in fact, they do not. The certification process for any security system is lengthy and expensive, and it must be conducted by a U.S. government agency. A class A system is not necessarily the most desirable solution for commercial environments—such a system is very expensive to purchase, and the overhead costs for implementing all of the security features are tremendous.

A newly installed NetWare operating system has a security classification of D (minimal protection) because the security features have not yet been activated. For example, there is not yet a password on the Supervisor account. A properly configured NetWare system has a class C security rating. In this chapter, you learn to implement the various security features of NetWare.

Using Log-in Security

At the very minimum, the log-in security of NetWare should be enabled. When a user invokes the LOGIN.EXE program from the SYS:LOGIN directory on the server, a copy of this program is transferred to the workstation memory. The LOGIN.EXE program acts as the guardian of the NetWare NOS.

In current NetWare releases, the user password is encrypted before transmission to prevent devices, such as protocol analyzers, from "seeing" the password in the clear. This encryption does not, however, prevent a clever user from capturing the encrypted password and replaying the log-in sequence from another workstation to gain unauthorized access to a user account. To foil such attempts, NetWare employs a special *log key* that is unique from session to session and is difficult to duplicate.

The complete log-in process is described in the following steps:

1. The LOGIN program asks for the user name.

2. The user inputs his user name, or enters the server/user name combination. If the user specifies a new server, LOGIN locates and attaches to the specified server. The details of the workstation attachment mechanism are discussed in Chapter 12.

3. The workstation then issues an NCP LOGOUT request to clear any connection information left from a previous session. This request is made because of a feature of the LOGIN program that automatically logs you out of the current session if you run LOGIN while logged in to the server.

4. The workstation requests the object ID of the user name account. This is the hexadecimal user ID number described in Chapter 10.

5. The workstation requests a log key from the server. This log key is unique for a given session. The server responds to this request by sending out an 8-byte variable log key.

6. LOGIN requests the user password, and then performs a non-reversible encryption using the user's object ID and password to calculate a 16-byte encrypted password value.

7. The workstation encrypts the 16-byte encrypted value and the variable 8-byte log key by using a non-reversible encryption algorithm to get a new 8-byte password value that is transmitted to the server for authentication. This process is essentially double-encryption.

8. The server repeats the double-encryption performed by the workstation to get an 8-byte password value.

9. If the values from the workstation and the server match, user access is granted; otherwise, the log-in attempt is rejected and the intruder lockout counter for that user is incremented. This counter limits the number of unsuccessful log-in attempts that can be made.

Using Password Security

In this section, you learn some general methods for selecting passwords and ways to safeguard password security. You also learn how to implement NetWare's password security restrictions.

Protecting Passwords

NetWare security is password-based. Passwords are the first line of defense. If a user knows or guesses your password, however, he can access your account. After the password is verified by the LOGIN utility, the intruder has access to all privileges for your account. (The user is limited only by the limitations imposed on the account.) If he manages to invade a Supervisor account, the entire network is in jeopardy. Therefore, Supervisor passwords must be guarded with extreme care and changed often. Unfortunately, many

Supervisors consider themselves exempt from the security restrictions imposed on normal users. Intruders who want to break into the system thus focus their attention on obtaining the Supervisor passwords.

Another important aspect of NetWare security is the physical security of the servers. The NetWare server machines must be kept in a physically secure location, with limited access. It is possible, however, to boot the server machine under DOS—perhaps when no one is logged in to the server—and use programs to obtain a *binary dump* of critical locations on the disk. These dumps can be used to decrypt the Supervisor password. (Novell will probably make this process more difficult in the future because of some adverse publicity.)

The following guidelines can be followed to protect passwords:

- Make passwords mandatory for all users. This control is accessed through SYSCON under NetWare.

- Change the defaults that come with the system. For example, the initial defaults for SUPERVISOR and GUEST are no password.

- Do not write down your password anywhere, especially on or near the PC. Take the extra trouble to remember your password.

- Do not type your password while others are watching, especially if you are not a touch typist. If you suspect that you are being observed as you type in your password, change your password at the first secure opportunity.

- Never let another user use or share your password. If your password is revealed—whether deliberately or inadvertently—change it as soon as you can.

Selecting Passwords

If the network administrator allows you to chose your own passwords, pick passwords that are not easy to guess. NetWare passwords can be up to 127 characters long. The following lists some general guidelines for creating good passwords:

1. Create passwords that are not found in any dictionary. Words that are found in a dictionary are subject to a "dictionary attack" program that can systematically try dictionary entries to obtain your password.

2. Avoid passwords that are names of people or pets (especially family members or family pets). Good hackers usually do their homework.

3. Passwords that are a mix of alphabetic and numeric characters are better than passwords that are made up of one or the other. Especially avoid all numeric passwords, such as phone numbers, birth dates, and social security numbers.

4. Create passwords that are relatively long—they should contain no fewer than eight characters. Short passwords are vulnerable to an automated attack in which all possible combinations can be tried. If you are a network administrator, you can implement a minimum password length through SYSCON (or when the user account is created with MAKEUSER). A longer password may take an extra second or two to enter, but the extra security is well worth the effort.

5. Do not use the names of machines and servers you access as passwords.

6. When making a password, use a combination of short words, special characters, and numbers. An example of such a password is **$lock;not9he**.

7. Avoid meaningless passwords that you are tempted to write in a book or some place for future reference.

8. To remember passwords, use contractions of phrases such as: "Better not forget this password" can be **Bet!fogt:pwd** or the phrase "Remember to water plants today" can be abbreviated as **Remb^wtr%plnts[tdy]**.

9. Pick passwords that are pronounceable such as: **Hick*Enuf**, **O2.beRich**, and **O2be.Sprt**.

Some security-conscious organizations insist that employees agree in writing to comply with documented guidelines for creating passwords and other security matters. Others use machine-generated passwords consisting of random letters and numbers. Again, the problem with this method is that users are tempted to write down these hard-to-remember passwords, providing the opportunity for discovery.

Implementing NetWare Password Security

Figure 11.1 shows the account balance/restrictions box for a user (in this case ANNE), which can be used to control password permissions.

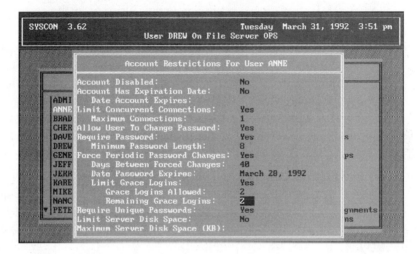

Figure 11.1:
Account Restrictions For User box.

To display this box, perform the following steps:

1. Log in to the server with a Supervisor account and invoke SYSCON.

2. Make the following menu selections:

   User Information

   Select a user

   Account Restrictions

From the box shown in the figure, the following password restrictions can be noted about the user named ANNE:

- The number of *concurrent connections*, or the workstations that USER1 can log in to simultaneously, is limited to one.

- ANNE can change her password, but the minimum password length is eight characters.

■ ANNE is required to change her password every 40 days, and her current password expires on March 28, 1992.

■ The number of *grace logins* are limited to two. That is, ANNE receives two warnings that her password is expiring and must be changed. If she fails to assign a new password after the second warning, it expires and a Supervisor must assign a new one.

■ ANNE cannot reuse old passwords when the current password expires. Passwords that differ from each other by two digits, such as the number of the month that the password is changed, should be avoided. These passwords are easy to guess.

Any of these restrictions can be changed for a user account. To change the default password restrictions for all users that will be created in the future, use the dialog box shown in figure 11.2. To display this dialog box, perform the following steps:

1. Log in to the server with a Supervisor account and invoke SYSCON.

2. Make the following menu selections:

   Supervisor Options

   Default Account Balance/Restrictions

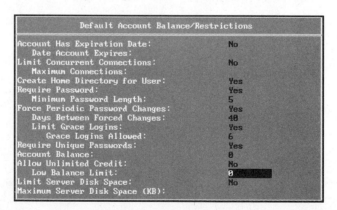

Figure 11.2:
Default Account Balance/Restrictions dialog box.

Understanding the Intruder/ Detection Lockout Feature

The Intruder Detection/Lockout feature of NetWare limits the number of unsuccessful log-in attempts a user can make. After a predefined number of attempts, NetWare assumes that the user is an intruder and locks the user out for a period of time set by the administrator. The Intruder Detection/ Lockout dialog box, shown in figure 11.3, controls the intruder lockout mechanism. To display this dialog box, perform the following steps:

1. Log in to the server with a Supervisor account and invoke SYSCON.

2. Make the following menu selections:

   Supervisor Options

   Intruder Detection/Lockout

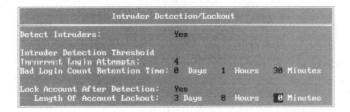

Figure 11.3:
Intruder Detection/Lockout box.

When an intrusion attempt is discovered, it is displayed on the server console and also logged in the NET$ACCT.DAT file, where it can be seen by using the PAUDIT utility (discussed in Chapter 10). The record indicates the user name, the date and time of the attempted log-in, and the physical node address from which the attempt was made. Intruder attempts are logged only for valid user names. If an invalid user name is used, NetWare password security rejects the log-in attempt, but no intrusion attempt is registered.

In the Intruder Detection/Lockout box, the Bad Login Count Retention Time field controls the sensitivity of the intruder detection/lockout mechanism; it can be defined as the time period over which unsuccessful log-in attempts are evaluated as intrusions. This sensitivity can be set between one minute and 40 days. The Length Of Account Lockout field defines the time for which the intruder is locked out and, just as the preceding setting, can be set to a value between one minute and 40 days. During this time, the user cannot log in unless reinstated by the Supervisor.

The intruder detection/lockout feature also can be used to foil the automated attacks discussed earlier in this chapter. This mechanism can be enabled for the Supervisor account; using it can be dangerous, however, if there is only one Supervisor account (SUPERVISOR). Anyone can then lock out the Supervisor account by deliberately trying out a few incorrect passwords. The Supervisor account is then locked out for the time delay specified by SYSCON—in the worst case, for up to 40 days!

Restricting Access Based on User Profile

The most effective way to secure system and user data is to correctly use the following features:

- Directory trustee assignment
- File trustee assignment (NetWare version 3.x only)
- Directory attribute security
- File attribute security
- File server security

The Directory trustee assignment feature controls access to files in a directory and can be set explicitly for users, or these assignments can be inherited by virtue of membership to a group. The File trustee assignment feature is defined in NetWare version 3.x and provides a finer level of control over individual files in a directory. Trustee assignments have the following meanings:

- Supervisory (NetWare version 3.x only)
- Read
- Write
- Create
- Modify
- File Scan
- Access Control

The Directory attribute and File attribute security features are flags that can be set on a directory and file to modify ways that files can be accessed. For example, all program files must be flagged with Copy Inhibit, Delete Inhibit, and Rename Inhibit, at least. For extreme security, the Execute Only flag also can be added, preventing the file from being copied and backed up (even by the Supervisor). When assigned, the Execute Only flag cannot be removed from the file, but the file can be deleted, and then reinstalled. Unfortunately, some programs do not operate correctly with the Execute Only flag, so care must be exercised in its use.

The Read audit (Ra) and Write audit (Wa) flags mentioned in the NetWare manuals are not implemented for NetWare version 3.11 and NetWare version 2.2.

Enabling Default Security Options

As previously discussed, most of NetWare's security features are not enabled when initially installed, which eases the job of initial system administration.

Figure 11.4 shows the Default Account Balance/Restrictions dialog box as seen by using the SYSCON utility. You can see that there is no account expiration date, no limit on concurrent connections, and no password requirements.

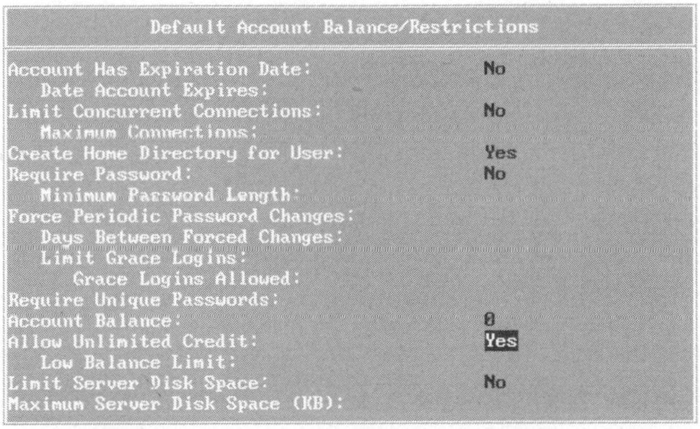

```
              Default Account Balance/Restrictions
Account Has Expiration Date:                No
    Date Account Expires:
Limit Concurrent Connections:               No
    Maximum Connections:
Create Home Directory for User:             Yes
Require Password:                           No
    Minimum Password Length:
Force Periodic Password Changes:
    Days Between Forced Changes:
    Limit Grace Logins:
        Grace Logins Allowed:
Require Unique Passwords:
Account Balance:                            0
Allow Unlimited Credit:                     Yes
    Low Balance Limit:
Limit Server Disk Space:                    No
Maximum Server Disk Space (KB):
```

Figure 11.4:
Default Account Balance/Restrictions box, with the Allow Unlimited Credit field set to Yes.

If the Limit Concurrent Connections: and Require Password fields are set to Yes, the Default Account Balance/Restrictions are changed to that shown in figure 11.5. The minimum password length is changed to five, but there is no requirement on unique passwords; that is, a user can reuse old passwords.

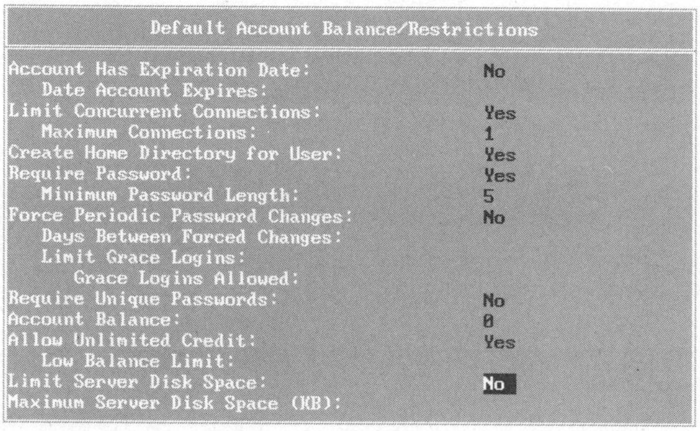

```
           Default Account Balance/Restrictions
Account Has Expiration Date:            No
    Date Account Expires:
Limit Concurrent Connections:           Yes
    Maximum Connections:                1
Create Home Directory for User:         Yes
Require Password:                       Yes
    Minimum Password Length:            5
Force Periodic Password Changes:        No
    Days Between Forced Changes:
    Limit Grace Logins:
        Grace Logins Allowed:
Require Unique Passwords:               No
Account Balance:                        0
Allow Unlimited Credit:                 Yes
    Low Balance Limit:
Limit Server Disk Space:                No
Maximum Server Disk Space (KB):
```

Figure 11.5:
Default Account Balance/Restrictions with the Limit Concurrent Connections: and Require Password: fields set to Yes.

If the Force Periodic Password Changes field is set to Yes, the defaults shown in figure 11.6 are displayed. You see that the days between forced changes of passwords is set to 40, and six grace log-ins are allowed after the password expires.

The intruder detection/lockout mechanism is not automatically enabled. It can be enabled by selecting Supervisor Options from SYSCON, and then selecting the `Intruder Detection/Lockout` option. When enabled, the default values, shown in figure 11.7 are selected. The intruder threshold is set to 7 attempts, the retention time is set to 30 minutes, and the length of lockout is 15 minutes. With these default settings, a clever intruder can try a maximum of 6 attempts every hour without completely locking up the account.

Although you should not be too liberal with threshold setting, keep in mind that everyone makes occasional typing errors. If the user is legitimate and simply makes a mistake, he should be able to enter the correct information on the second or third try. An intruder, however, may need several attempts to successfully open the account.

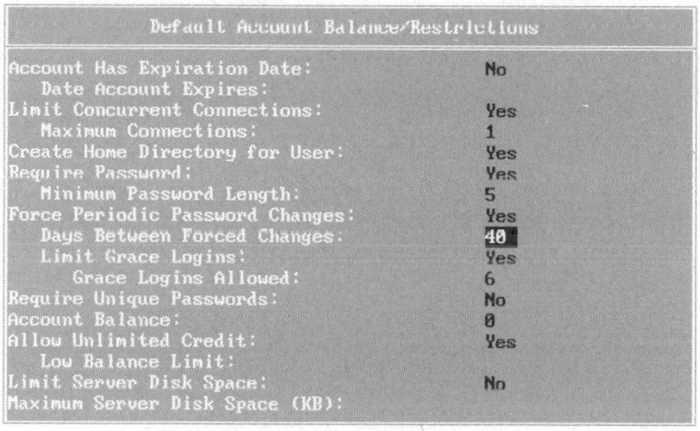

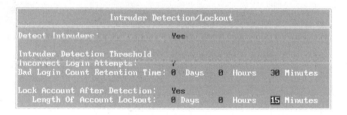

Figure 11.6:
Default Account Balance/Restrictions with the Force Periodic Password Changes field set to Yes.

Figure 11.7:
Default values in Intruder Detection/Lockout box.

Establishing a Class C Installation

The Default Account Balance/Restrictions settings are not adequate for secure installations. Instead, use the default settings shown in figures 11.8 and 11.9, which are adequate for most installations. By using these settings, the NetWare installation can be classified as a class C system.

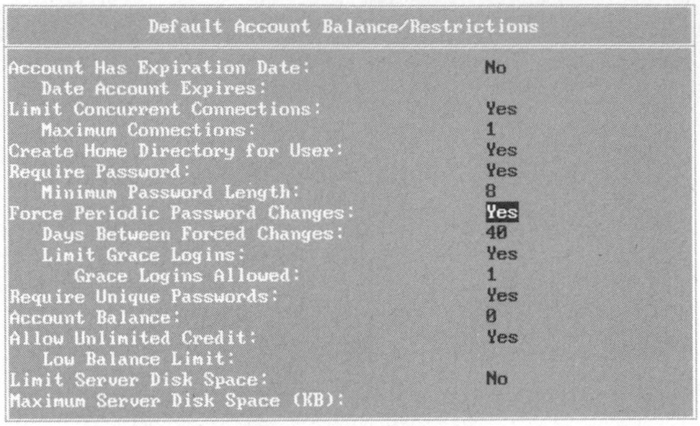

```
                Default Account Balance/Restrictions
Account Has Expiration Date:              No
    Date Account Expires:
Limit Concurrent Connections:            Yes
    Maximum Connections:                 1
Create Home Directory for User:          Yes
Require Password:                        Yes
    Minimum Password Length:             8
Force Periodic Password Changes:         Yes
    Days Between Forced Changes:         40
    Limit Grace Logins:                  Yes
        Grace Logins Allowed:            1
Require Unique Passwords:                Yes
Account Balance:                         0
Allow Unlimited Credit:                  Yes
    Low Balance Limit:
Limit Server Disk Space:                 No
Maximum Server Disk Space (KB):
```

Figure 11.8:
Recommended Default Account Balance/Restrictions settings for a class C security rating.

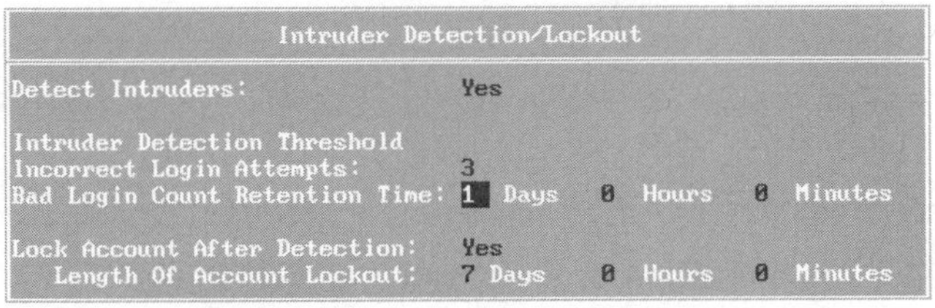

```
                Intruder Detection/Lockout
Detect Intruders:              Yes

Intruder Detection Threshold
Incorrect Login Attempts:      3
Bad Login Count Retention Time: 1  Days   0  Hours   0  Minutes

Lock Account After Detection:  Yes
    Length Of Account Lockout:  7 Days   0  Hours   0  Minutes
```

Figure 11.9:
Recommended Intruder Detection/Lockout default settings.

Using Bindery Audit Tools

Two excellent bindery audit tools are the SECURITY.EXE utility (which comes with NetWare) and BINDVIEW+ (available from the LAN Support Group, (713) 789-0882).

The SECURITY.EXE utility can be run by Supervisors to assist network administrators in determining how secure their NetWare configuration is. The utility must be run by a user with Supervisor privileges. It provides a list of potentially weak areas of the network's security, checks the bindery (system internal database) for user and group objects, and notifies you of potential problems due to excessive security imposed on a user or group (or due to unrestricted access because of no passwords).

The following report was produced by running the SECURITY utility. Notice that a number of security holes, or weaknesses, are reported; the main ones involve excessive rights to directories and the lack of passwords on many critical user accounts.

```
User AMAR (Full Name: AMAR RAMA)
  Has [ R  FA] rights in SYS:PUBLIC (maximum should be [ R  F ])
  Does not require a password
User DEI
  Account has not been used for more than 3 weeks
    Last Login: Thursday  October 24, 1992  9:45 am
  Does not require a password
  No Full Name specified
User ADMIN
  Is security equivalent to user SUPERVISOR
  Account has not been used for more than 3 weeks
    Last Login: Thursday  October 24, 1992  1:19 pm
  Does not require a password
  No Full Name specified
User USER15 (Full Name: USER NAME)
  Does not require a password
User KARANJIT (Full Name: Karanjit S. Siyan)
  Is security equivalent to user SUPERVISOR
  Account has not been used for more than 3 weeks
    Last Login: Friday  September 27, 1992  10:12 am
  Does not require a password
User GUEST
  Has no LOGIN_CONTROL property
  No Full Name specified
User SUPERVISOR
  Does not require a password
  No Full Name specified
```

In general, SECURITY reports the following problems (note that the word "object," when referring to security permissions in the NetWare bindery, means a user or a group):

- Objects without assigned passwords.

- Objects with insecure passwords (passwords that are easily guessed).

- Objects that have the security equivalence of Supervisor.

- Objects with privileges in the root directory of a volume.

- Objects without login scripts.

- Objects with excessive rights in standard directories. An object's rights in the standard directories must be limited, as follows:

Standard Directory	Trustee Assignment
SYS:PUBLIC	[R F]
SYS:SYSTEM	[ ]
SYS:LOGIN	[R F]
SYS:MAIL	[WC]

Another tool for generating bindery reports or for viewing the bindery is BINDVIEW+, which can automate security audits and locate major security holes on NetWare file servers. An auditor or network administrator can define a list of security-violation criteria called the *base line*; BINDVIEW+ searches for users, groups, files, directories, print queues, or print servers that violate this base line.

BINDVIEW+ comes with a *Query By Example* (QBE) report generator, which can be used to generate customized reports. It provides sample reports and templates that can be modified to your needs.

Traveling BINDVIEW+ is a customized version of the BINDVIEW+ report generator. It can select a large variety of security options for evaluating a LAN, such as the following:

- User password analysis (checks for insecure passwords)

- Data security analysis of user and directory of file data

- User rights analysis

- Virus security holes or security weaknesses that a virus can exploit

Restricting Log-ins: Time, Station, and Space

NetWare can restrict log-ins on certain days and times of the week, prohibiting users from working at certain times of the day or from logging in to the network from a remote location. In a secure environment, for example, you may not want users on the network after a certain time in the evening or on weekends.

Another useful capability restricts a user to a specific station only. A security problem in many organizations stems from users' unrestricted access to any workstation on the network. If a user is on a terminal that is not his regular workstation, he also may have access to sensitive papers and files lying on somebody's desk.

User accounts also can be assigned a disk quota to prevent them from "hogging" too much disk space.

The security restrictions discussed in this chapter must be balanced with ease of use. Excessive security can prevent intruders from accessing the network, but it also can be a great hindrance and annoyance to legitimate users.

Restricting Log-ins by Time

Figure 11.10 shows the Default Time Restrictions dialog box for users to log in to a server.

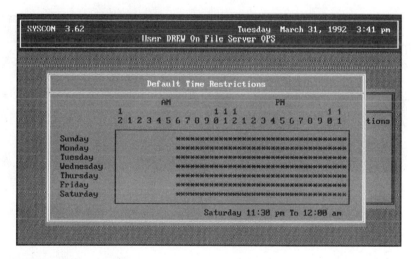

Figure 11.10:
Sample default time restrictions.

To display this dialog box, perform the following tasks:

1. Log in to the server with a Supervisor account and invoke SYSCON.

2. Make the following menu selections:

   Supervisor Options

   Default Time Restrictions

Each asterisk (*) represents a 30-minute interval. If a user is allowed to log in during a period, it is marked with an asterisk. A blank space indicates that the user is not allowed to log in. To disallow access during a half-hour time interval, press Del at the desired interval. To allow access, use Ins or type an asterisk. To toggle the state of the interval, press Enter. To delete a block of * values, mark the block by pressing F5, and then press Del.

In this example, you see that, by default, users are not allowed access to the file server on Saturday, or daily between 12:00 a.m. and 6:00 a.m.

Figure 11.11 shows the default time restrictions for all new users that are created. (These restrictions can be overridden for individual accounts.) This figure shows the time restrictions for a specific user (ANNE).

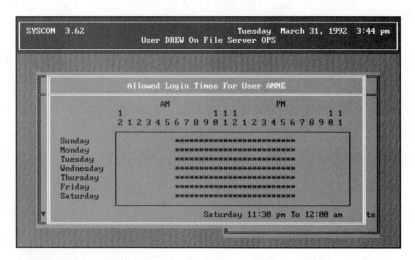

Figure 11.11:
Allowed Login Times For User screen, showing specific user.

To display the box, perform the following tasks:

1. Log in to the server with a Supervisor account and invoke SYSCON.

2. Make the following menu selection:

   User Information

3. Select a user name for time restriction and highlight:

   Time Restrictions

Restricting Log-ins by Station

Figure 11.12 shows the Allowed Login Addresses box, which restricts stations.

Figure 11.12:
Allowed Login Addresses box.

To display this dialog box, perform the following tasks:

1. Log in to the server with a Supervisor account and invoke SYSCON.

2. Make the following menu selections:

   User Information

   Select a user for station restriction

   Station Restrictions

Figure 11.12 shows an empty list of allowed log-in addresses for the user. This list is initially empty because there are no station restrictions for a user by default. To add station restrictions, press Ins at this screen. When prompted for the network address, enter up to an eight-digit hexadecimal network address for the workstation the user is allowed to access, and then press Enter. The screen in figure 11.13 is displayed.

Figure 11.13:
Station restriction choice.

To disallow access to all stations, select No; when prompted for the node address, as shown in figure 11.14, enter up to a 12-digit hexadecimal node address.

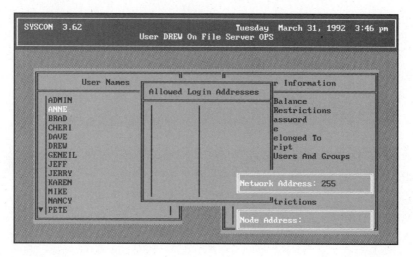

Figure 11.14:
Node Address prompt.

Figure 11.15 shows a station restriction on network address 00000255 and node address 000C00123456. The user can only log in from the listed station address.

Restricting by Space

Figure 11.16 shows the User Volume/Disk Restrictions box, which restricts disk space.

Figure 11.15:
Allowed Login Addresses box, showing restrictions.

Figure 11.16:
User Volume/Disk Restrictions dialog box.

To display this dialog box, perform the following tasks:

1. Log in to the server with a Supervisor account and invoke SYSCON.

2. Make the following menu selections:

   User Information

   Select a user for station restriction

   Volume/Disk Restrictions

   Select a volume to place the restriction

By default, the user's space is not limited. Change the Limit Volume Space?
field to Yes. Specify the Volume Space Limit field in kilobytes. Press Esc a
few times to exit SYSCON.

Ensuring Server Console Security

NetWare version 3.x has a server console security feature, ensuring that only
users with proper security can access the server. This protects the server
console from misuse.

The following features can be used:

- The SECURE CONSOLE command can be issued at the server console. This command does the following:

  Prevents loadable modules from being loaded from any directory other than SYS:SYSTEM.

  Prevents keyboard entry into the NetWare debugger.

  Prevents anyone but the console operator from changing the system date and time.

  Removes DOS from the file server. The intruder then cannot down the server, exit to DOS, and then run programs. With DOS removed, the system reboots if it is downed. You also can use a server machine with a power-on password feature.

- Select Lock File Server Console from MONITOR.NLM and supply a password to protect the server (see fig. 11.17).

- Protect RCONSOLE.NLM with a password so that a user cannot access the console remotely.

Finally, the best way to secure the server console is to place the server machine in a location that is not easy to access without detection, such as a locked room or office.

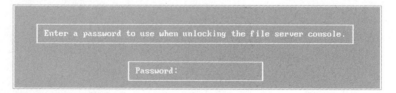

Figure 11.17:
Lock File Server Console in MONITOR.NLM.

Summary

In this chapter, you learned about different security classes and how NetWare can be used to implement a class C security system. Among the many NetWare security features are the following:

- Log-in security
- Password security
- Intruder detection/lockout security
- Time/Station/Space security
- Server console security

The NetWare Network Environment

PART THREE

Supporting DOS Workstations

A s far as the end user is concerned, the workstation is the most important component of the network. If the workstation is slow or does not have an adequate amount of RAM or disk space, users may not be able to do their work efficiently or even at all. Even if the network has the fastest server and a great deal of RAM, these do not help the user if the workstation is inadequate.

Chapter 3 shows you how to install NetWare routers; in Chapters 7 and 9, you learn to install NetWare servers. In this chapter, you learn how to manage the workstation. You also learn how to perform the following tasks:

- Generate IPX for NetWare workstations

- Install ODI components

- Use source routing drivers for IBM Token Ring networks

- Configure NetWare workstations for Ethernet II LANs

- Install OS/2 NetWare workstations

This chapter concludes with an in-depth discussion of the NetWare workstation connection mechanism. An understanding of this connection mechanism can help you solve problems, such as those that result in the `File server not found` message.

NetWare workstations comprise both hardware and software components. The following sections examine these components.

Understanding NetWare Workstation Hardware and Software

On a NetWare LAN, the workstations can be IBM personal computers or compatibles, Macintosh computers, or UNIX workstations. The PC is by far the most popular hardware platform for NetWare workstations; in fact, the PC is one of the earliest workstation platforms supported by Novell. (Historically, CP/M machines were the first.) This is not surprising when you consider that most computers in use today are IBM PCs and compatibles.

Other platforms, such as Macintosh and UNIX workstations, are increasing in popularity but are fewer in number than PCs. This chapter, therefore, focuses on the PC running DOS.

Eventually, Novell plans to develop NetWare so that it can run at the workstation- or server-level on every popular microcomputer or workstation architecture. Novell's strategic alliances with IBM, Apple, Sun, DEC, and Hewlett Packard are steps in that direction.

From a network manager's point of view, the capability of running NetWare on many hardware and operating system platforms is a welcome step toward multiple-vendor integration. An enterprise-wide network usually has a mix of different hardware and operating system platforms such as PCs, Macintoshes, engineering workstations that run UNIX, minicomputers, and mainframes. Users usually interact with PC, Macintosh, or engineering workstations, although terminals still are used in some instances.

Each workstation platform can use a variety of operating systems. Many operating systems have a preferred *Graphical User Interface* (GUI). Table 12.1 lists the dominant workstation/OS platforms of today. Note, however, that this list is not complete; many other OS and GUI choices are available, such as PC-MOS, PICK, DESQview, and NewWave, but a discussion of all these operating systems and GUIs is beyond the scope of this book.

Table 12.1
Popular Workstation/OS Combinations

Workstation	Operating System	GUI
IBM PC XT	DOS	No standard GUI
IBM PC AT 286	DOS OS/2 1.x	Microsoft Windows Presentation Manager
IBM PC AT 386	DOS OS/2 2.x UNIX	Microsoft Windows Presentation Manager and Microsoft Windows X Windows
Eng. workstations (SUN, HP, DEC, and so on)	UNIX	X Windows
Macintosh	System 7	System

The IBM PC Family and PC Compatibles

The IBM PC family currently includes the IBM PC XT, IBM PC AT 286, IBM PC AT 386, and IBM PS/2 microcomputers, as well as numerous compatible microcomputers produced by other manufacturers. The 486 and higher compatibles fall into the 386 category because the architecture of the Intel 80486 and 80586 machines is essentially the same as the Intel 80386 machine. The common denominator for all IBM PC platforms is DOS. DOS-based applications usually run in the Intel processors' real mode. By using tools such as the Phar Lap memory extender and special compilers, however, developers can write DOS applications that run in protected mode with the Intel 80286 and higher microprocessors.

The distinction between real and protected modes is important because the mode determines what size application can run on the workstation. Real mode exists in the Intel microprocessor architecture to maintain compatibility with Intel 8086-based machines (IBM PC and IBM PC XT).

In real mode (fig. 12.1), DOS and applications can run in 640K of RAM. An additional 384K—a total of 1024K—also is available, but typically is used by adapters in the workstation to carry out direct memory mapping of their internal buffers. This additional 384K is sometimes called *high memory*. More recent versions of MS-DOS and *Digital Research DOS* (DR DOS), use clever techniques to utilize unused RAM in this additional 384K high-memory range. This allows more space for applications that must run within the 640K. As applications have grown more complex, developers have taken many stop-gap measures to make as much RAM as possible available for applications. These techniques include the use of extended memory, the conversion of extended memory to expanded memory, and the use of high memory to load DOS, device drivers, and *Terminate-and-Stay-Resident* (TSR) programs.

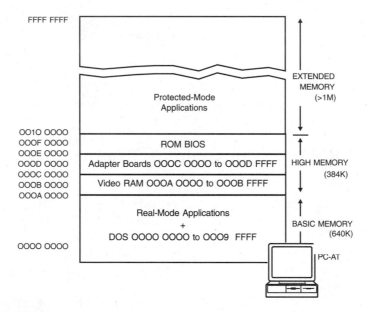

Figure 12.1:
Real-mode versus protected-mode applications.

Protected mode is available only on Intel 80286 and higher microprocessors. In protected mode, the Intel 80286 can use up to 16M of RAM corresponding to the 24-bit address lines of the microprocessor. The Intel 80386 provides up to 4G of RAM in protected mode; therefore, protected mode is the logical choice if you want to run large applications. But things are not as simple as they appear. Applications are dependent on DOS, and DOS runs in real mode. DOS applications, therefore, also must run in real mode. Even those DOS applications that use special techniques to run in protected mode—the Intel 80286 and higher—must switch to real mode to use DOS. A few other minor problems exist. For example, the BIOS in most PCs operates in real mode and is nonre-entrant. Protected-mode operating systems, such as NetWare, OS/2, and UNIX, bypass most real-mode services offered by the BIOS. (This explains why certain BIOS-based functions, such as Shift-PrtScrn, do not work under these operating systems.)

DOS continues to be a real-mode OS so that it can run the large installed base of DOS real-mode applications. If DOS ever becomes a protected-mode, multi-tasking OS, many applications may have to be recompiled or rewritten to run in protected mode.

The minimum requirements you need for an IBM PC NetWare workstation that runs DOS are as follows:

- At least 640K of RAM

- Workstation NIC with no conflicts with other hardware devices in the workstation

- Monochrome, EGA/VGA or higher display adapters (CGA adapters also can be supported but, because of their poor quality, are usually avoided)

- Floppy disk drive to boot DOS and run NetWare workstation software

- NICs with remote boot PROMs to boot with workstation operating system image kept on the server in the absence of floppy drives

DOS-based PCs must run DOS 3.x or higher. Support for DOS 2.x and below has been dropped.

To use a DOS machine as a NetWare workstation, you must run networking software at the workstation. This networking software ordinarily takes up 66K of space. Because DOS consumes about 64K of space, this leaves about 520K of space to run an application. In later chapters, you learn how MS-DOS 5 and DR DOS use even less memory.

The workstation's networking software (often called the *shell*) uses a certain number of software interrupts. Only applications that do not conflict with these software interrupts can run on the NetWare workstation. Conflicts of this type have become less frequent because of Novell's market dominance. Most application vendors maintain compatibility with Novell to avoid these conflicts, but if a conflict arises, the application vendor can usually be convinced to use some other software interrupt. Table 12.2 lists the software interrupts used by a NetWare workstation.

Table 12.2
Software Interrupts by NetWare Workstation

Network Component	Interrupts	Memory Size (Bytes)
IPX.COM	08 0B 2F 64 7A C8 F0 F3 F5 FD FF	19840
NET3.COM	10 17 1B 20 21 27	41472

OS/2 1.x runs on Intel 80286 or higher machines, but the future of OS/2 is with 2.x and higher versions. OS/2 2.x runs on Intel 80386-based and higher machines. The minimum requirement for OS/2 2.x is 4M.

To use OS/2 at a NetWare workstation, networking software must run in the form of device drivers. The most important piece of the networking software for OS/2 is the OS/2 NetWare requester. The NetWare requester allows OS/2 workstations to access the NetWare server.

Configuring DOS Workstations for NetWare

The workstation needs to be set up with the networking software before it can access the NetWare server. Two forms of network software exist for DOS workstations. The older combination of IPX and NETx remains the most common method used to configure DOS workstations. The newer *Open Data Link Interface* (ODI) approach represents Novell's future strategy and offers some advantages when multiple protocols must be supported. In DOS workstations, the networking software is loaded as TSR programs. For OS/2 workstations, the networking software is set up as device drivers.

IPX/NETx Workstation Software

Two major components make up the networking software for a DOS workstation. These are as follows:

- IPX.COM
- NETx.COM

Both IPX.COM and NETx.COM are TSR programs that must be loaded after you boot the workstation in DOS. IPX must be loaded at the workstation first, followed by NETx.COM. (The x refers to the major DOS rev number—3 for DOS 3.x and 5 for DOS 5.x.) These programs are typically run in the AUTOEXEC.BAT file or some other DOS batch file. Together, IPX.COM and NETx.COM set up the DOS NetWare workstation environment.

IPX.COM contains an implementation of the SPX/IPX protocols that are linked with the NIC drivers. That is, IPX.COM implements layers 3 (network) and 4 (transport) of the OSI model (see fig. 12.2). The IPX protocol interfaces with the rest of the network by using the NIC drivers linked with it. Figure 12.2 illustrates the IPX.COM in relationship to the NIC driver. Because workstations can have a variety of NICs, a different driver must be linked with IPX.COM for each NIC type. NetWare does not come with a separate IPX.COM for each driver type. NetWare gives you the pieces to create the IPX.COM, such as the object module IPX.OBJ and the network drivers for a number of NICs. Other network drivers not included with NetWare can be obtained from the NIC vendor or CompuServe. The NetWare installer must link these individual pieces together to create an IPX.COM file. Such a file implements the transport protocols necessary for packet transmission across the network.

The process of creating a new copy of IPX.COM by linking with an NIC driver is called *generating the shell*. This can be confusing because *shell* refers to NETx.COM rather than IPX.COM, but IPX.COM is the file being generated. The NETx.COM file does not have any NIC driver components and does not need to be generated. NETx.COM is a generic program for a specific DOS version x and is used with IPX.COM. NETx.COM is the workstation shell because it surrounds DOS and processes each command before the command is passed on to DOS or the network. The NETx.COM is a program that extends the workstation environment. Like IPX.COM, NETx.COM is loaded as a TSR at the workstation. NETx.COM must be loaded after IPX.COM is loaded. NETx.COM runs on top of DOS and creates a network environment for the user.

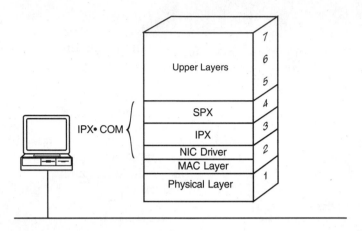

Figure 12.2:
IPX components.

The user can still use DOS commands while the shell is loaded because a NetWare workstation views the network as a series of DOS drives. Drives A to E usually are reserved for local hard disks and RAM drives at the workstation, and drives F to Z generally are assigned to the network.

The server's file system is accessible to the user by drive letters F to Z. The NetWare MAP command enables the user to map a drive letter to a directory on the server disk. This network drive letter can be used when a drive letter is needed for network and most DOS commands. In other words, the work environment of the client includes the server's file system. Access to the file server's system is not automatic; you need a valid user account and password on the server.

The x in NETx.COM stands for the DOS version being used at the workstation. NET3.COM is used for DOS 3.x, and NET5.COM is used for DOS 5.x. To simplify management of NetWare workstations, Novell now has a generic NETX.COM shell that can be used for all DOS 3.x and later versions. Support for earlier DOS versions has been discontinued.

NETx.COM is not bound to any drivers and runs on top of the IPX/SPX protocols implemented by IPX.COM; therefore, it is not generated by the shell or workstation generation process.

The shell can be viewed as a network traffic director. It distinguishes local commands from network commands. Local commands are sent to DOS where they are processed by the workstation operating system. Network commands are sent across the network. Consider the following command:

```
COPY C:\DATA.22 A:
```

The shell recognizes this as a local command that deals with local resources only. No network resources are referred to in the source (local hard disk file C:\DATA.22) or destination (floppy drive A). This command is processed locally by DOS.

Now, consider the following command:

```
COPY F:\USERS\DEI\DATA.22 A:
```

If you assume that the drive letter F refers to a network drive, this command means to copy the file DATA.22 from the network drive F:\USERS\DEI to the local floppy. The shell recognizes this as a network command and performs the file transfer from the network drive to the local floppy. The transfer involves software and hardware network components, including the shell (NCP requests and replies), IPX.COM (transport protocols IPX/SPX), network drivers, the workstation NIC, and the LAN. The user does not see all the behind-the-scenes work that satisfies a simple DOS COPY request. And herein lies the power of the system: the network is as easy to use as DOS commands.

Connecting to the Server

When the shell NET*x*.COM loads, it initializes the workstation environment. An important part of this initialization is finding a server to connect to. The shell broadcasts a SAP packet asking for the nearest server. The servers on the network that receive this SAP request respond with a Give Nearest Server SAP response.

The server's response tells the client how far away the server is (number of hops) and the name of the server. This information enables the client to attach to the server. This attachment is a logical connection for which control commands are sent to manage the client-to-server connection. This connection is not the same as being logged in to the server. Logging in to the server is done through the LOGIN.EXE command stored in the server's SYS:LOGIN directory.

After the initial handshake has formed an attachment to the server, the shell maps the first available network drive to the server's SYS:LOGIN directory. Drive F is usually the first available drive because it follows drive E—the default value of the LASTDRIVE parameter in CONFIG.SYS. Most workstations do not have the LASTDRIVE parameter set in their CONFIG.SYS file; therefore, the DOS system defaults to E for the LASTDRIVE parameter.

The SYS:LOGIN directory to which F is mapped contains the program files LOGIN.EXE and SLIST.EXE. LOGIN.EXE implements the LOGIN command, and SLIST.EXE implements the server list command that displays a list of all servers that can be reached by the workstation.

To invoke the LOGIN.EXE file, the user must change to the F drive and issue the LOGIN command. LOGIN.EXE then is downloaded to the workstation's RAM and runs on the workstation's CPU. The LOGIN command prompts the user for a log-in name and password. If this is entered correctly, the user is then logged in to the server.

Thus, the log-in commands take the following sequence:

```
IPX
NETX
F:
LOGIN
```

A more general form of the LOGIN command that specifies the user name is as follows:

LOGIN [[ServerName/]UserName]

For example, if you want to log in to a server named KSS, type the following command:

LOGIN KSS/UserName

The server name distinguishes between several servers on the network. When several servers are available, each one responds to the shell's initial request for the nearest server. The server that has the fastest response is the one selected for the attachment. This may not be the server on which you want to log in.

The IPX.COM Workstation Software

The workstation generation program, or WSGEN, is common to both NetWare 2.2 and NetWare 3.11 and later versions. Prior to these versions, a program called SHGEN was used. Older versions of NetWare, such as Advanced NetWare 2.0a, used a program called GENSH.

You can find WSGEN on the NetWare disk labeled WSGEN. The workstation generation process can be performed on any PC with a floppy drive and sufficient memory to run WSGEN. WSGEN runs from the DOS prompt.

WSGEN links the NIC drivers to the program file IPX.OBJ to produce an IPX.COM file that implements the SPX/IPX protocols. The IPX.COM file also contains the linked NIC driver that can communicate with the NIC. NETX.COM is a generic program that can be used with all linked IPX.COM versions; NETX.COM is not customized by WSGEN.

This section gives you a detailed look at the WSGEN process. You must have the following software/hardware components to perform these exercises:

- An IBM PC with 640K RAM and one floppy drive
- The WSGEN disk containing the generation program
- LAN driver disks such as LAN_DRV_001 or LAN_DRV_XXX
- DOS 3.x or higher to boot the PC

To prepare the NetWare Workstation for generation, take the following steps:

1. Boot the workstation with the DOS boot disk.

2. Place the disk labeled NetWare WSGEN in drive A. Enter the following command to start the generation process:

   WSGEN

   The WSGEN opening screen appears, as shown in figure 12.3.

3. Press Enter to continue workstation generation. After a few seconds of the Please Wait message, WSGEN displays a screen showing a list of the network drivers (see fig. 12.4).

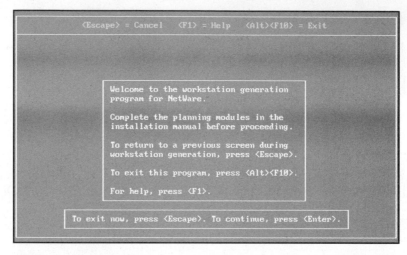

Figure 12.3:
The Workstation Generation program opening screen.

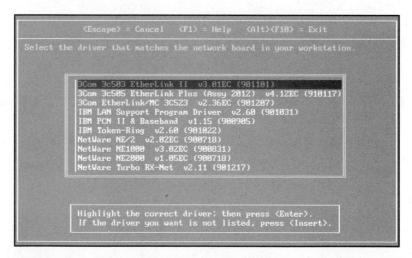

Figure 12.4:
The Workstation Generation select network driver screen.

4. If you find the driver for the NIC card installed at your workstation, select it by highlighting the LAN Driver. (If the driver you need is not listed, press Ins and proceed with step 5, or skip to step 9.)

5. A message appears asking you to insert a disk labeled LAN_DRV_???. Drivers not listed in the default list of drivers must be obtained from the driver manufacturer. These drivers come in disks labeled LAN_DRV_???. The symbol "???" is a code assigned to the manufacturer.

6. Insert the disk labeled LAN_DRV_XXX in a drive and press Enter to continue. A message that states the driver for the NIC was read successfully appears.

7. Press Enter to continue. A screen that displays the list of network card drivers on the LAN_DRV_XXX disk appears.

8. Use the cursor keys to scroll down the list of drivers and locate the NIC driver.

9. Highlight the NIC driver and press Enter.

10. A list of configuration options should appear. Figure 12.5 shows a sample screen of typical configuration options.

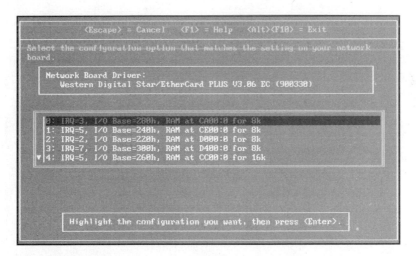

Figure 12.5:
The Workstation Generation configuration options screen.

11. Highlight the configuration option that matches the NIC setting and press Enter.

12. Highlight the *Yes, generate workstation software* option and press Enter.

13. If the disk WSGEN is not in a drive, insert it when prompted to do so.

    The following messages appear:

    ```
    Creating DOS Workstation.
    Novell Linker, Version 2.1
    Linking WSGEN:IPX.COM.
    Insert disk LAN_DRV_200 in any drive
    Strike a key when ready . . .
    ```

14. Insert the following disks, in this order:

    LAN_DRV_001 or LAN_DRV_XXX

    WSGEN

The following messages appear, as does the screen shown in figure 12.6:

```
Novell configuration utility:
Configuring WSGEN:IPX.COM
```

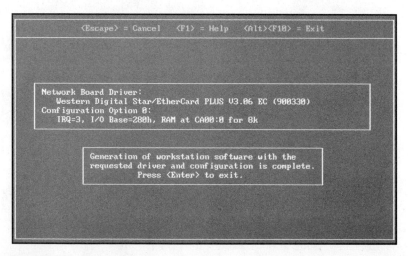

Figure 12.6:
The Workstation Generation complete screen.

15. Workstation generation is now complete. Press Enter to exit.

16. Copy the files IPX.COM and NET3.COM from the WSGEN disk onto a NetWare workstation boot disk. You can prepare this disk by using the DOS format command, as follows:

    FORMAT A: /S

    If you have a single floppy system, copy these files to your hard disk first, and then copy from the hard disk to the floppy.

17. Create a batch file NETLOG.BAT that has the following commands (or put the commands in the AUTOEXEC.BAT file):

    IPX

    NET3

    F:

    LOGIN

18. Use the batch file to log in to the NetWare server, as follows:

    NETLOG

    If you have an account on the server, you can log in to the server. If the workstation cannot find a server, a `File server not found` message appears.

NET and IPX Options

Both NET*x* and the IPX programs have options that can be used to alter their behavior. One useful option, the I option, reveals the following important information:

```
IPX I

Novell IPX/SPX v3.04 (910703)

Copyright 1985, 1991 Novell Inc. All Rights Reserved.

LAN Option: D-Link Pocket Ethernet DE-600  V2.01 (910321)
Hardware Configuration: Printer port & IRQ channel auto-
detected
```

```
NET5 I
```

```
NetWare V3.10 - Workstation Shell for PC DOS V5.x (910307)
```

```
(c) Copyright 1990 Novell, Inc. All Rights Reserved.
```

```
NETX I
```

```
NetWare V3.22 - Workstation Shell (910731) (c) Copyright
```

```
1991 Novell, Inc. All Rights Reserved.
```

The IPX I command in the preceding examples states the version number of the IPX module—version 3.04. The date stamp reveals that the driver was released on March 21, 1991 (910321). The NIC driver linked is the D-Link (David Systems) Pocket Ethernet DE-600 driver. The version number of the driver is V2.01, and the hardware configuration tells you that the printer port and the IRQ level are automatically detected by the driver.

The NET5 I and NETX I commands reveal similar information. You can tell that NETX is a more recent version—version 3.22 versus V3.10—than NET5. This fact is confirmed if you examine the date of release and the copyright year.

Whereas the I option was available for older versions of IPX and NET*x*, newer versions of these programs have more useful options. To find these options type the NET*x* /? and IPX /? commands, as follows:

```
IPX /?
```

```
Usage: IPX [options]
valid options:
   I or /I        Displays version information
   D or /D        Displays hardware options
   O or /O<num>   Load using hardware option <num>
   C or /C=[path]<filename>  Specifies an alternate
                                 configuration file
   ? or /?                   Displays this help screen
```

The option letters can be preceded by either the hyphen (-) or forward slash (/) character. The -I option is the information option. The /D option displays the hardware configuration. An example of the use of the /D option is as follows:

```
IPX /D
```

```
Novell IPX/SPX v3.04 (910703)(c)
Copyright 1985, 1991 Novell Inc. All Rights Reserved.

LAN Option: D-Link Pocket Ethernet DE-600  V2.01 (910321)
Hardware options available:

  *  0. Printer port & IRQ channel autodetected
```

Each driver has a number of selectable configuration options. The asterisk (*) is placed next to the option currently selected in the driver. You can load IPX with an alternate hardware option by using the /O parameter to specify the hardware option. IPX also can be loaded with a number of configurable options to be placed in the specified text file. If the text file is not specified, the configuration file has the default name NET.CFG.

NETX /?

```
NetWare V3.22  Workstation Shell (910731)
(c) Copyright 1991 Novell, Inc. All Rights Reserved.

Usage : NETX  [<option>]
Valid <options>:

/?                              Displays shell usage
/T                              Displays shell version
                                and type
/U                              Unloads the NetWare
                                shell from memory
/F                              Forcibly unloads the
                                NetWare shell, in spite
                                of TSRs loaded after
                                the shell (CAUTION: The
                                /F option can hang your
                                workstation.)
/PS=<server>                    Specifies a preferred
                                server
/C=[path\]<filename.ext>        Names your NetWare
                                shell configuration
                                file (For use with
                                DOS 3.0 through 5.0.)
```

The -I option is the information option.

The /U unloads the shell and releases the RAM space occupied by the shell. This enables you to experiment with memory configurations without having to reboot the workstation. Prior to the /U option, the only way to unload the shell—if third-party software or shareware utilities were not used—was to reboot the workstation.

Before the shell unloads, other TSRs that were loaded after the shell must be removed. Some TSRs cannot be unloaded. In this situation, you can force an unload of the shell by using the /F option. The /F option can create gaps of unused space in the workstation RAM and can cause your workstation to "hang."

The /PS=*server* option forces a connection to the specified server. This is useful when multiple servers are on the network. To reconnect to the desired server, use the LOGIN command that specifies the server name, or invoke NET*x* with the preferred server name. Therefore, to ensure a connection to the server named KSS, type the following:

```
NETX /PS=KSS
```

The /C option specifies the shell configuration file. If you do not specify the shell configuration file, the NET.CFG file in the current directory—if it exists—is used as the configuration file.

Shell Configuration Files: SHELL.CFG and NET.CFG

The shell configuration can be customized by placing commands in the NET.CFG file. These commands must be placed at the beginning of the NET.CFG file and also can be placed in the older SHELL.CFG file. Novell, however, is replacing the SHELL.CFG file with the more versatile NET.CFG file.

The configuration commands can be grouped into configuration options for:

- IPX
- NET*x*
- NETBIOS

Tables 12.3 to 12.5 summarize these parameters for your reference. For more detailed information, refer to the NetWare 2.2 *Using the Network* manual.

The following is a sample NET.CFG file for DOS workstations:

```
                                  ; IPX.COM configuration
options
CONFIG OPTION=1                   ; Uses configuration option 1
IPX RETRY COUNT-30               ; Increases retry count
IPX SOCKETS=60                    ; Increases IPX sockets
SPX CONNECTIONS=50                ; Increases SPX connections

                                  ; NETx.COM parameters
FILE HANDLES=60                   ; Increases file handles
LOCAL PRINTER=0                   ; Disables Shift PrtScrn
LONG MACHINE TYPE=KSS_PC          ; Changes %MACHINE
PREFERRED SERVER=KSS_SRV          ; Specifies server to connect
                                    to.
SEARCH MODE=2                     ; Never searches for data
                                    files
                                    in search drives
SET STATION TIME=OFF              ; Special timing clock at
                                    workstation
TASK MODE=0                       ; Plain Old DOS - no
                                    multitasking.

                                  ; NETBIOS parameters
NETBIOS COMMANDS=22               ; Increases command queue
NETBIOS RECEIVE BUFFERS=10        ; Increases IPX receive
buffers
NETBIOS SEND BUFFERS=10           ; Increases IPX send buffers
NETBIOS SESSIONS=20               ; Reduces sessions
```

Table 12.3
NET.CFG IPX.COM Parameters

Parameter	Value
CONFIG OPTION=*n*	Overrides the network driver configuration option selected by WSGEN or DCONFIG.
INT64=[ON I OFF]	Configures IPX to use software interrupt 64 hex. Primary purpose is for compatibility with earlier versions of NetWare. Default is ON.

continues

Table 12.3
Continued

Parameter	Value
INT7A=[ON I OFF]	Configures IPX to use software interrupt 7A hex. To be used for compatibility with NetWare 2.0a. Default is ON.
IPATCH=*a*	Fixes "bugs" in IPX>COM. Any location in IPX.COM can be replaced ("patched") with a specified value.
IPX PACKET SIZE LIMIT=*n*	Changes the maximum packet size set by a LAN driver—if the driver supports this.
IPX RETRY COUNT=*n*	Specifies number of times a workstation tries to resend a packet. Default is 20 retries.
IPX SOCKETS=*n*	Specifies maximum number of sockets that can be opened by the workstation. Default is 20 sockets.
SPX ABORT TIMEOUT=*n*	Specifies number of clock ticks SPX waits without receiving response from the remote side before it terminates the connection. Default is 540 ticks (about 30 secs).
SPX CONNECTIONS=*n*	Specifies number of simultaneous SPX connections allowed at a workstation. Default is 15 connections.
SPX LISTEN TIMEOUT=*n*	Specifies number of clock ticks SPX waits for a response from the remote side. If there is no response, it times out and sends "probe" packets to see if remote is still alive. Default is 108 ticks (about 6 seconds).
SPX VERIFY TIMEOUT=*n*	Specifies number of clock ticks SPX waits before sending a packet to the remote side to verify if a connection is still alive. Default is 54 ticks (about 3 seconds).

Table 12.4
NET.CFG NETx.COM Parameters

Parameter	Value
ALL SERVER= [ON | OFF]	Sends End of Task signal to all connected servers, if set to ON. If set to OFF, sends End of Task signal only to the servers interacting with the task. Default is OFF.
CACHE BUFFERS=n	Specifies number of cache buffers. Cache buffers are 512-byte buffers that the shell uses for local caching of non-shared, nontransactional files. Default is 5 buffers.
EOJ=[ON | OFF]	Specifies if files, locks, and semaphores are closed automatically at the end of the job. Default is ON.
FILE HANDLES=n	Specifies an upper limit on number of files the workstation can have opened at the network simultaneously. Default is 40 files. Local files are controlled FILES= in CONFIG.SYS.
HOLD=[ON | OFF]	Specifies if workstation files should be held open if they were opened and closed. Default is OFF.
LOCAL PRINTERS=n	Changes the BIOS setting for the number of local printers at a workstation. Setting n to 0 prevents the workstation from hanging if the Shift-PrtScrn key is pressed when no local printer exists.
LOCK DELAY=n	Specifies the number of ticks the shell waits before obtaining a lock. Default is 1.

continues

**Table 12.4
Continued**

Parameter	Value
LOCK RETRIES=*n*	Specifies the number of times the shell attempts to get a lock on a network resource.
LONG MACHINE TYPE=*typeName*	Changes the value of the %MACHINE login script variable. The default value is IBM_PC. The variable *typeName* is 6 characters or less.
MAX CUR DIR LENGTH=*n*	Defines the current directory length as a value that can be from 64 to 255. Default is 64.
MAX PATH LENGTH=*n*	Defines the network path length as a value that can be from 64 to 255. Default is 255.
MAX TASKS=*n*	Defines the maximum number of tasks that can be active simultaneously at the workstation. Used in DESQview and MS Windows environment. The value ranges from 20 to 128 with a default of 31.
PATCH=*n*	Patches any address in the shell.
PREFERRED SERVER= *serverName*	Forces the shell to attach to the specified server.
PRINT HEADER=*n*	Sets the size of the initialization string for the printer that is sent before each print job. The value ranges from 0 to 255 with a default of 64 bytes.
PRINT TAIL=*n*	Sets the size of the reset string for the printer that is sent after each print job. The value ranges from 0 to 255 with a default of 16 bytes.

Parameter	Value
READ ONLY COMPATIBILITY= [ON I OFF]	Specifies if a file marked Read Only attribute can be opened for read/write. Default value is OFF.
SEARCH MODE=*mode*	Specifies the search mode for the shell. Can be used to extend the normal DOS search for a data file on the search drives. The value can be from 1 to 7 with a default of 1. Search mode has the following meanings:

1. Search if path not specified for data file
2. Never search
3. Search if path not specified, and request is to read a file but not to modify it
4. Reserved
5. Always search
6. Reserved
7. Always search if request is only to read the file

Parameter	Value
SET STATION TIME= [ON I OFF]	Synchronizes the shell's workstation time to servers time when set to ON. Default is ON.
SHARE=[ON I OFF]	Enables a process to inherit all the resources of a parent process, such as file handles, when set to ON. Default is ON.
SHORT MACHINE TYPE=*typename*	Sets %SMACHINE log-in variable to the specified value. The default value is IBM. The variable *typeName* is 4 characters or less.

continues

Table 12.4
Continued

Parameter	Value
SHOW DOTS= [ON | OFF]	Enables shell to emulate the DOS FindFirstMatching and FindNextMatching calls for dot (.) and dot-dot(..) entries when set to ON. The default is ON. Must be ON for MS Windows.
SPECIAL UPPER CASE=[ON | OFF]	Causes the shell to call DOS to provide translation for ASCII characters above 128 when set to ON. Used for foreign language and special characters support. Default is OFF.
TASK MODE=n	Affects the manner in which the shell handles virtual machine task management. The default value of 2 works well with MS Windows 3.0. Earlier Windows versions used a task mode of 1. If you are not using multitasking, you can speed up the shell by using a task mode of 0.

Table 12.5
NET.CFG NETBIOS.EXE Parameters

Parameter	Value
NETBIOS ABORT TIMEOUT=n	Specifies the number of ticks to wait for an acknowledgment. After this time, NetBIOS times out and terminates the connection. Default value is 540 ticks (about 30 seconds).

Parameter	Value
NETBIOS BROADCAST COUNT=*n*	Specifies the number of times NetBIOS broadcasts a query/claim for a name. The value ranges from 2 to 65535. Default value is 4 if internet is ON, or 2 if internet is OFF.
NETBIOS BROADCAST DELAY=*n*	Specifies the number of ticks NetBIOS waits between query/claim broadcasts. Value can be from 18 to 65535. Default value is 36 if internet is ON, or 18 if internet is OFF. NOTE: When multiplied by NETBIOS BROADCAST COUNT, this determines the total time taken to broadcast a name resolution packet across the network.
NETBIOS COMMANDS=*n*	Specifies the number of outstanding NetBIOS commands that can be waiting for completion at the workstation. The values range from 4 to 250 with a default of 12.
NETBIOS INTERNET= [ON | OFF]	Sends claim-name packets to all stations on the internet if set to ON. If internet is OFF, NetBIOS sends name-claim packets to stations on the local network and ignores them from outside the local network. Claim name packets are sent to establish the uniqueness of the NetBIOS name of a station. The default value is ON. If more than one LAN segment is used or if a nondedicated server is used, this value must be ON.
NETBIOS LISTEN TIMEOUT=*n*	Specifies the number of ticks NetBIOS waits for a packet from a remote station before requesting the remote station to verify its connection. Value can be from 1 to 65535. Default value is 108 (about 6 seconds).
NETBIOS RECEIVE BUFFERS=*n*	Specifies the number of receive IPX buffers used by NetBIOS. Value can be from 4 to 20. Default value is 6 buffers.

continues

**Table 12.5
Continued**

Parameter	Value
NETBIOS RETRY COUNT=*n*	Specifies the number of times NetBIOS transmits a request to establish a connection or to retransmit a failed communication before it gives up. The value ranges from 10 to 65535 with a default value of 20.
NETBIOS RETRY DELAY=*n*	Specifies the number of ticks NetBIOS waits between packet transmissions while establishing a connection or resending a data packet. The value ranges from 10 to 65535 with a default value of 10 ticks (about 0.5 second).
NETBIOS SEND BUFFERS=*n*	Specifies the number of send IPX buffers used by NetBIOS. Value can be from 4 to 20. Default value is 6 buffers.
NETBIOS SESSIONS=*n*	Specifies the number of NetBIOS sessions the workstation can have. The values can range from 4 to 250 with a default of 32.
NETBIOS VERIFY TIMEOUT=*n*	Specifies the number of ticks NetBIOS waits before attempting to send a packet to the remote station to confirm the connection. Value can be from 4 to 65535. Default value is 54 ticks (abut 3 seconds).
NPATCH=*n*	Patches a location in the NETBIOS.EXE file.

ODI Shells and Drivers

Novell and Apple developed a specification called the ODI to support multiple protocols in a workstation and a server. Network drivers for NIC cards can be written to this ODI specification, and this enables multiple protocol stacks to share the same network driver. NIC drivers for NetWare 3.x servers are written to the ODI specification.

NetWare workstations can use either the generated workstation software or the ODI drivers. But if you need to run multiple protocol stacks, you must use the ODI drivers. An example of an application that uses ODI drivers is LAN Workplace for DOS. This product, available from Novell, enables a workstation to use SPX/IPX protocols to log in to a NetWare server or use TCP/IP protocols to log in to a TCP/IP host.

ODI offers a number of advantages, including the following:

- Multiple protocol support, such as TCP/IP, SPX/IPX, and AppleTalk, can be added to the same NIC driver without adding extra NICs.

- Sessions with a variety of servers and hosts using different protocol stacks at the workstation can be established. In general, you use a protocol stack at the workstation that the server or host understands.

- All protocol stacks written to the ODI specification can communicate with any NIC driver written to the ODI specification.

- Multiple protocols support is simplified because only one LAN driver exists. Improvements in the ODI LAN driver (or bug fixes) benefit all protocols that work with the improved LAN driver.

- More configuration choices are available through the NET.CFG configuration file. This makes it possible to change the workstation software configuration more easily.

The ODI Specification

The three important components that make ODI work at the workstation level are as follows:

- LSL.COM

- ODI LAN driver

- Protocol stacks

LSL.COM implements the *Link Support Layer* (LSL), and the ODI LAN driver constitutes layer 2 of the OSI model (data link layer). The protocol stacks implement layer 3 and above.

Understanding the ODI Driver Load Sequence

ODI drivers eliminate the need to generate the workstation software, but they still require the individual components to be loaded in a specific order.

In terms of workstation RAM and logical connections between the components, you must load the Link Support Layer first because when the ODI LAN driver is loaded, it expects to logically connect to the LSL layer. The LSL layer and the ODI LAN driver have interface points that dovetail with each other. Next, you load the ODI LAN driver. With the LSL.COM and the ODI LAN driver loaded, the data layer (OSI model) is complete.

You then load the communications protocols on top of the link support layer. When the communications protocol loads, it automatically binds itself to the link support layer. This completes the communications protocol stack down to the NIC interface. You also can load additional protocol stacks at this time.

To make use of the communications protocol, you must run an application or network program, such as the NetWare shell.

For DOS NetWare stations, the communications protocol SPX/IPX is implemented in the file IPXODI.COM.

To summarize the preceding steps, the commands that must be issued to set a NetWare station with an NE2000 NIC to log in to a NetWare server are as follows:

```
LSL
NE2000
IPXODI
NETX
F:
LOGIN
```

The NE2000.COM is the program name for the NE2000 ODI LAN driver.

ODI Component Options

All ODI components have optional parameters that can be used to modify their behavior. At the very least, they all have the ? parameter to obtain help, and the U parameter to unload the components. You must unload the ODI components in the reverse order of the loading sequence. The unload order is NET*x*.COM, IPXODI.COM, ODI LAN Driver, and LSL.COM.

The ODI components are on the NetWare Lite DRIVERS disk, or the disk labeled DOS ODI WORKSTATION SERVICES. LSL.COM, IPXODI.COM, and the LAN drivers accept a ? parameter which instructs them to display the file version and help list.

LSL ?

```
NetWare Link Support Layer  v1.10 (910625)
(c)Copyright 1991 Novell, Inc. All Rights Reserved.

Available command line options:

    LSL          Installs the LSL
    LSL U        Removes resident LSL from memory
    LSL ?        Displays this help screen
```

WDPLUS ?

```
Western Digital LAN Adapter MLID v1.02 (910621)
(c) Copyright Western Digital Corporation 1991, All Rights
Reserved.

Available command line options:

    WDPLUS       Installs the MLID
    WDPLUS U     Removes resident MLID from memory
    WDPLUS ?     Displays this help screen
```

IPXODI ?

```
NetWare IPX/SPX Protocol  v1.10 (910625)
(c)Copyright 1991 Novell, Inc. All Rights Reserved.

Available command line options:

    IPXODI       Installs IPX, SPX, and Diagnostic Responder
    IPXODI D     Installs IPX and SPX
    IPXODI A     Installs IPX
    IPXODI U     Removes resident IPXODI from memory
    IPXODI ?     Displays this help screen
```

The LSL and ODI LAN drivers have only the ? and U options for displaying help and unload from RAM.

IPXODI has a few other options besides the ? and U options. The IPXODI.COM file consists of the following three components:

- IPX (OSI Layer 3)

- SPX (OSI Layer 4)

- Remote Diagnostic Responder (OSI Layer 7)

Many applications do not need SPX or the Remote Diagnostic Responder. The Remote Diagnostic Responder is useful for some third-party applications that gather diagnostic information. By not loading these components, you can save workstation memory. The SPX and the Remote Diagnostic Responder each take up roughly 4K of RAM. If you need more memory to run applications, IPXODI can be invoked using the A or D option.

Table 12.6 shows the amount of memory consumed when IPXODI is running with various options:

Table 12.6
IPXODI Options Memory Usage

Command	Meaning	Memory Used (Bytes)	Memory Saved (Bytes)
IPXODI	Load full IP	15904	N/A
IPXODI D	Load IPX and SPX only	12272	3632
IPXODI A	Load IPX only	7088	5184

The Workstation ODI Boot Disk

To prepare the workstation boot disk containing the ODI drivers, perform the following steps:

1. To prepare a DOS bootable disk, type the following command:

    ```
    FORMAT A: /S
    ```

2. Copy the following files from the DOS ODI WORKSTATION SERVICES BOOT disk to the DOS bootable disk:

    LSL.COM
    IPXODI.COM

ODI Network Driver (such as NE2000.COM)
NET*x*.COM

3. Create a batch file and enter the following commands in the batch file:

```
LSL
ODI Network Driver
NETx
F:
LOGIN
```

(In your actual batch file, replace *ODI Network Driver* with the name of the appropriate driver file.)

4. Create AUTOEXEC.BAT and CONFIG.SYS files to suit your workstation environment. For instance, you can put a FILES= and BUFFERS= parameter along with any device drivers particular to your workstation. You also may want to increase the size of memory set aside for the DOS environment variables by placing the following in CONFIG.SYS:

```
SHELL=COMMAND.COM /P /E:800
```

The preceding statement in the CONFIG.SYS file increases the size of environment variable memory to 800 bytes for DOS 3.2 and higher versions.

In the AUTOEXEC.BAT file, you may want to add the PROMPT PG command to change the prompt to include the current working directory.

5. If your NIC card is set to a nondefault setting or if you need to support protocols other than SPX/IPX, you must create a NET.CFG file.

NET.CFG Configuration File Options for ODI Workstations

NET.CFG is a text file that contains commands to alter the behavior of ODI workstation components. SHELL.CFG also contains shell configuration information. Information in the SHELL.CFG file is now included in the more versatile NET.CFG file. The contents of the SHELL.CFG file can be placed at the beginning of the NET.CFG file. If both the SHELL.CFG and NET.CFG file exist on the workstation disk, both are processed, but any SHELL.CFG commands in NET.CFG are ignored.

The main section headings for NET.CFG are left-justified. The entries under each heading are indented by a space or a tab. The three section headings are as follows:

- LINK SUPPORT
- PROTOCOL
- LINK DRIVER

(Comments are preceded by a semicolon and statements in NET.CFG are case-insensitive.)

The LINK SUPPORT section establishes the number of communication buffers and the memory size set aside for those buffers.

The PROTOCOL section maintains the binding between a specific protocol and the ODI Network Driver. Some protocols maintain several simultaneous sessions. The PROTOCOL section also can be used to control the number of sessions.

The LINK DRIVER section changes the hardware configuration settings in the ODI Network Driver. Examples of hardware settings are DMA, Interrupt Line, Base Memory address, and I/O Port address. Use the LINK DRIVER section when the workstation NIC uses nondefault settings.

Not all main section headings need to be in the NET.CFG file. For example, if the Western Digital EtherCard PLUS must be set to the nondefault settings of IRQ=5, I/O Port address=300 (hex), memory base address of D8000, then NET.CFG looks something like the following:

```
LINK DRIVER WDPLUS
    ; Interrupt Request Line is set to 5
    int   5
    ; I/O Port address is 300 hex
    port 300
    ; Base memory address is D8000
    mem D8000
```

The PROTOCOL and LINK SUPPORT sections are not listed because the default protocol and link support settings need not be changed.

Link Support

You can change the BUFFERS and MEMPOOL parameters in the LINK SUP-PORT section.

The BUFFERS parameter takes the following general form of the BUFFERS parameter:

```
BUFFERS bufferNumber [bufferSize]
```

The BUFFERS parameter changes the number (*bufferNumber*) and size (*bufferSize*) of communication buffers for non-SPX/IPX protocols. SPX/IPX protocols implemented by the IPXODI protocol stack do not use the LSL buffers; they use a separate set of communication buffers. An example of a protocol that needs LSL buffers is TCP/IP, which needs at least two buffers. The size of a buffer must be large enough to hold the MAC header and the maximum data size encapsulated by the MAC header.

The *bufferSize* is optional and has a minimum value of 618 bytes and a default value of 1130 bytes. The total amount of buffer space for LSL buffers must not exceed approximately 59K:

bufferNumber x bufferSize <= 59K

The MEMPOOL parameter takes the following general form:

```
MEMPOOL memSize [k]
```

The MEMPOOL parameter specifies the size of the memory pool buffer (*memSize*) that is set aside. This number can be expressed in kilobytes by including the k after *memSize*. SPX/IPX protocols do not use memory pool buffers. Protocols such as TCP/IP need at least 2048 bytes of memory pool.

For the exact setting of BUFFERS and MEMPOOL, you must consult the third-party protocol settings.

Protocol

You can specify the BIND and SESSIONS parameters in the PROTOCOL section.

The PROTOCOL section main heading must specify the protocol name that the parameters BIND and SESSIONS apply to. An example of the protocol section is as follows:

```
PROTOCOL IPX
    BIND NE2000
```

The BIND parameter refers to IPX because this protocol was specified in the main section heading: PROTOCOL IPX.

The BIND parameter takes the following general form:

```
BIND networkDriver
```

BIND makes a logical association between the protocol specified in the PROTOCOL section heading and the ODI network driver (*networkDriver*). This logical association establishes a data path between the NIC and the protocol stack. The BIND parameter also is useful if a number of NICs are in a workstation. When the protocol stack IPXODI loads, it binds to the first NIC driver loaded. This may not be the NIC that you want to use with the SPX/IPX protocol stacks. To change the default binding, use the BIND parameter. For example, if a workstation has the EXOS215 board and the Token Ring board, and you want IPX to bind to the TOKEN ring driver, you can use the following statements in NET.CFG:

```
PROTOCOL IPX

    ; Force IPX binding to TOKEN ODI driver.
    bind TOKEN
```

Even if the TOKEN driver is loaded last, the IPX protocol binds to the TOKEN driver.

In the DOS environment IPX can be bound to only one NIC driver.

Some protocols can be used to establish multiple sessions. The SESSIONS parameter can be used to specify the number of sessions (*numberSessions*).

```
SESSIONS numberSessions
```

Link Driver

The *driverName* in the LINK DRIVER section heading must specify the ODI network driver name. All parameters included in the LINK DRIVER section heading apply to *driverName*. These parameters are described in table 12.7.

Table 12.7
Link Driver Parameters

Parameter	Meaning
DMA	DMA channel number
INT	Interrupt line number
MEM	Memory address range
PORT	I/O Port address
NODE ADDRESS	Assigns a new MAC address
SLOT	Associates NIC driver with a slot
FRAME	Specifies MAC layer frame encapsulation
PROTOCOL	Registers a new protocol
SAPS	Service Access Points for LANSUP driver
LINK STATIONS	Link Stations for LANSUP driver
ALTERNATE	Use alternate adapter for LANSUP, TOKEN, PCN2
MAX FRAME SIZE	Specifies maximum frame size for Token Ring
* DMA [#1 | #2]	*channelNumber*

The DMA parameter can be used to configure up to two DMA channels. Some NICs have two configurable DMA channels. The first configurable channel is number 1, and the second configurable channel is number 2. When the number is omitted, the first configurable channel is configured.

The *channelNumber* refers to the DMA channel value used by the NIC.

```
LAN DRIVER 3C505

        ; Set the DMA channel to 3.
        ; Since there is only one DMA configurable channel
        ; the #1 parameter can be omitted.
        DMA 3
```

```
LAN DRIVER DriverWithTwoDmaChannels

    ; The driver has two configurable DMA channels
    ; Set the second DMA channel to 4 and the first
    ; DMA channel to 3.
    DMA #2 4
    DMA 3
    ; Notice that since #1 or #2 was omitted, it
    ; refers to the first configurable DMA channel
```

* INT [#1 | #2] *interruptRequestNumber*

The INT parameter can be used to configure up to two interrupt lines. Some NICs have two configurable interrupt lines. #1 refers to the first configurable line, and #2 refers to the second configurable line. When the number is omitted, it is assumed that the first configurable line is being configured.

The *interruptRequestNumber* refers to the interrupt line value used by the NIC.

Examples:

```
LAN DRIVER EXOS05

    ; Set the interrupt line to 2.
    ; Since there is only one configurable
    ; interrupt line the #1 parameter can be omitted.
    int 2

LAN DRIVER DriverWithTwoInterruptLines

    ; The driver has two configurable interrupt lines
    ; Set the second interrupt line to 4 and the first
    ; interrupt line to 3
    int #2 4
    int 3
    ; Notice that since #1 or #2 was omitted, it
    ; refers to the first configurable interrupt line.
```

* MEM [#1 | #2] *hexStartAddr [hexLengthInParagraphs]*

The MEM parameter can be used to configure up to two memory address ranges. Some NICs may have two configurable address ranges. Number 1 refers to the first configurable range, and number 2 refers to the second configurable range. When the number is omitted, the first configurable memory address range is configured.

The *hexStartAddr* variable refers to the start address of NIC memory, and *hexLengthInParagraphs* refers to the size of the NIC memory in paragraphs. Paragraphs are memory blocks of 16 bytes. The *hexLengthInParagraphs* variable usually can be omitted because the ODI drivers can determine this length from the NIC.

Examples:

```
LAN DRIVER WDPLUS

        ; Set the base address to D8000 and
        ; the memory size to 4000 hex bytes
        ; (400 paragraphs).
        ; Because there is only one configurable
        ; address range the #1 parameter can be omitted.
        mem D8000 400

LAN DRIVER DriverWithTwoMemoryRanges

        ; The driver has two configurable memory ranges
        ; Set the second range to DC000 and the first
        ; range to D0000
        mem #2 DC000
        mem D0000
        ; Notice that since #1 or #2 was
        ; omitted, it refers to
        ; the first configurable range.
```

* PORT [#1 | #2] *hexStartAddr [hexNumberPorts]*

The PORT parameter can be used to configure up to two I/O port address ranges. Some NICs may have two configurable I/O ports. Number 1 refers to the first configurable port, and number 2 refers to the second configurable port. When the number is omitted, the first configurable port address range is configured.

The *hexStartAddr* variable refers to the start address of the I/O port, and *hexNumberPorts* variable refers to the number of I/O ports. The *hexNumberPorts* usually can be omitted because the ODI drivers can determine this number from the NIC, or it can be hard-coded in the NIC driver.

Examples:

```
LAN DRIVER NE1000

        ; Set the I/O port address to 300.
        ; Since there is only one configurable
        ; I/O port, #1 can be omitted.
        port 300

LAN DRIVER DriverWithTwoPorts

        ; The driver has two configurable I/O ports
        ; Set the first port to 280 and the second
        ; port to 300
        port #1 280
        port #2 300
```

* NODE ADDRESS *hexNodeAddress*

The NODE ADDRESS parameter overrides the MAC address that may be set for the NIC. Many NICs use the IEEE MAC layer addressing scheme. Examples of such NICs are IEEE 802.3, IEEE 802.4, IEEE 802.5, and FDDI NICs. These NICs allow a local addressing mode whereby the MAC address stamped on the NIC board can be replaced by a local address.

The *hexNodeAddress* variable refers to the new MAC address of the NIC. You must be careful when you set the *hexNodeAddr* because it may conflict with other NICs. In normal circumstances, the NIC address need not be changed. You may need to change the NIC address, however, if either of the following unusual circumstances exist:

1. A bug in the NIC causes two NICs to report the same MAC address. Normally, the NIC vendor sets MAC addresses. Occasionally, the NIC vendor can make an error and give two NICs the same MAC address.

2. Certain protocols—transparent bridge, Token Ring—may use contention schemes based on MAC addresses for their operation. If you change the MAC address, you can favorably alter the behavior of these protocols.

Examples:

```
LAN DRIVER 3C501

        ; Set the node address to C1002.
        node address C1002
```

* SLOT *slotNumber*

The SLOT parameter can be used to disable the default slot scan in Micro Channel or EISA machines. The LAN driver refers to the NIC in the specified slot.

The *slotNumber* variable refers to the slot number that is usually found on the back of these machines.

In the following example, two NE/2 NICs are being used in a workstation. They are inserted in slots 1 and 2. The NET.CFG file can contain the following lines:

```
LAN DRIVER NE2

        ; Set the slot number to 1.
        ; Actually, if the slot parameter was left out,
        ; the default scan would start with slot 1 and
        ; this would be OK
        slot 1
        ; Other parameters can be set for NE/2 in slot 1.
        ;

LAN DRIVER NE2

        ; Set the slot number to 2.
        ; The slot parameter is required to make a
        ; distinction
        ; between the NICs in slots 1 and 2.
        slot 2
        ; Other parameters can be set for NE/2 in slot 2.
        ;
```

If the NET.CFG is set up as indicated, the batch file to load the ODI components can then contain commands to load the two NE2 drivers:

```
LSL
NE2
NE2
```

FRAME *frameType*

The FRAME parameter specifies alternate MAC layer encapsulations for the NIC boards. Most Ethernet NICs can be set up to have IEEE 802.3 encapsulation or ETHERNET_II encapsulation. When the frame parameter is not specified, the default is IEEE 802.3 for Ethernet NICs. The differences between IEEE 802.3 and ETHERNET II frames are discussed in Chapter 2. Certain upper-layer protocols such as IP (from TCP/IP) or AppleTalk may require a different MAC layer encapsulation than the default value. The FRAME parameter changes the MAC framing used for the upper-layer protocols.

The *frameType* refers to frame type values, such as:

- ETHERNET_802.3
- ETHERNET_802.2
- ETHERNET_II
- ETHERNET_SNAP
- TOKEN_RING
- TOKEN_RING_SNAP
- IBM_PCN2_802.2
- IBM_PCN2_SNAP
- NOVELL_RX-NET

* PROTOCOL *uprotocolName hexProtocolId frameType*

The PROTOCOL parameter registers new protocols to be used with existing ODI drivers.

You can replace *protocolName* with the new protocol being registered. For example, replace *hexProtocolId* with the protocol ID assigned to the new protocol and replace *frameType* with a valid frame type to be used for MAC layer encapsulation.

If, for example, you want to add a new protocol NEWP to a EXOS215 NIC, the protocol ID assigned to NEWP is 99AF and the MAC encapsulation is ETHERNET_SNAP. The NET.CFG file contains lines similar to the following to register the NEWP protocol:

```
LINK DRIVER EXOS215
        frame ETHERNET_SNAP
        protocol NEWP 99AF ethernet_snap
```

If you use IPX and the new protocol, NEWP, you must specify the PROTO-COL parameter. Also, you must specify the protocol ID for IPX. The default frame of ETHERNET_802.3 has a protocol ID of 0. The NET.CFG file will look similar to the following:

```
LINK DRIVER EXOS215
        frame ETHERNET_SNAP
        protocol NEWP 99AF ethernet_snap
        frame ETHERNET_802.3
        protocol IPX 0 ethernet_802.3
```

Table 12.8 lists frame types and protocol IDs for IPX.

The SAPS and LINK STATIONS parameters are used for the LANSUP drivers to specify the number of service access points and link stations needed. They are specific for IBM LANSUP driver. If you do not use this driver, you do not need these parameters. These parameters must be set to values recommended by the IBM LAN Support Program documentation which comes with the NICs that use these drivers.

The LANSUP, TOKEN, and PCN2 drivers can be the primary or alternate adapter. If you use an alternate adapter, you must use the ALTERNATE parameter as shown in the following example:

```
LINK DRIVER LANSUP
        alternate
```

Table 12.8
Protocol IDs for IPX

Frame Type	Protocol ID (hex)
ETHERNET_802.3	0
ETHERNET_802.2	E0
ETHERNET_II	8137
ETHERNET_SNAP	8137
TOKEN-RING	E0
TOKEN-RING_SNAP	8137
IBM-PCN2_802.2	E0
IBM-PCN2_SNAP	8137

continues

Table 12.8
Continued

Frame Type	Protocol ID (hex)
NOVELL_RX-NET	FA
IP	800
ARP	806
RARP	8035

* MAX FRAME SIZE *frameSize*

This parameter specifies the maximum frame size (*frameSize*) used on the Token Ring LAN. For Token Ring NICs with 8K of shared RAM, this parameter has a default value of 2168 bytes. For larger shared-RAM sizes, the default value is 4216 bytes.

The value of *frameSize* must be a multiple of 8 and must be large enough to include the largest frame size plus 6 bytes of adapter overhead. The largest frame size must be the largest data packet plus the largest header. The largest header can be determined as follows:

MAC header	=	35 bytes
SNAP header	=	5 bytes
Upper layer protocol header	=	74 bytes
Largest header	=	114 bytes

If 2K data packets were to be sent, maximum frame size would be the following:

Data packet size	=	2048 bytes
Largest header	=	114 bytes
Adapter overhead	=	6 bytes
Largest frame size	=	2168 bytes

To obtain maximum frame size, the largest frame size must be rounded to a multiple of 8. This number is 2168. The NET.CFG entry looks similar to the following:

```
LINK DRIVER TOKEN
         max frame size 2168
```

ODI Workstation and Token Ring Source Routing

NetWare workstations that need to communicate across an IBM source routing bridge must run the IBM Token Ring Source Routing Driver contained in the file ROUTE.COM on the DOS ODI WORKSTATION SERVICES disk.

To install ROUTE.COM, copy it from the DOS ODI WORKSTATION SERVICES disk to the workstation boot disk. Include ROUTE.COM after you load the ODI NIC driver but before you load the protocol stack.

For workstations that use LANSUP driver, the ODI load sequence is as follows:

```
LSL
LANSUP
ROUTE
IPXODI
```

The ODI load sequence for workstations that use TOKEN driver is shown below:

```
LSL
TOKEN
ROUTE
IPXODI
```

ROUTE.COM can be loaded with a number of parameters specified on the command line. To obtain a brief list of these parameters, use the ROUTE ? command, as follows:

```
ROUTE ?

NetWare Source Routing Driver   v1.11 (910123)
 (c)Copyright 1991 Novell Inc. All Rights Reserved.

ROUTE
U,BOARD=dd,CLEAR,DEF,GBR,MBR,NODES=dd,REMOVE=xxxxxxxxxxxx
```

U   Unloads a previously installed Source
                           Router from memory.

BOARD=dd   A DECIMAL board number as Assigned by
                           ODI. Do NOT use this parameter if you
                           are using an OLD IPX Driver.

CLEAR   CLEAR ALL Nodes from a previously
                           loaded Source Router.

DEF   Send DEFault (Unknown) Node Addresses
                           ALL ROUTES Broadcast. If NOT entered,
                           SINGLE ROUTE Broadcast is ASSUMED.

GBR   Send Broadcast (FFFF FFFF FFFF)
                           Addresses ALL ROUTES Broadcast. If NOT
                           entered, SINGLE ROUTE Broadcast is
                           ASSUMED.

MBR   Send MultiCast (C000 xxxx xxxx)
                           Addresses ALL ROUTES Broadcast. If NOT
                           entered, SINGLE ROUTE Broadcast is
                           ASSUMED.

NODES=dd   The number of NODE Addresses to
                           support. dd is a DECIMAL number
                           between 0 and 255. If dd is LESS THAN
                           08, then 08 is ASSUMED. If NOT
                           entered, dd DEFAULTS to 16.

REMOVE=xxxxxx   A HEXADECIMAL NODE Address to REMOVE
                           from a previously loaded Source
                           Router. If LESS THAN 09 HEXADECIMAL
                           DIGITS are entered, 4000 xxxx xxxx is
                           ASSUMED.

All Parameters are optional, are not case-sensitive, and can be entered in any order. They can be used to set the Source Router being loaded to or change the configuration of a previously loaded Source Router.

Most of these parameters have default values that work with simple networks. For larger networks, some of the parameters can be changed to reduce network traffic on some paths. Table 12.9 describes these parameters. With the exception of the NODES parameter, these parameters can be entered on a second ROUTE command to alter the behavior of the ROUTE program already loaded.

For example, the following command means that source routing is done through board 2. Frames for stations that have addresses not in the source routing table are sent as *All Routes Broadcast* (DEF) frames. *General Broadcast*

(GBR) and *Multicast Broadcast* (MBR) frames also are sent as All Routes Broadcast frames. The source routing table has 20 entries:

```
ROUTE BOARD=2,DEF,GBR,MBR,NODES=20
```

If a major crash on the network affects many SR bridges, type the following command to force a rebuild of the source routing table:

```
ROUTE CLEAR
```

Table 12.9
ROUTE.COM Command Line Parameters

Parameter	Meaning
BOARD=*number*	Specifies a board number for the Token Ring board. The board number is determined in the order in which the LAN driver is loaded.
CLEAR	Forces a rebuild of the source routing table. Can be used if the SR (Source Routing) bridges are down or an alternate path is available.
DEF	Sends frames that do not have addresses in the Source Routing table as All Routes Broadcast frames, which prevents them from being forwarded across Single Route IBM bridges. When DEF is not specified, these frames are forwarded as Single Route Broadcast frames.
GBR	Sends General Broadcast frames as All Routes Broadcast frames. When GBR is not specified, GBR frames are forwarded as Single Route Broadcast frames.
MBR	Sends Multicast Broadcast frames as All Routes Broadcast frames. When MBR is not specified, GBR frames are forwarded as Single Route Broadcast frames.
NODES=*entries*	Specifies the number of entries in the source routing table. The value ranges from 8 to 255 with a default of 16.

continues

Table 12.9
Continued

Parameter	Meaning
REMOVE=*address*	Removes a specified node address from the source routing table. This forces the workstation to find an alternate route. Can be used when an SR bridge is down. The address is a 12-digit hex number. If fewer than 9 digits are entered, the IBM prefix of 4000 hex is added.

DOS NetWare Workstations and Ethernet II LANs

When a NetWare workstation is used to connect to a VAX host running NetWare for VMS, the workstation must be set up for Ethernet II encapsulation. This is because DEC uses Ethernet II encapsulation at the MAC layer. Many UNIX based LANs also use Ethernet II.

The default MAC layer encapsulation for NetWare Ethernet stations is IEEE 802.3. To work with LANs where hosts and servers are set up for Ethernet II encapsulation, the MAC layer encapsulation must be changed to ETHERNET II. In this section, you learn how to change the MAC encapsulation.

IPX.COM for Ethernet II

The utility ECONFIG can be used to change the frame encapsulation for IPX. This utility can be found on the WSGEN disk. When you type **ECONFIG** at the DOS prompt, you get the following information about its usage:

```
Usage: econfig [volume:]file [parameter list]
[parameter list] is one of the following:

SHELL:[configuration type]
AD:[configuration type]
[configuration type] = N, E [type constant]
[type constant] = 0 FFFF (8137 is Novell's assigned type
constant)
```

```
Example: econfig os.exe a:n; b:e 8137; c:e 15af
        econfig shell.com shell:e 8137
```

You can use ECONFIG to configure IPX.COM and NetWare 2.x NOS. You cannot use it with ODI workstation software or NetWare 3.x. For ODI workstations, the configuration must be done through the FRAME parameter in the NET.CFG file. For NetWare 3.x NOS, configuration must be done by the FRAME parameter on the LOAD command in file AUTOEXEC.NCF (see Chapter 8).

The steps outlined next show how to use ECONFIG to configure IPX.COM:

1. Copy the ECONFIG utility to the directory that contains IPX.COM, or make ECONFIG available through the DOS search path.

2. Type the following command to configure IPX.COM:

   ECONFIG IPX.COM SHELL:E 8137

   The constant 8137 is the Ethernet Type field value assigned to Novell.

3. To verify the configuration change, type the following:

   ECONFIG IPX.COM

   You will see the following message:

   ```
   SHELL: Ethernet Typefield: 8137 (Assigned Novell
   type constant)
   ```

   Type the following command to change the shell back to the Novell IEEE 802.3 encapsulation:

   ECONFIG IPX.COM SHELL:N

ODI Workstations for Ethernet II

To configure ODI workstations for Ethernet II, include the FRAME parameter in the NET.CFG file under the LINK DRIVER section. The NET.CFG file for NE2000 driver may look similar to the following:

```
LINK DRIVER NE2000
        frame ETHERNET_II
```

The frame ETHERNET_II parameter changes the MAC layer encapsulation to Ethernet II.

Windows 3.1

Installing Windows 3.1 on a NetWare-based network can be done by installing Windows individually at each workstation or by loading a copy of Windows onto a server, and then running setup to download and install Windows at each workstation. The latter approach is much easier and consists of running Windows setup with the /a option to install Windows on the server, and then running Windows setup with the /n option from each station logged in to the server. To do this legally, you should have a license for each Windows workstation you will be installing.

Depending on the location of the shared files, user files, and swap files, Windows can be installed at the workstation in four possible configurations.

Shared files are Windows utilities (TERMINAL.EXE, CLOCK.EXE, and so on), font files, device drivers, and help files. All of the shared files can take up to 16M of disk space. A Windows installation normally installs only those files needed by the workstation hardware configuration, and these can be anywhere between 8 to 11M. User files include INI, PIF, and GRP files that contain a user's system configuration, and these occupy about 300K of disk space. The swap file is used by the Virtual Memory Manager and can be on a local or network drive. Because keeping it on a network can generate a great deal of network traffic when this swap area is used, it is strongly recommended that you keep the swap file local. It also is best to allocate this file permanently in one contiguous chunk of disk space in order to speed up swap file access.

Installation Configurations

The four configurations mentioned earlier are as follows:

> Local installation only
>
> Network installation only
>
> Shared and user files on network
>
> Shared files on network, user files local

One can derive other permutations of these four basic configurations by keeping the swap file on the network; but as mentioned earlier, this is not a recommended option.

Local Installation Only

This configuration—shown in figure 12.7—has the largest amount of local disk space requirement and does not have any sharing of files on the server. This could be a valid option if sufficient disk storage space is available locally. The advantage of this approach is that all files needed to operate Windows in case of server down time are available locally.

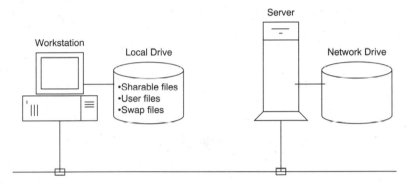

Figure 12.7:
Local Installation only

Network Installation Only

This configuration—shown in figure 12.8—is the complete opposite of the previous configuration in that all files are stored on the server. Shared files need to be on a shared directory on the server and marked with the share-able flag using FLAG. User files and swap space can be in the user's home directory. This configuration also implies that the swap file is kept on the server, which can slow down the network; Windows' performance will be a little slower when swapping is involved. This may be the only option for diskless workstations. The advantage of this approach is that it requires a minimal (zero, actually) local storage requirement.

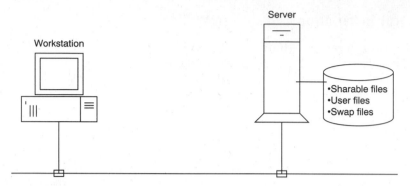

Figure 12.8:
Network Installation only.

Shared and User Files on Network

This configuration—shown in figure 12.9—is a variation of the "Network Installation Only" approach in the sense that the swap file is kept locally, and the shared and user files are stored on the server. Shared files need to be on a shared directory on the server and marked with the shareable flag using FLAG. User files and swap space can be in the user's home directory. Swap file is kept on a local disk so that swapping does not generate any additional network traffic that can slow down the network and reduce Windows' performance. This is the best option if there is local storage space, but you wish to conserve it for other uses.

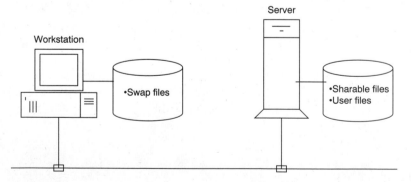

Figure 12.9:
Shared and user files on network.

Shared Files on Network, User Files Local

Figure 12.10 demonstrates this configuration choice. Shared files need to be on a shared directory on the server and marked with the shareable flag using FLAG. User files and swap space are on the local disk. This option is attractive if you wish to conserve server disk space. Unless the user workstation is secured by other means, this is a less secure configuration than the preceding one in which user files are kept on the server. Keeping the user files on the server implies that they are protected using the server network operating system permission. Keeping it local on a DOS workstation implies that any user can gain access to the user files.

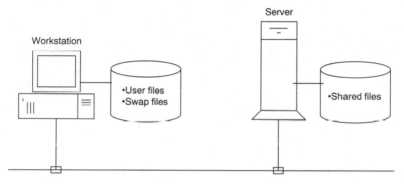

Figure 12.10:
Shared files on network, user files local.

Network Drivers

It is best to use ODI drivers that come with Windows because this gives you the flexibility of changing the IRQ, Base Address, Shared Memory, and other network settings easily. These drivers also can be obtained through the NetWire forum on CompuServe or through the Windows Resource Kit.

The Windows Resource Kit comes with a NEWIPX utility that can generate traditional (non-ODI) IPX.COM files conveniently during network log-in. NEWIPX determines if the workstation's IPX needs to be updated, and if it does, it generates a new IPX. To set up NEWIPX, do the following:

1. Create a directory on the server and give users [R F] privileges to this directory.

2. If you create the directory under SYS:PUBLIC, the [R F] rights will be inherited.

3. Copy the files IPX.OBJ and NEWIPX.EXE from the Windows Resource kit to the new subdirectory you have created.

4. Copy the NIC drivers to be linked with IPX.OBJ to the same directory.

Next, set up the following in the login script file for the user:

```
rem Invoke NEWIPX and pass it the directory containing the
user's IPX.COM
F:\PUBLIC\NEWIPX  C:\NETLOG

rem Check Error_Level codes:
rem
rem Error_Level    0          No upgrade necessary
rem Error_Level    1          Upgrade successful
rem Error_Level  > 1          Upgrade failed

if  "%ERROR_LEVEL" > "1" then begin
    rem  Problem running NEWIPX
    write "IPX upgrade failed. Please inform your
Supervisor"
    pause
end

if  "%ERROR_LEVEL" = "1" then begin
    rem  Ran NEWIPX with no problems
    write "New IPX installed"
    pause
end
```

NET.CFG Settings

The following parameter settings in the NET.CFG can alter Windows behavior:

SHOW DOTS

FILE HANDLES

ENVIRONMENT PAD

SEARCH DIR FIRST

Set SHOW DOTS=ON in NET.CFG. The default is OFF. This causes DOS System Calls FindFirstMatching and FindNextMatching to work correctly for current (.) and parent (..) directories.

The default setting for FILE HANDLES is 40. The recommended value is 60 for Windows. Using smaller values may cause error messages about files not being available.

When a *Virtual DOS Machine* (VDM) is created, it inherits the parent's environment space but does not allow for any growth in this environment space. The ENVIRONMENT PAD allows additional memory to be allocated for the environment space when a VDM session is created.

The SEARCH DIR FIRST parameter has a default value of OFF. This means that if handle-oriented directory searches are being done, the files are searched first, and then the directories. Setting SEARCH DIR FIRST=ON, causes the directories to be searched before files.

INI File Settings

Windows distribution contains additional NetWare related files:

NETWARE.DRV

NETWARE.HLP

NETWARE.INI

NWPOPUP.EXE

VNETWARE.386

VIPX.COM

TBMI2.COM

The NETWARE.DRV file contains program code to implement many of the NetWare-related command functions. For instance, setting NetWareHotKey=1 in the Options section of NETWARE.INI file causes the NETWARE.DRV command functions to be invoked by using the F6 hot key. NETWARE.HLP contains help information for NETWARE.DRV functions. The NETWARE.INI file controls the configuration for NETWARE.DRV.

The NWPOPUP.EXE program handles broadcast messages that appear in a Window pop-up screen. During Windows Setup of NetWare workstations, a LOAD= line is placed in WIN.INI file to cause this to be loaded when Windows runs.

The VNETWARE.386 file virtualizes multiple sessions to the NetWare server. VIPX.386 virtualizes IPX communications between sessions. The 386 extension indicates that this file can be used in 386 enhanced mode only.

The TBMI2.COM program is the task-switched buffer manager for IPX/SPX used to support non-Windows programs that need to talk directly to the SPX/IPX protocol stack.

NETWARE.INI

The NETWARE.INI file and its sections are discussed in tables 12.10 and 12.11.

Table 12.10
NETWARE.INI Options Section

Parameter	Description
NetWareHotKey=	Setting this enables the hot key to invoke the functions in the NETWARE.DRV. The following codes can be used:
	To use F6, set the value to 1. For other function keys, use the formula: 111 + Function Key Number. Therefore, to use the function key F10 as a pop-up, set the value to 111 + 10 = 121.
Messages=	A value of 0 blocks broadcast messages, and a value of 1 enables broadcast messages. Default value is 1.
RestoreDisplay/Timeout=	Specifies the number of seconds the "Restore Connections" message is to be displayed when reconnecting permanent drive and printer mappings. A value of 0 disables the message. The maximum value is 30 seconds.

Table 12.11
NETWARE.INI MSW30-PrtQ Section

Parameter	Description
MaxJobs=	This is the number of print jobs displayed by the Print Manager. The default value is 50 with a minimum of 1 and a maximum of 250.
MaxBufSize=	This is the buffer size in bytes for sending jobs to be queued. The default is 3500. The value can range from 3500 to 30,000 bytes.
UpdateSeconds=	This specifies the frequency in seconds that Print Manager should update the print queue display. The value can range from 1 to 65 seconds and has a default of 30 seconds.

SYSTEM.INI

The SYSTEM.INI file has a NetWare section that contains the parameters described in table 12.12.

Table 12.12
SYSTEM.INI NetWare Section

Parameter	Description
NWShareHandles=	If set to TRUE, drive mappings have a global effect on all DOS sessions. The default value is FALSE, which means drive mappings in a DOS session are local to that DOS session only.
RestoreDrives=	If set to TRUE, drive mappings are restored to their previous state when exiting Windows. The default value is TRUE.

WIN.INI

The WIN.INI can affect a NetWare station's behavior by setting parameters defined in the Windows and Network sections. Tables 12.13 and 12.14 document this behavior.

Table 12.13
WIN.INI Windows Section

Parameter	Description
NetWarn=	Specifies if a warning message should be displayed when the shell is not loaded. A value of 1 enables the warning and a value of 0 disables the warning. The default value is 1.

Table 12.14
WIN.INI Network Section

Parameter	Description
DriveMapping	This contains the drive mappings from the DOS session. These have the following entries: F:=[FS1/SYS:] APPS\DB F:= [FS1/SYS:APPS\DB] for root maps
LPT1:=	This contains the printer attachments from the DOS session.
LPT1-OPTIONS=	For each permanent printer attachment, there is an options entry that looks like the following: LPT1-OPTIONS=Flag,C,T,TO,F,BT,BN

Parameter	Description
	Flag = 8 (No Form feed sent at end of job)
	Flag = 16 (Notify On)
	Flag = 64 (Tabs Enabled)
	Flag =128 (Banner On)
	C = Number of Copies
	T = Tab Size
	TO = Timeout in Seconds
	F = Form Number
	BT = Banner Text
	BN = Banner Name

Using TBM12

TBMI2 is used for non-Windows applications that need to multitask and that make direct calls to the SPX/IPX stack. To determine if your application needs to use TBMI2, perform the following test:

1. Load TBMI2. Just type the name, and it becomes memory resident.

2. Run Windows.

3. Run the non-Windows applications.

4. Exit Windows.

5. Type the command to obtain diagnostic information on TBMI2

   ```
   TBMI2   /D
   ```

6. If the parameters "TBMI2 Old int usage count" or "TBMI2 Far call usage count" is non-zero, the application has made direct calls to the SPX/IPX stack.

The TBMI2's command line parameters are the following:

/? or **/H**	Help on program usage.
/Cfilename	Configuration file. If not specified, NET.CFG is used.
/D	Diagnostic information.
/I	Version information.
/U	Unload TBMI2 from memory.

The TBMI2 configuration parameters are as follows:

```
INT 64=[ON | OFF]
INT 7A=[ON | OFF]
```

The INT 64 parameter, if set to ON, allows applications to access SPX/IPX by the software interrupt INT 64 (hex). It is used to provide compatibility with earlier versions of IPX. The default value is ON. If an application needs to access interrupt 64 (hex), it can be set to OFF.

The INT 7A parameter, if set to ON, allows applications to access SPX/IPX by the software interrupt INT 7A (hex). It is used to provide compatibility with applications written for NetWare v2.0a. The default value is ON. If an application needs to access interrupt 7A (hex), it can be set to OFF.

Exploring the Workstation Connection Mechanism

This section explains the behind-the-scenes mechanism that makes a workstation connection possible. The actual connection mechanism is discussed first, and then the tables kept at the workstation and the server to manage the connection are discussed.

Making the Connection

When the NetWare shell or OS/2 NetWare requester loads, it has no knowledge of any servers on the network. Because all servers keep track of services available on the network through the SAP protocol (see Chapter 3), the shell can connect to any one server. Once this connection is made, the shell can query the server about other services on the network.

You must perform the following steps to make the connection:

1. Obtain a server's address

2. Obtain a route to the server

3. Request and negotiate a connection

Server's Address

To obtain a server's address, the shell issues a SAP broadcast request for the nearest server. All routers—including servers that act as internal routers—on the workstation's segment that have knowledge of the nearest server respond with a SAP response.

This sequence of events is illustrated by the first two packet transmissions in figure 12.11. Figure 12.11 also shows other packet transmissions necessary to complete a connection. The SAP request and SAP response packets are decoded by a LANalyzer in figures 12.12 and 12.13. Figure 12.13 shows that the SAP response contains the server name, its full internet address, and the number of hops required to reach the server.

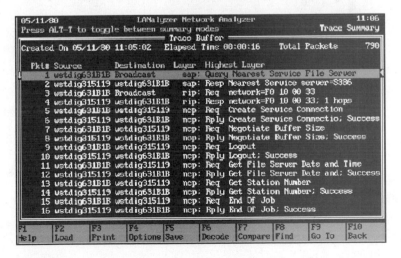

Figure 12.11:
Packet transmissions in making a connection.

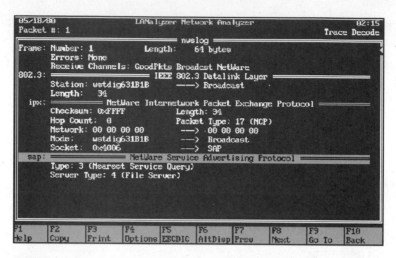

Figure 12.12:
A Get Nearest Server SAP request.

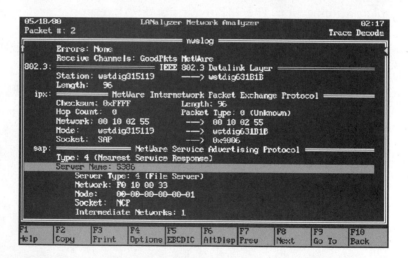

Figure 12.13:
A Give Nearest Server SAP response.

The Get Nearest Server/Give Nearest Server request/response also can be observed through the router tracking screen by typing **TRACK ON** at the server console.

The Get Nearest Server/Give Nearest Server information for NetWare 3.x has the following syntax:

```
InOut [LAN:NodeAddr] Time        Give Nearest Server

InOut [LAN:NodeAddr] Time        Give Nearest Server serverName
```

The NetWare 2.x Get Nearest Server/Give Nearest Server information, which does not have the Time field, has the following syntax:

```
InOut [LAN:NodeAddr]     Give Nearest Server

InOut [LAN:NodeAddr]     Give Nearest Server serverName
```

The NetWare 3.x TRACK screen displays Get Nearest Server/Give Nearest Server information as follows:

```
IN   [A:400000000010]    01:00:12pm   Get Nearest Server

OUT  [A:400000000010]    01:00:13pm   Give Nearest Server KSS
```

NetWare 2.x TRACK screen shows Get Nearest Server/Give Nearest Server information in this manner:

```
IN   [A:400000000010]    Get Nearest Server

OUT  [A:400000000010]    Give Nearest Server KSS
```

A Route to the Server

After the workstation has the name and internet address of the server, it determines the best route to the server. It sends a RIP request (Get Local Target) and waits for a RIP response (Give Local Target). The RIP protocol was discussed in Chapter 3. The RIP request and response are shown as packets 3 and 4 in figure 12.11. The details of these packets are shown in figures 12.14 and 12.15.

If the server's network number is the same as the workstation's number, the server and the workstation are on the same network. If the server's network number is different from the workstations network number, the shell broadcasts a RIP request for the fastest route to the server. If several routers respond with a route equal to the shortest route, the first response is selected.

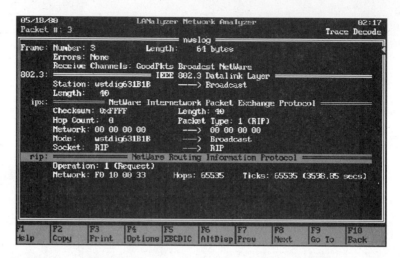

Figure 12.14:
A RIP request packet for best route to server.

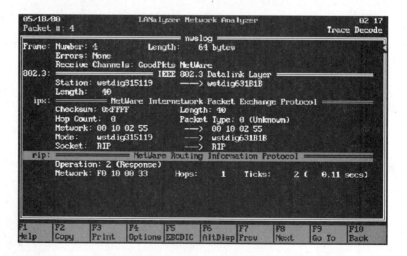

Figure 12.15:
A RIP response packet for best route to server.

The MAC address of the router or the server is used to forward the NCP connection request.

Connection Request and Negotiation

After the workstation knows the internet address of the server—and the router to get to it, if necessary—it issues an NCP connection request to create a connection to the server. The NCP connection request and response are shown as packets 5 and 6 in figure 12.11. These packets are shown decoded in figures 12.16 and 12.17.

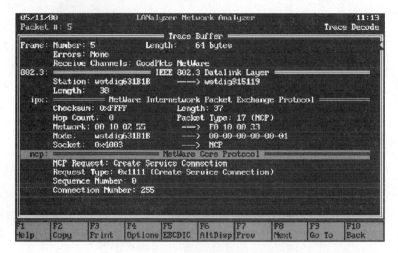

Figure 12.16:
An NCP service connection request packet.

After the connection to the server is established, the shell negotiates the maximum packet size it can use. Packets 7 and 8 show this negotiation. The shell issues an NCP Negotiate Buffer Size request (fig. 12.18), and the server responds with an NCP Negotiate Buffer Reply (fig. 12.19).

The Preferred Server Shell

The preferred server shell (v3.01 and higher) adds features not offered by older shells. The server to which an attachment is made can be specified by parameters on the command line (NET*x* PS=*serverName*) or by a parameter in the NET.CFG file.

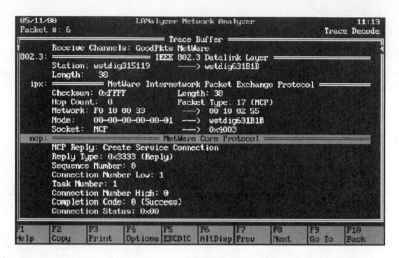

Figure 12.17:
An NCP service connection reply packet.

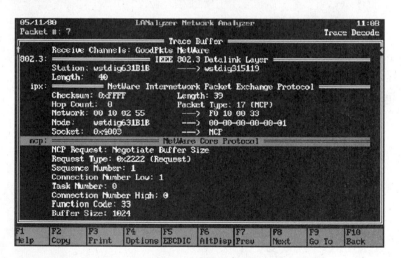

Figure 12.18:
NCP Negotiate Buffer Size request packet.

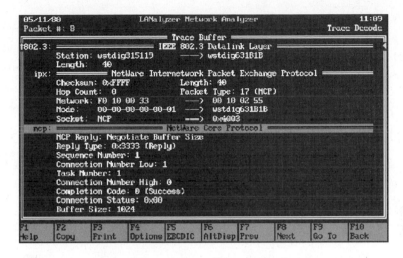

Figure 12.19:
NCP Negotiate Buffer reply packet.

The first eight steps in table 12.15 to make a connection are the same for the older shells and the preferred server. If the server that the preferred shell initially connects to is not the one specified by the user, you must perform several additional steps as shown in table 12.16. The preferred shell obtains the IPX internet address of the preferred server from the bindery of the attached server (steps 9 and 10). It then obtains a route to the preferred server (steps 11 and 12), creates the connection (steps 13 and 14), negotiates maximum packet size (steps 15 and 16), and destroys the service connection made in steps 5 and 6. Steps 11 to 16 repeat steps 3 to 8, except that the interaction takes place with the preferred server rather than the first attached server.

The preferred shell saves the Give Nearest Response up to four additional servers, in case the server that responds first does not have any free connection slots.

Table 12.15
Initial Connection Packet Sequence

Packet Type	Protocol	Source	Destination
1. Get Nearest Server	SAP	client	broadcast
2. Give Nearest Server	SAP	router	client
3. Route Request (GetLocalTarget)	RIP	client	broadcast
4. Route Response (GiveLocalTarget)	RIP	router	client
5. Create Connection	NCP	client	server
6. Connection Assigned	NCP	server	client
7. Negotiate Packet Size	NCP	client	server
8. Maximum Packet Size	NCP	server	client

Table 12.16
Connection Sequence for Preferred Server Shell

Packet Type	Protocol	Source	Destination
1. Get Nearest Server	SAP	client	broadcast
2. Give Nearest Server	SAP	router	client
3. Route Request (GetLocalTarget)	RIP	client	broadcast
4. Route Response (GiveLocalTarget)	RIP	router	client
5. Create Connection	NCP	client	server
6. Connection Assigned	NCP	server	client
7. Negotiate Packet Size	NCP	client	server
8. Maximum Packet Size	NCP	server	client

Packet Type	Protocol	Source	Destination
9. Query Server Bindery for Preferred Server	NCP	client	server
10. Address of Preferred Server	NCP	server	client
11. Route Request (GetLocalTarget)	RIP	client	broadcast
12. Route Response (GiveLocalTarget)	RIP	router	client
13. Create Connection	NCP server	client	preferred
14. Connection Assigned	NCP	preferred	client server
15. Negotiate Packet Size	NCP server	client	preferred
16. Maximum Packet Size	NCP	preferred	client server
17. Destroy Service Connection	NCP	client	preferred server

NetWare Core Protocol (NCP)

The NCP (layer 7) is used for all requests for services by the client and for the responses to these requests. The NCP provides its own session control and sequence control instead of relying on SPX—a transport layer protocol—to provide this function. This streamlines the NCP protocol that runs on IPX by avoiding the overhead of layers 4, 5, and 6.

The Request Type field determines the type of NCP packet, such as Connection Request or Negotiate Buffer Size. The client assigns the Sequence Number field starting with a value of one after the connection is established. Every request by the client is assigned a sequence number, one greater than the previous request. The server's NCP response contains the same sequence as the corresponding NCP request. This ensures that the client is receiving the correct response for its request. It also enables the shell and the server to determine when a packet is lost.

When a client establishes a connection to the server, a connection number is assigned for the duration of the session. This connection number is placed in the Connection Number field of every NCP request/response packet. The Connection Number field identifies NCP requests and responses as belonging to a specific session.

Connection Management

The connection between a client and the server is identified by a connection number that remains the same for the duration of the session. The client and the server keep track of this and other information in special tables. These tables enable the client and server to manage the session.

The Shell's Connection Table

The shell's connection table is used to keep track of the client's connections. A DOS client can support up to eight server connections. Each entry of the shell connection table contains the server name and the internet address of the server it connects to. If the packets need to be forwarded to a router to reach the server, the router's MAC address is stored in the table entry (Router Node Address). The current value of the NCP sequence number and the connection number for the session also are stored in the table.

Two timeout values are maintained for every connection: maximum timeout and receive timeout. The maximum timeout is the maximum time the shell waits for a response from the server before it resends the request. This timeout is based on the initial estimate of the time delay between the client and the server, obtained during the RIP response to the nearest server route request, and is measured in clock ticks.

```
Maximum Timeout = 16 × Td + 10
```

Td=Time delay between client and server. If the server and client are on the same LAN, Td equals one tick, and maximum timeout equals $16 \times 1 + 10 = 26$ ticks.

The receive timeout is dynamically adjusted based on current delays on the network. The initial value is set by the following formula:

```
Initial Receive Timeout = 4 × Td + 10
```

The receive timeout increases by 50 percent if the server does not respond within the current setting of the timeout value.

```
New Increased Receive Timeout = 1.5 × Current Receive
Timeout
```

The increase continues by 50 percent every time the server does not respond in the specified time, until the maximum timeout value is reached.

The shell reduces the receive timeout value every time the shell does not have to issue a retry request. To decrease the receive timeout, the shell takes the time necessary to receive a response to the last request that did not require a retry, multiplies that value by 2, and adds 10. The new receive timeout is set to the mean of this calculated value and the current receive timeout.

```
New Decreased Receive Timeout= [ (2 × Time to receive
response)+ 10)   + Current receive timeout ] / 2
```

The IPX Retry Count parameter determines the number of times the shell sends the request. This parameter can be set in the NET.CFG—previously SHELL.CFG—file. If this count is exceeded, the error message `Network error on server XXXX. Error XXXX from network. Abort, Retry?` appears. Some network drivers may ignore the IPX Retry Count parameter setting in the NET.CFG file and use a hard-coded default.

The Server Connection Table

A portion of the connection table keeps track of the clients it services. This table contains an entry for every connection to a client. The Network Address, Node Address, and Socket Number refer to the internet address of the client. Each time a connection request from a client arrives, the server compares the IPX internet source address with these fields. If these addresses do not match, a security breach has occurred.

The Sequence Number field keeps track of request/response packets between a client and the server. The NIC Number field holds the number of the NIC (A, B, C, D), or Network number of the NIC, used to send the packet to the client. If the server was reached by routers, the MAC address of the router on the server's segment is placed in the Intermediate Router Address field. Because of this, the server does not need to determine a route to the client. To send a reply to the client, the server simply copies the Intermediate

Router Address field in the packet's MAC destination address field. The packet's IPX destination address field contains the destination internet address of the client. The routers then route the server reply packet to the client.

The Watchdog Timer field is discussed a little later. A 100-byte Reply Buffer is maintained for every client connection. If the response to a client is less than 100 bytes, a copy of the response is kept in the Reply Buffer field. If the client does not receive a response and resends the request, the server uses the Reply Buffer field to reply to the client. The server then does not have to reprocess the client request because most server responses are less than 100 bytes.

Watchdog Process

The server maintains a watchdog process to monitor shell connections that may have crashed because of network problems or a workstation crash. At the end of the watchdog timer, files that were opened by the workstation before the crash are closed, and the connection information for the workstation in the server connection table is removed.

The server uses the watchdog process to poll clients not heard from in the last 5 minutes. Figure 12.20 shows the watchdog packets captured using the LANalyzer. An active shell responds to the watchdog packet request. Figures 12.21 and 12.22 show the details of the watchdog packet request and response. If the shell fails to respond, the server sends a watchdog request packet every minute until it has sent a total of 11 watchdog request packets. If the shell fails to respond to the last watchdog packet, the station is cleared.

NetWare 3.x servers enable you to set a parameter that monitors workstations cleared by the watchdog process. This parameter can be set by typing the following on the NetWare 3.x console:

```
SET CONSOLE DISPLAY WATCHDOG LOGOUTS=ON
```

NetWare 3.x watchdog parameters can be changed by typing the following SET commands:

```
SET NUMBER OF WATCHDOG PACKETS=numbWatchdogPackets
```

The preceding command, which can be placed in an NCF file, sets the number of times the server polls an inactive station before it terminates the connection. This value ranges from 5 to 100 and has a default value of 10.

```
SET DELAY BEFORE FIRST WATCHDOG PACKET=delayFirstWatchdogPacket
```

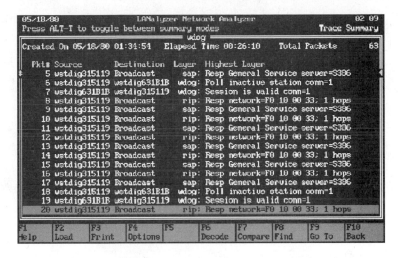

Figure 12.20:
Watchdog packets captured using the LANalyzer.

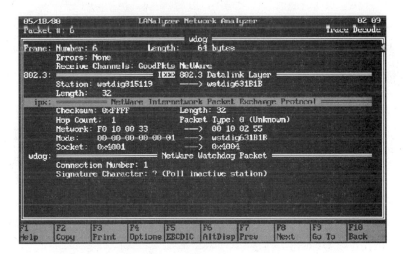

Figure 12.21:
Watchdog packet request.

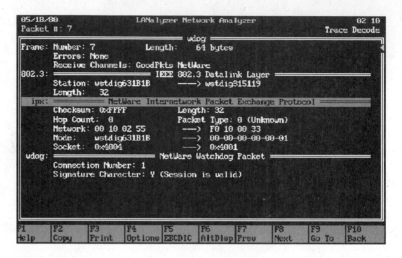

Figure 12.22:
Watchdog packet response.

In the preceding command, *delayFirstWatchdogPacket* is the normal delay between the time a watchdog poll packet is sent to an active station and a valid response is received from that station. This value ranges from 15.7 seconds to 20 minutes 52.3 seconds and has a default value of 4 minutes 56.6 seconds.

SET DELAY BETWEEN WATCHDOG PACKETS=*delayWatchdogPackets*

The *delayWatchdogPackets* command controls the time between repeated sendings of watchdog poll packets if no response is received. This value ranges from 9.9 seconds to 10 minutes 26.2 seconds and has a default value of 59.3 seconds.

In NetWare 2.2, the WATCHDOG command can be issued from the server console to change the watchdog process timing parameters. The general syntax of this command is as follows:

WATCHDOG [START=*n***] [INTERVAL=***n***] [COUNT=***n***]**

The START value designates the number of seconds the server waits to send a watchdog request packet to verify the connection. The value ranges from 15 to 1200 with a default of 300 seconds.

The INTERVAL represents the number of seconds the server waits to send repeated watchdog request packets after the client fails to respond. The value ranges from 1 to 600 with a default of 60.

The COUNT refers to the number of intervals the server waits after START before clearing the connection. The value ranges from 5 to 100 with a default of 10.

Preparing the PC as a Workstation

When DOS is used to boot a PC, the PC has no idea that it will be used as a workstation on a NetWare LAN. The CONFIG.SYS file does not contain network drivers. The network software that is needed to turn the PC into a workstation on a NetWare LAN is loaded as TSR programs. These TSRs are IPX.COM and NETX.COM. If ODI drivers are being used, then you need the ODI Driver.COM file, the Link Support Program LSL.COM, and the IPXODI.COM that implements the SPX/IPX protocols. The ODI drivers also are loaded as TSRs.

Although CONFIG.SYS does not contain commands that suggest that the PC is being used as a NetWare workstation, certain configuration commands in the CONFIG.SYS file can have an important effect on using the PC as a NetWare workstation.

The following discussion is for DOS-based workstations. For OS/2, the CONFIG.SYS file contains direct network driver support. OS/2 is discussed in Chapter 13.

Loading DOS

You might find that it is helpful to have a knowledge of what takes place behind the scenes when DOS first loads. Certain problems during the processing of network login scripts become clear when you understand the DOS load process.

When a system is first powered up, it automatically jumps to location 0FFFF0 hex, and begins executing the program starting at that location. This is a feature of all Intel 8086 family of microprocessors (the 80286, 80386, and 80486), and is independent of any operating system (such as DOS, OS/2, and

UNIX) that may be running on the PC. The special location 0FFFF0 hex lies in a location in the ROM of the PC, and performs a power on self-test (POST) that checks memory (RAM) integrity, the keyboard, system clock, and other devices. After a successful POST, control is transferred to the bootstrap program, which is part of the BIOS (see figs. 12.23, 12.24, and 12.25).

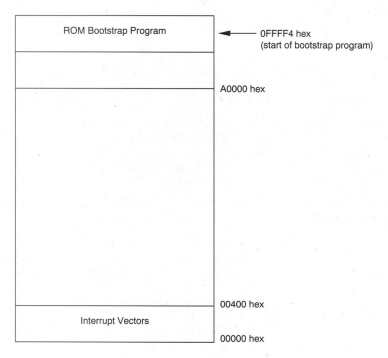

Figure 12.23:
Memory map when control is transferred to bootstrap program.

The bootstrap program reads the first sector on the boot media (either the floppy disk in drive A or hard disk in drive C), which contains the remainder of the bootstrap program and information on the disk. After reading the rest of the bootstrap program into an arbitrary location in memory, the system transfers control to it. The bootstrap program then checks for the existence of a copy of the operating system. For MS-DOS, this is done by checking for the two files IO.SYS and MSDOS.SYS in that order. For IBM PC-DOS, these two files are IBMBIO.SYS and IBMDOS.SYS. If these files are missing, the system responds with the following error message:

```
Non-System disk or disk error
Replace and strike a key when ready
```

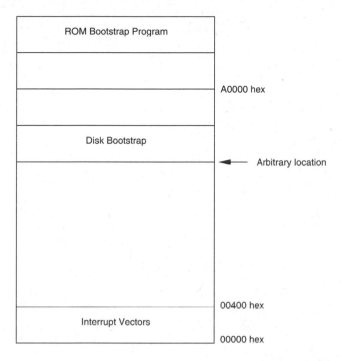

Figure 12.24:
Memory map on loading disk bootstrap.

You receive this message also when the NetWare workstation software is copied to a floppy disk that has not been properly prepared by using the FORMAT /S or SYS commands in DOS.

If the two system files are found, they are read into memory and control is transferred to the program in IO.SYS. In some systems, the IO.SYS loads first, and this in turn reads MSDOS.SYS in memory. The IO.SYS file actually consists of the following two parts:

- **BIOS.** Contains a linked set of resident device drivers for standard PC devices, such as CON, AUX, PRN, COM1, COM2, COM3, and NUL. Also, some hardware-specific initialization code is run to initialize certain devices.

- **SYSINIT.** Contains code from Microsoft and the BIOS supplied by the manufacturer of the PC. SYSINIT is called by the manufacturer's BIOS initialization code. It determines the amount of contiguous RAM, and then relocates itself so it can "get out of the way" of the DOS kernel that is loaded next.

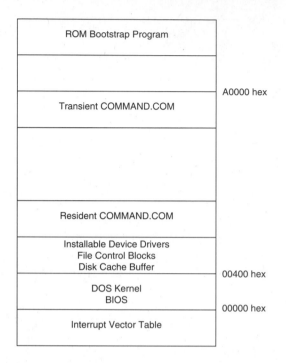

Figure 12.25:
Final DOS map showing COMMAND.COM components.

Next, SYSINIT executes the initialization code in MSDOS.SYS, to accomplish the following:

- Setting up internal system tables

- Setting up interrupt vectors in locations 20 hex to 2F hex

- Calling the initialization function for each resident device driver

After the system initialization code displays, the MS-DOS copyright message displays, and the basic MS-DOS system loads. SYSINIT uses the MS-DOS file services to open the CONFIG.SYS file. (CONFIG.SYS processing is discussed in more detail in the following section.) If it is found, the entire CONFIG.SYS file is loaded in memory and each line in the file is processed. Any device drivers loaded by DEVICE= or DEVICEHIGH= commands are processed in the order in which they are found and loaded in memory. For DR DOS, statements with a ? before them cause the system to prompt the user if that statement should be processed.

After all the installable device drivers are loaded, SYSINIT closes all the files it has opened. SYSINIT then opens the console (CON), printer (PRN), and auxiliary (AUX) devices as standard input, standard output, and standard error devices.

Finally, SYSINIT calls the MS-DOS EXEC function to load the command line interpreter COMMAND.COM, which is located on the boot media or specified by the SHELL= statement in CONFIG.SYS. To conserve memory, COMMAND.COM actually loads two parts. The *resident part* loads in lower memory, and the *transient part* loads just below the 640K limit.

The resident part of COMMAND.COM always is resident in RAM. The transient portion of COMMAND.COM can be written over by applications that are big enough to fill the entire 640K. After the application exits, DOS reloads the transient portion from a copy of COMMAND.COM. The location of COMMAND.COM is indicated by the COMSPEC environment variable, whose default value is set by the COMMAND.COM path in the SHELL= statement in the CONFIG.SYS file. The value of COMSPEC is important because an invalid COMSPEC can be the cause of the Invalid COMMAND.COM—System Halted error message that sometimes is encountered with NetWare LANs. This issue is discussed later on in this chapter. After SYSINIT performs its job, it is no longer needed and is discarded (see fig. 12.25).

If an AUTOEXEC.BAT file is in the root directory of the boot media, it is read into memory and processed by using the command line interpreter COMMAND.COM. If the AUTOEXEC.BAT file is not found, DOS prompts you for the date and time, which is a good reason to create an AUTOEXEC.BAT file and have at least a statement such as PROMPT PG in the file.

Understanding the CONFIG.SYS File

The following statements may appear in the CONFIG.SYS file and are important for a PC that you want to set up as a NetWare workstation:

```
SHELL=<pathname>/COMMAND.COM /P /E:<space>
FILES=<number of file handles>
BUFFERS=<number of buffers>
LASTDRIVE=<lastdrive>
DEVICEHIGH=<device path>
BREAK=[ON | OFF]
```

The SHELL= statement uses the /P switch to run AUTOEXEC.BAT and make the command line interpreter permanent. The /E switch tells DOS the amount of space it should reserve for the environment variables. In a NetWare environment in which many applications are being run, you might want to increase this value if you get the message `Out of environment space`. A good value to use is 800 bytes. The SHELL= statement, then, might look like the following:

```
SHELL=C:\DOS\COMMAND.COM /P /E:800
```

The C:\DOS\ statement specifies the *pathname* in which the DOS COMMAND.COM file can be found. If you are using an earlier version of DOS, such as DOS 3.1, the environment space is measured in number of paragraphs. Each paragraph is 16 bytes.

The FILES= statement controls the number of files the workstation can have open locally. It does not have any effect on the number of files opened on the network. FILES= still is important for applications that need to open a combination of local and network files. You can control the number of files that can be opened on NetWare servers by using the FILE HANDLES= statement in the NET.CFG (or older SHELL.CFG) file. The default is 40 open files on the network per workstation.

You can, for example, set the number of files a workstation can open locally to 30 by including `FILES=30` in the CONFIG.SYS file. You also can set the number of files that can be opened on the network to 50 by including `FILE HANDLES=50` in the NET.CFG file.

The BUFFERS= statement specifies the number of 512-byte blocks set aside for read and write operations. DOS reads and writes data in 512-byte sectors. If a sufficient number of buffers are in RAM, this can speed up file operations. In DR DOS, the HIBUFFERS= statement can be used to allocate buffers in high memory rather than conventional memory. A general rule of thumb is to have one buffer for every file you might want to open simultaneously.

The LASTDRIVE= statement specifies the last drive letters recognized by DOS. Its default value is E. This is the reason that the first network drive usually defaults to drive F. Under certain conditions, such as running NetWare Lite and NetWare on the same workstation, you might want to use the LASTDRIVE= statement to set a different last drive. If you set the LASTDRIVE= parameter to M, for examples, drives A to M can be used for local devices and network drives for NetWare Lite. Drives N to Z then can be used by NetWare.

When some applications are installed, they may add the LASTDRIVE=Z statement in the CONFIG.SYS file. Under these conditions, you do not have any assignable network drives for NetWare. You have to change the LASTDRIVE= statement to a value with which NetWare can work.

Another application for LASTDRIVE= is to use drive letters C, D, and E, which normally are used for local disks as network drives. You might want to do this for diskless workstations or workstations with floppy drives and no hard drives. In the latter case, if you have two floppy drives and no virtual RAM disks, you can use the statement LASTDRIVE=B so that the first available network drive is C. This setup is useful if you are running out of drive letters to assign to network directories.

The DEVICEHIGH= and DEVICE= statements load device drivers in memory. The DEVICE= statement loads device drivers in conventional memory. DEVICEHIGH= loads the drivers in upper memory, leaving more space for applications to run in conventional memory. If you want to conserve conventional memory for applications, you should load as many device drivers in upper memory by using DEVICEHIGH=. In DR DOS, the equivalent command for loading drivers in upper memory is HIDEVICE=.

By setting the BREAK= statement to BREAK=OFF, you cannot break out of programs by using the Ctrl-C or Ctrl-Break keys until the program performs an I/O operation on the screen or printer. Setting the BREAK=OFF statement can prevent users from breaking out of batch files.

This section has covered only the CONFIG.SYS parameters that have a more direct bearing on the network environment. For a more complete and comprehensive description of CONFIG.SYS parameters, consult your DOS manual. In general, most other CONFIG.SYS parameters can be specified in the CONFIG.SYS file without adversely affecting the network workstation environment.

The following is an example of a CONFIG.SYS file used in a network workstation. This example should give you a sense of what you can place in the CONFIG.SYS file without having any problems.

```
DEVICE=C:\DOS5.0\HIMEM.SYS
DOS=HIGH,UMB
DEVICEHIGH=C:\DOS5.0\SETVER.EXE
DEVICEHIGH=C:\DOS5.0\EMM386.EXE RAM
FILES=40
BUFFERS=40
SHELL=C:\COMMAND.COM /P /E:800
LASTDRIVE=M
```

In the preceding example, the LASTDRIVE= statement is set to M because the workstation also is used for NetWare Lite. The first available network drive then becomes N for NetWare LANs

Understanding the AUTOEXEC.BAT File

After the CONFIG.SYS file processes, DOS uses the command line interpreter to execute the commands in the AUTOEXEC.BAT file. DOS looks for the AUTOEXEC.BAT file in the root directory of the boot media. The statements that you can place in CONFIG.SYS files are fundamentally different than the ones you can place in AUTOEXEC.BAT files. The statements in CONFIG.SYS files are special statements dealing with system configuration. On the other hand, the statements in AUTOEXEC.BAT files can be any DOS internal or external commands and any applications that you normally load from the DOS command line.

You can, for example, place the following commands in your AUTOEXEC.BAT file to set up an automatic startup script for logging in to a NetWare network:

```
@ECHO OFF
PROMPT $P$G
PATH C:\LOCAL\APPS;C:\LOCAL\BIN
IPX
NETx
REM * Remove NETBIOS if applications do not need it
NETBIOS
REM * Next line is only needed, if NETBIOS applications are
REM * poorly written and check for IBM PC LAN product before
REM * running. Most of these applications have been
REM * fixed and you would not normally need the INT2F program
INT2F
F:
LOGIN serverName/userName
```

In DOS 3.3 or higher, the @ character instructs the batch file not to display that line. The ECHO OFF command stops the commands in the AUTOEXEC.BAT file from being displayed as they are executed. The PATH command sets up a local path environment. When the log-in processing continues, a special login script is processed that sets up the network environment. This login script contains commands to set up the network search path. In earlier versions of the shell (NETX.COM), the network search path would override the local path. This problem has been fixed in more recent releases so that, as new network search paths are added, the PATH in the AUTOEXEC.BAT file is preserved and added at the end of the search path.

In the preceding example, the NETBIOS and IN2F commands are optional and are needed only if you are running applications that need the NETBIOS protocol stack. Because of NetWare's popularity, most applications are written to make direct use of the IPX protocols. You should seldom have a need to use Novell's NETBIOS emulation.

If you are using the ODI drivers, then you probably want to use an AUTOEXEC.BAT file similar to the following:

```
@ECHO OFF
PROMPT $P$G
PATH C:\LOCAL\APPS;C:\LOCAL\BIN
LSL
REM * Replace SMCPLUS with the ODI driver for the
REM * network adapter.
SMCPLUS
IPXODI
NETx
F:
LOGIN serverName/userName
```

In the preceding example, the LSL is loaded first, which is followed by the ODI driver for the network adapter in the workstation. In the preceding example, the ODI driver for an SMC Elite 16T network adapter (*SMCPLUS*) is used. The IPXODI program that implements the SPX/IPX protocols is loaded next, and finally the NETx shell program. ODI drivers require that a NET.CFG file be set up appropriately as discussed in an earlier chapter.

You can load the IPX.COM and the NETX.COM in upper memory by using the LOADHIGH command from DOS 5.0, or the HILOAD command in DR DOS.

Examining the Log-In Process

When the NetWare shell (NETX.COM) loads, it sets up the first network drive to map to the SYS:LOGIN directory on the specified server. The first network drive usually is F. By changing to this drive and invoking the

LOGIN program, you can initiate the user authentication process. The user has to supply the correct log-in name and password before access to a NetWare server is granted.

After you log in, the commands that you type are checked by the shell to see if they are network commands. Network commands are sent to the server, where they are processed and the results sent back. Local commands are processed by the local workstation operating system. The advantage of this approach is that, as far as DOS is concerned, it has little awareness that the workstation is being used on a network. The networking software makes it appear as if the network is an extension of the workstation operating environment. This makes it possible for single-user applications to run on the network if they are set up correctly.

Figures 12.26 and 12.27 show the kind of processing that takes place at the workstation and the server to keep the network transparent to DOS.

When a DOS application wants to make use of DOS system services, such as request for file open, it issues a software interrupt by using the instruction INT 21H. When NETx loads, it takes over several software interrupts and steals the DOS interrupt by placing an address to its own code in the interrupt vector for 21 (hex). In this manner the shell can monitor all DOS system calls. If the DOS system call is for NetWare services, such as access to a file on a network drive, the shell directs this request across the network to the server. In this sense, the shell plays the role of a traffic policeman or a redirector.

The request is sent as an NCP packet encapsulated in an IPX datagram and passed on to the LAN drivers for the workstation. The LAN drivers encapsulate the IPX packet with data link headers and send this packet across the network to the server. The server's LAN drivers strip the data link header and pass the IPX packet to the IPX process on the server. The IPX process passes the IPX packet to the router process on the server. Remember, every NetWare server is capable of acting as an IPX router. The router process examines the destination address on the IPX packet and checks if the IPX packet is destined to a different network than the one on which the IPX packet was received. If the IPX packet belongs to a different network, the router process consults its routing table to determine to which router the IPX packet should be sent. The IPX header then is replaced by the address of the next router. This process continues until the IPX packet gets to its final destination.

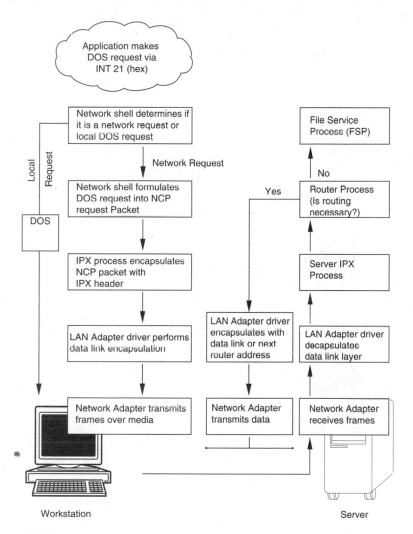

Figure 12.26:
NetWare workstation makes a system request.

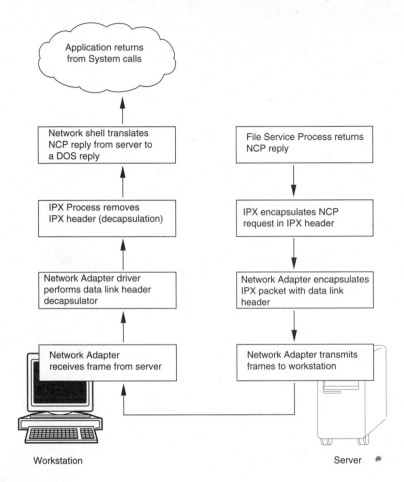

Figure 12.27:
NetWare server replies to workstation request.

If the router process discovers that no routing is necessary, it strips the IPX header and sends the original NCP request to the file server process on the server. The file server processes the request and sends an NCP reply packet to the router and IPX process. The router process determines whether or not the packet needs to be routed. The NCP packet is encapsulated in an IPX packet and sent to the LAN drivers, which send it back to the workstation that made the request. At the workstation, the LAN drivers strip off the data link header and pass it on to the IPX software running at the workstation (IPX.COM or IPXODI.COM). The IPX process at the workstation strips off the IPX header and sends the NCP reply packet to the NetWare shell, which translates the original DOS request to a DOS system reply. The application that was waiting for the DOS system service then resumes its work.

Summary

In this chapter, you learned how to manage the workstation setup, including the following activities:

- Generating IPX for NetWare workstations

- Installing ODI components

- Using source routing drivers for IBM Token Ring networks

- Configuring NetWare workstation for Ethernet II LANs

Toward the end of the chapter, you learned details of the NetWare workstation connection mechanism. Knowledge of this connection mechanism can help troubleshoot many configuration problems.

Supporting Non-DOS Workstations

NetWare has long provided services for DOS clients. This is not a DOS world, however, and a variety of other computer environments command significant user bases. Therefore, Novell has aggressively pursued the goal of enabling NetWare to provide services to a variety of computer environments.

Currently NetWare provides connectivity for Macintosh, OS/2, and UNIX computers. This connectivity is provided through a variety of protocol and file-support options. By adding AppleTalk protocol support for connectivity, Apple Filing Protocol support for file access, and AppleTalk Print Service Protocol support for printing, you enable your Macintosh users to access files on a NetWare server and print to NetWare printers as though the resources were installed on a standard Mac network.

This chapter discusses the support NetWare provides for Macintosh and OS/2 workstations. It also introduces you to Novell's UnixWare product, a UNIX environment that can utilize standard IPX/SPX protocols to access NetWare servers.

Macintosh

Every Macintosh station comes with a built-in LocalTalk adapter that communicates at speeds up to 254K per second. If you want higher communication speeds, Token Ring or Ethernet NICs can be used on Macintosh stations equipped with expansion slots. The protocol used by Macintosh workstations is AppleTalk. For a NetWare server to coexist with Macintosh workstations, the NetWare server must support AppleTalk protocols.

Figure 13.1 shows that the NetWare server runs a dual protocol stack that consists of the native NCP/SPX/IPX stack and the AppleTalk protocol stack. The Service Protocol Gateway (SPG) translates Apple File Protocol requests issued by Macintosh workstations to NCP requests at the server. The SPG then translates the NCP responses of the NetWare server to AFP responses before they are relayed to the requesting workstation. This procedure creates the illusion that the NetWare server is a Macintosh server.

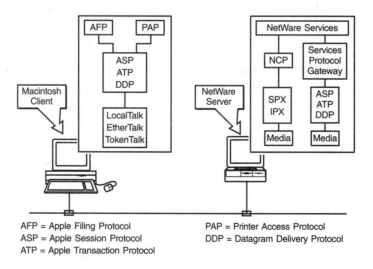

AFP = Apple Filing Protocol   PAP = Printer Access Protocol
ASP = Apple Session Protocol   DDP = Datagram Delivery Protocol
ATP = Apple Transaction Protocol

Figure 13.1:
Macintosh workstation. (Graphic courtesy of Learning Group International)

The AppleTalk protocol stack is implemented as an NLM on NetWare v3.x and as a VAP on NetWare v2.x. The client software that runs on Macintosh workstations is AppleShare. Macintosh workstations see the NetWare servers as AppleShare servers. This enables Macintosh users to use the familiar AppleShare interface; for instance, they can use the Chooser program to select the NetWare server.

From the Macintosh workstation's perspective, the NetWare server looks just like an AppleShare server, and the Macintosh user can use the familiar chooser program to log in to the NetWare server and access the NetWare volumes.

Most of the complexity of setting up Macintosh stations on a NetWare network is at the server. The discussion that follows is for configuring the NetWare v3.x server to act as an AppleShare server.

The sequence of steps necessary to configure a NetWare v3.x server to act as an AppleTalk server is outlined as follows:

1. At the file server, type the following to load the Macintosh name space and add it to the server volume:

    ```
    load mac
    add name space macintosh to volume SYS
    ```

    Replace SYS with the name of the server volume that will support Macintosh files.

2. Load INSTALL NLM and install NetWare for Macintosh. This involves copying the Macintosh support files to the server and can be done by selecting Product Options from the Installation Options screen.

3. Edit STARTUP.NCF file and add the following:

    ```
    load mac
    set minimum packet receive buffers=100
    ```

4. Edit AUTOEXEC.NCF and add the following:

    ```
    load appletlk net=50001 zone={"Admin"}

    load  ne2000 int=2  port=300  frame=ethenet_snap
    name=EtherNet1
    load  dl2000  int=3  port=200  name=LocalTalk1

    bind  appletlk EtherNet1 net=1-4 zone={"Admin", "Dept1"}
    bind  appletlk  LocalTalk1  net=6  zone={"Dept2"}

    load afp
    load atps
    ```

The APPLETLK.NLM contains the AppleTalk protocols and the AppleTalk router. The AFP.NLM and ATPS.NLM implement the Apple Filing Protocol and the Apple Print Services (see fig. 13.2). The AppleTalk routing in figure 13.2 is performed at the level of the *Datagram Delivery Protocol* (DDP) by the *Routing Table Maintenance Protocol* (RTMP).

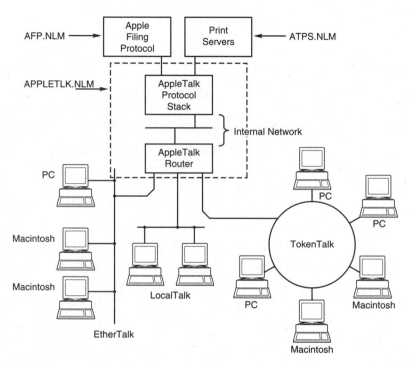

Figure 13.2:
AppleTalk modules and Internal Routing.

When the LOAD APPLETLK command is issued, the AppleTalk routing and communication protocols (ASP, ATP, DDP) are loaded.

The LOAD NE2000 and LOAD DL2000 commands load the drivers for Ethernet and LocalTalk respectively. This configuration is for a network of the type shown in figure 13.3 that has an Ethernet and LocalTalk board installed in the server. The Ethernet network must use the SNAP protocol for encapsulating upper-layer AppleTalk protocols, and, therefore, the FRAME=ETHERNET_SNAP parameter must be specified when the driver is loaded. Because the DL2000 driver uses the standard *LocalTalk Link Access Protocol* (LLAP), no frame parameter is required.

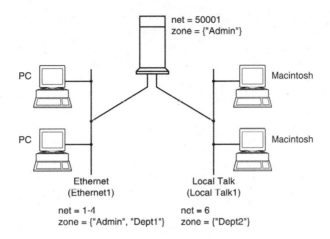

net = 50001
zone = {"Admin"}

PC

Macintosh

PC

Macintosh

Ethernet
(Ethernet1)

Local Talk
(Local Talk1)

net = 1-4
zone = {"Admin", "Dept1"}

net = 6
zone = {"Dept2"}

Figure 13.3:
Example AppleTalk network.

The BIND statements specify the binding of the AppleTalk protocols to the NIC drivers. The NET=1-4 may look peculiar but is used to refer to the fact that Extended network addressing is being used to support Extended Networks. Extended Networks were defined at the time AppleTalk Phase 2 protocols were defined to overcome the shortcomings of AppleTalk Phase 1 protocols. AppleTalk Phase 1 protocols could not have more than 254 node addresses per physical network segment. This was due to the fact that the network address field in LLAP is 8 bits long. Modern networks, such as Ethernet and Token Ring, can easily have more than 254 node addresses on a physical network segment. To support these networks, a network range was defined. The actual node address consisted of network number and a node number pair. Each network number could have associated with it 254 node addresses. Thus, a network range of NET=1-4 can have $4 \times 254 = 1,016$ node addresses. LocalTalk networks are unchanged in AppleTalk Phase 2. Thus, you see the NET=6, which is a single network number. This is semantically equivalent to using a NET=6-6 network range. The network range is a pair of numbers that must be between 1 and 65,279. Physical segments cannot have overlapping numbers, otherwise the AppleTalk router would get confused. All AppleTalk routers connected to the same physical network must have the same network-number range. This is similar to the rule for connecting IPX routers to the same physical network.

The BIND parameters specify a zone parameter. Zones are a logical grouping of devices on an AppleTalk network that make it easier to locate devices through the Chooser panel. Searches for resources on a network are always done in the context of the currently selected zone. The user is free to pick other zones through the Chooser panel. Normally, the current zone is the same as the default zone. The default zone can be changed by the user through the Macintosh Control Panel.

The LOAD AFP and LOAD ATPS commands load the AppleTalk Filing Protocol and Print Service protocols.

One of the areas of potential confusion experienced by network administrators for Macintosh networks is the assignment of zone names. The following discussion will clarify some of these issues.

Zones are used to narrow the search for resources on the network. A user belonging to the "Engineering" department, for example, normally needs to see only those resources belonging to his department and should not be presented with resources for other departments. Occasionally, a user may need to access network resources belonging to another department, in which case, a facility exists to make the selection. In this discussion, departments of an organization are used to logically divide the network. Other logical groupings are possible such as grouping by physical location for "Building1," "Building2," and so on. These logical divisions have a name assigned to them called the *zone name*.

In the example of the AUTOEXEC.NCF file, several zone names are used. The first is the zone name used with the LOAD APPLETLK command. This zone name refers to the internal AppleTalk network within the server. This internal network number must have a network number and a zone name assigned to it. It is treated as a non-extended Phase 2 network and, therefore, has a single network number assigned to it. It is a good idea to choose network numbers with a high value for internal network numbering to distinguish between other network numbers. The internal network is contained within the AppleTalk module (fig. 13.2) and does not have any physical components. When the internal AppleTalk receives a file request for the AppleTalk server, it routes it as it would any other packet. Because the AppleTalk server is in the same module as the AppleTalk router, the packet is sent directly through the internal network to the server. The AppleTalk server with the given zone name and its print services will show up in the list for the zone name they belong to. Zone names are represented as quoted (") strings. They can be 32 characters long and can even include spaces.

Zone names also must be specified in the BIND command. For extended networks, multiple zone names (up to 255) are possible. This is seen in the BIND NE2000 example. For non-extended networks (Phase 1 networks), a single zone name must be used as seen in the BIND DL2000 example. In extended networks, the first zone name listed becomes the default zone. If there are several routers connected to the same physical network segment, they must agree about the zone name or zone list assigned to it. Because the default zone is the first zone name, the zone list for each router must begin with the same zone name.

For complex networks, the number of possible zones—the zone list, in other words—can be become potentially large. Because there is a limit of 82 characters for the BIND command, it is not always possible to list all the zone names on the command line. To solve this problem, the -z option can be used when the AppleTalk protocol stack is loaded:

```
LOAD APPLETLK  NET=5001 -Z
```

The -z option causes the LOAD APPLETLK command to look for the file ATZONES.CFG in the SYS:SYSTEM directory. This file can be created by a text editor and is a list of the network range and zone list pairs. An example of an ATZONES.CFG file is shown as follows:

```
net=50002 zone={"Control"}
net=50003 zone={"Control"}
net-50004 zone-{"Control"}

net=10-15 zone={"Control", "Building1", "Building2"}
net=16-20 zone={
"Building3",
"Building4",
"Building5"
}

net=21-25 zone={"Manufacturing", "Marketing }
```

Essentially, the ATZONES.CFG file contains a mapping between net numbers and associated zone names.

Typically, a user selects the zone name as top-level organizer for accessing the network resources in the Chooser Panel. After a zone name is selected, the user clicks on the service icon. This causes the Macintosh station to send

Name Binding Protocol (NBP) broadcasts for the service in the selected zone. Any intervening routers will re-broadcast the NBP request to the appropriate networks. The routers directly connected to the selected zone broadcast the NBP request to all nodes in that zone. The nodes that provide the service send an NBP reply packet containing their names. These names are then displayed in the Chooser panel.

Zone names are maintained by the AppleTalk network routers. After a router discovers a new router through the RTMP protocol, it sends a *Zone Information Protocol* (ZIP) request to that router querying it for its zone information. The zone information is cached by all the routers, and as long as the router has a good entry in the RTMP table, another zone query is not issued. Routers are not automatically informed about changes in zone configuration. This becomes a problem if the zone name is deleted; it will show up as a valid zone name in the Chooser for Macintosh computers, even though it does not exist. The only way to update zone information in the list is to force the RTMP tables to change. This can be done by isolating a network segment and waiting for the RTMP protocol to detect the change. This procedure can take between 10 to 20 minutes, or longer, in a large AppleTalk internet. The other approach is to reset all routers by bringing them down and up again.

OS/2 LAN Requester and Drivers

The components of an OS/2 NetWare workstation resemble the ODI architecture discussed for DOS workstations because OS/2 NIC drivers are based on the ODI specification. The Link Support Layer provides a logical network interface for the protocol stacks to bind to. Protocol support includes IPX, SPX, and Named Pipes. The NetWare LAN requester assumes the role of the NetWare shell in DOS workstations.

To install an OS/2 NetWare station follow these steps:

1. Install OS/2 at the workstation. (Follow the instructions that come with OS/2.)

2. Install OS/2 NetWare requester and workstation drivers on the OS/2 workstation.

3. Install NetWare utilities for OS/2 on the file server.

4. Optionally, install *Remote Initial Program Load* (RIPL) capability for diskless workstations.

The NetWare OS/2 Requester

Before you install the NetWare OS/2 requester, you must install OS/2 on the workstation. OS/2 requires a hard disk for installation. Consult the OS/2 documentation to learn how to install OS/2.

To install the NetWare requester, the associated drivers for link support, and the SPX/IPX protocols, run the INSTALL program located on the REQUESTER disk. Install the NetWare OS/2 components in the C:\NETWARE directory on the OS/2 workstation hard disk.

To install the OS/2 NetWare requester follow these steps:

1. Boot the workstation with OS/2 and select either OS/2 window or OS/2 full screen from the Group-Main window.

2. Insert the REQUESTER disk in drive A and type the following at the OS/2 prompt:

   `A:INSTALL`

3. Follow the instructions to select the installation directory. The default is C:\NETWARE. The installation program guides you through the process.

4. Edit the CONFIG.SYS file to enable the network driver for the NIC in the OS/2 workstation. You usually must remove the REM (remark) comment that precedes the *DEVICE=* statement for the NIC driver.

The following list shows the CONFIG.SYS file for an OS/2 NetWare workstation. The CONFIG.SYS statements are grouped for easy identification. Most of the CONFIG.SYS commands deal with OS/2 configuration. Toward the end of the CONFIG.SYS are the NetWare requester components. Before the NetWare requester component (NWREQ.SYS) is activated, a number of support components, such as link support, NIC driver, and protocol stack, must be activated. A number of statements dealing with other protocols such as SPX, Named Pipes, and NetBIOS are commented out. If these components are needed for the OS/2 NetWare workstation, the REM that precedes them must be removed.

The NetWare requester components and protocol stacks are all implemented as device drivers. For example, IPX is implemented by the IPX.SYS device driver, SPX by the SPX.SYS device driver, Named Pipes by the NMPIPE.SYS device driver, and NetBIOS by the NETBIOS.SYS device driver. This contrasts with DOS workstations that implement these components by terminate-and-stay resident (TSR) programs.

```
IFS=C:\OS2\HPFS.IFS  /CACHE:512 /CRECL:4 /AUTOCHECK:C
PROTSHELL=C:\OS2\PMSHELL.EXE
SET USER_INI=C:\OS2\OS2.INI
SET SYSTEM_INI=C:\OS2\OS2SYS.INI
SET OS2_SHELL=C:\OS2\CMD.EXE
SET AUTOSTART=PROGRAMS,TASKLIST,FOLDERS,CONNECTIONS
SET RUNWORKPLACE=C:\OS2\PMSHELL.EXE
SET COMSPEC=C:\OS2\CMD.EXE
LIBPATH=.;C:\OS2\DLL;C:\OS2\MDOS;C:\;C:\OS2\APPS\DLL;C:\NETWARE;
SET
PATH=C:\OS2;C:\OS2\SYSTEM;C:\OS2\MDOS\WINOS2;C:\OS2\INSTALL;C:\
;C:\OS2\MDOS;C:\OS2\APPS;L:\OS2;P:\OS2;C:\NETWARE;
SET
DPATH=C:\OS2;C:\OS2\SYSTEM;C:\OS2\MDOS\WINOS2;C:\OS2\INSTALL;C:\
;C:\OS2\BITMAP;C:\OS2\MDOS;C:\OS2\APPS;C:\NETWARE;P:\OS2;
SET PROMPT=$i[$p]
SET HELP=C:\OS2\HELP;C:\OS2\HELP\TUTORIAL;
SET GLOSSARY=C:\OS2\HELP\GLOSS;
SET IPF_KEYS=SBCS
PRIORITY_DISK_IO=YES
FILES=20
DEVICE=C:\OS2\TESTCFG.SYS
DEVICE=C:\OS2\DOS.SYS
DEVICE=C:\OS2\PMDD.SYS
BUFFERS=30
IOPL=YES
DISKCACHE=64,LW
MAXWAIT=3
MEMMAN=SWAP,PROTECT
SWAPPATH=C:\OS2\SYSTEM 2048 2048
BREAK=OFF
THREADS=256
PRINTMONBUFSIZE=134,134,134
COUNTRY=001,C:\OS2\SYSTEM\COUNTRY.SYS
SET KEYS=ON
REM SET DELDIR=C:\DELETE,512;D:\DELETE,512;
BASEDEV=PRINT01.SYS
BASEDEV=IBM1FLPY.ADD
```

```
BASEDEV=OS2DASD.DMD
SET EPMPATH=C:\OS2\APPS
SET FAXPM=C:\OS2\APPS
DEVICE=C:\OS2\APPS\SASYNCDA.SYS
PROTECTONLY=NO
SHELL=C:\OS2\MDOS\COMMAND.COM C:\OS2\MDOS /P
FCBS=16,8
RMSIZE=640
DEVICE=C:\OS2\MDOS\VEMM.SYS
DOS=LOW,NOUMB
DEVICE=C:\OS2\MDOS\VDPX.SYS
DEVICE=C:\OS2\MDOS\VXMS.SYS /UMB
DEVICE=C:\OS2\MDOS\VDPMI.SYS
DEVICE=C:\OS2\MDOS\VWIN.SYS
DEVICE=C:\OS2\MDOS\VCDROM.SYS
REM DEVICE=C:\OS2\PCMCIA.SYS
REM DEVICE=C:\OS2\MDOS\VPCMCIA.SYS
BASEDEV=OS2CDROM.DMD /Q
IFS=C:\OS2\CDFS.IFS /Q
BASEDEV=OS2SCSI.DMD
BASEDEV=NECCDS1.FLT
BASEDEV=AHA154X.ADD
DEVICE=C:\OS2\MDOS\VMOUSE.SYS
DEVICE=C:\OS2\POINTDD.SYS
DEVICE=C:\OS2\MOUSE.SYS SERIAL=COM2
DEVICE=C:\OS2\COM.SYS
DEVICE=C:\OS2\MDOS\VCOM.SYS
CODEPAGE=437,850
DEVINFO=KBD,US,C:\OS2\KEYBOARD.DCP
DEVINFO=SCR,VGA,C:\OS2\VIOTBL.DCP
SET VIDEO_DEVICES=VIO_VGA
SET VIO_VGA=DEVICE(BVHVGA)
DEVICE=C:\OS2\MDOS\VSVGA.SYS

REM — NetWare Requester statements BEGIN —
DEVICE=C:\NETWARE\LSL.SYS
RUN=C:\NETWARE\DDAEMON.EXE
DEVICE=C:\NETWARE\NE2000.SYS
DEVICE=C:\NETWARE\IPX.SYS
DEVICE=C:\NETWARE\SPX.SYS
RUN=C:\NETWARE\SPDAEMON.EXE
```

```
rem DEVICE=C:\NETWARE\NMPIPE.SYS
rem DEVICE=C:\NETWARE\NPSERVER.SYS
rem RUN=C:\NETWARE\NPDAEMON.EXE NP_COMPUTERNAME
DEVICE=C:\NETWARE\NWREQ.SYS
IFS=C:\NETWARE\NWIFS.IFS
RUN=C:\NETWARE\NWDAEMON.EXE
rem DEVICE=C:\NETWARE\NETBIOS.SYS
rem RUN=C:\NETWARE\NBDAEMON.EXE
DEVICE=C:\NETWARE\VIPX.SYS
DEVICE=C:\NETWARE\VSHELL.SYS
REM — NetWare Requester statements END —
```

OS/2 NetWare Utilities

OS/2 NetWare workstations cannot use the DOS NetWare utilities installed during the server installation. Novell has written OS/2 versions of utilities, such as SYSCON, FCONSOLE, FILER, and SESSION. These utilities are on disks labeled OS2UTIL-1, OS2UTIL-2, and so on. The utilities must be installed on the server for OS/2 NetWare workstations to use them. This must be accomplished as a separate step.

To install the OS/2 NetWare utilities complete the following steps:

1. Boot up the workstation with OS/2 and select either OS/2 window or OS/2 full screen from the Group-Main window.

2. Insert the OS2UTIL-1 disk in drive A and use the LOGIN program to log in as SUPERVISOR to the NetWare server (*serverName*):

   A:\LOGIN\LOGIN *serverName*/SUPERVISOR

   (Replace *serverName* with the name of the server.)

3. Change to the drive that contains the OS2UTIL-1 disk and type the following command:

   SERVINST *serverName*

4. Follow the instructions until the OS/2 NetWare utilities are installed.

After the OS/2 NetWare utilities are installed, the OS/2 utilities are located in the directories indicated in the preceding list. The separate directories SYS:LOGIN/OS2, SYS:PUBLIC/OS2, and SYS:SYSTEM/OS2 are created to avoid name conflicts with DOS utilities.

When the OS/2 NetWare workstation logs in to a NetWare server that has the NetWare utilities installed, drive L is mapped to the SYS:LOGIN/OS2 directory. This enables you to invoke the OS/2 LOGIN program in that directory. SYSCON must be used to modify the user's login script to include drive mappings to SYS:PUBLIC/OS2.

To invoke the OS/2 LOGIN program, when attached to a NetWare server without the OS/2 NetWare utilities installed, you must copy the OS/2 LOGIN program onto the OS/2 workstation's hard disk.

NET.CFG for OS/2 NetWare Workstations

To configure the NetWare requester for non-default settings, you must use the NET.CFG configuration file. The NET.CFG file for OS/2 is similar to that used for DOS workstations, but some differences exist. The main section headings for the OS/2 NET.CFG file are left-justified, and the entries under each heading are indented by a space or a tab.

The BUFFERS parameter can be changed in the LINK SUPPORT section.

The general form of the BUFFERS parameter is as follows:

```
BUFFERS bufferNumber [bufferSize]
```

The BUFFERS parameter changes the number (*bufferNumber*) and size (*bufferSize*) of communication buffers.

The *bufferSize*, which is optional, has a default value of 1130 bytes. The total amount of buffer space for LSL buffers must not exceed 64K:

bufferNumber × bufferSize <= 64K

The *protocolName* in PROTOCOL STACK can be IPX or SPX. Each of the protocol stacks—IPX and SPX—has a different set of parameters. Tables 13.1 and 13.2 describe the parameters for IPX and SPX.

Examples:

```
PROTOCOL STACK IPX

        socket 128   ; Increase socket count to max of 128
        bind trxnet  ; Bind IPX to Novell RX-Net driver

PROTOCOL STACK SPX

        sessions 19  ; SPX session to 19
        abort timeout 450000   ; Abort time out to 45 secs.
```

```
verify timeout 20000    ; Verify time out to 40
secs.
listen timeout 15000    ; Listen timeout to 15 secs.
retry count 10    ; Reduce retries to 10
```

Table 13.1
OS/2 IPX Parameters for Protocol Stack

Parameter	Meaning
socket count	Specifies the maximum number of sockets (count) that IPX can have open at a workstation. The number of sockets can be from 9 to 128. The default value is 32.
router mem size	Specifies the memory size in bytes in the router memory pool allocated for routing. Default value is 450.
bind name	Specifies the NIC driver name that is bound to the IPX protocol stack. Primarily used for workstations with several NICs.

Table 13.2
OS/2 SPX Parameters for Protocol Stack

Parameter	Meaning
sessions count	Specifies number of SPX connections (count) to be supported. Acceptable values are between 8 and 256 with a default of 16.
abort timeout val	Specifies the number of milliseconds (val) SPX must wait for an acknowledgment before terminating a connection. Minimum value is 10 milliseconds, and the default is 30000 milliseconds (30 seconds).
verify timeout val	Specifies the number of milliseconds (val) SPX must wait between packet transmissions before asking for an acknowledgment that the connection is still intact. Minimum value is 10 milliseconds, and the default is 3000 milliseconds (3 seconds).

Parameter	Meaning
listen timeout val	Specifies the number of milliseconds (val) SPX waits for a packet from the connection. Minimum value is 10 milliseconds and the default is 6000 milliseconds (6 seconds). If no packet arrives in the specified time, SPX includes a request for immediate acknowledgment in every packet sent. If no acknowledgment is received, SPX uses the abort timeout value.
retry count val	Specifies the number of times (val) the workstation attempts to resend a packet. Acceptable values are from 1 to 255 with a default of 20.

The NETWARE REQUESTER Section

The OS/2 NetWare requester can be configured in the NETWARE REQUESTER section. The parameters that can be controlled are described in table 13.3.

Example:

```
NETWARE REQUESTER

        sessions 15              ; Set to 15 sessions
        cache buffers 20         ; 20 read/write buffers
        request retries 5        ; Reduce retries to 5
        preferred server KSS     ; Attach to server with name
                                   KSS
```

Table 13.3
OS/2 NetWare Requester Parameters

Parameter	Meaning
cache buffers cnt	Specifies number of buffers (cnt) at workstation to be used to cache data from open files. Acceptable values range from 0 to 128 with a default of 8.

continues

Table 13.3
Continued

Parameter	Meaning
sessions cnt	Specifies number of file server connections (cnt) that the requester supports. Acceptable values range from 8 to 20 with a default of 8. (Each connection uses at least 3 IPX sockets.)
request retries cnt	Specifies number of times (cnt) the requester tries to resend a request following a communication error. Minimum value is 5 and the default value is 20.
preferred server sn	Specifies the server name (sn) to attach to when the NetWare requester loads.

The NETWARE NETBIOS Section

The NETWARE NETBIOS section is used only if the NetBIOS protocol stack is loaded (DEVICE=NETBIOS.SYS in CONFIG.SYS). Configuration of NetBIOS protocol includes name management, session creation, and session management. Table 13.4 describes the NetBIOS parameters.

Example:

```
PROTOCOL NETBIOS

        names 28        ; Name table size 28
        sessions 20     ; NetBIOS sessions
        internet off    ; Turn claim-name packets off across
                          internet
```

Table 13.4
OS/2 NetWare NetBIOS Parameters

Parameter	Meaning
names *cnt*	Specifies the number of names (*cnt*) the workstation can have in its name table. The values can range from 4 to 128 with a default of 26.

Parameter	Meaning
sessions *cnt*	Specifies the number of NetBIOS sessions (*cnt*) the work station can have. The values can range from 4 to 128 with a default of 32.
commands *numb*	Specifies the number of outstanding NetBIOS commands (*numb*) that can be waiting for completion at the workstation. The values range from 4 to 128 with a default of 12.
sessions *cnt*	Specifies the number of NetBIOS sessions (*cnt*) the workstation can have. The values range from 4 to 128 with a default of 32.
retry delay *numb*	Specifies delay in milliseconds (*numb*). If no response is received to a NetBIOS connection request or a packet transmission, it waits for the specified amount of time before trying again. The default value is 500.
retry count *numb*	Specifies the number of times (*numb*) NetBIOS tries to establish a connection or send data, if there is no response the first time. The default value is 20.
internet [on | off]	The internet parameter determines the behavior of the claim-name packet. NetBIOS requires all stations to have a unique logical name. Claim-name packets establish a unique NetBIOS name. When set to ON, NetBIOS broadcasts claim-name packets to all stations on the internet to establish the uniqueness of the claim-name packet. When internet is OFF, NetBIOS sends name-claim packets to stations on the local network only. It ignores responses from outside the local network.
broadcast count *N*	Specifies the number of times (*N*) NetBIOS broadcasts a claim for a name. Minimum value is 1. Default value is 4 if internet is ON, or 2 if internet is OFF.
broadcast delay *N*	Specifies delay in milliseconds (*N*). NetBIOS waits for the specified time between a query and claim broadcasts. Value can be from 100 to 65,535. Default values is 2000 if internet is ON or 1000 if internet is OFF.

continues

Table 13.4
Continued

Parameter	Meaning
abort timeout *N*	Specifies timeout value in milliseconds (*N*). If no acknowledgment is received in the timeout interval, NetBIOS terminates the connection. Minimum value is 500. Default value is 30,000.
verify timeout *N*	Specifies the timeout in milliseconds (*N*). NetBIOS waits for at least the specified value before sending a "probe" packet to the remote station to confirm the connection. Value can be from 100 to 65,535. Default value is 3000.
listen timeout *N*	Specifies timeout in milliseconds (*N*). NetBIOS waits for the specified time for a packet from a remote station. It then send a "probe" packet to verify its connection. Value can be from 200 to 65,535. Default value is 6000.

The LINK DRIVER driverName Section

The *driverName* in the LINK DRIVER section heading must be replaced with the OS/2 network driver name. All parameters included in the LINK DRIVER section heading apply to *driverName*. These parameters are as follows:

1. DMA

2. INT

3. MEM

4. PORT

5. NODE ADDRESS

6. SLOT

7. FRAME

8. PROTOCOL

These parameters have the same meaning and syntax as described for ODI LINK DRIVER parameters. Refer to the section on ODI drivers to see how to use these parameters. The only difference is the SLOT parameter. SLOT has an additional option—the "?" parameter. The SLOT ? parameter tells the OS/2 NetWare requester to find the first board corresponding to the board designated in the LINK DRIVER *driverName*.

If OS/2 NetWare stations are used with IBM Source Routing bridges, the source routing driver must be enabled by placing the following statement in the OS/2 CONFIG.SYS file:

```
DEVICE=C:\NETWARE\ROUTE.SYS
```

The router parameters can be configured through the PROTOCOL ROUTER main-section in the OS/2 NET.CFG file. The general syntax of the parameters for this section is shown as follows:

```
PROTOCOL ROUTE
        source route def gbr mbr nodes n board n
```

The parameters for the source route are DEF, GBE, MBR, NODES N, and BOARD N. These parameters have the same meaning as the corresponding DOS ODI source routing parameters. For details about these parameters, consult Chapter12.

For example, to enable DEF, GEBR, and MBR at the OS/2 NetWare station, place the following in the NET.CFG file:

```
protocol route
        source route def gbr mbr
```

The NetWare SPOOLER Section

The NetWare spooler controls print jobs initiated at the workstation.

The NetWare SPOOLER section takes the following general syntax:

```
netware spooler
    form n
    copies n
    [keep | no keep]
    size n
    [tabs | no tabs]
```

```
file s
name s
[banner | no banner]
[form feed | no form feed]
maxsetup n
maxreset n
```

Table 13.5 explains each of the parameters of the NetWare SPOOLER syntax.

Table 13.5
OS/2 NetWare SPOOLER Parameters

Parameter	Value
form *n*	Specifies the form number (*n*) to be used for printing. Default is form 0.
copies *n*	Specifies the number (*n*) of copies to be printed. Default is 1 copy.
[keep	no keep]	Specifies that printing should continue (keep) even if capture is interrupted. Default is keep.
space *n*	Specifies the number (*n*) of spaces in a tab. Default is 8.
[tabs	no tabs]	Spooler expands tab to the number of spaces specified in the space n parameter. Default is tab.
file *s*	Specifies the filename (*s*) to be printed in the banner.
name *s*	Specifies the user name (*s*) to be printed in the banner.
[banner	no banner]	Enables/disables printing of banner.
[form feed	no form feed]	Enables/disables form feed at end of job.
maxsetup *n*	Specifies the maximum number of characters (*n*) setup string that is sent to the printer.

Parameter	Value
maxrest *n*	Specifies the maximum number of characters (*n*) in the reset string that is sent to the printer.

UNIX Workstations

UNIX is an operating system that runs on a broad range of hardware platforms. UNIX was originally used on minicomputers, mainframes, and supercomputers before becoming available on engineering workstations and the IBM PC.

Most engineering workstations that run UNIX use the Motorola 68000 family of microprocessors. Many UNIX vendors also have ported their version of UNIX to the Intel 80XXX microprocessor. At one time, a version of UNIX ran on an IBM PC/XT—an Intel 8086 microprocessor. Today, most of the interest in the Intel family is focused on the Intel 80386 or higher. These microprocessors have the power to run UNIX efficiently.

Because UNIX runs on a variety of hardware platforms and because so many varieties of UNIX exist, UNIX hardware requirements cannot be generalized. The UNIX vendor can help to determine the hardware requirements you need. Minimum RAM for most UNIX versions that run on the PC family is 4M. Experts recommend that you use at least 12M of RAM for serious work. Hard disk size depends on the UNIX components installed, but generally a 200M or larger disk is best.

Because UNIX workstations commonly use TCP/IP as the transport protocol for networking, integration with NetWare requires that NetWare also run TCP/IP. Currently, TCP/IP support is available only in NetWare 3.11 or higher. NetWare v3.x enables the server to act as a NFS server and an IP router (see Chapter 3).

UnixWare

UnixWare is UNIX System V Release 4 that supports a built-in NetWare SPX/IPX protocol stack. This product has been developed by UNIVEL, a joint venture of USL and Novell. Because USL has been purchased by Novell from AT&T, it is now a wholly owned subsidiary of Novell. The UnixWare product comes in two main versions: a personal edition and an Application Server. The personal edition is meant for the end-user who needs to run 32-bit UNIX applications on a desktop and has no need for the complexity of a full UNIX version with its development tools. The Application Server is meant for developers who want to write client/server applications with the server applications running on the UnixWare Application server back-end. The Application Server provides the developer with the full range of UNIX development tools.

One of UnixWare's attractive features is its ease of installation. It can be installed from CD-ROM and is much simpler to install compared to other UNIX versions. An X-Windows-based graphical interface is provided. The user has a choice of using either MOTIF or OpenLook interface. UnixWare uses the term MOOLIT to describe its MOTIF and OpenLook option.

Figure 13.4 shows UnixWare used on a NetWare network. The UnixWare Application Server also is positioned as a down-sizing platform for Mainframe-based applications. It comes with a complete set of development tools such as COBOL compilers, linkers, and libraries to port mainframe applications. The down-sized applications or new server applications can serve as back-ends to either DOS-based applications running an SPX/IPX stack or to other UnixWare Personal Edition desktops. The UnixWare desktop has built-in SPX/IPX protocol stack and a NetWare requester. It can be used as a NetWare client to a NetWare server by making a connection through the SPX/IPX protocol stack. Because UnixWare supports TCP/IP, this can be used to access other UNIX servers and NetWare running NetWare for NFS. NetWare for NFS provides NFS, FTP, and remote XCONSOLE services.

From a user's perspective, UnixWare provides the following features:

- **Graphical desktop.** Choice of MOTIF or OpenLook.

- **NetWare networking.** You can access a NetWare server using SPX/IPX.

- **Application compatibility.** Thousands of UNIX applications, including those that run on the popular SCO UNIX.

- **Multitasking.** This enables the user to run several applications simultaneously.

- **Multiuser capability.** The Personal Edition supports 2 users and the Application server has an unlimited number of users.

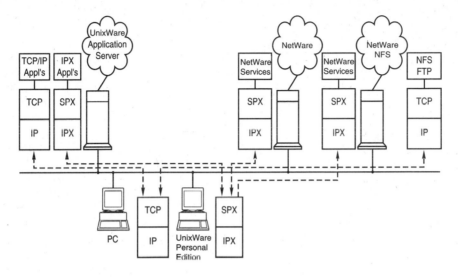

Figure 13.4:
Example UnixWare network.

Summary

This chapter discussed NetWare's support for Macintosh and OS/2 workstations and introduced you to Novell's UnixWare product, a UNIX environment that can access NetWare servers by means of standard IPX/SPX protocols.

Managing Sessions

## 14

The network environment is where the user lives and breathes on the network, and therefore must be configured with a great amount of planning and attention to detail. This chapter discusses the different types of start-up files for the individual DOS workstation and the network environment. Network start up files are called *login scripts*.

The following sections discuss the login script commands and script variables that make up the network start-up files. Recommendations are presented on how to organize the login scripts to keep them simple and understandable. You also learn about the NetWare MENU system.

Understanding Login Scripts

After the user logs in successfully, a network login script is processed, which sets up the network environment. The login script file is kept on the server and plays a role similar to that of the AUTOEXEC.BAT file for a single-user PC. Two types of login scripts are used: *system* and *user*.

When a user logs in to a server, login scripts associated for that user are executed. First, the system login script is executed. The system login script sets up a global environment for the user. Next, an individual login script for that user is executed. The individual login script sets up a user-specific network environment.

System and User Login Scripts

After the LOGIN utility authenticates a user's log-in request, it looks for a file called NET$LOG.DAT in the SYS:PUBLIC directory (see fig. 14.1). This file contains the location of the system login script. A *system login script* is used for commands that affect all the users. Examples of the commands that can be placed within the system login script are commands for displaying messages, mapping network drives, search drives, and setting environment variables. Because the system login script file can be viewed by other users, do not keep sensitive information in this file. The system login script can be created or edited by using SYSCON. The system log-in is stored as a text file in NET$LOG.DAT for the current releases of NetWare.

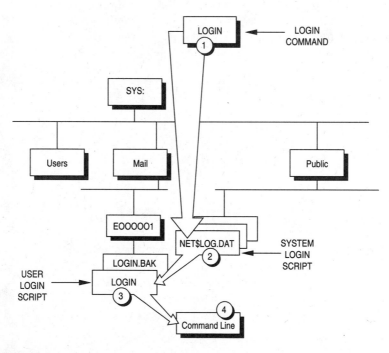

Figure 14.1:
The order of login script processing. (Graphic courtesy of Learning Group International)

After the system login script is executed, the user login script is processed. The *user login script* is kept in a text file called LOGIN in the MAIL directory for that user. Earlier in this book, you learned that the MAIL directory was originally created for a Novell electronic mail program that has been discontinued. The MAIL directory is a subdirectory in the SYS:MAIL directory and has the user's internal hexadecimal ID.

The individual login script serves to customize the user environment even further. The same type of commands that can be executed in the system login script file also can be placed in the individual login script file. The LOGIN.BAK file holds a backup version of the LOGIN script file, which is created when the LOGIN script file is changed by using the SYSCON utility.

After the user's individual login script utility is executed, control is returned to the DOS prompt, and the user's environment is considered to be set.

Default Login Script

The first time the Supervisor logs in to the server, no login script files have been set. The server uses a default login script file so that the supervisor can perform basic functions. If a user is created and the Supervisor forgets to set up a login script file for the user, the default login script file is executed. The default login script is executed only if no individual login script exists and is ignored if the system finds an individual login script.

The default login script file looks similar to the following one. Comments have been added to illustrate certain points.

```
REM This sets up a greeting for the user
WRITE "Good %GREETING_TIME, %LOGIN_NAME."

REM This is similar to the DOS ECHO OFF command.
REM It stops the display of commands as they are executed.
MAP DISPLAY OFF

REM Error processing is not shown
MAP ERRORS OFF

REM Map the first network drive (*1:) to the
REM user's home directory, which by default is the
REM user's name under the root directory on volume SYS:
MAP *1:=SYS:%LOGIN_NAME

REM Map the first search drive to the SYS:PUBLIC directory
REM which contains some basic system utilities that can
REM be executed by the user.
```

```
MAP S1:=SYS:PUBLIC

REM Turn on display of commands as they are processed
REM so that when the MAP command is executed, a list
REM of the current drive mappings is displayed.
MAP DISPLAY ON
MAP
```

You can see that the MAP command in the preceding file can be executed from the command line as well as directly in the login script. Some login script commands, such as WRITE, MAP DISPLAY ON, and MAP DISPLAY OFF, cannot be executed from the DOS prompt.

The commands in the login script files are interpreted by the LOGIN utility, including the MAP command. The MAP command is in the SYS:PUBLIC directory. The first time you execute the MAP command in the login script, you do not have a search drive mapping to the SYS:PUBLIC directory. The MAP commands, however, still work, regardless of the absence of a search path to the SYS:PUBLIC directory. The reason for this is that the MAP command is interpreted and not invoked as an external program.

If you want to invoke external utilities, you must precede them with the # character. To invoke the utility CHKVOL, for example, use the following command in the login script file:

#CHKVOL

Another item to notice in the preceding login script file example is the use of the %GREETING_TIME and %LOGIN_NAME variables. These are called *login script identifier variables* and are examined later in this chapter. These variables evaluate to character strings which then can be used in commands, such as WRITE Good %GREETING_TIME, %LOGIN_NAME. This statement, for example, may produce the following message:

```
Good Morning, KARANJIT.
```

The %GREETING_TIME evaluates to Morning and %LOGIN_NAME evaluates to the user's login name, in this case, KARANJIT. When you use these variables in a string, such as **Good %GREETING_TIME, %LOGIN_NAME.,** the script variables must be in uppercase letters to evaluate correctly. Outside string variables, the script variables can be in upper- or lowercase.

Complex Login Script Files

One of the more powerful commands that can be used in a login script is the IF ... THEN conditional statement. This type of statement has the following general form:

```
IF expression THEN BEGIN
    statements
ELSE
    statements
END
```

or

```
IF expression THEN statement
```

The IF statement in the login script file gives you the power of conditionally executing statements; that is, the IF statement executes statements only if a certain condition is true. It can be used to customize a login script. The login script, however, might become too complicated when you use the IF ... THEN statement, such as the following one:

```
MAP DISPLAY OFF
BREAK OFF
FIRE PHASERS 3 TIMES
WRITE " "
WRITE "Good %GREETING_TIME, %LOGIN_NAME"
WRITE " "
WRITE "You have logged in to file server %FILE_SERVER"
WRITE "from station %NETWORK_ADDRESS:%P_STATION."
WRITE " "
WRITE "Your connection number is %STATION and you are"
WRITE "using shell %SHELL_TYPE on machine %SMACHINE."
WRITE "Your internal userid is %USER_ID"
WRITE " "
WRITE "Today is %DAY_OF_WEEK %MONTH_NAME, %DAY %YEAR"
IF MEMBER OF "NONCIVILIAN" THEN
    WRITE "System time is %HOUR24:%MINUTE:%SECOND"
ELSE
    WRITE "System time is %HOUR:%MINUTE:%SECOND %AM_PM"
END
```

```
IF MONTH = "1" AND DAY = "1" THEN BEGIN
   WRITE "Happy new year %YEAR, %FULL_NAME"
END

IF SHORT_YEAR = "00" THEN WRITE "Have a nice new century!"

IF NDAY_OF_WEEK = "6" THEN
   WRITE "Have a good weekend!"

IF NDAY_OF_WEEK > "1" AND NDAY_OF_WEEK < "7" THEN
   FDISPLAY SYS:MESSAGES/DAILY.MSG

ELSE
   DISPLAY SYS:MESSAGES/WEEKEND.MSG
END

IF MEMBER OF "ENGINEERING" THEN BEGIN
   IF DAY_OF_WEEK="TUESDAY" THEN
      WRITE "STAFF MEETING AT 3:00 PM"
   IF DAY_OF_WEEK="FRIDAY" THEN BEGIN
      WRITE "STATUS MEETING AT 3:30 PM."
      WRITE "BE THERE OR BE SQUARED!"
   END
END

MAP INS S1:=SYS:PUBLIC
MAP INS S2:=SYS:PUBLIC/%MACHINE/%OS/%OS_VERSION

IF MEMBER OF "PAYROLL" THEN BEGIN
   IF DAY_OF_WEEK="MONDAY" THEN
      WRITE "STAFF MEETING AT 1:00 PM IN CONF.RM. 303"
   IF DAY_OF_WEEK="FRIDAY" THEN
      WRITE "REVIEW MEETING AT 11:00 AM."
   END

   ATTACH LAKSHMI/%LOGIN_NAME
   MAP L:=LAKSHMI/SYS:USERS/%LOGIN_NAME
END

COMSPEC=S2:COMMAND.COM

IF MEMBER OF "ACCOUNTING" THEN
   MAP INS S16:=SYS:APPS/AMRIT
END

IF MEMBER OF "WPUSERS" THEN
   MAP INS S16:=SYS:APPS/WP
END
```

```
IF MEMBER OF "PAYROLL" OR MEMBER OF "ACCOUNTING" THEN BEGIN
   MAP INS S16:=SYS:APPS/ADP
   MAP *2:=SYS:PAYROLL
END

IF LOGIN_NAME = "SUPERVISOR" THEN BEGIN
   MAP *1:=SYS:USERS/SUPER
   MAP *2:=SYS:SYSTEM
   MAP INS S2:=*2:
   MAP INS S3:=SYS:SYSTEM/NMUTILS
END

IF MEMBER OF "ACCOUNTING"
   #CAPTURE Q=ACCT_LASERQ NB TI=25

IF MEMBER OF "ENGINEERING" THEN BEGIN
   #CAPTURE Q=ENG_LASERQ NB NT TI=15
   IF ERROR_LEVEL <> "0" THEN BEGIN
      SEND "ERROR IN CAPTURE" TO TOM
      #EMAIL TOM "ERROR IN CAPTURE FOR %LOGIN_NAME"
   END
END

IF <EDITOR>="BRIEF" THEN
   MAP INS S16:=SYS:APPS/BRIEF
END

DOS SET X = "1"
ALOOP:
   SET X = X + "1"
   WRITE "VICTORY PARADE!"
IF <X> IS LESS THAN 7 THEN GOTO ALOOP

DRIVE *2:
DOS VERIFY ON
SET PROMPT = "$P$G"
MAP DISPLAY ON
MAP
EXIT "MENU *1:TOPAPPS"
```

The preceding system login script resembles a BASIC program more than a simple login script. Its only redeeming feature, besides the fact that it may work for a specific environment, is that it makes use of almost every type of script variable and log-in statement. The system login script's complexity makes it difficult to maintain. When making changes for a specific group, an inadvertent mistake is easy to make, which can affect all the users on the system.

Recommendations for Organizing Script Files

Over a period of time, the system login script file can get complex (such as the one in the preceding section) as you try to adapt a common system login script file to a changing network environment. You can, however, organize script files in a way that avoids most of the preceding complexity and yet provides a flexible mechanism that can be adapted as new needs arise. Figure 14.2 shows a recommended organization.

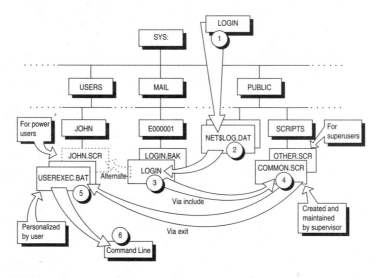

Figure 14.2:
Recommended structure for user login scripts. (Graphic courtesy of Learning Group International)

The system login script file is kept as simple as possible. IF ... THEN statements should not be used in the system login script. The system login script file can contain statements to display messages that are system wide, such as:

```
REM  ****************************************************
REM  *                                                  *
REM  * The system login script can only have            *
REM  * simple statements of the type FDISPLAY            *
REM  *                                                  *
REM  ****************************************************

REM * Send a global display message
FDISPLAY SYS:MESSAGES/GLOBAL.MSG
```

When the preceding system login script file is processed, it displays any global system messages that the supervisor may have kept in the message file SYS:MESSAGES/GLOBAL.MSG. Control then is transferred to the individual login script file.

The individual login script can contain a statement such as the following:

```
INCLUDE SYS:PUBLIC/SCRIPTS/COMMON.SCR
```

The INCLUDE statement means that the contents of the specified file, in this case SYS:PUBLIC/SCRIPTS/COMMON.SCR, are processed as login script commands. If all the users have a common script file, the COMMON.SCR statement can be used for them. The advantage of using the INCLUDE statement is that if the login script for the users is to be changed, only the COMMON.SCR file needs to be changed once. Suppose, for example, that you are not using the INCLUDE statement. Then, to change the login script for users, you have to use SYSCON to change every login script for all the users. This can become a tedious process and can be avoided entirely by using the INCLUDE statement and a common script file.

The first few statements can be greeting statements. These are followed by drive mappings, including search drives. The COMSPEC variable then must be set to point to the correct copy of COMMAND.COM.

Next, individual messages can be printed. Avoid using too many IF .. THEN statements, otherwise the statements can become too complex. If you want to use conditional statements, such as IF MEMBER OF GROUP THEN ...., you can create a separate *group*.SCR file and specify it in the INCLUDE statement in the login script file for members of the group, as follows:

```
INCLUDE SYS:PUBLIC/SCRIPTS/group. SCR
```

In the preceding example, you can replace *group* with a name of the group for which special processing needs to be done. The users must have read and file scan rights ([R F]) in the SYS:PUBLIC/SCRIPTS directory.

Within members of the group, most of the login script commands are the same, but a small amount of customization may need to be done for individual users. This customization can be placed in a batch file called USEREXEC.BAT that is kept in the home directory for every user as in the following example:

```
EXIT * USEREXEC.BAT
```

The EXIT statement terminates processing of the login script. If an argument such as *1:USEREXEC.BAT is specified, the argument is treated as a command that is executed immediately when the login script terminates. The *1 refers to the first network drive. The *1 drive is mapped by using the MAP command and, in this case, points to the home directory for the user:

```
MAP *1:=SYS:USERS/%LOGIN_NAME
```

The home directory for the user contains the USEREXEC.BAT file. This USEREXEC.BAT file can contain any customization commands for the user.

As an administrator, you may have to deal with users who like to play with and customize their own login script files. These users often are called *power users*, and they probably will balk at being placed in the same category as common users through the COMMON.SCR file. For these users, you can create a login script file containing the following command:

```
INCLUDE SYS:USERS/%LOGIN_NAME/%LOGIN_NAME.SCR
```

The preceding command looks in the user's home directory for processing a file that has the same name as the user's log-in name with a SCR extension. The SCR extension is the author's convention for SCRipt files. You can use your own, if you prefer.

Because the power users have rights to their home directory, they can freely edit their script files. If they make a mistake that hurts them, they only have themselves to blame and not you.

When To Use the EXIT Command

Avoid using the EXIT command in all but the last line in the individual login script because the EXIT command terminates the processing of the login script, and this may not be what you want to do.

If used in the system login script file, the EXIT command stops the processing of the system login script and returns control to the DOS prompt. The individual login script file is bypassed.

The EXIT command sometimes can be placed in the individual login script file to serve as a convenient means of escaping to the DOS prompt. For properly designed script files, however, this should not be necessary.

Understanding Login Script Commands

The following commands can be used in login scripts:

# (Execution of external commands)	FIRE PHASERS
ATTACH	GOTO
BREAK	IF ... THEN ... ELSE
DOS BREAK	INCLUDE
COMSPEC	MACHINE
DISPLAY	PAUSE
FDISPLAY	PCCOMPATIBLE
DOS SET or SET	REMARK or REM
DOS VERIFY	SHIFT
DRIVE	WRITE
EXIT	

The following sections discuss these commands.

The # Character

When placed before an external command, the # character provides external program execution. The following is the general syntax of the command:

```
# [path]filename parameters
```

The [*path*]*filename* statement specifies the full path name of the external command. The # character must be the first character in the command line. Under DOS, you can execute any EXE and COM file. To execute a DOS batch file or a DOS internal command, you must invoke the command line processor by using the following command:

```
#CCOMMAND /C batch or internal
```

In the preceding command, *batch or internal* is replaced by the name of a batch file or an internal command. To clear the screen from the login script, you can use the DOS CLS internal command, as shown in the following command:

```
#COMMAND /C CLS
```

When executing an external command, you must make sure that the proper drive mappings and search drives have been set. This is because the external command executes in the context of the NetWare environment set up at the time of execution. You must have sufficient network rights in the directory where the program is located—minimum rights should be [R F].

When the external command is executed, the log-in program still is resident in RAM and is not released until termination of the login script processing. Therefore, do not load TSRs during log-in processing because it will leave a hole in memory (where the log-in program was) when login script processing terminates.

The ATTACH Command

The ATTACH command, which can be executed as a NetWare command from the DOS prompt, enables you to attach to other servers. You can attach to a maximum of eight file servers. This command enables you to attach to other file servers without interrupting the current execution of the login script. The general syntax of the command is as follows:

```
ATTACH [fileserver[/username[;password]]]
```

If the *fileserver*, *username*, and *password* are not specified, you are prompted for them.

You need to be careful about including password information in the login script file. Anyone with read access to the login script file can read the password, which compromises the security of your network.

The BREAK Command

The BREAK ON command enables you to terminate the execution of your login script. The general syntax of the command is as follows:

```
BREAK [ON | OFF]
```

If the command is set to BREAK ON, the command enables you to terminate the processing of your login script by pressing Ctrl-C or Ctrl-Break. The default value is OFF.

The BREAK command is different from the DOS BREAK command, which is explained next.

The DOS BREAK Command

If DOS BREAK is set to ON, it enables Ctrl-Break checking for DOS. With the Ctrl-Break checking enabled, whenever a program sends a request to DOS, it can be terminated by pressing Ctrl-Break. This command is equivalent to the BREAK command, which is available under MS-DOS.

The COMSPEC Command

COMSPEC specifies the directory that DOS should use to load the command-line processor COMMAND.COM. The general syntax is the following:

```
COMSPEC=[path]COMMAND.COM
```

You can use a command line processor other than COMMAND.COM, but such implementations are rare. The COMSPEC command directly sets the COMSPEC DOS environment variable.

Earlier, this chapter described the sequence of events when DOS loads. It was explained that a transient portion of COMMAND.COM is loaded in the area of memory just below 640K.

When a large program loads, it can overwrite the transient portion of DOS. When this program exits, the transient portion of COMMAND.COM needs to be restored. DOS makes use of the COMSPEC environment variable to obtain a copy of COMMAND.COM. If the COMMAND.COM in memory and the one indicated by COMSPEC are for different versions of DOS, the workstation will crash with an `Invalid COMMAND.COM` message. On a network, chances are that users may be using different versions of DOS, and therefore COMSPEC may be pointing to an incorrect version of DOS. The COMSPEC variable should be set to the correct directory. This can be done by using the following commands:

```
MAP S2:=SYS:PUBLIC/%MACHINE/%OS/%OS_VERSION
COMSPEC=S2:COMMAND.COM
```

In the first command, for example, you can use the following command for MS-DOS 5:

```
SYS:PUBLIC/IBM_PC/MSDOS/V5.00
```

You can place in this directory the MS-DOS utilities that will be used by the users on the network, and also place a copy of MS-DOS 5.0 COMMAND.COM. This enables you to share DOS 5 utilities on the network and have a single place where you can locate COMMAND.COM.

Another technique that can be used for users who boot from the hard disk is to set COMSPEC as follows:

```
COMSPEC=C:\COMMAND.COM
```

This preceding command takes care of different versions of DOS on the workstation's hard disk.

The DISPLAY Command

This command shows the contents of the specified file on the workstation screen. The exact characters are displayed, including any control codes for printer and word processing formats. The following is the general syntax:

```
DISPLAY [pathname]file
```

The [*pathname*]*file* statement is the name of the file whose contents are displayed.

The FDISPLAY Command

The FDISPLAY command shows the contents of the specified text file on the workstation screen. The text is formatted and filtered so that only the text is displayed. The general syntax is the following:

```
FDISPLAY [pathname]file
```

The [*pathname*]*file* statement is the name of the file whose contents are displayed.

The DOS SET or SET Command

This command can be used to set a DOS environment variable from within a login script. The general syntax is as follows:

```
[option] [DOS] SET name = "value"
```

The [*option*] parameter can be replaced by an optional keyword, such as TEMP, TEMPORARY, or LOCAL, to signify that the variable is set only during the login script processing and does not affect the DOS environment. Replace *name* with the name of the environment variable and *value* with its actual value. The *value* must always be enclosed in quotation marks (").

The following are examples of the use of the SET command:

```
SET PROMPT = "$P$G"          For setting DOS prompt

SET FNAME =                  For removing the definition of
                             the environment variable

SET Y = "1"

SET Y = <Y> + 1

SET UDIR = "*1:\\USERS\\%LOGIN NAME"
```

If you want to use the backslash character (\) in a string value, you must specify two backslashes, as shown in the following example:

```
SET FILENAME = "F:\\PUBLIC\\TEMP\\KSSFILE"
```

The reason for providing two backslashes is that the single backslash character is used to indicate special character codes, as shown in the following list:

\r	Indicates a carriage return
\n	Specifies a new line
\"	Embeds quotation marks in string
\7	Generates a beep sound (bell)

The DOS VERIFY Command

When set to ON, the DOS VERIFY command verifies that the data copied to a local drive can be written without errors. The default is OFF and the general syntax is the following:

```
DOS VERIFY [ON|OFF]
```

The NCOPY command automatically does a read-after-write verify check and can be used to copy files to floppy disks. If you want to use the MS-DOS COPY command, you should have the following command in your login script for added reliability in making copies to floppy disks:

```
DOS VERIFY ON
```

The /V option also can be used with the MS-DOS COPY command to produce the same effect.

The DRIVE Command

The DRIVE command can be used to specify which network drive is the default drive. The general syntax is as follows:

```
DRIVE [driveletter: | *n:]
```

Replace the *driveletter* statement with a drive letter, and *n* with the network drive number, such as ***1**, ***2**, and so on. The first network drive *1 is the default drive, but you can change this by specifying the new default drive in the DRIVE command.

The EXIT Command

Normally, execution of the login scripts terminates at the end of processing the individual user login script. The EXIT command can be used to prematurely terminate the login script processing or to specify the command to be executed on termination. The general syntax is the following:

```
EXIT [filename]
```

Replace the *filename* statement with the program name plus arguments of any command to be executed after the login script terminates. If an error message about limitations in the size of the command string that can be executed is displayed, you can try to minimize the characters in the command string by leaving out file extensions.

Examples of the use of the EXIT command are the following:

EXIT	Terminates log-in processing
EXIT MENU	Executes the MENU utility on termination
EXIT "F:USEREXEC.BAT"	Executes USEREXEC.BAT in the default drive on termination

The FIRE PHASERS Command

The FIRE PHASERS command produces sound effects of firing phasers. It does not work from the DOS command line. The general syntax is as follows:

```
FIRE PHASERS n TIMES
```

Replace *n* with a number from 1 to 9. Some of examples of this command follow:

```
FIRE PHASERS 4 TIMES

FIRE PHASERS %NDAY_OF_WEEK TIMES
```

The GOTO Command

Use the GOTO command to repeat processing of portions of the login script. The following is the general syntax:

```
GOTO label
```

You can replace the *label* with an identifier, but it must be specified in the current login script. The following example shows how to use the command:

```
SET X = "1"
REM The line below shows how labels can be defined
LOOP:
    REM The indentation shown below is for purposes
    REM of clarity and readability of the login script.
    REM It is not a requirement.

    REM Placing <> around X tells the login processor
    REM that this is an environment variable whose value
    REM needs to be evaluated.
    SET X = <X> + "1"

    REM Do whatever login script processing
    REM that needs to be repeated, here.

    REM Place a condition for terminating the loop, otherwise
    REM you will repeat this loop indefinitely!
    IF <X> <= "10" THEN GOTO LOOP
```

Set BREAK ON in the login script before experimenting with loops, just in case you want to break out of a loop you create unintentionally.

The IF ... THEN ... ELSE Command

This statement enables you to execute certain commands conditionally. The general syntax is as follows:

```
IF conditional(s) [AND|OR|NOR] conditional(s) THEN
    command
ELSE
    command
END
```

If the command is a series of statements, then you must include the BEGIN command on the previous line.

In the preceding syntax, the *conditional(s)* statements can be generated by using the following operators:

Any of the following operators are equivalent to Equal:

    =

    ==

    EQUAL

    EQUALS

Any of the following operators are equivalent to Not Equal:

    !=

    <>

    Not equal

    Does not equal

    Not equal to

The following are used as greater-than and less-than relational operators:

>   Is greater than

<   Is less than

>=   Is greater than or equal to

<=   Is less than or equal to

The INCLUDE Command

The INCLUDE command is used to indicate a level of indirection for processing login scripts. The content of the file specified in the INCLUDE statement is to be processed next, after which processing returns to the statement following the INCLUDE command. The general syntax is as follows:

```
INCLUDE [pathname]filename
```

The *[pathname]filename* statement is the location of the file to be processed.

You can nest INCLUDE commands up to any level limited only by the memory available for processing. As a practical matter, do not use more than two levels of nesting, or your login script will be difficult to figure out by others. You must have a minimum of [R F] rights to the INCLUDE file.

The MAP Command

The MAP command has the same syntax and meaning as the NetWare MAP command found in the SYS:PUBLIC directory, with only a few extensions. Use the following extensions to the MAP command for login script processing:

```
MAP DISPLAY [ON|OFF]
```

```
MAP ERRORS [ON|OFF]
```

The MAP DISPLAY ON command shows the drive mappings when you log in. This is the default setting. To disable the MAP processing, messages use MAP DISPLAY OFF.

MAP ERRORS ON displays error messages, that occur, for example, if the path to which you are mapping does not exist (not relocatable). The default setting is ON. To disable the display of MAP errors, you can use MAP ERRORS OFF. You should leave the MAP ERRORS command to its default setting of ON.

The PAUSE or WAIT Command

This command pauses the execution of the login script. Its general syntax is the following:

```
PAUSE
```

or

```
WAIT
```

This command can be used to pause the execution of the login script so that the messages do not scroll by before you have time to read them.

The PCCOMPATIBLE or COMPATIBLE Command

This command is used to indicate that the workstation PC is IBM PC compatible. Its general syntax is as follows:

```
PCCOMPATIBLE
```

or

```
COMPATIBLE
```

If your machine is IBM PC-compatible, but you have changed the long machine or short machine name by using the LONG MACHINE TYPE= or SHORT MACHINE TYPE= statements in the NET.CFG (older SHELL.CFG) file, you must use the PCCOMPATIBLE command to indicate to the shell that your machine is IBM PC compatible. If you do not do this, graphic NetWare utilities, such as SYSCON and FILER, which use the C-Worthy library routines, will not work correctly.

The REMARK or REM Command

This command is used to place comments in the login script file for enhancing the readability of the login script. You can use REMARK or REM. The general syntax is the following:

```
REM [text]
```

or

```
* text
```

or

```
; text
```

The SHIFT Command

The LOGIN command can be used to pass variables after the LOGIN *servername/username* command. These variables are referred to as %0, %1, %2, and so on.

In the LOGIN command, you might have typed something like the following:

```
LOGIN WE_SERVE/LYDIA PUBS GRAPHIC
```

The following shows how the variables of the general syntax are replaced with statements in the preceding command:

%0 = **WE_SERVE**

%1 = **LYDIA**

%2 = **PUBS**

%3 = **GRAPHIC**

The %0 variable always is assigned to the file server being logged in to, even if the file server name is not explicitly specified in the LOGIN command. The %1 variable always is mapped to the user's log-in name. The %2 variable and other variables are mapped to the additional arguments on the LOGIN command line.

The SHIFT command shifts the variable assignments. Its general syntax is as follows.

```
SHIFT [n]
```

The *n* variable can be a positive number for the number of variables you want to shift to the right, or it can be a negative number for shifting to the left. If *n* is left out, the default value of 1 is assumed.

The primary use of the SHIFT command is to sequence through the parameters specified in the command line. The following loop, for example, can be used to assign %2 to each of the parameters specified in the LOGIN command line after the user name.

```
LOOP:
    IF "%2" = "VAL1" THEN Command
    IF "%2" = "VAL2" THEN Command
    IF "%2" = "VAL3" THEN Command

    SHIFT 1
IF "%2" <> "" THEN GOTO LOOP
```

The preceding loop checks each of the parameters against a specific value and, if a match is found, performs the action specified. The SHIFT 1 command causes the %2 variable to be assigned to the next parameter to the right until no more parameters are left to process. When no more parameters are left, the conditional expression in the IF statement evaluates to false, and execution proceeds to the statement following the IF statement.

The WRITE Command

The WRITE command is used to display a text message on the screen. Its general syntax is the following:

```
WRITE text
```

You can use the semicolon (;) to concatenate text strings. The following two WRITE commands, for example, result in the same output:

```
WRITE Good ; GREETING_TIME; , %LOGIN_NAME

WRITE Good %GREETING_TIME, %LOGIN_NAME
```

Login Script Variables

This chapter has made many references to log-in variables and many examples have been used throughout the chapter. Table 14.1 gives a formal definition of each of these script variables. The script variables also are sometimes referred to as log-in macros, because they evaluate to a specific value. When used as part of a string or a path name, the percent character must be used before the script variable name.

Table 14.1
Identifier Variables

Conditional Items	Screen Display
ACCESS_SERVER	Displays TRUE if access server is functional. Displays FALSE if not functional.
ERROR_LEVEL	Displays the number of errors. If 0, no errors are found.
MEMBER OF *group*	Displays TRUE if the user is a member of a specified group. Displays FALSE if the user is not a member of a specified group.

Date	Screen Display
DAY	Displays the day from 01 to 31.
DAY_OF_WEEK	Displays the day of the week.
MONTH	Displays the month from 01 to 12.
MONTH_NAME	Displays the name of the month.
NDAY_OF_WEEK	Displays the number of the weekday.
SHORT_YEAR	Displays the year in short format, such as 92, 93, and so on.
YEAR	Displays the year in full format, such as 1992, 1993, and so on.

DOS Environment	
<>	Enables you to use any DOS environment variable as a string.
NETWORK_ADDRESS	Displays the network number of the cabling system in eight hex digits.
FILE_SERVER	Displays the name of the file server.

Time	
AM_PM	Displays the time as day or night, using a.m. or p.m.
GREETING_TIME	Displays the time of day as morning, afternoon, or evening.
HOUR	Displays the time of day in hours, from 1 to 12.
HOUR24	Displays the hour in 24-hour time, from 00 to 23.
MINUTE	Displays the minutes from 00 to 59.
SECOND	Displays the seconds from 00 to 59.

continues

Table 14.1
Continued

User	Screen Display
FULL_NAME	Displays the full name of the user by using SYSCON information.
LOGIN_NAME	Displays the user's log-in name.
USER_ID	Displays the ID number of each user.

Workstation	
MACHINE	Displays the machine for which the shell was written, such as IBMPC.
OS	Displays the workstations operating system, such as MS-DOS.
OS_VERSION	Displays the DOS version of the workstation.
P_STATION	Displays the station address or node address in 12 hex digits.
SMACHINE	Displays the name of the machine in short format, such as IBM.
STATION	Displays the connection number.

Novell Menus

All NetWare versions ship with the MENU utility. This utility takes as its input a text file containing a description of how the menus should appear. This text file has a MNU extension and can be created with any text editor. The basic syntax of this text file is as follows:

```
%Title V,H,C

Option1
     Executable commands
```

```
Option2
     Executable commands

Option3
     Executable commands

Option4
     %Sub Menu

%Sub Menu,V,H,C

OptionSub1
     Executable commands

OptionSub2
     Executable commands
```

The following sample menu script is an example of a menu text file:

```
%Dei's Menu,0,0,1

File Manager
     FILER
System Configuration
     SYSCON
File Console
     FCONSOLE
Applications
     %Applications

%Applications,14,60,1
WordProcessing
     MAP G:=SYS:APPS\WP
     G:
     WP
     F:
Database
     MAP G:=SYS:APPS\DBX
     G:
     DB
     F:
Spread Sheet
     MAP G:SYS:APPS\SS
     G:
     SS
     F:
```

As can be seen in the preceding examples, main and submenu titles always are preceded by the percent (%) character placed on the left margin. The percent character serves as an indication to the MENU parsing function that what follows is the title of the menu.

The menu title is followed by three numbers separated by commas. The first number is the distance (measured in lines) of the center of the menu from the top of the screen. The second number represents the distance (measured in columns) of the center of the menu from the left edge of the screen. These two numbers represent the vertical (V) and horizontal (H) coordinates of the center of the menu. A value of zero indicates that the menu is to be centered with respect to that coordinate. Thus, in the preceding example, you can see that Dei's main menu has the coordinates of 0,0, which means the menu is to be placed perfectly in the center. The third number is the color palette. The color palette is the color scheme for the foreground and background.

The color palette can be changed or a new one defined by using the utility COLORPAL. For most situations, the default color palette should suffice. There are 5 predefined color palettes, and these are numbered 0 to 4. If the color palette number is left out, a default color palette of 0 is used.

The option lines are placed on the left margin also, but without the "%" character. One or more commands are placed below each option line. The commands are placed on separate lines and must be indented. The menu utility can be invoked by using the command:

```
MENU MenuFile
```

If you leave out the menu file, the default menu file MAIN.MNU which is defined in the SYS:PUBLIC directory is used. It is customary to define a menu file for each user name and to give the menu file the same name as the user's log-in name. Therefore, for the user DEI, the menu file could be DEI.MNU. This menu for the user can be invoked by using the command:

```
MENU DEI
```

This command can be placed in the user's login script by using the following:

```
#MENU DEI
```

or

```
EXIT "MENU DEI"
```

or

```
EXIT   "MENU %LOGIN_NAME"
```

The last EXIT command automatically expands to the file name that has the same name as the user's log-in name.

If the EXIT command exits to a batch file called USEREXEC.BAT, defined in the user's home directory, then the USEREXEC.BAT file can contain the MENU FileName command:

```
EXIT "F:USEREXEC.BAT"
```

When designing menus, an important consideration is the placement of the menus. This can be done in an ad hoc fashion by trial and error until one gets the placement desired. Or better still, a more systematic method can be used. The systematic method consists of using the following formulas in which V and H are the coordinates specified in the menu title definition:

V = number of lines above menu + (number of lines in height of menu)/2

H = number of columns to left of menu + (number of columns in width of menu)/2

Suppose, for example, that the height of the menu is 8 lines, and its width is 20 columns. Also, you have decided to place the top of the menu 10 lines from the top of the screen and the left edge of the menu 50 columns to the left of the screen. Using the preceding formulas, you get the following values:

V = 10 + 8/2 = 10 + 4 = 14

H = 50 + 20/2 = 50 + 10 = 60

The title would then be placed as:

```
%Title,14,60,0
```

If the `File Missing` message appears when the MENU command is invoked, it indicates that the file cannot be found in the current directory or on the search path. In this case, you need to make sure that the file exists in the current directory or in the search path.

Sometimes it is useful to give the user the option to enter information on the commands. An example of this would be an option to copy files or send messages. A portion of the menu script file could then be the following:

```
%Interactive Commands,10,20,1
File Copy
     NCOPY @1"Source file name" @2"Destination"
Send Message
     SEND @1"Type a message" @2"Send to?"
```

The variables @1 and @2 in the preceding example become place-holders for whatever value the user types. The user is prompted to type these values. The text that follows the @ variables is displayed so that the user knows what kind of information is expected by the MENU system.

When the MENU utility displays the options, it sorts the options in alphabetical order. This can sometimes lead to undesirable consequences when the options appear in a different order from the one intended. Some system administrators, therefore, resort to prefixing the option title with a number such as:

```
%Title,0,0

1. Option A
     Executable

2. Option B
     Executable

3. Option C
     Executable
```

Using this approach sorts the menu titles in the order of the numbers. This scheme works well for options that do not exceed 9. An option number of 10, for instance, will appear between option 1 and 2. You can of course resort to using two or more digit numbers, such as 01, 02, 03, and so on, to solve this problem.

Summary

In this chapter, you learned the different types of startup scripts that are necessary to set up a NetWare workstation. These include the familiar DOS startup files CONFIG.SYS and AUTOEXEC.BAT. Certain statements in these files can be specifically configured for the network environment.

Two types of login scripts are used: system and user. The relationship between these files was discussed in this chapter, along with details of the login script commands and variables that can be used to set up a customized network environment.

Finally, you saw how the Novell MENU system can be used to make it easier for users to access network services.

The NetWare File System

## 15

The NetWare server provides a remote file system that can be accessed by NetWare clients. Because many users share this remote access file system, the following points are important:

- The server's remote file system must be well-organized and easy to maintain.

- Users must share the server's file system without violating system security or another user's privacy.

- Access to the file system must be intuitive and consistent with the workstation operating system used by the client.

- Access to the file system must be nearly as fast as access to a workstation's local hard disk.

NetWare combines all of these features. The NetWare system and utilities are organized into standard directories, such as LOGIN, SYSTEM, and PUBLIC. Users can be assigned a home directory to store their personal files. If a directory contains system programs used for network administration, access to these programs can be restricted. Access to the network files is simple and intuitive; you can access the server files by using the workstation's operating system commands. And because most LANs operate at speeds of megabits per second, access to the server's file system is fast. You can read and write to a network file about as fast as you can read and write to a local disk.

Looking at Directory Organization

The server's disk is an important component of the server. A high-performance disk subsystem has a dramatic effect on the server's overall performance. Many types of disk subsystems exist. A knowledge of disk subsystem features helps you to choose the correct disk to improve a server's performance.

The user sees a logical view of the server disk. This logical view must be consistent with the workstation operating system used by the client. For example, a user of a Macintosh station sees the remote file system by using the FINDER interface, and a user of a DOS workstation sees the file system as a number of remote drives designated by letters, such as F, G, H, and so on.

Disk Subsystems

Disk systems are internal or external. The computer's chassis houses the internal disk; you can access internal disks only by removing the chassis, which usually involves powering down the computer. External disk systems exist outside the computer. A host bus adapter in the computer acts as a bus interface for the external disk. External disks are more convenient for the network administrator because you do not have to turn off the computer to access an external disk.

A good disk subsystem for a server has the following characteristics:

- Large capacity
- High data throughput—fast disks and system bus
- Low cost
- Capability to withstand long periods of use
- Reliability

Choose a disk subsystem based on how well it satisfies the preceding criteria.

Because the server is a repository for programs and data shared by many network users, it should have as large a disk system as is practical based on drive cost and drive support. A fast disk system improves server performance as long as other factors, such as LAN speed and server system bus, are not bottlenecks. The type of system bus must be considered carefully if fast disk performance is required because the data has to travel through the system bus. AT-style buses currently handle 4 Mbps to 8 Mbps data rates. These data rates can become bottlenecks for disk subsystems that transfer at higher data rates—ESDI and SCSI drives. Faster disks are better suited for the EISA—Enhanced Industry Standards Architecture—Micro Channel buses.

Because the disk acts as a repository for applications and data, reliability is one of the most important criterion of the servers disk subsystem. If the disk subsystem fails, the network may be unusable. Loss of critical data on the server can result in loss of revenue for an organization. To avoid this, proper backups must be made.

Table 15.1 shows the results of a study done by the Yankee Group concerning the cost of system down time for over 250 U.S. corporations. From this you can see that disk subsystems must be very reliable to keep network down-time costs low. For this very reason, Novell has defined its *SFT System Fault Tolerant* architecture. SFT Level II—discussed in Chapter 6—enables a secondary disk to act as a backup to the primary disk for all operations. If the primary disk fails, the secondary disk can be used without any loss in network downtime.

Table 15.1
Cost of System Downtime

Cost per Hour	Percentage of U.S. Corporations
$1,000	42 %
$10,000	26 %
$50,000	5 %
$50,000	4 %
Unknown	23 %

The common disk subsystems for microcomputers are ISA, IDE, SCSI, and ESDI.

Be sure that you purchase the disk controller and adapter from the same source or vendor. If you try to mix and match disk controllers and drives, you may not get optimum performance.

Data Encoding Techniques

Some disk controllers use special encoding techniques to place more data per disk track. These disk controllers work with specially designed disks that have the capability to retain high-density data. If you use these controllers with a disk that is not designed for high-density encoding, you can lose data. An understanding of data encoding techniques helps you recognize these problems.

A disk is composed of platters that have magnetic surfaces divided into tracks. The tracks are divided into sectors, which are further subdivided into bytes of information. Sectors are preceded by sector IDs set during the low-level format of a disk. High level formats deal with the logical organization of the disk sectors.

Disk drives encode the data on magnetic media inside the tracks on each disk platter. The type of magnetic media can be oxide, plated, or sputtered. The bit information is stored in terms of magnetic charges on the disk. The disks rotate at speeds of 3600 to 7200 revolutions per minute (RPM). As the disk rotates, the disk controller electronically positions the heads—one per surface—to the correct track so that sectors can be read or written. As the track spins under the disk head, the magnetic media is read as a series of digital pulses. These pulses are decoded as a binary digit of 1 or 0. An encoding scheme represents data on the disk.

Table 15.2 shows an encoding scheme used for *Modified Frequency Modulation* (MFM) drives. In this scheme, every bit of information is represented as two half-bits on the disk. A half-bit is defined as a *silence* (no magnetic charge) or a *pulse* (magnetic charge). To represent a data bit of 1, the half-bits are defined as a silence followed by a pulse. To represent a 0, two half-bit combinations are used: if the previous half-bit was a pulse, two half-bits of silence are used; if the previous half-bit was a silence, the half bits are a pulse followed by a silence.

Table 15.2
MFM or RLL 1,3 Encoding

Data	Half-Bit encoding
0	1 0 (if previous half-bit is 0)
	0 0 (if previous half-bit is 1)
1	0 1

Table 15.3 shows the half bit encodings for any two consecutive data bits. With two data bits, only four combinations exist: 00, 01, 10, and 11. From this table you see that the minimum number of silence bits is 1, and the maximum number of silence bits is 3. This type of encoding is called *Run Length Limited* (RLL) *1,3*. MFM uses RLL 1,3 encoding. Drives in IBM-XTs and earlier IBM-ATs are MFM drives. ESDI drives use RLL 2,7 or RLL 3,9 and can pack more bits of information. Because the sector size is usually 512 bytes, more sectors can be used per track.

Table 15.3
RLL 1,3 Half-Bit Patterns

Data pattern	Half-Bit encoding
0 0	0: 1 0 1 0 (previous bit 0)
	1: 0 0 1 0 (previous bit 1)
0 1	0: 1 0 0 1 (previous bit 0)
	1: 0 0 0 1 (previous bit 1)
1 0	0: 0 1 0 0 (previous bit 0)
	1: 0 1 0 0 (previous bit 1)
1 1	0: 0 1 0 1 (previous bit 0)
	1: 0 1 0 1 (previous bit 1)

Table 15.4 shows the encoding for a RLL 2,7 drive. With this type of encoding, drives can pack 26 sectors per track. Twenty-five sectors are used for data, and the remaining sector can be used to remap a bad sector on the track. This technique—called *sector sparing*—accepts up to $25 \times 512 = 12{,}800$ bytes per sector, which is nearly double that of MFM drives that have 17 sectors per track. Another technique—*track sparing*—marks the entire track as bad, but this results in an inefficient utilization of disk space.

Table 15.4
RLL 2,7 Encoding

Data pattern	Half-Bit encoding
0 0	1 0 0 0
0 1	0 1 0 0
1 0 0	0 0 1 0 0 0
1 0 1	1 0 0 1 0 0
1 1 1	0 0 0 1 0 0
1 1 0 0	0 0 0 0 1 0 0 0
1 1 0 1	0 0 1 0 0 1 0 0

ST-506/412 Disk Subsystems

ST-506/412 disk subsystems are the most common disks found in microcomputers. Shugart Technologies, which later changed its name to Seagate Technologies, originally developed this interface standard.

The disk controller for ST-506 supports two disks. A 34-pin ribbon cable carries control signals that connect to the hard disks, and a 20-pin ribbon cable carries data. Up to two disks can be daisy-chained—that is, connected in a series—on the same control cable.

Some controllers employ a 34-pin cable with a twist in the middle that causes wires 24 and 29 to be "twisted." This twist enables both hard drives to be jumpered to identical settings. The twist makes one drive appear to be drive 0 (the first drive), and the other drive appear to be drive 1 (the second drive) despite the identical jumper settings.

5T-506 disk controllers typically use MFM encoding to store data.

IDE Disk Subsystems

In the 5T-506 disk interface, the controller electronics are on a separate adapter installed in an expansion bus slot. Disk manufacturers have come up with a scheme to integrate the disk controller electronics in the system board. Cables from the system board connect to disks. IDE stands for Intelligent Device Electronics or Integrated Device Electronics.

IDE drives are faster than 5T-506 drives, but appear to NetWare to be ST506 drives. Both usually use the same NetWare drivers as the ISADISK.DSK driver program.

ESDI Disk Subsystems

Maxtor developed the Enhanced Small Devices Interface (ESDI) in 1983, and a number of disk drive manufacturers have adopted it since then. The I/O interface used for many minicomputer environments is the foundation of the ESDI.

ESDI drives use 2,7 or 3,9 RLL encoding that enables them to compress more sectors per track. The number of sectors per track can be 26, 53, or a higher number. Because ESDI drives can use different RLL encodings, make sure that you buy a matched disk controller and disk—that is, buy them from the same source.

Many ESDI controllers implement track buffering. When a request for a single sector is made, the entire track is read and cached in fast RAM on the disk controller. This is done in anticipation of subsequent sector requests from the same track. ESDI track buffering works only for read operations, not write operations.

Track buffering does not replace NetWare's file caching mechanism, but complements it. NetWare's file caching mechanism provides cache buffering for both read and write operations, which improves the file system's overall performance.

SCSI Disk Subsystems

The *Small Computer Systems Interface* (SCSI), pronounced "Scuzzy," is a *bus interface* for peripheral devices. SCSI enables devices such as disk drives and tape drives to be connected to an external I/O bus. Developed by Adaptec, SCSI became an *American National Standards Institute* (ANSI) standard in 1982. Apple's Macintosh PLUS and later models made the SCSI popular. These machines are equipped with a SCSI port that enables you to plug in disk drives and tape units externally.

Because the SCSI is a bus interface, I/O devices are connected serially—or daisy-chained—to the bus. Up to eight such devices can be connected to the bus. Some SCSI products integrate the device controller with the SCSI adapter; others integrate the device controller and the SCSI adapter on the drive itself. The latter solution is called an embedded SCSI disk drive. Although these solutions reduce the cost of the product, they impose a limit on the number of devices that can be connected to the SCSI adapter.

The SCSI architecture is based on the block-multiplexor I/O channel interface of IBM mainframes and can transfer data at rates up to 32 Mbps. A new SCSI-II architecture that is faster and more efficient has been proposed and is being implemented by some device manufacturers.

Logical View of Disk Subsystem

The NetWare NOS presents a logical view of the server's disk. A NetWare client sees the server's disk as being organized into volumes, directories, and files. Internally, NetWare manages the disk as a sequence of disk blocks of fixed size. This block size is 4K for NetWare v2.x and is available for NetWare v3.x at installation time with values of 4K, 8K, 16K, 32K and 64K. Because NetWare manages the disk as a sequence of blocks, NetWare remains independent of the physical disk structure, such as number of sectors per track, number of cylinders, and number of disk platters (surface area).

To use the server's disk, unused drive letters (usually F to Z) are assigned to directories on the server. After this logical association is made, you can treat the server directories as extensions to the local disk subsystem. Access to the server's remote file system can be made with the workstation operating system commands by using a network drive letter.

Volumes

A server's disk is organized into *volumes*. Volumes are a logical division of the space available on a server's disk.

In NetWare v2.x, a volume has a maximum size of 254M. If a disk is smaller than or equal to 254M, a volume can span the entire disk. This is the preferred way to make volume assignments for the NetWare v2.x—that is, whenever possible a volume spans an entire disk.

If the disk is larger than 254M, it must be divided into volumes no larger than 254M. Figure 15.1 shows a NetWare v2.x disk with a capacity of 680M. It is divided into three volumes: two volumes of 254M, and one volume of 172M. The 254M volume size limitation also limits the maximum file size to 254M because a file cannot exceed volume size. For applications that use very large files, this can be a serious limitation.

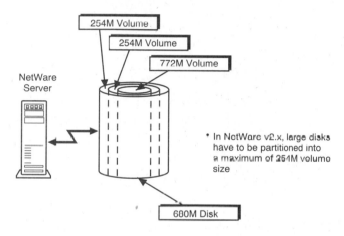

254M Volume

254M Volume

772M Volume

NetWare Server

• In NetWare v2.x, large disks have to be partitioned into a maximum of 254M volume size

680M Disk

Figure 15.1:
NetWare v2.x partitioning of large disk.

In NetWare v3.x, a server supports 64 volumes that have a maximum size of 32TB. Because this is greater than the size of disks available today, you do not need to partition a large disk into logical volumes in NetWare v3.x. In the example in figure 15.1, the entire 680M disk can be assigned to a single volume.

In NetWare v3.x, a logical volume can span several server disks, which is called *volume spanning*. A volume consists of up to 32 volume segments. Each volume segment can be a disk partition or an entire disk. The volume segments are defined by using the Disk Options in the INSTALL NLM.

To perform volume spanning, you must follow these steps:

1. After you load INSTALL.NLM, select the following choices:

    Installation Options

    Volume Options

2. After a list of volumes appears, press Ins to add a new volume. If you have more than one hard disk that potentially can be used for volume spanning, a list of these partitions appears.

3. From the Free Space Available for Volume Segments list, select the disk to be used as a volume segment.

4. In the New Volume Information menu, enter the Volume Name, Volume Block Size, and Initial Segment Size fields.

    The Initial Segment Size field holds the total number of blocks available for that volume segment. If you want to use a smaller value, you can compute the new block size by using the formula:

    Disk blocks = (Amount of space to be allocated in M × 1024) / Block size in K

    If you want to use only 25M for a volume configured with 4K blocks, the number of disk blocks for Initial Segment Size is:

    Disk blocks = 25 x 1024 / 4 = 6400 blocks

    The block size must be the same for all volume segments.

5. Press Esc, and save the volume definition.

The *Volume Definition Table* stores the details of volume name, size, and segments. Every volume contains a Volume Definition Table in its partition.

Volume spanning enables applications to have large files that cannot fit on a single disk. Another advantage is that multiple simultaneous I/O operations can be done on the volume in *parallel* because the volume now has a number of separate disks and disk controllers that provide concurrent access to it. This also means that requests to access a volume do not have to be queued up as long as they refer to an area of the volume on a separate disk because the requests can be processed by the separate disk controllers and drives.

The disadvantage to volume spanning is that if any of the disks comprising a volume fails, the entire volume fails. Novell recommends that you use SFT Level II to avoid this problem, but this approach can be expensive when very large disks are involved.

The first volume in a NetWare server always is named SYS:. This volume holds the NetWare NOS and its program and data files. Other volumes can have names consisting of from two to 15 characters. Try to keep volume names simple and easy to remember. For instance, the first volume after SYS: can be labeled VOL1:, the next one VOL2:, and so on.

Volumes hold data in blocks that have a size of 4K. In NetWare v2.x the block size is fixed to 4K, but in NetWare v3.x you can select larger block sizes, such as 8K, 16K, 32K, or 64K.

Larger block sizes provide more efficient file access for large files because fewer blocks must be accessed for a given file. Larger disk blocks also require fewer entries in the *File Allocation Tables* (FATs) and, therefore, less RAM to keep track of them. Smaller size disk blocks use more RAM for their FAT tables.

If you have a volume intended for large database files, you can configure it for larger block sizes to provide more efficient file access. If you have a large number of small files on a volume, larger block sizes waste space because the last block is on the average only half full. After you select a block size, you cannot change it without destroying the data on the disk. You must be careful, therefore, if you select a nondefault block size when you install NetWare v3.x. If you are not sure about the size you want, leave the block size at the default value of 4K.

Directories and Files

A volume can be further divided into directories and files. NetWare supports a hierarchical file structure. Figure 15.2 illustrates the hierarchy of dividing a volume into directories and files. For DOS workstations, the files and directories follow the 8.3 naming rule—that is, 8 characters, a period, and a 3-character extension.

To specify a file on a particular server, the full path name of the file is used. Use the following syntax:

```
[serverName/]volName:dir1{/dir2}/fileName
```

The directory separator delimiter character is / or \. The following are examples of NetWare path names:

```
KSS/SYS:PUBLIC/SCRIPTS/STUDENTS.SCR
SYS:APPS\README.DOC
VOL1:BRIGHT/DOC\MANUAL.DOC
```

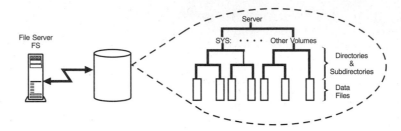

Figure 15.2:
Logical organization of NetWare server file system.

In the first example, the path name includes the name of the server KSS. The server name is separated from the rest of the path name by either the / or \ character. This example uses /. The volume name is SYS:. The first directory is PUBLIC, and the subdirectory name is SCRIPTS. The file name is STUDENTS.SCR.

In example two, the optional server name is left out. This implies that the name of the default server is used. The directory APPS that contains the file README.DOC is under the volume name SYS:.

In example three, the optional server name is left out. The volume name is VOL1:. The directory name is BRIGHT. BRIGHT has a subdirectory named DOC, which contains the file MANUAL.DOC. In example 3, both / and \ are used as directory separators. As a matter of style, one or the other character should be used consistently.

Drive Mappings

To use the NetWare server's file system, the user assigns an network drive to a directory on the server. The process of assigning a workstation drive letter to a server directory is called *mapping a network drive*. Figure 15.3 shows the available drive letters. Driver letters from A to E usually are reserved for local drives because the default LASTDRIVE parameter for CONFIG.SYS is drive E. Drives F to Z are used for network drives.

Figure 15.4 shows drive mappings to the file system on the server. Use the MAP command to set up the drive mappings. The syntax of the MAP command is as follows:

```
MAP [INS | DEL | ROOT] driveName: [ = networkDirectory]
```

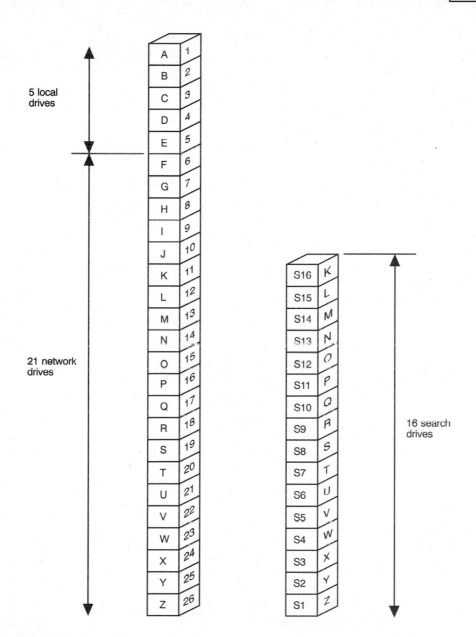

Figure 15.3:
Search drives. (Graphic courtesy of Learning Group International)

DriveName is a drive letter or a search drive (see next section). The [= *networkDirectory*] means that the assigned network directory is optional if the DEL option is used.

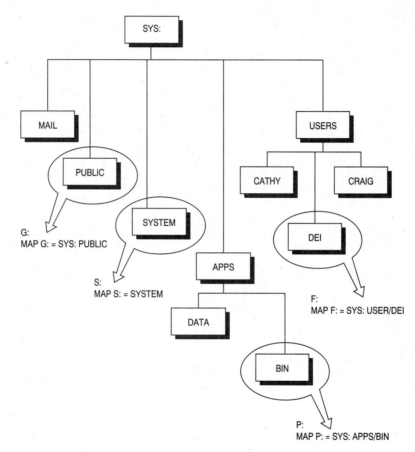

Figure 15.4:
Drive mappings to server's file system.

Examples of how to use the MAP command are as follows:

```
MAP F: = SYS:PUBLIC
MAP ROOT G: = KSS/VOL1:DEVELOP/BIN
MAP DEL F:
```

Example one maps drive F to SYS:PUBLIC on the default server.

Example two maps drive G to VOL1:DEVELOP/BIN on server KSS. In addition, G is *rooted* (ROOT) to the network directory KSS/VOL1:DEVELOP/BIN. When a drive is rooted to a network directory, the network directory acts as the root of the file system. Because the root directory is the top-level directory, you cannot go up the directory by using the following DOS command:

```
CD ..
```

This fake root protects the security of the network directory. You also can use the fake root to install single user applications on the NetWare server. Some single user applications are installed in the root directory. If these applications are installed on the server, they can clutter up the root directory on the server volume. A fake root enables you to install a single user application in a subdirectory on the server. To legally install a single user application on the server, you must have a license for every user of the application on the network.

Example three deletes (DEL) the drive mapping for F. If you delete a drive mapping, the [= *networkDirectory*] is omitted.

You cannot map to a network directory unless you have access rights to that directory. If you attempt to map to a network directory for which you do not have access rights, the error message DIRECTORY XXX NOT LOCATABLE appears.

Search Drives

In DOS, the PATH command specifies the order that directories are searched if a program file is not found in the current directory. The directories specified in the PATH command are stored in a DOS environment variable of the same name (PATH).

You cannot include NetWare directories as part of the DOS PATH command by using the NetWare syntax for a directory. For example, a DOS station has the following setting for the PATH environment variable before logging into a NetWare server:

```
PATH=C:\WP51;C:\BIN;C:\BC\BIN;C:\WC386\BIN
```

To add the NetWare directory SYS:PUBLIC\UTIL to the beginning of the search path, you might be tempted to try the following DOS PATH command:

```
PATH=SYS:PUBLIC\UTIL;C:\WP51;C:\BIN;C:\BC\BIN;C:\WC386\BIN
```

This DOS PATH command does not work. DOS cannot process the NetWare syntax SYS:PUBLIC\UTIL in the PATH environment variable because DOS only recognizes a one letter drive in this location. To solve this problem, NetWare uses *search drives* to specify network directories as part of the search path.

Figure 15.3 shows search drives. Sixteen search drives exist, and they are labeled SEARCH1 to SEARCH16. You can abbreviate SEARCH by using S. The first search drive, therefore, is abbreviated as S1, and the sixteenth search drive is abbreviated as S16. Use the MAP command to make search drive assignments. Search drives specify the order that directories, including network directories, are searched. This is similar to the way the DOS PATH command operates, except that search drives enable you to work with network directories.

In the preceding example, therefore, if you want to include the network directory SYS:PUBLIC\UTIL as part of the search path, you can use the following MAP commands:

```
MAP S1:=SYS:PUBLIC\UTIL
```

or

```
MAP INS S1:=SYS:PUBLIC\UTIL
```

The first MAP command maps search drive 1 (S1) to the network directory SYS:PUBLIC\UTIL, and this directory is searched first. The second MAP command inserts (INS) SYS:PUBLIC/UTIL as the first search drive. If the first search drive was assigned previously, the INS option pushes it down the list to become the second search drive. Figure 15.5 illustrates this "push-down" effect. This figure shows the search drives before and after the user issues the MAP INS command.

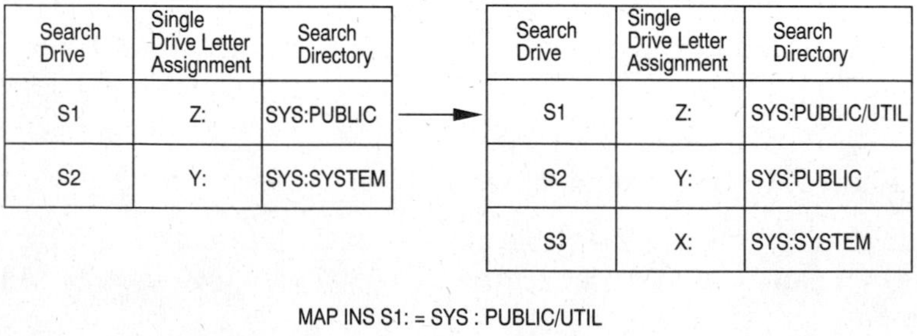

Search Drive	Single Drive Letter Assignment	Search Directory		Search Drive	Single Drive Letter Assignment	Search Directory
S1	Z:	SYS:PUBLIC	→	S1	Z:	SYS:PUBLIC/UTIL
S2	Y:	SYS:SYSTEM		S2	Y:	SYS:PUBLIC
				S3	X:	SYS:SYSTEM

MAP INS S1: = SYS : PUBLIC/UTIL

Figure 15.5:
The push-down effect of the MAP INS command.

When the user issues the **MAP S1:=SYS:PUBLIC\UTIL** command to map search drive 1, the DOS PATH environment variable changes also. It assigns an unused drive letter starting with Z to the network directory, and inserts Z in the DOS PATH environment variable. Therefore, the DOS PATH environment variable before the MAP S1:=SYS:PUBLIC/UTIL command looks like this:

```
PATH=C:\WP51;C:\BIN;C:\BC\BIN;C:\WC386\BIN
```

After using the MAP command, the DOS PATH environment variable looks like this:

```
PATH=Z:.;C:\WP51;C:\BIN;C:\BC\BIN;C:\WC386\BIN
```

DOS recognizes the single letter Z as another directory letter, and it searches drive Z as it does any local drive. The period (.) stands for the current directory, and when used in the PATH environment variable, it indicates that the current directory Z, mapped to SYS:PUBLIC\UTIL, is to be searched.

NetWare assigns search drive letters beginning with Z and moving backward through the alphabet to K. Figure 15.3 illustrates this—search drive 1 uses Z, and search drive 16 uses K. Letter assignments for applications usually begin with F: and move through J. The reverse order of letter assignment for search drives minimizes conflicts between the applications and search drives. Applications drive letters are assigned safely up to drive J. If applications use drives beyond J, you will have a conflict when you reach the maximum of 16 search drives because search drive 16 also uses K. This situation is not uncommon in complex NetWare user environments, and the network manager may wish that the English alphabet had more than 26 letters or that DOS used a different scheme.

Search drive mappings affect the user's current session only. When a user issues a MAP command to map to a network directory, the mapping is only for the user who issues the command. Other users on the network are not affected by this drive mapping. The shell holds the drive mappings only for a session. When the user logs out of a server by using the LOGOUT command, the drive mappings disappear from the drive map table. To make the drive mappings permanent, the user must automate the execution of the MAP commands. One way to do this is with a login script. MAP commands used to build a network search path can be placed in a login script file. A *login script* defines a user's network environment and is the equivalent of the DOS AUTOEXEC.BAT file. Login scripts are discussed in detail in Chapter 14.

Network Drive Assignments

The best way to learn about network drive assignments is to experiment with them. This section gives you hands-on experience with drive mappings.

To follow the exercises listed in this section, you must have access to the user SUPERVISOR account and a non-supervisor user account. If you want to create a user to follow the exercises in this section, refer to Chapter 10.

1. Log in as SUPERVISOR or use a valid user account. (See Chapter 12 if you are not sure how to log in to a server.)

2. Type:

   MAP

   The MAP command examines the current drive mappings. The response to this command looks like the following output. The details depend on the way your login script (see Chapter 14) is set up.

   ```
   Drive  A:    maps to a local disk.
   Drive  B:    maps to a local disk.
   Drive  C:    maps to a local disk.
   Drive  D:    maps to a local disk.
   Drive  E:    maps to a local disk.
   Drive  F: = S386\SYS:  \


   SEARCH1:  = Z:. [S386\SYS:  \PUBLIC]
   SEARCH2:  = Y:. [S386\SYS:  \PUBLIC\IBM_PC\MSDOS\V3.31]
   ```

3. Issue a MAP command to map drive I to SYS:PUBLIC:

   MAP I:=SYS:PUBLIC

   To verify that your mapping has been successful, type:

   MAP

4. Try to map to a directory that does not exist.

   MAP J:=SYS:DEVELOP

   The `Directory SYS:DEVELOP is not locatable` message appears.

5. Map to a directory for which you do not have access rights. To perform this step you must create a directory called SYS:DEVELOP/

BIN using a supervisor account, and then log in as a user that does not have SUPERVISOR rights. Type:

```
MAP J:=SYS:DEVELOP/BIN
```

If you do not have access to this directory, you will get an error message that states that the directory is not locatable.

You also can log in as a supervisor, assign Read and File scan rights of SYS:DEVELOP to the user you are working with, and then map drive H to the directory SYS:DEVELOP while logged in as a non-supervisor user:

```
MAP J:=SYS:DEVELOP/BIN
```

This time the mapping is successful.

6. To delete the drive J mapping, type:

```
MAP DEL J:
```

7. To map drive J to the same directory as I, type:

```
MAP J:=I:
```

Use the MAP command to verify this mapping.

8. You do not need to use the NetWare network directory syntax to specify the volume name to map to a network directory. Try the following:

```
MAP H:=F:\PUBLIC
```

The preceding command maps H to the same volume as F, starting from the root, and going down to the PUBLIC directory.

9. You can experiment with search drives in the next few sections.

To note the current search drives, type:

```
MAP
```

Current drive mappings and search drive mappings similar to the following appear:

```
Drive  A:   maps to a local disk.
Drive  B:   maps to a local disk.
Drive  C:   maps to a local disk.
Drive  D:   maps to a local disk.
Drive  E:   maps to a local disk.
```

```
Drive  F: = S386\SYS:  \
Drive  H: = S386\SYS:  \PUBLIC
Drive  I: = S386\SYS:  \PUBLIC
Drive  J: = S386\SYS:  \PUBLIC
  ──
SEARCH1:  = Z:. [S386\SYS:  \PUBLIC]
SEARCH2:  = Y:. [S386\SYS:  \PUBLIC\IBM_PC\MSDOS\V3.31]
```

In the preceding example, search drive 1 is mapped to
S386\SYS:\PUBLIC.

To display the current DOS search path, type:

PATH

The following response appears:

```
PATH=Z:.;Y:.;
```

Notice that the PATH command is consistent with the current search
drive mappings.

10.   Insert SYS:DEVELOP/BIN as the first search drive. Type:

MAP INS S1:=SYS:DEVELOP/BIN

To examine the changed drive mappings, type:

MAP

The following response appears:

```
Drive  A:    maps to a local disk.
Drive  B:    maps to a local disk.
Drive  C:    maps to a local disk.
Drive  D:    maps to a local disk.
Drive  E:    maps to a local disk.
Drive  F: = S386\SYS:  \
Drive  H: = S386\SYS:  \PUBLIC
Drive  I: = S386\SYS:  \PUBLIC
Drive  J: = S386\SYS:  \PUBLIC
  ──
SEARCH1:  = X:. [S386\SYS:  \DEVELOP\BIN]
SEARCH2:  = Z:. [S386\SYS:  \PUBLIC]
SEARCH3:  = Y:. [S386\SYS:  \PUBLIC\IBM_PC\MSDOS\V3.31]
```

Compare the search drive mappings with those in step 9.

To examine the DOS PATH environment variable type:

PATH

The following results appear:

```
PATH=X:.;Z:.;Y:.;
```

Compare the DOS PATH environment variable with that in step 9. Notice that the DOS PATH environment variable reflects the changed search drive mappings.

11. Delete the first search drive mapping:

MAP DEL S1:

To examine the new search drive mappings and the DOS PATH environment variable, use the commands outlined in step 10. These should have the same values, as in step 9.

12. Try to delete a drive that does not exist:

MAP DEL S16:

If the search drive S16 does not exist, an error message appears.

13. Add a search drive at the end.

You probably have fewer than 16 search drive mappings for your current log-in session. If you do, type the following command:

MAP INS S16:=SYS:DEVELOP

To examine the search drive mappings, type:

MAP

Notice that you did not create search drive 16, but you did create a search drive with a number one greater than the last search drive. When you want to create a search drive, but do not know the number of the last search drive, use the MAP INS S16: command. This command automatically assigns the next available number to the new search drive.

14. The MAP command also can be applied to a local directory:

MAP INS S16:=C:

To examine the new search drive mappings and the DOS PATH environment variable, use the MAP and PATH commands. Notice that directory C:\ is now in the search drive list and the DOS PATH environment variable.

If you do not have a hard drive, you can use floppy drive A. If you have a diskless workstation, you cannot perform this part of the exercise.

15. To map drive H to SYS:PUBLIC type:

    ```
    MAP H:=SYS:PUBLIC
    ```

    Make H the current drive, and use the DOS change directory command to go one level up to the root SYS:.

    ```
    H:
    CD ..
    ```

    Type the MAP command to find out the current search drive mappings.

    The change directory command changes the drive mapping of drive H.

16. Repeat step 15 with a fake root MAP command. For instance, to map drive H to SYS:PUBLIC with a fake root, type:

    ```
    MAP ROOT H:=SYS:PUBLIC
    ```

    Make sure that H is the current drive, and use the DOS change directory command to move up one level to the root SYS:.

    ```
    H:
    CD ..
    ```

    Now use the MAP command to find out the current search drive mappings. Unlike step 15, the change directory command does not go above the fake root.

17. If you inadvertently wipe out the DOS PATH environment variable, the search drives also are deleted.

    To delete the DOS PATH, type:

```
F:
CD \
SET PATH=
```

Unless your current directory is SYS:PUBLIC, which stores the MAP command, type **MAP**. The following message appears:

```
Bad command or file name
```

To change to the SYS:PUBLIC directory that holds the MAP.EXE (command program file) type:

```
CD \PUBLIC
```

Next, type **MAP**. Note that the search drive mappings also have been wiped out.

Alternate Name Space Support

NetWare v3.x also supports alternate file systems, such as the Macintosh file system. These alternate file systems also are called *alternate name spaces*. Macintosh workstations see the NetWare file systems in terms of folders. A Macintosh file has two components—a *data fork* and a *resource fork*. A data fork holds the data portion of the file and the resource fork contains file attributes, such as the icon used to display the file and access rights to a file. To support the Macintosh file system, NetWare v2.x must run the Macintosh VAP, and NetWare v3.x must run the Macintosh Name Space NLM (MAC.NAM). When you select a backup utility for a NetWare server that implements the Macintosh name space, make sure that it can back up both data forks and resource forks.

In addition to the Macintosh name space, NetWare v3.x supports OS/2 name space and UNIX name space. These name spaces have longer file and directory names (typically 254 characters). If OS/2 uses the FAT file system (a DOS-compatible file system), the OS/2 name space is *not* needed. The OS/2 name space *must* be installed if the HPFS (High Performance File System) is used.

To add name space support, load the name space module in the STARTUP.NCF file and use the ADD NAME SPACE command in the AUTOEXEC.NCF file.

For example, to add name space support for a Macintosh file system, perform the following steps:

1. Load the disk driver and add the following line in STARTUP.NCF:

   LOAD MAC

2. After you mount the volume to which you want to add the name space, type the following line in AUTOEXEC.NCF:

   ADD NAME SPACE MACINTOSH TO VOLUME SYS

   To add name space support for a volume other than SYS, replace SYS with the volume name. To examine current name-space modules use the command:

   ADD NAME SPACE

   After you add the Macintosh name space, you must run the MACINST program to complete the Macintosh installation on the file server.

   To add name space support for OS/2, NFS, or FTAM, replace MACINTOSH with OS2, NFS, or FTAM.

Organizing a Directory

Upon its installation on the server, NetWare creates a standard directory structure to store its program and system files. To install applications and user's data on the server, you can augment this directory structure. This section examines how the standard directory structure can be augmented.

Default Directory Organization

During installation, NetWare creates a standard directory structure shown in figure 15.6. The SYSTEM, PUBLIC, LOGIN, and MAIL directories are created on volume SYS: for both NetWare v2.x and NetWare v3.x.

In addition to these directories, NetWare v3.x creates a directory called ETC under SYS:SYSTEM. The ETC directory holds tables and configuration information for TCP/IP support. This directory is modeled after the UNIX /etc directory.

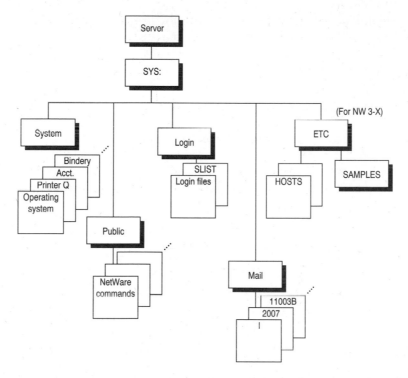

Figure 15.6:
Server SYS: structure as installed. (Graphic courtesy of Learning Group International)

The root directory also has a file called DELETED.SAV that holds the names of the files that have been deleted but can be recovered by the SALVAGE command.

In the sections that follow, you learn about the kinds of files in each of these directories.

LOGIN Directory

The LOGIN directory contains the NetWare utilities LOGIN.EXE and SLIST.EXE. The LOGIN directory also holds the operating system boot images created by the DOSGEN program for diskless workstations. Some LAN managers use this directory to store other programs that they want to be widely available to users without restrictions. An example of such a program is a virus scan program.

The default access rights to the SYS:LOGIN directory prevent modification of programs in this directory. You must make sure that these default access rights are not changed. Otherwise, the LOGIN directory can become a place through which a virus can spread.

PUBLIC Directory

The PUBLIC directory contains the NetWare utilities that are most commonly used. It also holds a copy of LOGIN.EXE and SLIST.EXE as a backup in case they are corrupted in the LOGIN directory. Again, care must be exercised to limit access to SYS:PUBLIC so that NetWare utilities may be run but not modified.

For a description of the utilities in the PUBLIC directory, refer to the NetWare *User's Manual*. A description of these utilities is beyond the scope of this book, but the more important files in SYS:PUBLIC are listed in table 15.5 for your ready reference. This list is for NetWare v3.x. The program files for NetWare v2.x are similar to those for NetWare v3.x

Table 15.5
Important Files in SYS:PUBLIC for NetWare v3.x

File name	Description
ALLOW.EXE	Enables user to view, edit, set, or modify IRM for a directory or a file.
ATTACH.EXE	Attaches to a server other than the one that you are logged in on—up to a maximum of eight servers.
CAPTURE.EXE	Redirects local printer output to a network printer. Used for single-user applications that print to the local printer only.
CASTOFF.EXE	Blocks the receipt of messages, except those sent by a supervisor through FCONSOLE.
CASTON.EXE	Enables the receipt of messages through the SEND command.
CHKVOL.EXE	Displays statistics on volume usage.

File name	Description
COLORPAL.EXE	Selects the color palettes to be used with NetWare graphic utilities.
DSPACE.EXE	Sets disk space restrictions for directories and network paths.
ENDCAP.EXE	Ends redirection of local printer output to network printer.
FCONSOLE.EXE	Monitors server utilization and performance statistics. (Limited in NetWare v3.x because these functions are performed by the MONITOR NLM.)
FILER.EXE	Manages files and directory rights, rights mask, and attributes.
FLAG.EXE	Sets file attributes.
FLAGDIR.EXE	Sets directory attributes.
GRANT.EXE	Grants rights to directories and files for users and groups.
LISTDIR.EXE	Lists all subdirectories below the current directory.
LOGIN.EXE	Authenticates users' request to log in to the server and executes the log-in.
LOGOUT.EXE	Logs out from the server.
MAKEUSER.EXE	Adds or deletes users from directives in a script file.
MAP.EXE	Assigns drive letters to network directories.
MENU.EXE	Runs menu script files.
NBACKUP.EXE.	Backs up server files to various backup devices.
NCOPY.EXE	Copies network files. More efficient than DOS COPY commands.
NDIR.EXE	Lists network information about directories and files. Similar to DOS DIR commands, but gives network-specific information on files.

continues

Table 15.5
Continued

File name	Description
NPRINT.EXE	Prints on network printers.
NVER.EXE	Lists NetWare version on server.
PCONSOLE.EXE	Configures and manages shared printers and queues.
PRINTCON.EXE	Creates and modifies print job configurations.
PRINTDEF.EXE	Configures form and printer device driver information.
PSTAT.EXE	Displays printer status.
PSC.EXE	Controls/displays status of network printers.
PSERVER.EXE	Sets up a dedicated print server at a workstation.
PURGE.EXE	Removes files erased in the current log-in session.
REMOVE.EXE	Removes a user or group from the list of trustees for a path.
RENDIR.EXE	Renames a directory.
REVOKE.EXE	Revokes directory or file rights for a user or group.
RIGHTS.EXE	Displays effective rights of a user for directories and files.
RPRINTER.EXE	Sets up a remote nondedicated printer.
SALVAGE.EXE	Recovers deleted files.
SEND.EXE	Sends a message to other stations.
SESSION.EXE	Manages session parameters, such as drive mappings, and sends messages.
SETPASS.EXE	Sets or changes user passwords.
SETTTS.EXE	Sets transaction tracking level.
SLIST.EXE	Displays a list of file servers on the network.
SMODE.EXE	Sets the search mode of an executable file.

File name	Description
SYS$ERR.DAT	System error data file.
SYS$HELP.MSG	System help data files.
SYS$MSG.DAT	System message data files.
SYSCON.EXE	Manages user accounts and groups.
SYSTIME.EXE	Displays server time and synchronizes workstation time to server time.
TLIST.EXE	Displays a directory's trustee list.
USERDEF.EXE	Provides a menu-driven front end to MAKEUSER.
USERLIST.EXE	Lists users logged in.
VERSION.EXE	Displays version of utility.
VOLINFO.EXE	Displays real-time volume utilization.
WHOAMI.EXE	Displays information about your connection.

SYSTEM Directory

The SYSTEM directory contains the NetWare operating system files and system programs. Access to SYS:SYSTEM must be limited to system administrators and special management utilities that may need to access SYS:SYSTEM. The print spooler queues are implemented as subdirectories in the SYS:SYSTEM directory. Certain types of print servers may therefore need access to these directories.

For a description of the utilities in the SYSTEM directory, refer to the NetWare *Supervisor's Manual*. A detailed description of these utilities is beyond the scope of this book, but table 15.6 lists the more important SYS:SYSTEM files for your reference. The list is for NetWare v3.x. The program files for NetWare v2.x are similar to the NetWare v3.x files. The fundamental difference is that NetWare v3.x SYSTEM directories contain NLMs, and NetWare v2.x SYSTEM directories contain VAPs.

The SYSTEM directory for NetWare v3.x also contains a subdirectory called ETC that contains configuration files and tables for TCP/IP support.

Table 15.6
Important Files in SYS:SYSTEM for NetWare v3.x

File name	Description
ACONSOLE.EXE	Provides remote console connection over an asynchronous link.
ATOTAL.EXE	Generates an accounting summary of server resource usage.
AUTOEXEC.NCF	Contains system configuration information. See NetWare Command File (NCF) in Chapter 8.
BCONSOLE.EXE	(Btrieve console.) Executes Btrieve operations and observes Btrieve status.
BINDFIX.EXE	Attempts to repair damaged bindery (system database).
BINDREST.EXE	Restores bindery to previous state. Used when BINDFIX does not work.
BROUTER.EXE	Routes Btrieve record manager requests.
BSTART.NCF	Loads Btrieve NLM from the server console—a NetWare Command File.
BSTOP.NCF	Unloads Btrieve NLM—a NetWare Command File.
BTRIEVE.NLM	Provides Btrieve Record Management service.
CLIB.NLM	Supports utilities requiring C library routines and functions.
DCB.DSK	Disk Coprocessor Board driver NLM.
DOSGEN.EXE	Creates boot image files for diskless stations.
EDIT.NLM	Text editor NLM that can be run from server console.
INSTALL.NLM	Installs and configures v3.x NOS.
IPCONFIG.NLM	NLM for configuring IP addressing.
IPXS.NLM	STREAMS interface to IPX protocols.

File name	Description
ISADISK.DSK	ISA disk driver NLM.
MAC.NAM	Macintosh file system Name Space support NLM.
MATHLIB.NLM	Math library routine interface for the Intel 80387 coprocessor.
MATHLIBC.NLM	Math library routine emulation of the Intel 80387 coprocessor. Used if coprocessor does not exist.
MONITOR.NLM	Monitors server resources.
NET$REC.DAT	Contains bindery data.
NMAGENT.NLM	Manages multiple LAN drivers on server.
PAUDIT.EXE	Displays server accounting log.
PROTO.NLM	Views protocol identification numbers.
PSERVER.NLM.	Loads printer server on file server.
REMOTE.NLM	Monitors server console remotely in Remote Management Facility.
ROUTE.NLM	Supports source routing for IBM Token Ring bridges.
RS232.NLM	Support for remote console connection over an asynchronous link.
RSETUP.EXE	Creates custom server boot disk to support remote server control.
RSPX.NLM	Supports remote management of server console.
SECURITY.EXE	Reports security holes on the server.
SNMP.NLM	SNMP Agent on server.
SPXCONFG.NLM	Provides configuration of SPX parameters.
SPXS.NLM	SPX protocol for STREAMS.
STREAMS.NLM	Implements STREAMS protocol. Used as a common transport interface for multiple transport protocols.

continues

Table 15.6
Continued

File name	Description
SYS$ERR.DAT	System error message file.
SYS$ERR.LOG	System error log file.
SYS$MSG.LOG	System messages file.
TCPIP.NLM	Implements TCP/IP protocols on NetWare v3.x server.
TLI.NLM	Transport Layer Interface NLM. Common transport interface.
TCPCONFG.NLM	Configures TCP/IP.
TOKENRPL.NLM	Enables remote boot for IBM Token Ring network boards.
UPGRADE.EXE	Upgrades from NetWare v2.x to NetWare v3.x.
UPS.NLM	Implements the software link between server and UPS (Uninterrupted Power Supply) device.
VREPAIR.NLM	Repairs minor volume problems.
WSUPDATE.EXE	Updates shell files from the file server.

MAIL Directory

The MAIL directory contains the login scripts for the users who are defined on the NetWare server. Every object on the system, including users, has a unique internal hexadecimal ID, called the *user ID*. This user ID is an internal reference variable used to keep track of user information in the system bindery. When a user account is created on the server, a subdirectory with the same name as the user ID also is created in the SYS:MAIL directory. Access rights to the user ID directory in SYS:MAIL are set up automatically. The user ID subdirectory contains the user's login script in a file called LOGIN. If a login script file is changed, NetWare keeps a copy of the old login script, in a file called LOGIN.BAK.

Earlier versions of NetWare distributed an electronic mail program called MAIL. The electronic mail messages were stored in the user ID subdirectory in SYS:MAIL along with the user's login script. Distribution of the electronic mail program was discontinued, but the name of the directory MAIL remains.

Command Reference: On-Line Help by Means of the HELP Utility

Because all NetWare commands and utilities are found in the SYS:PUBLIC or SYS:SYSTEM directory, tables 15.5 and 15.6 are a summary of the command reference. By using this table and the NetWare HELP utility, you can learn about any command.

For instance, if you want to learn about the NetWare command PSC, perform the following steps. (The screens shown are for a NetWare 3.11 server, but the help utility is similar for NetWare 2.2. The help utility was written using NFOLIO from Folio Corporation of Provo, Utah.)

1. Log in to the server and type:

    HELP

    A screen similar to figure 15.7 appears.

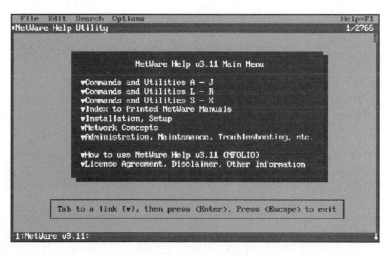

Figure 15.7:
NetWare 3.11 Help Main Menu.

2. Press Tab to get to the first link help option. Then use the arrow keys to move the cursor to the desired help section and press Enter. For getting information about the command PSC, for instance, move to the `Commands and Utilities L - R` option and press Enter (see fig. 15.8).

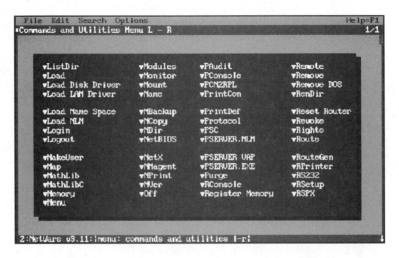

Figure 15.8:
NetWare 3.11 Commands and Utilities Menu L - R.

3. Now use Tab and the arrow keys to position the cursor on the command you want to learn about, and press Enter.

   To find out more about the PSC command, for example, select it by moving the cursor to the `PSC` option, and then press Enter. The main PSC help screen appears, as shown in figure 15.9.

4. You can explore a number of items in detail on this screen. If you select the Parameters field, for example, a screen displays that shows you how to format parameters to the PSC command (see fig. 15.10).

5. If you select the `Notes` option from the PSC main help screen, the screen illustrated in figure 15.11 is displayed.

6. If you select the `Examples` option from the PSC main help screen, the information illustrated in figure 15.12 is displayed.

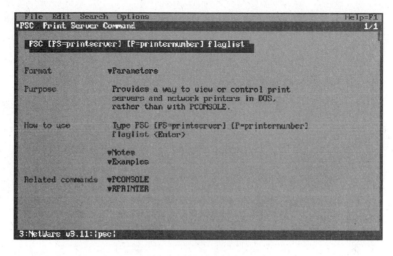

Figure 15.9:
The NetWare 3.11 PSC (Print Server Command) screen.

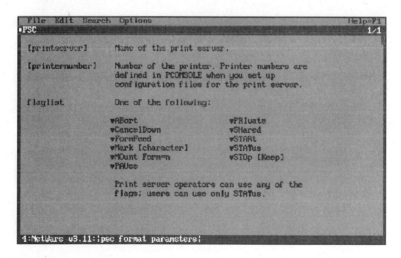

Figure 15.10:
The NetWare 3.11 PSC format parameters screen.

The preceding screen shows you many examples. If you want to see how to use PSC to view the status of all printers, select the `View status of all printers` option. Figure 15.13 shows the information that appears.

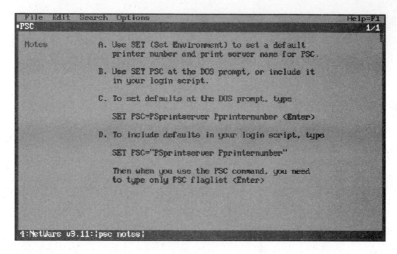

Figure 15.11:
The NetWare 3.11 PSC Notes screen.

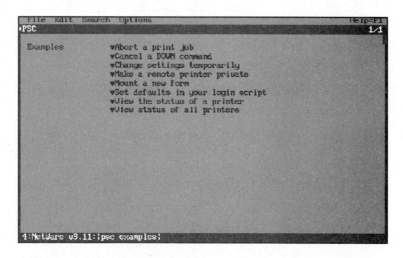

Figure 15.12:
The NetWare 3.11 PSC Examples screen.

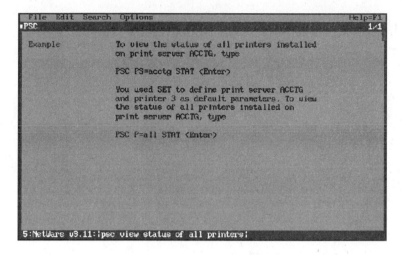

Figure 15.13:
The NetWare 3.11 PSC view status of all printers screen.

7. Press Esc to return to the main PSC help menu. Notice the links to Related Commands near the bottom of the screen display (in this case, RCONSOLE and RPRINTER). You can examine these commands by using HELP.

8. To exit HELP, press Esc several times.

As you can see, with only a few keystrokes, you can obtain a wealth of information about PSC or any command.

Applications Directories

In the previous section, you learned about the standard directory structure created by NetWare during installation. When you want to install applications or user's directories, you must define directories to keep these applications separate from the NetWare NOS files. This separation results in easier maintenance and upgrades of NetWare and application programs.

Directory Organization for Few Applications on Server

Figure 15.14 shows application directories installed directly under the root directory of a volume. For instance, the network version of WordPerfect 5.1 can be installed in a directory called SYS:WP51; dBASE can be installed in a directory called SYS:DBASE. This approach works only when relatively few applications are installed on the server. If many applications are installed on the server, the root directory becomes cluttered with a large number of directories. If you keep the number of directories in the root small, the directory structure is easy to comprehend and manage.

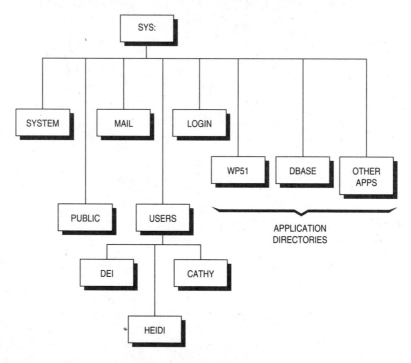

Figure 15.14:
Directory organization for few applications on server.

An application directory can have many subdirectories for data and programs, or a single application directory can store all programs and data.
Applications may require a specific structure for the application directory.

Directory Organization for Many Applications on Server

When many applications are installed on the server, a two-level structure
for defining application directories is best. Similar applications are grouped
together in a directory named to reflect the specific kind of application.
Figure 15.15 illustrates this concept.

Consider a server that needs more than one word processor, for instance. A
class directory called SYS:WP can be created, within which individual application directories for the separate word processors can be created. Word
Perfect 6.0 can be installed in the directory SYS:WP/WP60, Microsoft Word
can be installed in the directory SYS:WP/WORD, and a text editor such as
Brief can be installed in SYS:WP/BRIEF.

Another example is a software developer who uses C compilers from different vendors. The class directory can be SYS:C. Microsoft C compiler can be
installed in the directory SYS:C/MSC, and the Borland C++ compiler can be
installed in SYS:C/BC.

In these examples, the volume SYS: is used for the application directories. If
other volumes are available, they also can be used to install applications. In
general, applications used simultaneously can be distributed across multiple
volumes. This improves performance because disk controller and device
electronics are not shared by all the applications. Some applications enable
you to store data files in more than one data directory. If frequently used
data files are stored on separate server physical disks, the application's
speed increases.

Other OS Applications: OS/2, Mac, and Windows

If the server supports more than one kind of workstation operating system,
you must keep the applications for the different operating systems separate.
This improves organization and makes installation and removal of applications on the server easier. Figure 15.16 shows a sample directory organization that has OS/2, DOS, Mac, and Windows applications installed on the
server. In many instances, a spreadsheet, such as Excel, also is installed for
different operating system platform types.

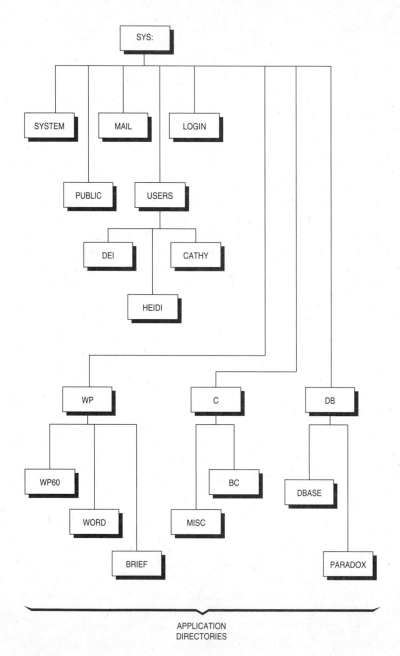

Figure 15.15:
Directory organization for many applications on server.

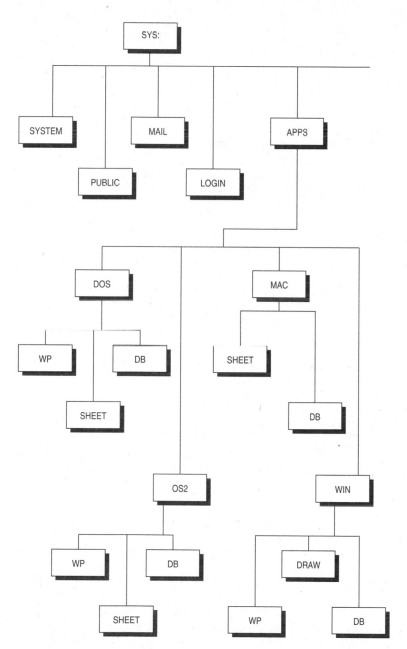

Figure 15.16:
Multiple OS application support on server.

Home Directory Organization

A *home directory* on the server disk stores a user's personal files. Users usually have unrestricted access to their home directories because the home directory is an extension of the local disk space at the user's workstation.

NetWare uses a default home directory structure of SYS:HOME (HOME is directly under SYS:). Users have subdirectories under the SYS:HOME directory named after their log-in names. With this approach, user TOM has a home directory of SYS:HOME/TOM. The home directory also can have a directory structure of SYS:USERS. This is a common name for home directories used by many operating systems. In this case, the user TOM has a home directory of SYS:USERS/TOM.

Figure 15.17 shows the home directories for a number of users. Within the home directories, users create subdirectories to organize their files.

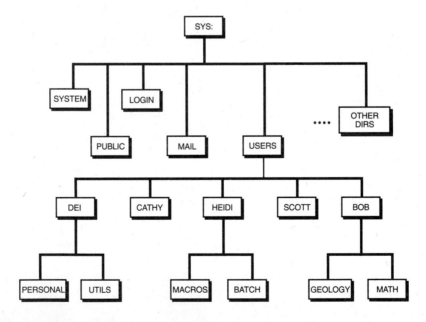

Figure 15.17:
Home directory organization on server.

The NetWare utility SYSCON creates home directories as part of a user account. See Chapter 10 for details on how to use SYSCON.

DOS Directories

A copy of the DOS program files should be kept on the server. This simplifies access to DOS programs when the user logs in to the server. You also should include the network directory that contains the DOS programs as one of the search drives so that DOS programs can be invoked from any directory.

Because many versions of DOS can be used by users on the network, Novell recommends that you use the directory structure shown in figure 15.18 to store DOS programs. To support this directory structure, NetWare defines a number of script variables shown in figure 15.18 by the % sign (see Chapter 14). These script variables are used to specify directories in the login script and are mapped into values as shown in figure 15.18. Thus the script variable %MACHINE can map into values IBM_PC or COMPAQ; the script variable %VERSION can map into version numbers such as V3.20, V3.31, V5.0. Depending on the DOS version and machine type, the appropriate network directory can be specified by using the generic script variables. The LONG MACHINE TYPE parameter in the NET.CFG workstations configuration file determines the value of script variables like %MACHINE (see Chapter 12).

Ordinarily, the network administrator strives to have one version of DOS for all users on the network. Conflicts between DOS versions and applications, and DOS versions tailored to the workstation hardware and specific DOS applications, make it difficult to have only one version of DOS. Under these circumstances, you can use the directory structure in figure 15.18.

If you use the scheme shown in figure 15.18, you must make sure to avoid license infringements. That is, you must have a license for each user who could use DOS workstations at any time.

File System Performance

Several factors can improve a disk subsystem's performance. These factors include optimum selection of disk block size, file caching, directory hashing and caching, and the use of Turbo FATs.

Disk Block Size

In NetWare v3.x, you have the option to select a disk block size different from the default. You select this block size at the time you define a volume by using INSTALL NLM. The disk block size values that are legal in NetWare v3.x are 4K (default), 8K, 16K, 32K, and 64K.

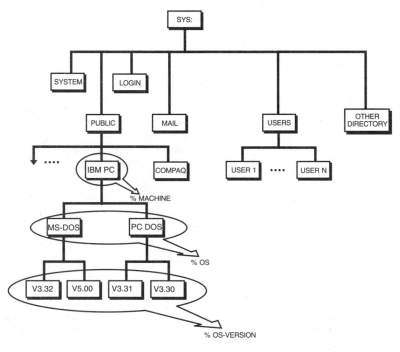

Figure 15.18:
DOS directory structure on server.

In a database consisting of a small number of very large data files, a large disk block size is best. Database operations typically are executed in a local region of a data file. If the disk block size is large, fewer blocks must be fetched compared to a volume that has a smaller disk block size. In addition, the fewer the disk blocks you have in a volume, the smaller the size of the FAT to keep track of them in RAM.

In a system that contains many files, large disk block size results in a higher proportion of unused disk space. In this situation, a smaller disk block size gives better space utilization.

Memory for File Caching and Directory Caching and Hashing

Server RAM left over after allocation has been made to the NOS is used for file caching. The larger the amount of RAM that is used in the server, the greater the amount of space that is left for file caching. Additional file cache results in better server performance. Directory hashing and caching are enabled by default, and they speed up directory access.

In NetWare v3.x, the SET command controls some of the parameters that affect file and directory caching. Chapter 9 discusses these parameters in greater detail.

Turbo FATs

If a file is more than 2M in size, and you flag it with an indexed attribute, a separate index table is built for every indexed file. These special index tables are called *Turbo FATs*. The FLAG command flags a file with an indexed attribute. NetWare v3.x automatically indexes files having over 64 regular FAT entries. The indexed file attribute can be used in NetWare v3.x but has no effect.

Disk Space Management

Because users share disk space on the server, you can limit disk space per user. In NetWare v2.x, you must enable the option to limit disk space during installation in NetWare v3.x. Disk-space limiting enables individual disk quotas to be assigned by using SYSCON or DSPACE utilities.

One reason to restrict disk space is to prevent a user from using an inordinate amount of disk space. Suppose that a user runs an application that has a software bug. This bug causes it to go in a loop while it writes to a data file. The data file can become large enough to consume all available disk space on the server and to prevent others from using the server's disk. In the NetWare v3.x, the SET command monitors volume usage.

NetWare v3.x SET Command for Volume Utilization

You can use the SET VOLUME command to set thresholds and warnings for volume utilization. These commands are as follows:

SET VOLUME LOW WARN ALL USERS

SET VOLUME LOW WARNING THRESHOLD

SET VOLUME LOW WARNING RESET THRESHOLD

The SET VOLUME LOW WARN ALL USERS command warns all users that the volume is almost full. The values can be set to either ON or OFF, but ON is the default. Some LAN managers turn this value to OFF so that the beginning network user is not confused by unfamiliar system messages. In this case, you must run the utility CHKVOL or VOLINFO for the server volumes on a daily basis.

Example:

```
SET VOLUME LOW WARN ALL USERS=OFF
```

The SET VOLUME LOW WARNING THRESHOLD command controls how many free disk blocks remain on a volume before NetWare issues a warning. To estimate this number, you must divide the desired free space threshold by the disk block size. The value for this parameter ranges from 0 to 100,000 blocks, with a default value of 256.

If you want to set the threshold to 1M, for a nondefault disk block size of 8K, for example, the number of free blocks is estimated by:

Free blocks = Free disk space/Disk block size = 1M/8K = 128

The SET command would be as follows:

```
SET VOLUME LOW WARNING THRESHOLD=128
```

For a disk block size of 4K (default), the free block count will be 1M/4K = 256—the default value.

The SET VOLUME LOW WARNING RESET THRESHOLD command determines how many disk blocks must be freed up before a second warning is issued. This parameter prevents repeated warning messages from being sent if the free space hovers around the limit established by SET VOLUME LOW WARNING THRESHOLD. When the first warning is issued (SET VOLUME LOW WARN ALL USERS), and the users reduce disk space to just below the threshold, you may not want another warning message to appear if the disk space utilization soon rises above the threshold again. This process of dipping below the threshold and then rising again can occur repeatedly, and a repeated warning message is very annoying to the user. The value for this parameter ranges from 0 to 100,000 blocks, with a default value of 256.

To set this threshold value to 256 blocks (1M for 4K size blocks), the command is as follows:

```
SET VOLUME LOW WARNING RESET THRESHOLD=256
```

These SET values can be recorded in the STARTUP.NCF file.

CHKVOL and VOLINFO

CHKVOL and VOLINFO commands monitor disk space. CHKVOL is a command-line utility similar to the DOS's CHKDISK utility, and it displays the results just once. As illustrated in figure 15.19, you can use CHKVOL to quickly find out how much disk space is available. VOLINFO is an interactive utility that displays disk utilization in real-time. VOLINFO monitors disk space and directory entries available on server volumes. You can change the time intervals at which the information is updated in the Available Options box (see fig. 15.20).

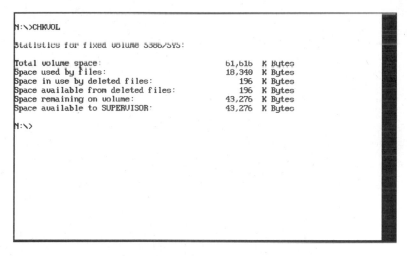

Figure 15.19:
The CHKVOL utility.

DSPACE

DSPACE is a disk space management utility that limits the maximum size of a directory and its subdirectories on a per user basis.

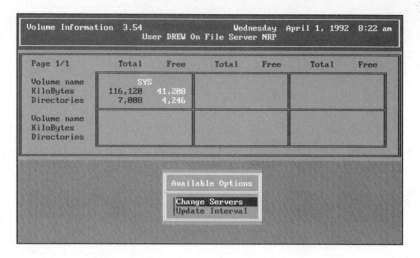

Figure 15.20:
The VOLINFO utility.

To invoke this utility perform the following steps:

1. Log in to a server as a SUPERVISOR, and type **DSPACE**.

2. Select User Restrictions. When a list of users appears, select the user that you want to work with. Then, when a list of volumes appears, select the volume that you want to work with.

3. A screen similar to the one shown in figure 15.21 appears:

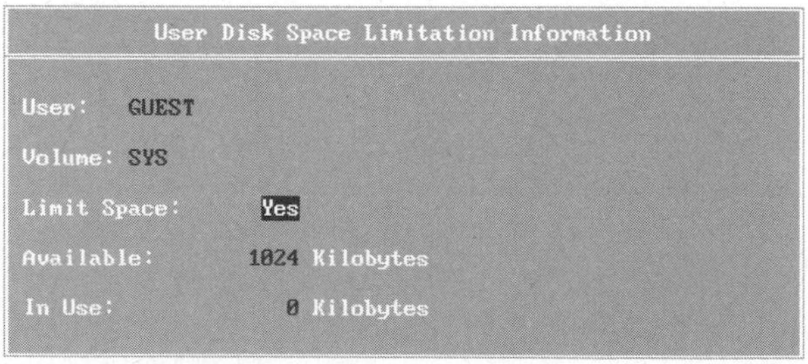

```
┌─────────────────────────────────────────────────┐
│      User Disk Space Limitation Information       │
├─────────────────────────────────────────────────┤
│                                                   │
│  User:    GUEST                                   │
│                                                   │
│  Volume:  SYS                                     │
│                                                   │
│  Limit Space:    Yes                              │
│                                                   │
│  Available:    1024 Kilobytes                     │
│                                                   │
│  In Use:          0 Kilobytes                     │
│                                                   │
└─────────────────────────────────────────────────┘
```

Figure 15.21:
User Disk Space Limitation Information screen.

The Limit Space field tells you if the disk space limitation is enabled for that user. The Available field tells you the current disk space restriction for the user, and the In Use field shows the amount of space used by the user.

4. From the Available Options menu, select Directory restrictions. (You may need to press Esc a few times to get this menu to appear.)

5. A window appears that contains the current directory. Enter the directory for which you want to perform the restriction, and press Enter. Or, use Ins to build the directory path one level at a time.

6. A screen similar to that shown in figure 15.22 appears with the following fields

   ■ The Path Space Limit specifies the minimum size limit for all the directories along the selected path. If a directory above the selected directory has a smaller space limit, that limit applies to the current directory.

   ■ The Limit Space field specifies if any restrictions exist on the current directory. Enter Yes for restriction or No for no restriction.

   ■ The Directory Space Limit specifies the space restriction on the selected directory.

   ■ The Currently Available field specifies the space currently available for the selected directory.

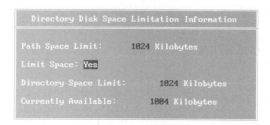

Figure 15.22:
Directory disk space limitation information.

SYSCON

The utility SYSCON restricts space on a per user basis. The steps to perform this task are as follows:

1. Log in to a server as a SUPERVISOR, and type **SYSCON**.

2. Select User Information and, when a list of users appears, select the user you want to work with. From the User Information window, select Volume/Disk Restrictions, and then select the volume that you want to restrict. A screen similar to figure 15.23 displays.

Figure 15.23:
User/Volume Disk Restrictions screen.

Change the Limit Volume Space? field from No to Yes, and specify the amount of disk space in kilobytes in the Volume Space Limit field. The Volume Space In Use field reports the space currently used by the user.

Rights Access

After a user successfully logs in to the server, NetWare controls access to directories and files on the server. In this section, NetWare v3.x rights security are discussed first. Because NetWare v3.x rights security is a superset of NetWare 2.2 security, you easily can understand both NetWare v3.x security and NetWare 2.2 security. Toward the end of this section, you learn the differences between NetWare v3.x and NetWare 2.2 security.

Trustee Rights

In NetWare, users are assigned rights to perform operations such as Read, Write, Create, and Erase in files in a directory. The user entrusted with these rights is called a *Trustee,* and the actual rights assigned are called *Trustee Assignment*—or TA.

A user can be given a trustee assignment explicitly. In other words, the trustee assignment can be given on an individual-user basis. To set individual rights for a large number of users, however, is very tedious and difficult to maintain. In addition, many users have similar needs; they access the same directories and files on the server. For instance, all engineers in the engineering department need access to the same directories. To help with the management and administration of users with similar needs, NetWare uses groups.

A *group* is a collection of network users who has the same access privileges to directories and files on the server. For instance, all engineers are members of a group called ENGINEERS. The group ENGINEERS can be given a trustee assignment in a manner similar to that for individual users. The difference is that all members of the group automatically inherit the trustee assignments for that group (see fig. 15.24). If new members are added to the engineering department, they are made members of the group ENGINEERS. If engineers leave the department, they are removed from the group ENGINEERS. This automatically removes the privileges for the user as a member of the group ENGINEERS.

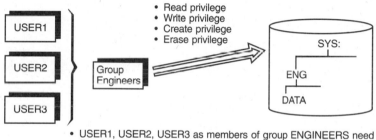

- USER1, USER2, USER3 as members of group ENGINEERS need Read, Write, Create, Erase privileges to SYS:ENG/DATA

- The group ENGINEERS is given Read, Write, Create, Erase trustee assignment to SYS:ENG/DATA

Figure 15.24:
Trustee assignment on a group basis. (Graphic courtesy of Learning Group International)

Most users are members of more than one group. They are at least members of a predefined group called EVERYONE. The total rights for a group is the sum of all the rights inherited by virtue of membership to all groups. Therefore, if a user has Read and Write TA (trustee assignment) to directory SYS:COMMON/DATA because of membership in group EVERYONE and Read, Create, and Erase TA to the same directory because of membership in group ENGINEERS, then the user has a TA of Read, Write, Create, Erase to SYS:COMMON/DATA—that is, the sum of the user's rights by virtue of membership to groups EVERYONE and ENGINEERS. Groups and their membership are defined through the NetWare utility SYSCON.

Directory Rights and File Rights

Table 15.7 shows the NetWare v3.x directory rights, and table 15.8 shows the differences between NetWare v3.x and pre-NetWare 2.2 rights. NetWare 2.2 rights are similar to NetWare v3.x rights except that NetWare 2.2 does not have supervisory rights.

Table 15.7
NetWare Directory Trustee Rights

Name	Description
S*	*Supervisory* rights to all directory/subdirectories/files
R	*Read* rights to open files in a directory, read contents, and execute
W	*Write* rights to open and write (modify) contents of files
C	*Create* rights to create files and subdirectories in a directory
E	*Erase* rights to delete a directory, its files, and its subdirectories
M	*Modify* rights to change directory and file attributes and rename
F	*File scan* rights to view names of subdirectories and files
A	*Access Control* rights to other users, modify trustee rights, and IRM

* NOTE: NetWare 2.2 does not have supervisory rights.

Table 15.8
Comparison Between NetWare v3.x and Pre-NetWare 2.2 Rights

v3.x	pre 2.2	Comments
S		No equivalent concept of supervisory rights in pre-NetWare 2.2
R	R O	Read includes opening and writing to a file in NetWare 3.2

v3.x	pre 2.2	Comments
W	W O	Write includes opening and writing to a file in NetWare v3.x
C	CP	Parental rights eliminated in NetWare v3.x and 2.2
E	DP	Parental rights eliminated in NetWare v3.x; name different
M	M	Modify is same in pre-NetWare 2.2 and NetWare v3.x
F	S	Names different; concept is same
A		Closest concept in pre-NetWare 2.2 is parental rights

The Read and Write rights in table 15.7 enable the user to read and write files in a directory. The user needs both of these rights to perform updates on files in a directory. Reading and writing also imply that the user has a right to open files in a directory. Earlier versions of NetWare (pre-NetWare 2.2) had an explicit Open right that always had to be set to do anything useful with a file. Newer versions of NetWare do not have an explicit Open right—it is implied by the Read and Write rights.

The User needs the Create and Erase rights to create and remove files and subdirectories. Modify rights can be used to change file attributes. Without Modify rights, you cannot use NetWare commands, such as FLAG, to change file attributes.

The File Scan right enables a user to view names of files and subdirectories. If you do not want a user to see file names in a directory, you can remove the File Scan right. With this right removed, the user can issue DIR or NDIR (NetWare DIR command) but cannot see the name of files in the directory.

The Access Control right enables other users to modify trustee rights and the IRM (Inherited Rights Mask). IRM is discussed a little later in the chapter. This means that a user who has Access Control rights to a directory can use a NetWare utility, such as FILER, to assign rights to other users for this directory. Access Control rights must be assigned only to trusted users.

Table 15.9 shows file level rights for NetWare v3.x. In NetWare v3.x Trustee Assignment can be made at the file level. This is unlike NetWare v2.x in which a TA can be made only at the directory level. NetWare v3.x gives you more control over files in a directory. In most situations, such a high level of control is not needed, but this control is nice to have if you do encounter a situation that needs it. Trustee rights for files are similar to those for directories, except that the scope of these rights is limited to an individual file. File trustee rights use the same symbols as directory trustee rights. The Create right for a file gives the user the right to salvage a file after it has been deleted. This is different from the Create right for a directory, which enables you to create files and subdirectories in a directory.

Table 15.9
NetWare v3.x File Trustee Rights

Name	Description
S	*Supervisory* rights to all rights to the file
R	*Read* rights to open a file, read contents, and execute the program
W	*Write* rights to open and write (modify) contents of a file
C	*Create* rights to salvage a file after the file has been deleted
E	*Erase* rights to delete a file
M	*Modify* rights to change a file's attributes and rename the file
F	*File Scan* rights to view name of a file and its full pathname
A	*Access Control* rights to modify file's trustee assignments and IRM

You can determine Trustee Assignments by using the utilities SYSCON and FILER or the command-line utilities GRANT and REVOKE. You also can use a batch utility for creating users called MAKEUSER to assign TA. SYSCON and MAKEUSER are discussed in Chapter 10.

The following examples illustrate the use of the command-line utilities GRANT and REVOKE.

To give user BALI a Trustee Assignment of Read, Write, Create, Erase, and File Scan to directory SYS:WP/DATA, type the following command:

```
GRANT R W C E F FOR SYS:WP/DATA TO BALI
```

To remove from user MOTI the Trustee Assignment of Write, Create, and Erase for directory SYS:WP/DATA type:

```
REVOKE   W  C  E   FOR SYS:WP/DATA FROM MOTI
```

Inherited Rights Mask

In NetWare v3.x, the *Inherited Rights Mask* (IRM) is the filter that blocks the inheritance of rights from parent directories. NetWare v3.x assigns an IRM to each subdirectory and file.

When a user creates a new directory (or file), the maximum potential rights that it can inherit from the parent directory are all rights. That is, the Inherited Rights Mask is [SRWCEMFA]. (The individual letters in the square brackets represent the first letter of the individual right.) The IRM can be restricted to limit the effective rights a user has to a directory (or file).

You can use the NetWare utility FILER or the command-line utility ALLOW to modify the Inherited Rights Mask.

The following example illustrates the use of the ALLOW command. To see the IRM for a directory for the user KIPLING, type the following:

```
ALLOW SYS:USERS/KIPLING
```

To assign an IRM of Read, Write, Create, File, Scan, and Access Control for user KIPLING, type:

```
ALLOW SYS:USERS/KIPLING TO INHERIT R W C F A
```

Effective Rights

Figure 15.25 illustrates how effective rights can be determined from Trustee Assignments and the Inherited Rights Mask by applying some *rules of combination*. These rules of combination are illustrated in figures 15.26 and 15.27 for directories and files.

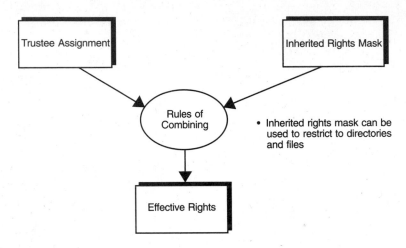

Figure 15.25:
Effective Rights and Inherited Rights Mask. (Graphic courtesy of Learning Group International)

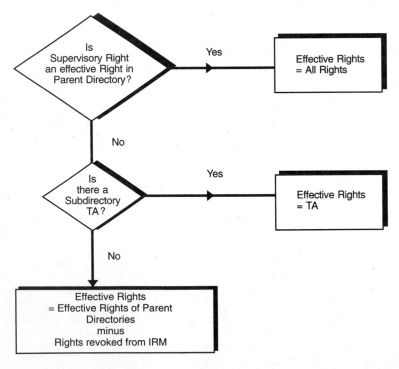

Figure 15.26:
Effective Rights for directories.

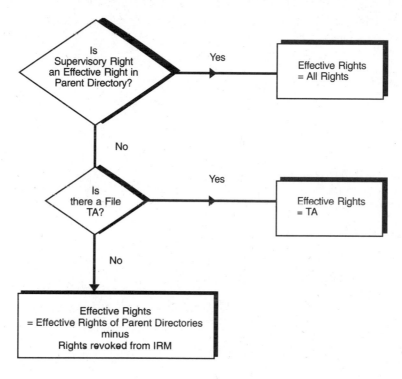

Figure 15.27:
Effective Rights for files.

At first glance, the rules of combination look complex, but after you study a few examples, you can appreciate the logic behind them. The examples that follow determine effective rights for directories.

Example 1: If no explicit Trustee Assignment has been granted to a subdirectory, the effective rights for the subdirectory are determined by the *logical* AND of the subdirectory's Inherited Rights Mask and the parent directory's effective rights. The effective rights of SUBDIR01 and the logical AND operation are shown in figure 15.28.

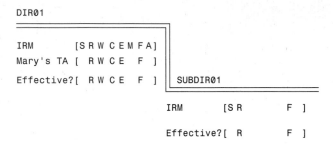

```
DIR01

IRM        [S R W C E M F A]
Mary's TA [ R W C E    F  ]
Effective?[ R W C E    F  ]   SUBDIR01

                              IRM        [S R        F  ]

                              Effective?[ R          F  ]
```

Figure 15.28:
No explicit trustee assignment in subdirectory. (Graphic courtesy of Learning Group International)

Example 2: If explicit Trustee Assignment has been granted to a subdirectory, the effective rights for the subdirectory are the same as the explicit Trustee Assignment regardless of the subdirectory's Inherited Rights Mask. In other words, an explicit TA overrides any IRM setting. The effective rights to subdirectory SUBDIR02 are shown in figure 15.29.

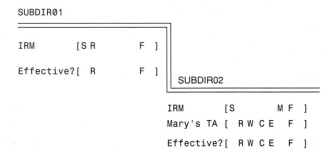

```
SUBDIR01

IRM        [S R        F  ]

Effective?[ R          F  ]   SUBDIR02

                              IRM        [S        M F  ]
                              Mary's TA [ R W C E    F  ]
                              Effective?[ R W C E    F  ]
```

Figure 15.29:
Trustee rights in subdirectory. (Courtesy of Learning Group International)

Example 3: If Supervisory Rights are granted to the parent directory, the user has all rights for the subdirectories and files regardless of a subdirectory's Trustee Assignment and Inherited Rights Mask (see fig. 15.30). (You must be careful when you assign Supervisory rights.)

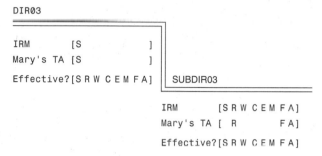

Figure 15.30:
Supervisory rights in parent directory. (Graphic courtesy of Learning Group International)

You can examine the effective rights by using the NetWare utility FILER or the command-line utility RIGHTS.

To view the effective rights for the current directory for the user issuing the command, type:

    RIGHTS

To view the effective rights of user ATHENA for directory SYS:USERS type:

    RIGHTS SYS:USERS/ATHENA

The rules of combination are designed so that effective rights flow down subdirectories. If no explicit TA is made, the effective rights are modified by the IRM. When an explicit TA is made, a new set of effective rights flows down subdirectories. This is different from pre-NetWare 2.2 versions in which Trustee Assignments rather than Effective Rights flow down subdirectories. When this happens, unexpected rights can be inherited by users when they create new subdirectories. The Inherited Rights Mask and the rules of combination were introduced in NetWare 2.2 and NetWare v3.x to overcome these problems. If you are familiar with NetWare v2.1x, the Inherited Rights Mask replaces the Maximum Rights Mask used in the earlier NetWare versions.

Attribute Security

Individual files or directories can be assigned attributes that override a user's effective rights (see fig. 15.31). USER1 has Read, Write, Create, Erase effective rights to SYS:PUBLIC/DATA. But the file is flagged with a Delete Inhibit attribute that prevents the file from being deleted even though the user has the Erase effective right for the directory.

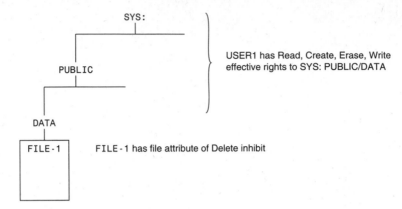

Figure 15.31:
Attribute security. (Graphic courtesy of Learning Group International)

Tables 15.10 and 15.11 illustrate directory attributes and file attributes. Use the FLAGDIR command to set directory attributes and the FLAG command to set file attributes.

Table 15.10
Directory Attributes for NetWare v3.x

Directory Attribute	Meaning
D	The *Delete Inhibit* attribute prevents directory from being erased.
H	The *Hidden* attribute hides a directory from a DOS DIR command.
P	The *Purge* attribute purges all files in directory when deleted.
R	The *Rename Inhibit* attribute prevents a directory from being renamed.
Sy	The *System* attribute similar to H; used for system directories.

Table 15.11
File Attributes for NetWare v3.x

File Attribute	Meaning
A	The *Archive Needed* attribute is automatically assigned to files modified after backups.
CI	The *Copy Inhibit* attribute restricts copy rights for Macintosh users.
DI	The *Delete Inhibit* attribute prevents file from being erased.
X	The *Execute Only* attribute prevents files from being copies; is permanent.
H	The *Hidden* attribute hides a file from a DOS DIR scan.
I	The *Indexed* attribute speeds access to large files; automatically assigned for files with over 64 FAT entries.
P	The *Purge* attribute purges a file when deleted.
Ra	The *Read audit* attribute audits reads to a file.
Ro	The *Read only* attribute cannot write to, erase, or rename files.
Rw	The *Read Write* attribute is the default setting for a file.
R	The *Rename Inhibit* attribute prevents a file from being renamed.
S	The *Sharable* attributes file can be used by more than one user.
Sy	The *System* attribute is similar to H; used for system files.
T	The *Transactional* attribute protects against incomplete operations on files.
Wa	The *Write audit* attribute audits writes to a file.

To set an attribute security of Sharable and Delete Inhibit, and to flag a file as Transactional, type:

```
FLAG FileName S D T
```

To place an attribute security on a directory so that all files in the directory are purged—that is, they cannot be recovered by the SALVAGE command after they are deleted—type:

```
FLAGDIR DirName P
```

SALVAGE and FILER

NetWare comes with two utilities to manage the file system—SALVAGE and FILER. SALVAGE restores files that have been deleted. In NetWare v2.x, SALVAGE has a command-line interface and can recover files that were deleted in the last delete command for the current log-in session. The NetWare v3.x SALVAGE is more flexible and enables the recovery of files that have been deleted but whose disk space has not been reallocated for other purposes.

The FILER utility can be used to change a user's rights to a file or a directory. FILER enables you to set a Trustee Assignment to a directory (or file) and to modify the Inherited Rights Mask. As mentioned earlier, the Trustee Assignment and the Inherited Rights Mask can be used to determine effective rights.

SALVAGE

NetWare 2.2's SALVAGE command enables you to select a volume and then recover files last deleted. NetWare v3.x's SALVAGE utility is more powerful and a superset of the NetWare 2.2's SALVAGE utility. This section discusses the NetWare v3.x SALVAGE utility.

The SALVAGE utility can be used to:

■ Recover or purge a file

■ Restore files

■ View/Recover deleted files

When SALVAGE is invoked from the command line, the Main Menu Options screen shown in figure 15.32 displays.

Figure 15.32:
NetWare 3.11 Salvage main menu options.

Salvage From Deleted Directories—recovers erased files from directories that do not exist.

Select Current Directory—enables you to change to another directory or volume/server to view the files that can be salvaged.

Set Salvage Options—enables you to change the way files are displayed on the screen. For example, you can display files sorted by deletion date, file size, file name, or owner name.

View/Recover Deleted Files—enables you to view files in the current directory. You can then recover or purge these files.

Recovered files are placed in the directory from which they were deleted. But if the directory has been deleted, the recovered files are placed in a hidden directory in the root called DELETED.SAV. NetWare currently does not track deleted directories, but it does track files by date and time. Because of this, you can have several versions of a file with the same name. If the file being recovered to a directory already exists, SALVAGE prompts you to rename the file being salvaged.

When you select View/Recover Deleted Files, the screen shown in figure 15.33 appears. The default pattern (*) is all files. Figure 15.34 shows a list of files in the SYS: directory. This list shows 11 salvageable files. When you highlight a file for recovery and press Enter, information appears that tells you when the file was deleted, when it was last modified, who the owner of the file was, and who deleted it (fig. 15.35). To restore the file choose Yes when the question Recover This File? appears. Notice that the screen in figure 15.34 shows several salvageable files with the same name BACKOUT.TTS.

Figure 15.33:
The NetWare 3.11 Salvage menu to specify files to be viewed for recovery.

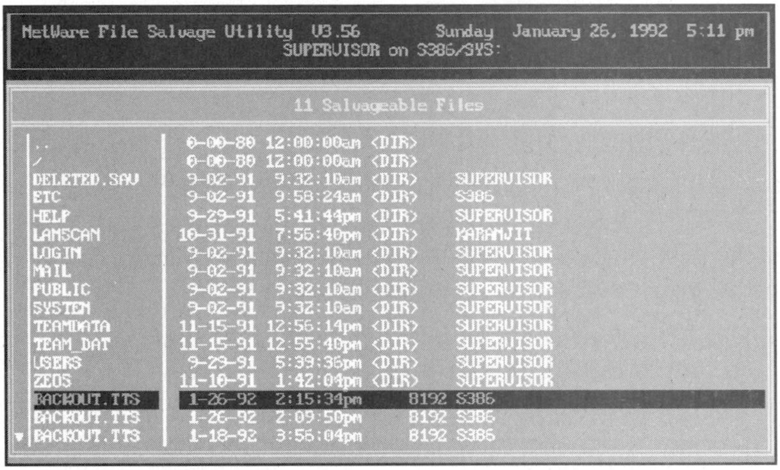

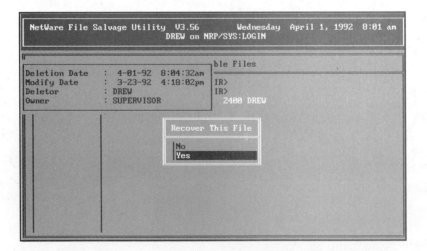

Figure 15.34:
The NetWare 3.11 Salvage screen showing files that can be recovered.

Figure 15.35:
The NetWare 3.11 Salvage screen showing details on a salvageable file.

To purge a file, highlight the file and press Del. Figure 15.36 shows the purge screen.

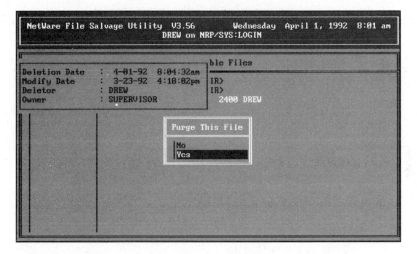

Figure 15.36:
The NetWare 3.11 Salvage purge screen.

The files to be viewed can be sorted by a number of options shown in figure 15.37. Use Set Salvage Options in the SALVAGE main menu to determine these options.

Figure 15.37:
The NetWare 3.11 Salvage file list options.

FILER

The FILER utility is used to control volume, directory, and file information, to change directories, and to set file security.

To invoke the utility, type **FILER**. Figure 15.38 shows the screen that appears. The main options are briefly explained in the following list:

Figure 15.38:
FILER main menu.

Current Directory Information—displays information about a directory such as:

Creation date

Directory owner

Inherited Rights Mask

Maximum Rights Mask (pre-NetWare 2.2)

Trustee Assignments

Effective Rights

Directory Contents—shows information on files and subdirectories for the current directory. Your effective rights determine which files and directories you can see.

Select Current Directory—enables you to change the current directory from FILER.

Set Filer Options—enables you to change the defaults for Directory Contents.

Volume Information—enables you to view the following information on the volume on which the current directory is located:

Total size of volume

Free space on volume

Maximum number of directories allowed

Unused directory entries

Figure 15.39 shows the screen that appears when you select Current Directory Information from the FILER main menu. If you can highlight a field, you can change the field.

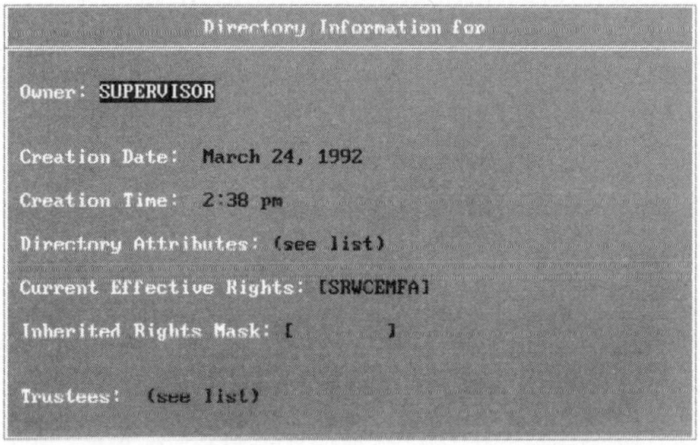

Figure 15.39:
FILER directory information.

On the screen in figure 15.39, the following fields can be changed:

Owner

Creation Date

Creation Time

Directory Attributes

Inherited Rights Mask

Trustees

When FILER runs on pre-NetWare 2.2 versions, it displays the Maximum Rights Mask information instead of the Inherited Rights Mask.

To change directory rights for a current directory, select the Directory Attributes field, and press Enter. A list of Current Attributes displays. To add an attribute, press Ins; to delete an attribute, highlight it, and press Del. Figure 15.40 shows the list of directory attributes that can be added to SYS: directory. Table 15.10 describes these attributes.

The Inherited Rights Mask field can be changed in a manner similar to the Directory Attributes. Figure 15.41 shows the screen that appears after you highlight this field and press Enter and Ins. The rights displayed were discussed earlier in this chapter.

Figure 15.40:
FILER Setting directory rights.

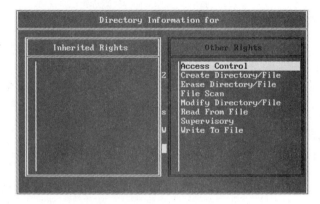

Figure 15.41:
FILER Setting Inherited Rights Mask.

The Trustees field can be used to change the trustees (users or groups) assigned to the directory. Figure 15.42 shows the screen that displays after you highlight this field and press Enter and Ins. The list of users and groups that can become trustees to this directory appears.

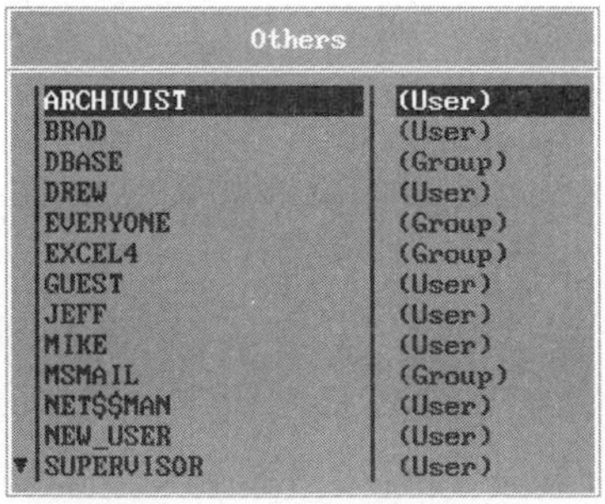

Figure 15.42:
FILER Setting trustees.

The Directory Contents option on the FILER Available Topics menu can be used to display a list of the subdirectories and files that are contained by the current directory. Figure 15.43 shows a list of subdirectories and files that was displayed by selecting Directory Contents.

```
                        Directory Contents
  APPS                              (subdirectory)
  ETC                               (subdirectory)
  LOGIN                             (subdirectory)
  MAIL                              (subdirectory)
  MSMAIL                            (subdirectory)
  NET_UTIL                          (subdirectory)
  PUBLIC                            (subdirectory)
  SYSTEM                            (subdirectory)
  TNA                               (subdirectory)
  USERS                             (subdirectory)
  ACCESSOR.APP                      (file)
  APPS.APP                          (file)
  MAIN.APP                          (file)
  TREEINFO.NCD                      (file)
▼ TTS$LOG.ERR                       (file)
```

Figure 15.43:
FILER Directory Contents.

To manage subdirectories, highlight the subdirectory name, and press Enter. This action displays the Subdirectory Options menu shown in figure 15.44. Selections in this box enable you to copy, move, and view subdirectories as well as enter subdirectory rights. This menu also has the Make This Your Current Directory option, which is an easy way to change FILER's current directory.

```
            Subdirectory Options
  Copy Subdirectory's Files
  Copy Subdirectory's Structure
  Make This Your Current Directory
  Move Subdirectory's Structure
  View/Set Directory Information
  Who has rights here
```

Figure 15.44:
FILER Subdirectory Options.

If a file is highligted in the Directory Contents box, FILER displays the menu shown in figure 15.45. This menu supports copying, moving, and viewing of files as well as setting file rights and file information.

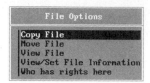

Figure 15.45:
FILER File Options.

Figure 15.46 shows the screen when Set Filer Options is selected from the FILER main menu. If you can highlight a field, you can change the field.

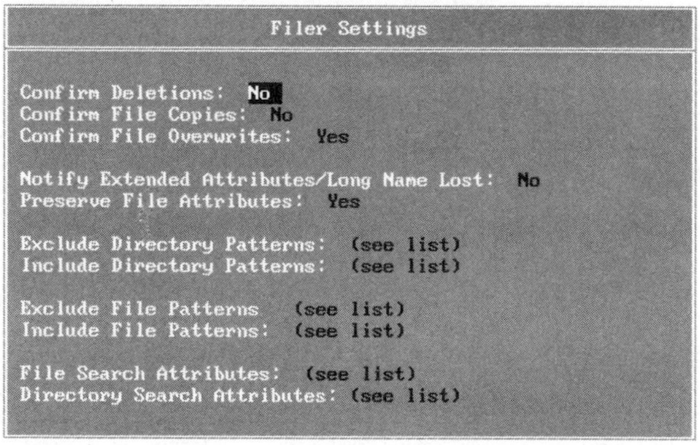

Figure 15.46:
FILER File Settings.

On this screen, the following options can be changed:

Confirm Deletions

Confirm File Copies

Confirm File Overwrites

Notify Extended Attributes/Long Name Lost

Preserve File Attributes

Exclude/Include Directory Patterns

Exclude/Include File Patterns

File/Directory Search Attributes

Figure 15.47 shows the screen that appears when you select Volume
Information from the FILER main menu.

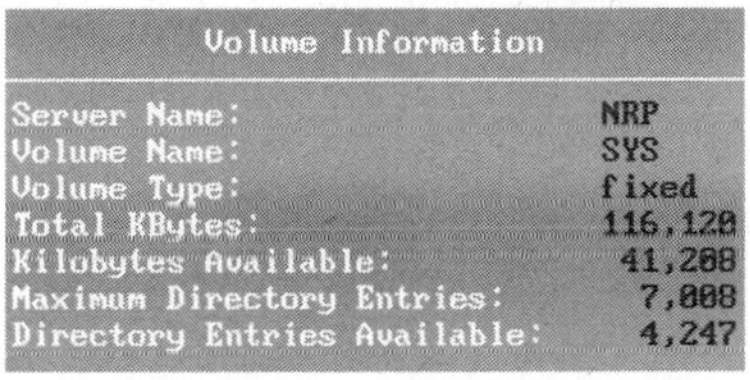

```
              Volume Information
Server Name:                   NRP
Volume Name:                   SYS
Volume Type:                   fixed
Total KBytes:                116,120
Kilobytes Available:          41,208
Maximum Directory Entries:     7,008
Directory Entries Available:   4,247
```

Figure 15.47:
FILER Volume Information.

Summary

In this chapter, you have learned about the organization of the NetWare file
system. The NetWare file system resides on physical hard disks at the server
and is, therefore, effected by the performance of the server hard disk. You
learned the characteristics of common server hard disks such as MFM, IDE,
ESDI, and SCSI. This chapter also covered the use of the NetWare file system
through network drives. Drive mappings and search drives were discussed,
as well as NetWare's HELP utility and file security system.

Printing

In this chapter, you learn the fundamental concepts behind NetWare printing. You learn about the NetWare printing model, how to install print servers and remote printers, and how to configure core print services. You also are shown how to use NetWare printing utilities. As in previous chapters, some of the more important and intricate steps of network printing are covered in several examples.

Understanding NetWare Printing

NetWare enables a printer to be shared by several users. An entire print job must be completed before another can start; otherwise, you get unreadable output consisting of characters from different print jobs. To be printed in a serial fashion, the jobs might have to wait in a queue.

NetWare enables users to share printers attached either to servers or workstations. Figure 16.1 shows a simple model for printing to a network printer attached to the file server. In the case of intelligent print devices such as the HP LaserJet III Si, the printer can be attached directly to the network because it has the network interface and processing power to participate as a station on the network.

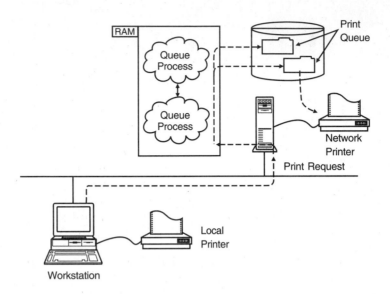

Figure 16.1:
Network printer attached to the file server.

In earlier versions of NetWare, the only way a printer could be shared was to attach it to a server. Up to five printers could be attached in this manner. This type of configuration is called *core print services*. Core print services still are available in NetWare v2.2, but NetWare v2.2 uses a more flexible approach that enables most of the configuration to be done by console commands.

In earlier versions of NetWare (version 2.15 and below), the only way to configure the core print services was to bring down the server and run NETGEN in the custom mode, and then select Printer Options from the Miscellaneous Options box. It was difficult to manage NetWare Core Printing Services, so many outside vendors have produced utilities to fill this gap. These products work in conjunction with the NetWare printing mechanism and provide many useful features.

With the release of NetWare v3.x and NetWare v2.2, a more flexible technique has been added that enables you to configure print servers at the server, a bridge, or a dedicated print server PC.

The print server configurations that currently are available in NetWare are as follows:

Print server VAP

Print server NLM

Dedicated print server at workstation

Nondedicated print server at workstation

Core print services

These print server configurations are examined in the sections that follow.

NetWare printing requests can be made from the workstation in several ways:

Using NPRINT

Using PRINTCON

Using CAPTURE and ENDCAP

NetWare-aware applications

Figure 16.2 also shows these methods.

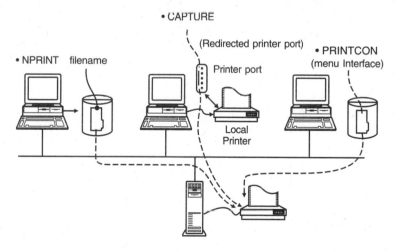

Figure 16.2:
Common methods of printing from workstations.

In each of these methods, the data to be printed is directed from the work-station to a queue on the connected server. A print server process services the queue and directs the print job to a local printer or a remote printer (see fig. 16.3).

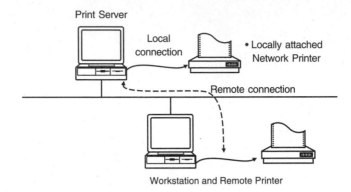

Figure 16.3:
Network printers can be local or remote.

Using Local and Network Printers

Figure 16.4 shows a network that has a combination of local and network printers. Local printers can be used only by the workstations to which they are attached. Network printers can be shared by more than one user on the network.

After a print job leaves a workstation, it is stored temporarily in a print queue at the file server, and then is sent to the print server. If the print server is on a different machine than the file server, the print job is sent from the queue on the file server across the network to the printer. Figure 16.5 illustrates this concept.

Print Queues

Every print job sent to a network printer is sent to a print queue on the file server first. The queue stores the print job temporarily until the network printer is ready.

The print queues are created as subdirectories on the file server under the SYS:SYSTEM directory. The print jobs are stored as files in the print queue subdirectory. After the print job is completed, the file containing the print job is removed.

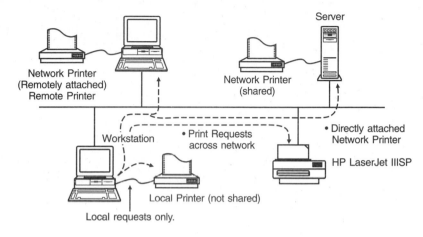

Figure 16.4:
Local and network printers.

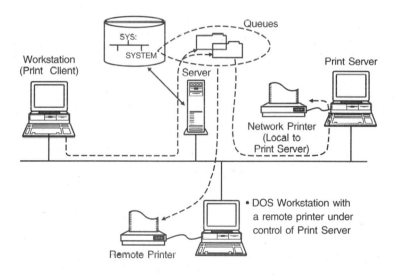

Figure 16.5:
Routing print jobs from a print queue to a printer through a print server.

Print queues must be created by using the PCONSOLE utility or the
NetWare 2.2 QUEUE command, and they must be created before defining a
print server. Before queues can be created on a NetWare 2.2 server, core
printing services must be installed by the INSTALL program.

The important concept to remember is that print queues are serviced by print servers; a *logical association* or *assignment* exists between a print queue and printers defined by the print server. The print server also can be considered a queue server because it prints jobs in the queue.

For the sake of simplicity and ease of management, it often is best to keep this logical association between a queue and a printer on a one-to-one basis, as shown in figure 16.6. Other types of logical associations, such as many-to-one, one-to-many, or many-to-many, also are possible. These are illustrated in figures 16.7 and 16.8.

Figure 16.6:
One-to-one queue-to-printer assignment.

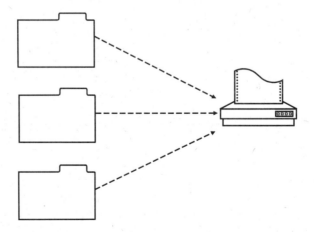

Figure 16.7:
Many-to-one queue-to-printer assignment.

In complex logical associations, you might need to use the *queue priority feature*. When a printer is assigned to a queue through PCONSOLE, you can select a priority number, from 1 to 10, which determines the order in which the queue is serviced. Figure 16.9 shows a many-to-one printer setup in which queues are assigned at different priorities. The higher priority queue is serviced first, and the lower priority queues are serviced only when no print jobs are in the higher priority queues.

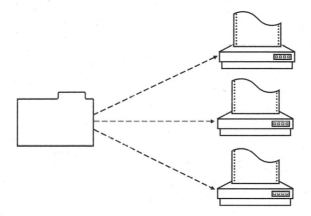

Figure 16.8:
One-to-many queue-to-printer assignment.

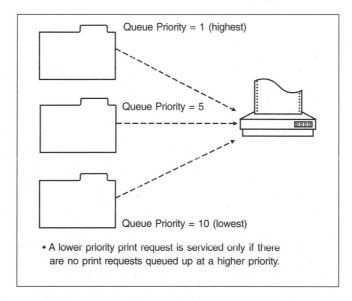

Figure 16.9:
Queue priorities.

It is best to keep a one-to-one logical association between print queues and printers; that is, one print queue is serviced by one printer. Print queues and print servers should be given names that make it easy to identify this logical association. Also, the names selected must be indicative of the type of print jobs associated with print queues and print servers.

Queue Operators and Queue Users

Queues are managed by queue operators. Queue operators can perform the following tasks:

> Assign other users to be queue operators
>
> Edit a print job in the queue
>
> Delete a print job, even while it is being printed
>
> Modify queue status of the print job
>
> Change the order in which print jobs are printed from the normal *First Come First Serviced* (FCFS) basis

After a print queue is created, the user SUPERVISOR is automatically assigned as a queue operator, and members of the group EVERYONE are assigned as print queue users. This is the default setup and works well for small networks.

In larger networks, it might become necessary to delegate responsibility for managing queues to other users. The supervisor can assign other users as queue operators through the PCONSOLE utility.

Figure 16.10 shows a print queue assigned for the group engineers located on the second floor of a building. The queue is defined on a file server located on the second floor, and the print server that services this queue also is on the second floor. The printing device might use special print paper, and because you do not want all users on the network to print to the engineering print server, the queue users will be members of group ENGINEERING and not group EVERYONE. These changes can be made by using the PCONSOLE utility.

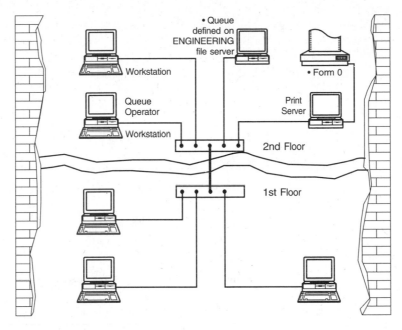

Figure 16.10:
Organizing printers for groups and users.

Only users who are designated as queue users can submit jobs to the print queue.

In larger networks, delegate responsibility to queue operators for a department and make only the members of this department queue users. The queue operators then can manage the print jobs for their department. The queue can be defined on the departmental file server. If such a server does not exist, the queue might have to be defined on a central file server.

Print Servers

A print server can be a workstation or a file server that has printers attached to its parallel or serial ports. A remote printer configuration also can be defined so that the print server sends the print job to a printer attached to another workstation. This workstation must be running the RPRINTER utility.

The print server takes the print jobs out of the queues assigned to it and sends them to the appropriate network printer. The print server must be created by using the PCONSOLE utility, *after* creating the print queues it will service. Before running the print server, you must use PCONSOLE to provide the following configuration information for the print server:

The queues that will be serviced by the printers

The file servers the print server must attach to service the queues

The print server operators

The printers that a print server will support

A print server can service queues from as many as eight file servers. If the print server must serve queues on other file servers, you must create a print-server user account on each file server so you can attach to them to access the queues on that file server.

Normally, any user can examine the status of a print server; you do not need special privileges to do this. If you want to print to a print server, however, you must be a *queue user* to insert your job in the queue serviced by the print server.

A *print server operator* is a special user who can perform the following tasks by using PCONSOLE:

Change queues serviced by the printer

Change queue priority

Attach print server to other file servers

Assign users to be notified if printer needs service

Change forms for the printer

Issue commands to the printer

Down the print server

A print server can specify and support up to 16 printers, including local and remote printers.

For local printers, you need to specify to which port the printer is connected. Up to five local printers can be defined. Most IBM PCs and compatibles can support up to three parallel printer ports (LPT1, LPT2, and LPT3) and two serial ports (COM1 and COM2). For serial printers, you must define the communication parameter settings in your printer configuration. These include the following:

Baud rate (bits per second)

Data bits (8 or 7 bits)

Stop bits (1 or 2)

Parity (Odd, Even, or None)

XON/XOFF (for flow control)

Remote printers are workstations that run a terminate-and-stay-resident (TSR) program called RPRINTER. A remote printer accepts the print jobs sent to it by the print server and directs them to the printer attached to the workstation.

NetWare Printing Utilities

Table 16.1 shows a list of NetWare's printing utilities with a brief summary of their functions. These utilities are used depending on the situation at hand. These situations are discussed later in this chapter.

Table 16.1
NetWare Printing Utilities and Commands

Utility	Function
PCONSOLE	Print Console. Creates or modifies print queues and print server definitions, controls network printing, and views information about network printing.
PRINTDEF	Printer Definition. Creates a database to store print device definitions and print forms.
PRINTCON	Printer Console. Uses information stored in PRINTDEF to create customized print job configurations that control the way a job is printed. These print job configurations can be used with CAPTURE, NPRINT, and PCONSOLE.

continues

**Table 16.1
Continued**

Utility	Function
CAPTURE	Captures local ports. Redirects output to local printer ports to printer queues on the file server. Used for applications and situations that do not have an understanding of printer queues.
ENDCAP	Ends capture of local printer ports. A printer attached to a local port can be used as a local printer.
SPOOL	Maps a network printer number to a printer queue to support older applications that print to a network printer number.
NPRINT	Network Print. Modeled after the DOS PRINT command but works with network print queues. Used from the command line to submit a job to a file to be printed on a network printer.
PSC	Print Server Command. Controls print server from the command line as opposed to using PCONSOLE.

Print servers can be set up in one of four major ways. These methods correspond to the programs PSERVER.EXE, PSERVER.NLM, PSERVER.VAP, and RPRINTER.EXE. These print server configurations are described in table 16.2. RPRINTER.EXE can be used only if a print server has been set up in one of the other three ways. Technically, RPRINTER.EXE is not a print server program because it relies on either PSERVER.EXE, PSERVER.NLM, or PSERVER.VAP to act as a print server. RPRINTER.EXE supports a remote printer connection to a print server.

Table 16.2
NetWare Print Server Programs and Configurations

Print Server	Function
RSERVER.EXE	Runs at a DOS workstation in the nondedicated mode. Workstation can be used for running applications while printing takes place in the background. Must be used in conjunction with the PSERVER program running at a workstation or server.
PSERVER.EXE	Runs on a dedicated workstation and converts the workstation to a dedicated print server.
PSERVER.NLM	Print Server NetWare Loadbale Module. Runs on a NetWare v3.x server that can act as a print server.
PSERVER.VAP	Print Server Value Added Process. Runs on a NetWare v2.2 server that can act as a print server.

One easy way to remember which print server program corresponds to which machine platform is to examine the extension of these file names. The EXE print server programs run at the workstation. PSERVER.EXE runs at a dedicated station and converts it to a print server as the name of the program suggests. The R in RPRINTER.EXE stands for *remote*. This program is called RPRINTER, not RSERVER as it often is mistakenly referred to. This underscores the point made earlier, that RPRINTER is not really a print server program. It relies on the other PSERVER programs to direct a print job to it. The program with an NLM extension is a NetWare loadable module and can run only on a NetWare v3.x server. The program with a VAP extension is a value added process and can run only with a NetWare v2.x server.

Installing Print Servers

Figure 16.11 shows an outline of the steps necessary to install a print server. In greater detail, these steps are as follows:

1. Create network print queues on the file server by using PCONSOLE.

2. Assign queue operators and queue users to the printer queue.

3. Create a print server definition.

4. Specify the file servers that have the queues that the print server will service.

5. Define printers used by the print server.

6. Assign queues to printers defined for the print server.

7. Optionally, set up printing for additional file servers.

8. Run one of the print server programs: PSERVER.EXE, PSERVER.VAP, or PSERVER.NLM on the appropriate hardware platform.

9. If a remote printer was assigned to the print server, run RPRINTER.EXE at the workstation (see fig. 16.11).

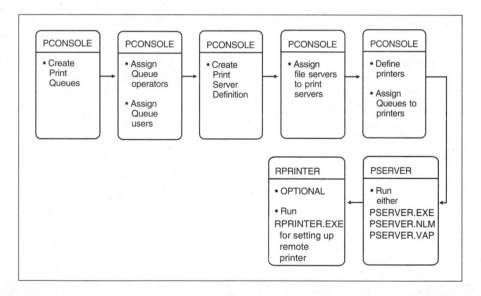

Figure 16.11:
Print server installation chart.

Using PRINTDEF for Printer and Form Definitions

PRINTDEF is used to define forms and printer definitions. The printer definitions include different modes of printer operation, such as letter quality, standard print mode, courier, and so on. The functions necessary to place the printer in a certain mode are defined in terms of escape code sequences that are sent to the printer.

NetWare comes with standard printer definitions for the major brands of printers. You can import and include them in the printer definition database, as follows:

1. Log in as a supervisor to a NetWare server. (This exercise shows the screens for a NetWare v3.11 server.) Type **PRINTDEF** to invoke the PRINTDEF utility. A screen similar to the one in figure 16.12 appears.

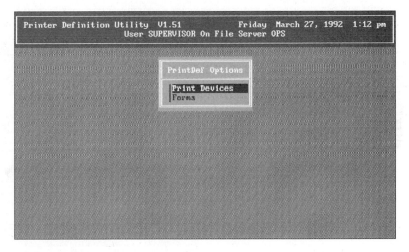

Figure 16.12:
The PrintDef Options box.

2. Highlight the Forms option and press Enter. A screen showing a list of forms that have been defined appears (see fig. 16.13).

Figure 16.13:
The Forms box.

3. The screen shows a form that already has been defined. To add a new form, press Ins. A Form Definition box similar to the one shown in figure 16.14 displays.

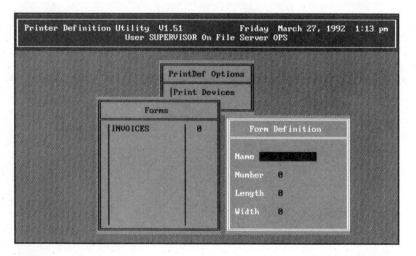

Figure 16.14:
Form Definition box.

4. Use the cursor keys to enter the following values:

      Name of form

      Form number

Length of form in number of lines per page

Width of form in number of characters per line

After entering the name of the form, press Esc and answer Yes to save the changes.

The new form that has been added appears (see fig. 16.15).

Figure 16.15:
The Forms box.

5. Press Esc to go back to the PrintDef Options list. You now are finished creating a new form that can be used later on.

NetWare comes with several printer device definitions for most standard printers. The printer definition you want probably has already been defined in the *Printer Definition Files* (PDF) that can be found in SYS:PUBLIC. The PDF files are easily recognizable because they have a PDF extension. Even if you want to create a new printer definition file, you can almost always start with an existing PDF file and customize it to suit your needs.

6. From the PrintDef Options box, select the `Print Devices` option. The Print Device Options box is displayed (see fig. 16.16).

The `Edit Print Devices` option can be used for editing an existing definition. It also can be used for viewing an existing definition. The `Import Print Device` option can be used to insert a previously exported printer definition into the printer database. The `Export Print Device` option can be used to save a printer definition in the database to an external PDF file that can be used later on for importing to another printer definition database.

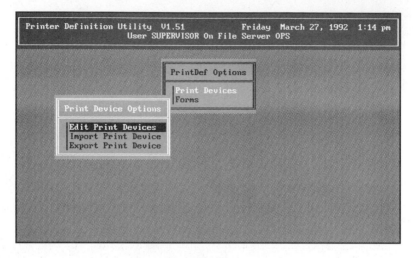

Figure 16.16:
The Print Device Options box.

7. Select the Import Print Device option. When prompted for the Source Directory, enter SYS:PUBLIC or the name of the directory containing the PDF files, and press Enter. A list of available PDFs displays (see fig. 16.17).

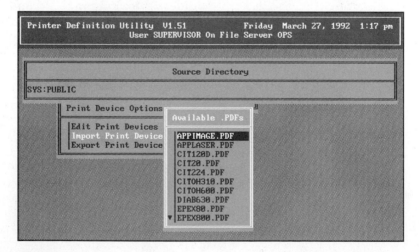

Figure 16.17:
The Available .PDFs box.

8. Highlight the PDF file that you want to import and press Enter. For this exercise, import the APPLASER.PDF file.

9. You should be back to the Print Device Options list after the selected PDF file has been imported. Select the `Edit Print Devices` option to view the printer definitions. You should see a list of printer definitions in the database. In figure 16.18, for example, you also see an Epson Ex-800 printer definition that already was defined in this printer definition database.

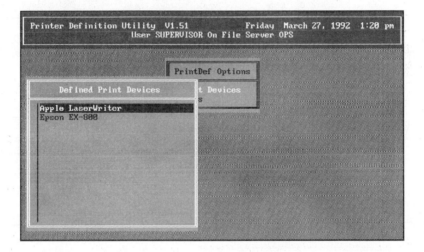

```
 Printer Definition Utility  V1.51          Friday  March 27, 1992  1:20 pm
                          User SUPERVISOR On File Server OPS


                                    PrintDef Options

              Defined Print Devices        t Devices
                                          s
            Apple LaserWriter
            Epson EX-800
```

Figure 16.18:
The Defined Print Devices box.

10. Highlight the newly defined printer and press Enter to see its definition. The Edit Device Options box displays (see fig. 16.19).

11. Select the `Device Modes` option. A list of device modes for the selected printer definition displays (see fig. 16.20).

12. Select one of the device modes and press Enter. The functions defined in the selected device mode appear (see fig. 16.21).

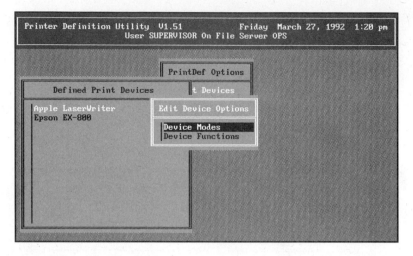

Figure 16.19:
The Edit Device Options box.

Figure 16.20:
Device modes for the selected printer definition.

13. Select one of the functions and press Enter. The escape codes defined for that function are listed, as shown in figure 16.22.

Diablo 630 Courier ... Functions
INITGRAPH
START630
COURIERFONTS
10PITCH
END630
DOIT

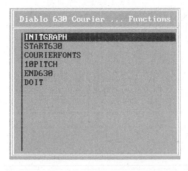

Figure 16.21:
Device mode functions.

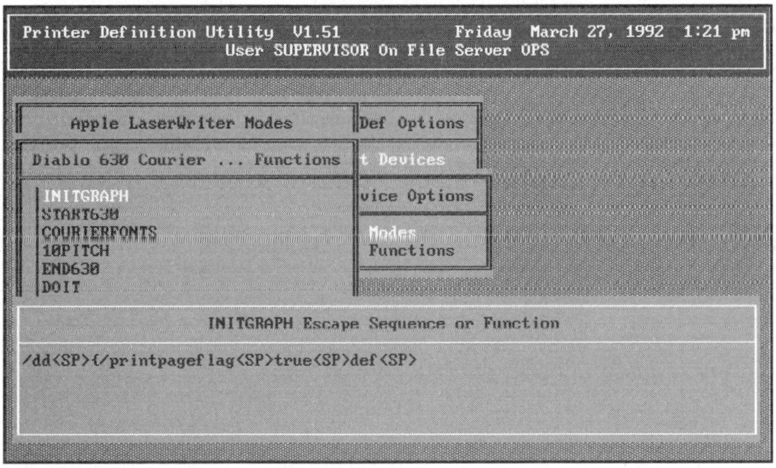

Printer Definition Utility V1.51 Friday March 27, 1992 1:21 pm
User SUPERVISOR On File Server OPS
Apple LaserWriter Modes
Def Options
Diablo 630 Courier ... Functions
t Devices
INITGRAPH
START630
COURIERFONTS
10PITCH
END630
DOIT
vice Options
Modes
Functions
INITGRAPH Escape Sequence or Function
/dd<SP>{/printpageflag<SP>true<SP>def<SP>

Figure 16.22:
The Escape Sequence or Function box.

14. Press Esc enough times to get back to the Edit Device Options box and select `Device Functions`. The list of functions and their corresponding escape codes are listed, along with the function you viewed earlier (see fig. 16.23).

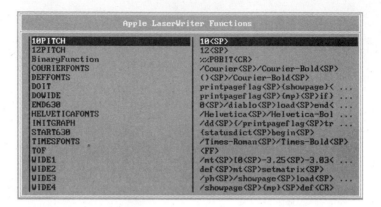

Figure 16.23:
Functions and escape codes.

The ellipses (...) indicate more escape codes are available, which can be viewed by highlighting the function and pressing Enter.

15. Press Esc enough times until the Exit PRINTDEF query appears. Answer Yes, select Save Data Base, and then select Exit.

Using PRINTCON

The PRINTCON utility can be used to define printer job configurations that can be used in utilities such as CAPTURE, NPRINT, and PCONSOLE. Use the following steps:

1. Log in as a supervisor to a NetWare server. (This exercise shows the screens for a NetWare v3.11 server.) Type **PRINTCON** to invoke the PRINTCON utility. The Available Options box displays (see fig. 16.24).

Figure 16.24:
The Available Options box.

2. To create a print job configuration, select the `Edit Print Job Configurations` option. The Print Job Configurations box appears (see fig. 16.25).

Print Job Configurations

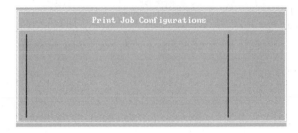

Figure 16.25:
The Print Job Configurations box.

3. Press Ins to define a new printer configuration, and enter the name (up to 31 characters) of the print job configuration. A screen showing details of the print job configuration appears, as shown in figure 16.26.

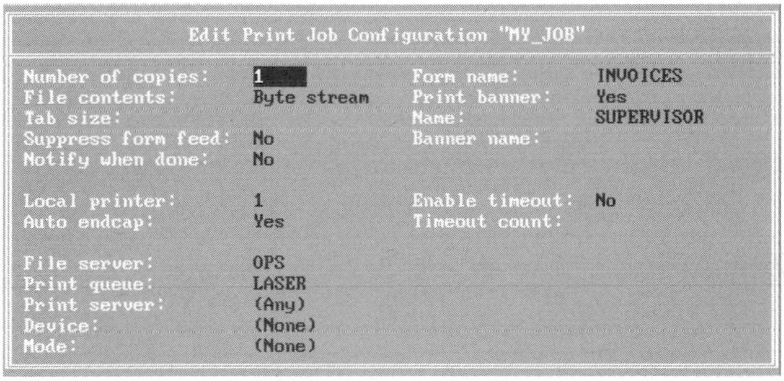

Edit Print Job Configuration "MY_JOB"
Number of copies: 1
File contents: Byte stream
Tab size:
Suppress form feed: No
Notify when done: No
Form name: INVOICES
Print banner: Yes
Name: SUPERVISOR
Banner name:
Local printer: 1
Auto endcap: Yes
Enable timeout: No
Timeout count:
File server: OPS
Print queue: LASER
Print server: (Any)
Device: (None)
Mode: (None)

Figure 16.26:
The Edit Print Job Configuration box.

The important fields and their meanings are described in table 16.3.

Table 16.3
Edit Print Job Configuration Box Fields

Field	Meaning
Number of copies	The number of copies to be printed for a print job.
File Contents	The type of print job. Values are Text and Byte stream. For jobs containing graphic data, Byte stream should be selected. For jobs consisting of text files, Text should be selected. If Text is selected, you can define the Tab size field that has a default value of 8.
Suppress form feed	After the print job ends, should a form feed be suppressed (Yes) or issued (No)?
Notify when done	After the print job ends, should the workstation be notified (Yes) or not (No)?
Local printer	Which LPT printer (1, 2, or 3) should be used for the CAPTURE command by default?
Auto endcap	Should the shell wait until ENDCAP is run before printing (No), or should it print whenever a program is exited (Yes)?
File server	The target file server where the print job should be sent.
Print queue	The queue on the specified target file server to which the print job should be sent. The print queue is defined by PCONSOLE.
Print server	Which print server associated with the print queue should service the print job? Default is (Any), but a specific print server can be specified.
Device	The print job must be customized for the specified printer.
Mode	After the Device field is selected, you can specify the print mode that was defined for the printer (using PRINTDEF).

Field	Meaning
Form name	The default form name (form 0) is shown here. An alternate form (defined by PRINTDEF) can be selected.
Print banner	Should a banner be printed before printing every job?
Name	If Print banner is set to Yes, the name on the banner can be specified here. When left empty, the name of the user printing the job is used; otherwise, whatever text is entered in this field is printed in the banner name.
Banner name	The banner includes the name of the file being printed. This field specifies the name of the file to be included in the banner. If the field is left blank, the name of the file being printed will be in the banner. If text is included here, that text will be printed in the banner, instead of the file name.
Enable timeout	When set to Yes, the shell automatically prints captured data after the time specified in the Timeout count field. When set to No, captured data is printed based on what the Auto endcap is set to. If the Auto endcap is set to Yes, printing occurs only after exiting the program. If Auto endcap is set to No, printing begins immediately.
Timeout count	Specifies the number of seconds the shell waits before printing saved data if nothing has been sent to the captured LPT. Timeout count is only applicable if Enable timeout field is set to Yes.

4. After making the desired changes to the print job, press Esc and answer Yes to save changes. A screen showing a list of print job configurations including the new one just defined appears, as shown in figure 16.27.

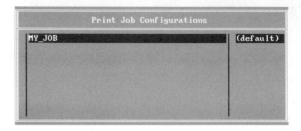

Figure 16.27:
The Print Job Configurations box.

5. Press Esc to return to the Available Options box. To select the default print job configuration, select `Select Default Print Job Configuration` from the Available Options box.

6. To copy the print job configuration to another user, select `Copy Print Job Configuration`. A screen showing the source user to copy the print job from is displayed.

7. Enter a user for whom a print job configuration has already been defined and saved in the database. A screen displays the target user to copy the print job to.

8. Enter a user to which the print job configuration needs to be copied. This user must have been defined already. The `Copy Print Job Configuration` option is a quick way to replicate a print job configuration to other users.

9. Press Esc until the Exit Printcon query appears. Answer Yes to exit and Yes again to save changes in the database.

Using PCONSOLE To Define Queues and Print Server Definitions

The PCONSOLE utility can be used to set up print queues and print servers, control network printing, and view information about network printing, as follows:

1. Log in as a supervisor to a NetWare server. (This exercise shows the screens for a NetWare v3.11 server.) Type **PCONSOLE** to invoke the PCONSOLE utility. The Available Options box appears (see fig. 16.28).

Figure 16.28:
The Available Options box.

The options in the PCONSOLE box perform the following tasks:

Change Current File Server:

Selects the current file server

Attaches to file servers

Changes to a different user name on additional file servers

Logs out of additional file servers

Print Queue Information:

Creates/deletes/renames print queues

Assigns/removes queue operators

Assigns/removes queue users

Changes operator flags

Assigns print server to service a queue

Removes a print server from a queue

Views currently attached print servers

Lists the jobs in a queue

Prints a file

Sets/changes print job parameters

Deletes a print job

Changes order of print jobs

Places a hold on a print job

Views print queue status, queue object ID, print queue servers

Print Server Information:

Creates/deletes/renames print servers

Selects the password for the print server

Assigns the print server's full name

Attaches file servers to a print server

Views print server information, object ID

Downs a print server

Adds printers to the print server

Removes printers from the print server

Temporarily sets service mode of printer and mounted form number

Sets notify list of users for printers

Lists printers and queues serviced by printer

Assigns/removes print server operators

Assigns/removes print server users

Assigns queues to printers

Removes queues from printers

As you can see, PCONSOLE can perform a wide variety of tasks. In this exercise, only the tasks necessary to set up a new print server are performed.

2. To create a print queue, select Print Queue Information. A screen showing the print queues should be displayed. The Print Queues box appears (see fig. 16.29).

3. To create a queue, press Ins. When prompted for a print queue name, enter a queue name with a maximum of 47 characters, and press Enter. The name of the print queue should now appear in the Print Queues box, as shown in figure 16.30.

Figure 16.29:
The Print Queues box.

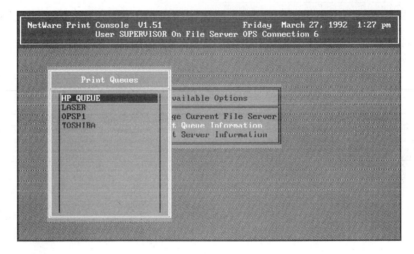

Figure 16.30:
Displaying the name of the print queue.

4. Highlight the name of the print queue you just created and press Enter. The Print Queue Information box appears, as shown in figure 16.31.

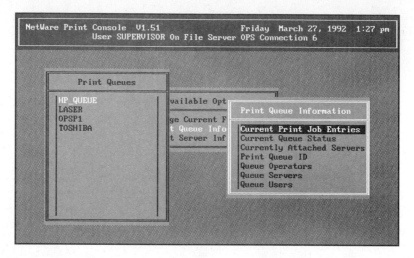

Figure 16.31:
Print Queue Information box.

5. Explore the options that follow. Most of these should indicate that no print jobs and entries in the queues exist. The Print Queue ID name can be recorded because it is the name of the subdirectory in SYS:SYSTEM that implements the print queue.

> **Current Print Job Entries**
>
> **Current Queue Status**
>
> **Currently Attached Servers**
>
> **Print Queue ID**

6. Select the Queue Users option. The Queue Users box displays (see fig. 16.32).

   By default, group EVERYONE (all users) can submit jobs to the print queue. This usually is adequate. If you want to restrict the queue users, highlight group EVERYONE and press Del. You can press Ins to add additional users.

7. Press Esc to return to the Print Queue Information box.

8. Select the Queue Operators option. A screen showing the list of queue operators appears (see fig. 16.33).

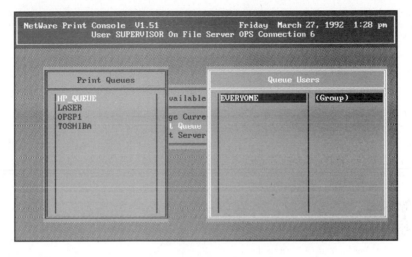

Figure 16.32:
The Queue Users box.

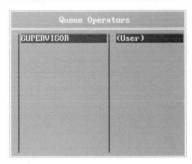

Figure 16.33:
The Queue Operators box.

> By default, SUPERVISOR is always a queue operator. To assign other queue operators press Ins.

9. Press Ins at the Queue Operators list. A list of potential queue operators appears, as shown in figure 16.34.

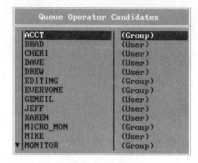

Figure 16.34:
The Queue Operator Candidates box.

10. Mark the users to be made queue operators by pressing F5 and then pressing Ins. The selected users and groups that are the new queue operators appear in the Queue Operators box (see fig. 16.35).

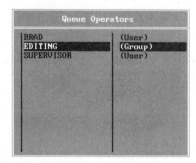

Figure 16.35:
Displaying new queue operators in the Queue Operators box.

11. Press Esc to return to the Print Queue Information box.

12. Select the Queue Servers option. A screen showing the list of queue servers (print servers) appears, as shown in figure 16.36.

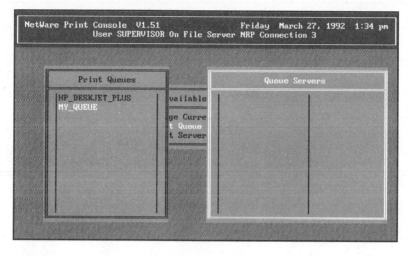

Figure 16.36:
The Queue Servers box.

This list initially should be empty. If queue servers, which are the same as print servers, have been defined, they can be assigned to service the queue at this point by pressing Ins.

13. Press Esc until you return to the Available Options box. The print queue has been defined at this point. The next step is to define a print server.

14. Select the `Print Server Information` option. The Print Servers box displays, showing a list of the print servers that already are created (see fig. 16.37).

15. To create a print server, press Ins. When prompted for a print server name, enter a name with a maximum of 47 characters, and then press Enter. The name of the print server you just created appears, as shown in figure 16.38.

16. Highlight the name of the print server you just created and press Enter. The Print Server Information box displays (see fig. 16.39).

Figure 16.37:
The Print Servers box.

Figure 16.38:
Displaying the new print server.

Figure 16.39:
The Print Server Information box.

17. Explore the `Print Server ID` option. The print server is the name of the subdirectory in SYS:SYSTEM that holds the print server information.

18. Select the `Print Server Users` option. The Server Users box, which shows the list of print server users, appears on-screen (see fig. 16.40).

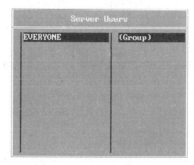

Figure 16.40:
The Server Users box.

By default, all users (group EVERYONE) are users of print servers. This is adequate in most circumstances. If you want to restrict the print server users, highlight group EVERYONE and press Delete to delete group EVERYONE from the list of print server users. You can press Ins to add additional users.

19. Press Esc to return to the Print Server Information box.

20. Select the `Print Server Operators` option. A box showing the list of print server operators appears, as shown in figure 16.41.

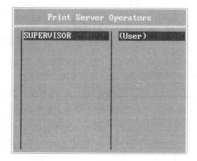

Figure 16.41:
The Print Server Operators box.

By default, SUPERVISOR is always a print server operator. To assign other print server operators, press Ins.

21. Press Ins at the Print Server Operators list. A list of the potential print server operators displays (see fig. 16.42).

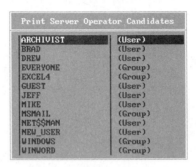

Figure 16.42:
Print Server Operator Candidates box.

22. Press Esc enough times to get back to the Print Server Information box.

23. Select Change Password and enter a print server password for added security.

24. Select Full Name and enter a descriptive name for the print server.

25. Select Print Server Configuration and press Enter. The Print Server Configuration Menu box displays (see fig. 16.43).

Figure 16.43:
The Print Server Configuration Menu box.

26. Select the File Servers To Be Serviced option. A screen similar to the one shown in figure 16.44 appears.

Figure 16.44:
The Configured Printers box.

The default server is displayed. This is the server mapped to by the current default network drive. The available file servers can be obtained by pressing Ins.

27. Press Esc to return to the Print Server Configuration Menu. The print server has been created. The printer(s) for the print server must be defined at this point.

28. Select the `Printer Configuration` option. A list showing the configured printers appears. Initially, this list shows that no printers have been installed, as shown in figure 16.44.

    You now must configure a printer, as follows:

Printer	0
Type	Parallel
Port	LPT1
IRG	7
Forms	0
Queue service mode	Change forms as needed

29. Highlight the first item on the list and press Enter. A screen showing the printer configuration appears (see fig. 16.45).

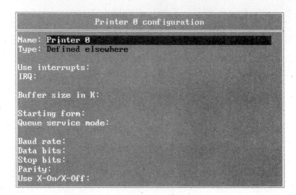

Figure 16.45:
The Printer Configuration box.

The Printer Configuration box fields have the meanings as shown in table 16.4.

Table 16.4
Printer Configuration Box Fields

Fields	Meaning
Name	Enter a name for the printer, with a maximum of 47 characters.
Type	Defines a local or remote printer. In each category you have a choice of three parallel printer ports (LPT1, LPT2, LPT3) and four serial ports (COM1, COM2, COM3, COM4).
Use Interrupts	Enables the use of interrupts when you answer Yes. Interrupts are more efficient than polling techniques. The only reason to disable printer interrupts is to solve interrupt conflict problems.
IRQ	The Interrupt Request Line setting for the printer.

Fields	Meaning
Buffer size in K	The size of the print server's internal buffer. 3K is adequate for most purposes. If the printer does not run smoothly, increasing the print buffer size might help.
Starting form	Denotes the number of the form that must be mounted on the printer when the print server starts.
Queue Service Mode	Defines the queue service modes, as follows: Change forms as needed, Minimize form changes across queues, Minimize form changes within queues, and Service only currently mounted form.

The baud rate, data bits, stop bits, parity, and Use X-On/X-Off (flow control) are defined for serial printers and define the serial printer configuration.

30. Make the changes to the printer configuration. Press Esc once and answer Yes to the Save Changes query.

31. Return to the Print Server Configuration Menu by pressing Esc once.

    Now that a printer has been defined for the print server, you can designate a list of users that can be notified should the printer require service. For defining additional printers, you can repeat the previous steps for defining printers.

32. Select the `Notify List for Printer` option. When the defined printers list appears, highlight a printer and press Enter. A box similar to the one shown in figure 16.46 displays with a box that initially is empty.

33. Press Ins and the Notify Candidates box appears. Mark the users/group by pressing F5, and then press Enter. A screen indicating the notify intervals appears, as shown in figure 16.47.

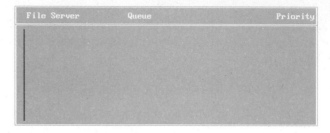

Figure 16.46:
File server notification list display.

Figure 16.47:
The Notify Intervals box.

The First field defines the time in seconds the first notification is sent. The Next field defines the intervals at which this message should be sent.

34. Press Esc to save changes. A box similar to the one shown in figure 16.48 displays.

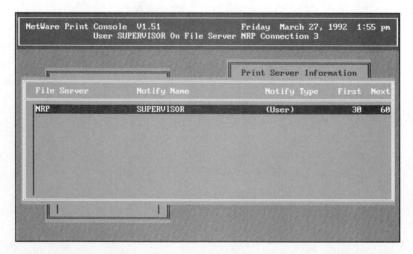

Figure 16.48:
File server notification list display.

35. Press Esc enough times to get back to the Print Server Configuration Menu. The next step is to assign a queue to the printer just defined.

36. Select the Queues Serviced by Printer option. After a list of defined printers appears, highlight a printer and press Enter. A screen similar to the one shown in figure 16.49 appears.

37. Press Ins. After the list of available queues appears, highlight the queue to be serviced by the printer and press Enter. Repeat this process for additional queues to be serviced by the printer attached to the print server.

Figure 16.49:
File server queues display.

After making the queue assignment for a printer, you are prompted for a priority. The priority value is from 1 to 10, with 1 being the highest priority.

After completing the queue assignment for a printer, a screen similar to the one shown in figure 16.50 appears.

38. Press Esc until the Exit Pconsole box appears. Select Yes to exit PCONSOLE.

The printer definition is complete. The next step is to install a print server. The print server program can be installed using any of the three PSERVER programs.

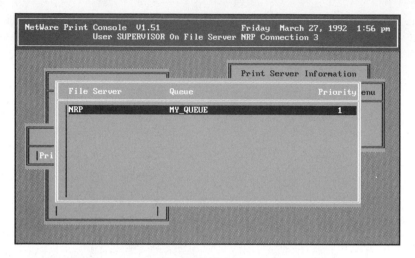

Figure 16.50:
File server queues display.

Running the PSERVER Program

The PSERVER program can be installed at the NetWare v3.x server, NetWare v2.x server, or a dedicated workstation. To install the program, follow these steps:

1. At the NetWare v3.x server console, enter the following command:

   LOAD PSERVER *fileserver/printserver*

   The LOAD PSERVER command loads the PSERVER.NLM at the NetWare v3.x server. The arguments specify the name of the print server. The file server name can be left out.

2. For a dedicated workstation, create a user with the same name as the print server. Set the SPX connections to 60 or more. You can do this by entering the following line in the NET.CFG file:

   SPX Connections=60

   Load IPX and the shell with the new value for SPX connections. Log in to the file server on which the print server was defined and enter the following command:

   PSERVER *fileserver/printserver*

3. For a NetWare v2.2 server, make sure that the PSERVER.VAP is in the SYS:SYSTEM directory. Then bring down the server and bring it up again. During the boot process, it asks if you want to load the VAPs. Answer Yes and enter the server name when prompted to do so.

4. If prompted for the password, enter the password set for the print server through PCONSOLE. A screen similar to the one shown in figure 16.51 displays.

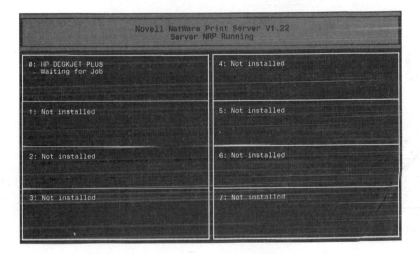

Figure 16.51:
PSERVER activity display.

To see the next group of printers (8–15), press the spacebar.

Installing Remote Printers

To install a remote printer, you must have defined a remote printer as one of the printers in the print server definition by using PCONSOLE. A maximum of 16 printers, including local and remote printers, can be defined for each print server.

The print server that is defining the remote printer must be running.

Perform the following steps to set up a remote printer at the workstation:

1. Attach a printer to be configured as a remote printer at the workstation. The printer settings must match those selected when defining the remote printer through PCONSOLE.

2. Log in as a user at the remote printer workstation and invoke the remote printer command by typing **RPRINTER**.

3. Select the print server that defines the remote printer. A list of remote printers assigned to the selected print server displays.

4. Select the remote printer. You should see a message informing you that the remote printer is installed.

The RPRINTER program takes up approximately 9K at the workstation.

Using Core Print Services

Core print services are available only in the NetWare v2.x version. In NetWare v2.2, core print services can be configured at the server console without bringing the server down. In earlier versions of NetWare (v2.15 and below), the server had to be brought down and the NETGEN utility used to configure print services.

Core Print Services Console Commands

The NetWare 2.2 console commands for managing core print services are as follows:

QUEUE *queuename* CREATE

PRINTER *n* CREATE *port*

PRINTER *n* ADD *queuename* [[AT] [PRIORITY] *nn*]

SPOOL *n* *queuename*

The first keyword in these commands can be abbreviated using the first letter of the keyword—P for PRINTER, Q for QUEUE, and S for SPOOL.

These commands can be placed in the AUTOEXEC.SYS file in the SYS:SYSTEM directory so that they can be executed each time the server is booted. If a command is issued to create a queue or print definition that already exists, a harmless error message is generated on the server console.

Creating Print Queues

The create queues command (QUEUE *queuename* CREATE) creates a queue with the name you provide on the NetWare server. Issuing this command creates a subdirectory with a name that is the queue ID (hexadecimal number) in SYS:SYSTEM. This subdirectory holds the print jobs submitted for printing. Some examples follow:

```
Q ENG_QUEUE CREATE
Q ACCT_QUEUE CREATE
Q URGENT_QUEUE CREATE
```

These commands create print queues named ENG_QUEUE, ACCT_QUEUE, and URGENT_QUEUE.

Creating a Printer Definition

The printer definition command (PRINTER *n* CREATE *port*) creates a printer definition for the specified print number at the server's printer ports. The value of *n* specifies one of five printers and must be between 0 and 4. The ports could be serial (COMx) or parallel ports (LPTx). Issuing this command creates a subdirectory whose name is the print server ID (hexadecimal number) in SYS:SYSTEM. This subdirectory holds the printer definition. When a serial port (COMx) is specified, a default configuration is installed with the following values:

```
Poll            15
XONXOFF         No
Baud            9600
Stopbits        1
Wordsize        8
Parity          None
```

To change any of the default settings, specify any of the preceding parameters following the PRINTER *n* CREATE *port* command. The following is an example:

```
P 0 CREATE COM1 XONXOFF=YES WORDSIZE=7 PARITY=EVEN
```

Notice that the PRINTER command is abbreviated by the letter P. The XON/XOFF parameters are set to Yes, meaning XON/XOFF flow control is used. The word size is set to 7 bits, with even parity.

Other examples are as follows:

```
P 0 CREATE LPT1
P 1 CREATE COM2
```

These create printer numbers 0 and 1, which are defined on ports LPT1 and COM2

Assigning Printers to Queues

The assign printers to queues command (PRINTER *n* ADD *queuename* [[AT] [PRIORITY] *nn*]) assigns a printer to a queue. When this assignment is made, the priority level at which the queue will be serviced can be specified. This priority (*nn*) can have a value between 1 and 10, with 1 the highest priority.

Queues at the highest priority are serviced before those at lower priorities. Normally a queue is assigned to one printer to keep this logical association simple. As explained earlier in this chapter, more complex mappings such as one-to-many, many-to-one, and many-to-many are possible.

Examples of the assign printers to queues command follow:

```
P 0 ADD ACCT_QUEUE
P 1 ADD ENG_QUEUE AT PRIORITY 4
```

The first command assigns printer number 0 to the queue ACCT_QUEUE. The second command assigns printer 1 to the queue ENG_QUEUE at a priority level of 4.

Using the SPOOL Command

The SPOOL command (SPOOL *n queueName*) supports older applications that send their print jobs to print numbers rather than queues. If the printer number *n* is specified, the spooler with the name *queueName* is used. Printer number 0 is the default printer, so at least one SPOOL command must be given with printer number 0. The NPRINT and CAPTURE commands also have a default printer number when not explicitly specified.

Examples of the SPOOL command follow:

```
S 0 ENG_QUEUE
S 1 MY_QUEUE
```

The printer number 0 (default network printer) is assigned to the ENG_QUEUE, and printer 1 is assigned to MY_QUEUE. This assignment means that older applications that use printer numbers to direct the printer output will have their jobs directed to these queues and will be printed by the printers assigned to service this queue.

Using One Printer with Multiple Queues

Figure 16.52 shows an example of one printer that services four queues. The queues are set to priority levels ranging from 1 to 4. Applications generate print jobs that can go in either one of these queues. When a high-priority job enters QUEUE_1, which is to be serviced at the highest priority level of 1, the current print job in progress is completed, and the new high-priority job is sent to the printer.

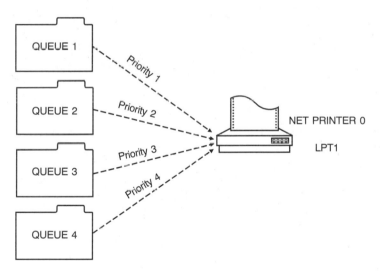

Figure 16.52:
One printer with multiple queues.

To implement this queue structure, the following commands should be issued at the server console:

```
Q QUEUE_1 CREATE
Q QUEUE_2 CREATE
Q QUEUE_3 CREATE
```

```
Q QUEUE_4 CREATE
P 0 CREATE LPT1
P 0 ADD QUEUE_1 AT PRIORITY 1
P 0 ADD QUEUE_2 AT PRIORITY 2
P 0 ADD QUEUE_3 AT PRIORITY 3
P 0 ADD QUEUE_4 AT PRIORITY 1
```

This is an example of one-to-many mapping

Using One Queue with Multiple Printers

Figure 16.53 shows an example of one queue being serviced by three printers. The printers are identical and assigned to ports LPT1, LPT2, and LPT3. Applications generate print jobs that can go in the single queue. The print job is serviced by the next printer that becomes free.

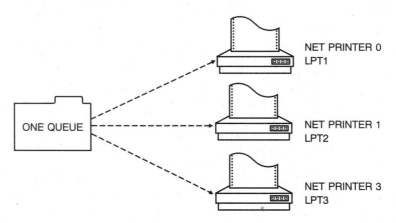

Figure 16.53:
One queue with multiple printers.

To implement this queue structure, the following commands should be issued at the server console:

```
Q ONE_QUEUE CREATE
P 0 CREATE LPT1
P 1 CREATE LPT2
P 2 CREATE LPT3
P 0 ADD ONE_QUEUE
P 1 ADD ONE_QUEUE
P 2 ADD ONE_QUEUE
```

This is an example of many-to-one mapping

Using Multiple Queues with Multiple Printers

Suppose that three queues are serviced by two printers. The printers are identical and assigned to ports LPT1 and LPT2. Applications generate print jobs that can go in the queues. The print jobs are serviced by the next printer that becomes free. QUEUE_2 is serviced by both PRINTER_1 and PRINTER_2 and is serviced at a higher priority than the other queues.

To implement this queue structure, the following commands should be issued at the server console:

```
Q QUEUE_1 CREATE
Q QUEUE_2 CREATE
Q QUEUE_3 CREATE
P 0 CREATE LPT1
P 1 CREATE LPT2
P 0 ADD QUEUE_1 AT PRIORITY 2
P 0 ADD QUEUE_2 AT PRIORITY 1
P 1 ADD QUEUE_2 AT PRIORITY 1
P 1 ADD QUEUE_3 AT PRIORITY 2
```

This is an example of many-to-many mapping

Generating Print Jobs

Print jobs are generated by applications running at the workstation or using print utilities to print files. These print jobs are sent to queues defined on a file server. From the queues, they are processed by the print servers assigned to the queue and sent to local or remote printers.

The utilities to generate print jobs are as follows:

CAPTURE and ENDCAP

NPRINT

PCONSOLE

Using CAPTURE and ENDCAP

Applications designed to work with NetWare are compatible with the NetWare print queue and print support mechanisms. During the installation of these applications, you can define the interface to network printers. This should be all the printer configuration necessary.

Many applications, however, do not have a direct interface to NetWare printers; they require additional support and configuration. The command-line utilities CAPTURE and ENDCAP provide this support.

After you issue the CAPTURE command, it captures printer output directed at a parallel local port and sends it across the network to a print queue.

In earlier versions of NetWare, the print job from CAPTURE had to be redirected to a network printer. With NetWare v2.2 and NetWare v3.x, Novell has made the print queue the focal point for submitting jobs. The print job in the queue is printed on a network printer depending on how print queues have been assigned to print servers. This is a more flexible approach. The SPOOL command bridges the gap for applications that do not have awareness of print queues.

The SPOOL command must be used to associate a print number with a print queue if CAPTURE on pre-NetWare v2.2 or older applications is being used.

To associate the default printer (network printer 0) with the queue DEFAULT_QUEUE, for example, issue the following command at the server console:

```
S 0 DEFAULT_QUEUE
```

After the CAPTURE command is issued, it controls the print jobs sent to the local parallel port until another CAPTURE or ENDCAP command is issued or the user logs out. It is common to place the CAPTURE command in the login script file so that it holds for the duration of the session. If placed in the login script, CAPTURE (and external commands, in general) must be preceded by the numeral character (#) to indicate to the log-in processing that this is an external program or utility.

The following command directs printer output sent to the local port to the print queue HIGH_SPEED by using the job configuration MY_JOB.

```
CAPTURE L=1 Q=HIGH_SPEED J=MY_JOB
```

The following command is the same as the earlier CAPTURE command but is executed from the login script.

```
#CAPTURE L=1 Q=HIGH_SPEED J=MY_JOB
```

Job configurations contain many of the parameters that can be specified in the CAPTURE command. If the job configuration is set up appropriately, the other parameters are not necessary. If the parameters are specified explicitly on the command line, they override any settings in the job configuration.

Table 16.5 shows a list of parameters (options) that can be set up for both CAPTURE and NPRINT command (discussed later). Only the abbreviated forms of these parameters are shown because they tend to get used more often. The full form of these parameters can be determined from the description column. Unless explicitly stated or implied in the description, many of the parameters are common to both CAPTURE and NPRINT.

Table 16.5
CAPTURE and NPRINT Options and Parameters

Option	Description
SH	Shows the current CAPTURE settings.
?	Shows the list of options for CAPTURE.
NOTI	NOTIfies when the print job is done.
NNOTI	NoNOTIFY. Does not notify when print job is done (default setting).
TI=n	TImeout. Specifies timeout period n in seconds before job is printed. Default is TI=0 (disabled). Only for CAPTURE.
AU	AUtoEndcap. ENDCAP is automatically issued when application exits. Default setting. Only for CAPTURE.
NA	No AutoEndcap. ENDCAP is not automatically issued when application exits. Only for CAPTURE.
L=n	Specifies the Local parallel printer n to be used for capturing. Only for CAPTURE.

continues

Table 16.5
Continued

Option	Description
S=*fs*	Server. Specifies the file server *fs* where the print job should be sent. Default is the default file server.
PS=*ps*	PrintServer. Specifies the print server *ps* where the print job should be sent. Only for NPRINT.
Q=*qn*	Queue. Specifies the queue name *qn* where the print job is sent. If queue name is not specified, the print job is sent to the queue that spooler 0 has been assigned to.
CR=*path*	Create. Specifies the path for the file that will store the print job, instead of being sent to the print queue. Only for CAPTURE.
J=*jc*	Job. Specifies the job configuration *jc* to be used for printing.
F=*n*	Form. Specifies the form number or name to be used for printing.
C=*n*	Copies. Specifies the number of copies (1 to 999) for printing. Default is 1.
T=*n*	Tabs. Specifies the tab size in the text mode of printing. Default is 8.
NT	No Tabs. Specifies no tabs should be used for the byte stream mode of printing.
NB	No Banner. No banner separator pages are generated.
NAM=*n*	NAMe. Indicates the text *n* that appears on the banner page instead of the default user name.
B=*n*	Banner. Specifies the banner name to be printed in the lower part of the banner instead of the default value of the file name being printed or LST: (for CAPTURE).
FF	FormFeed. Generates a form feed at the end of a print job. Default is form feed enabled. Only for CAPTURE.

Option	Description
NFF	NoFormFeed. Disables form feed at end of print job. Only for CAPTURE.
K	Keep. Keeps the received portion of the print job on the file server until it is printed, even if the workstation crashes. Only for CAPTURE.
D	Delete. Automatically erases the file after printing. Only for NPRINT.

The following are some other uses of the CAPTURE command:

In the following command, the local parallel port LPT1 is redirected to the print queue assigned by the Spooler 0 command (S 0 *queueName*):

```
CAPTURE NOTI
```

In the following command, the local parallel port LPT1 is redirected to the queue HP_QUEUE on file server KSS:

```
CAPTURE S=KSS Q=HP_QUEUE
```

In the following command, the local parallel port LPT2 is redirected to the queue and file server specified by the job configuration MY_JOB (set by using PRINTCON) and two copies of the print job are to be printed:

```
CAPTURE J=MY_JOB L=2 C=2
```

In the following command, the local parallel port LPT3 is redirected to the queue EPSON_QUEUE on the default file server and no form feed is to be issued at the end of the print job. Also, the job should be printed on form number 2. If this form is not mounted, a notification message is sent to mount the correct form.

```
CAPTURE L=3 Q=EPSON_QUEUE F=2 NFF
```

In the following command, the local parallel port LPT1 is redirected to the queue HP_QUEUE on the default file server, and the tab size to be used for text printing is 8. You should use tabs for text jobs to speed up printing.

```
CAPTURE L=1 Q=HP_QUEUE T=8
```

In the following command, the local parallel port LPT1 is redirected to the queue HP_QUEUE on the default file server, and the tabs and other control characters have special meanings for the application. This is the byte stream mode and is slightly slower than the text mode.

```
CAPTURE L=1 Q=HP_QUEUE
```

In the following command, the local parallel port LPT1 is redirected to the queue HP_QUEUE on the default file server, and the banner page separating print jobs is suppressed.

```
CAPTURE Q=HP_QUEUE NB
```

In the following command, the local parallel port LPT2 is redirected by using the job configuration SPL_JOB, and the banner page separating print jobs has the text SPECIAL_JOBS printed on top. Instead of the default LST: that appears below the banner name, the string SPELL appears.

```
CAPTURE J=SPL_JOB L=2 NAM=SPECIAL_JOBS B=SPELL
```

In the following command, the local parallel port LPT1 is redirected to the file REPORT.1 in the directory SYS:APPS/DATA:

```
CAPTURE CR=SYS:APPS/DATA/REPORT.1
```

In the following command, the local parallel port LPT1 is redirected to the queue MY_QUEUE and the job is sent to the queue after a timeout period of 12 seconds, if no further output is received. Also, the print job is kept in queue for printing, in case the workstation crashes.

```
CAPTURE Q=MY_QUEUE TI=12 K
```

To end the capture of the local parallel port, use the ENDCAP command. A number of options can be specified by using the ENDCAP command. These are listed in table 16.6.

Table 16.6
ENDCAP Options and Parameters

Option	Description
L=n	Local. Ends the capture for parallel port n. When not specified, local port LPT1 is assumed.
A	All. Ends capture for all local parallel ports.
C	Cancel. Ends capture of LPT1 and discards any data without printing.

Option	Description
CL	CancelLocal. Ends capture for LPT port *n* and discards any data without printing.
CA	CancelAll. Ends capture for all LPT ports and discards any data without printing.

The following are some examples of how to use the ENDCAP command:

The following command ends the capture of LPT1 port:

```
ENDCAP
```

The following command ends the capture of LPT3 port:

```
ENDCAP L=3
```

The following command ends the capture of LPT1 port and discards any spooled data without printing:

```
ENDCAP C
```

The following command ends the capture of LPT2 port and discards any spooled data without printing:

```
ENDCAP CL=2
```

The following command ends the capture of all parallel ports:

```
ENDCAP A
```

The following command ends the capture of all parallel ports and discards any spooled data for printing:

```
ENDCAP CA
```

NPRINT

The NPRINT command is similar to the DOS PRINT command, in that it can be invoked from the command line to print a file. The parameters for NPRINT were discussed in table 10.3, together with the parameters for CAPTURE. As was explained in that section, many of these parameters are the same as that for CAPTURE, and many of the examples of CAPTURE command in the preceding section also can be used with NPRINT.

The following examples make use of parameters that are unique to NPRINT or that behave differently from CAPTURE.

The following command prints the FILE.TXT file to the queue HP_QUEUE on file server KSS to be processed by HP_PSERVER. The banner name is SCS and the tab size is set to 4 for text printing. The lower part of the banner shows the file name FILE.TXT being printed.

```
NPRINT FILE.TXT Q=HP_QUEUE PS=HP_PSERVER S=KSS NAM=SCS T=4
```

The following command prints the FILE.TXT file to the queue set by the Spooler 0 command and suppresses the banner page:

```
NPRINT FILE.TXT NB
```

PCONSOLE for Printing

The versatile PCONSOLE utility also can be used for printing jobs, as shown in the following steps:

1. Type **PCONSOLE**.

2. Make the following selections:

   Print queue information

   Select a queue for printing

   Current print job entries

3. A list of print jobs in progress displays.

4. To print a job, press Ins. Enter the directory to be used for printing, and a list of files in that directory displays. Highlight a file to be printed and select it. To print several files, mark them by using F5 and press Enter to select them.

5. Select the print job configuration to be used for printing. The job configuration screen appears. You can edit any of the job configuration parameters. When done, press Esc to select the current settings and to submit the files for printing.

6. You can highlight any job in the print queue to obtain more detailed information on that job. The meanings of the individual fields are described in table 16.7.

Table 16.7
Print Queue Entry Information

Field	Description
Print job	Denotes job number of print job in queue
File size	Denotes size in bytes of print job
Client	Denotes user who sent the print job
Description	Denotes name of job
Status	Denotes condition of job
User hold	Indicates if job is held in queue by user or queue operator
Operator hold	Indicates if job is held by queue operator
Service Sequence	Specifies the order in which the job is printed
Number of Copies	Specifies number of copies to be printed
File contents	Specifies text or byte stream mode, text mode converts tabs to spaces, byte stream enables application to determine printer codes
Tab size	Specifies number of spaces per tab
Suppress form feed	Controls form feed generation at end of print job
Notify when done	Determines if user is notified at end of print job
Target server	Denotes print server that can process print job
Form	Denotes form type used for print job
Print Banner	Controls banner generation
Name	Specifies name to be printed in upper part of banner

continues

Table 16.7
Continued

Field	Description
Banner name	Specifies name to be printed in lower part of banner
Defer printing	Enables you to defer printing
Target date and time	If printing is to be deferred, it sets the date and time for printing (default is 2:00 am on the following day)
Job entry date and time	Information on when the job was submitted

Monitoring and Controlling Print Jobs

The following are commands that you can use to monitor and control print jobs:

> PSTAT
>
> PSC
>
> PCONSOLE

Printer Status: PSTAT

The printer status command PSTAT can be used only for core print services. PSTAT reveals information on printers attached directly to the NetWare v2.x server, such as the following:

> Ready status: on-line and off-line
>
> Active status: active and stopped
>
> Forms: Form number and name currently mounted

Print Server Command: PSC

The PSC command is a quick way of controlling print servers and network printers. It can be used for monitoring and controlling printers. Many of the functions in PSC also can be done by PCONSOLE. The difference is that PSC is used at the command line, whereas PCONSOLE is interactive.

Table 16.8 shows the list of flags that can be used with the PSC command. The general form of the PSC command is as follows:

```
PSC [PS=printserver] [P=printnumber] flaglist
```

Table 16.8
PSC Flags and Options

Flags	Description
STAT	STATus. Shows status of connected printers.
PAU	PAUse. Stops the printer temporarily.
STAR	STARt. Restarts a printer that was paused or stopped.
AB	Abort. Aborts the print job.
STO [K]	STOp [Keep]. Stops the printer. To resubmit the job, specify Keep.
MA [*char*]	Mark. Marks an asterisk (*) at print head. To use another character, specify the *char* value. Used for form alignment.
FF	FormFeed. Sends a form feed to the printer. The printer must be paused or stopped to do a form feed.
MO F=*n*	Mount Form=*n*. Specifies a different mount form.
PRI	PRIvate. Specifies that the printer is private. It removes the remote printer from the list of network printers used by a print server and changes the remote printer to a local printer.
SH	Shared. Undoes the PRIvate option. Makes the remote printer available to others.
CD	CancelDown. Cancels the command to down the server if `Going down after current jobs` was selected in PCONSOLE.

You can use the DOS SET command to define the environment variable PSC to set the default values of the PS (print server) and P (printer). This simplifies the use of the PSC command by reducing the number of keystrokes that you have to enter.

At the DOS prompt, you can use the following command to set PSC:

```
SET PSC=PSprintServer PprinterNumber
```

To specify PSC in a login script, use the following command:

```
SET PSC="PSprintserver PprinterNumber"
```

Replace printserver and printerNumber with the name of the print server and printer number. Then, you can issue the following command without having to specify the PS and the P parameters:

```
PSC flagList
```

The following are examples of using the preceding commands. The following command sets the print server to HP_PSERVER and the printer number to 0:

```
SET PSC=PSHP_PSERVER P0
```

To pause the printer, use the following command:

```
PSC PAU
```

To restart the printer, use the following command:

```
PSC STAR
```

In the preceding commands, the print server is HP_PSERVER and the printer number is 0 because these parameters were set in the DOS environment variable.

To display statistics on print server EP_PSERVER and printer 1, use the following command:

```
PSC PS=EP_SERVER P=1 STAT
```

The explicit use of PS and P parameters at the command line override any default settings.

Form Control and Management

The PRINTDEF utility can be used to create and manage a database of forms. You were shown how to use PRINTDEF earlier in the chapter. Forms are useful when there is a need to share a printer with different types of forms, such as sales invoices, checks, and word processing documents. The print server keeps track of the current form that is in use at the printer. When a print job specifies a different type of form, it waits until the right form is mounted. Once the correct form is mounted on the printer, any of the following commands can be issued to indicate to the print server that a new form has been mounted:

```
PRINTER n MOUNT formnumber
```

or

```
PSC PS=printsever P=printernumber MO=formnumber
```

The formnumber parameter in the preceding commands can be replaced by a numeric value for the form number or by the form name.

PCONSOLE

You also can use the PCONSOLE to view the status of print queues, as shown in the following steps:

1. Enter PCONSOLE.

2. Make the following selections:

   Print queue information

   Select a queue for printing

   Current queue status

3. The current queue status of the selected queue appears on-screen.

Summary

In this chapter, you have learned how to use and set up NetWare's printing mechanisms. NetWare supports a variety of printing methods to suit the needs of different printing applications. NetWare-aware applications designed to make use of the NetWare printer function APIs (Application

Programming Interfaces) require very little configuration support. Applications that do not work as intimately with the NetWare printing mechanisms, however, require additional support.

Most of the printing chores can be done by using the PCONSOLE utility. A detailed guided tour of how to use PCONSOLE was presented in this chapter, along with examples on using many of NetWare's command-line utilities for printer support.

Internetworking

This chapter examines considerations for connecting NetWare in an internet environment that consists of non-NetWare networks and devices. The topics discussed include communications connectivity of NetWare LANs to the following networks:

- TCP/IP networks
- X.25 networks
- T1 networks
- Asynchronous links
- Synchronous links
- IBM SNA networks
- OSI networks
- UNIX networks

This chapter also discusses the installation of Novell's LAN WorkPlace for DOS, NetWare for NFS, and NetWare for FTAM.

NetWare Communications Connectivity

Novell has made a strong commitment to support the current major networking architectures. Some of these network architectures (such as IBM SNA) are proprietary, others (such as TCP/IP networks) are industry standards, and some (such as the OSI networks) are international standards.

These different networks are likely to coexist in the near future, so the capability to integrate multivendor networks is a key requirement for many network environments.

TCP/IP Connectivity

TCP/IP has become a de facto protocol standard for connecting different computing platforms, and it currently has the largest support among communication vendors. It is predicted that TCP/IP protocols will eventually be replaced by OSI protocols, but meanwhile, TCP/IP-based products, and the vendor and user support for them, show no signs of declining.

TCP/IP is not one protocol; it consists of the two protocols TCP and IP. *Transmission Control Protocol* (TCP) is a transport protocol that fits into layer 4 of the OSI model. The *Internet Protocol* (IP) is a network protocol that fits into layer 3 of the OSI model. Often, *TCP/IP* is used as a term to describe the transport and network protocols and also the application protocols that make use of it. The basic TCP/IP protocols are shown in figure 17.1. The OSI model comparison is meant for categorizing the functions of the protocols and does not indicate OSI compliance.

In the figure, TCP represents a transport protocol that provides reliable communications through *virtual circuits*. This means that any errors occurring in the underlying network are corrected by TCP. TCP provides automatic acknowledgments and retransmissions of data (in case of errors), so that the users of the TCP layer do not have to worry about unreliable transmissions. In many ways, TCP is similar to Novell's SPX protocol, but it also is designed to work effectively over WANs (wide area networks). Besides data-transmission integrity, TCP also provides software addressing (port numbers) for applications that make use of it.

The *User Datagram Protocol* (UDP) in figure 17.1 provides a "best-efforts" datagram delivery service. It is used for network environments that are essentially quite reliable, such as LANs. If greater reliability is desired, the network application layer is responsible for implementing it. UDP is used by the *Simple Network Management Protocol* (SNMP), *Network File System* (NFS), and *Trivial File Transfer Protocol* (TFTP). It also is used to encapsulate NetWare IPX packets for IP tunneling.

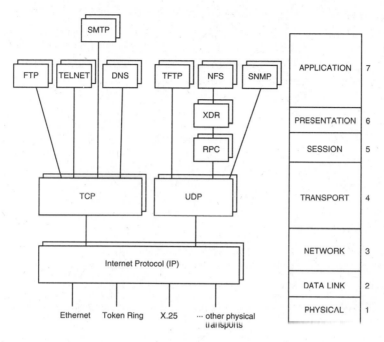

Figure 17.1:
TCP/IP protocols and the OSI model.

The IP protocol can run on a wide variety of networking technologies, such as LANs, X.25, Frame Relay, Packet Radio, and Point-To-Point links. It provides a uniform interface to these networking technologies, as well as a uniform network address, routing of the transport protocols, fragmentation, and reassembly for long messages.

Novell provides a variety of products for TCP/IP networks, which makes it easy to integrate NetWare-based networks with TCP/IP-based networks. Novell obtained much of its TCP/IP experience through its merger with Excelan. Novell's TCP/IP products enable different operating system platforms (DOS, OS/2, Macintosh, and UNIX) to be integrated. On the workstation side, these products are known collectively as the LAN WorkPlace products.

The goal of these TCP/IP-based products is to provide high-speed communications between dissimilar computers, which is the first step for running distributed applications across multiple dissimilar computers. Many vendors have begun providing this capability because they realize that they cannot lock a customer into one application architecture. Novell calls this concept *Network Integrated Computing Architecture* (NICA), which also means that applications written to TCP/IP can be distributed over the network.

Novell also provides MultiNet, a hardware-independent implementation of TCP/IP networking, for remote connectivity to VAX/VMS environments. NetWare v3.11 and above includes the TCP/IP Transport, a collection of NLMs that provides NetWare with TCP/IP transport protocols, application programming interfaces (APIs)—such as BSD Sockets, STREAMS, and AT&T's TLI (Transport Layer Interface)—and tools for managing those protocols. The IP routing that the TCP/IP Transport provides enables TCP/IP packets to be routed from one NetWare v3.x network to another. Tunneling IPX packets through IP subnets enables NetWare v3.11 (and above) servers to be connected through a TCP/IP internet.

TCP/IP support is provided through the *Open Data-Link Interface* (ODI) drivers. These drivers can support multiple protocols, such as IPX and TCP/IP, through a single network adapter. This is valuable for the workstation that needs to run several client applications to communicate with servers using different protocols through a single network adapter. Without ODI (or a similar scheme) you would need multiple adapters in the workstation to provide multiple protocol stack functionality, resulting in higher cost and fewer free adapter slots at the workstation.

LAN WorkPlace for DOS

LAN WorkPlace for DOS provides access to TCP/IP hosts for DOS workstations and for Windows 3.x users who have DOS workstations. As mentioned in the previous section, TCP/IP has become a vendor-independent protocol, so the communications subnet and hardware can be implemented with products from a variety of sources.

The TCP/IP host machines can be UNIX systems, Digital VAXs running VMS or Ultrix, IBM mainframes running MVS or VM, or NetWare running NetWare for NFS. For DOS users, access is provided by a command-line interface; for Windows users, access is provided by the Windows graphical user interface (GUI).

Besides the basic TCP/IP application services, LAN WorkPlace can be used to run other TCP/IP-based applications, such as Quarterdeck's DESQview/X, VisionWare's X-Vision (a Windows-based X-Server), ORACLE's SQL*Net TCP/IP for MS-DOS, and the SYBASE PC Net-Library for DOS. Memory (RAM) space available for running these applications on the workstation is critical. Currently, the combined TCP/IP and ODI network drivers consume about 45K of conventional RAM. IPX and the NetWare shell require an additional 16K on machines that support extended or expanded memory. By using ODI, protocol stacks can be dynamically loaded or unloaded from memory without having to reboot.

The capabilities provided by LAN WorkPlace (for DOS and OS/2) are listed in table 17.1.

Table 17.1
LAN WorkPlace Features

Features	Description
FTP	*File Transfer Protocol* enables clients to transfer files between TCP/IP hosts supporting an FTP server. The FTP server can be a UNIX host or NetWare running the FTPSRV NLM.
TFTP	*Trivial File Transfer Protocol* utilities provide a simplified version of the FTP protocol using UDP/IP services.
rcp	A UNIX-like command-line utility, *remote copy* (rcp) provides an alternate method of file transfer.
Telnet VT220	Terminal emulation through *Telnet*. DEC VT100 and terminal emulators are included for both Windows and DOS. These emulators support up to 10 concurrent sessions to multiple hosts. *Telnet Application Programming Interface* (TelAPI) can be used to employ other vendors' communications programs and terminal emulators for communicating with TCP/IP-equipped hosts through Telnet.

continues

Table 17.1
Continued

Features	Description
Remote execution	UNIX-style commands including *remote shell* (rsh) and *remote execute* (rexec) enable users to invoke programs on remote systems from the DOS prompt and see the results on their own screen.
Remote printing	*Remote Printing* (rpr) provides printing of files to UNIX and VMS hosts.
NetBIOS on TCP/IP	The recommendations of standard documents RFC-1001/RFC-1002 NetBIOS API (B-node implementation) that provide a standard NetBIOS session layer interface over TCP/IP.

For users running MS Windows v3.x for DOS, LAN WorkPlace provides the following features:

- Up to 10 Telnet sessions can be provided through one workstation. The Host Presenter provides up to 10 simultaneous Telnet session windows (emulating a VT220, VT52, or VT100 terminal) to multiple TCP/IP-equipped hosts. It supports data transfer to and from the Telnet session through the Windows Clipboard. The Host Presenter also includes a scripting language called *Script Director*. Script Director makes conventional host-based applications easier to use.

- FTP server (FTPd—daemon) that runs in the background under Windows and accepts file requests from multiple FTP clients.

- File Express provides a graphical front end, instead of the traditional command-line user interface.

LAN WorkPlace uses ODI driver interfaces to run TCP/IP and NetWare IPX/SPX protocols concurrently on Ethernet, Token Ring, and ARCnet LANs. Because NetWare v3.11 (and above) can act as an IP router, LAN WorkPlace can connect NetWare clients on ARCnet and Token Ring LANs to TCP/IP hosts on Ethernet segments (see fig. 17.2). NetWare 2.x IPX routers do not support IP routing and must be on the same network segment as the target TCP/IP host.

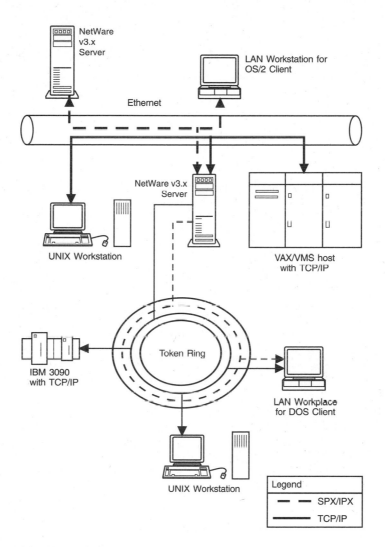

Figure 17.2:
LAN WorkPlace for DOS.

LAN WorkPlace supports the Internet Standards listed in table 17.2. This list applies to the LAN WorkPlace products for DOS, OS/2, and Macintosh.

Table 17.2
Standards Supported by LAN WorkPlace

Standard Name	Standard Number
IP (Internet Protocol)	RFC 791
IP Subnet Extension	RFC 950
IP Broadcast Datagrams	RFC 919IP
Broadcast Datagrams with Subnets	RFC 922
TCP (Transmission Control Protocol)	RFC 793
UDP (User Datagram Protocol)	RFC 768
IP-IEEE (Internet Protocol on IEEE 802)	RFC 1042
NetBIOS (NetBIOS Service Protocol on TCP/IP)	RFC 1001, 1002
ARP (Address Resolution Protocol)	RFC 826
RARP (Reverse Address Resolution Protocol)	RFC 903
ICMP (Internet Control Message Protocol)	RFC 792
DNS (Domain Name System) Resolver	RFC 1034, 1035
TELNET (Telnet Protocol)	RFC 854
FTP (File Transfer Protocol)	RFC 959
TFTP (Trivial File Transfer Protocol)	RFC 783

LAN WorkPlace for OS/2

LAN WorkPlace for OS/2 (see fig. 17.3) provides the capabilities of LAN WorkPlace for DOS on an OS/2 workstation. Because OS/2 is a multitasking operating system, multiple concurrent TCP/IP connections are easy to provide at an OS/2 workstation.

LAN WorkPlace for OS/2 supports the features listed in table 17.1 and the standards documents listed in table 17.2.

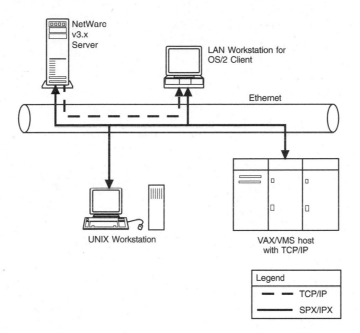

Figure 17.3:
LAN WorkPlace for OS/2.

For third-party developers, an OS/2 developer's kit provides an application programming interface to the TCP/IP interface. The API can access the network drivers and the TCP/IP protocols through the BSD socket interface.

LAN WorkPlace for Macintosh

LAN WorkPlace for Macintosh provides Macintosh users with access to TCP/IP hosts such as IBM mainframes, VAX minicomputers, and PCs (see fig. 17.4). The users use the familiar Macintosh interface to access the remote hosts. The product consists of the TCPport transport system software, HostAccess, and NetStat desk accessory. HostAccess provides Telnet and FTP capability.

The physical transport mechanism for LAN WorkPlace for Macintosh can be EtherTalk (Ethernet) or LocalTalk. The Macintosh Plus can use the built-in LocalTalk connection, whereas the Macintosh SE, SE30, II, IIcx, and so on can use either LocalTalk or EtherTalk.

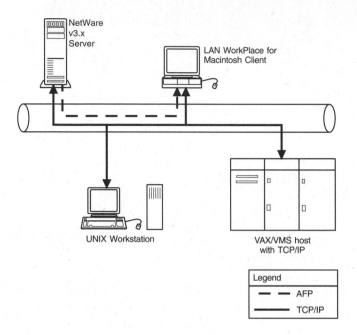

Figure 17.4:
LAN WorkPlace for Macintosh.

The features and standards supported by LAN WorkPlace for Macintosh are listed in tables 17.1 and 17.2.

Installing and Configuring LAN WorkPlace for DOS

This section presents you with a specific method for installing LAN WorkPlace for DOS. Follow these steps:

1. Install the ODI driver programs for your LAN NIC in the root directory or a directory that is on the DOS search path. Start the installation by running the program INSTALL from the LAN WorkPlace for DOS disk, in drive A, as follows:

   ```
   A:INSTALL
   ```

2. When the installation screen appears, do the following:

   Select drive for installing LAN WorkPlace (C: or D:).
   Install LAN WorkPlace Windows applications.

To install Windows applications, you must have Windows 3.x installed because several Windows INI files need to be modified.

3. If the Windows directory is not on the DOS search path, you will be prompted for the directory path that contains Windows.

   If you do not have sufficient disk space to do a full installation, you are asked whether or not you want to stop the installation. If you are reinstalling LAN WorkPlace for DOS, and you know that the installation will overwrite existing files, select No.

4. The list of information you need to know to complete the installation is shown in figure 17.5.

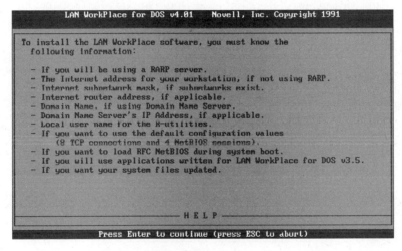

Figure 17.5:
Information needed for LAN WorkPlace software installation.

5. After you know the answers to the configuration information, press Enter to continue.

6. If you are using a *Reverse Address Resolution Protocol* (RARP) to specify your IP address, you do not need to specify your IP address. Otherwise, you are asked to specify your IP address.

7. If you selected No for RARP server, you must specify your IP address, which must be unique. (Consult your network administrator for a unique IP address.)

   IP addresses are entered in the dotted decimal notation as four decimal digits, separated by a period (.).

8. If you are using *subnets* to logically partition your network, you must specify a *subnet mask*. The IP address is a two-part address, consisting of a network ID and a host ID, as shown in figure 17.6. There are different IP address formats (Class A, B, C, D, and E) that determine how many bits of the 32-bit IP address are used for the network ID and the host ID. For instance, a class B address in figure 17.6 has 16 bits for the host ID, enabling it to have 64,000 hosts (computers) on one network. Because this number is so large for most single networks, it is much easier to logically partition a single IP network into subnetworks. This can be done by superimposing your own meaning on the host ID. For example, in figure 17.7 the host ID can be further divided into a subnet field and a host ID field. The subnet field is the logical address you assign to a network smaller than the original single network, consisting of 64,000 hosts.

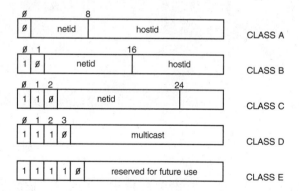

Figure 17.6:
Internet addressing.

The subnet mask is also specified in the dotted decimal form, in which a binary 1 in the mask corresponds to the network and a binary 0 corresponds to the host. For instance, a subnet mask of

255.255.255.0 means that the last 8 bits are assigned to the host ID (computer), and the remaining 24 bits are split between the net ID and the subnet ID. If you are using a class B address, the first 16 bits are used for the net ID, leaving 8 bits for the subnet ID.

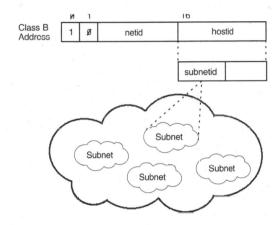

Figure 17.7:
Subnet addressing.

9. If you answered Yes for subnet masks, you must specify the subnet mask and press Enter. You are then asked if you have an IP router.

10. If you are connecting to another TCP/IP internetwork, you probably have at least one IP router. You must specify the IP address of the default router. All packets with IP addresses not known to the current network are then sent to this default IP router.

11. If you answered Yes for an IP router, enter the IP router internet address.

12. You are asked if you want to accept the default TCP/IP configuration parameters. If you are not sure about these parameters, accept the defaults. Otherwise, specify TCP/IP parameters. If you need to have more than eight TCP connections or four NetBIOS sessions, you have to override the default parameters. The configuration parameters that can be changed are the following:

    TCP connections

    UDP sockets

> IP raw connections
>
> NetBIOS sessions
>
> NetBIOS commands

13. You are asked if your network has a *Domain Name Server* (DNS), which automatically translates symbolic names to their equivalent IP addresses. For many UNIX-based hosts, this is popularly implemented by the *Berkeley Internet Name Domain Server* (BIND) program. If you have such a server, you must specify its IP address.

14. If you selected Yes to the DNS server, you must enter its IP address.

15. If you want to load NetBIOS to run applications developed by third-party vendors, you can answer Yes to the question on loading NetBIOS during system boot.

16. If you answer Yes to the question on using applications from an earlier release of LAN WorkPlace, a converter program will be loaded through AUTOEXEC.BAT to support the older applications.

17. Enter the user name you use to run the R-utilities (rcp, rsh, rexec, rpr, rpd, rps) to access a remote host. The user name you enter is stored in the DOS environment variable NAME, using the set NAME= command in your AUTOEXEC.BAT file.

18. To save your configuration information, answer Yes to update system files. System files are AUTOEXEC.BAT, CONFIG.SYS, NET.CFG, PROGRAM.INI, SYSTEM.INI, and WIN.INI.

19. Follow the instructions for inserting the LAN WorkPlace disks until the installation is complete.

Public Data Network Connectivity

When LANs are separated by large distances, connecting them together requires a physical transport medium. Because it is not always possible to install cables to span large distances separating LANs, it is easier and cheaper to use existing facilities to connect the LANs.

A common facility that most LANs have access to is the telephone circuit. Telephone lines are normally used for voice (analog) signals. *Modems* can be used to convert the digital data in packets to an analog signal for transmission across telephone lines. When *Integrated Services Digital Network* (ISDN) becomes widely available, the modem device will no longer be necessary because data will be sent in digital form across the physical transport. Telephone circuits can be used on a dial-up basis or the telephone circuit can be dedicated for data connections. The dedicated telephone circuits are called *leased lines*, and can be cheaper if they are in use constantly. A disadvantage of the telephone circuit is its limited data bandwidth. For higher data-transfer rate, synchronous circuits such as T1 can be used to connect LANs.

Another type of technology that is popular for transporting data across long distances is the X.25 network, which is traditionally used for terminal access to remote hosts (minicomputers and mainframes) and file transfers. X.25 speeds are not adequate for network-intensive LANs (the typical maximum is 64 Kbps), but they can be used for file transfer between LANs. X.25 is an international standard and is implemented by many public data networks. Many countries have public X.25 data networks, called *Public Data Networks* (PDNs).

This section explores Novell-based solutions for connecting LANs across large distances. The products that implement these solutions are the following:

- NetWare Link/X.25
- NetWare X.25 Gateway
- NetWare Asynchronous Remote Router
- NetWare Link/64
- NetWare Link/T1

NetWare Link/X.25

In figure 17.8, NetWare Link/X.25 simultaneously connects a NetWare network with up to 11 remote networks. The X.25 connection provides NetWare with access to a packet-switching PDN. Any host or computer system connected to the X.25 network, as well as any public or private databases, can be accessed by NetWare users.

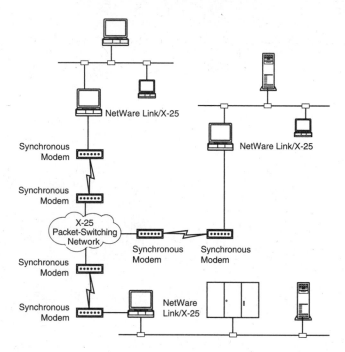

Figure 17.8:
NetWare Link/X.25.

An example of a public database is CompuServe, which has information on stock market prices, airline schedules, computer forums, and so on. Novell's NetWire forum also is on CompuServe. The CompuServe forum can be reached by ordinary dial-up lines using local telephone access numbers. Asynchronous modems can be used for dialing from your PC, but your data eventually goes into a *Packet Assembler/Disassembler* (PAD) or a synchronous modem for transmission across the X.25 network.

The NetWare Link/X.25 connection acts as a router and enables NetWare users to be connected to other NetWare LANs and users. Figure 17.8 illustrates three NetWare LANs connected by X.25 networks using NetWare Link/X.25. A maximum of 11 remote networks can be connected in this manner. The PDN multiplexes up to 11 connections (virtual circuits) over a single line, and it performs routing functions to send the traffic for each virtual circuit to its proper destination. NetWare X.25 works with private networks and public networks, such as SprintNet and Tymnet. Some of the PDN networks supported are listed in table 17.3.

Table 17.3
Certified Public Data Networks for NetWare/X.25 Products

Country	Network Name
Australia	Austpac
Austria	Radaus Data
Belgium	DCS
Canada	Datapac
Canada	Infoswitch CNCP
Chile	Entel
Denmark	Datapak
Finland	Datapak
Finland	Digipak
France	Transpac
Germany	Datex-P
Hong Kong	Datapak
Hong Kong	Intelpac
Netherlands	Datanet-1
New Zealand	Pacnet
Norway	Datapak
Portugal	Telepac
Singapore	Telepac
Spain	Iberpac
Sweden	Datapak
Switzerland	Telepac
UK	Packet Switch Stream
US	Accunet

continues

Table 17.3
Continued

Country	Network Name
US	CompuServe
US	Infonet
US	SprintNet (formerly Telenet)
US	Tymnet

The X.25 protocol recommendations are published every four years. NetWare X.25 supports the 1980 and 1984 CCITT recommendations for X.25 and X.75 (for connecting X.25 networks). Because most PDNs support these recommendations, NetWare Link/X.25 can be used with most of the international PDNs.

NetWare Link/X.25 operates as an external router that runs in either dedicated or nondedicated mode. The actual router interface and mechanisms are transparent to the user, enabling local network users to access remote resources as if they were local. Router connections are established or terminated using the X.25 CALL, ANSWER, and HANGUP commands.

Though any IBM PC, XT, AT, PS/2, or compatible can be used for NetWare Link/X.25, an 80286- or 80386-based machine is recommended. The minimum RAM requirements are 320K. For installation, one floppy disk drive is needed. Network connections include a network adapter for the local network and an X.25 board for the WAN link. The X.25 board is called the Novell *X.25 Extended Adapter*. The X.25 adapter is connected to a synchronous modem by means of a modem cable.

The external connections that are supported through the synchronous modem include leased lines and dial-up connections with speeds of 56 or 64 Kbps. For LAN-to-LAN connections the transport protocol is SPX/IPX. This is not surprising because this is the native protocol used to connect NetWare workstations to servers. Because of limited speeds, this type of network connection limits the applications to file transfers and terminal access. For situations in which remote-server-based applications are run at the workstation, the X.25 speeds are inadequate.

NetWare X.25 Gateway

NetWare X.25 Gateway software, running on a PC workstation with a Novell X.25 adapter, can turn the workstation to an X.25 Gateway for NetWare users. Gateway software enables multiple NetWare users to share a single link to a public or private X.25 Packet Data Network (PDN) and can be used by most major public data networks. Table 17.3 contains a list of X.25 networks that are also supported by the NetWare X.25 Gateway.

The NetWare X.25 Gateway can communicate with any host device that supports X.25 communications for asynchronous sessions. NetWare users must run terminal-emulation software in order to enable PCs to emulate asynchronous terminals, which are used to access other X.25 hosts. Many vendors, including Hewlett-Packard, IBM, Digital Equipment Corporation, Data General, Prime, Stratus, and Tandem, support X.25 communications on some or all of their computers. The X.25 Gateway supports a variety of terminal emulation packages. Depending on the emulation software used, a workstation can have up to eight simultaneous sessions. The terminal emulation software uses SPX/IPX or NetBIOS protocol to access the Gateway. The terminal emulation software selected must support the interrupt 14h (BIOS level) interface. Table 17.4 lists terminal-emulation packages that support the interrupt 14h interface and have been tested with the NetWare X.25 Gateway.

Table 17.4
Terminal-Emulation Software Tested with NetWare X.25 Gateway

Product	Vendor
AdvanceLink	Hewlett-Packard
CROSSTALK Mk.4	DCA/Crosstalk Communications
PROCOMM PLUS	Datastorm Technologies, Inc.
Reflection /+	Walker Richer & Quinn, Inc.
SimPC Master	Simware, Inc.
Softerm PC	Softronics
ZSTEM 240	KEA Systems, Ltd.

Figure 17.9 shows an X.25 Gateway connection to a NetWare LAN. The Gateway is typically connected to the packet-switching network through a high-speed synchronous modem. The X.25 Gateway PC provides the connection to the X.25 network, which is then shared by multiple LAN users.

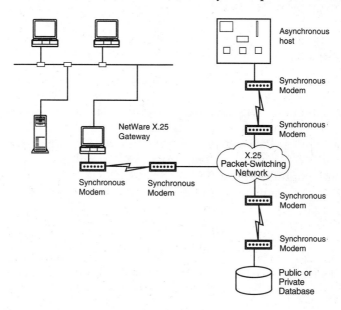

Figure 17.9:
NetWare X.25 Gateway.

The NetWare X.25 Gateway supports speeds from 1.2 Kbps to 64 Kbps. At speeds of 56 Kbps and above, the X.25 Gateway is usually connected to the packet-switching network through a *Channel Service Unit/Data Service Unit* (CSU/DSU). If the CSU/DSU is equipped with a V.35 interface, a V.35-to-RS-232-C converter is used. The data transfer rate across the X.25 Gateway is considerably faster than the 19.2 Kbps maximum speed of asynchronous gateways.

There are a number of considerations for selecting software for communicating with an X.25 Gateway.

- **Choice of supported terminal-emulation software.** To work with the NetWare X.25 Gateway, the software must support the interrupt 14h (BIOS level) interface.

- **Multiple gateway support.** In large installations, multiple gateways may be necessary for performance, reliability, and higher availability.

- **Number of host-terminal sessions.** Some terminal-emulation software enable a single user to access multiple hosts.

- **Script language.** Automating the login connection to a host is a very useful feature. A script language within an asynchronous terminal-emulation package can be used to implement this and many common chores, such as interacting with menus on the host.

- **Keyboard mapping.** Differences usually exist between the keyboard of a PC and an asynchronous terminal that the host expects to communicate with. Most terminal-emulation products provide a mapping of terminal function keys to keys on the PC keyboard. Macro-mapping features also can enable users to represent a sequence of keystrokes with a single keystroke.

- **International language support.** If NetWare workstations are to be used in an international network, the terminal emulation product should have translation tables for international language support.

- **Management.** Remote management of the connection is an important issue in host connectivity. Both the host system manager and the PC network supervisor need information about gateway activity, which can be used to solve gateway-related problems.

- **File transfer.** Users who need a host connection often need to transfer files between their workstation and the host. At least XMODEM and Kermit transfer protocol should be supported.

- **Memory constraints.** Memory requirements can become critical in a network environment. Terminal-emulation software can take up to 100K of PC memory, in addition to memory used by DOS and network software. The NetWare shell requires about 50K of memory. Because of the 640K restriction of DOS, users can quickly run out of memory necessary for running applications. OS/2 workstations do not suffer from the 640K restriction, but the OS/2 operating system and applications require more memory themselves, further increasing the need for memory. In any environment, memory-efficient terminal-emulation software is needed to optimize available memory.

Other features of NetWare X.25 Gateway include utilities for frame and packet-level statistics with trace capabilities; support for up to eight simultaneous sessions per workstation; assignment of *Switched Virtual Circuits* (SVCs); and support for dial-up X.25 connections, which offer occasional users a less-expensive alternative to leased lines. The transport protocols used to access the NetWare X.25 Gateway are SPX/IPX or NetBIOS. The maximum number of workstations and X.25 sessions supported by using Novell SPX/IPX are 97 users and 97 virtual circuits (sessions). If NetBIOS is used, the limits are 97 users and 254 virtual circuits. The X.25 line speeds are 1.2 Kbps to 64 Kbps, and the CCITT specifications supported are 1984 LAPB CCITT Recommendations X.25, X.3, X.28, X.29, and X.121. All 22 X.3 parameters are supported, both for mandatory and optional values. Parameters 1, 6, and 11 support the mandatory values only.

NetWare X.25 Gateway software requires an IBM PC, PS/2, or compatible with a network adapter, a connection to the network, at least one disk drive, and 512K of RAM. The NetWare X.25 Gateway also requires a synchronous modem and the Novell X.25 Extended Adapter.

NetWare Asynchronous Remote Router

The NetWare Asynchronous Remote Router software enables LANs to be connected over asynchronous dial-up lines to form a wide area network (see fig. 17.10). This product enables multiple asynchronous communications lines to be installed on a network, providing connections with other remote networks at speeds of up to 9.6 Kbps.

The link is transparent to users on either network from a procedural point of view, but because of its low speeds, users are usually aware of the longer time it takes to transfer data. Also, because of the lower speeds, applications requiring direct file access, such as databases, should not be run across asynchronous communications lines.

With NetWare Asynchronous Remote Router, the physical connections are made over voice-grade dial-up telephone lines. Because such connections are widely available, the network connections can be installed and reconfigured quickly; that is, networks can be connected to the WAN without waiting for installation of leased lines. With dial-up circuits, connections are made on demand, and if the usage is low, this can be an economical solution. For constant usage, leased lines (dedicated circuits) may turn out to be more economical.

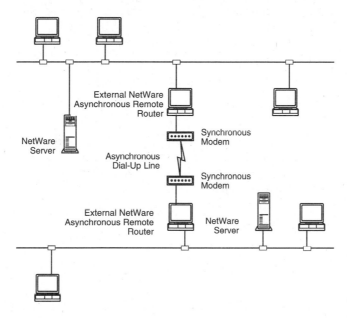

Figure 17.10:
NetWare Asynchronous Remote Router.

The NetWare Asynchronous Remote Router can be configured in any one of the following ways:

- A COM1 or COM2 port of a NetWare External Router can be used as a single-line asynchronous router.

- A communications adapter, called the *Wide Area Network Interface Module+* (WNIM+) can be installed in a NetWare file server. Each WNIM+ has an onboard processor, memory, and four asynchronous ports. A maximum of one WNIM+ can be installed in a NetWare file server.

- The WNIM+ can be installed in a network workstation, turning the workstation into an external router. A maximum of two WNIM+ adapters can be installed in a single external router, bringing the total number of lines supported to eight.

Support for both the server and external asynchronous router using COM1, COM2, or the WNIM+ is bundled with NetWare v2.x and NetWare v3.x.

Additional copies of the NetWare Asynchronous Remote Router are required for additional external routers and must be purchased separately.

Novell does not recommend that the NetWare file server be used as a remote router, except in very small networks that use low-line speeds. The NetWare operating system has to process every character or group of characters it receives. For a high volume of asynchronous traffic, the server performance for other operations is seriously degraded.

When installing the NetWare Asynchronous Remote Router software in an external router, an IBM PC, XT, AT, or compatible can be used to run the router software. Novell recommends using an 80286- or 80386-based machine. The asynchronous router needs a network adapter for the local network and an asynchronous port. The asynchronous port can be COM1 or COM2 serial ports or the ports on WNIM+ adapters. The WNIM+ is connected to asynchronous modems through RS-232 cables. If COM1 or COM2 ports are used, the maximum speeds are 2400 bps. With WNIM+ boards, speeds up to 9600 bps are possible.

A dedicated router operating in real mode requires a minimum of 512K of RAM, and a nondedicated bridge operating in real mode requires a minimum of 640K. Dedicated 80286 and 80386 bridges running in protected mode require a minimum of 1M of RAM.

NetWare Link/64

NetWare Link/64 enables remote NetWare LANs to be connected through synchronous communications lines (see fig. 17.11). This product supports speeds from 9600 bps to 64 Kbps. NetWare Link/64 routes SPX/IPX and NetBIOS protocols over wide area networks. NetWare routing protocol (RIP) dynamically determines the shortest path for each packet, based on the current network topology. Inactive links are automatically bypassed.

NetWare Link/64 software can run in the file server with NetWare or in an external router. The external router can run in either a dedicated or non-dedicated mode. The Link/64 software communicates with a synchronous adapter that can support the V.35, RS-422, and RS-232 interfaces. Any one of the following synchronous adapters can be used:

■ Novell Synchronous/V.35+ (up to 2.048 Mbps)

■ Novell Synchronous/RS-422+ (up to 2.048 Mbps)

■ Novell Synchronous/RS-232+ (19.2 Kbps)

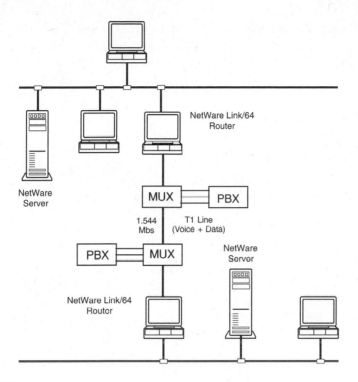

Figure 17.11:
NetWare Link/64.

These Novell products can work with existing customer equipment, including Data Service Units/Channel Service Units (DSUs/CSUs), synchronous modems, multiplexers, and data switches. A summary of the functions and features of NetWare Link/64 follows:

- Diagnostic programs for installation verification and on-line trouble-shooting.

- Utilities for generating network loads and checking error rates under normal loads or stress testing.

- Support for V.35, RS-422, and RS-232 interfaces.

- NetWare Link/64 can work with any NetWare-supported network, including Ethernet, Token Ring, and ARCnet.

NetWare Link/64 is designed to run at a maximum speed of 64 Kbps. If applications requiring high throughput are used on the network, the higher performance provided by NetWare Link/T1 may be needed.

NetWare Link/T1

NetWare Link/T1 enables remote NetWare LANs to be connected by a T1 network. If a T1 network is not available, a point-to-point T1-circuit can be used. The connection is by synchronous communications lines over speeds ranging from 9,600 bps to 1.544 or 2.048 Mbps. In North America, T1 speeds are 1.544 Mbps, whereas in Europe they are set to 2.048 Mbps.

Figure 17.12 shows NetWare LANs connected by using NetWare Link/T1. This product enables connectivity at LAN speeds (greater than 1 Mbps), which means that applications can run across remote LANs connected by NetWare Link/T1. NetWare Link/T1 is designed for users who need high-speed LAN-to-LAN communications. Examples of these communications are applications requiring high throughput, such as databases, direct-file access, and rapid file transfers.

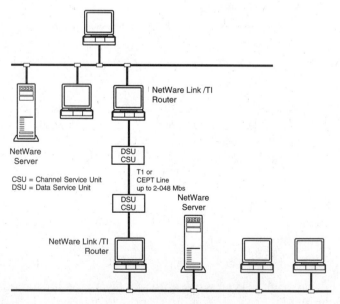

Figure 17.12:
NetWare Link/T1.

The T1 circuit acts as the physical transport medium on which IPX/SPX and NetBIOS packet traffic can run. NetWare routing protocols (RIP—Routing Information Protocol) are used to dynamically determine the shortest path and fastest route for each packet, based on the current network topology. Failed links are automatically bypassed by the routing protocol.

NetWare Link/T1 software can run in the file server with NetWare (internal router) or in an external router. If performance is a consideration, the external router configuration gives better performance. The external router can run in either a dedicated or nondedicated mode. When running in an external router, the NetWare Link/T1 software requires DOS 3.x or higher. It also can run on the NetWare v3.x as an NLM or on NetWare v2.x server as a VAP.

NetWare Link/T1 software can be used with T1 network adapters, such as Novell's Synchronous/+ Adapters, which support the V.35, RS-422, and RS-232 interfaces. These adapters are the following:

- Novell Synchronous/V.35+ (up to 2.048 Mbps)

- Novell Synchronous/RS-422+ (up to 2.048 Mbps)

- Novell Synchronous/RS-232+ (19.2 Kbps)

These network adapters can work with existing customer equipment such as DSU/CSUs, synchronous modems, multiplexers, and data switches.

NetWare Link/T1 comes with diagnostic programs that can be used for installation verification and on-line troubleshooting. Utilities are provided for generating network loads and checking error rates under normal loads or stress loads. NetWare Link/T1 can be used to connect any NetWare-supported network such as Ethernet, Token Ring, and ARCnet.

IBM Host Connectivity

Novell provides a variety of products to connect with IBM's *Systems Network Architecture* (SNA) network environment. These products have made NetWare LANs acceptable in the IBM network environment. Novell gained much of its earlier expertise in SNA products through the acquisition of CXI, which was known for its SNA connectivity products.

This section discusses solutions for connecting NetWare LANs to IBM minicomputers and mainframes. Before discussing these solutions, a few words concerning IBM's SNA architecture and the vocabulary and terminology used to describe their communication products will make the discussion that follows more understandable.

The network architecture used by IBM for connecting its mainframe computers, IBM hosts, to terminals is called *SNA*. Figure 17.13 shows an example of an IBM SNA network that has a single domain. A *domain* consists of an IBM host and the communications network that provides access to it. Users interact to IBM hosts through terminals such as the IBM 3278 and IBM 3279. The terminals are managed by a specialized device called the *cluster controller*. The cluster controller (*terminal controller* in other network architectures) is needed because, by themselves, the terminals are "dumb"; the cluster controller handles the networking and connectivity chores on behalf of the terminals. The cluster controllers are managed by a *Front End Processor* (FEP) called the *communications controller*. The communications controller talks to the IBM host and offloads many of the communications functions that would otherwise have to be performed by the IBM host. The communication in this type of architecture is managed by the *Virtual Telecommunication Access Method* (VTAM) program, which runs on the host, and/or the *Network Control Program* (NCP), which runs on the communications controller.

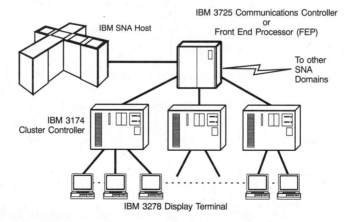

Figure 17.13:
IBM SNA network.

Many of the techniques that are used to provide connections to the IBM SNA network involve some form of device emulation. The devices that are popularly emulated are the IBM 3278 and 3279 terminals, and the IBM cluster controller. Emulating the IBM terminals is called *3270 emulation*. When you hear a product name, such as the NetWare 3270 CUT Workstation, you can tell from the use of the 3270 that this product involves terminal emulation.

The device that emulates an IBM cluster controller is called an *SNA gateway* because it can be connected to the IBM communications controller, and it can provide access to an SNA network from a non-SNA network.

NetWare for SAA

NetWare for SAA provides LAN-to-host connectivity for SNA networks. These connectivity options are integrated with the NetWare v3.x operating system. The host communications are managed by NLMs running on the NetWare server. At the heart of this product is the *Communications Executive* (see fig. 17.14), which provides communications-specific extensions to the NetWare operating system. Other services, such as X.25, wide area network routing, and remote LAN access, run on top of the Communications Executive.

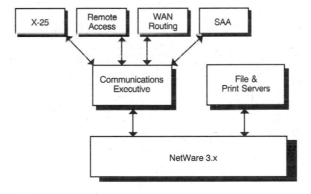

Figure 17.14:
NetWare for SAA Communications Executive.

The Communications Executive provides a core set of functions available to applications services located on the server and to client applications running on workstations. The Communication Executive and NetWare for SAA are implemented as *NetWare Loadable Modules* (NLMs). These NLMs can be configured to run in conjunction with file and print services on a single server, or they can be installed on a NetWare v3.11 server dedicated to communications services (see fig. 17.15). NetWare for SAA comes with a kernel version of NetWare v3.x that does not provide any file services. The NetWare kernel can be used to configure dedicated communications services, as shown in figure 17.15.

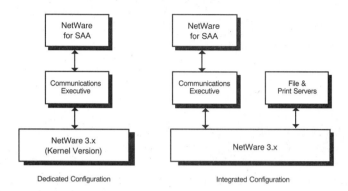

Figure 17.15:
Dedicated versus integrated configuration for NetWare for SAA.

The network connections supported by NetWare for SAA are either Token Ring or SDLC connections to the host. Token Ring connections can be made through 3174 cluster controllers, 37xx front-end processors, or integrated Token Ring controllers on the 9370 and AS/400 systems. SDLC connections can use synchronous modems to a 37xx front-end processor at speeds of up to 64 Kbps.

Access to the NetWare for SAA services can be made by using the NetWare 3270 LAN Workstation for DOS. The total number of host connections supported by NetWare for SAA can be up to 64. These sessions can be any combination of display, printer, or *Advanced Program-to-Program Communications* (APPC) sessions.

Additionally, NetWare for SAA can emulate a PU 2.0 (cluster controller) device when accessing host applications. It also can emulate PU2.1 (smart cluster controller) peer-to-peer connections between LAN workstations hosts and workstations on the Token Ring LAN.

Because NetWare for SAA runs on a NetWare server, any workstation that can access the server can make use of its services. This access can be provided by any of the LANs supported by NetWare such as ARCnet, Ethernet, and Token Ring. The native NetWare protocols such as SPX/IPX are used to provide a connection to NetWare for SAA. Figures 17.16 and 17.17 show NetWare for SAA configured for a Token Ring and an SDLC connection.

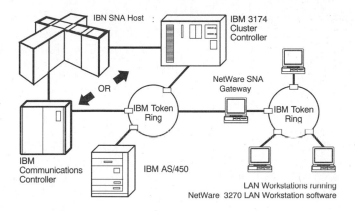

Figure 17.16:
NetWare for SAA configured for Token Ring.

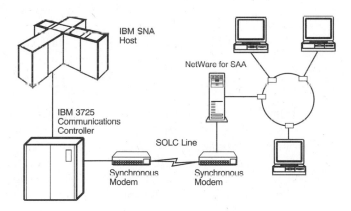

Figure 17.17:
NetWare for SAA configured for SDLC.

In function, the NetWare for SAA acts as a gateway, but it is more versatile than the NetWare Gateway products. The features and functions of NetWare for SAA are enumerated in the following list:

■ Integrated with NetWare v3.x. Because NetWare v3.x is a multi-tasking operating system, the limitations of running on a DOS platform are eliminated. NetWare for SAA is implemented as a collection of NLMs.

■ There is a choice of dedicated or nondedicated configurations for NetWare for SAA. The dedicated configuration uses a NetWare kernel version that does not have the overhead of file services; it provides better performance than the nondedicated configuration.

■ The NetWare for SAA NLM configuration can be done dynamically—the NLMS can be loaded and unloaded even while the server is running.

■ Because it runs on a NetWare v3.x platform, NetWare for SAA can make use of the fault-tolerance capabilities of NetWare v3.x, including SFT Levels I, II, III, and TTS, and the security and management services of NetWare.

■ The 64 host sessions can be any combination of display, printer, and APPC sessions.

■ Support for both pooled and dedicated LUs. *LU Groups* are pools of LUs for which a user or group of users has access rights. A user can reference these LU Groups by name when requesting host sessions. Based on the user's access rights, the LUs are dynamically allocated from the named group on a first-come, first-served basis. With dedicated LUs, LUs are allocated to specific users, and they can simultaneously access LU Groups and dedicated LUs.

■ Communication-specific security. Besides NetWare security, administrators also can implement communication-security measures through the use of *Access Control Lists* (ACLs). ACLs are lists of NetWare users or groups authorized to use communications resources, such as specific host connections, LU Groups, and dedicated LUs. The communication-security mechanism is integrated with the NetWare bindery for ease of management.

■ NetView interface. NetWare for SAA includes an interface to IBM's NetView so that management can be integrated with the host-based network-management system. The interface to NetView is based on IBM's Entry Point model and makes the server running the NetWare Communication Services software appear to the host as an IBM device.

■ Name service. NetWare for SAA extends NetWare Name Service to address communications resources such as hosts and links by name. This enables access to a communications resource without knowing which route to take. It also supports single network logins.

- Diagnostic trace utility. The trace utility enables a network manager to request a trace for all LUs or for a specific LU.

- Menu-driven CSCON configuration utility.

Configuring NetWare for SAA involves configuring the connected mainframes to recognize NetWare for SAA. The *Virtual Telecommunications Access Method* (VTAM) software on the host—which controls the host network, and/or the *Network Control Program* (NCP) software, running on a front-end processor—must be configured to recognize the server running NetWare for SAA and the sessions it supports. Configuration information about the host and the host link must be entered through the CSCON configuration utility.

NetWare for SAA requires an IBM PC 386 (or higher) or a PS/2 (or compatible), installed with the NetWare v3.x operating system. The server must have a minimum of 6M of RAM. In addition, the server must have a LAN adapter for communicating with the workstations on the network and a communications adapter for the host connection.

Novell has tested a variety of hardware configurations for the NetWare for SAA product. Before installing the product, you might wish to obtain the most recent list of tested hardware from Novell. For host connections, Novell recommends the following:

- Novell Synchronous Adapter for the PC or the IBM Multiprotocol Adapter/A for Micro Channel for speeds up to 19.2 Kbps.

- Novell Synchronous/V.35 Adapter for the PC for speeds up to 64 Kbps.

For Token Ring connections, Novell recommends the following:

- Cabling type: Type A (shielded twisted pair) cabling in the IBM Cabling System or an equivalent.

- Two Token Ring adapters to split loads on a heavily used NetWare for SAA computer. One adapter can be used for host communications and the second can be used for LAN communications.

- Host connections to Token Ring: A 3174 cluster controller with the Token Ring Network Gateway Feature (IBM Feature #3025); a 3720/25/45 front-end processor with a Token Ring Interface Coupler or Token Ring Adapter; an IBM AS/400 with the IBM Token Ring Network Adapter (#6160) or the IBM Token Ring Network Subsystem (#6240); or a 937x with the IBM Token Ring Subsystem Controller Option.

Users who need to access the host device through NetWare for SAA need the NetWare 3270 LAN Workstation for DOS software, which enables their workstations to emulate 3270 terminals and 3287 printers, transfer files to and from the host, and run LU6.2 transaction programs. The limits for NetWare for SAA are currently 64 remote connections to the host and 64 connections through Token Ring. Up to 250 users can be defined as users of the communications services but no more than 64 can simultaneously access NetWare for SAA. Maximum line speeds supported are 64 Kbps for remote SDLC and 16 Mbps for Token Ring.

NetWare for SAA provides access to IBM AS/400 minicomputers through the Token Ring Connection. The AS/400 must be connected with an IBM or compatible Token Ring Adapter. Although most AS/400 applications are supported by NetWare for SAA, the following applications have been certified by Novell:

- IBM OfficeVision/400

- IBM AS/400 Query

- IBM AS/400 Online Education

- IBM AS/400 Utilities

NetWare SNA Gateway

The NetWare SNA Gateway software can run on any IBM PC or PS/2 and convert it into an SNA Gateway server. The NetWare SNA Gateway emulates an IBM cluster controller, and enables DOS machines on a LAN, such as Token Ring, to connect to the NetWare SNA Gateway and, through it, to the SNA host. Essentially, the NetWare SNA Gateway emulation is that of a Node Type 2.0 (PU) or 2.1 device, such as a cluster controller.

Depending on the type of host connection used, the NetWare SNA Gateway enables as many as 97 PCs or PS/2s on a LAN to communicate with an IBM or compatible SNA mainframe or midrange computer. The DOS machines communicate with the NetWare SNA Gateway software by using SPX or NetBIOS protocols. The NetWare SNA Gateway itself supports four different host connection options: Coaxial, CoaxMux, Remote, or Token Ring. Selecting the right option is an issue of cost and budget. These four options are discussed in the following sections:

- **Coaxial.** This option supports up to five host display and 3287 printer sessions through a coaxial connection between an emulator adapter in the Gateway server and an SNA DFT port on a 3x74 cluster controller. This connection is illustrated in figure 17.18.

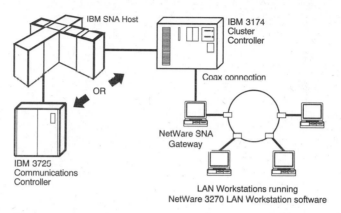

Figure 17.18:
NetWare SNA Gateway: Coaxial connection.

■ **CoaxMux.** This option supports up to 40 display and printer sessions. The required PC-emulation adapter is connected through coaxial to a 3299 multiplexer port on a 3x74 cluster controller. This type of connection enables the gateway to multiplex eight five-session DFT lines over a single coaxial connection. This connection is illustrated in figure 17.19.

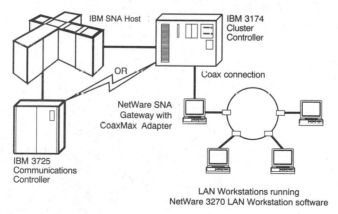

Figure 17.19:
NetWare SNA Gateway: CoaxMux connection.

■ **Remote.** This option supports up to 128 SNA host display and
printer sessions on up to 97 workstations by means of an asynchronous modem connection to a 37xx front-end processor at speeds of
up to 64 Kbps. This connection is illustrated in figure 17.20.

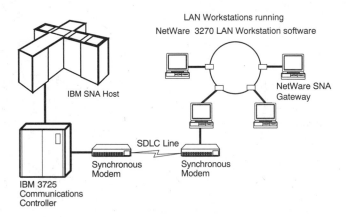

Figure 17.20:
NetWare SNA Gateway: Remote connection.

■ **Token Ring.** Up to 128 host terminal and printer sessions are
available to 97 workstations on a Token Ring network. The host
connection can be made through the IBM 3174, 3720, 3725, 3745,
9370, or AS/400 if they are capable of Token Ring access. This
connection is illustrated in figure 17.21.

For Coaxial connections, the Novell Coax Adapter for the PC or PS/2 can be
used. This adapter is connected to an IBM 3x74 or compatible cluster controller with coaxial cable such as RG-62 A/U. Alternatively, the IBM 3278/79
Adapter, the IBM 3270 Connection Adapter, the IRMA Convertible, or an
IRMA I prom-based adapter with Novell-supplied IRMA PROMS can be
used. The cluster controller must be configured for *Dual Function Terminal*
(DFT) mode.

For CoaxMux connections, the Novell CoaxMux Adapter for the PC can be
used. This adapter is connected to a 3299 port on an IBM SNA 3174 or 3274
controller by means of a RG-62 A/U coaxial cable.

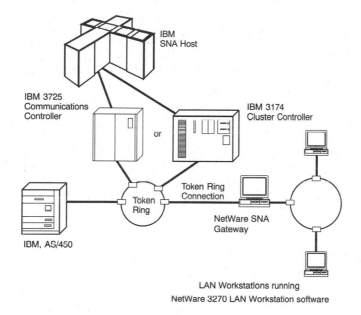

Figure 17.21:
NetWare SNA Gateway: Token Ring connection.

For Remote connections, you can use a remote communications adapter that connects by means of synchronous, externally clocked modems over SNA/SDLC lines to an IBM 37xx front-end processor or equivalent. Depending on the adapter, it is either connected to the modem by means of an RS-232 modem cable or a V.35 cable.

The Novell Synchronous Adapter for the PC or the IBM Multiprotocol Adapter/A for the Micro Channel can be used for speeds of up to 19.2 Kbps. For speeds of up to 64 Kbps, the Novell Synchronous/V.35 Adapter for the PC can be used. Tests have shown that both the Novell Synchronous Adapter and the Novell Synchronous/V.35 Adapter perform best when used in a 386-based or better machine. Although this configuration can support up to 97 workstations and 128 sessions, decreasing the number of host sessions frees more memory and processing power for gateway operations.

For Token Ring connections, an IBM or compatible Token Ring adapter can be used. The Token Ring Network requires Type A (shielded twisted pair) cabling in the IBM Cabling System or an equivalent. One of the following host devices must be connected to the Token Ring network: a 3174 cluster controller with the Token Ring Network Gateway Feature (IBM Feature #3025); a 3720/25/45 front-end processor with a Token Ring Interface Coupler or Token Ring Adapter; an IBM AS/400 with the IBM Token Ring Network Adapter (IBM Feature #6160) or the IBM Token Ring Network Subsystem (IBM Feature #6240); or a 937x with the IBM Token Ring Subsystem Controller Option.

For a Token Ring connection to the SNA network, the IEEE 802.2 protocol is used to communicate with the host. This means that the NetWare SNA Gateway must be on the same ring as the host device or connected to the host ring through an IBM Token Ring Bridge using source routing.

For workstation-to-NetWare gateway communications, SPX/IPX or NetBIOS protocols are used.

Any one of these adapters must be placed in the PC to act as the NetWare SNA Gateway. A second LAN adapter must also be placed in the gateway for LAN communications. For reasonable performance, a realistic number of host sessions must be used. Configuring with a maximum of 97 workstations and 128 sessions usually results in sluggish performance.

NetWare SNA Gateway includes NetWare LU6.2 for supporting distributed applications that operate in a peer-to-peer fashion using the *Advanced Peer to Peer Communications* (APPC). LU 6.2 is an implementation of IBM's APPC architecture, which supports peer-to-peer connections to PU2.1 devices. The NetWare SNA Gateway product includes keyboard files, templates, and documentation to facilitate connection to an IBM AS/400 through a Token Ring attachment. A Gateway Status utility provides status information on available host sessions, host-link status, session (LU) identification, and workstation status. There are management tools that include an internal trace facility for quick diagnosis and a self-test that isolates LAN problems between the gateway and the workstation.

NetWare SNA Gateway uses the *Service Advertising Protocol* (SAP) to broadcast its existence, meaning that all interconnected NetWare LANs are aware of the existence of the NetWare SNA Gateways and can make use of their services.

Multiple NetWare SNA Gateways can coexist on a single LAN, which enables access to multiple hosts and the capability to distribute the session load across several gateways. The NetWare SNA Gateway also enables implementation of backup gateways for redundancy and load-sharing among several gateways connected to a heavily used host.

Access to the SNA Gateway for PC users is provided by Token Ring LANs, which provide high-speed IBM host access and gateway capabilities to other LAN topologies. The NetWare SNA Gateway can bridge Novell-supported environments, such as Ethernet, by using both a Token Ring and an Ethernet adapter in the gateway machine.

NetWare SNA Gateway supports both pooled and dedicated LUs. Pooled LUs can be accessed by users on a first-come, first-served basis. Dedicated LUs enable network supervisors to assign LUs to specific users. The SNA gateway can be run as either a dedicated or nondedicated server. Because of the processing power needed to perform the gateway functions, it is recommended that the dedicated server configuration be used.

Before the gateway can be connected to the SNA host, the *Virtual Telecommunications Access Method* (VTAM) software on the host, which controls the host network and the *Network Control Program* (NCP) software, which runs on a communications controller (IBM 37XX), must be configured to recognize the SNA Gateway and the sessions it supports. This may require the help of the SNA host personnel. The product does come with worksheets that help the NetWare SNA Gateway installer to obtain information on the SNA host.

One key decision to make before installing NetWare SNA Gateway is the type of connection that makes the most sense for your environment— remote, coaxial, or Token Ring. This decision dictates the type of communications hardware to use with the gateway software. The same software package works with all three connections.

In general, a remote connection is required whenever the SNA host is at a distance from the users and cannot be easily connected by other means.

Coaxial connections provide a middle ground for connecting to local hosts, and they provide higher performance than remote connections (and usually cost less than Token Ring connections).

Token Ring connections provide the highest performance currently available, but they also have the highest cost. They give greater flexibility because the Token Ring also can be used for general LAN connectivity.

Regardless of the type of connection used, all configurations of the NetWare SNA Gateway require an IBM PC, PS/2, or recommended compatible with a network adapter and a connection to the SNA network. Because the performance of the gateway machine affects both gateway throughput and performance, this should be a high-performance machine, such as an 80486-based PC. The gateway configuration can operate in nondedicated mode in any workstation. Although the nondedicated gateway makes the solution more economical, the gateway is at the mercy of the workstation users and is susceptible to rebooting when it is used in nondedicated mode. The software requires 202K to 502K of RAM, depending on the connectivity option chosen and the number of sessions for which the software is configured.

Novell publishes a list of PCs and network hardware for which the SNA Gateway has been tested. Before buying the hardware, it is a good idea to obtain the most current list to avoid hardware/software compatibility problems.

In addition to the NetWare SNA Gateway software that provides connection to the SNA environment, users need to run the NetWare 3270 LAN Workstation software, which enables workstations to emulate 3270 terminals, and 3287 printers, and to transfer files to and from the host. The applications tested and certified by Novell that can be run at the workstations are the following: IBM OfficeVision/400, IBM AS/400 Query, IBM AS/400 Online Education, and IBM AS/400 Utilities.

Optional software for AS/400 communications also can be used, which includes the AS/400 Token Ring Gateway connection with additional keyboard files to create 5250 keyboard layouts on the NetWare 3270 LAN Workstations. The keys supported are 3270 keys, with the exception of special function keys provided by the IBM 3270 Remote Attachment Feature. Novell also recommends the use of Spectrum Concepts' XCOM6.2 File Transfer software for file transfer between the 3270 LAN Workstations and the AS/400 through a separate NetWare SNA Gateway configured for LU6.2. The XCOM6.2 software is required on the PC and on the AS/400.

NetWare 3270 LAN Workstation for DOS

In the discussion on NetWare SNA Gateway, it was mentioned that the user needs terminal-emulation software to access the SNA host. The NetWare 3270 LAN Workstation for DOS provides this terminal-emulation capability, along with printer emulation. This product can be used with NetWare SNA Gateway or NetWare for SAA.

The emulation software supports up to five host sessions per workstation, which can be any combination of display, printer, *Advanced Program-to-Program Communications* (APPC) sessions, DOS session, file transfer, and keyboard-remapping utility. The data traffic from the workstation is sent across the LAN by using SPX/IPX or NetBIOS. The product is currently sold on a server license, which allows one copy of the software per file server, regardless of the number of workstations that use it.

File transfers between workstation and host are accomplished by using the SEND/RECEIVE or TRANSFER utilities, which are included with the software. The SEND/RECEIVE utilities upload and download files to and from the host by working with IBM's IND$FILE host file-transfer software in the TSO, CMS, and CICS environments. The TRANSFER utility can be used for the transfer of RFT and FFT data between the PC and the host when running SAA office applications, such as OfficeVision and DISOSS.

The features and functions of NetWare 3270 LAN workstation for DOS include the following:

- NetWare LU6.2 for support of LU6.2 applications.

- Automatic reattach that can reestablish the connection between the workstation and gateway if the gateway fails and is brought back up.

- Printer-session customization, which enables users to assign a printer to either a network or local printer, specify the number of lines-per-page, and configure software to automatically invoke a host printer session whenever it is loaded.

- Emulation of IBM 3270 terminals and 3287 printers.

- Support for up to five display and printer sessions per LAN workstation. These five sessions can be established with multiple hosts simultaneously when using NetWare for SAA.

- SEND/RECEIVE or TRANSFER software enables files to be transferred between the PC and the host.

- Support for commonly used APIs such as IBM's EEHLLAPI and Low-Level API, as well as for Novell's NetWare 3270 API.

- Keyboard-mapping capability and international language keyboard support.

- Redirection of host screen prints and 3287 printing-to-network printers.

- Support for extended data stream, including reverse video, underlining, highlighting, and seven colors.

- Internal trace and diagnostic facility.

■ Support for pointing devices, such as light pens and Microsoft mouse-compatible devices.

NetWare 3270 LAN Workstation for DOS software emulates up to five display (LU2), printer (LU1 or LU3), and APPC (LU6.2) sessions per workstation. These LUs must be defined in the VTAM software, which runs on the host and controls the host network; and/or the Network Control Program, which runs on a front-end processor.

The NetWare 3270 LAN Workstation software is designed to work with NetWare operating systems v2.x and above by using SPX or any IBM NetBIOS network. At the workstation, DOS 3.1 or above and the appropriate NetWare adapter driver are required. For PS/2 workstations, DOS3.3 or above must be used.

When loaded at the workstation, the software takes up a minimum of 121K of RAM for a single session to a NetWare SNA Gateway or NetWare for SAA. More memory is required to support additional sessions and functionality.

An option in the NetWare 3270 LAN Workstation for DOS is the NetWare 3270 Vector Graphics Option, which adds graphics capability to one host display session. The Vector Graphics Option supports the features and functions of an IBM 3179G color graphics terminal and of the IBM 3270 PC G. This option enables the use of host graphics applications such as GDDM, SAS/GRAPH, DISSPLA, and TELLAGRAF.

Remote user connection can be provided by using the *NetWare Access Server* (NAS), which allows up to six remote users to dial in to a NetWare network and run NetWare 3270 LAN Workstation for DOS software.

Application developers can make use of the development tools and APIs provided by the NetWare 3270 Tools. The API support includes DOS-supported APIs, such as NetWare 3270 API, IBM EEHLLAPI, and IBM Low-Level API.

NetWare 3270 CUT Workstation

The NetWare 3270 LAN products require workstations to be connected by a LAN. If a single stand-alone PC workstation needs to be connected to an SNA host, the LAN solution can become cost-prohibitive. A product called the *NetWare 3270 Control Unit Terminal* (CUT) *Workstation* can be used instead (see fig. 17.22). It is a software package that provides 3270 terminal-emulation and enables IBM PC, PS/2, and compatible work-stations to emulate an IBM display terminal for communications with IBM mainframes.

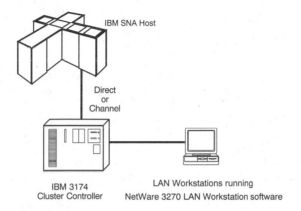

Figure 17.22:
NetWare 3270 CUT Workstation.

The workstation communicates with the host by means of a direct coaxial connection to a 3x74 or compatible cluster controller. Users can transfer files to and from the host by using the SEND/RECEIVE utilities. The SEND/RECEIVE utilities upload and download files to and from the host, by working with IBM's IND$FILE host file transfer software in the TSO, CMS, and CICS environments. Other features and functions of the product include the following:

- Stand-alone PC users can access and run 3270 applications.

- Support for an extended data stream, including reverse video, underlining, highlighting, and seven colors.

- Support for common application-programming interfaces, including NetWare 3270 API, IBM EEHLLAPI and LLAPI, and DCA IRMA Subroutines.

- Support for one host and one DOS session.

- Support for file transfer through NetWare 3270 SEND/RECEIVE commands.

- Keyboard-mapping utility and international language keyboard support.

■ Support for pointing devices, such as light pens and Microsoft-compatible mice.

A coaxial interface adapter is required for each workstation that needs access to the host. This adapter is connected to an IBM 3x74 or compatible cluster controller with coaxial cable, such as the RG-62 A/U. The coaxial interface adapter can be the Novell Coax Adapter (for the PC or PS/2),the IBM 3278/79 Adapter, the IBM 3270 Connection Adapter, or the IRMA Convertible.

The NetWare 3270 CUT Workstation software is designed to run in a stand-alone workstation running DOS 3.1 or above; it takes up a minimum 58K of RAM.

NetWare 3270 Multiworkstation

The NetWare 3270 CUT Workstation software enables only a single session to the SNA host. The *NetWare 3270 Multiworkstation* is designed to overcome the single-session limitation. It is a single station terminal-emulation software, but it enables IBM PC, PS/2, and compatible workstations to emulate up to five IBM display terminals and printers for communications with IBM mainframes.

These workstations are directly connected to the host by means of one of three connectivity options: coaxial, Token Ring, or SDLC (see fig. 17.23). The product includes file-transfer support, support for multiple application-programming interfaces, and workstation-customization tools.

The coaxial option requires a coaxial adapter for each PC that needs a host connection. This adapter is connected to an IBM 3x74 or compatible cluster controller with coaxial cable, such as the RG-62 A/U. The coaxial adapter can be the Novell Coax Adapter for the PC or PS/2, the IBM 3278/79 Adapter, the IBM 3270 Connection Adapter, or the DCA Convertible Adapter. An IRMA I prom-based adapter with Novell-supplied PROMS also can be used. The cluster controller must be configured for DFT mode.

A remote connection to the host also is possible, requiring a remote communications adapter that connects through synchronous, externally clocked modems over SNA/SDLC lines to an IBM 37xx communications controller. This adapter is connected to the modem through an RS-232 modem cable. For PC and AT bus machines, the Novell Synchronous Adapter for the PC is required. The IBM Multiprotocol Adapter/A for the Micro Channel Architecture bus can be used in PS/2 or compatible machines.

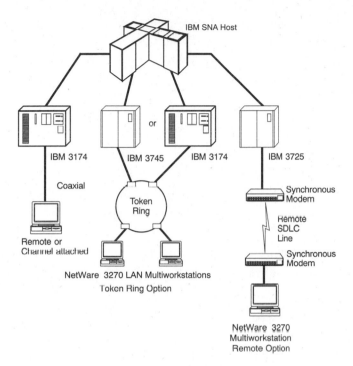

Figure 17.23:
NetWare 3270 Multiworkstation.

An IBM Token Ring stand-alone connection requires an IBM or compatible Token Ring adapter. The Token Ring Network requires Type A (shielded twisted pair) cabling in the IBM Cabling System or an equivalent. One of the following host devices must be connected to the Token Ring network: a 3174 cluster controller with the Token Ring Network Gateway Feature (IBM Feature # 3025); a 3720/25/45 front-end processor with a *Token Ring Interface Coupler* (TIC) or *Token Ring Adapter* (TRA); or a 937x with the IBM Token Ring Subsystem Controller Option. The IEEE 802.2 protocol is used to communicate with the host. Because of this, users of the Token Ring connection option must be on the same ring with the host device or be connected to the host ring through the 802.3 bridge using source routing.

With the NetWare 3270 Multiworkstation option, users can transfer files to and from the host by using the SEND/RECEIVE or TRANSFER utilities. The SEND/RECEIVE utilities upload and download files to and from the host by working with IBM's IND$FILE host file-transfer software in the TSO, CMS, and CICS environments. The TRANSFER program enables the transfer of RFT and FFT data between the PC and the host when running *Systems Application Architecture* (SAA) office applications such as OfficeVision and DISOSS. Features and functions of the multiworkstation product include the following:

- Emulation of IBM 3278/9 terminals and 3287 printers and support of up to five concurrent host terminal and printer sessions and a DOS session on a single workstation.

- File Transfer Utilities. SEND/RECEIVE or TRANSFER software.

- Support for many common application programming interfaces, including NetWare 3270 API, IBM EEHLLAPI and LLAPI, and DCA IRMA Subroutines.

- Keyboard-mapping utility and international language support.

- Redirection of host screen prints and 3287 printing-to-network printers.

- Extended data stream, including reverse video, underlining, highlighting, and seven colors.

- Internal trace facility for problem diagnosis.

- Support for pointing devices such as the light pen and Microsoft mouse-compatible devices.

For a large number of users, installing a LAN and a gateway may be more cost-effective than the Multiworkstation option.

The NetWare 3270 Multiworkstation requires an IBM PC, PS/2, or recommended compatible, with at least one disk drive and 256K of RAM. The type of communications hardware needed for the software depends on the type of connection: coaxial, SDLC, or Token Ring.

An option of the NetWare 3270 Multiworkstation and the Token Ring Server Option supports the use of the NetWare 3270 Vector Graphics Option, which adds graphics capability to one host display session. The Vector Graphics Option supports the features and functions of an IBM 3179G color graphics terminal, as well as those of the IBM 3270 PC G. This allows network users to run host graphics applications such as GDDM, SAS/GRAPH, DISSPLA, and TELLAGRAF.

NetWare 5250 Gateway

The NetWare 5250 Twinax Gateway turns a PC or PS/2 on a NetWare LAN into a gateway server that can be used to access an IBM AS/400 or System/3X minicomputer (see fig. 17.24). The gateway communicates with the AS/400 or System/3X through a local twinaxial or remote SDLC connection. IBM PCs on a NetWare LAN can then use this gateway to access information and applications on the minicomputer. In essence, the NetWare 5250 Gateway enables AS/400 or System/3X users to combine the functions of their personal computer with those of a midrange terminal.

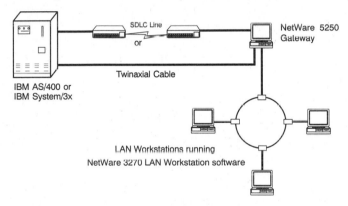

Figure 17.24:
NetWare 5250 Gateway.

The NetWare 5250 Gateway supports up to seven local or nine remote concurrent display or host-addressable printer sessions to PCs attached to the network, with up to five of those available concurrently to any single workstation.

The features offered by the NetWare 5250 Gateway include the following:

■ Connects NetWare LANs to IBM minicomputers through local twinaxial or remote SDLC connections. The NetWare 5250 Gateway distributes up to seven local or nine remote concurrent 5250 display and host-addressable printer sessions to PC and PS/2 workstations on a NetWare network.

■ Allows multiple gateways to run on a single LAN. Additional gateways can be used for redundancy, load sharing, and support for multiple minicomputers.

■ NetWare SPX transport protocol is used by workstations to communicate with the NetWare 5250 Gateway. Use of the SPX protocol eliminates the need for the NetBIOS protocol, which avoids the overhead of NetBIOS. Also, SPX is a higher-performance protocol.

■ The NetWare 5250 Gateway can be configured in the dedicated or nondedicated mode of operation. You can choose to run the gateway server as a dedicated server or as a combination gateway server and NetWare 5250 LAN Workstation. Dedicated mode delivers optimal performance and reliability; nondedicated mode reduces the amount of equipment required.

To use the NetWare 5250 Gateway, users must run the NetWare 5250 LAN Workstation software on their workstations (described in the next section). Also, the AS/400 or System/3X minicomputers need to be configured to understand the NetWare 5250 Gateway.

The NetWare 5250 Gateway requires an IBM PC, PS/2, or compatible computer with a network adapter, a communications adapter, and a connection to the network. The communications link to the host is provided by a twinax adapter or an SDLC adapter. These adapters must be installed in the gateway server PC.

The twinax adapters supported are the Novell Twinax Adapter (for PCs) and the Micro-Integration STwinax MCA Adapter (for PS/2s).

The SDLC adapters supported are the Novell Synchronous Adapter for PCs, the Novell Synchronous/V.35 Adapter for PCs, and the IBM Multiprotocol Adapter/A. In addition to the adapter for host communications, a network adapter is necessary to connect the gateway PC to the NetWare LAN and the workstations.

Novell has published a list of hardware components that have been tested by Novell and recommended for use with its NetWare 5250 Gateway. Before proceeding with the installation you may wish to consult the most recent version of this list.

To summarize the sessions capability of the NetWare 5250 Gateway, the maximum number of host sessions-per-connection is seven for local twinax connections and nine for remote SDLC connections. The maximum number of NetWare 5250 Gateways that can be specified on a NetWare 5250 LAN Workstation is four. The maximum line speed supported for local twinax connection is one Mbps, 56 Kbps for remote SDLC connection. The RAM requirement on the gateway PC is 355-370K for running the Gateway software.

NetWare 5250 LAN Workstation

To use the NetWare 5250 Gateway on a NetWare LAN, terminal-emulation software must be used on the NetWare workstations. The NetWare 5250 LAN Workstation provides this terminal-emulation capability, as shown in figure 17.24. The product provides PCs and PS/2s on a NetWare LAN with access to IBM AS/400 or System/3X minicomputers.

The NetWare 5250 LAN Workstation provides multisession capability. It supports five host display and printer sessions per workstation, hot-key transfer of control to and from DOS, and normal operations from the DOS session. The NetWare 5250 LAN Workstation features include the following:

- Multiple device-emulation types for the IBM AS/400 and System/3X environments. Current support includes IBM 3180, 3196, 5251, 5291, and 5292 displays; and IBM 3812, 5219, 5224, 5225, and 5256 printers.

- Capability to run multiple AS/400 and System/3X applications and utilities.

- Support for up to seven local or nine remote host sessions and one DOS session per workstation when used with NetWare 5250 Gateway.

- Keyboard-remapping capability enables an entire keyboard to be easily mapped to a 5250 or PC layout.

- Keyboard macro support enables users to record and play back frequently used keystroke sequences.

- Support for file transfer to AS/400 or System/3X hosts.

The NetWare 5250 LAN Workstation is sold on a per-server basis; it may be loaded on a file server or on individual 5250 LAN Workstations. Each host session must be configured on the minicomputer before it can be activated. The terminal emulation requires the use of the NetWare SPX transport protocol.

Asynchronous Servers

Asynchronous servers enable dial-in or dial-out access to a LAN. A problem that has to be solved for dial-in access is that the communications links have low speeds (compared to LAN speeds) and are inadequate for direct data file or program access. Invoking a 500K program from a remote PC connected to the network over a 19.2 Kbps link can take over three minutes. These delays are unacceptable to most users.

One solution is to use workstations on the LAN as proxy for the remote user. When the remote user, connected by a low-speed link, makes a direct network request for a data or program file, the request is executed on the proxy workstation. Only the screen changes are transferred to the remote workstation. Keystrokes generated at the remote workstation appear as if they are generated by the proxy workstation.

NetWare Asynchronous Communications Server (NACS)

The *NetWare Asynchronous Communications Server* (NACS) turns any IBM PC, AT, or compatible into an asynchronous communications server that enables up to 16 network workstations to simultaneously dial in or out of a NetWare LAN. The NACS software enables a pool of asynchronous modems, attached to the NACS, to be shared for a variety of communications tasks (see fig. 17.25).

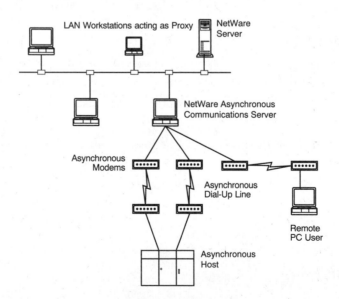

Figure 17.25:
NetWare Asynchronous Communications Server (NACS).

Users run terminal-emulation software and access asynchronous hosts by means of the NACS: the NACS Control Program, which runs in a communications server PC, and the *NetWare Asynchronous Interface* (NASI) software, which runs in a user's workstation. The *NACS Control Program* manages the serial ports and all connection activities; the NASI software provides the application interface that enables workstation software, such as asynchronous terminal-emulation packages, to access the ports managed by the Control Program. The NASI software enables the NACS to work with a variety of asynchronous communications software packages.

Access to the communications server is simplified by the use of the *Distributed Asynchronous Name Service* implemented by the NACS program. Users can access a connection simply by requesting it by name. When users request a connection by name, the NACS software connects them with that resource, wherever it is located on the network, making the support of multiple NACSs simple and transparent. Other features and functions include the following:

- 16 asynchronous connections per NACS.

- Line speeds up to 19.2 Kbps-per-port.

- Multiple NACSs on a single network.

- Dial-out capability, so that users can share access to host computers and public computer services.

- Resource names defined through the Distributed Asynchronous Name Service.

- Communications ports are rotored across groups of ports and NACSs. Connection requests are pooled among groups of ports and NACS servers.

- A workstation can access multiple NACSs simultaneously.

- Support for a variety of asynchronous communications packages.

- User has full modem control, including hardware-flow control.

- Inactive session timeout feature frees up ports for other users.

The NACS server software requires a dedicated IBM PC or compatible with 256K of RAM, a network adapter, and a connection to the network. Asynchronous communications are implemented by the *NetWare Wide Area Network Interface Module+* (WNIM+), a communications adapter that supports up to four asynchronous ports. As many as four WNIM+ adapters can be installed in a single NACS, bringing the total number of supported ports to

16. Asynchronous modems are connected to the WNIM+ through RS-232 modem cables.

Users who want to access the NACS as an asynchronous gateway to dial-out need an asynchronous terminal-emulation software package. Novell recommends any one of the following terminal-emulation packages:

- Columbia University—MS Kermit

- Crosstalk/DCA—Crosstalk Mark IV

- Crystal Point Software—PCTerm

- Datastorm—ProComm

- Diversified Computer Systems—EM 220, EM 4010, or EM 4105

- Dynamic Microprocessor Associates—ASCOM IV

- The M/H Group—VSComm

- Persoft—SmarTerm

- Polygon Software—PolyTerm

- Relay Communications—Relay Gold

- Softklone—Mirror

- Softronics—Softerm PC

- Telemark—PC TEK

- Walker, Richer and Quinn—Reflection Series

Remote PC users who need to dial in to the LAN through the NACS can use either of the two following supported packages:

- Dynamic Microprocessor Associates—pcANYWHERE

- Triton Technologies—Cosession

NetWare Access Server

The NetWare Access Server software runs on an Intel 80386 or higher machine and enables up to 15 remote users to dial in to a NetWare network and access all the services and files available on the network—including applications, electronic mail, and access to mainframes and minicomputers. In addition to the 15 remote user sessions, a single session is reserved for network supervisors, enabling them to manage the network and remote connections.

A security feature in the NetWare Access Server prevents unauthorized remote access. Figure 17.26 illustrates a network configuration using the NetWare Access Server.

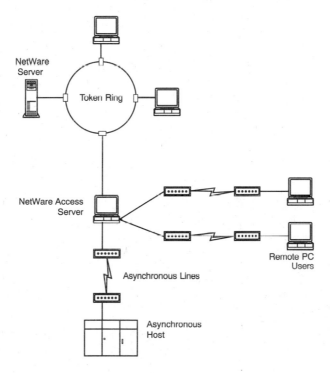

Figure 17.26:
NetWare Access Server.

The NetWare Access Server software runs in the protected mode of the Intel 80386 microprocessor. It divides the CPU and RAM into virtual Intel 80386 machines, with each machine using 640K of RAM. The total number of such machines is 15. When a remote user dials in, one or more of the virtual machines is used for executing user requests.

Remote users can dial in to the NetWare Access Server through asynchronous modems. Software for remote PC connections is included with the NetWare Access Server.

Network requests sent by remote users are executed by one of the virtual 8086 machines on the NetWare Access Server. Only screen updates and keystrokes travel over the asynchronous lines; data file and program access occur at LAN speeds.

NetWare security access is controlled by the security features of the NetWare file server. An optional dial-back feature is included, which enables the Access Server to grant a network session to a remote user only after the server has called the user back (after initial contact) at a number specified by the network supervisor. This makes it difficult for unauthorized users to gain access to the network from a remote dial-up link. Other features and functions of NAS include the following:

- Support for 15 remote users and one supervisor session.

- Designed for heavy dial-in use without tying up local network workstations for executing remote requests.

- Dial-back capability for additional security. This feature can be implemented on a user-by-user basis.

- Audit trails are maintained on the NetWare Access Server, enabling the administrator to review remote access.

- Monitoring utilities. Session and status control utilities enable supervisors to monitor, the NAS server, session, and modem status; to view the work being done by a user; and to disconnect a user when necessary.

- Remote users can disconnect from the NAS server after starting long-running tasks and call back later to take follow-up action.

- Print jobs can be directed to network or remote printers.

- File-transfer capability.

The NetWare Access Server requires a network adapter and an asynchronous communications adapter for remote dial-up links. The amount of RAM needed can be estimated by the following rule of thumb: 3M of RAM is required for every 4 active sessions. For a total of 15 sessions, 12M of RAM is necessary.

The asynchronous connections can be provided by Novell's WNIM+ adapter, which is a high-performance asynchronous communications adapter that supports up to 4 asynchronous connections. As many as 4 WNIM+ adapters can be installed in a single NetWare Access Server for a total of 16 connections (15 remote users and one supervisor). The WNIM+ adapters are connected to asynchronous modems by means of RS-232 cables.

Distributed File System and NetWare Integration

Novell offers two products that offer solutions to the problem of interoperability between multivendor platforms: *NetWare for NFS* and *NetWare for FTAM*.

One of the most important resources that needs to be shared in a multivendor network is a universal file system. Such a file system can be distributed across a variety of platforms and provide transparent access to files anywhere on the network. Also, if this access is transparent to the user, the user does not have to be concerned about the location of the files. The two products, NetWare for NFS and NetWare for FTAM, implement a distributed file system that is transparent to the users, but they do this using fundamentally different approaches.

NFS was originally developed by Sun Microsystems. It was designed to enable file systems on UNIX hosts to be distributed and shared in a LAN environment. Sun Microsystems made the specifications to NFS and some key source code available to other vendors. There are over 150 vendors, including Novell, that have licensed the NFS technology. Novell's implementation of NFS is called NetWare for NFS. NFS is not an international standard the way FTAM is, but it has become a popular de facto standard.

FTAM (File Transfer Access Management) is an application layer (layer 7) international standard from the International Organization of Standards (ISO) committee. It is part of *Government Open Systems Interconnect Profile* (GOSIP).

GOSIP is a procurement standard for all federal agencies; different countries have their own GOSIP standard. For example, there is a US GOSIP, a UK GOSIP, a JAPAN GOSIP, and so on. GOSIP makes sure that network equipment purchased by different federal agencies can interoperate.

FTAM, which is part of GOSIP, implements a common virtual store capability that can be accessed by other computers. This *virtual store capability* can be used as a distributed file system, just as NFS can. The protocols used by FTAM are OSI protocols; NFS is based on TCP/IP protocols. Another difference is that NFS uses a typically connectionless mechanism; FTAM requires connections to be established between any two computers involved in an FTAM exchange.

NetWare NFS

NetWare NFS runs on NetWare v3.x servers and provides a distributed file system that can be used by any computer that has a client implementation of NFS. Specifically, it allows UNIX workstations transparent access to the NetWare v3.x file system and other services. NetWare NFS implements the protocols listed in table 17.5. Therefore, any NFS client that implements these protocols can access the files exported by the NetWare server running NetWare for NFS.

Table 17.5
Protocols Supported by NetWare for NFS

Protocol Abbreviation	Protocol's Full Name
XDR	Sun Microsystems External Data Representation Protocol
RPC	Sun Microsystems Remote Procedure Call (RPC)
NFS v.2	Sun Microsystems, Inc. Network File System version 2
MOUNT	Sun Microsystems, Inc. Mount Protocol
PORTMAPPER	Sun Microsystems, Inc. Portmapper Protocol
LPD	Berkeley UNIX Line Printer Daemon Protocol
FTP	DARPA (RFC 959) File Transfer Protocol

NetWare NFS consists of several NLMs that add NFS server capability to the NetWare server. Once NetWare NFS is installed, workstations with NFS client services can share files with other NetWare clients. These clients include DOS, Macintosh, OS/2, and UNIX workstations. The clients issue a MOUNT command to share the files exported by NetWare NFS. Besides file services, NetWare print services are also available, which enables a NetWare v3.x server to function as the single, centralized repository for all client files and to simplify file management in a complex network environment.

NetWare NFS runs on any server machine that can run the NetWare v3.x operating system; that is, a PC using an Intel 80386 or higher microprocessor. The minimum server RAM is 5M, and 3M of disk space are required on the volume that will support NFS name space. Because NFS makes use of the TCP/IP protocols, the TCP NLM must be loaded and running prior to activating NetWare for NFS.

NetWare NFS provides the following services over the TCP/IP transport:

- NFS for file sharing

- Line Printer Daemon (LPD) for print services

- File Transfer Protocol Daemon (FTPD)

- LOCKD, a standard UNIX file- and record-locking service

NetWare NFS features are described in the following list:

- The NFS Server NLM provides the mechanism that enables UNIX clients to view the NetWare v3.x file system as an extension of their native NFS environment. UNIX clients use the standard UNIX/NFS mount command to access NetWare volumes. Key NFS Server elements include transparent support of authentication, file-attribute mapping, file-name mapping, file locking, permissions mapping, and remote server-based system administration.

- The UNIX Namespace NLM provides the NetWare v3.x file system with native UNIX file attributes and naming conventions, enabling transparent file access from UNIX environments and file sharing across all NetWare v3.x supported name spaces, including DOS, Macintosh, and OS/2.

- The LPD NLM enables UNIX-TCP/IP clients to submit print jobs to NetWare v3.x print queues.

- The FTPD NLM enables any FTP client with valid NetWare access to connect to a NetWare v3.x server and to initiate file transfers to and from any NetWare volume or directory.

- The Lock Manager NLM supports file and record locking in the NFS environment. Applications that perform UNIX advisory file and record locking are fully supported through the Lock Manager program within NetWare NFS.

- NFSCON NLM management and configuration utility enables monitoring of the NFS server. The tasks performed by management utilities include the following:

     System configuration and parameter initialization

     Statistics on NFS server utilization

     Fine-tuning of software parameters to enhance server performance

     Logging of error conditions

     Manipulation of the NFS file and directory permissions

DOS clients can access NetWare NFS services by using the following NFS client implementations for DOS:

- Sun Microsystem's PC-NFS

- Beam & Whiteside's DOS NFS

- FTP Software's Interdrive that comes with the PC/TCP Plus package

Installing NetWare NFS

The following steps are a guided tour for installing NetWare NFS:

1. From the server console, load the INSTALL NLM.

2. Select Product Options and press Ins.

3. When prompted for the drive/path name of the product source media, enter it. This is normally the floppy disk containing NetWare for NFS, unless you have copied it to NetWare volume. In that case, enter the source path name on the volume (example: **SYS:NFS**, if NetWare for NFS has been copied to this path).

4. When prompted to do so, enter the path name of the directory containing the SERVER.EXE program. This enables the installation process to copy the NFS name space to the DOS partition used to boot NetWare.

5. Select the INSTALL option from NFS Installation Options, which copies the NFS files to the proper directories (**SYS:SYSTEM**, for example) until the screen in figure 17.27 appears.

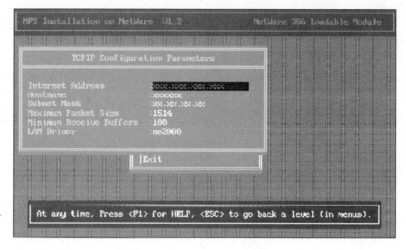

Figure 17.27:
NFS TCP/IP Configuration Parameters.

6. Fill out the TCP/IP Parameters, based on your network setting, and press Esc, and the answer Yes to update configuration files.

7. When asked if you want to activate the following services, answer Yes (unless you do not want the services because of lack of RAM at server). You are prompted for the following services:

    UNIX to NetWare Print Service

    NetWare to UNIX Print Service

    Remote Console for UNIX (XCONSOLE)

    FTP Server

    Lock Manager

8. If you are reminded to restart the server to install the NFS name space, take note and press Esc.

9. Exit NFS INSTALL, and the list of NFS products that have been installed should appear.

10. Use Alt-Esc to switch to the system console. If you are doing the install from a remote console, use the asterisk (*) key on the numeric keypad.

11. Add the NFS name space from the system console. Execute the following commands to perform this step:

    ```
    LOAD NFS
    MOUNT volumeName
    ADD NAME SPACE NFS TO SYS
    ```

12. Return to the INSTALL screen, by pressing Alt-Esc (or the * key on the numeric keypad).

13. Select the NetWare for NFS product name to invoke the NFSADMIN to be used for configuring the NetWare server.

    At this point, you must configure the user and group tables, NFS exports, host tables, file attributes for exported NetWare directories, and NetWare-to-UNIX LPR Gateway. The configuration information is kept in SYS:ETC and follows the UNIX/NFS style and convention as closely as possible.

14. Answer Yes to modify the following files in SYS:ETC.

    NFSUSERS

    NFSGROUP

    HOSTS

    EXPORTS

    LPR$PSRV.NAM (LPR Print Gateway, NetWare-to-UNIX print service)

15. Add user names of NetWare users to the list of NFS users by pressing Ins. This list is used by NetWare to map the NFS uid (user ID) to the NetWare user name to determine the user's trustee rights. When finished adding users, press Esc and confirm changes.

    Add group names of NetWare groups to the list of NFS groups by using the Ins key. This NFSGROUP file is used by NetWare to map the NFS gid (group ID) to the NetWare group name. When finished adding groups, press Esc and confirm changes.

    Add the host names (file HOSTS) and the internet address of each computer that is explicitly authorized to mount the NetWare file system by the EXPORTS file. When finished adding groups, press Esc and confirm changes.

16. Add the directories that can be exported from the NetWare file system to other computers. This list is written out to the file EXPORTS. This file is read automatically by the mounted NLM. Exported names must follow the UNIX naming convention and be entered in lowercase. All exported names in a volume must begin with /*volname*. To export the SYS: root directory, use **/sys/**.

17. Configure the LPR Gateway. For this part you must know the Printer Description, UNIX Host Name, UNIX Printer Name, and NetWare Print Queue Name.

18. When finished configuring printers, exit NFSAdmin and INSTALL.

19. If you missed a step, you can use LOAD NFSADMIN from the console to configure any of the configuration files in SYS:ETC.

NetWare FTAM

File Transfer Access and Management (FTAM) provides a network-wide common view of a *virtual file store system* (see fig. 17.28). The virtual file store system provides a common view of the file system to all FTAM clients, who are called *initiators*. The virtual store file system is mapped to the real file system by FTAM. In general, the FTAM system enables copying of files to another system, reading and writing of individual records in the file, and changing attributes of a virtual store file.

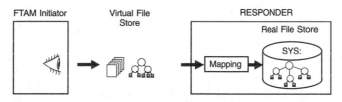

Figure 17.28:
File transfer, access, and management (FTAM).

NetWare FTAM is an OSI FTAM server that runs on top of NetWare v3.x and enables a variety of FTAM clients to access the NetWare v3.x file system. In OSI terminology, the FTAM server is called the *responder* and the FTAM client is called the *initiator*. NetWare FTAM implements all seven layers of the OSI protocol suite and enables file transfer between NetWare and any other complementary OSI FTAM initiator, regardless of the hardware or software platform being used. FTAM initiators also can send files to NetWare print queues.

Figure 17.29 shows the NetWare FTAM components. The FTAM.EXE program runs on a NetWare workstation and communicates with the FTAM initiator, implemented by the FTAMCLI.NLM. The FTAM responder is implemented by the FTAMSVR.NLM. The FTAM initiator and responder can run on a single NetWare v3.x server or on different servers.

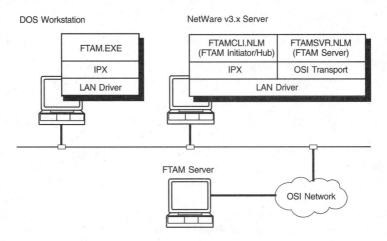

Figure 17.29:
NetWare FTAM components.

NetWare FTAM is implemented as a set of NLMs that runs on the NetWare v3.x operating system (see fig. 17.30).

The data flow between a FTAM user and FTAM initiator is shown in figure 17.31.

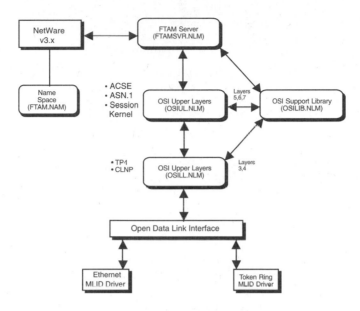

Figure 17.30:
Data flow between NetWare v3.x and FTAM server.

NetWare FTAM complies with U.S. GOSIP; it can be used with third-party X.400 mail gateways to satisfy the basic profile and service requirements of GOSIP 1.0. It implements the standard OSI protocol specifications for FTAM, ACSE, ASN.1, OSI Session, TP Class 4, and CLNP, and it conforms to the following *National Institute of Standards and Technology* (NIST) specifications:

FTAM T1 and M1
Directory Access: NBS-9 document type

U.S.GOSIP
Conforms to limited FTAM specification
Interoperates with full FTAM implementation

TOP 3.0
Conforms to limited FTAM specification
Interoperates with full FTAM implementation

U.K. GOSIP
Interoperates with U.K. GOSIP-conformant implementations

Standards Conformance:

Directories:	NBS-9 document type
FTAM:	ISO 8671 (file types 1 and 3, limited and enhanced management)
ACSE:	ISO 8650
Presentation:	ISO 882x3
ASN.1:	ISO 8825
Session:	ISO 8327
Transport:	ISO 8072 (COTP), ISO 8602 (CLTP)
Network:	ISO 8473 (CLNP), ISO 9542 (ES/IS)
Link:	ISO 802.2
Physical:	ISO 802.3 (CSMA/CD), ISO 802.5 (TR)

NetWare FTAM features include the following:

■ Provides file storage, retrieval, and management services to FTAM clients, depending on the capabilities of their FTAM client software:

Users can transfer and retrieve whole files to the servers disk for storage.

Users can delete files from the server's disk.

Users can read a file's attributes.

Users can rename files.

■ Clients using NBS-9 can create and delete directories and list directory contents.

■ NetWare FTAM enables FTAM clients to send files to NetWare print queues.

■ NetWare FTAM runs on NetWare v3.x and requires at least 6M of memory and 1M of free disk space. The NetWare server must be connected to an Ethernet or Token Ring network and configured for IEEE 802.2 framing.

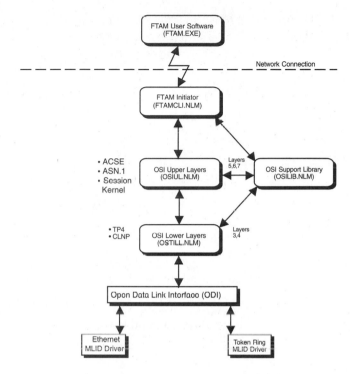

Figure 17.31:
Data flow between FTAM user and FTAM initiator.

Installing NetWare FTAM

The following steps give you a guided tour for installing NetWare FTAM:

1. From the server console, load the INSTALL NLM.

2. Select Product Options, then press Ins.

3. When prompted for the drive/path name of the product source media, enter it. This is normally the floppy disk containing NetWare for FTAM, unless you have copied it to NetWare volume. In that case, enter the source path name on the volume.

   You have a choice of installing the FTAM server, FTAM client, or both. These instructions assume that you want to install both.

4. When prompted to do so, enter the path name of the directory containing the SERVER.EXE program. This enables the installation process to copy the FTAM name space to the DOS partition used to boot NetWare.

   You see a screen for NetWare FTAM configuration.

5. Select Volumes for FTAM Name Space.

6. Press Ins and add the volumes that you want to use for FTAM.

7. Select Set Configuration File Parameters from NetWare FTAM Configuration.

8. Select Set Default Directory from Configuration File Options. Accept the default SYS:LOGIN directory if you want user files to be stored there. Otherwise, select another directory.

9. Select Set Default NSAP from NetWare FTAM Configuration. The default NSAP address, as shown in figure 17.32, displays. Press Esc to select it.

Figure 17.32:
FTAM default NSAP address.

10. Back out of the menus by selecting the Return option and save configuration changes. Press Esc until asked if you want to exit NetWare for FTAM installation. Answer Yes.

    The screen shown in figure 17.33, showing the installed products, displays.

11. Exit INSTALL.

12. Run the script ADDFTMNS.NCF to load the FTAM name space and add it to the volumes selected.

        ADDFTMNS

Figure 17.33:
FTAM installed products.

13. Load the LAN driver with IEEE 802.2 encapsulation. For example, you can load the NE2000 driver on port 340 (hex), interrupt 4 by using the following:

    ```
    LOAD NE2000 PORT=340 INT=4 FRAME=ETHERNET_802.2 NAME=OSI
    ```

14. Load the NetWare FTAM NLMs in the following order:

    LOAD OSIINIT

    LOAD OSILIB

    LOAD OSILL

    BIND CLNP TO *NAME*

    LOAD OSIUL

    LOAD FTAMSVR

    LOAD FTAMCLI

    Replace *NAME* with the value used in the BIND command.

15. Add the following command to load the FTAM name space to STARTUP.NCF:

    ```
    LOAD FTAM
    ```

16. To load FTAM automatically, add the commands in step X to Y in the AUTOEXEC.NCF file.

17. Use the OSICON utility to perform configuration or maintenance tasks for FTAM clients and FTAM server. OSICON also can be used to configure ISO Lower Layers, Local NSAP, and Local OSI

environment. For example, the screen in figure 17.34 is obtained by using OSICON -> FTAM Client. The P-Selector, S-Selector, and T-Selector are used to support multiple protocol entities at a given OSI layer. In NetWare FTAM, the T-Selector values can be changed to support multiple applications by using the OSI transport layer.

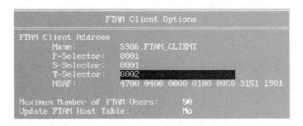

Figure 17.34:
FTAM client options.

18. To Update the FTAM Host table, use the following selections:

OSICON -> FTAM Client -> Update FTAM Host Table = Yes

-> Select FTAM Host.

The screen shown in figure 17.35 shows the FTAM Host Information that can be changed. The addressing format is OSINET. Other formats are possible and can be selected by setting the field Change NSAP Format to Yes. These address formats are shown in figure 17.36. One of these address formats, the U.S.GOSIP format, is shown in figure 17.37.

Figure 17.35:
FTAM host information.

Figure 17.36:
FTAM NSAP format options.

Figure 17.37:
FTAM U.S.GOSIP format.

NetWare Ports to Other Platforms

It is Novell's intention to port NetWare on every major computing platform.
The agreement with Hewlett-Packard to do a native port of NetWare v3.x to
the HP High Precision Architecture is an example of Novell's strategy. As
other RISC platforms become more dominant, you can expect to see more
NetWare ports to these platforms.

This section examines ports of NetWare to the VMS and UNIX environments.

Port of NetWare to VAX/VMS

A company called Interconnections has ported NetWare to the VMS platform. NetWare runs as a process on top of the VMS operating system on a
VAX. File services, server management, and NetWare security are mapped
to equivalent functions on the VMS operating system.

NetWare for VMS enables a DEC VAX/VMS system to function as a NetWare server, which enables the integration of PC-based LANs and VAX/VMS-based minicomputer networks. DOS and OS/2 users can share data, applications, and printer services with VAX terminal users. DOS users also can make use of *Terminal Emulation Service* (TES) to access VMS applications. The VAX can be used as a large and secure disk storage with reliable and regular file backups. NetWare files are stored as standard RMS files, with automatic and dynamic translation of differences in file attributes and naming conventions among DOS, OS/2, and VMS.

NetWare for VMS enables as many as 254 DOS and OS/2 users to access the server concurrently. SPX/IPX packets can be transported across DECnet by using tunneling. This gives NetWare PC users on DECnet transparent access to remote VAXs or NetWare file servers by using the wide area networking features of DECnet. The SPX/IPX packets are encapsulated in DECnet packets that are then carried to any NetWare for VMS file server on the DECnet network. Once received, the DECnet envelope is removed and the SPX/IPX packets are forwarded to the desired NetWare server. This effectively creates a virtual IPX network over DECnet.

NetWare for VMS is installed on the VAX by using the standard VMSINSTAL utility, and it requires a minimum of 2M of memory (4M is recommended). It requires 10,000 blocks of disk space to operate, but 20,000 blocks are needed temporarily during installation.

A DEC Ethernet controller and the DEC-supplied Ethernet controller driver must be installed in the VAX, providing an Ethernet connection to the network. The NetWare workstations must be configured to use Ethernet II frame encapsulation, rather than the default IEEE 802.3 encapsulation. For ODI drivers, the frame encapsulation can be specified in the NET.CFG file. For non-ODI drivers, the ECONFIG utility can be used to configure the IPX.COM file for Ethernet II encapsulation. The TES feature on workstations requires 33K of RAM, but it can be unloaded when not in use. TES supports third-party emulation software written to use interrupt 14, including the following products:

> EM 220 by Diversified Computer Systems, Inc.
> poly-STAR by Polygon Software, Inc.
> PCTerm by Crystal Point Software, Inc.
> Reflection Series by Walker, Richer and Quinn
> SmarTerm by Persoft, Inc.
> SofTermPC by Softronics, Inc.

TNET-05 by Grafpoint
ZSTerm by KEA Systems Ltd.

NetWare for VMS supports DEC's standard DEC Ethernet controllers, including the DEUNA, DELUA, DESQA, DELQA, DEQNA, DESVA, DEBNT, DEBNI, and DEBNA controllers.

Digital Equipment Corporation also has a product called PATHWORKS for NetWare. This product implements NetWare on VMS and Ultrix operating systems and enables NetWare users to make use of high-performance server hardware.

NetWare for UNIX

With the development of NetWare v3.x, the NetWare operating system was written in the portable C language and compiled using a 32-bit C compiler (Watcom C compiler). Figure 17.38 illustrates that NetWare services can be considered to be independent of the multitasking features of the NetWare operating system. Because the NetWare services were rewritten in the portable C language, the multitasking NetWare operating system can be replaced by some other general-purpose operating system such as UNIX, VMS, or OS/2. Several of Novell's strategic partners have done that, but have focused their attention on porting NetWare services to the UNIX operating system. This version of NetWare was called Portable NetWare; its new name is NetWare for UNIX.

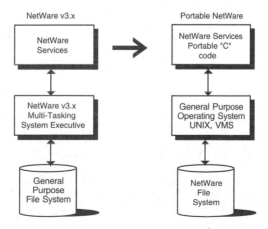

Figure 17.38:
Portable NetWare.

Novell's strategic partners in the effort to run NetWare on UNIX platforms include NCR, Prime, Data General, Unisys, Hewlett-Packard, Innovus, Wang Labs, Mips, Altos Computers, Pyramid, ICL, Interactive, Integraph, and Rational Data.

Summary

This chapter has examined solutions for connecting NetWare to non-NetWare networks and devices. The topics discussed include the communications connectivity of NetWare LANs to TCP/IP networks, X.25 networks, T1 networks, Asynchronous Links, Synchronous Links, IBM SNA networks, OSI networks, and UNIX networks.

This chapter also discussed distributed file system solutions such as NetWare NFS, NetWare FTAM, and NetWare support on other platforms such as VMS and UNIX.

Viruses and Networks

A very unfortunate problem in the computer world is the computer *virus*—a program designed to attack and destroy other programs, data, and systems. Viruses can take advantage of the widespread popularity of networks in order to transport themselves and infect other systems on the network.

In this section, you learn about the different types of computer viruses and the methods and techniques you can use to detect and control them.

Understanding the Virus Threat

Understanding viruses can help you understand the nature of the threat and help you take preventive measures to control the spread of viruses.

A *virus* is a program code that copies itself into other programs and modifies them. This process is called *infecting*. A virus can make an exact copy of itself or, when copying, can generate a slight variation of itself while infecting the target program. In other words, a virus can self-mutate as it spreads. Self-mutating viruses are more difficult to detect, because their signatures often change when they mutate.

A *virus signature* is a consistent binary pattern that appears in a virus program. This signature can be identified by virus-detecting programs.

A virus causes the infected computer systems to function in ways not originally intended. These actions can be harmless (printing "funny" messages on the screen) or vicious (destroying programs and data).

When an infected program runs, the virus code is executed with the same privileges as the original program. As the virus code executes, it can perform a number of tasks, as in the following:

1. Search for other programs to infect and propagate (copy) itself or a variation of itself to other programs.

2. Destroy data indiscriminately or selectively. In the worst case, all the information on the hard disk can be destroyed. In some situations, only selected data might be destroyed, making it difficult for the user to know about the attack.

3. Introduce time bombs, which cause damage at a specified time. Dates such as Friday the 13th are very popular. These viruses try to replicate themselves at every opportunity, so that they can do more damage during their scheduled "explosion."

Because of the damage viruses can cause, they could more accurately be called *vandalware*, *programmed threats*, or *rogue programs*. Viruses are a form of terrorism, usually aimed at destroying data and programs. They seldom destroy hardware equipment directly. In one well-known case, however, a virus altered the scan rate of an IBM PC monitor's electronic beam and caused the monitor to burst into flames.

Viruses try to protect themselves by hiding their identity, operating only at specific times, and covering their tracks so that they can wipe out all evidence of their wrongdoing.

Understanding Worms, Rabbits, Trojan Horses, and Other "Wild Life"

In addition to viruses, other types of programs pose a security risk. In this section, the worm and other such programs are briefly defined.

- **Worm.** An independent program that replicates by copying itself from one computer to another across a network. Unlike a virus that attaches itself to other programs, a worm maintains its independent existence. It usually does not destroy data or modify programs, which leads some people to conclude that worms are benign. However, worms can tie up computer resources, causing extensive network down time.

The individual components of a worm that run on computers are called *segments*. These segments form a chain or the body of the worm. If a segment fails, the remaining pieces find another computer to replace the failed segment. As additional segments join the worm, it appears as if the worm itself moves through the network.

Worms are rarely found on DOS workstations because DOS is single tasking and does not lend itself to background processing. Worms are more likely to exist on multitasking operating systems, such as OS/2, UNIX workstations, and the NetWare server.

A highly publicized worm attack took place on November 2, 1988, on Internet—a network that links hundreds of universities, research organizations, and businesses. The worm crawled through the communications lines and, as it multiplied itself, created processes that used up most of the computing resources. The infected networks and computer systems ground to a halt. As a result, hundreds of hours of research time was wasted, electronic mail messages were lost, and important deadlines were missed. Total loss estimates from this worm attack ranged from $1 million to $100 million.

- **Trojan horse.** A program code fragment that hides itself inside another program and performs a disguised function. Trojan horses are used by viruses and worms to escape detection. Just as the Greeks came out from hiding after their wooden horse was brought inside Troy, once inside the system, the virus or worm does its damage.

- **Bomb.** A special type of Trojan horse that remains hidden and is used as a launch pad for releasing a virus or worm attack. A particular date, time, or condition triggers the attack. If the trigger is based on a date or time, it is called a *time bomb*. An example of a time bomb is the Friday the 13th Virus that was triggered on the first Friday the 13th in 1988. A *logic bomb* is triggered by an event or logic condition. Some software developers, for example, have installed logic bombs that explode if an illegal copy is made of their software.

- **Trap door** or **back door.** A mechanism that allows the software developer to sneak back into the system, circumventing normal system protection. Sometimes programmers design these trap doors for testing and debugging the system. Although ordinarily removed before the system is released, back doors are sometimes left by accident or design. In the 1983 movie *War Games*, for example, the protagonist enters into the NORAD computer system through a trap door left by its creator.

- **Spoof.** A program that tricks a user into giving away privileges. A spoof is usually implemented by a Trojan horse. Prime targets for spoof programs are the network log-in or authentication mechanism. A spoof that pretends to be another user is called a *masquerade*.

  In the case of NetWare, the masquerade can be a program running on another workstation on the network that has the understanding of SAP protocols, and then responds to a GetNearestServer query with a fake GiveNearestServer reply. In other words, the spoof goes through the entire log-in sequence only to steal the user's password. Passwords are encrypted in current versions of NetWare, but *cryptology* (the science of encryption/decryption) also can be used to decrypt passwords. It is possible to play back the log-in sequence to the NetWare server from another workstation and obtain unauthorized access. NetWare uses some undocumented methods to protect itself from playback attacks.

- **Bacteria.** Programs that make copies of themselves. Otherwise, they do nothing. Their goal is to consume all available resources on your system, such as disk space or memory. Programs that rapidly reproduce themselves are called *rabbits*. If the NetWare server disk space fills up unaccountably, you might want to search the server for bacteria programs.

- **Crab.** A program that attacks the data display on the computer terminal. A well-known example is a crab program for DOS machines that causes letters to drop to the bottom of the screen.

- **Creeper.** A worm-like program that is designed to spread across computer monitors and display "funny" messages on computer screens. An example of a creeper program that was popular on the ARPANET in the 1970s displayed the message *I'm the creeper, catch* *me if you can!* It was designed to spread from terminal to terminal until it was eradicated by a program called the reaper.

■ **Salami.** A program that slices away tiny pieces of data. For example, it can change the decimal point position in a spreadsheet or shave pennies from an account. These errors are likely to go undetected; you might attribute them to a computer glitch or error-rounding in arithmetic calculations.

The great variety of viruses should underscore the seriousness of the virus problem. There are a number of preventive measures that can be used to reduce the risk of being victimized by these programs. These measures are described later in this chapter.

As of the writing of this book, there have been no major viruses known to have penetrated NetWare security. One reported incident involved the distribution of some infected disks by Novell. This virus did not penetrate NetWare's operating system security, however. The problem was 5 ¼-inch disks containing the Network Support Encyclopedia (NSE), released on December 12, 1991, for North American distribution. This release contained a variation of the "stoned" virus. Novell has since corrected this problem and instituted stricter measures for detecting viruses in the disk-duplication process.

Other virus incidents have usually resulted from workstations logged in with Supervisor accounts. Because there is usually no restriction on Supervisor accounts, these workstations are particularly vulnerable to virus attacks.

Novell keeps the implementation details and the source code for its security and the password-encryption mechanism under close wraps, making it difficult for potential virus writers to create effective viruses. Developers interact with NetWare through well-defined APIs, and the APIs provide controlled access to NetWare services. When the internal structure of an operating system is highly publicized, viruses can easily be created to exploit the system's security weaknesses. This problem has particularly been true with UNIX, whose implementation details are well-known.

Understanding Virus Methods of Attack

A virus can infect programs or data on a floppy drive, RAM, or network drive or tape. The computer virus emulates biological viruses by attacking other organisms—in this case, software. Besides infecting software on a network drive, it can spread itself through communication links, such as telephone lines, bulletin boards, LAN communications, or WAN communication links.

Although a virus can attach itself to virtually any program, certain programs and areas of a disk are especially popular targets for a virus attack, as follows:

- **Command shell.** For DOS workstations, this shell is the COMMAND.COM program. Because the command shell runs every time a program is invoked, this is a popular target for virus infection.

- **Network authentication software.** For NetWare, this is the LOGIN.EXE program that resides in the SYS:LOGIN and SYS:PUBLIC directories.

- **Device drivers.** In many operating systems, device drivers work closely with the operating system kernel. If a device driver is infected, the chance of operating system kernels becoming infected becomes greater. If the kernel is infected, nothing on the system is safe because the kernel controls the operating environment.

- **Boot record image.** The boot record image is found on a floppy disk or hard disk. When the system is booted, the boot sector is responsible for loading the operating system into memory. If the boot program contains a virus, the virus exists from the time the system is initialized.

After you identify programs that may be the target of attacks, certain steps can be taken to prevent or reduce your vulnerability. For instance, you now know that two programs, COMMAND.COM and LOGIN.EXE, are potential targets. If a virus attaches itself to one of these programs, the program size changes. The program sizes of COMMAND.COM and LOGIN.EXE, therefore, should be noted and checked periodically; to be most effective, the check should be automated.

You can note the date and time stamps on these programs, but it is easy for viruses to keep the date and time stamps unchanged. In fact, clever viruses can keep the program size the same by exploiting the structure of the executable program fiie and by using compression techniques. A number of commercial programs can vaccinate executable files by seeing whether or not they have been modified.

Managing the Virus Threat for NetWare

You can use a number of techniques to contain the virus threat. For the purposes of this book, these techniques are discussed in the context of a NetWare LAN; however, some of the principles discussed also can be applied to stand-alone workstations and other networks.

Virus-Prevention Techniques

Many virus-prevention techniques are procedural in nature—they involve a set of recommended actions or ways to accomplish a task to reduce the risk of being infected by a virus. These techniques include:

1. When testing or installing new programs, always boot from a good, write-protected boot floppy disk. The boot floppy disk should have a trusted copy of the operating system boot programs. Because many viruses try to modify the operating system programs, they can be foiled by write protection. Unfortunately, this method is not fool proof—workstations such as the IBM PC use a software flag to indicate that the disk is write-protected. The software flag is normally set by a disk drive mechanism that reads the setting of the write-protect tab on the disk. Virus programs can deliberately change the setting of this software flag.

2. Install only licensed copies of software from reputable vendors. Be aware that, although most vendors have quality control that checks for viruses and other problems, they can fail to detect a virus.

3. Do not install software from bulletin boards or "out of the box" if you suspect that the software package has been tampered with. This advice against bulletin boards may be too restricting for many organizations because there are excellent tools and utilities that can be obtained from bulletin boards. If you install programs from such sources, use a commercial anti-virus package to thoroughly test a program before installing it.

   Many bulletin-board programs come with source code. If source code is available, compile this code to produce an executable copy of the program if possible. Viruses do not usually infect source code; instead, they concentrate on executable programs. Few network administrators have the resources necessary, however, to compile source code to produce an executable image of the program. If you must use a bulletin board to download programs, do so from a reliable bulletin board—one that is concerned about the spread of viruses and has a known system for checking for viruses.

4. Prevent network users from experimenting with shareware or freeware programs on the network.

5. Perform regular backups of your data. If you do succumb to a virus, your recovery process will be much easier.

6. Make judicious use of diskless workstations. Because viruses can enter by means of programs installed from workstations, users with diskless workstations cannot introduce viruses.

7. Directories that contain program files on the server should have the minimum rights necessary for program execution. For a NetWare server, the minimum trustee assignment is Read and File scan (R F).

8. Train users to be vigilant with security risks and viruses. Most users are willing to cooperate with network administrators to reduce the virus threat.

9. Put your organization's security policy in writing. Obtain cooperation and agreement on this policy from all levels of management and from all users of the network.

10. Monitor users' security practices, including informal checks on the kind of activity a user typically performs on the network.

11. Do not run experimental programs or tests while logged in to the server with Supervisor privileges because there are no restrictions to the Supervisor account. Test new programs on workstations that are disconnected from the network.

12. Use passwords that are difficult to guess as a first line of defense against viruses. Chapter 11 discussed different techniques for creating good passwords. Other precautions also can be taken to improve password security, such as requiring users to have unique passwords and to change them periodically, having a minimum password length restriction, and locking an account if a user fails to log in correctly after a predetermined number of tries.

13. When booting the server from a floppy drive or a DOS partition, be sure that the DOS programs and the boot sector have been disinfected. A virus that exists before the server is booted can modify the NetWare volume because NetWare security is not operational before NetWare is booted. Most viruses are aimed at DOS—they have an understanding of the DOS boot sector and file structure. Because they do not have an understanding of NetWare volume format and file structure, they are unlikely to corrupt NetWare volumes. Although there are no known viruses that are aimed specifically at NetWare, it is possible, however, for such viruses to exist. If they have an intimate knowledge of the volume format, for example, they can infect the volume while the server machine is booted under DOS.

14. Make use of NetWare's directory and file attributes. Because they are extensions of DOS file attributes, DOS-based virus programs are not able to penetrate NetWare security very easily. For example, if the Read-Only attribute is set for NetWare version 3.x, the Delete Inhibit and Rename Inhibit flags are automatically set. The Copy Inhibit flag prevents a file from being copied. The most effective attributes for preventing the spread of viruses are the Read-Only and Copy Inhibit flags. Directory and file attributes can be modified by the FLAGDIR and FLAG commands. To flag the LOGIN.EXE file as read-only with Copy Inhibit, enter **FLAG LOGIN.EXE RO CI**.

15. Remove Modify Rights for directories containing program files. Having access to Modify Rights enables users and virus programs to change the file attributes for files in a directory or subdirectory, rendering the Read-Only and Copy Inhibit flags ineffective.

16. Sensitive directories and files should be marked with the Purged flag so that when files are deleted, they are automatically purged. Deleted files are not removed from the server disk until purged. A clever virus program aimed specifically at NetWare can corrupt deleted files that have not been purged. Then, if these corrupted files are later salvaged, the virus is salvaged along with the infected files.

Detecting Viruses

A number of excellent utilities are available for detecting and correcting software viruses (by removing them or rendering them harmless). Correcting for viruses also is known as *disinfecting* a program. For DOS machines, many of these utilities run as TSRs that run periodic checks in the background or monitor the execution of programs.

No general virus detection algorithm exists. Most virus-checking programs look for signatures of known viruses. These programs work quite well most of the time because most viruses are variations of old ones. Developers of anti-virus programs are constantly looking for new virus types to add to their lists. If you have an anti-virus program, but you have not received updates for it on a regular basis, your program is probably out of date and cannot detect newer virus types. Contact the program's manufacturer or your local dealer to inquire about anti-virus updates.

Table 18.1 lists a representative sample of the virus-detection packages available today.

Table 18.1
Virus Detection Packages

Software	*Company*	*Phone*
Anti-Virus Kit	1stAid Software	617-783-7118
Certus	Foundation Ware	216-752-8181
SiteLock	Brightwork Dev, Inc.	201-544-9258
Quarantine	OnDisk Software	212-254-3557
VIRUSCAN, NETSCAN	McAfee and Assoc.	408-988-3832

Known viruses can be detected with anti-virus programs; unfortunately, new viruses are created all too often. These viruses may not be found by the current version of your commercial virus-detection software. For those viruses that escape detection by these programs, you can monitor your system for unusual occurrences, such as those listed here. The following occurrences may signal that an undetected virus is lurking somewhere in your network:

- **Unexpected change in a volume label, file size, or date.** As discussed earlier, beware of changes in the following files: LOGIN.EXE, SYSCON.EXE, NETCON.EXE, MAKEUSER.EXE, FILER.EXE, SERVER.EXE, or NET$OS.EXE. These programs interact with the NetWare operating system security mechanism and must be guarded against virus attacks.

- **Bad sectors.** Some viruses hide themselves in fake bad sectors. If a virus is hiding here, a large number of bad sector errors are reported.

- **Floppy disk light on when default directory is some other drive.** This can mean that the virus is busy snooping and infecting other drives, even though you are not performing operations on those drives.

- **Flag attributes for program and data files change from Read-Only to Read-Write.** This was discussed in the preceding section.

- **Unusual corruption of the server bindery.** For example, look for changes in trustee assignments for directories and files or the inability to perform operations, such as group and trustee assignments.

Eliminating Virus Attacks

If a virus attacks the network, the action that a network manager performs to detect, contain, and exterminate the virus is critical. You should have a written plan of action prepared, in the event that you become the victim of a virus attack. Your plan can be modeled after the steps that follow, adding instructions for the special situations of your own network:

1. If you suspect that a workstation is infected, isolate the workstation from the rest of the network by removing all network cables, modems, and other connections. Intelligent peripheral devices, such as LaserJet printers that have RAM or storage capacity, also should be disconnected.

2. Turn off the workstation to deactivate viruses that can be lurking in RAM. Some viruses survive a warm boot, so pressing Ctrl-Alt-Del is not guaranteed to deactivate viruses running in RAM.

3. Isolate all removable media that may have been infected, including floppy disks and tapes. The suspected media should be write-protected as a precaution. Floppy disks, because of their lower cost,

can be discarded (shredded or physically destroyed). If floppy disks will be reused, they should be erased with a bulk eraser because a DOS FORMAT may not remove the virus. Because hard disks are more expensive, you may wish to keep infected hard disks around so that you can disinfect and reuse them.

4. When disinfecting the hard disks, boot up from the disk containing the original version of the operating system. Remember to write-protect the disks before using them.

5. Be aware that some viruses are able to survive a high-level disk format. It may be necessary to apply a low-level format to the hard disks.

6. If files are inconsistent, even after disinfecting the storage media, restore data from the most recent backup (assuming you have been implementing a regular backup policy). As previously discussed, backups are vital to recovery from a virus attack.

7. If you have not done so already, think seriously about installing virus-protection software. In many cases, anti-virus software can disinfect the affected media.

The key to survival after a virus attack is preparedness. Panic should be avoided because the actions you take after a virus attack can help you to recover data and restore order. Preparedness also can help eliminate the panic that usually follows after a virus attack.

Using the McAfee Associates Toolkit

The McAfee and Associates anti-virus software are shareware programs that can be used to detect and eliminate viruses.

Using NETSCAN and SCAN

NETSCAN is a virus detection and identification program for local and wide area networks. NETSCAN searches for both known and unknown viruses on any network drive that is accessible as a DOS device. It works by searching the system for instruction sequences or patterns that are unique to each known computer virus, and then reporting their presence, if found. To detect unknown viruses, NETSCAN appends a validation code or "CRC check" for COM and EXE files. If the file has been modified in any way, NETSCAN reports that an infection might have occurred. NETSCAN also checks for new viruses by means of a user-supplied list of search strings.

Figure 18.1 shows the NETSCAN options and figure 18.2 shows the use of NETSCAN in searching for viruses on a network drive. The /M option, shown in figure 18.2, searches the RAM of the workstation for any viruses that may be lurking in RAM. At this writing, NETSCAN /M can identify the following viruses in RAM:

197	Anthrax	Form	Phantom
512	Brain	Invader	Plastique
1253	Dark Avenger	Joshi	Polish-2
1554	Disk Killer	Microbes	P1R (Phoenix)
2100	Doom-2	Mirror	Taiwan-3
3445-Stealth	EDV	Murphy	Whale
4096	Fish6	Nomenclature	Zero-Hunt

```
F:\LANSCAN>NETSCAN
NETSCAN V77 Copyright 1989-91 by McAfee Associates.  (408) 988-3832

To scan entire disk(s), just specify the disk(s) you want to scan.
Examples:
        NETSCAN F:
        NETSCAN F: G:
        NETSCAN F:

To scan a single directory, specify the directory.
Examples:
        NETSCAN \newstuff
        NETSCAN F:\unknown\things

To scan a single file, specify the file.
Examples:
        NETSCAN prog.com
        NETSCAN F:\there\unknown.exe

To remove infected files, use the /d option.
Example:
        NETSCAN F:\here /d


F:\LANSCAN>
```

Figure 18.1:
NETSCAN options.

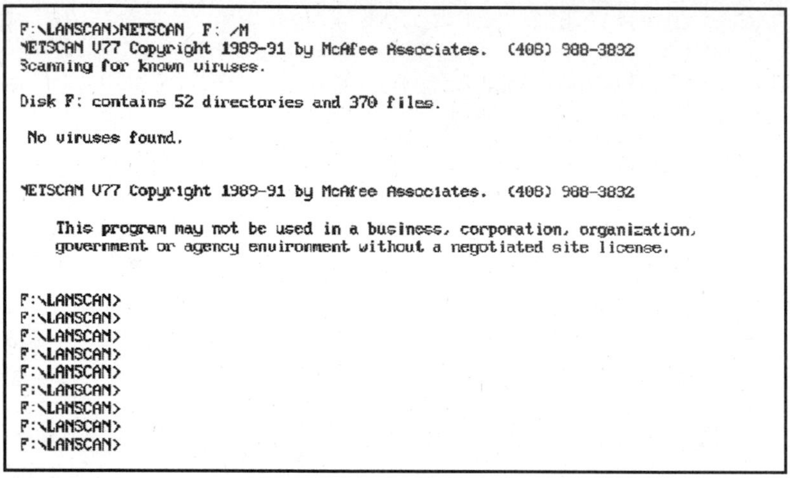

```
F:\LANSCAN>NETSCAN  F: /M
NETSCAN V77 Copyright 1989-91 by McAfee Associates.  (408) 988-3832
Scanning for known viruses.

Disk F: contains 52 directories and 370 files.

 No viruses found.


NETSCAN V77 Copyright 1989-91 by McAfee Associates.  (408) 988-3832

     This program may not be used in a business, corporation, organization,
     government or agency environment without a negotiated site license.


F:\LANSCAN>
F:\LANSCAN>
F:\LANSCAN>
F:\LANSCAN>
F:\LANSCAN>
F:\LANSCAN>
F:\LANSCAN>
F:\LANSCAN>
F:\LANSCAN>
```

Figure 18.2:
NETSCAN search results.

The SCAN utility is similar to NETSCAN, but it is more appropriate for DOS disks. SCAN searches the DOS boot sector for viruses.

Using McAfee CLEAN-UP

CLEAN-UP is a virus-disinfection program for IBM PC and compatible computers. CLEAN-UP searches the partition table, boot sector, or files of a PC and removes viruses specified by the user. In most instances, CLEAN-UP is able to repair the infected area of the system and restore it to normal usage. CLEAN-UP works on all viruses identified by the current version of the VIRUSCAN (SCAN) program.

CLEAN-UP runs a self-test when executed. If it has been modified in any way, a warning is displayed. The program does continue to remove viruses, however. If CLEAN-UP reports that it has been damaged, you should obtain a clean copy of the program.

CLEAN-UP is packaged with the VALIDATE program to ensure the integrity of the CLEAN.EXE file. The VALIDATE program distributed with CLEAN-UP can check all further versions of CLEAN-UP.

Figure 18.3 shows how the CLEAN-UP options can be used to disinfect a drive. The name of the virus to search for is specified by its ID in square brackets. The virus ID is reported by running NETSCAN or SCAN.

```
F:\LANSCAN>CLEAN
CLEAN 7.2V77 Copyright 1989-91 by McAfee Associates.  (408) 988-3832

To clean entire disk(s), specify the disk(s) and the virus.
Examples:
          CLEAN C: [virus name]
          CLEAN C: D: [virus name]
          CLEAN A: [virus name]

To clean a single directory, specify the directory and virus.
Examples:
          CLEAN \newstuff [virus]
          CLEAN C:\unknown\things [virus]
          CLEAN A:\ [virus]
          CLEAN . [virus]

To clean a single file, specify the file and the virus.
Examples:
          CLEAN \unknown\prog.com [virus]
          CLEAN A:\unknown.exe [virus]


F:\LANSCAN>
```

Figure 18.3:
CLEAN-UP options.

Summary

This chapter discussed viruses and how to secure a network system against viruse attack. First, you learned to distinguish not just viruses but various members of the extensive "virus family," including worms, rabbits, Trojan horses, bombs, trap doors, spoofs, bacteria, crabs, creepers, and salami.

Second, you learned about different virus methods of attack, especially such popular virus targets as the command shell and the boot record.

Then you were shown some effective strategies for preventing virus attack, as well as how to detect the presence of viruses and how to eliminate viruses after they have been identified in your system

Network Management

As LANs grow in scope, you can encounter significant problems in managing the user environments and operating the network. This chapter examines the tools you can use to manage larger networks.

Many third-party tools use proprietary schemes to manage a NetWare LAN. Some interesting developments have occurred in network management based on standard protocols. Products that comply with these standards can be mixed on a NetWare LAN and should be compatible. This section discusses these network management protocols.

Simple Network Management Protocol (SNMP)

The *Simple Network Management Protocol* (SNMP) is perhaps the most widely implemented vendor-independent network management protocol. SNMP originated in Internet, which is used to connect universities, government, and commercial organizations. Internet primarily uses the TCP/IP-based suite of protocols and is the largest computer network in the world.

SNMP has seen rapid deployment since it was first published. It is based on an earlier protocol called *Simple Gateway Monitoring Protocol* (SGMP). One reason for SNMP's popularity is that it is easier to implement than other competing protocols, such as OSI's CMIS/CMIP. Perhaps another subtle reason for its popularity is that the SNMP document (RFC 1098) is easier to read and understand than the OSI management protocol documents.

Many network vendors, including Novell, offer SNMP-based network management products. Today, most LAN hub vendors proudly announce that their hubs are SNMP-compliant. In fact, SNMP compliance has become a determining factor in many a network manager's decision to buy a specific product. Vendors such as DEC (which has its own proprietary network management protocols) or AT&T (which was interested only in OSI network management protocols) have announced or reengineered their products to implement SNMP.

With SNMP's popularity, it seems to have unstoppable momentum. It will be interesting to see if SNMP can be replaced by the more comprehensive and complex OSI management protocols.

Introduction to SNMP

The SNMP protocol is a layer 7 protocol. SNMP reports network management information over the network itself, but in case the network is down, it is possible to report management information over serial links such as RS-232 by using the *Serial Line Interface Protocol* (SLIP).

SNMP's attraction is its simplicity. Only four operations are defined that operate on SNMP objects. These operations are shown in table 19.1.

Table 19.1
SNMP Operations

Operation	Meaning
GET	Retrieves specific management information
GET-NEXT	Retrieves by traversal the next item of management information
SET	Manipulates the management information
TRAP	Reports events

Device parameters that describe management information are called *managed objects*. The collection of managed objects describe a *virtual store*. You can view this virtual store as a database. This database is called the *Management Information Base* (MIB). The MIB objects are described in a formal language called *Abstract Syntax Notation, Rev 1* (ASN.1). ASN.1 also is used to represent application layer data in the OSI model and is part of the presentation layer (layer 6).

Vendors can add device-specific MIBs through private enterprise extensions. MIB compilers are available to compile these definitions for inclusion in the SNMP managers. The MIB definitions (both I and II) are oriented toward management of TCP/IP-based networks; therefore, many vendors add private enterprise extensions to manage the features of their products. Ethernet and Token Ring parameters are managed by SNMP extensions. Vendors such as Synoptic Communications and Racal Interlan have published their extensions so that third-party SNMP managers can include these extensions.

Though SNMP originated on the TCP/IP-based Internet, RFC standards exist for use on OSI and SPX/IPX (Novell)-based networks. For example, RFC-1298 describes how SNMP can run over SPX/IPX protocols.

SNMP Agents and Managers

The nodes in a network that are to be managed run an implementation of the SNMP protocol that enables an external entity to manage the device. An *SNMP agent* enables these nodes to be managed by an external entity called an *SNMP manager*. The Novell LANtern product, discussed later in this chapter, is an example of an SNMP manager.

All managed devices do not need to directly support SNMP protocols. Repeaters and amplifiers on the network, for example, may not have sufficient processing capability to run SNMP protocols. Other devices on the network may implement other management protocols. These devices are called *foreign devices*. Foreign devices and devices that do not support SNMP can be managed by proxy SNMP agents.

SNMP agents and managers communicate through specially formatted messages called *Protocol Data Units* (SNMP PDUs). SNMP PDU requests are sent by managers to agents, and the agents respond with the requested values. Communication is driven by the managers, but agents are expected to respond. Because network events occur asynchronously, agents use the SNMP trap operation to report these events to the manager. The SNMP protocol is symmetrical; that is, SNMP GetRequest messages can be initiated by any SNMP device.

SNMP defines the notion of a community. A *community* is a relationship between an SNMP agent and one or more of its SNMP managers. All SNMP messages contain this community name. The community name is used to authenticate if the message is sent by an SNMP entity that belongs to the community.

SNMP agents are popularly implemented on, but not limited to, network hubs, concentrators, bridges, routers, and gateways. SNMP commands can be issued to disable malfunctioning concentrator ports, filter packets based on source or destination address, and report on packet statistics.

The SNMP protocol is concerned with the transfer of SNMP messages. The way that the MIB information is presented to the user and stored for analysis is an implementation issue left for the SNMP manager. This is where product differentiation between the SNMP managers take place. PC-based SNMP managers tend to use the Microsoft Windows graphical user interface (GUI), and UNIX-based SNMP managers use X-Windows.

SNMP Tools and Utilities

SNMP building blocks in the form of tools, compilers, and utilities are available from a number of vendors, such as Epilogue Technology Corp., Performance Systems International, and SNMP Research.

SNMP Research offers NETMON, which can run on a PC-based or UNIX workstation platform and displays a real-time geographical or logical map of the network. NETMON displays the status of links that are up or down (green for up and red for down), and then logs events to a disk. The SNMP manager requires support for UDP/IP. In most cases, this support is an appropriate TCP/IP driver that can work with the network interface. TCP/IP drivers include support for UDP.

SNMP can be used with non-TCP/IP-based networks. Only the SNMP managers and agents use UDP/IP, but other devices on the network can use their own protocols that coexist with UDP/IP. SNMP managers and agents, for example, can be used in a NetWare LAN. The NetWare nodes can use SPX/IPX and the SNMP devices can use UDP/IP. Both sets of protocols can coexist on the same Ethernet or Token Ring LAN.

To demonstrate that SNMP is not restricted to computers running TCP/IP, some vendors have gone to extreme lengths. At an Interop show, Epilogue Technology demonstrated an SNMP agent controlling a toaster. SNMP Research demonstrated a SNMP-controlled electronic dog complete with a canine MIB! Users clicking on an X-Windows icon could cause this dog to bark.

Novell's LANtern

Novell's LANtern system contains the LANtern Network Monitor and the LANtern Services Manager. The LANtern Network Monitor is an SNMP agent from Novell that is designed to work with one or more SNMP managers to manage Ethernet networks. Novell's SNMP manager is called LANtern Services Manager.

The LANtern Network Monitor

The LANtern Network Monitor acts as a dedicated listener that gathers comprehensive statistical information about network performance utilization. Alarms implemented as SNMP trap messages also report the status of a network or warn you when parameter values exceed a predefined threshold. Communication with the LANtern monitor takes place over the network. In case of network failure, this communication also can be performed through an RS-232 serial interface. The LANtern monitor's hardware specifications are described in table 19.2.

Table 19.2
LANtern Network Monitor Hardware Specifications

Parameter	Description
CPU	Motorola 68020, 16 MHz with zero wait states
RAM	Up to 2M dual ported RAM; 8K of battery-backed static RAM
EPROM	256K of flash EPROM (expandable to 512K) for program storage
NIC	Intel 82586 LAN coprocessor (Ethernet)

continues

Table 19.2
Continued

Parameter	Description
Serial Port	CCITT V.24/V.28. DB-9 IBM AT compatible RS-232
Power	30 Watts. 95 to 264 VAC

The primary communication to a LANtern network monitor takes place over the network. You also can use a secondary communication channel over the serial interface port.

The LANtern monitor requires three pieces of information to communicate over the monitored network: its own IP address (adminNetworkIPAddr), the subnet mask (adminNetworkSubnetMask), and the address of one (any) directly connected gateway (adminNetworkGateway). When power is first applied to the LANtern monitor, it does not have this information. It obtains it by employing either the *Bootstrap Protocol* (BOOTP) or *Reverse Address Resolution Protocol* (RARP).

For LANtern monitors on an isolated remote LAN segment, the serial link running a data link protocol is specified in MIB object adminSerialDataLink. The default encapsulation is SLIP.

LANtern monitors all network traffic and gathers statistics on general network events and station-to-station traffic. A *network event* is any activity on the network that can cause the carrier sense (Ethernet) to be active for more than 0.5 microseconds. Table 19.3 lists the network events.

Table 19.3
LANtern Monitors General Network Events

MIB variable	Meaning
eGoodPackets	Total number of good packets
eBroadcastPackets	Broadcasts
eMulticastPackets	Multicasts

MIB variable	Meaning
eUnicastPackets	Unicasts
eCRCAlignmentErrors	Faulty CRC
eOversize	Frame > 1518 bytes with good CRC
eUndersize	Frame < 64 bytes with good CRC
eJabbers	Frame > 1518 bytes with bad CRC
eLocalCollisions	Local collision or Signal Quality Error
eCollisionFragments	Frame < 64 bytes with bad CRC

The LANtern monitor keeps statistics for transmitting and receiving stations that include total packets transmitted, total bytes transmitted, total errors transmitted, protocols used, the date and time of first transmission, and the date and time of most recent transmission. The MIB defines two tables, eStnToStnTableSD and eStnToStnTableDS, through which this information can be accessed. These tables are identical, except that eStnToStnTableSD is organized with the source address as the major key and the destination address as the minor key and that eStnToStnTableSD is organized with the destination address as the major key and the same address as the minor key. You can use these tables to get statistics on packets received by a station or transmitted from a station.

The LANtern Services Manager

LANtern Services Manager (LSM) is an SNMP manager that runs on a standard 80386, 80386SX, or 80486 IBM-compatible PC under the MS-Windows environment. Designed to work with the LANtern Monitor, the LSM can communicate with the LANtern Monitors through the monitored network or an RS-232 interface.

LSM detects and polls LANtern monitors, looks for stations, and can gather long-term trend data at user-definable intervals. LSM polls LANtern for real-time statistic data only if requested to do so, so that the impact of SNMP traffic on normal network activity is minimized. LSM stores information about alarms, events, station configuration, and long-term trends in Novell's popular Btrieve database.

Figure 19.1 shows the data flow between LANtern monitors and an LSM. This figure shows that LSM connections can be made through the monitored LAN, modem, or direct RS-232 link. The modem uses the RS-232 interface on the LANtern monitor and LSM. Real-time data can be displayed by means of messages, graphs, or tables. LANtern configuration data is stored in a configuration database that can be edited through LSM. Alarms and trend data are stored in the Btrieve database and can be displayed as trend table, trend graph, and alarm log.

You enable real-time data gathering by selecting the network segment and requesting the data that you want to display. LSM displays the data in the form of a graph or a table. As long as the data window is active, LSM continues to gather and update the display. Even if you minimize the real-time data window (turn it into an icon), the LSM continues to gather and store information in the background. LSM gathers and displays data in the form of counters, gauges, conversations, and station information.

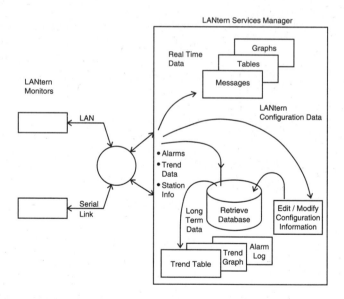

Figure 19.1:
LANtern service manager data flow.

Nineteen counters are available that can keep track of numbers of certain events. You can display the counters individually, in combination, or by profiles. *Profiles* contain several counters of the same type, such as packet counts broken by packet size. Gauges measure percentages of utilization, broadcast packets, collisions, and errors, and can be defined with an alarm threshold. If activity exceeds the threshold, an alarm notice can be generated. Conversations to and from a station can be monitored in the form of packets sent to and received from a station. These packets are displayed in the form of a table that can be updated at the rate you want or sorted by any column as a key.

Long-term trend data can be gathered and stored by the LSM in user-definable intervals. LSM displays this data as trend graphs or trend tables. A *trend graph* is a line graph that displays trend data in percentages for a selected network segment. The same counters and profiles are available as are available for real-time data. The trend data can be stored for 25 hours (100 15-minute intervals) before it is overwritten. The trend table lists the information gathered in the form of a table. It can be sorted automatically using any column as the sort key.

LSM provides two forms of alarm notices: gauge threshold alarms and activity event alarms. *Gauge threshold alarms* occur whenever the percentage value (gauge) exceeds the predefined threshold for utilization, broadcasts, collisions, and errors. *Activity event alarms* are related to specific lists of events or conditions that the LANtern monitor can detect. These events are listed in table 19.4.

Table 19.4
General Events Reported by LANtern Monitors

Event	Meaning
New station	Indicates when a station first starts transmitting
Duplicate IP address	Indicates two stations with same IP address
Station active	Indicates when a critical active station begins transmitting again
Authentication failure	Indicates an invalid community name in SNMP message

continues

Table 19.4
Continued

Event	Meaning
Cable failure	Indicates a cable fault on Ethernet or transceiver drop
Ping notification	Indicates when a LANtern monitor receives response to an echo-test message sent to a station
Warm start	Indicates that the LANtern was warm started
Utilization	Indicates that utilization exceeds threshold
Broadcasts	Indicates that broadcast packets exceed threshold
Collisions	Indicates that collisions exceed threshold
Errors	Indicates that packet errors exceed threshold

Figures 19.2 to 19.5 depict a scenario in which the LSM can be used to manage a network. The MIS manager sees a bright red alarm on the LSM console. A glance at the LSM gauges (fig. 19.2) reveals that the alarm was caused by a high number of CRC/Alignment errors. The MIS manager selects Station Monitor from the pull-down menu and sorts the table by using the Errors out column (fig. 19.3). The first six lines on this table show an unusually large number of errors. The MIS manager double-clicks on the icons that represent these stations (fig. 19.4). The location field indicates that the six stations are in the same building. Closer examination of the 10BASE-T network in the building (using a 10BASE-T tester) network reveals that faulty twisted-pair wiring is causing the errors (fig. 19.5).

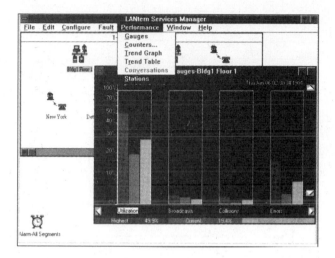

Figure 19.2:
LANtern Services Manager reveals a high number of CRC/Alignment errors.

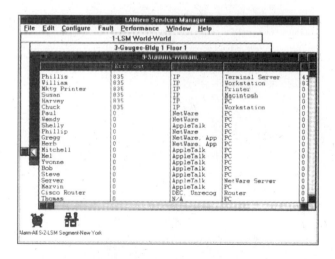

Figure 19.3:
Sorting of station table by Errors out reveals six stations with a high amount of errors.

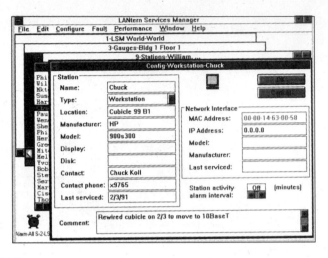

Figure 19.4:
Detailed view of stations reveal that they are in the same location connected by 10BASE-T.

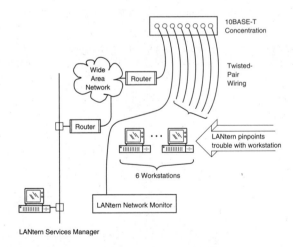

Figure 19.5:
LANtern Services Manager pinpoints trouble with twisted-pair wiring.

Remote Monitoring (RMON)

A number of organizations, including Novell, support an extension to SNMP MIBs that can be used for remote monitoring. This extension is called the RMON MIB. RMON specifies the way in which data can be monitored remotely from a central site. Although this process sounds similar to what SNMP does, SNMP MIBs typically focus on device configuration.

The RMON MIB defines more comprehensive monitoring and analysis than SNMP MIBs. A network vendor can implement RMON MIBs in devices such as hubs, bridges, and routers. The RMON MIB will provide the kind of information that Novell's LANtern product currently provides, which may lessen the need for dedicated probes such as LANtern Network Monitor. Gathering information for RMON MIBs is a process-intensive task, however, and the market for dedicated probes will still exist.

RMON defines nine categories of MIB objects. A vendor needs to implement only one category to comply with the RMON specification. Newer versions of Novell's LANtern monitor implement these categories.

OSI-Based Management

OSI network management is ambitious and complex. It makes use of a protocol called *Common Management Information Protocol* (CMIP). In concept, it is similar to the SNMP-based approach except that it has a wider scope. Comparisons between these two sets of protocols have resulted in heated debates. Proponents of both systems realize that each protocol has a role to play in managing future networks. Both protocol families use a management-information base and vendor-specific extensions to the MIB.

Scope of OSI Management

Figure 19.6 shows the OSI network management model. The *Network Management Application Process* (NMAP) implements the network management services consisting of five elements:

- Fault management
- Performance management
- Security management
- Configuration management
- Accounting management

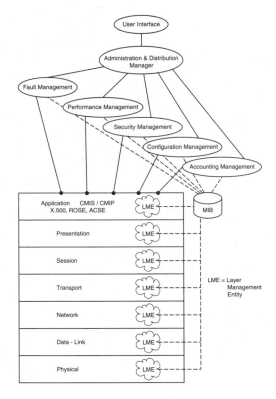

Figure 19.6:
OSI network management model.

Each layer of the OSI model has a *Layer Management Entity* (LME) that sends management information on these five aspects to the NMAP. This management information is stored in the MIB, which is a virtual store that describes the different parameters to be managed.

The management operations that you can perform on MIBs are similar in concept to SNMP, but more complex. SNMP has four operations, but CMIP includes operations such as M-INITIALIZE, M-GET, M-SET, M-ACTION, M-ABORT, M-CREATE, M-DELETE, M-EVENT-REPORT, and M-TERMINATE.

OSI Management Protocols

Common Management Information Services (CMIS) and *Common Management Information Protocol* (CMIP) are the protocols used at the application layer. CMIS describes the management services provided to NMAP. The implementation of CMIS is done by the CMIP, which is a peer-to-peer protocol used to exchange management information (fig. 19.6).

The CMIP protocols make use of other OSI protocols. *Application Common Services Element* (ACSE) is used to provide communications binding, and *Remote Operation Services Element* (ROSE) implements a *Remote Procedure Call* (RPC) mechanism. At the other layers, full OSI-based services are used.

An Interim Approach: CMOT

Because full OSI-based services are implemented on few networks, an attempt has been made to run OSI network management protocols on TCP/IP-based networks. TCP/IP was chosen for this experiment because it is a de facto industry standard, and it is the hope of OSI advocates that TCP/IP will be replaced by OSI protocols. Implementing CMIP on TCP/IP-based networks will make the transition to full OSI management protocols easier. The management protocol for this interim approach is called *Common Management Over TCP/IP* (CMOT).

The networking model for a CMOT management system is shown in figure 19.7. Only a minimal set of presentation-layer services needed for connection establishment, release, and data exchange are implemented. These minimal presentation services are referred to as *Lightweight Presentation Protocol* (LPP). The LPP services run on the TCP/UDP at the transport layer, which in turn run on *Internet Protocol* (IP) at the network layer. The CMIP protocol is implemented by *Common Management Information Services Element* (CMISE). A peer-to-peer session exists between CMISE on management systems over which CMIP messages are exchanged.

Although there is a large commercial interest in SNMP, there is little in CMOT. CMOT may have missed its window of opportunity because SNMP delivered a working network management protocol with a powerful functionality that is much faster.

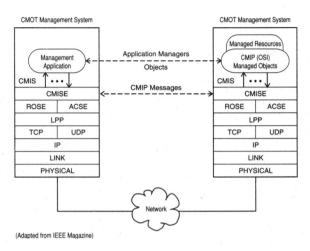

(Adapted from IEEE Magazine)

Figure 19.7:
CMOT Management System.

SNMP versus CMIP

Both SNMP and CMIP have strong proponents. Although CMIP offers features missing in SNMP, SNMP is widely deployed, and CMIP implementations are few at this time.

CMIP is association-oriented and requires that two CMIP application entities be connected before they can exchange management information. Although management information is sent reliably, there is greater overhead in CMIP. SNMP, on the other hand, does not need an established connection to send information. It has less protocol overhead and is faster than CMIP. You cannot be assured, however, that SNMP messages will reach their destination. You may have to build an acknowledgment strategy for certain applications.

CMIP enables multiple-object selection with conditional commands. For example, in CMIP you can request port information for all bridges that have a badPacketCount >= 50. SNMP does not support this capability directly. In SNMP, every bridge must be queried separately for badPacketCount, and the SNMP manager must check to see if the badPacketCount >= 50. CMIP returns more information from a single command than is needed in some situations, and filtering would have to be done anyway. SNMP tends to deliver just the information requested and nothing else.

Both CMIP and SNMP can specify multiple operations of the same type within a single request. In SNMP, the requests are carried out, in an atomic fashion—either they are all done, or none are carried out and an error code is returned. In CMIP, a best-efforts approach is used to carry out operations on multiple instances of the same object.

You can use CMIP to send a single request to get large amounts of data. If the data cannot be accommodated in a single reply, the data is sent in a series of linked replies. SNMP does not support linked replies and can be inefficient for retrieving large amounts of data, such as addressing tables. SNMP proponents argue that the need for transfer of tables of information is less frequent than reading or writing to a simple MIB object.

You can use CMIP and SNMP to sequence or browse through an MIB. In CMIP, you can use wild cards to get multiple-object selection capabilities. With SNMP, the GET-NEXT command can traverse the MIB in a column-row order. To support the complex CMIP operations, MIB object organization gets more difficult and complex. SNMP GET-NEXT operation and MIB object organization is simpler.

CMIP uses object-specific commands such as "reboot system." SNMP makes use of the SET operation to set a Boolean flag to reboot the system.

CMIP event reports can be confirmed or unconfirmed. SNMP events are always unconfirmed. CMIP objects are more complex and comprehensive than SNMP objects. On the other hand, CMIP objects are more difficult to implement.

SNMP uses a polling method to access critical MIB parameters. CMIP uses an event-based reporting mechanism, which expects the managed device to report events. Polling introduces traffic overhead when the number of managed devices become large. Polling, however, keeps the SNMP-managed devices simple. CMIP is more efficient for managing large numbers of network devices, but these devices tend to be more complex because they have to take care of reporting events.

In general, CMIP more efficiently communicates large amounts of management information of the type that occurs between two CMIP managers. SNMP is better suited for manager-to-managed-device communications.

Summary

This chapter discussed a number of network management schemes, including SNMP, CMOT, and CMIS/CMIP. SNMP is the most widely supported technology. Novell has two products, the LANtern Services Manager and the LANtern Monitor, that implement SNMP.

Network Applications

Before LANs became popular, most applications for DOS were written under the assumption that only one user would be operating the machine at a time. Because there was no way to share resources under DOS on a single machine, this seemed like a reasonable assumption. After LANs became commonplace, many users tried to run these single-user applications on a network. They discovered that sometimes the applications ran without any problems, but they sometimes crashed or lost data. This chapter explores why these problems occur with single-user software and how multiuser software overcomes these problems. The different types of multiuser software also are examined.

Running Single-User Software on a Network

Normally, single-user applications are designed to run on machines without any network connections. Is it then possible for the single-user application to run on a network? Consider a single-user application that is stored at the workstation. When the name of the startup program for the application is typed at the DOS prompt, the DOS loader loads the application from the local media on which it is stored, and control is then transferred to the application that runs on the workstation.

If the single-user application is stored on a directory on the server, the user must first log in to a server on the network to run the application. The user must have a minimum of Read and File scan privileges in the directory in which the single-user application is stored. That directory can be set in the user's search path. The search path can be set making use of the MAP command at the command line, or the MAP commands can be placed in the login script files, as discussed in Chapter 14. Alternatively, the user can change the current directory to the directory in which the application is stored by using the MAP command or the DOS CD command.

When the name of the startup file for the application is typed, DOS does not know that the application is stored on a network directory; DOS issues a request to load the application program in the workstation's memory. The NetWare shell monitors all DOS system calls by placing itself between the request for DOS services—by means of the INT 21 (hex) interrupt—and the DOS services. If the NetWare shell determines that the request is for a file on the server, it issues a *NetWare Core Protocol* (NCP) packet to implement this request. The server (on which the file resides) processes the NCP request and returns an NCP reply indicating the status of the processed request.

When DOS issues a request to load the application program into memory, that request is translated by the NetWare shell into an NCP request to fetch a copy of the application program from the server (see fig. 20.1). A number of *packet transmissions* are performed to get the entire application program from the server directory to the workstation. The application program is then loaded in the workstation memory, and execution takes place without DOS being aware that the program was downloaded from the server.

When the single-user application loads from the NetWare server, a typical operation is to access a data file. The data file may be on the network, and the single-user application is not aware that it is opening a network file. (It issues a DOS request to open a file.) The NetWare shell intercepts this request. After determining that the open file request is for a data file on the network, the NetWare shell directs the request to the server. The file is opened on the server, and the application is ready to perform file operations on it.

If the application needs to read a portion of a data file, it can open the file, read the data, and close the file again. The application also can open the file, and then keep it opened until the application ends normally.

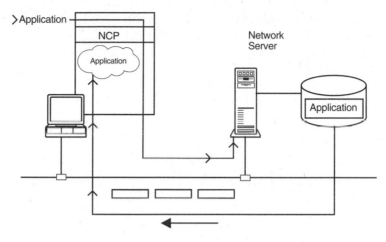

Figure 20.1:
Loading an application from a NetWare server.

If the application has been written to perform the first option, another station on the network running the same single-user application can open the file after it has been closed (see fig. 20.2) and modify the data in the file. When the first station reopens the file, the file will have been changed by the second station, but the first station will not be aware of this change. The two applications can easily step over each other and destroy each other's changes.

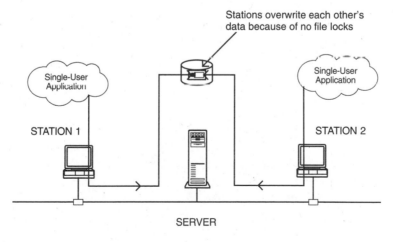

Figure 20.2:
Data file conflicts when multiple users use a single-user application on a network.

The real problem is that there is no mechanism to enable the applications to communicate with each other when sharing data. Each application runs independently of other applications and is not aware of changes made to shared data.

To solve the single-user data access problem, there must be a concurrency-control mechanism that enables an application to place a lock on a data file so that other applications cannot modify the data file. A *lock* is a mechanism that is placed on a shared resource. It grants control over the resource to the application issuing the lock.

If the second option is being used by the application software, the single-user application can lock the data file by making use of NetWare features. When a data file is copied or created on a NetWare server, it has the default Non-sharable Read Write attributes. (This means that the file can be opened for read/write operations but, as long as the file is open, NetWare locks the file for you.) Therefore, if the file has Non-shareable Read Write attributes, the first station that opens the file locks the file (other stations are denied access to this file). This is one way to ensure that single-user applications can operate on a NetWare LAN.

To enable single-user applications to have the same file opened by a number of applications, the data file must have the Shared attribute. File attributes for NetWare files can be changed by using the FLAG command or the FILER utility.

Running Multiuser Applications

Multiuser applications are designed with *concurrency control* mechanisms. This means that applications are able to share data without writing over each other's data. Examples of applications that require this type of concurrency control are database applications, spreadsheets, electronic mail, and group productivity tools.

Concurrency-Control Mechanisms

Three concurrency-control mechanisms can be used for data file sharing:

- File locking
- Record locking
- Field locking

Figure 20.3 presents a conceptual view of these mechanisms. *File locking* makes the entire file unavailable to other users. If a word processor locks a file, for example, the file is unavailable for update operations. It may still be available for viewing (read operation), but other users cannot update the file in use. This is how networking versions of word processor applications, such as WordPerfect, implement file locks.

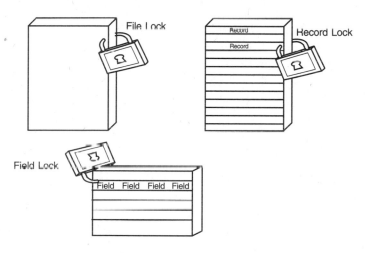

Figure 20.3:
Concurrency-controlled mechanisms.

Record locking locks a range of bytes, rather than the entire file. This is a very useful feature in database applications in which different workstations may be working on different parts of the same data file. DOS 3.3 and later versions contain system services to support record locking. If the DOS record-locking services are used, the NetWare shell translates them into NCP requests that implement the locking through NetWare APIs. NetWare provides record-locking APIs that can be used directly by multiuser applications.

Field locking is a further refinement of the record-locking concept. Several users may be working on the same record but on different fields of that record. In an employee database, for example, one data-entry clerk can be updating the address and phone numbers of an employee while someone else is updating salary information for that employee. You also can have a higher-level lock so that certain fields can be viewed and updated by certain users only. A good example of this is the employee database, in which the salary information can be hidden from most users.

Logical Records versus Physical Locks

NetWare provides two types of locking mechanisms that are important for applications: logical and physical locks.

You can implement a *logical lock* by assigning a logical name to a resource and locking that name. Other applications check for a lock on the name before accessing the resource. A logical record is enforced by applications. It is not enforced by the NetWare operating system.

Physical locks are different from logical locks because they are enforced by the network operating system. Physical locks can be used to lock a range of bytes in a file. (This is the way to implement record and field locking.) If another user attempts to access a range of bytes that is physically locked, the user receives an `Access denied` message.

Logical and physical locks on a NetWare v3.x server can be displayed by using the MONITOR NLM. NetWare defines the following types of physical locks:

- **Locked Exclusive.** Locked so that no one else can read or write to the specified range of bytes

- **Locked Shareable.** Locked so that reads are OK but only one station can write

- **Locked.** Logged for future locking

- **TTS Holding Lock.** Unlocked by application, but still locked by TTS because transactions are not complete

SET Parameters That Control Application Locks

NetWare v3.x has a number of record-locking parameters that are important for applications that make use of file and record locking. You can use the SET command to set these parameters on the server console. These parameters are as follows:

- MAXIMUM RECORD LOCKS

- MAXIMUM FILE LOCKS

- MAXIMUM RECORD LOCKS PER CONNECTION

- MAXIMUM FILE LOCKS PER CONNECTION

Limits are placed on the total number of system-wide and per-connection file and record locks because implementing locks takes up server resources that can be used for other functions. In most situations, the default limits are adequate for applications that make use of record and file locking. If applications fail because of messages about insufficient file and record locks, consider increasing these limits.

MAXIMUM RECORD LOCKS sets a limit on the total number of record locks that are possible on a NetWare server at the same time.

MAXIMUM FILE LOCKS sets the limit on the total number of opened and locked files NetWare can simultaneously handle at the server.

MAXIMUM RECORD LOCKS PER CONNECTION controls the maximum number of record locks a station can use per connection.

MAXIMUM FILE LOCKS PER CONNECTION controls the maximum number of opened and locked files a station can use per connection.

Database Applications in a LAN Environment

Databases that run on LANs must be able to support multiple-user access to the database. This means that all of the network and database protocols needed for remote access of the database must be supported. For NetWare LANs, the preferred protocols are the SPX/IPX for transport. Because the database software makes use of NetWare files to implement its database, the NetWare Core Protocols also are used. Database servers, such as SQL Server from Microsoft, require the Named Pipes protocol. (This must be supported at the workstation that accesses the SQL Server.)

The database also must be able to implement file and record locking and, optionally, field-level locking. Security mechanisms should be in place that enable access to files, records, and fields on a per-user or per-user group basis.

Another important requirement is the automated recovery and backup facility. If data files get corrupted, there should be a way of making the data files consistent. A transaction tracking capability, as implemented in the NetWare SQL product, also is desirable. Such *transaction tracking services* (TTSs) are available in NetWare. When used in the context of databases, TTS means that a log is made of the transaction before the transaction is actually executed. This transaction log is called the *transaction backout file*. If the transaction fails because of a server, workstation, or network crash, the transaction can be rolled back to the point before the transaction, so that the integrity of the database is preserved.

There are two types of technologies used to implement databases on a LAN: file server-based technology and database server-based technology.

File Server-Based Technology

Figure 20.4 shows a LAN in which file server-based technology is used. In this technology, the file server provides remote file services used for storing the database files. Most of the database processing is done at the workstation. The file server provides only reading/writing of data blocks and support for record and file locks. The algorithms for record manipulation are executed at the workstation.

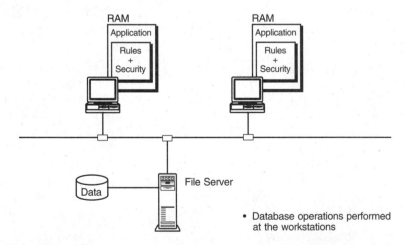

Figure 20.4:
File server-based technology.

With file server-based databases, records have to be transported from the file server to the workstation for processing. Tasks that require processing many records at a time can generate a large amount of traffic. The network bandwidth and the delays involved in record transfer can easily become a bottleneck. For every record update, the record must first be transferred to the workstation. The record copy is changed at the workstation and then sent back to the server to be written into the database, which results in at least two record transfers per update operation. If the record is larger than the maximum packet size configured for the LAN, additional packet transfers may occur as the record is broken into smaller pieces and sent across the network.

Consider a situation in which the database consists of 500,000 employee records. A query is sent to the file server-based database asking for a list of all employees who earn more than $200,000 per year. Although only a few individuals satisfy this criterion, this query still means that each of the 500,000 records is transported to the workstation, where the salary field is compared to the $200,000 criterion. This is not a very efficient way to process this information.

Database files on the server are implemented as B+ or B* trees, which are database technologies in which the indices used to access the records are kept in pages of a fixed size and organized in the form of a tree. As part of the database operation, it may be necessary to perform operations, such as splitting and recombining, on these index blocks. In file server-based databases, the index block operations have to be performed at the workstation. This creates its own traffic, and when splitting and recombining lead to other blocks being split or recombined, the network traffic increases.

File server-based technology, though not very efficient, is adequate for small databases. For larger databases, a different type of technology is needed: database server-based technology.

Examples of file server-based products are Paradox, dBASE from Borland, Rbase from Microrim, ZIM from Zanthe, Foxbase from Fox Software, Clipper from Nantucket, Focus from Information Builders, Dataflex from Data Access, and DataEase from DataEase International.

Database Servers

In database servers (see fig. 20.5), database operations are split into front-end and back-end operations. The back end is run on a server and performs all database operations. The front end is used to provide a graphical interface to the user and to perform minor processing. Actually, this is very similar to the way traditional database processing takes place on mainframe databases, in which all processing is done on the mainframe.

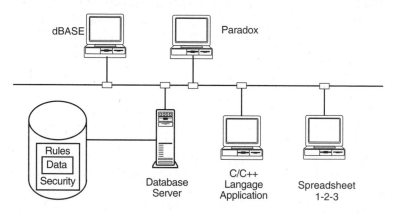

- Database operations performed on the database server

Figure 20.5:
Database servers.

In many ways, database servers are a happy marriage of mainframe database technology and PC technology. The PC used as a workstation performs all graphical user interface processing, and database operations are performed on a centralized machine. The rules and integrity checks for database processing are kept on a central computer, which provides the best kind of security.

Consider the example in which the database consists of 500,000 employee records and a query is sent to the file server-based database for a list of all employees that have a salary greater than $200,000 per year. In the database server example, because all database processing takes place at the database server, there is no requirement to transfer each one of the 500,000 records to the workstation. The database server can sequence through each record and compare the salary field against the $200,000 criteria. Only the handful of records that satisfy the criterion is sent to the workstation. This is a much more efficient way of processing this information.

Another advantage of using a database server is not having to transfer B+/B* tree index pages to the workstation for splitting and recombining.

Examples of database server products are NetWare SQL from Novell, LAN Server from Oracle, SQL Server from Microsoft, INGRES from Ingres Corporation, SQL Base from Gupta Technologies, and XDB Server from Novell.

LAN-Based Word Processing

The advantages of using network versions of word processors is that PC users can easily share files across the network. A network operating system such as NetWare can be used for implementing security and file sharing, so that personal information is kept safe from others. Figure 20.6 shows a LAN-based word processing application.

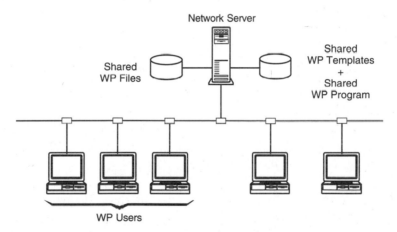

Figure 20.6:
LAN-based word processing.

The NetWare server can be used for sharing common document templates and group documents, and for document consolidation. Popular LAN-based word processing applications are WordPerfect, Microsoft Word, and many others.

LAN-Based Spreadsheets

The NetWare server can be used to share spreadsheets among several users (see fig. 20.7). At the basic level, at least file locking should be implemented, which prevents users from updating the spreadsheet at the same time. If users are working on different areas of a large spreadsheet, it may be desirable to have cell-level locking, so that individual users can work on the same spreadsheet without overwriting each other's work.

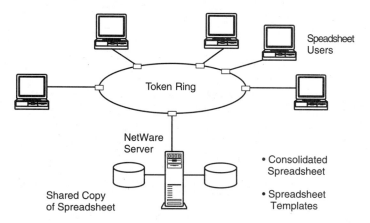

Figure 20.7:
LAN-based spreadsheets.

Some LAN spreadsheets support intelligent consolidation, in which groups of spreadsheets can be rolled up and consolidated across the network. The NetWare server also enables the sharing of common templates and financial models that have all the formulas predefined—all that is required is data entry.

Electronic Mail

Figure 20.8 shows the model for electronic mail running on a LAN. The NetWare server acts as a post office where the mail boxes for the users are kept. Electronic mail is sent by posting a mail message to the server. Users can log in to the server at any time and run the electronic mail application, which enables them to read the messages waiting for them.

Figure 20.8 shows that mail-gateways are necessary to access other electronic mail systems. It also is possible for users to dial in to the LAN to read their electronic mail.

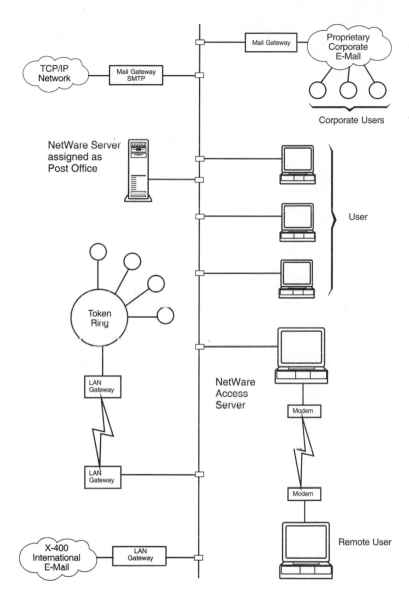

Figure 20.8:
A large LAN-based electronic mail configuration.

The most popular electronic mail protocol for LANs is *Message Handling System* (MHS). MHS was originally developed by Action Technologies of Emeryville, California, but its specification and future evolution is now under the control of Novell.

Some of the popular electronic mail products include Da Vinci Mail from Da Vinci Systems, Banyan Mail from Banyan Systems, Higgins Mail from Enable/Higgins Group, Herald Mail from Emissary Systems, Quick Mail from CE Software, and ALL-IN-1 mail from DEC.

Many of the electronic mail systems provide electronic mail gateways to other systems such as IBM PROFS, IBM DISOSS, DEC ALL-IN-1, X.400, and SMTP. For international mail networks, the standard is X.400. When evaluating electronic mail systems, support for X.400 gateways should be on the top of your list because this is the way most electronic mail systems are evolving.

Many electronic mail packages are feature-rich. Some of the features that are supported are the following:

- Carbon copy and blind copy. *Carbon copy* is sent to the designated user. A *blind copy* of the message is sent to other recipients that do not show up in the electronic mail.

- Distribution list. These can be personal or system wide.

- Attachments. Files, graphic data, and screen captures can be attached and sent.

- File folders. For organizing personal mail.

- Delivery receipt and read receipt on a per-electronic-mail basis.

- Auto forwarding and express delivery.

- Message encryption and compression.

- Pop-up notification of new mail.

- Electronic mail gateways to other electronic mail systems.

- Remote user access.

Workgroup Software

Workgroup software enables a group of users to coordinate their efforts as a team. It has a combination of features such as electronic mail, word processing, to-do-list, project tracking/management/scheduling, financial planning, and electronic accessories (calculators, notepads, clocks, alarms).

Examples of such applications include Notes from Lotus, Office Vision from IBM, WordPerfect Office from WordPerfect Corporation, Rhapsody from AT&T, and Total Office Manager from Network Technology.

MHS

Do not confuse Message Handling System—originally created by Action Technologies—with MHS specified in the X.400 MHS standard, even though they have the same name.

MHS does not provide a user interface; it is a messaging standard that specifies the mechanism as to how messages are to be represented and exchanged. It can be used by application developers to develop distributed applications. MHS handles the collection, routing, and delivery of any message or file across dissimilar environments. Applications that use MHS do not have to worry about the mechanics of data transfer such as transport protocols, error checking, sequencing, and so on. MHS handles these low-level details by properly interfacing with appropriate transport protocols. MHS provides transparent store and forward capabilities. It is designed to run on Novell networks, though stand-alone versions of MHS for DOS also are available. When MHS is run on a server, it takes approximately 300K of RAM.

Because the communication method is store-and-forward, a message can be held at an electronic post-office box before it is transmitted. Therefore, MHS is not suited for realtime interprocess communication. When implemented on a server, MHS provides a back-end store-and-forward message server.

MHS is similar in concept to X.400, but is much simpler. It does not require the extensive computing resources required by X.400, and it has a much simpler API. It is typically used to transmit electronic messages, but also can be used for transmitting text and binary files. To send mail from an MHS system to a non-MHS system such as ALL-IN-1, Easylink, X.400, or SMTP, you need a mail gateway to convert the different mail formats.

Details of the MHS structure are documented in the NetWare MHS Developer's Kit which contains a description of the *Message Control Block* (MCB), and *Standard Message Format* (SMF) interface.

An example of an MHS-based network is shown in figure 20.9. The MHS post offices also are called MHS hubs because they act as a central site for exchanging electronic mail.

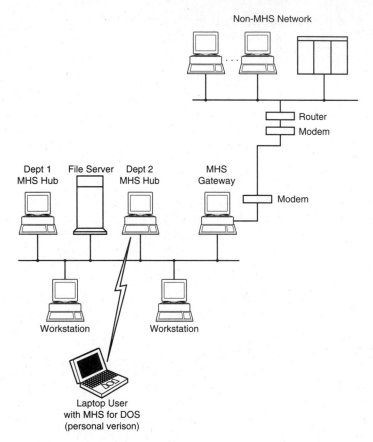

Figure 20.9:
An example of an MHS network.

This network shows that a mobile user can dial into the network with a laptop and a modem and receive or send mail on the MHS network. The laptop user needs the personal edition of MHS up and running on his system; this enables the user to log in to the network at any one of the hubs and collect or send mail. The mail is stored at an MHS hub from which it is sent to the destination directly or through intervening MHS hubs.

Electronic mail can be composed and sent by the laptop user while the user is logged in to the network. However, this approach can be costly in terms of long-distance telephone charges. A better way is to configure the MHS on the laptop so that long-distance connection time is reduced to electronic-mail transfer only. This can be done by setting up default routing information in configuration files on the laptop.

The following sample batch file can be used to start the MHS connectivity manager on your laptop:

```
@echo off
rem Go to the MHS directory installed on your laptop
cd  \ mhs\exe
rem Invoke MHS
mhs -l
rem Invoke the E-mail user agent
call uagent.bat
rem Save log files and then delete them
copy \sdrege.*    \log\*.*   >  nul
del  \sdrege.*   >  nul
```

The use of the -l option causes the MHS program to run and terminate if there is no more mail to deliver. The connectivity manager (user agent) is run after the electronic-mail transfer. The log files are then backed up and deleted for the next session.

To set up a menu driven system using Novell menus, one can set up a menu script similar to the following:

```
%MHS Dialup,10,60
SCS Corporate Office
    @echo off
    set MHSPHONE=1,406-333-4471
    call MHSCON.BAT    CORPMHS   2
    set MHSPHONE=
Your MHS Choice
    @echo off
    set MHSPHONE=@1"Please enter the MHS dial number"
    call MHSCON.BAT    CORPMHS   2
    set MHSPHONE=
```

The MHSCON.BAT file can use the MHSUSER command and accept arguments to make the connection. The phone number is passed as an environment string variable to the MHSCON.BAT batch file to make it possible to pass comma (,) values for delays. The use of commas is useful when dialing out using the number 9 or causing delays for credit card numbers.

BTRIEVE

The Btrieve record manager was originally developed by Softcraft which was later purchased by Novell in the mid-1980s. Btrieve is bundled with every version of NetWare. It is a complete record manager system that enables you to build in an indexed data file. You can build a master index and several supplementary indexes for each data file. The indexed files are maintained in the same file as the data file. Btrieve has been used as the basis for building applications by many third-party vendors (including many accounting packages) primarily because it is fast. Some of Btrieve's features are the following:

- Up to 24 indexes per file

- 14 different data types (Integer, String, Zstring, Float, BCD, Money, Date, and so on)

- Ascending/Descending keys with user-defined collating sequences

- 4G data-file size

- Volume spanning

- Data-file encryption and file ownership

- Single and multiple record-level locks

- File-level locks

- Defining atomicity of operations using Transaction Tracking

- Logging and Rollforward processes to recover from corrupt files

- Dead-lock detection in a server-based environment

Integrated into Btrieve is its own cache manager that can be used for optimizing I/O performance. When Btrieve is loaded at the workstation, you can specify the size of this cache. The cache can dramatically improve I/O performance. If cache space is overcommitted, a least-recently-used (LRU) algorithm is used.

Btrieve can run either as a server-based program or a workstation-based program. The workstation-based program has to be purchased separately, whereas the server-based is bundled with NetWare. At the workstation, Btrieve can run on DOS/MS Windows and OS/2 platforms. Future support for other dominant workstation operating system platforms is expected.

In the workstation-based version, Btrieve is loaded as a TSR for DOS and as a device driver for OS/2. The application program calls the Btrieve interface through a system call. These system calls are trapped by Btrieve. This approach allows an application written in any language that can issue a system call to access the Btrieve record manager. Btrieve comes with software wrappers (libraries or DLLs) for languages such as C, Pascal, COBOL, and BASIC.

In the server-based version, Btrieve runs on the NetWare server and is accessed by workstations that must run the Btrieve requester component. The Btrieve requester is responsible for sending data requests to the Btrieve server component and receiving results from the Btrieve server and communicating it to the application. Figure 20.10 shows the possibilities of the different workstation clients communicating with the NetWare Btrieve server component.

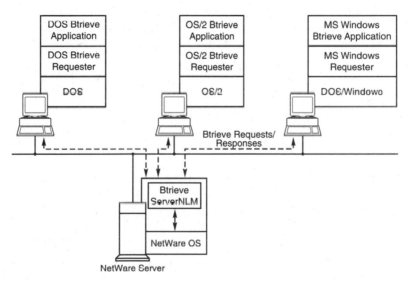

Figure 20.10:
Btrieve requester/server architecture.

Btrieve Programs

The NetWare Btrieve package consists of the following programs:

BSERVER

BROUTER

Btrieve Requester

BSERVER is the Btrieve record manager, which runs at the server. It can be set up to run using the console LOAD command in the AUTOEXEC.NCF file. The BROUTER also loads at the server and allows other server-based applications loaded at the server to communicate with the BSERVER. Essentially, it provides server-to-server Btrieve operation. The Btrieve requester must be loaded at each workstation, and its name is specific to the workstation operating system on which it runs. The BSERVER and BROUTER programs are available as NLMs for NetWare v3.x and VAPs for NetWare v2.x.

In addition to the preceding components, a utility called BSETUP.EXE is available that runs at a workstation and can be used for configuring the BSERVER and BROUTER programs. Some of the parameters BSETUP can configure are the following:

■ Number of open files, handles, locks, transactions, files per transaction, sessions

■ Largest record size, page size, compressed record size

■ Create file as transactional

■ Logging of selected files

NetWare SQL

NetWare SQL comprises a number of components that can be used to convert a NetWare server to an SQL server. Figure 2.11 shows the architecture of the NetWare SQL server.

NetWare SQL relies on the Btrieve NLM component (BSERVER NLM) to perform the record manager operations. NetWare SQL runs on top of this and provides an SQL database server functionality. This SQL server can accept SQL requests from other workstations that must be running the SQL requester. An XQLI program is available that can run at the workstation and be used to compose and issue SQL queries against NetWare SQL.

Client applications can be written to make use of embedded SQL queries to the NetWare SQL server.

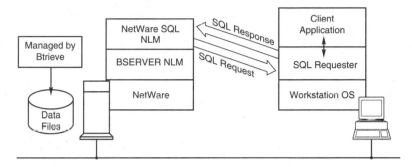

Figure 20.11:
NetWare SQL architecture.

Although NetWare SQL is available from Novell, its performance is lower than that of other SQL servers from database vendors such as Oracle and Gupta Technologies.

SBACKUP

A very important consideration in managing applications and their associated data files is preserving files in case of catastrophic events such as a disk crash, fire, or earthquake. Backup is a very traditional means for assuring that one can recover from these unfortunate events.

Novell's SBACKUP utility runs as an NLM on the NetWare v3.x (or higher) server and is used to provide a server-based backup. This means that the tape-drive hardware can be attached directly to the NetWare server instead of to a workstation, and the server's file system can be backed up locally. Prior to the availability of SBACKUP, the only backup option available from Novell was to use a workstation as a backup. There were and still are a variety of third-party backup methods that provide server-based backup, such as ArcServe from Cheyenne Software.

The distinction between server-based and workstation-based backup methods is seen in figure 20.12. In workstation-based backups, the file system has to be backed up across the network. This generates a large amount of network traffic that can seriously impact the normal work of other users on the network. For this reason, workstation-based backup methods are confined to the early hours of the morning when there are likely to be few users on the network. If the workstation and server are separated by router and bridge devices, performing workstation-based backups can stress these components and further reduce the throughput of the network. In a server-based backup, the file system is backed up using the bus used to connect the backup device to the server. The server bus is generally faster than most common networks in use today, and, therefore, backups can be performed at speeds generally not possible using workstation-based methods. For SBACKUP, transfer rates have been reported that are four times faster than backing up a remote server. If the server disk and backup device are attached to the same internal bus, and the backup is done at the same time as heavy access to the server's disk subsystem by other users, there will be a small performance degradation because of bus contention.

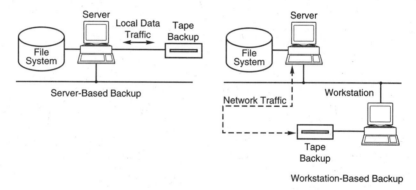

Figure 20.12:
Server-based versus workstation-based backup.

In addition to performing server-based backup, SBACKUP can file systems of other NetWare servers across the network. The comments made earlier about backups across the networks apply to backing up other servers; however, this feature is a great convenience to the network administrator because it makes remote backups of other servers possible.

The SBACKUP architecture consists of a number of components necessary to perform local and remote backups. Figure 20.13 illustrates the SBACKUP architecture. The server that is connected to the backup device is called a *host*. Other servers that can be backed up across the network are called *targets*. A backup device needs to be connected only to the host and not to the targets. However, for the host to back up its own file system, it must have the host and target components loaded.

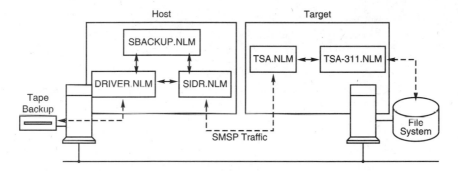

Figure 20.13:
SBACKUP architecture.

The host server backup system consists of the following NLM components:

SBACKUP.NLM

SIDR.NLM

DRIVER.NLM

The SBACKUP.NLM provides the user interface to SBACKUP and also serves as the backup engine. It interfaces with the disk driver NLM. The DRIVER.NLM is a generic name; the actual driver NLM name is specific to the tape drive being used. Examples of tape driver NLMs are WANGTEK.NLM, ASPIDIBI.NLM, and TAPEDC00.NLM.

For the host server to back up the target server, it needs to establish a network connection to the target server. A special NLM called SIDR.NLM provides this capability. SIDR.NLM is a backup requestor very much like the requestor and redirector components used in NetWare DOS or OS/2 workstations. It makes the connection to the target server and uses Novell's Storage Management Services Protocol (SMSP) to backup the target server's file system. The SMSP protocol has the capability of specifying parent data sets, child data sets, trustee information, bindery information, disk space restriction, and directory and file attributes. The *parent data set* is a term used to describe a directory, subdirectory, or a bindery. A parent data set has subordinate data sets such as child data sets. *Child data sets* do not have any subordinates. An example of a child data set would be a file.

The TSA.NLM is the target server agent and provides the end point to the connection request from the SIDR.NLM. It provides the link between the

SIDR data requester and the target-specific module running on the target called TSA-311.NLM. The TSA-311.NLM has the awareness of the target's file system data structure and passes this information on to the TSA.NLM.

A number of auxiliary NLMs are needed to support the operation of SBACKUP. These NLMs are installed when the file server is installed, and include the following:

STREAMS.NLM

SPXS.NLM

TLI.NLM

CLIB.NLM

NUT.NLM

The STREAMS, SPSX, and TLI NLMs provide the communications components needed to connect the host SIDR and target TSA NLMs. The CLIB is the base C-Language library and OS interface. The NUT NLM provides an interface for other NLMs in the form of a template so that NLMs can call up a menu interface.

If the host server needs to back up its own file system, it must have the host and target components loaded.

All of the SBACKUP components together consume a fairly substantial chunk of server memory. You need at least 3M of memory above and beyond the server's requirements to run the SBACKUP system on the host.

NetWare comes with drivers for most of the major backup devices. The current trend is to use backup devices that connect using SCSI controllers. SCSI devices give higher transfer data rates and provide the ability to daisy-chain several SCSI devices. SBACKUP supports the following tape devices:

- Devices that use a DIBI-2 certified driver

- Wangtek tape drive with Quik O2 controller

- Wangtek tape drive with PC36 (60, 125, or 150/125) controller

Although the operation of SBACKUP is similar to NBACKUP, the two use different data-storage formats and, therefore, are incompatible with each other. For this reason, you should never mix the two storage formats. Data backed up using SBACKUP must be restored with SBACKUP only, and data backed up with NBACKUP must be restored with NBACKUP. NBACKUP supports DOS and Macintosh file-name spaces only, whereas SBACKUP supports these and additional name spaces such as NFS and OS/2.

The SBACKUP can be run in parallel with other console commands you can issue from the server. You must, therefore, never accidentally mount or dismount a volume while SBACKUP is in progress. Doing so can permanently damage the volume, corrupt the data, or crash the server.

SBACKUP Installation Issues

SBACKUP is automatically installed during NetWare installation. It is contained on the disks labeled BACKUP. Device driver and parameter information are stored in the directory SYS:SYSTEM\DIBI under the file name DIBI2$DV.DAT. This file also contains information about all the supported device drivers and can be edited using a text editor run from a workstation. Alternatively, you can use the EDIT NLM from the server console to edit this file. The following is an example of the command that enables you to edit from the server console:

```
LOAD EDIT SYS:SYSTEM\DIBI\DIBI2$DV.DAT
```

New device driver information can be added by adding a line for the driver. You can use existing driver information as an example for adding new drivers.

To load SBACKUP, you must perform the following load sequences from the server console:

1. `LOAD TSA` (This loads all applicable modules and configuration files.)

2. `LOAD SBACKUP`

3. Enter the user name (SUPERVISOR or backup operator) and password

4. If more than one backup device driver is loaded, you will be prompted to select one of the device drivers

To back up a server you must have SBACKUP NLM loaded and running. Then you need to perform the following tasks:

1. From the Main menu use the `Select Target to Backup/Restore` option.

`Select the target server` appears. Only those servers that have the target component NLMs loaded appear on the list. If you select a target server that is different from the host server, you must provide a user name and password to log in to the server.

2. Select the `Backup Menu` option from the Main Menu.

3. From the Backup Menu, choose the `Select Working Directory` option.

   Enter the path name of the working directory. This is the working directory that must be in the host file server.

4. From the Backup Menu, select `Backup Selected Directory`.

   When the Backup Options window appears, enter the following information:

What to backup:	(Directory name)
Session Description:	(For documentation purposes)
Exclude Options:	(See list)
Include/Exclude Options:	(See list)
Clear modify bit:	No
Append This Session:	Yes

5. Back out of this screen by pressing Esc. Save the settings and answer Yes to proceed with the backup.

6. From the Start Backup Menu prompt, select the option to back up now or later.

Note that if files are in use by users, they will not be backed up and will be reported in the SBACKUP error log. You can use the `View Error Log` option from the SBACKUP Main Menu to view the error log.

To restore a server, you must have SBACKUP NLM loaded and running and perform the following tasks:

1. Select the `Restore Menu` option from the Main Menu.

2. From the Restore menu, choose the `Select Working Directory` option.

Enter the path name of the working directory. This is the working directory which must be in the host file server.

3. From the Restore Menu, select either the `Restore Session` or `Restore Without Session Files` option.

   The `Restore Without Session Files` option checks through a backup of entries on tape to find a session to restore.

4. When the Restore Options window appears, select the desired option:

Overwrite Existing Parent:	Yes
Overwrite Existing Child:	Yes
Include Exclude Options:	(See List)
Destination Paths:	None

   The default is to restore all trustee, attributes, and data as they were during backup.

5. Back out of the preceding screen by pressing Esc, and save the settings. Answer Yes to proceed with the restore.

6. At the Start Restore prompt, select Yes.

Summary

In this chapter, you learned about the basic differences between single-user and multiuser software and the different concurrency-control mechanisms that are needed to support multiuser applications.

The different types of application technologies, such as file server-based databases and database servers, also were discussed. The kinds of services offered by LAN-based versions of spreadsheets and word processing software were examined.

Command Reference

## PART FOUR

NetWare
Command Reference

ADD NAME SPACE   :

Purpose

Stores non-DOS files, such as Macintosh files, on a NetWare volume. This command is available only at the file server console.

Syntax

```
ADD NAME SPACE name TO VOLUME volumename
```

Options

Macintosh	Use for Macintosh files
OS2	Use for OS/2 files
NFS	Use for UNIX files
FTAM	Use for UNIX files

Rules and Considerations

To set up a volume for the storage of non-DOS files, make sure that the appropriate NetWare Loadable Modules (NLMs) for the non-DOS files have been loaded. Next, configure the volume for the new name space.

Before you can use this command, you must load the appropriate name space module. Extra server memory is required for each name space you add to a volume. Use the ADD NAME SPACE command once for each non-DOS naming convention you intend to store on a NetWare volume.

To use Macintosh files on your NetWare 3.11 server, you must run MACINST and specify your server as a target file server after you have added name space.

Examples

To add Macintosh name space support to the NetWare volume SYS, type the following form of the command at the console:

```
ADD NAME SPACE MACINTOSH TO SYS
```

To see the name space support currently set up on your server, type the following command at the file server console:

```
ADD NAME SPACE
```

The screen displays the following message:

```
Missing name space name
Syntax: ADD NAME SPACE <name space name>
[TO [VOLUME]] <volumename>

Loaded name spaces are:
DOS
MACINTOSH
```

Notes

After you set up a NetWare volume to store non-DOS files, you can reverse the name space only by loading and running the VREPAIR utility and destroying all non-DOS file data.

You must use the ADD NAME SPACE command for every volume that needs to store non-DOS files.

See also

LOAD NAME SPACE   STARTUP.NCF

MACINST   VREPAIR

ALLOW

F> 3.11

Purpose

Enables you to change, view, or set the inherited rights mask (IRM) of a file or directory. The ALLOW command resides in the SYS:PUBLIC directory.

Syntax

```
ALLOW path\filename rightslist
```

Use the following rights in place of the *rightslist* variable. Except for ALL, use the first letter only.

Options

ALL	Specifies all rights
No Rights	Specifies no rights, does not remove Supervisory
Read	Opens and reads files
Write	Opens and writes to files
Create	Creates and writes to files
Erase	Deletes a file or directory
Modify	Renames files or directories; modifies file or directory attributes
File Scan	Views files and directories
Access Control	Enables changes to security assignments

You may use only the boldfaced letters rather than the entire word. Add a space between rights.

Rules and Considerations

You must change all of the IRM rights of a directory or file at the same time. Each time you use the ALLOW command to change the mask, it overrides the previous mask; you cannot change the mask incrementally.

You cannot remove the S(Supervisory) right from the IRM of a directory or file.

Examples

To change the IRM of subdir1 to Read and File Scan, type the following:

```
ALLOW SUBDIR1 R F
```

To change the IRM of file1 in subdir1 to Read, Write, and File Scan, type the following:

```
ALLOW SUBDIR1\FILE1 R W F
```

Important Messages

NetWare may display the following message when you issue the ALLOW command:

```
No Entries Found!
```

If this message appears, make sure that you specified a file or directory that exists and that you spelled it correctly. Also, make sure that you specified the correct path, and that you have File Scan rights in the directory.

The following message may appear if the Access Control right is not set correctly:

```
Directory Name (mask) Not Changed.
```

If this message displays with the name of your directory, make sure that the Access Control right is set in the directory.

Notes

When you change the IRM of a directory or file, you are changing the effective rights of all users in that directory or file.

See also

RIGHTS

ATOTAL   F> Purpose

The ATOTAL utility is designed to be used with Novell's Accounting feature. ATOTAL lists the following accounting totals:

- Connect time in minutes
- Service requests

- Blocks read
- Blocks written
- Disk storage in blocks per day

Syntax

```
ATOTAL
```

Rules and Considerations

Before you run ATOTAL, make sure that NetWare's accounting feature has been installed. See Syscon for information on installing the accounting feature. This command must be run from the SYS:SYSTEM directory.

Important Message

NetWare may display the following message when you attempt to issue the ATOTAL command:

```
ACCOUNTING SERVICES TOTAL UTILITY, Version 2.02
Unable to open sys:system\net$acct.dat
file not found. Perhaps accounting is not
enabled?
```

If this message appears, make sure that the accounting has been installed on your file server. Also, make sure that accounting has been running for at least one-half hour and that you have logged out of the server and then logged back in.

Example

To generate a summary list of the accounting services, from SYS:SYSTEM (or with a search drive mapped to SYS:SYSTEM), use the following command:

```
ATOTAL
```

This displays the summary list on the workstation's screen.

Notes

ATOTAL generates a great deal of data, and you may not derive much value from simply displaying the data on-screen. A much more practical idea is to redirect the output data to a file, using standard DOS redirection commands, and then print the file.

To redirect ATOTAL data to a file, type the following:

```
ATOTAL > filename.ext
```

In this generic syntax, *filename.ext* is the name of the file in which you want to direct the ATOTAL data. To print the file, type **NPRINT** *filename.ext*. This command sends the ASCII text file *filename.ext* to the default print queue on your file server.

The DOS redirection procedure creates a standard ASCII file, which you can import into a word processing or spreadsheet program for further processing.

See also

SYSCON

ATTACH   F>

Purpose

Provides access to services provided by another file server after you have logged into a file server.

ATTACH.EXE is stored in SYS:LOGIN and SYS:PUBLIC

Syntax

```
ATTACH fileserver_name/username /P /G
```

Options

fileserver_name	The name of the file server to which you want to attach.
fileserver_name\username	The file server name and user name for the file server to which you are attaching.
private	For OS/2 sessions only. This option enables you to attach to a server in single session.
global	For OS/2 sessions only. This option enables you to attach to a server in all sessions.

Rules and Considerations

The ATTACH command assigns a connection number to a workstation and attaches the workstation to an additional file server. ATTACH does not execute the system login script. After you are attached, however, you have access to files, applications, and other resources. If you do not include the file server name and user name in the command, NetWare prompts for them. If the user name requires a password, NetWare prompts for the password, as well. You can attach to as many as seven file servers other than the one you currently are using.

You can use the ATTACH command without entering the file server name or user name. After you type **ATTACH**, NetWare displays the message `Enter server name` to prompt for the file server name. NetWare then displays the message `Enter user name` to prompt for the user name. Enter the name of the user for that file server. If that file server requires a password, NetWare prompts for the password by displaying the message `Enter your password`. When you enter the password, NetWare should display the following message:

`Your station is attached to server servername`

If you do not know the name of the file server to which you want to attach, use the SLIST command to obtain a list of file servers that are available.

You can attach to seven file servers at one time. Log in to the first file server and attach to seven others.

Important Message

If the ATTACH command fails, NetWare may display the following message:

`No response from file server.`

If this message appears, a bad connection may exist between the file server onto which you are connected and the file server to which you are trying to attach.

Example

To attach the user Jacob to the file server FS1, issue the following command:

`ATTACH fs1\jacob`

Notes

If you try to attach to an eighth file server, NetWare displays the following message:

```
The limit of 8 server connections has been reached
```

If you already are attached to seven file servers and you want to attach to another one, you must first log out from one of the servers to which you are attached. Log out by issuing the following command:

LOGOUT *fileserver_name*.

You then you can attach to another file server.

Too many file server attachments can affect your system's performance. If performance is slow, log out from the file servers whose services you do not need, then re-attach when you need those services.

You also can use the MAP command to attach to another file server. Simply issue the MAP command and NetWare prompts you for the file server name, user name, and a password (if one is required for the user name you specify). NetWare runs the MAP command and attaches you to the file server at the same time.

One final way to attach to another server is to issue the CAPTURE or NPRINT commands with the */S=servername* switch. You will be asked for a user name and password if the user guest has a password or has been deleted.

See also

LOGIN	SLIST
MAP	WHOAMI

BIND : 3.11

Purpose

Links the LAN drivers to a communication protocol and to a network board in the file server. The communication protocol must be linked to the board, or it will be unable to process packets. Each network board and protocol is bound separately.

Syntax

BIND *protocol to board_name protocol_parameter*

or

```
BIND protocol to LAN_driver [driver_parameters]
protocol_parameter
```

Options

protocol	Normally, you would use IPX, Internetwork Packet Exchange, protocol although you may use other protocols such as IP.
LAN_driver	The Name of driver you loaded for the network board.
board_name	The board name you assigned when you loaded the driver.
DMA=*number*	The DMA channel the network board is configured to use (if any).
FRAME=*name*	Frame type the driver is to use for this network board.
INT=*number*	The hardware interrupt the network board is configured to use.
MEM=*number*	The Shared memory address the network board is configured to use (if any).
PORT=*number*	The I/O port address (in hex) the network board is configured to use.
SLOT=*number*	The slot in which the network board is installed (valid only for EISA and IBM Micro Channel equipped machines).
driver_parameter	You should include a driver_parameter when you have more than one network board of the same type in the file server.
NET=*number*	The unique network address number for the cabling system that is attached to the board.
protocol_parameter	Use for the parameters unique to the selected communications protocol. IPX has only one: NET.
ADDR=*number*	The unique IP address for that machine.

Refer to the documentation that comes with other third-party protocols for their specific protocol parameters.

Rules and Considerations

The following information applies when you load multiple network boards of the same type. When binding a protocol to a board name, you do not need to include the driver_parameters because each board has a unique name that identifies its hardware settings. If you choose not to name the boards, you must let the operating system know which protocol goes to which board. This is accomplished by binding the protocol to the LAN driver, then specifying which board to bind to by listing that board's hardware settings. These settings, or driver_parameters, should be enclosed in square brackets.

If you loaded the driver with more than one frame type for a single network board, select a hexadecimal number that is different from all other network numbers (IPX internal network numbers and cabling systems).

Do not use the same number that was used for another frame type on the cabling system.

Before you use BIND, you must install the board and load the driver.

Unless a communication protocol has been linked (bound) to the network board, that board cannot process packets.

Bind a protocol to each LAN driver you load. If you load a LAN driver more than once, bind a protocol for each set of driver parameters.

Examples

To bind IPX to the NE2000 LAN card, with a network address of 105, type the following:

```
BIND IPX to NE2000 NET=105
```

Repeat the process for each LAN driver in the file server.

To bind the IPX protocol to the NE2000 LAN card, with a network address of 105, a port address of 340, an interrupt of 4, and a frame type of Ethernet_802.3, use the following command:

```
BIND IPX to NE2000 [PORT=340 INT=4 FRAME=ETHERNET_802.3] NET=105
```

You must issue this command each time the file server is booted; otherwise, you can place the command in the AUTOEXEC.NCF file. Include complete LAN-card configuration information in this file. Add the line after the LOAD LAN driver command.

Important Message

To determine which LAN drivers need a protocol bound to them, type **CONFIG** at the file server console. Bind a protocol if the LAN driver information ends with the following message:

```
No LAN protocols are bound to this LAN board
```

Notes

If the network board is attached to an existing cabling system, NET=*number* must use that system's network address. Failure to comply results in router-configuration errors on other file servers and routers on the network.

NET=*number* is always required when binding the IPX protocol. If you fail to enter this parameter at the command line, the network operating system prompts for the network address.

See also

ULOAD

BINDFIX

Purpose

Helps solve problems with the NetWare bindery files. In v3.x, the bindery files are called NET$OBJ.SYS, NET$PROP.SYS, and NET$VAL.SYS. In v2.1x to v2.2, the bindery files are called NET$BIND.SYS and NET$BVAL.SYS. You may encounter one or several problems with the bindery, such as the following:

- You cannot change a user's password.

- You cannot change or modify a user name.

- You cannot modify a user's rights.

- You receive the unknown server error message during printing, even when you are printing on the default file server.

- At the file server console, you see error messages that refer to the bindery.

- Most symptoms occur in the SYSCON utility.

BINDFIX.EXE and the bindery files are stored in the SYS:SYSTEM directory. Invoke the BINDFIX command from the SYS:SYSTEM directory.

Syntax

```
BINDFIX
```

Rules and Considerations

Log in to the file server as user SUPERVISOR. Make sure that all other users are logged out of the file server. Before running BINDFIX, disable LOGIN at the file server console or in the FCONSOLE utility.

Important Messages

BINDFIX closes down the bindery files and then rebuilds them. After it rebuilds the files, it displays a list of the tasks it is performing. After it rebuilds the files, BINDFIX reopens them.

BINDFIX displays the following prompt:

```
Delete mail directories for users that no longer exist? (y/n):
```

If you answer Yes, BINDFIX deletes all corresponding mail directories for nonexisting users from the SYS:MAIL directory. BINDFIX then prompts as follows:

```
Delete trustee rights for users that no longer exist? (y/n):
```

If you answer Yes, BINDFIX scans all mounted volumes on the file server and deletes nonexisting users from all trustee lists.

BINDFIX renames the NET$OBJ.SYS, NET$PROP.SYS, and NET$VAL.SYS files to NET$OBJ.OLD, NET$PROP.OLD, and NET$VAL.OLD, and creates new NET$OBJ.SYS, NET$PROP.SYS, and NET$VAL.SYS files in v3.x. In v2.1x and v2.2, the NET$BIND.SYS and the NET$BVAL.SYS are renamed to NET$BIND.OLD and NET$BVAL.OLD. If BINDFIX run on v2.x finishes successfully, the following message appears:

```
Please delete the files NET$BIND.OLD and NET$BVAL.OLD after you
have verified the reconstructed bindery.
```

Do not delete the .OLD files immediately. If you delete the .OLD files, you will not be able to restore the bindery if a problem occurs.

Notes

Make sure that all users are logged out of the file server before you run BINDFIX.

After BINDFIX reconstructs the bindery files, do not delete the .OLD files from the SYS:SYSTEM directory. Keep these files, so that you can restore the bindery if a problem arises with the newly constructed bindery files.

After all of your users' groups and trustee assignments have been made with a new installation, you might want to execute BINDFIX to get an original backup copy of your bindery files. Copy .OLD files onto a floppy disk for safe keeping. If BINDFIX is unable to reconstruct the bindery files, and if BINDREST is not restoring the bindery, copy the .OLD files back into the SYS:SYSTEM directory and try BINDREST again.

See also

BINDREST	DISABLE LOGIN
BROADCAST	FCONSOLE
CLEAR STATION	MONITOR

BINDREST   F>

Purpose

Reverses the effect of the BINDFIX command. The BINDREST command restores the backup bindery files created by BINDFIX. The backup bindery files are called NET$OBJ.OLD, NET$PROP.OLD, and NET$VAL.OLD in v3.x. In v2.1x and v2.2, the files are called NET$BIND.OLD and NET$BVAL.OLD. BINDREST returns these files to their original versions and names (NET$OBJ.SYS, NET$PROP.SYS, and NET$VAL.SYS in v3.x or NET$BIND.SYS and NET$BVAL.SYS). You only need to use BINDREST if BINDFIX fails. If you lose your bindery files and you have a backup copy of the bindery files on floppy disk, copy these files to the SYS:SYSTEM directory and execute BINDREST.

Syntax

```
BINDREST
```

Rules and Considerations

Before using the BINDREST command, log in to the file server as user SUPERVISOR and make sure that all other users are logged out of the file server. Use the FCONSOLE or USERLIST command to ensure all users are logged out of the file server. Use FCONSOLE or CLEAR STATION to clear all logged in users. Use DIS-ABLE LOGIN to prevent users from logging in to the file server while BINDREST is running.

Important Messages

If you invoke BINDFIX then delete the .OLD files after BINDFIX runs, you cannot use BINDREST to restore the bindery files.

If you delete the old v3.x bindery files, NetWare displays a message similar to the following:

```
ERROR: File NET$OBJ.OLD does not exist.
ERROR: File NET$PROP.OLD does not exist.
ERROR: File NET$VAL.OLD does not exist.

Unable to restore old bindery files.
```

If you have a backup of the .OLD files on a floppy disk, copy them to the SYS:SYSTEM directory and rerun BINDREST.

Note

Make sure that all users are logged out of the file server before you invoke the BINDREST.

See also

BINDFIX	FCONSOLE
BROADCAST	MONITOR
CLEAR STATION	USERLIST
DISABLE LOGIN	

BROADCAST

Purpose

Sends a message to all users logged in or attached to the file server or to a list of connection numbers. You must issue the BROADCAST command from the file server console.

Syntax

```
BROADCAST "message" TO username
```

Options

username	The user's login name.
connection number	The connection number listed by the USERLIST command.
Press Space	Enter a space on the same line as the command to specify another user name or connection number. Place the space between user names or connection numbers.

Rules and Considerations

To determine a connection number, refer to Connection Information in the MONITOR screen at the file server console, or use the USERLIST command from your workstation.

The message can be up to 55 characters long. If you do not specify the connection number or user name, NetWare sends the message to all attached users.

All logged in users receive the messages, except the following:

- Users who have used the CASTOFF ALL command.
- Users who logged in using an ACS or NACS.
- Users who are logged in on a remote workstation.

Some graphics applications that are being used will not show the message you received, but you will hear a beep. Press Ctrl-Enter to continue.

Users who receive the message will see it appear on the 25th line of the screen. The message should not interfere with the screen display. The workstation locks and nothing happens until the user clears the message by pressing Ctrl-Enter.

Examples

Suppose that you want to send the message "Meeting in room 1A in 10 minutes" to all users. Issue the following command:

```
BROADCAST Meeting in room 1A in 10 minutes
```

You do not need to enclose the message in quotation marks when you are sending a message to all users.

If you want to send the same message to Tim, Jane, Jacob, and connection number 6, issue the following command:

```
BROADCAST "Meeting in room 1A in 10 minutes" to Tim, Jane,
Jacob, and 6
```

Notes

A message received at a workstation prevents further work until the message is cleared from the screen.

Use the CASTOFF ALL command at the workstation to prevent it from receiving messages.

See also

CASTOFF ALL

MONITOR

CAPTURE   F>

Purpose

Redirects printed output from applications not designed to run on a network or from the screen to a NetWare print queue. CAPTURE also can save printed data to a file.

Syntax

`CAPTURE` *options*

Options

The optional switches used by CAPTURE consist of one or more of the following:

AU (AUtoendcap)
Automatically closes out a print job when you exit an application. Autoendcap is enabled by default.

NA (NoAutoendcap)
Requires the use of the ENDCAP utility to terminate the effects of CAPTURE. Use NoAutoendcap to move in and out of your applications without prematurely closing the print queue file(s) you are creating.

B (Banner)
A banner name can be any word or phrase up to 12 characters in length that you want to appear on the lower part of the banner page. To represent a space between words, use an underline character; the underline character will print. The default is LST.

NB (NoBanner)
Tells NetWare not to print a banner page.

C (Copies=*n*)
Replace *n* with with the number of copies you want to print (1 to 999). The default is 1 copy.

CR (CReate=*filespec*)
Creates a print file in which to store instead of sending the print job to a file server's print queue. *Filespec* can be any legal DOS file name and can include path information; you can create the print file, however, only on a network drive.

FF (FormFeed)
Sends a form-feed code to the printer at the end of each print job so that the next print job can start at the top of the next sheet of paper. If your application sends a form-feed code at the end of the print job, an extra page will be fed through the printer wasting paper. Form feeding is enabled by default.

NFF (NoFormFeed)
Disables the sending of form-feed codes at the end of a print job.

F (Form=*formname* or *n*)

Replace *formname* with the name of the form on which you want your print job to print. Replace *n* with the form number onto which you want your print job to print. Use the PRINTDEF utility to define form names or numbers (or both) before using this option.

J (Job=*jobconfig*)

Replace *jobconfig* with the name of a predefined print job configuration you want to use. You must use the PRINTCON utility to define print jobs before using this option.

K (Keep)

Tells CAPTURE to keep all data it receives during a print capture in case your workstation locks up or loses power while capturing data. This option is useful if you capture data over a period of several hours. If your workstation loses its connection to the file server, the server sends the data to the print queue after the server realizes your station is no longer connected to it.

L (Local=*n*)

Indicates which local LPT ports you want to capture. Valid choices are 1, 2, or 3. The default is 1. The local LPT ports defined here are "logical" connections, not "physical" ports. You can print to and capture from all three LPT ports even though your workstation might only have one physical LPT port installed.

NAM (NAMe=*name*)

name can be any word or phrase, up to 12 characters in length, that you want printed on the upper part of the banner page. The default is the user's name used when you logged in to the file server. The NoBanner option defeats the purpose of using this switch, because no banner page is printed.

Q (Queue=*queuename*)

queuename is the file server queue name to which you want to send the print job. This option is useful if multiple queues are mapped to one printer. If you fail to specify a queuename, CAPTURE defaults to the queue to which Spooler 0 has been assigned.

S (Server=*name*)	*name* is the name of the file server to which you are sending the print job and the server on which the print queue is located. The default is the default server you first logged in to.
SH (SHow)	Displays a list of the currently captured LPT ports. SH does not affect the capture status of an LPT port. It merely returns the currently active CAPTURE options (if any). You cannot use SH with other CAPTURE options.
T (Tabs=*n*)	Use this option only if your application program does not support print formatting; most do. *n* is the number of characters in each tab stop, from 0 to 18. The default is 8.
NT (NoTabs)	Ensures that all tabs arrive at the printer unchanged. By default, this option also specifies the file to be a binary or "byte stream" file. Use this option only if your application program has its own print formatter. Most applications produce embedded printer-specific codes. This option ensures that those codes arrive at the printer intact.
TI (TImeout=*n*)	Enables you to print from an application without forcing you to exit it. It sends the print data to the print queue in a specified number of seconds after the application finishes writing to the file or after waiting the specified number of seconds for additional print output. After the specified amount of time, CAPTURE begins again. For best results TI should not be set to less than 5 seconds or greater than 60. *n* = number of seconds, 1 to 1,000. Timeout is disabled by default.

You can list multiple options.

Rules and Considerations

The create=*filespec* switch must use a network drive.

The FormFeed switch might not be necessary on some laser printers that are installed as network printers. Many laser printers automatically issue a form feed at the end of a page or partial page of text.

You must use the PRINTDEF utility to define forms before you use the Forms switch.

You cannot use SH with any other CAPTURE options. It must be used alone.

If your TI setting is not long enough, you might experience printing problems, especially if you are printing graphics. Increase the TI setting if parts of files are being printed or if files do not print at all.

You can define commonly used CAPTURE options in PRINTCON as job configurations and use the Job option to indicate which configuration profile to use.

If you fail to specify options with the CAPTURE command, data is printed according to the default print job configuration defined in PRINTCON.

Output should be sent to print queues rather than printers. Printer numbers and print server names are not supported in CAPTURE.

The data you capture is not printed or sent to a file unless you end the CAPTURE command and send your data to a network printer or a file. This can be done by using either the AU or TI switch, or by using the ENDCAP utility.

To use the ENDCAP utility effectively to send captured print jobs to the printer, disable AUtoendcap and TImeout in the CAPTURE command.

Example

To capture print jobs to the queue called Laser on the file server Training Solutions, type the following:

```
CAPTURE S=TRAINING_SOLUTIONS Q=LASER_Q NB TI=5 NFF
```

The job does not print a banner, the timeout is five seconds, and no form feed follows the print job.

For best results, and to prevent your workstation from possibly hanging, use the CAPTURE command in your login script.

If you use the CAPTURE command at the DOS prompt, it overrides the command issued in your login script, unless you merely issue a CAPTURE SHow.

Notes

Use AU to save several different screen prints or printouts from the same application to a single print-queue file. AU does not automatically terminate the capture of an LPT port. To terminate an active LPT capture, you must issue the ENDCAP command.

If you experience problems (such as half-completed pages) when printing from your application, increase the value of TI until the problem stops or until you reach 60, whichever comes first. It is extremely rare when an application, even an intense database query, will pause longer than 45 seconds between print output bursts.

Your workstation might hang if you press Shift-Print Screen when none of your LPT ports are captured and no local printers are attached to your workstation. To prevent this, include the following line in the NET.CFG file on your boot disk:

```
LOCAL PRINTERS = 0
```

You can save data in a print file to a server to which you are not attached. If you specify a server to which you are not attached, CAPTURE attaches you as the user GUEST unless GUEST requires a password, or GUEST has no effective rights to any of the server's print queues or disk space. You cannot create a file or send a file to a queue without rights.

It often is preferable to capture to a print file when you are plotting from CAD packages in the NetWare environment. This usually causes far fewer problems than trying to capture the plot output to a file server queue. After the plot file has been created, you can use the NPRINT utility to send the plot file to the queue.

See also

ENDCAP	NPRINT
NET.CFG	SPOOL

CASTOFF   F>

Purpose

Prevents messages sent from the file server console or other workstations from reaching your station and interrupting unattended operations (such as printing or compiling).

Syntax

```
CASTOFF
```

or

```
CASTOFF ALL
```

Options

A or ALL   Blocks messages from both the file server console and other workstations on the network

Rule and Considerations

The CASTOFF command blocks messages sent by other workstations. CASTOFF ALL blocks all messages, including those sent from the file server console.

Before starting any process that can run unattended (such as compiling, printing, remote LAN hookup, and so on), you should use CASTOFF ALL to prevent messages from interrupting the unattended process.

Example

```
CASTOFF ALL
```

Note

To enable your station to receive incoming messages again, use the CASTON utility.

See also

CASTON

SEND

CASTON

F>

Purpose

Enables your workstation to resume receiving messages if you used the CASTOFF utility to block incoming messages.

Syntax

```
CASTON
```

Rules and Considerations

When a workstation receives a message, the station cannot continue processing until the user acknowledges the message by pressing Ctrl-Enter.

Important Message

The following message appears on-screen after CASTON is invoked:

```
Broadcast messages from the console and other stations will now
be accepted.
```

See also

CASTOFF

SEND

CHKDIR   F> 3.11

Purpose

Lists information about directories and volumes. When invoked, CHKDIR displays the following types of information:

- Directory space limitations for the file server, volume, and directory
- The volume's maximum storage capacity in kilobytes, and the directory's maximum storage capacity (if the directory has a space restriction in effect)
- Kilobytes currently in use on the volume and in the specified directory
- Kilobytes available on the volume and in the specified directory

Syntax

CHKDIR *path*

Option

path   The directory path leading to and including the path you want to check.

Rules and Considerations

The *path* option must be a legal DOS path name. You can substitute NetWare volume names for DOS drive letters.

Example

Suppose that you want to see information about a directory named SYS:DATA. Enter the following command:

```
CHKDIR SYS:DATA
```

NetWare displays information similar to the following:

```
Directory Space Limitation Information For:
TRAINING_SOLUTIONS/SYS:DATA

         Maximum      In Use Available
         631,600K     452,693K      178,907K Volume Size
         38,776K      178,907K \DATA
```

See also

CHKVOL

CHKVOL   F>

Purpose

Shows the amount of space currently in use and the amount of space available on the volume. The CHKVOL command displays volume space in bytes, the byte count taken by files, the number of bytes available on the volume, and the number of directory entries left. You can view this information on all volumes, and all file servers to which you are attached.

Syntax

```
CHKVOL fileserver_name\volume_name
```

Options

fileserver_name	The name of the file servers volume to view
volume	The name of the volume to view
*	Specifies all file servers you are attached to, or all volumes

Rules and Considerations

The use of CHKVOL is not limited by security; you may view CHKVOL to view volume information for any file server to which you are attached.

Important Messages

The CHKVOL command displays information similar to the following:

```
Statistics for fixed volume TRAINING_SOLUTIONS/SYS:

Total volume space:              640,048 K Bytes
Space used by 7,105 files:       152,672 K Bytes
Space remaining on volume:       487,376 K Bytes
Space available to username:     487,376 K Bytes
Directory entries available      2,121
```

`Directory entries available` does not refer to the number of directories you still can create on this volume. One directory entry is used by a DOS file, subdirectory, and trustee list. Macintosh files use two directory entries.

Examples

To check the volumes called SYS on all file servers to which you are attached, issue the following command:

```
CHKVOL */SYS
```

You can express wild cards in many different ways. If you want to see volume information for all the volumes on the file server named TRAINING, for example, issue the following command:

```
CHKVOL TRAINING/*
```

If you want to see the SYS volumes on file servers named TRAINING and SOLUTIONS, issue the following command:

```
CHKVOL */SYS
```

If you want to see information about all volumes on all the file servers to which you are attached, issue the following command:

```
CHKVOL */*
```

You also can specify drive letters that are mapped to volumes that you want to view.

Note

If NetWare displays the message `The specified volume not found`, either you mistyped the volume name or the volume does not exist. Check the volume name and try again.

See also

> ATTACH
> FILER (Volume Information)
> WHOAMI

CLEAR MESSAGE : 2.2

Purpose

Clears the message at the bottom of the file server's display when you are using the MONITOR command.

Syntax

```
CLEAR MESSAGE
```

Rules and Considerations

The CLEAR MESSAGE command clears a message from the bottom of the file server's display. The command does not clear the entire screen and does not affect the MONITOR screen.

The CLEAR MESSAGE command is coded into the operating system.

See also

BROADCAST

SEND

CLEAR STATION

Purpose

Removes all file server resources from the specified workstation, and breaks the link between the file server and the workstation.

Syntax

```
CLEAR STATION station_number
```

Rules and Considerations

The CLEAR STATION command is coded into the operating system. When you invoke CLEAR STATION, all the workstations' open files are closed and the communication link to the file server is broken. If the workstation had drive mappings to other file servers, the user can continue working on those file servers' drive mappings. If no drive mappings exist to other file servers, however, the user must reboot the workstation and reload IPX and NETx before accessing any file server.

Example

To clear station number two, issue the following command:

```
CLEAR STATION 2
```

To view a list of station numbers, you can issue the MONITOR command at the v3.11 file server console or use USERLIST at a workstation. The connection number is listed in the screen's left margin.

Note

Because the CLEAR STATION command closes open files, data may be lost when you use the command. CLEAR STATION normally is used when a workstation locks up and leaves open files on the file server.

See also

FCONSOLE

USERLIST

CLIB   :LOAD 3.11

Purpose

Provides NetWare Loadable Module (NLM) developers with a set of global functions and routines that an NLM can utilize. This global library of C routines and functions should be used if you are using an NLM, such as the BTRIEVE NLM or the PSERVER NLM which relies on CLIB to function properly.

CLIB is not fully functional unless the STREAMS NLM is loaded. If you fail to load STREAMS prior to loading CLIB, the NetWare v3.11 operating system attempts to load STREAMS for you.

Syntax

```
LOAD path CLIB
```

Option

path   The full DOS path name to the directory that contains the CLzIB NLM. The path name can begin with either a valid DOS drive letter or a valid NetWare volume name. If you do not specify a path, NetWare v3.11 attempts to locate and load the NLM from the SYS:SYSTEM subdirectory.

Rules and Considerations

NetWare sets a time zone for CLIB when the utility loads. By default, NetWare uses the Eastern Standard time zone. Use the SET TIMEZONE command to set the time zone so that it is appropriate for your geographical area.

Be sure to save the command in the AUTOEXEC.NCF file so that CLIB is loaded and the appropriate time zone is set each time the file server is rebooted.

Examples

To load the CLIB utility, issue the following command:

```
LOAD CLIB
```

To make sure that the additional modules necessary for CLIB to operate are loaded at boot time, add the following commands to the server's AUTOEXEC.NCF file:

```
LOAD STREAMS
LOAD CLIB
```

This example assumes the STREAMS and CLIB NLMs are located in the SYS:SYSTEM subdirectory.

Notes

You must load the CLIB NLM before you load any NLM that requires CLIB. If you want, you can place the STREAMS and CLIB NLMs on the DOS partition of the file server's hard disk.

The CLIB NLM is just one example of a loadable function library module. Some NLMs depend on other NLMs to function properly. To improve system performance and reliability, Novell recommends that you load the following NLMs in addition to CLIB. If you are using non-Novell supplied third-party NLMs that are incompatible with the current version of NetWare v3.11, these additional NLMs prevent the offending NLM from loading and/or corrupting the network operating system. It is strongly recommended that you load these NLMs in the following order:

LOAD STREAMS

LOAD CLIB

LOAD MATHLIB

LOAD TLI

LOAD IPXS

LOAD SPXS

To automatically load these NLMs at boot time, edit your AUTOEXEC.NCF file to include these commands.

See also

LOAD

SET TIMEZONE

CLS   : 3.11

Purpose

Clears the file server's console screen.

Syntax

CLS

Rules and Considerations

The cleared screen shows only the command prompt and the cursor.

See also

OFF

COMCHECK   F>

Purpose

Tests the communication between network stations, file servers, and routers. The command does not require the file server or router to be running. Use COMCHECK to help locate possible cable problems, duplicate node addresses, and potential problems with cable linking devices. COMCHECK checks the entire communications path before the network is up and running.

Syntax

COMCHECK

Rules and Considerations

Before you execute COMCHECK, make all cable connections to workstations, file servers, routers, and cabling devices. IPX must be loaded first. COMCHECK uses IPX to communicate to each cabled node on the cable system. Each node requires a unique ID. As you execute COMCHECK on the node, the utility prompts for a unique ID. You can use any name, such as NODE1, FILESERVER1, ROUTER3, and so on.

Example

```
IPX
COMCHECK
```

COMCHECK prompts you to enter a unique node name to identify the station. You can find the COMCHECK program on the disk labeled WSGEN. If you experience problems loading IPX, make sure that IPX is configured for the LAN card you are using, and that the setting on the LAN card matches that of IPX. The following message should appear on the screen:

```
NetWare Communication Check v2.00 Friday October 30, 1991 2.00
pm
Network     Node   Unique User  Yr Mo Dy Hr Mn Sc *
00000000    000000F3     Node1 91/10/30 02:09:21 *
00000000    00001A34     File Server  91/10/30 02:14:12
00000000    000000BF     Node2 91/10/30 02:18:01
```

- **Network.** Displays 0s if the shell is not loaded.

- **Node.** Displays the node ID of the LAN card installed.

- **Unique User.** Displays the unique name you gave to this node.

- **YrMoDy Hr Mn Sc.** Shows the time and date. The time is updated every 15 seconds to show that the node is communicating.

- ***.** Indicates that this is the current workstation.

If the station does not show any of this information after 15 seconds, check all cabling, connectors, cabling devices, and LAN cards. Make sure that each of the nodes has a unique node ID.

You can change the broadcast delay period by pressing Esc and selecting Broadcast Delay from the menu. This is specified in seconds, and tells the system the number of seconds or broadcasts from a particular station. The default setting is 15 seconds.

The Dead Timeout Period specifies the amount of time COMCHECK waits after a workstation does not send out packets and then declares the node dead. This time period must be at least 10 seconds greater than the broadcast delay period. A workstation that is declared dead will appear on the other workstations as a bold entry. The default Dead Timeout Period is 60 seconds.

See also

IPX

COMPSURF :Down 2.1

Purpose

Performs a low-level format and surface analysis (or integrity test) on standard MFM, RLL, ARLL, ESDI, and SCSI hard disks and prepares them for use under Novell NetWare.

Syntax

```
COMPSURF
```

Rules and Considerations

The COMPSURF utility may require several hours to test each hard disk properly. Be sure to allow sufficient time.

You must install hard disks before you execute the COMPSURF utility.

You should use COMPSURF to reformat disks only as a last, extreme measure to attempt to correct major disk drive problems (such as when it has become impossible to write and read data to and from the disk). COMPSURF destroys all data contained on a hard disk.

Do not execute COMPSURF on NetWare Ready drives because any NetWare ready information on the disk will be erased.

New hard disks no longer require testing with COMPSURF. The INSTALL command prepares new hard disks by using the ZTEST (track zero test) utility rather than COMPSURF.

Most hard disks are shipped with a manufacturer's bad block table that identifies, by head and cylinder number, any media defects (such as bad blocks) found by the manufacturer prior to shipment. If the hard disk you will be formatting (or reformatting) with COMPSURF has a manufacturer's bad block table, you should enter the bad blocks from this list prior to running COMPSURF.

If you are using SCSI hard disks, you also must run DISKSET, or an equivalent third-party utility, to configure the Host Bus Adapters (HBA) connected to any installed SCSI disk subsystems.

Important Message

The following message appears when you issue the COMPSURF command:

```
The COMPSURF command destroys all data on the hard disk!
```

Make sure that you have a backup of the disk's data before you execute the command.

Examples

You can run the COMPSURF utility by issuing the following command:

```
COMPSURF
```

Prepare to execute the COMPSURF utility by backing up the existing disk files and downing the file server. This step is only required on existing NetWare installations.

Locate the disk manufacturer's test printout. This will contain a list of media defects (such as bad blocks) detected by the manufacturer at the time of assembly. You are prompted to enter these blocks after you enter the COMPSURF utility. The manufacturer's bad block list is usually printed on a sticker attached to the hard disk housing. Often the list will be duplicated on a paper printout shipped with the disk.

If you do not have a hard copy printout of the bad block table, you might have to remove the cover from the file server or disk subsystem to locate the bad block table sticker on the hard disk housing. These defects should be entered into COMPSURF to enable COMPSURF to map out known media defects and prevent their use under NetWare. This will ensure greater data integrity.

If you want a printout of the media defects detected by COMPSURF, prepare and install a parallel printer. The printer must be connected to the first parallel port

(LPT1) on the file server. You will be given an opportunity to print the media defect list before exiting COMPSURF.

COMPSURF can run without a parallel printer attached. If you run COMPSURF without a printer, however, you must refrain from selecting any option that indicates printing test results. If you do select a print option when no printer is attached, COMPSURF might hang up the computer.

Before executing COMPSURF on a problem disk, you should try to copy as many data files as possible to a disk that is operational.

Be sure you have correctly identified all network hard disks in your server's hardware configuration, including disks both inside the file server and inside external disk subsystems. If necessary, execute DISKSET to identify SCSI hard disks in external disk subsystems or inside the file server. If necessary, run the SETUP (or similar) utility supplied by the computer manufacturer to identify internal disk drives.

Before executing COMPSURF, make sure that you can identify the disk drive on which you want to run COMPSURF by channel number, controller address, and drive number.

If needed, refer to the documentation accompanying your hardware for information on how to determine controller addresses and drive numbers.

If you are using a disk that is defined in the CMOS of your computer, most likely you will be using the ISADISK driver. If this is true, this unit functions on Channel 0.

You can low-level format and test only one hard disk at a time. Execute COMPSURF on each disk you want to be low-level formatted and tested.

Start COMPSURF by locating the program. Under NetWare v2.1x, it usually is located on the UTILEXE diskette. Under NetWare v2.2 and NetWare v3.11, it is located on the SYSTEM-2 diskette.

To load and execute COMPSURF, insert the appropriate disk into drive A, and type **COMPSURF** at the DOS prompt.

The Comprehensive Surface Analysis header appears on the screen, along with a list of the hard disk drives COMPSURF can find attached to the file server.

Select the hard disk you want to test. Do not be concerned if the head, cylinder, and sectors-per-track values displayed on the screen do not correspond to the actual values for the disk. Certain types of disk drives do not supply this information, and COMPSURF uses default values for these disks.

Select the appropriate program operational parameters for the drive you have selected. The parameters that appear depend on the type of disk you are testing and whether or not it has been previously formatted with COMPSURF. For most disks, the list will be similar to the following:

- Specify whether or not to format the disk.
- Specify whether or not to keep the current bad block list.
- Specify if you want to enter the media defect list.
- Select the number of passes for the sequential read/write test.
- Select the number of reads and writes to be performed in the random test.
- Confirm the operation parameters you have just selected.

A more detailed discussion of each prompt follows:

- `Format the disk:` This prompt appears only when you are retesting a disk that has been previously low-level formatted by COMPSURF. Any hard disk that has never been low-level formatted or tested with COMPSURF will be formatted automatically. If you answered Yes to the Format disk prompt and if the hard disk you have selected requires an interleave factor value, select the appropriate interleave factor. Interleave should be selected based on the following criteria:

  1. For internal hard disks in all NetWare file servers and IBM PC/AT-type file servers that run off original IBM or Western Digital 1003 series controllers, use the default interleave value of 2.

  2. For internal hard disks in all IBM PC/AT and 100 percent compatible NetWare file servers that run off Western Digital 1006 series controllers (or 100 percent compatibles), select an interleave value of 1.

  3. For internal hard disks in all IBM PC/AT and 100 percent compatible NetWare file servers that run off Western Digital 1007 series ESDI controllers (or 100 percent compatibles), select an interleave value of 1.

  4. For internal hard disks in an IBM PS/2 file server, select an interleave value of 1.

  5. For other types of hard disks (such as embedded SCSI or third-party external disks), check with the disk supplier to determine the appropriate interleave value.

  6. For internal hard disks in all IBM PC/AT and 100 percent compatible NetWare file servers that run off controllers not listed above, check with the controller manufacturer to determine the appropriate interleave value.

- **Current bad block list:** Each hard disk drive maintains a list of media defects. These media defects are areas of the disk that are physically unable to hold data reliably. This list is sometimes referred to as the bad block table. Answer Yes if you want COMPSURF to keep the current list of bad blocks or rebuild a new bad block table. If you answer No, the media defect list is cleared.

- **Media defect list:** The media defect list also is known as the bad block list. If the disk you are testing was not shipped with a manufacturer's media defect list, answer No to the prompt and go on to the next section. If the disk was shipped with a manufacturer's media defect list, enter the bad block list manually at the file server's keyboard when prompted.

  The bad blocks you enter from this list, as well as any additional bad blocks found by the COMPSURF utility, will be written to the disk's bad block table. It is important to enter the manufacturer's bad block list, if possible, to ensure that these blocks are included in the NetWare-compatible bad block table stored on the disk. This will prevent NetWare from using these potentially unreliable areas of the disk to store your valuable data.

- **Sequential Test:** This COMPSURF routine writes and reads various patterns to the disk sequentially to analyze the integrity of the disk's surface. Any bad blocks that are found during this process are added to the disk's bad block table so that the file server will not attempt to store data in them.

  Each pass of the sequential test takes roughly 30 to 45 minutes for the average 20M hard disk—and longer for hard disks with larger storage capacity.

  You can specify that the sequential test be performed from zero to five times. The COMPSURF criteria used to determine the reliability of the disk is based on three passes of the sequential test, however. It is strongly recommended that you not skip this section of COMPSURF.

- **Random Test:** This COMPSURF routine writes and reads data patterns to random locations on the disk to locate additional bad blocks. This procedure also will test the head positioning mechanics of the disk. As with the sequential test, any bad blocks that are found are included in the disk's bad block table so that the file server will not attempt to store data on them.

  The default number of write/reads (I/Os) shown in the prompt is the recommended minimum number of random I/Os to ensure an adequate sampling of the disk's head-positioning mechanism. You can increase or decrease this number of I/Os.

It takes approximately three minutes for the random test to perform 1000 I/Os. As an example, a random test performed on an average 20M hard disk would require 16,000 random I/Os and would take 45 to 50 minutes.

• **Enter the bad block list:** If the COMPSURF OPERATIONAL PARAMETERS window shows that media defects will be entered by hand, you must enter the manufacturer's bad block list from the file server's keyboard. An empty bad block window appears on the screen.

Bad blocks are identified by head and cylinder number. Each hard disk has a specific number of read/write heads and cylinders. The number of heads and cylinders for the currently selected disk should be displayed on the second line of the COMPSURF screen header.

Media defects can be added to the list by performing the following:

1. Press Insert. The following prompt should appear:

   ```
   Enter head number:
   ```

2. Type the head number of one of the bad blocks on the manufacturer's bad block list. Heads are usually numbered starting with zero, such as zero relative. If your disk has seven heads, for example, they are numbered from zero to six.

3. After you have typed the head number, press Enter. The following prompt should appear:

   ```
   Enter cylinder:
   ```

4. Type the cylinder number of the bad block as it appears in the manufacturer's list. Like heads, cylinders are also numbered starting with zero (such as zero relative).

5. After you have typed the cylinder number, press Enter. The head and cylinder numbers should be displayed in the list on the screen. If you make a mistake and type an incorrect head or cylinder number, you can correct it by simply highlighting the incorrect entry and pressing Delete.

6. Repeat these steps until you have entered all of the bad blocks on the manufacturer's bad block list.

7. Confirm the bad block list. After you have entered all of the bad blocks from the manufacturer's bad block list, press Esc. If you need to add or delete bad blocks to or from the table, answer No and return to the `Enter the bad block list` prompt. If the table is complete and correct, answer Yes to the prompt and continue.

- **Format and test the disk:** You do not need to make any more keyboard entries until the COMPSURF testing process is complete, but you should monitor the progress of the test as outlined in the process that follows. The information for each test assumes that you selected the recommended COMPSURF operational parameters, such as low-level formatting the disk and repeating the sequential surface analysis three times.

- **Formatting the disk:** While the disk is being low-level formatted, the following message should appear on the screen:

```
The Drive is Being Formatted
Please Wait
```

The formatting process can last anywhere from a few minutes to several hours, depending on the storage capacity and the type of hard disk being tested. The average 20MB hard disk, for example, takes roughly 15 to 25 minutes to low-level format.

```
The track zero test:
```

After the disk has been successfully low-level formatted, the track zero integrity test begins. This test ensures that track zero on the selected disk is 100 percent free from any media defects. Any defects on track zero would render the drive unbootable under NetWare, and might render the drive unusable altogether.

During this test, the screen displays information in a format similar to the following:

```
Track Zero Test
Block # Pattern Pass BadBlocks
0    a5a5  1/20    0
```

As the track zero test progresses, the numbers displayed in each column change to reflect what is occurring on the drive. This test will make 20 passes of track zero writing and reading various binary patterns to ensure it has no media defects.

```
Run the Sequential Test:
```

When the track zero test is successfully completed, the sequential test begins. This test searches the entire disk surface for media defects (such as bad blocks). Media defects are defined as blocks on the disk that cannot reliably store data.

The disk's bad block table consists of both bad blocks that you entered by hand and those discovered during the sequential test sequence. While the sequential test is running, you should see a screen similar to the following:

```
Sequential Test
Block # Pattern Pass BadBlocks
0    a5a5  1/20    0
```

The `Block #` column indicates the block currently being tested. This number counts down to zero for each of the five binary data patterns.

The `Pattern` column indicates the binary data pattern currently being written to the disk.

The `Pass` column indicates the number of passes of the sequential test that have been completed out of the total number of passes specified in the program operational parameters.

The `Bad Blocks` column indicates the number of bad blocks on the disk. This number is a total of those entered by hand and those located during the sequential test. This number might increment during the sequential test.

You can interrupt the sequential test at any time to view or to print a list of the bad blocks that have been located so far. You also can turn off the screen update to slightly speed up the execution of the program.

- **Display the bad block table:** This information appears on the screen in a format similar to the following. Do not worry about duplicate entries in the list; this is common and results from the fact that one track can have one or more bad blocks:

```
Head Cylinder

1    234
2    476
```

Program execution continues while you view the list.

- **Print the bad block table:** If you have attached a parallel printer to the first parallel printer port (LPT1) on the file server, you can print a list of the bad blocks found so far. After the testing process is complete, you will have another opportunity to print the complete bad block list.

Do not select the `Print the bad block table:` option if you have not attached a parallel printer to the file server. The computer will disconnect if you do, resulting in the loss of all located bad blocks and requiring you to restart COMPSURF from scratch.

- **`Turn off the screen update:`** Turning off the screen update enables the sequential test to proceed without constantly refreshing the screen display. This can marginally reduce the time required to complete the sequential test. You can exercise this option at any time during the sequential test. Updates to the screen information cease until you re-enable screen updating.

- **`Turn on the screen update:`** Resumes updates to the various columns on the screen.

- **`Run the Random Test:`** After the sequential test successfully completes, the random test automatically begins. If you specified zero passes of the sequential test, a random test initialization procedure will be executed before the actual random test begins. This initialization procedure prepares the disk's data storage area to prepare for the random I/O test.

  As with the sequential test, you can interrupt the random test at any time to view or to print a list of the bad blocks that have been located so far. You also can turn off the screen update to marginally speed up the operation of the program.

- **`Record the final bad block table:`** When all of the COMPSURF formatting and testing procedures have successfully concluded, a message similar to the following appears:

  ```
  Surface Analysis Completeddisk passed.

  Display Bad Block Table
  Print Bad Block Table
  ```

  If the disk did not successfully pass the COMPSURF testing series, this also is indicated on the screen. Failure to successfully pass a COMPSURF test requires replacing the hard disk.

  After completing the COMPSURF testing, press Esc to exit the program. You can display the bad block table on the screen and record the information by hand if you want, or, if you have a parallel printer attached to the file server, you can print a hard copy of the final bad block table.

  You should maintain a permanent record of the disk's bad block table. If you do not, you will be unable to reenter the bad block table should it ever be deleted.

Notes

Some manufacturers ship hard disk drives with the designation "NetWare Ready." You do not need to use the COMPSURF utility on the drives. In addition, advances in NetWare v2.2 and NetWare v3.11 Hot Fix techniques, as well as the ZTEST utility in NetWare v2.2, have made the COMPSURF utility somewhat unnecessary.

Beginning with NetWare v2.2, COMPSURF supports formatting the hard disk with a 1:1 interleave.

See also

DISKSET   INSTALL
HOT FIX   ZTEST

CONFIG

Purpose

Lists the following information about the file server:

- File server name; internal network number (NetWare v3.x).

- Loaded/Linked LAN drivers.

- Hardware settings on network boards.

- Node (station) addresses (ID) of network boards.

- Communication protocol bound to the network board (NetWare v3.x).

- Network number of the cabling scheme for a network board.

- Frame type assigned to the board (NetWare v3.x). Ethernet and Token-Ring boards can have more than one.

- Board name assigned (NetWare v3.x).

- Number of File Server Processes (NetWare v2.x).

- Linked active disk driver and settings (NetWare v2.2).

Syntax

```
CONFIG
```

Rules and Considerations

Use the CONFIG command to view a list of hardware settings on network boards before installing additional memory cards, network adapters, or disk coprocessor boards in the server. This will help you avoid conflicts before installation.

Under NetWare v2.x, use CONFIG to list the number of file server processes.

Use CONFIG to list all assigned network numbers and node addresses.

Under NetWare v3.x, use MODULES and MONITOR to display information about NetWare loadable modules (NLM) linked to the core operating system.

Under NetWare v3.x, use INSTALL to display configuration information about disk drivers (look in either the STARTUP.NCF or AUTOEXEC.NCF file).

Under NetWare v3.x, use DISPLAY NETWORKS to list all network numbers being used by other file servers on your network. This will help avoid router errors and internal IPX network number conflicts.

Example

To use CONFIG, issue the following command at the console:

```
CONFIG
```

Under NetWare v2.2, CONFIG displays information similar to the following:

```
Hardware Configuration Information for Server TRAINING_SOLUTIONS

Number of File Server Processes: 7

LAN A Configuration Information:
Network Address: [19910ACE] [ 32]
Hardware Type: NetWare RX-Net
Hardware Settings: IRQ = 9, I/O = 2E0, RAM Buffer at D000:0

LAN B Configuration Information:
Network Address: [19910ACE] [01A034845D1B]
Hardware Type: Novell NE1000
Hardware Settings: IRQ = 3, I/O = 300, No DMA or RAM
```

Under NetWare v3.11, CONFIG displays information similar to the following:

```
File server name: TRAINING_SOLUTIONS386
IPX internal network number: BADCAFE

NE-2000 LAN Driver V3.10 (900308)
 Hardware setting: I/O Port 300h to 31Fh, Interrupt 3h
 Node address:00001B0280A3
```

```
Frame type: ETHERNET_802.3
Board name: BACKBONE
LAN protocol: IPX network 00000001
```

See also

DISPLAY NETWORKS (NetWare v3.x)

INSTALL (NetWare v3.x)

MONITOR

CONSOLE   F> 2.2

Purpose

Switches a non-dedicated file server or router to the Console screen. Once in the Console screen, you can issue console commands.

Syntax

`CONSOLE`

Rules and Considerations

After using the CONSOLE command to switch the file server or router to console mode, use the DOS command to switch back to the work station mode.

See also

DOS

DCONFIG   : 2.2

Purpose

Changes the configuration options of the IPX.COM file and NET$OS.EXE operating system file. Enables you to modify the IPX.COM to match the configuration setting of the network board in the workstation should it require change after generation.

Also enables modification of various parameters in the NET$OS.EXE operating system file after generation.

Syntax

>   **DCONFIG** *filename options*

You can specify more than one option on a command line.

Options

>   *-i volume/drive: filename*   Uses input from specified file. This option is valid for IPX.COM only.
>
>   **SHELL:** *node address,*   Valid for IPX.COM only.
>   *configuration #;*

Rules and Considerations

You cannot use the DCONFIG command to insert or delete network card drivers from NET$OS.EXE, or to change the network card for which IPX.COM was originally generated.

When you issue DCONFIG with just the filename (such as IPX.COM or NET$OS.EXE), NetWare displays a list of the adjustable parameters' current settings.

If you type DCONFIG alone (with no options) on the DOS command line, NetWare displays a brief list of the available options.

Although the SHELL option shown previously lists a node address option, this is seldom used. Most network cards used today determine the node address automatically.

If you do not want to change part of an option (such as net address), leave that field blank.

Examples

To change the configuration of the LAN adapter used by IPX.COM to option 2, type the following:

>   **DCONFIG IPX.COM SHELL:, 2;**

To change the configuration of the LAN adapter used by NET$OS.EXE to option 3., type the following:

>   **DCONFIG NET$OS.EXE A: ,,3;**

To change the IPX.COM file at the workstation, change to the directory containing the boot files. To view the current configuration for the IPX.COM file, type:

```
IPX I
```

NetWare should display an informational screen similar to the following:

```
Lan Option: NetWare Ethernet NE2000 V1.00EC
(801004)
Hardware Configuration:IRQ=3, I/O Base=300h,
no DMA or RAM
```

You also can type `DCONFIG IPX.COM` to receive an informational screen similar to the following:

```
 Shell Driver: NetWare Ethernet NE2000 V1.00EC (801004)Node ad-
dress is determined automatically.
 * 0: IRQ = 3, I/O Base = 300h, no DMA or RAM
   1: IRQ = 3, I/O Base = 280h, no DMA or RAM
   2: IRQ = 3, I/O Base = 2A0h, no DMA or RAM
   3: IRQ = 3, I/O Base = 2C0h, no DMA or RAM
   4: IRQ = 4, I/O Base = 300h, no DMA or RAM
   5: IRQ = 4, I/O Base = 2A0h, no DMA or RAM
   6: IRQ = 4, I/O Base = 2C0h, no DMA or RAM
   7: IRQ = 5, I/O Base = 300h, no DMA or RAM
   8: IRQ = 5, I/O Base = 280h, no DMA or RAM
   9: IRQ = 5, I/O Base = 320h, no DMA or RAM
  10: IRQ = 7, I/O Base = 280h, no DMA or RAM
```

The asterisk (*) indicates that the active configuration option in IPX.COM is active, and displays the other options and the option numbers associated with each setting. To change IPX.COM to a different option number, such as option 4, type:

```
DCONFIG IPX.COM SHELL:,4
```

Following are examples of common changes made to NET$OS.EXE using the DCONFIG utility:

```
DCONFIG NET$OS.EXE BUFFERS:xxx
```

The *xxx* variable represents the desired number—150 is the maximum you can select in NETGEN. You can add more here. INSTALL in v2.2 enables you to use up to 1000 communications buffers.

To change a LAN adapter to another available configuration, use the command:

```
DCONFIG NET$OS.EXE A:,,xx
```

The *xx* variable represents the desired configuration # for LAN A Adapter configuration and network address can be changed simultaneously if you want.

Notes

Type `DCONFIG` *`filename.ext`* to display the current configuration of the selected file (IPX.COM or NET$OS.EXE). Before making any changes to the file, use this option and redirect it to a printer to create a handy reference. For the OS, this command would be `DCONFIG NET$OS.EXE > LPT1`.

If you want to make temporary changes to the IPX.COM configuration, you also can use the O# option in NET.CFG or SHELL.CFG, or load IPX.COM using the desired option number on the command line (such as IPX O#4). After the correct option is selected, you can use the ADCONFIG utility to make it permanent.

See also

INSTALL   SHELL.CFG

NET.CFG   WSGEN

NETGEN

DISABLE LOGIN

Purpose

Prevents users from logging in to the file server.

Syntax

```
DISABLE LOGIN
```

Rules and Considerations

The DISABLE LOGIN command does not affect users who already are logged in to the file server. It only prevents a user from logging in after you issue the command at the file server console.

Important Message

After you issue `DISABLE LOGIN` command, NetWare should display a message similar to the following:

```
Login is now disabled.
```

This confirms that the command has worked.

See also

ENABLE LOGIN
FCONSOLE (Status)
LOGIN

DISABLE TRANSACTIONS   : 2.2

Purpose

Manually disables the NetWare Transaction Tracking System (TTS). This command is used primarily by application developers who need to test transactional applications while TTS is disabled.

Syntax

```
DISABLE TRANSACTIONS
```

Rules and Considerations

The NetWare TTS uses only 40 bytes of memory; it can, however, use as much as 400K of memory if it is handling extremely large records. TTS is an integral part of the file server operating system that will protect the bindery and other files that have been flagged as transactional from becoming corrupted. TTS will remain disabled until you issue the ENABLE TRANSACTIONS command or reboot the file server.

Disabling transactions is not an effective way to increase memory at the file server. The protection TTS provides you is worth the additional memory used at the file server.

See also

ENABLE TRANSACTIONS   FLAG

FCONSOLE (Status)   SETTTS

DISABLE TTS   : 3.11

Purpose

Manually disables the NetWare Transaction Tracking System (TTS). This command is primarily used by application developers who need to test transactional applications while TTS is disabled.

Syntax

```
DISABLE TTS
```

Rules and Considerations

The NetWare Transaction Tracking System uses only 40 bytes of memory; it can, however, use as much as 400K of memory if it is handling extremely large records. TTS is an integral part of the file server operating system that protects the bindery and other files that have been flagged as transactional from becoming corrupted. TTS will remain disabled until you issue the ENABLE TTS command or reboot the file server.

Disabling transactions is not an effective way to increase memory at the file server. The protection TTS provides you is worth the additional memory used at the file server.

See also

ENABLE TTS FLAG

FCONSOLE (Status) SETTTS

DISK

: 2.2

Purpose

Monitors and displays the status of network disk drives. Shows which disks and disk channels are functioning normally and which ones are not.

Syntax

    DISK *volumename*

or

    DISK *

Options

When you issue the DISK command alone (without switches), NetWare displays a screen that provides information on all known disks and disk channels installed in the server.

volumename	Causes DISK to display information specific to the volume you specify
*	Displays an overview of disk volumes

When you issue the DISK command alone (without switches), NetWare displays information about all known disks and disk channels installed in the server.

Rules and Considerations

You must issue the DISK command from the file server console.

Examples

The following three examples demonstrate the use of the DISK command by itself, with the * switch, and with a specific volume name.

If you want to check the status of all the disks on your system, issue DISK by itself, as follows:

    DISK

NetWare displays information about all the system's disks, as follows (your system information may be different from the example shown here):

```
PHYSICAL DISK STATUS AND STATISTICS
        cha   con   drv   stat    IO Err   Free   Used
00       1     0     0    OK        0       699     8
01       1     0     1    OK        0         0     8
02       2     0     0    NO HOT    0         0     0
03       2     0     1    OFF       0         0     0
```

This table includes the following types of information:

First column	The physical drive number
cha	The channel number on which the interface board is installed
con	The address of the controller for that disk
drv	The disk address (as seen by the controller)
stat	The disk's operational status; the following values are possible:

	OK	Drive set for Hot Fix and not mirrored
	NO HOT	Hot Fix turned off for this drive (Reinstall Hot Fix as soon as possible; the drive will shut down automatically.)
	DOWN	Drive is out of service or not operating (Repair if possible, or remove from system if necessary.)
	M xx	Drive is part of a mirrored pair; xx is the number of the other drive in the pair
	D xx	Drive was originally set up for mirroring, but is now dead (Repair or replace drive and remirror.)

IO Err	The number of input/output errors that have occurred on this drive
Free	The number of unused blocks in the Hot Fix redirection area
Used	The number of used blocks in the Hot Fix redirection area (Hot Fix uses 6 blocks by default.)

If you want to see a list of all the file server's installed volumes, use the * switch, as follows:

DISK *

NetWare displays the following information (your list may be different from the one shown in this example):

```
                   FILE SERVER VOLUMES

Volume Name Phy Drv      Mir Drv
SYS           00           01
VOL1       02
ACCT       03
```

This table includes the following types of information:

Volume Name	The name assigned to each file server volume
Phy Drv	The physical drive number assigned to each drive
Mir Drv	The physical drive number of the secondary drive in a mirrored-pair set

If you want to see information about a specific volume, include the volume's name with the DISK command. In the following example, the volume is named SYS:

DISK SYS

NetWare displays the following information:

```
Information For Volume SYS
Physical drive number                     : 00
Physical drive type                       : ISA Disk type 09
IO errors on this drive                   : 0
Redirection blocks available              : 223
Redirection blocks used                   : 9
Mirror physical drive number              : 01

Other volumes sharing these
physical drive(s):
VOL1
```

NetWare first displays information about the unmirrored or primary disk on the controller that contains the requested volume. If the disk is part of a mirrored pair, NetWare also reports information about the secondary disk.

Note

In the preceding examples, the physical drive numbers are the drive numbers assigned to each disk by the operating system.

DISKSET   A> :LOAD

Purpose

Loads identification information about external hard disks attached to a Novell Disk Coprocessor Board (DCB) into the DCB's EEPROM chip.

You can load DISKSET at any time on a downed file server to perform the following functions:

- Place configuration information about the hard disks attached to the DCB into the DCB's EEPROM chip. This configuration information enables the file server to communicate with the attached hard disks through the DCB.

- Back up the NetWare Ready configuration information from a NetWare Ready drive to a floppy disk.

- Restore NetWare Ready configuration information from a backup floppy disk to the NetWare Ready drive.

Syntax

Use the following syntax for v2.2:

```
DISKSET
```

Use the following syntax for v3.11:

```
LOAD DISKSET
```

Rules and Considerations

If you are running v2.2, the file server must be downed before running the disk setup program.

If you are running v3.11, the file server must be up and running to load the disk setup program.

Example

A:DISKSET

In this example, the DISKSET utility loads from a DOS disk in drive A. When the utility is loaded, NetWare prompts you to specify the address of the controller you want to use. The system then presents a screen similar to the following:

```
Choose Controller Address
        1
        2
        3
        4
        5
        6
        7
```

After you select the DCB, you are ready to select a disk and controller type from the menu list. The screen should look similar to the following:

```
Select a DISK/CONTROLLER
CDC WRENII HALF-HEIGHT
CDC WRENIII/EMBEDDED SCSI
FJ-M2243/A4000
FJ-M2243/A4000 , FJ-M2243/A4000
Fujitsu M2246AS/EMBEDDED SCSI
Generic SCSI
Generic SCSI , Generic SCSI
MAXTOR-1140/A4000
MAXTOR-1140/A4000 , MAXTOR-1140/A4000
MAXTOR-1140/A4070
MAXTOR-1140/A4070 , MAXTOR-1140/A4070
MAXTOR-3280/EMBEDDED SCSI
MINISCRIBE 4020
MINISCRIBE 4020 , MINISCRIBE 4020
Pyxis 27/A4000
NETWARE READY/EMBEDDED SCSI
Pyxis 27/A4000 , Pyxis 27/A4000

Toshiba MK56/A4000
Toshiba MK56/A4000 , Toshiba MK56/A4000
Toshiba MK56/A4070
Toshiba MK56/A4070 , Toshiba MK56/A4070
```

```
Vertex V150/A4000
Vertex V150/A4000  , Vertex V150/A4000
Vertex V150/A4070
Vertex V150/A4070  , Vertex V150/A4070
Vertex V170/A4000
Vertex V170/A4000  , Vertex V170/A4000
Vertex V170/A4070
Vertex V170/A4070  , Vertex V170/A4070
Vertex V185/A4000
Vertex V185/A4000  , Vertex V185/A4000
Vertex V185/A4070
Vertex V185/A4070  , Vertex V185/A4070
```

If you have a NetWare Ready or other generic embedded SCSI hard disk, select `NetWare Ready/Embedded SCSI` or `Generic SCSI` from the list of options.

Repeat the preceding steps to configure the remaining hard disks and DCBs installed in your system.

Notes

The DISKSET program that ships with NetWare v2.x should be located on the SYSTEM-1 disk.

The controller address (for Novell's DCB) is controlled by a PAL chip on the board. If you require a different setting, you must contact your Novell reseller or Novell's After Market Products division.

The Novell DCB is controlled by an 80188 CPU chip, which is located on the board. This chip loads instructions from ROM that also is contained on the DCB. Newer versions of NetWare (especially NetWare v3.x) require specific versions of this ROM to operate properly. For more information, contact your Novell reseller or Novell's After Market Products division.

DISMOUNT

Purpose

Dismounts a NetWare drive partition or disk, rendering that volume unavailable to users. When a partition or disk is dismounted, you have the opportunity to maintain or repair the volume, or (in the case of NetWare v3.x) upgrade the disk drivers while the server is running.

Syntax

```
DISMOUNT volumename
```

Option

volumename   The name of the volume you want to take out of service

Rules and Considerations

Use the BROADCAST console command to inform users that you are dismounting the volume before you actually take the volume out of service. This warning will enable users who are using that volume to close any files they have in use.

If you have a NetWare volume that is not used very often, dismount it until you need it. Mounted volumes take up memory and reduce overall system performance.

Example

Suppose that you want to dismount a NetWare volume named VOL1. To take the volume out of service, use DISMOUNT as follows:

```
DISMOUNT VOL1
```

This command enables you to service the drive or change disk drivers.

See also

MOUNT

DISPLAY NETWORKS

Purpose

When entered at the server console, the DISPLAY NETWORKS command displays the following information on the server console's screen:

- Network numbers, both cable and internal IPX (NetWare v3.x only)
- The number of hops (networks crossed) required to reach the network (0 hops is the server at which you issue the command)

- The estimated time in ticks (each tick equals 1/18 second) required for a packet to reach the other network

- The total number of networks recognized by the internal router

Syntax

```
DISPLAY NETWORKS
```

Rules and Considerations

You must issue DISPLAY NETWORKS from the file server console.

Example

To make sure that your file server can read all the network numbers, type the following command at the file server console:

```
DISPLAY NETWORKS
```

This command displays the total number of networks recognized by the internal router.

Note

On a Novell NetWare network, each file server maintains an internal router table. This table lists the network and node addresses of each file server and router that this server recognizes. If you have trouble using the LOGIN and ATTACH commands, try using the DISPLAY NETWORKS command to determine whether the server or network in question is "visible" to the other servers and routers on the network.

See also

DISPLAY SERVERS
RESET ROUTER

DISPLAY SERVERS ⠇

Purpose

When entered at the server console, the DISPLAY SERVERS command displays the following information on the server console's screen:

- The file servers recognized by the internal router

- The number of hops (networks that must be crossed) required to reach the server

Syntax

`DISPLAY SERVERS`

Rules and Considerations

You can issue the DISPLAY SERVERS command only at the file server's console.

Example

If you are having trouble attaching to a file server, you can issue the DISPLAY SERVERS command as follows, to determine whether all the system's file servers recognize one another:

`DISPLAY SERVERS`

Note

On a Novell NetWare network, each file server maintains an internal router table. This table lists the network and node addresses of each file server and router that this server recognizes. If you have trouble using the LOGIN and ATTACH commands, try using the DISPLAY SERVERS command to determine whether the internal router table recognizes the server in question.

See also

DISPLAY NETWORKS
RESET ROUTER

DOS

: 2.2

Purpose

This command switches a nondedicated file server or router from console mode to DOS mode.

Syntax

DOS

Rules and Considerations

This command is valid only at a file server that is running NetWare v2.x in nondedicated mode. NetWare v3.x file servers cannot run in nondedicated mode.

If the workstation session (or task) hangs, the file server or router task also may hang, breaking any and all connections maintained by the file server or router. The loss of connection causes users to lose files and access to their applications, printers, disk storage, and other services.

If a nondedicated file server or router hangs when in DOS or console mode, ask all users to try to save their work (to a local disk, if necessary) and log out. Then bring the nondedicated machine up again to see if the problem is corrected.

Even if the nondecicated file server or router is still operating and functional, you must reboot the computer to return the workstation task to normal operation. As a result, however, the nondedicated file server or router will go down.

Example

After you have issued console commands, you may want to switch back to the DOS session and continue using your applications. To move back to the DOS session, issue the DOS command at the nondedicated file server or router console, as follows:

DOS

Notes

On a nondedicated file server running NetWare v2.x, the DOS session has the highest service priority. In other words, virtually all other service requests generated by other users are serviced after the nondedicated DOS session. Further, because the DOS session is polled (not interrupt-driven, as are the network adapter cards), this overhead exists even if no programs are executed in the DOS session. If at all possible, you should change your server to run in dedicated mode.

If you are running your NetWare v2.x file server in nondedicated mode, you are sacrificing approximately 30 percent or more of your server's performance. You can determine the system's minimum performance sacrifice by switching the file server to console mode (with all users logged out) and observing the server's utilization. The utilization data is displayed in Monitor mode. The percentage displayed represents the amount of overhead required just to maintain the DOS session on your nondedicated file server.

If the file server locks up and its keyboard does not respond, go to another workstation on the network and log in as supervisor. When you are in the system, issue FCONSOLE and select Down The Server. This command shuts down the server in an orderly fashion and should help avoid the corruption of files that might have been left open. This procedure may take several minutes.

See also

> CONSOLE
> FCONSOLE
> MONITOR

DOSGEN   F>

Purpose

DOSGEN creates a boot image file called NET$DOS.SYS in the SYS:LOGIN directory. NET$DOS.SYS is a copy of the files on the system's book disk. This file enables diskless workstations to boot from remote boot image files, which reside on the server's hard disk.

Syntax

```
DOSGEN source filename
```

Options

source	The drive in which DOSGEN can find the boot disk. If you omit this drive indicator, NetWare assumes that you want to use drive A.
filename	The output file name. If you do not specify an output file name, NetWare use the name NET$DOS.SYS.

Rules and Considerations

For proper operation, DOSGEN requires you to map two drives, as follows:

```
MAP F:=SYS:SYSTEM

MAP G:=SYS:LOGIN
```

If your network has several servers, copy the Remote Boot image files onto each server that may come up as the Remote Boot station's default server. Then, if the default server is busy when a Remote Boot station boots, the next available server becomes the default server.

Important Messages

If NetWare displays the `Error opening boot disk image file` error message, you probably are attaching to another file server that does not contain the Remote Boot image file. Either log in to the other possible default file servers as supervisor and run DOSGEN on each, or copy the SYS and BAT files in SYS:LOGIN from the default file server to the other file servers on the network.

If you receive the `Batch file missing` error message, make sure that the AUTOEXEC.BAT file is in SYS:LOGIN for every file server to which you can attach.

Example

The following form of the DOSGEN command should be run from drive G. This example retrieves the boot files from drive A and uses the files to create a remote boot image file called NET$DOS.SYS in the LOGIN subdirectory:

```
F:DOSGEN A:
```

To use this command to create a remote boot image file, complete the following steps:

1. Boot a suitable workstation from a floppy or hard disk, and log in as supervisor.

2. Insert the configured boot disk for the Remote Boot workstation into drive A.

3. Map drive F to SYS:SYSTEM.

4. Map drive G to SYS:LOGIN.

5. Change to SYS:LOGIN by making drive G current.

6. To run DOSGEN, type **F:DOSGEN A:**, as shown earlier. During the program's execution, your screen should contain the following information:

```
Floppy Type f9 = Quad Density, 15 Sectors per track
Total Floppy Space 2400 Sectors
Setting Up System Block.
Setting Up FAT Tables.
Setting Up Directory Structures.
Traversing Directory Structures.
Processing IBMBIO   COM
Processing IBMDOS   COM
Processing CONFIG   SYS
Processing COMMAND COM
Processing IPX      COM
Processing NET3     COM
Processing AUTOEXECBAT
Processing NET      CFG
Transferring Data to "NET$DOS.SYS"
```

7. Copy the AUTOEXEC.BAT file from the boot disk in drive A into the SYS:LOGIN subdirectory. NetWare may display the Batch file missing error message when you log in, if the AUTOEXEC.BAT file is not copied to SYS:LOGIN and the default user directory.

8. Copy the AUTOEXEC.BAT file from the boot disk to the default directory specified in the user's login script (usually the user's home directory).

9. Flag the NET$DOS.SYS file in SYS:LOGIN Shareable Read/Write.

The next example, which also should be run from drive G, assumes that you will be creating several remote boot image files. Like the first example, this form of the DOSGEN command retrieves the needed files from a disk in drive A, and uses the data to create a remote boot image file in the LOGIN subdirectory. This form of the DOSGEN command, however, names the new file ARCNET.SYS:

```
F:DOSGEN A: ARCNET.SYS
```

To use this command to create a remote boot image file, complete the following steps:

1. Boot a suitable workstation from a floppy or hard disk, and log in as supervisor.

2. Insert the configured boot disk for the Remote Boot workstation into drive A.

3. Map drive F to SYS:SYSTEM.

4. Map drive G to SYS:LOGIN.

5. Change to SYS:LOGIN by making drive G current.

6. To run DOSGEN, type **F:DOSGEN A: ARCNET.SYS**, as shown earlier. During the program's execution, your screen should contain the following information:

   ```
   Floppy Type f9 = Quad Density, 15 Sectors per track
   Total Floppy Space 2400 Sectors
   Setting Up System Block.
   Setting Up FAT Tables.
   Setting Up Directory Structures.
   Traversing Directory Structures.
   Processing IBMBIO   COM
   Processing IBMDOS   COM
   Processing CONFIG   SYS
   Processing COMMAND COM
   Processing IPX      COM
   Processing NET3     COM
   Processing AUTOEXECBAT
   Processing NET      CFG
   Transferring Data to "ARCNET.SYS"
   ```

7. Copy the AUTOEXEC.BAT file from the boot disk in drive A to the SYS:LOGIN subdirectory. NetWare may display a `Batch file missing` error when you log in if the AUTOEXEC.BAT file has not been copied to SYS:LOGIN and the default user directory. In the example, the AUTOEXEC.BAT file should contain only the name of a second batch file. This second batch file should contain the true desired contents of a boot AUTOEXEC.BAT. Because you are configuring for several remote boot image files, give a unique name and BAT extension (such as ARCNET.BAT) to each AUTOEXEC.BAT file from each boot disk, and copy them all into the SYS:LOGIN subdirectory. When each Remote Boot workstation boots, the

operating system reads the AUTOEXEC.BAT file and goes to the renamed batch file to execute the desired boot commands.

8. Copy the renamed AUTOEXEC.BAT file from SYS:LOGIN to the default directory specified in the user's login script (usually the user's home directory).

9. Flag the ARCNET.SYS file in SYS:LOGIN Shareable Read/Write.

10. Record the network number and node address of the station that will use the Remote Boot image file you just created. You will need this information when you create the BOOTCONF.SYS file.

When you create multiple Remote Boot image files, you also need a BOOTCONF.SYS file in the SYS:LOGIN directory. The BOOTCONF.SYS file lists the names of all the custom Remote Boot image files (except the default NET$DOS.SYS file), and the network and node address of each station that uses the customized remote boot image file. It is nothing more than an ASCII text file in the SYS:LOGIN subdirectory that routes the correct remote boot image file to the correct workstation. Take the following steps to create the BOOTCONF.SYS file:

1. Move to the SYS:LOGIN directory.

2. Use a DOS text editor (such as EDLIN) to create the BOOTCONF.SYS file in the SYS:LOGIN directory. The file should contain a line for each Remote Boot image file you created. Use the following format for entering the required information:

   0x (the number zero plus x)

   The network address

   A comma (,)

   The node or station address

   An equal sign (=)

   The remote boot image file name

   Following this format, your file should look something like this:

   ```
   0xBADCAFE,02F=ARCNET.SYS
   ```

   This example is for an ARCnet workstation. An Ethernet workstation would have a much longer node address.

3. To complete the setup, flag the SYS and BAT files in SYS:LOGIN as Shareable Read/Write. For example:

```
FLAG *.SYS SRW

FLAG *.BAT SRW
```

Notes

If one user can successfully log in but other users are unsuccessful when trying at the same time, verify that the *.SYS files were flagged Shareable Read/Write. You may also need to grant users the Modify right to the SYS:LOGIN subdirectory.

Use the TRACK ON command at the server console and watch for GET NEAREST SERVER REQUESTS from the workstation. This will give you an idea as to whether the boot ROM on the workstation is successfully sending packets to the file server.

Load MONITOR at the file server console and see if the diskless workstations are opening the BOOTCONF.SYS file, the NET$DOS.SYS file, or other boot disk image files.

If a workstation using a boot ROM does not boot, and you have another workstation with a disk drive configured the same as the first workstation (that is, if both have the same type of network board using the same configuration options), see if the second station will boot with the boot disk you used during DOSGEN. By booting with the boot disk in the second workstation, the booting proecedure should execute in the same manner as booting from the server with the Remote Boot image file on the first workstation.

DOWN :

Purpose

The DOWN command shuts down the NetWare operating system so that you can safely turn off the file server. When you issue the DOWN command, the following events occur:

- All cache buffers are written to disk.

- All open files are closed.

- All directory and file allocation tables are updated (if appropriate).

Syntax

DOWN

Rules and Considerations

Make sure that all users are logged out before you issue the DOWN command. Use the MONITOR command to make sure that all users have logged out and all files are closed.

Do not issue the DOWN command or turn off the server if database or word processing files are still open. Close these files from within the appropriate application, and then use DOWN.

Example

Before you can perform any kind of hardware maintenance to the file server, you must turn it off. Before turning off the server, issue the DOWN command, as follows:

DOWN

When you issue the command, NetWare should display a message similar to the following:

```
Server Training-Solutions has been shut down. Please reboot to
restart.
```

Notes

If you fail to use the DOWN command before turning off the file server, you will corrupt any files that may be open. Further, you may cause irreparable damage to the File Allocation Table (FAT) and Directory Entry Table (DET) on the hard disks. If the FAT and DET become corrupted, you probably will not be able to reboot the server and access your data.

Any changes to data files remain in cache buffers and are not written to disk until a minimum time (the default is three seconds) has elapsed or the files are closed. These changes are lost if you do not use DOWN before turning off the file server.

If the MONITOR screen shows a list of the files that are still open, it also should display the station connection numbers that opened them. If files remain open after all users have logged out, you can close these files from the server by using the CLEAR CONNECTION command. You should use this procedure, however, only as a last resort! If the files are not closed by the application that opened them, they may become corrupted.

See also

BROADCAST
CLEAR CONNECTION
MONITOR

ECONFIG   F>

Purpose

The ECONFIG command lists Ethernet configurations, configures workstation shells to use the Ethernet II protocol standard, and embeds NetWare's unique protocol number (8137) in the workstation shell file IPX.COM.

Syntax

```
drive1: ECONFIG drive2: IPX.COM SHELL:packet protocolnumber
```

Options

drive1:	Indicates the location of the ECONFIG.EXE file.
drive2:	Indicates the location of the IPX.COM file.
packet	Specifies the data that is to be transmitted, and its form of transmission. A packet can be one of the following:
	NetWare. Use **N** if the driver is to use the IEEE 802.3 standard frame format.
	Ethernet II. Use **E** if the driver is to use the Ethernet standard frame format.
protocolnumber	Specifies the Ethernet protocol number. By default, this is Novell's IPX protocol number (8137). You can specify any number currently registered with your server.

Example

This example assumes that the WSGEN disk (which contains ECONFIG.EXE) is in drive A, and that the IPX.COM file is in drive B. The following form of the command lists the current Ethernet configuration for IPX.COM:

```
A:ECONFIG B:IPX.COM
```

If the shell file is Ethernet-configurable, but has not yet been configured, you should see the following information on your screen:

```
SHELL: Novell Ethernet (IEEE 802.3 compatible)
```

If the shell file already has been configured with ECONFIG, you should see the following information:

```
SHELL: Ethernet Typefield: 8137 (Assigned Novell type constant)
```

To embed NetWare's protocol number 8137 into the IPX.COM file, type the following form of the ECONFIG command:

```
A:ECONFIG B:IPX.COM SHELL:E
```

NetWare displays the following information:

```
SHELL: Ethernet Typefield: 8137 (Assigned Novell type constant)
```

EDIT :LOAD 3.11

Purpose

The EDIT command creates or modifies an ASCII text file from the NetWare v3.11 file server console.

Syntax

```
LOAD path EDIT
```

Option

path   Determines the full path to the directory containing the EDIT module. You may begin with either a DOS drive letter or a NetWare volume name. If you do not specify a path, the operating system looks for EDIT in SYS:SYSTEM. You can use the SEARCH command to set up additional paths for automatic searching.

Rules and Considerations

You may find EDIT particularly useful when you want to create NCF batch files that automatically execute file server commands. Although you can edit such files in the INSTALL NLM, EDIT provides an alternative means to create or edit them.

You can use EDIT with ASCII text files on either DOS or NetWare partitions. The EDIT NLM can edit ASCII files up to 8K.

Example

To load the editor at the file server, issue the EDIT command as follows:

```
LOAD EDIT
```

At the `File to Edit` prompt, enter the complete directory path for the ASCII file that you want to create or edit. After you create or edit the file, press Esc to exit from EDIT. When the confirmation box appears, select Yes to save the file with the changes you have made during this editing session. Otherwise, you can select No to abort and exit without saving the changes.

See also

SEARCH

EMSNETX.COM or EMSNETX.EXE

Purpose

The EMSNET*x* command loads the NetWare shell driver and moves most of the commands in NET*x*.COM from DOS memory to LIM expanded memory. This arrangement frees approximately 34K of the DOS 640K base memory. About 6K must remain in base memory to handle various interrupts and some data.

Syntax

```
EMSNETX
```

Options

-I   Enables you to see which version of the shell driver you are using, without actually loading it into memory

-U   Unloads the shell driver from memory, but must be the last TSR program loaded for this to function properly

Rules and Considerations

IPX.COM must be loaded before you attempt to load EMSNETX.EXE.

Older versions used the *X* to represent the version of DOS you are running at the workstation; for example, MS-DOS v5 requires you to issue the command as **EMSNET5**.

All NETX.COM parameters in the shell configuration files SHELL.CFG and NET.CFG work with the expanded memory shell.

Example

Issue the following form of the command to load the shell driver into expanded memory:

```
EMSNETX
```

Notes

For ease of use, copy the EMSNETX.EXE (or COM) file to the workstation's boot disk and include the file name (EMSNETX) in the AUTOEXEC.BAT file. This automatically loads the shell driver when you boot your workstation.

The expanded memory shell works with all NetWare versions and operates under the same conditions as the regular NetWare DOS shell v3.01 and above.

The expanded memory shell replaces the current NETX.COM shell option and is intended for use by users who have LIM expanded memory.

You can use the following parameter in the SHELL.CFG or NET.CFG file to determine the number of times you can reenter the expanded memory shell:

```
ENTRY STACK SIZE
```

See also

NET.CFG
SHELL.CFG
XMSNETX

ENABLE LOGIN ：

Purpose

After you have used the DISABLE LOGIN command, you must use ENABLE LOGIN to enable the system's users to log in to the file server.

Syntax

```
ENABLE LOGIN
```

Rules and Considerations

The ENABLE LOGIN function is built into the file server's operating system.

When you disable login and then down the file server, you do not need to issue ENABLE LOGIN. The command is issued automatically when you reboot the file server.

Example

To reverse the DISABLE LOGIN command, issue the following:

```
ENABLE LOGIN
```

See also

> DISABLE LOGIN
> FCONSOLE (Status)
> LOGIN

ENABLE TRANSACTIONS : 2.2

Purpose

If the NetWare Transaction Tracking System (TTS) has been disabled—either automatically or manually—you must manually re-enable TTS by using the ENABLE TRANSACTIONS command.

Syntax

```
ENABLE TRANSACTIONS
```

Rules and Considerations

ENABLE TRANSACTIONS is a part of the operating system. During normal operation, TTS is enabled. The file server automatically disables TTS if the TTS backout volume (usually SYS) becomes full, or if the file server does not have enough memory to run TTS. You also can manually disable TTS by using the DISABLE TRANSACTIONS command. Transactions that were initiated while TTS was disabled cannot be backed out after TTS is re-enabled.

If the file server is rebooted while TTS is disabled, TTS is automatically re-enabled when the file server is rebooted.

Example

If you have disabled TTS and want to re-enable it, issue the following command:

```
ENABLE TRANSACTIONS
```

See also

DISABLE TRANSACTIONS
FCONSOLE (Status)
SETTTS

ENABLE TTS   : 3.11

Purpose

If the NetWare Transaction Tracking System (TTS) has been disabled—either automatically or manually—you must manually re-enable TTS by using the ENABLE TTS command.

Syntax

```
ENABLE TTS
```

Rules and Considerations

ENABLE TTS is a part of the operating system. During normal operation, TTS is enabled. The file server automatically disables TTS if the TTS backout volume (usually SYS) becomes full, or if the file server does not have enough memory to run TTS. You also can manually disable TTS by using the DISABLE TTS command. Transactions that were initiated while TTS was disabled cannot be backed out after TTS is re-enabled.

If the file server is rebooted while TTS is disabled, TTS is automatically re-enabled when the file server is rebooted.

Example

If you have disabled TTS and want to re-enable it, issue the following command:

```
ENABLE TTS
```

See also

DISABLE TTS

FCONSOLE (Status)

ENDCAP
F>

Purpose

Use the ENDCAP command to terminate the capturing of one or more of your workstations' LPT ports. Always use the CAPTURE command before using the ENDCAP command.

Syntax

```
ENDCAP option
```

Options

ENDCAP ends capturing to LPT1, unless you enter one of the following options:

`Local n`	Indicates the LPT port from which you want to end capturing. Replace *n* with the number of the desired parallel port, such as 1, 2, or 3.
`ALL`	Ends the capturing of all LPT ports.
`Cancel`	Ends the capturing of LPT1 and deletes the data without printing it.
`Cancel Local n`	Ends the capturing of the specified LPT port and deletes data without printing it. Replace *n* with the number of the desired parallel port, such as 1, 2, or 3.
`Cancel ALL`	Ends the capturing of all LPT ports and deletes the data without printing it.

Rules and Considerations

Use the ENDCAP command only after having issued the CAPTURE command.

Important Message

`LPTx set to local mode.`	Indicates that port LPT*x* (LPT1, 2, or 3) has been set to local operation and the CAPTURE function has been canceled

Examples

To end capturing to LPT1, issue the following command:

ENDCAP

To end capturing to LPT2, issue the following command:

ENDCAP L=2

To end capturing to LPT1 and delete the print job without printing it, issue the following command:

ENDCAP CL=1

See also

CAPTURE

EXIT
: 3.11

Purpose

Returns the file server console to DOS after you have used the DOWN command. EXIT enables you to access files on the DOS partition, or to reload SERVER.EXE with new parameters.

Syntax

    EXIT

Rules and Considerations

If you use the console command REMOVE DOS to remove DOS from memory, you cannot use the EXIT command to return to DOS.

Example

After you have shut down the file server, you can return to the DOS prompt by issuing the following command:

    EXIT

Note

You can use EXIT to warm boot the file server if you have issued the REMOVE DOS command.

See also

    DOWN
    REMOVE DOS

FLAG
F>

Purpose

Displays or changes files attributes.

Syntax

```
FLAG path flaglist
```

Options

path
: Designates directory path that leads to the name of the file you want to view or change.

flaglist
: Specifies one or more of the following attributes (use the bold character to express the attribute):

Shareable
: Allows a file to be opened by more than one person at a time. Shareable is often used in conjunction with Read Only and is also used to mark application programs (that is, EXE or COM files).

Read **O**nly
: Prevents you from writing to, deleting, or renaming a specified file. The Read Only flag often is used in conjunction with Shareable on application program files.

Read/**W**rite
: Specifies the file as a data file, which means that data can be written to it. This is a default setting for files.

Normal
: Specifies the NonShareable and Read/Write flags together. All files loaded on the network are set this way by default.

Transaction **T**racking **S**ystem
: Specifies the file is transactional. This flag is designed to be used with NetWare's Transaction Tracking feature, which prevents database corruption in case of system failure. The Transaction Tracking System ensures that when a file is modified, either all changes are made or no changes are made, thus preventing data corruption.

`Indexed`	Forces NetWare to keep a special File Allocation Table to speed data access. Used with data files using more than 64 cache blocks. Automatic in v3.11.
`Hidden`	Prevents a file from displaying when a DOS DIR command is executed. The file will appear, however, if you have the File Scan right in that directory, and you use the NDIR command. You cannot copy or erase Hidden files.
`SYstem`	Flags a file as a system file and is used for the system function. A system file does not appear when you use the DOS DIR command, but it will appear when you use the NetWare NDIR command if you have the File Scan right. You cannot copy or delete system files.
`Archive`	Attaches automatically to all files that have been modified since the last backup was performed.
`Execute Only`	Allows the program file to execute, but prevents it from being copied. This special flag is attached to COM and EXE files. Files with this flag set are not backed up, nor can this flag be removed. The file must be deleted and reinstalled to remove this attribute. This attribute can only be set by the supervisor in the FILER utility.
`SUBdirectory`	Displays or changes file attributes in the specified directory and its subdirectories.

Rules and Considerations

You must be attached to the file server before you can view or change file attributes of files on that server.

You cannot change file attributes in a directory unless your effective rights in that directory include the Read, File Scan, and Modify privileges.

Use the - or + constants to add or delete all file attributes except Normal and SUBdirectory. When attributes are added or deleted in the same command, keep the + attributes separate from the - attributes.

Example

If you want to flag as Shareable Read Only every file on the CDI server in the MS-DOS v5.00 directory under Public, enter the command:

```
FLAG CDI\SYS:PUBLIC\IBM_PC\MSDOS\V5.00\*.* SRO
```

Notes

MS/PC-DOS files should be flagged as Shareable Read Only.

If you enter the command FLAG /?, a help screen displays.

The *filename* parameter in the syntax also supports standard DOS wild-card characters.

Use the Execute Only flag with extreme care. Some application programs will not execute correctly if they are flagged with this option. If you are going to use this flag, make sure you have a copy of the EXE or COM file before you set this flag. The only way to remove this flag is to delete the file.

See also

> FILER
> NDIR

FLAGDIR   F> 3.11

Purpose

Lists or changes the attributes of directories and subdirectories.

Syntax

```
FLAGDIR path flaglist
```

Options

path   Specifies the path to the directory you want to view or change.

flaglist   Specifies one or more of the following attributes (use the bold character to specify the attribute):

        Normal   Cancels all other directory attributes. Normal is automatically overridden if you include any other option.

        Hidden   Prevents a directory from listing when the DOS DIR command is used. The directory will appear if you have the File Scan right and you use the NetWare NDIR command. With these privileges, you can access a Hidden directory, but you cannot copy or delete Hidden directories.

        SYstem   Flags a directory as a System directory, which stores the network's operational files. A directory flagged as System will not appear when you use the DOS DIR command. A System directory will appear if you use the NetWare NDIR command and if you have the File Scan right.

        Private   Protects data from casual directory-browsers. You can use the Private option to hide the directory names of all directories below the flagged directory. Although you cannot see any files on the system because you have no rights, you can see directories and use the DOS CD command to move through the directory structure. Can be used only in v2.2.

        Delete Inhibit   Prevents users from erasing a directory even if they have Erase rights for that directory. Can be used only in v3.11.

Rename Inhibit	Prevents users from renaming directories even if they have Modify rights for that directory. Can be used only in v3.11.
Purge	Marks files that you want to purge immediately after deletion. These files cannot be recoved by using SALVAGE. Can be used only in v3.11.
Help	Displays the FLAGDIR help text.

Rules and Considerations

You cannot set attributes on local drives.

You cannot copy or delete system directories.

Example

To flag the TGEN subdirectory as private and to prevent other users from seeing the subdirectories under it when they use the DOS DIR command, type the following:

```
FLAGDIR TRAINING_SOLUTIONS\SYS:USERS\TGEN P
```

See also

FILER

GRANT   F>

Purpose

Grants trustee rights to a user or a group.

Syntax

```
GRANT rightslist FOR path TO USER username
```

or

```
GRANT rightslist FOR path TO GROUP groupname
```

Note that the specifiers USER and GROUP are required if the user or group to be modified has the same name as another user or group.

Options

path	Specifies the path for granting trustee rights
username	Specifies the name of a valid user on the file server to whom you want to grant trustee rights
groupname	Specifies the name of a valid group on the file server that is to be granted trustee rights
rightslist	Represents one or more of the following options (use the bold character to express the desired option):

All	Grants all rights except supervisory rights in v3.11
Create	Enables users to create files but not to write to them
Erase	Enables users to delete or erase files
Modify	Enables users to modify file names or attributes
Access Control	Enables a user or a group to control access to the directory
Read	Enables users to read from a file in the directory
File Scan	Enables users to "see" file names during a DOS DIR command
Write	Enables users to write to files
Supervisor	Gives all available rights to user. 3.11 only.
ALL BUT or ONLY	Switches that you can use before the *rightslist* option

Rules and Considerations

You must be attached to a server before you can grant trustee rights on the server.

Before you can grant rights to a user (or group), the user must exist on the network.

If you elect to grant rights to a user, you can grant rights to only one user with each GRANT command.

If you revoke trustee rights, the user remains a trustee of the directory unless he or she is removed from the trustee list.

Example

The following example grants the Read, Write, File Scan, and Modify rights to the user TGENDREAU for the PUBLIC subdirectory on the file server TRAINING_SOLUTIONS:

```
GRANT R W F M FOR TRAINING_SOLUTIONS\SYS:PUBLIC TO TGENDREAU
```

See Also

ATTACH	REVOKE
MAP	SESSION
REMOVE	SYSCON

HELP   F>

Purpose

Enables you to view on-line information about NetWare. HELP provides information on NetWare concepts, system messages, and utilities. You can use HELP to search for information in databases or infobases.

Syntax

```
HELP command
```

Option

command   Specifies the command that you would like more information about.

Rules and Considerations

The HELP utility is placed in the SYS:PUBLIC directory during NetWare installation. Use the cursor keys to move around in HELP, or use the following keys:

+ or -	Rotates windows without closing them
Tab	Moves the cursor to the next link
Shift-Tab	Moves the cursor to the previous link
Esc	Closes windows, exits a search or exits the help utility

If your workstation has graphics support, you can use the left-right arrow keys to access graphics screens. If you have a mouse, point and click on the menu name. If you use a keyboard, access the menus with the following keystrokes:

Alt-S plus arrow keys	Enables you to scan menus
Alt-F	Accesses the file menu
Alt-D	Activates menus at the top of the screen

Following Links

Links are used to connect related information from different parts of the infobase. Use the TAB and SHIFT-TAB keys to position the cursor on the link, and then press ENTER. A new window will display the information.

Searching for Words or Phrases

When the cursor is in a window and not under a link, press the spacebar. The search window appears and the query window will be active. Type the word or phrase you want to find (enclose phrases in quotation marks), and then press ENTER. A new window appears displaying the segments of the infobase where the searched words occur. You can use the TAB or SHIFT-TAB keys to move through the information. If you want to see where the information appears in the complete infobase, press ENTER at the marker.

The following operands illustrate the different types of searches you can specify. These operands can be typed in upper- or lowercase letters.

- **AND**. Use the AND operator to search for combinations of words. You can use a space between each word to represent the AND operator. For example, to search for all occurrences of print and queues together in a segment, type `print queues`.

- **OR**. Use the OR operator to search for occurrences of words either together in the segment or separately. Use the forward slash character (/) to represent the OR operator. For example, to search for all occurrences of the words print or queues or both in the same segment, type `print/queues`.

- **NOT**. Use the NOT operator to search for all occurrences of a word except when it is used with another specific word. Use the circumflex symbol (^) to represent the NOT operator. For example, to search for all occurrences of the word print, except when it is used with the word queues, type `print^queues`.

- *** and ?**. Use the asterisk (*) and question mark (?) to search for variations or words. For example, to search for all words that begin with prin followed by more than one unspecified character, type `prin*`.

You also can perform a proximity search in a specific order to search for words that occur within a certain number of words from each other. Place the words that you want to search for inside quotation marks, followed by the number of words that you want to search within. For example, to search for the words print and queues within four words, type `"print queues"4`.

You can use the ampersand (@) symbol to perform a proximity search in any order. For example, to search for the words print and queues within five words in any order, type `"print queues"@5`.

You can print the information you find in HELP in several ways. Follow these steps to print information:

1. Press Ctrl-B to begin blocking text.

2. Use the cursor keys or a mouse to group the text together.

3. Press Ctrl-Printscrn after you block the text.

4. Select PRINT and highlight the desired settings, then press Enter.

   The block of text will print.

Blocks of information can also be sent to a file and printed later by choosing the menu option Redirect document to ____.

Example

```
HELP NPRINT
```

By typing HELP followed by a command you need help with, the HELP utility will display information on the command that you typed.

Note

If you need help using the HELP utility, press the F1 key inside the HELP window.

See also

NFOLIO

HOLDOFF

Purpose

Enables you to close a file that you have been using so that other users can access it. HOLDOFF reverses the effects of the HOLDON command.

Syntax

```
HOLDOFF filename.ext
```

Rules and Considerations

You do not need to use the HOLDOFF command unless you previously used the HOLDON command.

Example

```
HOLDOFF LOTUS.COM
```

The preceding example reverses the effects of the HOLDON command that was issued on the file LOTUS.COM.

See also

HOLDON

HOLDON

Purpose

Holds a file open while you use it and prevents other users from writing to the current file.

Syntax

```
HOLDON filename.ext
```

See also

HOLDOFF

INSTALL   :LOAD 3.11

Purpose

Enables you to install the v3.11 operating system on a file server's hard disk drive(s). INSTALL also is used to load the SYSTEM and PUBLIC files onto the file server; format and mirror hard disks; and create NetWare partitions, volumes, and file server boot files. Use the F1 key for help while the install utility is active. Press F1 twice for an overview of the installation process.

Syntax

```
LOAD path INSTALL
```

Option

path   Specifies the path or drive letter that the computer uses to load the install utility.

Rules and Considerations

Before you can use the INSTALL command, you must execute the SERVER program to bring up the v3.11 file server. The SERVER program can be found on the SYSTEM-1 disk. To execute the server command, insert the SYSTEM-1 disk in drive A and type **SERVER**. After you press Enter, information similar to the following will appear on the screen:

```
Novell NetWare 386 v3.11
Processor speed: 265
(Type SPEED at the command prompt for an explanation of the
speed rating)
Total server memory: 8 Megabytes
```

File server name:

Give the file server a unique name from 2 to 47 characters. The name cannot contain a period or spaces. After you name the file server, you will be asked to enter an internal network number. The internal network number must differ from other network numbers. The internal network number is a hexadecimal number (base 16) that uses 0-9 and A-F. The number can be 1 to 8 digits long.

Next, load the appropriate disk driver modules. Type `LOAD` *path disk driver*. Your disk driver should be either an ISADISK for AT type controllers, DCB for Novell Disk Coprocessor Boards, or PS2ESDI, PS2MFM, or PS2SCSI for PS/2 type controllers. The manufacturer of the disk controller you are using will provide you with these drivers. Consult your controller and disk drive documentation for more detailed information.

Now you are ready to load the INSTALL utility. To do so, insert the SYSTEM-2 disk in drive A in the file server and type `LOAD INSTALL` at the prompt.

Example

`LOAD A:INSTALL`

The preceding example loads INSTALL.NLM from drive A.

See also

DISKSET

LOAD

IPX.COM

Purpose

The Novell IPX (Internetwork Packet eXchange) is a communication protocol that creates, maintains, and terminates connections between network devices such as workstations, file servers, and routers.

Syntax

```
IPX options
```

Options

I   Enables you to see how the IPX file is configured. The I option does not load IPX into memory.

Additional switches for the v3.02 shells include the following:

D   Display hardware options

Onum   Loads IPX using the hardware option (*num*)

C=path filename   Use an alternate configuration file

?   Display this help screen

Rules and Considerations

At each workstation, two components in combination often are called the *shell*.

The first component is the *Internetwork Packet Exchange/Sequenced Packet Exchange (IPX/SPX)* interface. This interface provides the hardware communications routines that enable the workstation to communicate with its installed network card. The network card communicates with other network devices such as file servers.

The other component, called *NETX*, monitors DOS calls from the application that is running on the workstation. NETX determines whether the DOS calls are for a file server or the local PC.

NETX intercepts and prepares requests. Before NETX hands requests to IPX, IPX.COM uses a LAN driver routine to control the station's network board and address. The LAN driver routine also is used to route outgoing data packets for delivery on the network. IPX reads the assigned addresses of returning data and directs the data to the proper area within a workstation's shell or the file server's operating system.

Notes

The following message appears if you type IPX after you loaded the IPX.COM file at the workstation:

```
IPX/SPX already loaded.
```

Try to execute the NETx.COM file or log in to the file server or do both to use the IPX command.

See also

NETX

PROTOCOLS

IPXS :LOAD 3.11

Purpose

Used by other loadable modules that require STREAMS-based IPX protocol services.

Syntax

```
LOAD path IPXS
```

Option

path   Defines the full directory path to the directory that contains the
            loadable module. You can use DOS drive pointers such as A: or B:, or
            use a NetWare volume name. If no path is specified, the operating
            system assumes that the loadable module is in the SYS:SYSTEM
            subdirectory.

Rules and Considerations

Before you unload a protocol-stack NLM such as IPXS, unload all other loadable
modules that may potentially use IPXS.

If your loadable module requires STREAMS-based IPX protocol services, load the
following additional modules in the order listed before you load IPXS:

1. Load the STREAMS module

2. Load the CLIB module

3. Load the TLI module

Example

```
LOAD IPXS
```

The preceding example loads STREAMS-based IPX protocol services.

LISTDIR

F>

Purpose

Lists subdirectories and subdirectory information.

Syntax

```
LISTDIR path options
```

Options

path   Specifies the directory path for which you want more information. The path can include the volume, directory, and subdirectory.

option   Specifies one or more of the following options:

/Rights   Lists the Inherited Rights Masks of all subdirectories in a specific directory.

/Effective rights   Lists the effective rights for all subdirectories of the specified directory.

/Date or /Time   Lists the date or time or both that a subdirectory was created.

/Subdirectories   Lists a directory's subdirectories.

/All   Lists all subdirectories, their Inherited Rights Masks, effective rights, and their creation dates and times.

Example

To list all subdirectories, inherited rights masks, effective rights, and creation dates for everything in the WP51 directory, enter the command:

```
LISTDIR TRAINING_SOLUTIONS\SYS:APPS\WP51 /A
```

LOAD
: 3.11

Purpose

This command loads NetWare Loadable Modules (NLMs) at the file server console.

Syntax

```
LOAD path NLM parameter
```

Options

path	Represents the full path to the directory that contains the loadable module. The path variable can begin with either a valid DOS drive letter or a valid NetWare volume name. If you do not specify a path and the SYS: volume has not been mounted, the operating system (OS) assumes that the NLM is in the default DOS partition or directory. After the volume SYS: has been mounted, the OS assumes the loadable module is in the SYS:SYSTEM directory.
NLM	Specifies the name of one of the following types of NLMs:

> Disk drivers
>
> LAN drivers
>
> Name space
>
> NLM utilities

Consult either NETWARE, your reseller, or a third-party dealer for other available NLMs.

parameter	Settings are specific to each NLM. Refer to the NLM's documentation for more information.

Rules and Considerations

To load modules automatically each time the server boots, store the appropriate LOAD commands in the AUTOEXEC.NCF or STARTUP.NCF file. See AUTOEXEC.NCF and STARTUP.NCF for more information.

All NLMs should be certified by Novell, Inc. If you run any third-party NLMs, check with NETWARE or your Novell Authorized Reseller for a list of Novell-approved

NLMs. If you load a module that is not approved, your server may ABEND (an ABnormal END) and data may become corrupted.

NLMs will not load under any of the following conditions:

- The server cannot find the loadable module.
- The server does not have enough free memory.
- The module is dependent on another module that is not loaded.
- You used an invalid parameter.
- LOAD is not entered before the module name.
- You used an invalid command in the NCF files.

Example

To load the industry standard disk drive that supports many different hard disk drive controllers, enter the command:

```
LOAD ISADISK
```

Notes

An NLM links itself into the OS and allocates a portion of server memory for its own use.

Some NLMs will check the system memory for the existence of required NLMs at load time and automatically preload the required NLMs if necessary.

LOGIN   F>

Purpose

Accesses the named or default server and invokes your login script on that particular file server.

Syntax

```
LOGIN option fileserver/login_name scriptparameters
```

Options

option	May be one or more of the following:
	/Script
	/NoAttach
	/Clearscreen
fileserver	Identifies the file server you want to log into
login_name	Specifies your user name or login name (account name, for example)
scriptparameters	Specifies the parameters set in your login script

Rules and Considerations

You may include a LOGIN command in your AUTOEXEC.BAT file. Then when you boot your workstation, it will attach itself to the logically closest file server. This becomes your default server.

If you automatically log in to several servers simultaneously, you can synchronize your password on all the servers where you use the same login or user name. If you change the password, LOGIN prompts if you want to synchronize passwords on all servers.

A LOGIN implies a LOGOUT, and thus logs you out of other servers. To access another server and remain logged in to your default server, use the ATTACH command instead.

Notes

LOGIN shows the last time the user logged into the file server.

If the password notification is set to yes in SYSCON, users are notified when their passwords will expire each time they log on.

See also

ATTACH

LOGOUT

LOGOUT
F>

Purpose

Logs you out of file servers you are attached to.

Syntax

    LOGOUT *fileserver*

Option

Replace *fileserver* with the name of the server you want to log out of. If you do not specify a file server, you will be logged out of all file servers you are attached to.

Rules and Considerations

When you log out of a server, drive mappings to that server disappear. You must have a search drive mapped to the PUBLIC directory of at least one of the servers you are still attached to, or you cannot execute any NetWare utilities.

See also

ATTACH

LOGIN

MAKEUSER
F>

Purpose

This utility creates and deletes user accounts on a regular basis. Makeuser is commonly used to set up user accounts for new students each semester, create accounts for temporary employees, or to batch add many users at once. Workgroup managers often use MAKEUSER to create their users.

Syntax

    MAKEUSER

Rules and Considerations

To create and delete users with the MAKEUSER command, you first must create a USR script file. This file contains the keywords necessary to create the user(s), assign rights, assign trustee restrictions, assign a home directory to new users, or delete existing users from the system.

To modify or process a USR file, you must be in the directory where that file is located. You can use any ASCII text editor to create USR files, but the file must be saved in ASCII format and have a USR extension.

You must process the USR file with MAKEUSER before the accounts are created or deleted.

The keywords used in a USR file to create and delete users in MAKEUSER are as follows:

#ACCOUNT EXPIRATION month day year

#ACCOUNTING balance, lowlimit

#CLEAR or #RESET

#CONNECTIONS number

#CREATE user name [option ...]

#DELETE user name

#GROUPS group

#HOME_DIRECTORY path

#LOGIN_SCRIPT path

#MAX_DISK_SPACE vol, number

#PASSWORD_LENGTH length

#PASSWORD_PERIOD days

#PASSWORD_REQUIRED

#PURGE_USER_DIRECTORY

#REM or REM

#RESTRICTED_TIME day, start, end

#STATIONS network, station

#UNIQUE_PASSWORD

Important Messages

If USR file contains errors, you might see a message similar to the following:

```
Error  :  Line 001, Undefined keyword
Warning:  Line 002, Group expected
Please fix the error in the file and try it again.
```

Note

Create a directory for all USR files. When you create a USR file, the MAKEUSER command places the file in the current directory.

See also

USERDEF

MAP
F>

Purpose

Lists, creates, or changes logical drive mappings in the NetWare environment.

Syntax

MAP *parameters drive:=path*

Options

parameters can be one of the following:

INSert	Alters search drive mappings
DELete	Deletes a drive mapping
REMove	Deletes a drive mapping
Next	Maps next available drive letter to the specified path
ROOT	Maps the drive as fake root (useful for Windows applications)
drive	The drive letter mapped to the directory you want to work with
path	Directory path you intend to work with

Rules and Considerations

When attempting to map a drive to a specified path, the path named in the MAP command must exist.

You must be attached to a file server before you can map drives to it.

Examples

To list all currently active mappings, type the following:

```
MAP
```

Your screen display should resemble the following:

```
Drive A:  maps to a local drive
Drive B:  maps to a local drive
Drive C:  maps to a local drive
Drive D:  maps to a local drive
Drive E:  maps to a local drive

Drive F:= TRAINING_SOLUTIONS/SYS:
Drive G:= TRAINING_SOLUTIONS/SYS:USERS/GUEST /
SEARCH1:=Z:. [TRAINING_SOLUTIONS/SYS: /PUBLIC/]
SEARCH2:=Y:. [TRAINING_SOLUTIONS/SYS: /PUBLIC/IBM_PC/MSDOS/V5.00]
```

To map a fake root for applications (such as Windows applications) that write files to or create directories off the root directory, type the following:

```
MAP NEXT ROOT SYS:WINAPPS
```

If you then type **MAP** to view the active drive mappings, you should see the following screen display:

```
Drive A:  maps to a local drive
Drive B:  maps to a local drive
Drive C:  maps to a local drive
Drive D:  maps to a local drive
Drive E:  maps to a local drive

Drive F:= TRAINING_SOLUTIONS/SYS:
Drive G:= TRAINING_SOLUTIONS/SYS:USERS/GUEST /
Drive H:= TRAINING_SOLUTIONS/SYS:WINAPPS /

SEARCH1:=Z:. [TRAINING_SOLUTIONS/SYS: /PUBLIC/]
SEARCH2:=Y:. [TRAINING_SOLUTIONS/SYS:/PUBLIC/IBM_PC/MSDOS/V5.00/]
```

The space between the end of the path and the last slash indicates that this is a fake rooted drive.

To map an additional search drive, type the following:

```
MAP S16:=SYS:APPS\FOXPRO
```

By typing `S16:` for the search drive, you automatically assign it to the last available search drive position open.

Notes

Drive mappings are valid only for the active session unless you save them in your login script.

From a fake root, you cannot use the DOS CD (change directory) command to return to the original root directory. To change to the original root, you must remap the drive. Or you can type the CD command and reference the volume level as follows:

```
CD SYS:TRIVIA
```

The MAP command accepts either forward slashes (/) or backslashes (\) as part of the path. To maintain consistency with DOS, however, it is suggested you use only backslashes (\) in the path designation.

See also

SESSION

MATHLIB   :LOAD 3.11

Purpose

Loads a library of support routines, if your server has a math coprocessor (such as a 386 machine with a math coprocessor or a 486DX machine).

Syntax

```
LOAD path MATHLIB
```

Option

path   Specifies the path to the directory containing the NLM. Can begin with either a DOS drive letter or a NetWare volume name.

Rules and Considerations

If you do not specify a path, the operating system assumes the NLM is in SYS:SYSTEM.

If you need MATHLIB, the following modules need to be loaded in the exact order listed as follows:

> CLI
> MATHLIB
> STREAMS

Notes

To make sure that the modules necessary for MATHLIB load automatically when the file server boots, add the following commands to the AUTOEXEC.NCF file.

> LOAD STREAMS
>
> LOAD CLIB
>
> LOAD MATHLIB

See also

> INSTALL

MATHLIBC   :LOAD 3.11

Purpose

Loads a library of support routines if your server does not have a math coprocessor (such as a 386 machine without a math coprocessor).

Syntax

> `LOAD` *path* `MATHLIBC`

Option

> *path*   Represents the full path to the directory containing the NLM. Can begin with a valid DOS drive letter or NetWare volume name.

Rules and Considerations

You must load CLIB before you load MATHLIBC.

The following modules must be loaded in the exact order listed as follows:

STREAMS

CLIB

MATHLIBC

If you do not specify a path, the operating system assumes that the NLM resides in SYS:SYSTEM. (Use SEARCH to set up additional paths for searching.)

Note

To make certain that the NLMs necessary to support MATHLIB load when the file server boots, add the following commands to the AUTOEXEC.NCF file:

```
LOAD STREAMS
LOAD CLIB
LOAD MATHLIBC
```

See also

INSTALL

MEMORY   : 3.11

Purpose

Views the total amount of the memory the operating system can address in the file server.

Syntax

```
MEMORY
```

Rules and Considerations

NetWare v3.x addresses all memory installed in an EISA computer. If you have either a microchannel or ISA computer, the operating system only addresses up to 16M of memory. Use the REGISTER MEMORY command to enable the operating system to address the memory above 16M.

Example

To display all of the memory the operating system can address, type the following:

```
MEMORY
```

See also

REGISTER MEMORY

MENU   F>

Purpose

Invokes a custom menu that you have created. See Chapter 9 for information on creating custom menus.

Syntax

```
MENU filename
```

Rules and Considerations

When using the MENU command, you must specify the extension of the option file name unless you use the extension MNU.

Example

```
MENU main
```

MODULES   : 3.11

Purpose

Displays information about the modules currently loaded at the file server. You see the short name of the module, the long name of the module, and version information about your LAN and DISK driver modules.

Syntax

```
MODULES
```

See also

```
LOAD
```

MONITOR   :

Purpose

Locks the console, enables the screen saver, and enables you to monitor how efficiently the network is operating. When used with NetWare 3.11, the MONITOR command displays the following:

```
Utilization and overall activity
Cache memory status
Connections and their status
Disk drives
Mounted volumes
LAN xdrivers
Loaded modules
File lock status
Memory usage
```

Syntax

```
LOAD path MONITOR parameter
```

Options

path   Full path beginning with a DOS drive letter or NetWare volume name. If you do not specify a path, and volume SYS has been mounted, the operating system assumes the module is in SYS:SYSTEM unless other search paths have been added.

parameter can be one of the following:

ns   (No screen saver). Disables the screen saver option. If you do not use ns, a utilization snake appears on the screen after a few minutes of console keyboard inactivity. To redisplay the MONITOR screen, press any key.

nh   (No help). Prevents MONITOR HELP from loading.

p   Displays information about the file server microprocessor.

Important Message

```
This module is ALREADY loaded and cannot be loaded more than
once.
```

If MONITOR is already loaded, the preceding message appears. If it does, do one of the following:

Press Alt-Esc to move through the activated screens until the MONITOR screen appears.

Press Ctrl-Esc and select Monitor Screen from the list of available screens.

Notes

The MONITOR command can perform the following tasks:

- List active connections
- List physical record locks
- Clear a connection
- List open files
- List system disk drives
- List volume segments per drive
- Change the "Read After Write Verify" status

- Flash the hard disk light
- Activate/deactivate a hard disk
- Mount/dismount a removable media device
- Lock/unlock a removable media device
- List LAN drivers and statistics
- List system modules
- List resources used by system modules
- Lock the console
- Unlock the console
- Check file status
- View mounted volumes
- View memory statistics
- View tracked resources
- Exit

MONITOR
: 2.2

Purpose

Tracks and displays the activities of all workstations that are logged in to or attached to the file server. Also displays the activities of VAPs and enables you to see what files each station is using and possibly locking. MONITOR also displays the file server's utilization.

Syntax

```
MONITOR number
```

Option

Replace *number* with the station you want to monitor. If you omit *number*, stations 1 through 7 are displayed by default.

Rules and Considerations

Include a station number if you want to monitor the activities of one specific workstation. This information can be obtained using the FCONSOLE command.

The MONITOR command screen displays information on six stations at once.

MONITOR also displays the operating system version and the percentage of file server utilization.

When a workstation requests a transaction, MONITOR displays up to five files and a file status message. A file server running NetWare in dedicated mode also can display two status letters. File status also can have an identifier, and the request area often will display a message.

Example

```
MONITOR
```

Notes

Execute MONITOR if you suspect an application has crashed at a particular workstation. The display might show W for 20 minutes on a small file, indicating a Write operation has locked the workstation.

Every file shown has an accompanying DOS task number to the left of the status field.

The request area to the right of each station number indicates the most recent file server request the workstation made. The following is a list of valid requests that NetWare might display:

```
Alloc Resource Record
Begin Trans File
Clear File
Clear File Set
Clear Record Set
Close File
Clr Phy Rec
Clr Phy Rec Set
Copy File
Create File
Dir Search
```

End of Job
End Trans
Erase File
Floppy Config
Get File Size
Lock File
Lock Phy Rec Set
Lock Record
Log Out
Log Pers File
Log Phy Rec
Log Record
Open File
Pass File
Read File
Rel Phy Rec
Rel Phy Rec Set
Rel Record Set
Rel Resource
Release File
Release File Set
Release Record
Rename File
Search Next
Semaphore
Set File Atts
Start Search
Sys Log
Unlock Record
Win Format
Win Read
Win Write
Write File

See also

OFF

MOUNT

Purpose

Places the volume in service. By mounting the volume, users have access to the information about that volume. The MOUNT command can be used while the file server is running.

Syntax

    MOUNT volume_name or ALL

Options

volume_name	Specifies the volume name you want to put into service or mount
ALL	Enables you to mount all volumes without specifying the names of each volume

Rules and Considerations

If you have volumes that are not used often, it is wise to leave them dismounted until you need them. When you mount a volume, it uses file server memory; this lessens the amount of memory you have available for file caching.

Important Messages

    Volume volume_name could NOT be mounted.
    Some or all volume segments cannot be located.

This message is displayed if the volume you specified does not exist or has a problem.

See also

DISMOUNT

NAME
:

Purpose

Displays the name of the file server.

Syntax

NAME

Rules and Considerations

When you invoke the NAME command, you see the name of the file server in a format similar to the following:

```
This is server TRAINING_SOLUTIONS
```

NCOPY
F>

Purpose

Copies one or more files from one location to another.

The NCOPY command works much like the DOS COPY command. The big difference between the two is that NCOPY performs the copy at the file server itself. The DOS COPY command reads data from the file server and then writes the data back to the file server over the network. The NCOPY command is much faster and does not slow down the network as much as the DOS COPY command would.

The NCOPY command is placed in the PUBLIC directory during installation.

Syntax

NCOPY *path* **FILENAME** *to path FILENAME option*

Leave a space between the source file name and the destination directory path. The NCOPY command supports wild-card characters and up to 25 directory levels. When the copied file lands in the destination directory, it retains the original's date and time.

Options

/A	Copies only files that have the archive bit set. Will not reset the archive bit.
/COPY	Copies files without preserving the attributes or name space information.
/EMPTY	Copies empty subdirectories when you copy an entire directory with the /S option.
/FORCE	Forces the operating system to write sparse files.
/INFORM	Notifies you when attributes or name space information cannot be copied.
/M	Copies only files that have the archive bit set, and will reset the archive bit after copying.
/PRESERVE	Copies SYSTEM and HIDDEN files and preserves attributes.
/SUBDIRECTORIES	Copies all the files and subdirectories.
/VERIFY	Verifies that the original file and the copy are identical.
/Help /?	Displays usage guide.

Rules and Considerations

You may use wild cards to copy more than one file at a time. The NCOPY command automatically preserves a file's attributes.

Examples

To copy all the dbf files from drive G: to drive H:, type the following:

```
NCOPY G:*.dbf H:
```

To copy all of the dat files from the REPORTS directory to the ARCHIVE\JULY directory, type the following:

```
NCOPY SYS:DATA\REPORTS\*.DAT SYS:ARCHIVE\JULY
```

You then see the source and destination of the file as well as the names of the files being copied; it should resemble the following:

```
From    TRAINING_SOLUTIONS/SYS:DATA/REPORTS
To      TRAINING_SOLUTIONS/SYS:ARCHIVE/JULY
```

```
MASTER.DAT    to   MASTER.DAT
MAILING.DAT   to   MAILING.DAT
2 files copied.
```

See also

FILER

NDIR   F>

Purpose

Lists detailed file and subdirectory information, including NetWare specific information. The NDIR command can perform the following functions:

List files and subdirectories

Search a volume for a file

List specific files

Use wild cards to list related files

Use an option to list files

Use several options to list files

List Macintosh files

Syntax

NDIR *path option . . .*

Options

path	Identifies the directory path leading to and including the directory and file you want to list. You can include a file chain of up to 16 file names.
option	Can be one of the following:
	Attribute options
	Format options

Restriction options

Sort options

A list of the more commonly used options follows. Use a space between multiple options.

RO Lists files that have the read only attribute set.

S Lists files that have the shareable attribute set.

A Lists files that have their archive attribute set. Files are displayed in the backup format, which lists the last modified and last archived dates. The archive flag is set whenever a file is modified.

EX Lists files that are flagged as execute only.

H Lists files or directories that have the hidden attribute set.

SY Lists files or directories that have the system attribute set.

T Lists files that have been flagged as transactional.

I Lists files that have been flagged as index files.

P Lists files or directories that have the purge attribute set. (NetWare 3.x only.)

RA Lists files flagged as read audit. (NetWare 3.x only.) (Not currently implemented.)

WA Lists files flagged as write audit. (NetWare 3.x only.) (Not currently implemented.)

CI Lists files flagged as copy inhibited. Restricts copyrights of users logged in from Macintosh workstation. Only valid for files.

DI Lists files or directories flagged as delete inhibited. Prevents users from erasing directories or files even if they have the erase right.

RI Lists files and directories flagged as rename inhibited. Prevents users from renaming directories and files even if they have the Modify right.

D Lists time and date stamp information about files. Shows the date last modified, last archived, last accessed, and the date created.

R Lists your access rights on selected files (NetWare 3.11 only), lists inherited and effective rights on files and subdirectories, and shows file flags. On NetWare 2.x systems, no rights are associated with files, therefore the rights field will be empty.

MAC	Lists Macintosh subdirectories or files in a search area. When you list only Macintosh files or subdirectories, they appear with their full Macintosh names.
LONG	Lists all Macintosh, OS/2, and NFS long file names for the file under all loaded name spaces in a given search area.
HELP	Lists the NDIR command format and available command options.
OW	Lists files created by a specific user.
SI	Lists files by their sizes.
UP	Lists files by their last update date.
CR	Lists file by their creation date.
AC	Lists file by their last accessed date.
AR	Lists files by their archive date.
FO	Lists only files in a directory.
DO	Lists only subdirectories in a directory.
SUB	Applies the NDIR command to all subdirectories and subsequent subdirectories in a directory.

Rules and Considerations

Use a forward slash (/) before the first element of the option list and backslashes (\) in path names.

Each NDIR command can include up to 16 file names.

Example

To list all files in all subdirectories on the NetWare volume SYS, type the following:

```
NDIR SYS:*.* /SUB FO
```

The FO option excludes the listing of any subdirectory names found during the directory search.

Note

You may combine several restriction options in a single NDIR command line. For a full listing of all options and logical operators supported, use NDIR /HELP or refer to the documentation included with NetWare.

See also

FILER

FLAG

NETBIOS   F> 3.11

Purpose

Enables workstations to run applications that support IBM's NETBIOS networking calls. You also can view NetWare NETBIOS version information, determine whether NETBIOS has been loaded, determine which interrupt it is using, or unload NETBIOS.

Syntax

```
NETBIOS options
```

Options

Inquire   Views version information, whether NETBIOS has been loaded, and which interrupt it is using. Using this switch will not reload NETBIOS.

Unload   Unloads NETBIOS from memory.

Example

```
NETBIOS
```

NETX.COM   F> 3.11

Purpose

Provides an interface between the application and DOS. NETX intercepts all interrupt 21h DOS requests and inspects each one. After inspection, the shell either passes the request to the DOS interrupt routine or keeps it and converts the request into the appropriate NCP request, and sends it to IPX/SPX for transmission to the file server.

Older versions of the shell included NETx.COM. The X in NETx.COM is replaced with the version of DOS you are using at the workstation—NET3.COM for DOS 3.x, NET4.COM for DOS 4.x, and NET5.COM for DOS 5.x. There is a generic version of NETx.COM called NETX.COM.

Syntax

`NETX` *option*

Options

`/I`	Displays information about the shell type and the revision level of the NETx file.
`/U`	Unloads the NETx shell from the workstation's memory. NETx must be the last terminate-and-stay-resident (TSR) program loaded.
`PS=`*servername*	Specifies your preferred server. The shell attempts to attach you to the server you specify rather than the first available.

Rules and Considerations

NETX.COM must be loaded after IPX.COM has been loaded.

Important Message

```
Not running on top of DOS 3.x.
```

This message means you tried to load the wrong version of NETX. Use the VER command to find the version of DOS you are using and execute the proper NETX.COM command.

See also

IPX/SPX

NMAGENT.NLM   :LOAD 3.11

Purpose

Manages LAN drivers by collecting and storing information about them as they are loaded.

Syntax

```
LOAD path NMAGENT
```

The path should be specified only if the NMAGENT.NLM file is not in the SYS:SYSTEM directory.

Rules and Considerations

The NMAGENT (Network Management Agent) command must be loaded prior to any LAN drivers being loaded to enable it to register the LAN drivers. If NMAGENT has not been loaded, NetWare will attempt to load NMAGENT before it honors a request to load a LAN driver.

Examples

To load NMAGENT from the SYS:LOGIN directory, type the following:

```
LOAD SYS:LOGIN/NMAGENT
```

To load NMAGENT from the SYS:SYSTEM directory of file server FS1, type the following:

```
LOAD NMAGENT
```

Note

See the Netware System Administration manual for a list of the resources that are tracked by NMAGENT.

NPRINT

F>

Purpose

Sends a file from the disk to a NetWare print queue. The NPRINT command is the NetWare substitute for the DOS PRINT command.

Syntax

```
NPRINT filespec options
```

Options

NPRINT supports the following options:

Banner=*banner name*
Determines whether a banner (a word or phrase up to 12 characters) is printed. Spaces are entered by using the underscore character (above the minus on most keyboards). The default is the name of the file you are printing.

Copies=*n*
Specifies the number of copies to print from 1 to 999.

Delete
Deletes a file immediately after it is printed.

Form=*frm*
Specifies the name or number of a previously defined form. The default is the form specified in your default print job configuration if it has been defined.

Form**F**eed
Sends a form feed to the printer after the job has printed. The default is enabled.

Job=*jobname*
Specifies which print job configuration to use. Print job configurations can be created using PRINTCON. A single print job configuration can define the settings for all of the options for NPRINT with a single option.

NAMe=*username*
Specifies the name that appears on the top part of the banner page. The default is the user's login name.

`NoBanner`	Prints without the banner page. The default is for the banner page to print.
`NoFormFeed`	Does not send a form feed to the printer after the job has printed. The default is to send a form feed to the printer after a job has printed.
`NoNOTIfy`	Prevents the operating system from notifying you when a print job has finished printing. (This option is only necessary if NOTIfy is enabled in your print job configuration and you want to ignore it.)
`NoTabs`	Stops NetWare from altering your tabs before they are sent to the printer.
`NOTIfy`	Notifies you when the print job has been sent to the printer.
`Queue=queuename`	Identifies which queue the job is sent to. Queues may be defined with PCONSOLE.
`Server=servername`	Specifies which server the print job should be sent to for printing. The default is the current server.
`Tabs=n`	Indicates the number of spaces between tabs, ranging from 0 to 18. The default is 8 spaces.

Rules and Considerations

To use the NPRINT command, you first must create print queues. You can manage print queues with the PCONSOLE menu utility program.

If you execute NPRINT with the filespec to print and no options, the file will be sent to the print queue specified in the default print job configuration. If no default print job configuration has been set, the print job will be sent to, for example, PRINTQ_0, or the name of your default queue.

Print job configurations should be created with the PRINTCON menu utility program before use.

Forms should be defined with the PRINTDEF menu utility program prior to using them in print job configurations.

Important Messages

```
Access to the server FS1 denied.
```

This error occurs if you attempt to use NPRINT to print to server FS1 using the `Server=FS1` option, and you were denied access to the server. The GUEST account is usually used to attach to another server for printing purposes. If the GUEST account has a password assigned, you will get this error message.

To correct the error, attach to the server you are trying to print from and supply your correct user name and password for that server, or get the supervisor to remove the password requirements for the GUEST user.

```
Illegal banner specification. (length 1 - 12)
```

This error occurs if you attempt to use the `banner=` option without entering a banner name, or if you enter a banner longer than 12 characters.

To print a print job without a banner use the NB option instead of trying `banner=(nothing)`.

Examples

To send 10 copies of the OLDMEMO.TXT file in the root directory of drive A: to the printer serviced by the print queue HPLASER, type the following:

```
NPRINT A:\OLDMEMO.TXT Q=HPLASER C=10 NB NOTIFY
```

The print job prints without a banner, and the user is notified when the print job has been completely sent to the printer.

To send one copy of the MYMEMO.TXT file in the current directory to the printer serviced by PRINTQ_1, type the following:

```
NPRINT MYMEMO.TXT Q=PRINTQ_1
```

The print job prints with a banner showing the user's name on the upper half and MYMEMO.TXT on the lower half. The user will not be notified when the print job is completed.

To send the number of copies of the file 123DATA.PRN in the current directory to the printer serviced by the print queue defined in the print job configuration called TOSHIBA, type the following:

```
NPRINT 123DATA.PRN J=TOSHIBA
```

This print job configuration contains settings for tabs, notification, form feeds, banners, copies, and so on. Print job configurations are created with the PRINTCON utility.

Notes

Be careful when using the Delete option when printing a file you cannot reproduce. In the case of a paper jam, or even in some instances when a printer is turned off, when you send something to its print queues, you could be left without your printout and without the file necessary to re-create the printout.

Use the NB (NoBanner) option when sending EPS (Encapsulated PostScript) files to a PostScript printer to be certain that the banner information does not interfere with the printing of the PostScript information.

Use the NFF option when the file you are printing contains a form feed as the last character. If so, an extra blank page is printed after your print file. If this is the case, print the file with the NFF option.

Use PCONSOLE to cancel erroneous print jobs you have started printing using NPRINT.

Refer to Chapter 8 for information on setting up print jobs using the following NetWare Menu Utilities: PCONSOLE, PRINTCON, and PRINTDEF.

See also

CAPTURE

NVER   F>

Purpose

Reports the versions of NetBIOS, IPX/SPX, LAN driver, workstation shell, workstation DOS, and file server operating system for your file server and workstation.

Syntax

NVER

Example

NVER

The NVER displays the following sample output:

```
NETWARE VERSION UTILITY, VERSION 3.12
IPX Version: 3.02
SPX Version: 3.02

LAN Driver: NetWare Ethernet NE2000 V1.03EC (891227) V1.00
            IRQ - 2, I/O Base - 340h, no DMA or RAM

Shell:     V3.10 Rev. A
DOS:       MSDOS V5.00 on IBM_PC

FileServer: FS1
Novell Dedicated NetWare V2.2(100) Rev. A (02/11/91)
```

Notes

Use DOS redirection (>) to redirect NVER output to a file or printer. You will find the version information handy when trying to diagnose software problems or find differences between two workstations.

Refer to the NetWare manuals for information on the SYSCON and FCONSOLE menu utilities, which report file server software version information and performance statistics.

See also

IPX

NETx

OFF

Purpose

Clears the file server console screen, similar to CLS in DOS.

Syntax

```
OFF
```

Example

```
OFF
```

Note

Using OFF to clear an active MONITOR screen adds to the life of your video display and increases performance slightly.

PAUDIT   F>

Purpose

Displays the system's accounting records including login time, logout time, service charges, and intruder detection information.

Syntax

```
PAUDIT
```

Rules and Considerations

To use PAUDIT, the accounting services first must be installed on your file server using SYSCON.

Example

To display systems information, type the following:

```
PAUDIT
```

The screen returns information such as the following:

```
12/15/92 21:34:37  File server FS1
   NOTE: about User DKLADIS during File Server services.
   Login from address 99000001:00001B0ACD9C.
12/15/92 22:40:07  File Server FS1
   NOTE: about User DKLADIS during File Server services.
   Logout from address 99000001:00001B0ACD9C.
12/16/92 7:49:12  File Server FS1
   NOTE: about User SUPERVISOR during File Server services.
   Login from address 99000001:0080C820A5FB.
```

```
12/16/92 9:23:56  File Server FS1
   NOTE: about User SUPERVISOR during File Server services.
   Logout from address 99000001:0080C820A5FB.
12/16/92 9:24:36  File Server FS1
   NOTE: about User LBUCK during File Server services.
   Login from address 99000001:00001B0ACD9C.
```

Notes

PAUDIT.EXE is located in SYS:SYSTEM. Make sure you change to SYS:SYSTEM before you try to run PAUDIT.

Press Pause on newer 101-key keyboards to stop the scrolling, or press Ctrl-S on older keyboards.

You can redirect output from PAUDIT to a file with the DOS redirection operator (>), such as: **PAUDIT > TODAY.AUD**.

You can reset the accounting detail by erasing the NET$ACCT.DAT file in the SYS:SYSTEM directory.

See also

ATOTAL

PRINTER   :

Purpose

The PRINTER console command enables many options for controlling NetWare printers. This command is available in NetWare 286 only. Most of these functions may be performed using PRINTCON under both NetWare 286 and 386.

Syntax

PRINTER *options*

or

P *options*

Options

The PRINTER command has many functions, as shown in the following list. Be sure to substitute a valid printer number for the variable *n*. Valid printer numbers range from 0 to 4.

`PRINTER`	Lists information about printers attached to the file server, including on-line status, mounted forms, form number mounted, and the number of queues that are being serviced.
`PRINTER HELP`	Lists printer commands available from the file server console.
`PRINTER n ADD QUEUE queuename [AT PRIORITY]`	Adds an existing queue to printer *n*.
`PRINTER n CONFIG`	Shows the configuration for printer *n*.
`PRINTER n CREATE port`	Creates a NetWare printer process for a particular port. Valid port options are COM1, COM2, LPT1, LPT2, and so on.
`PRINTER n CREATE COMx options`	Changes configuration of a serial printer *n* attached to the file server's serial printer port *x*.

The options that are not specified remain unchanged. These options include the following:

Baud is the baud rate in bits per second

Wordsize is the number of data bits

Parity is the type of parity

XonXoff is handshaking

Stopbits is the number of stop bits

Poll is the polling period

`PRINTER n DELETE QUEUE queuename`	Stops a printer from servicing a particular queue temporarily. The queue may be added again with `PRINTER n ADD QUEUE queuename`.
`PRINTER n FORM FEED`	Sends a form feed to printer *n*.

`PRINTER n FORM MARK`	Prints a line of asterisks (*) marking the current top of form for printer *n*.
`PRINTER n MOUNT FORM frm`	Changes the type of form mounted in printer *n* to form number *frm*. Use PRINTDEF to define forms.
`PRINTER n POLL period`	Sets the polling period (amount of time the printer process waits to check printer queues for print jobs). The polling period default is 15 seconds and may be set from 1 to 60 seconds.
`PRINTER n QUEUE`	Displays a list of printer queues and priority levels.
`PRINTER n REWIND p PAGES`	Restarts the current print job on printer *n*, first rewinding the print job *p* number of pages. If the print job does not contain form feeds, or you attempt to rewind more than 9 pages, the print job will restart at the beginning.
`PRINTER n START`	Restarts a printer that has been stopped with `PRINTER n STOP`.
`PRINTER n STOP`	Stops printer *n*. The printer can be restarted with `PRINTER n START`.

Rules and Considerations

Valid printer numbers range from 0 to 4.

Examples

To use the PRINTER console command to set up NetWare core printing for a laser printer attached to LPT1: as printer 0 on the file server and assign it to an existing print queue named HPLASER, type the following:

```
PRINTER 0 CREATE LPT1

PRINTER 0 ADD HPLASER
```

To print a line of asterisks at the top of the page to check form alignment on a matrix printer attached to the file server as printer 2, type the following:

```
PRINTER 2 FORM MARK
```

To restart a printout a couple of pages back after a printer jam on a printer attached to the file server as printer 1, type the following:

```
PRINTER 1 REWIND 2 PAGES
```

Note

The PRINTER command controls and creates print jobs that also are controlled through several NetWare menu utilities. Information on these menu utilities can be found in Chapter 8. See PCONSOLE, PRINTDEF, PRINTCON, and SYSCON for more information on creating and controlling printer processes and print jobs.

See also

PSC   PSERVER (loadable module)

PSERVER (DOS executable)   PSTAT

PSC   F> 3.11

Purpose

The PSC command offers many of the same features as the NetWare PCONSOLE menu utility regarding printer status checking and print server control. If you use PSC, these status checking and print server control features are available from the DOS command line.

Syntax

```
PSC PS=printservername P=printernumber options
```

Replace `printservername` with the name of the print server you want to check or manage.

Replace `printernumber` with the number of the printer you want to check or manage.

See the Switches section for a list of valid options.

Options

Option	Meaning	Description
AB	ABort	Cancels the current print job and continues with the next print job in the queue.
CD	CancelDown	Use this option to reverse the effects of the "Going down after current jobs" selection in PCONSOLE
STAT	STATus	Displays the status of the printer.
PAU	PAUse	Pauses printing temporarily.
STO	STOp	Stops the printer. Use **STOP Keep** to resubmit the current job. Without Keep, the current job is deleted.
STAR	STARt	Starts the printer after it has been paused or stopped.
M	Mark	Prints a line of asterisks on the current line.
FF	Form Feed	Advances the printer to the top of the next page. The printer first must be paused or stopped.
MO F=n	MOunt Form	Replaces n with the number of a form that has been defined in PRINTDEF.
PRI	PRIvate	Changes a remote printer to a local printer so that network users cannot access it.
SH	SHared	Changes a private printer back to shared status.

Rules and Considerations

Print server operators can use any of the PSC features; regular NetWare users can use only the status checking features.

You can include PS– or P– or both with the PSC command.

Printer numbers are defined first using the PCONSOLE menu utility when the print server is set up. They may then be used with PSC from the DOS command line.

Important Messages

```
You must specify the print server name.
```

In the preceding message, PSC requires that you specify a print server name. If you want to set a default print server, use the SET PSC command. The following message appears if a syntax error appears in the PSC command:

```
The specified action is not supported.
```

To correct this problem, retype the PSC command line carefully and check spelling and syntax.

Examples

To stop an unwanted printing of the current job on print server ACCTNG, enter the following:

```
PSC PS=ACCTNG P=1 STOP
```

To notify NetWare that you have changed the type of paper loaded in printer 2 on printserver ADMIN to a paper type of 35, enter the following:

```
PSC PS=ADMIN P=2 MO F=35
```

Note

Many of these functions can be performed with PCONSOLE if a menu-driven utility is preferred. PSC is particularly helpful in batch files.

See also

PRINTER

PSERVER.EXE (DOS executable)

A>DOS EXECUTABLE

3.11, 2.2, 2.1x

Purpose

Use PSERVER to configure a personal computer as a dedicated print server.

Syntax

```
PSERVER fileservername printservername
```

The *fileservername* parameter is optional. Specify a valid print server name for the *printservername* parameter.

Rules and Considerations

Before you can run PSERVER, you must first use the NetWare PCONSOLE command to configure the print server.

Print servers created with the PSERVER command can support up to 16 printers and can service queues up to 8 file servers.

To run PSERVER, you must have access to IBM$RUN.OVL, SYS$ERR.DAT, SYS$HELP.DAT, and SYS$MSG.DAT.

See the Chapter 8 for more information on the PSERVER.EXE program.

Important Messages

If you have a print server named LASERS and the following message appears, you already started a print server named LASERS:

```
There is already a print server named LASERS running.
```

If you want to load a second print server with the same configuration as LASERS, create another print server and give it a different name.

If the following message appears when you try to print from your workstation on the network, your workstation does not have enough SPX connections:

```
There are not enough SPX connections to run the print server.
```

To create more SPX connections, add the following line to the SHELL.CFG file in the workstation's boot directory:

```
SPX CONNECTIONS=60
```

Example

To load a print server named ACCTNG on the ADMIN file server, enter:

```
PSERVER ADMIN ACCTNG
```

Note

Use the PCONSOLE command from any workstation to shut down a print server that was started with the PSERVER command.

See also

> PSC
>
> PSERVER.NLM (loadable module)

PSERVER.NLM   :LOAD 3.11

Purpose

Loads a print server on a NetWare 3.11 file server. PSERVER is a loadable module.

Syntax

> `LOAD` *path* `PSERVER` *printservername*

The path should be specified only if the PSERVER.NLM file is not in the SYS:SYSTEM directory.

Rules and Considerations

Before you can load PSERVER, you must use the PCONSOLE NetWare menu utility to set up print queues, print servers, and printers.

The PSERVER.NLM command can support a total of 16 printers, including as many as 5 local printers depending on the number of parallel and serial ports on the server. The PSERVER.NLM command can support up to 16 remote printers run using the RPRINTER command.

Example

To start a print server called MAIN that has already been configured with the PCONSOLE menu utility, switch to the file server console and enter the following command:

> `LOAD PSERVER MAIN`

Note

It is usually desirable to load PSERVER automatically each time you boot the file server. To do so, use the INSTALL command to include a `LOAD PSERVER` *printservername* command in the server's AUTOEXEC.NCF file. Replace *printservername* with the name of the print server you want to load.

See also

PSERVER.EXE (DOS executable)

PSTAT   F> 2.2

Purpose

Displays printer status information.

Syntax

PSTAT S=servername P=printer

Options

S=*servername* Designates the name of a valid file server.

P=*printer*   Designates *printer* is either a valid printer name or printer number.

Rules and Considerations

Before you can use the PSTAT command to check printers on a server, you must first attach or log in to the server.

You do not need to supply the name of the server (S= option) if it is the default server.

Notes

An off-line printer will be listed as on-line until you attempt to print to it.

Use the PCONSOLE NetWare menu utility to obtain individual print job status.

See also

PRINTER

PSC

PURGE
F>

Purpose

Prevents previously erased files from being salvaged.

Syntax

```
PURGE filepath /ALL
```

Options

filepath	An optional parameter that accepts wild-card characters.
/ALL	Deletes all recoverable files in the current directory and in all subdirectories.

Rules and Considerations

If you type `Purge` with no options, all of the recoverable files in the current directory will be removed. The Purge command used with no options has the same effect as entering a file path with the *.* wild cards.

Examples

To permanently remove all recoverable erased files on a file server volume, log in as SUPERVISOR and enter the following command at the volume root directory:

```
PURGE /ALL
```

To purge only your DOC files in the SHAREDOC directory on file server FS2 on volume DATA, enter the command:

```
PURGE FS2/DATA:SHAREDOC\*.DOC
```

Note

See related information in Chapters 9 and 10 on the SALVAGE and FCONSOLE
menu utility programs.

QUEUE : 2.2

Purpose

Creates and maintains NetWare print queues. Displays a list of print queues including information about the number of jobs in each print queue, print queue name, and
the number of printers servicing each queue.

Syntax

```
QUEUE options
```

or

```
Q options
```

Options

HELP	Displays a list of valid options.
queuename CHANGE JOB *jobnumber* TO PRIORITY *prioritylevel*	The *quename* variable is the name of a valid print queue. The *jobnumber* variable is replaced by a particular print job whose priority you want to change. The *prioritylevel* variable is the new priority level for the print job that you want to change. A priority level of 1 will move the print job to the top of the queue; a priority level of 1 plus the number of jobs in the queue will move the job to the end of the queue.
QUEUE *queuename* CREATE	Use the *queuename* variable for the name for the new print queue. Used in lieu of PCONSOLE to create print queues from the console instead of a workstation.

`QUEUE queuename` `DELETE JOB jobnumber`	In the *queuename* location, specify the print queue that contains the print job(s) you would like to cancel. The *jobnumber* is the actual number of the particular print job. If you type an asterisk for the job number, all print jobs in the queue will be deleted.
`QUEUE queuename DESTROY`	Completely destroys the print queue *queuename* and all of its print jobs.
`QUEUE queuename JOBS`	Displays a list of print jobs for the *queuename* print queue.

Rules and Considerations

Do not use the QUEUE command on a network running the NetWare Name Service.

Important Messages

If the message `Queue already exists.` displays after you enter the QUEUE command, you are attempting to create a queue with the same name as an existing queue. Change the name and reenter the command.

The message `The specified Queue does not exist.` displays if you enter the name of a queue that does not exist on this server. Correct the name and reenter the command.

The message `Unknown Queue Command.` displays if you enter the QUEUE command incorrectly. Retype the command and then check the syntax.

Examples

To create a print queue for dot-matrix printers, enter the following at the console:

```
QUEUE MATRIX CREATE
```

To create a print queue specifically for the sales staff, enter the following at the console:

```
QUEUE SALES CREATE
```

To list all the print jobs in a print queue named HPLASER, enter the following command at the console:

```
QUEUE HPLASER JOBS
```

To display a list of queues and their current status at the console, enter the command:

```
QUEUE
```

Notes

Use the PCONSOLE utility instead of the QUEUE command on NetWare Name Service (NNS) Networks.

See related information in Chapter 8 on the PCONSOLE menu utility.

See also

PRINTER

PSC

REGISTER MEMORY   : 3.11

Purpose

Enables NetWare to recognize more than 16M of system memory.

Syntax

```
REGISTER MEMORY memstart memlen
```

Rules and Considerations

The memory length *memlen* must end on an even paragraph boundary divisible by 0x10.

Example

To make the file server recognize 4M of additional memory starting at the 16M boundary, enter the following command at the console:

```
REGISTER MEMORY 0x1000000 0x100000
```

REMIRROR   : 2.2

Purpose

Restores a duplexed or mirrored drive pair when one drive has been replaced.

Syntax

```
REMIRROR drivenumber
```

Rules and Considerations

In the *drivenumber* place, specify the drive that needs to be updated. The REMIRROR command updates the hard disk drive to contain the same information as the mirrored drive.

Important Messages

```
Mirror drive will be auto remirrored.
```

If the preceding message appears after the system boots, the file server noticed during the boot that the mirror drive had been replaced or had previously failed. The file server automatically attempts to REMIRROR the drive if the drive previously failed or was replaced; you do not have to enter REMIRROR manually in this situation.

The following sample error message indicates that mirroring has failed on the file server CSOS drive 01, which affects the SYS volume:

```
Mirroring turned off on CSOS. Drive 01 failed. Mirroring turned
off on SYS.
```

To correct this problem, you enter `REMIRROR 01`

Example

To update drive 01 so that it matches drive 00 in a mirrored pair, enter the command:

```
REMIRROR 01
```

Notes

Remirroring hard disk drives is often a slow process. During the remirror operation, file server response is slow because one drive's information is being copied in the background.

If you do not shut down the file server after a mirrored drive pair has failed, REMIRROR will need to copy only the information that has changed since the mirror process failed. If you shut down the server, REMIRROR must copy the entire contents of one drive to the other drive, which is a lengthy process.

See also

UNMIRROR

REMOTE   :LOAD 3.11

Purpose

Enables you to use the RCONSOLE utility to run the file server console from a workstation.

Syntax

LOAD *path* **REMOTE** *remotepassword*

Option

remotepassword   Replace this variable with the password that you want all remote administrators to use.

Rules and Considerations

The path need only be specified if REMOTE.NLM is not found in the SYS:SYSTEM directory.

The *remotepassword* variable defaults to the SUPERVISOR password if no password is specified.

You can load RSPX only after REMOTE is loaded so that you can access the RCONSOLE utility.

Examples

To load remote file server console support using the password "SECRET," enter the following command at the console:

```
LOAD REMOTE SECRET
LOAD RSPX
```

To load remote file server console support using the SUPERVISOR password, enter the following at the console:

```
LOAD REMOTE
LOAD RSPX
```

To load remote file server console support from the SYS:NLM subdirectory using the password ABCDEFG, enter the following at the console:

```
LOAD SYS:NLM/REMOTE ABCDEFG
LOAD RSPX
```

Note

You can access the remote console even when the file server console is in use, and both can display different information.

See also

RS232

RSPX

REMOVE   F>

Purpose

Deletes users and groups from file and directory trustee lists.

Syntax

REMOVE USER *username* FROM *path option*

or

REMOVE GROUP *groupname* FROM *path option*

The *username* and *groupname* variables indicate either a user or a group that is to be removed from a directory or file trustee list. Indicate the path to the directory or file in the *path* variable.

Options

/S   Removes the user or group from all subdirectories in the specified path.

/F   Removes the user or group from files in the specified path.

Rules and Considerations

The USER and GROUP specifiers are only necessary when users and groups have the same name; otherwise the REMOVE command automatically distinguishes between users and groups.

If you enter REMOVE with only a user or group name, the user or group is removed from the trustee list of the current directory.

Important Messages

```
User or group "HORST" not found.
```

In the preceding example, the message indicates that no user or group named HORST exists on this server. Reenter the command with the correct name.

```
CSOS/APPS:ALLDOCS
User "FRED" no longer a trustee to the specified directory.

Trustee "FRED" removed from 1 directories.
```

The preceding example message confirms that the user FRED was successfully removed as a trustee from the directory ALLDOCS on disk volume APPS of file server CSOS.

```
CSOS/APPS:DATENTRY
Group "TEMPS" no longer a trustee to the specified directory.

Trustee "TEMPS" removed from 1 directories.
```

The preceding example message confirms that the group TEMPS was successfully removed as a trustee from the directory DATENTRY on disk volume APPS of file server CSOS.

```
CSOS/SYS:JUNK
No trustee for the specified Directory.
```

The previous sample error message displays when a user or group exists, but they are not a trustee of the specified directory or file.

Examples

To remove the group TEMPS as a trustee from the DATENTRY subdirectory on volume APPS of server CSOS, enter the command:

```
REMOVE GROUP TEMPS FROM CSOS\APPS:DATENTRY
```

To remove the user FRED from the trustee list of the ALLDOCS subdirectory on volume APPS of file server CSOS, enter the command:

```
REMOVE FRED FROM CSOS/APPS:ALLDOCS
```

To remove tthe user FRED from the trustee list of all the subdirectories of the ALLDOCS directory on volume APPS of file server CSOS, enter the command:

```
REMOVE FRED FROM CSOS/APPS:ALLDOCS /S
```

Notes

Refer to the Netware documentation on SYSCON and FILER NetWare menu utilities for related information.

The /S option only removes the user or group from the trustee lists of every subdirectory of the specified directory path; the /S option does not affect the trustee rights to the specified directory.

See also

GRANT   REVOKE
MAKEUSER   TLIST

REMOVE DOS   : 3.11

Purpose

Removes DOS completely from a NetWare 3.11 file server memory, eliminating access to DOS.

Syntax

```
REMOVE DOS
```

Rules and Considerations

After you remove DOS from the file server, the system will perform a warm boot when you issue the EXIT command at the file server console; the system does not return to DOS.

If you remove DOS from the file server, Network Loadable Modules (NLMs) cannot be loaded from floppy disk drive partitions or the server's DOS hard drive partitions.

Important Message

```
DOS access has been removed from file server.
```

The previous message displays after DOS is successfully removed from memory. To reload DOS access, you must shut down the file server and reboot.

Example

To remove DOS access from the file server, enter the command:

```
REMOVE DOS
```

Using this command ensures that unauthorized NLMs cannot be loaded at the file server console.

Note

If you use the REMOVE DOS command to disable DOS access on the file server, you still can copy NLMs into the SYS:SYSTEM subdirectory from a workstation.

RENDIR   F>

Purpose

Renames a file server subdirectory without affecting the trustee rights to that directory.

Syntax

```
RENDIR dirpath newname
```

Rules and Considerations

If you have no trustee rights to a directory, you cannot change its name.

The RENDIR command renames a directory, but it does not affect the directory's trustee or user rights.

Important Messages

```
Directory renamed to DEPTDOCS.
```

The preceding message confirms that you successfully renamed a sample directory to DEPTDOCS.

```
The path specification (directory name) was incorrect.
```

The preceding message displays if you try to rename a subdirectory that does not exist or one that does not exist on the specified directory path. Correct the original directory path and name and retry the command.

Examples

To rename the MYDOCS subdirectory to DEPTDOCS on the DOCS partition of file server FS3, type the command:

```
RENDIR FS3/DOCS:MYDOCS DEPTDOCS
```

If you want to give the current directory a new name, you can use a period (.) to specify the current directory path. To duplicate the previous example, use the Change Directory command (CD) to make the FS3/DOCS:MYDOCS subdirectory current, and then enter:

```
RENDIR . DEPTDOCS
```

Notes

Changing directory names with RENDIR does not update MAP commands in DOS batch files or NetWare login scripts. If you do use RENDIR to rename a directory that you previously accessed using MAP commands, rewrite any affected MAP commands in the login scripts and batch files.

You can find additional file management capabilities in the NetWare FILER menu utility. This utility is described in Chapter 6.

RESET ROUTER

Purpose

Updates inaccurate or corrupted router tables that result from file server or network bridge failure.

Syntax

```
RESET ROUTER
```

Rules and Considerations

The RESET ROUTER command is used only when inaccurate or corrupted router tables must be rebuilt.

Important Message

```
Router has been reset.
```

According to the preceding message, the router table for this server has been rebuilt.

Example

To rebuild the router on a NetWare file server, go to the file server console and enter the command:

```
RESET ROUTER
```

Note

The router tables are automatically updated every two minutes. Use the RESET ROUTER command on every network file server to update the router table sooner than the automatic two minute time period.

See also

TRACK OFF
TRACK ON

REVOKE

F>

Purpose

Enables you to revoke individual trustee rights for files or directories from users and groups.

Syntax

REVOKE *rightslist* *path* FROM USER *username* /SUB or /FILE

REVOKE rightslist *path* FROM GROUP *groupname* /SUB or /FILE

Options

rightslist   The rightslist can consist of one or several of the following rights attributes. Each attribute must be separated by a space:

Right	Description	NetWare 2.2 or 3.11
ALL	All	BOTH
A	Access Control	BOTH
C	Create	BOTH
E	Erase	BOTH
F	File Scan	BOTH
M	Modify	BOTH
R	Read	BOTH
S	Supervisor	3.11
W	Write	BOTH

path   Optional variable that defaults to the current directory if no path is specified.

username   Specifies a single existing user who will have his or her rights revoked.

groupname   Specifies a single existing group that is to have its rights revoked.

/SUB	Affect subdirectories of the selected directory.
/FILE	Affect files of the selected directory.

Rules and Considerations

The *rightslist* variable can consist of one or several rights separated by spaces.

If the path is omitted, REVOKE will default the current directory.

The /FILE and /SUB flags may not be use in the same command.

The /SUB (subdirectory) flag used with REVOKE affects only subdirectories of the selected directory; the directory is not affected.

You must include the USER or GROUP identifiers only if the user or group you want to modify has the same name as another user or group.

Important Messages

```
No trustee for the specified directory.
```

The preceding message displays if the specified directory does not exist. Check the spelling and retry the command.

```
User or group "ACCNTG" not found.
```

In the preceding example, no user or group was found with the name ACCNTG. Check the user or group name and retry the command.

```
CSOS/DOCS:SPECDOCS
Trustee's access rights set to [RWC MFA]

Rights for 1 directories were changed for DEDE.
```

The preceding example confirms the E (Erase) trustee right was successfully revoked from user DEDE in the SYS:SPECDOCS directory.

Examples

To block the user DEDE from erasing files in the SPECDOCS subdirectory on volume DOCS of the default file server, enter the command:

```
REVOKE E DOCS:SPECDOCS FROM USER DEDE
```

To remove completely the user STEPHEN from the subdirectory SHAREDOC on the VOL1 volume on file server SP1, enter the command:

```
REVOKE ALL SP1/VOL1:SHAREDOC FROM USER STEPHEN
```

Continuing with the last example, to revoke the erase right for all the files in the SHAREDOC subdirectory for group ADMIN, enter the command:

```
REVOKE E SP1/VOL1:SHARDOC FROM GROUP ADMIN /FILE
```

Notes

When you revoke rights, make sure you do not alter the rights for the EVERYONE group in the LOGIN, MAIL, and PUBLIC system directories. If these rights are changed, the system will not work as expected.

For more information on the SYSCON menu utility, see Chapter 7. This chapter lists additional features for maintaining trustee rights for users and groups.

See also

GRANT

REMOVE

RIGHTS   F>

Purpose

Displays your effective rights to a file or subdirectory.

Syntax

RIGHTS

or

RIGHTS *path*

Option

path   Specifies a valid NetWare volume, a directory, subdirectory, or file path. The path can be listed, for example, as **FS1/SYS:SYSTEM**.

Important Message

```
Specified path not locatable.
Usage:  RIGHTS [path]
```

```
Rights = All    | Read | Write | Create | Erase | Modify
                | Filescan | Access Control
```

If the previous message appears, you specified a directory path that does not exist. Correct the directory path and try again.

Examples

The following sample output lists a user with all rights to the MISCDOCS directory of volume PROGS on file server CSOS:

```
CSOS\PROGS:MISCDOCS
Your Effective Rights for this directory are [RWCEMFA]

           May Read from File.(R)
           May Write to File. (W)
           May Create Subdirectories and Files.   (C)
           May Erase Subdirectories and Files.    (E)
           May Modify File Status Flags.   (M)
           May Scan for Files.(F)
           May Change Access Control.      (A)

           You have ALL RIGHTS to this directory area.
```

The following example output lists a user with limited rights to the PUBLIC directory of volume SYS on file server CSOS:

```
CSOS\SYS:PUBLIC
Your Effective Rights for this directory are [R    F ]

           May Read from File.(R)
           May Scan for Files.(F)
```

Note

See the NetWare menu utilities SYSCON and FILER for menu driven access to directory and file rights.

See also

GRANT
REMOVE
REVOKE

RPRINTER

F>

Purpose

Connects a workstation printer to the network as a remote printer. RPRINTER also is used to disconnect workstation printers from the network.

Syntax

```
RPRINTER printservername printer flag
```

Options

`printservername`	Specify the print server that includes the printer you want to connect to the network.
`printer`	Specify the printer number for the remote printer. This number represents the printer configuration that was defined using the PCONSOLE command.
`-R`	Disconnects the remote printer
`-S`	Displays the status of the remote printer
	No flag connects the remote printer

Rules and Considerations

RPRINTER runs as a TSR (terminate-and-stay-resident) program on the user's workstation. For this reason, the RPRINTER utility requires workstation memory.

If a user's local printer is connected to the network as a remote printer, the user must print to a captured network printer port rather than print directly to the local printer port.

If more than one remote printer is attached to a workstation, the RPRINTER TSR must be loaded for each printer.

The NetWare shells must be loaded on the workstation before the RPRINTER TSR is loaded.

To run RPRINTER, the workstation must have access to the following files:

IBM$RUN.OVL

RPRINT$$.EXE

RPRINTER.HLP

SYS$ERR.DAT

SYS$HELP.DAT

SYS$MSG.DAT

Important Messages

```
No print servers are operating.
```

If the preceding message appears, no printer servers are running. Start a printer server and try to connect the remote printer.

```
RPRINT$$.EXE not found.
```

If the preceding message appears, the RPRINTER utility was not installed with the capability to access all the necessary files. Reinstall RPRINTER so that all the files listed in the Rules and Considerations section are available when you run RPRINTER.

Examples

To load RPRINTER on a workstation that has been set up properly for remote printer 2 on print server ADMIN, enter the command:

RPRINTER ADMIN 2

To remove the remote printer defined in the previous example, enter the command:

RPRINTER ADMIN 2 -R

To check the status of remote printer number 2 on print server ADMIN, enter the command:

RPRINTER ADMIN 2 -S

Notes

To support a remote printer, the workstation must not be rebooted. If a workstation supporting remote printers is rebooted, the RPRINTER TSR must be reloaded for each remote printer connected to the workstation.

The commands for connecting remote printers can be loaded by the AUTOEXEC.BAT file of the workstation if the NetWare shells are loaded before the RPRINTER utility is run.

For example, include the following commands in AUTOEXEC.BAT:

```
CD\NET
IPX
NETX
RPRINTER ADMIN 2
CD \
```

The preceding example assumes that IPX, NETX, RPRINTER, and all required files are located in C:\NET.

RS232   :LOAD 3.11

Purpose

Enables you to access the file server console over asynchronous communications ports or a modem. The RS232 command is used with the REMOTE.NLM.

Syntax

```
LOAD RS232 comport speed
```

Options

comport   Valid options for this variable are 1 for COM1 or 2 for COM2.

speed   Valid options for this variable are 2400, 4800, or 9600 for the data transfer rate of the modem.

If you do not enter the *comport* or *speed* variables when RS232 is loaded, you will be prompted to do so.

Example

To load remote support for a 9600 bps modem attached to COM2 on the file server, enter the command:

```
LOAD RS232 2 9600
```

Notes

REMOTE.NLM must be loaded before RS232 so that you can use the RS232 NLM as a remote console.

See the Remote Management section of the *NetWare System Administration* manual for more information on the RS232 NLM.

See also

REMOTE

RSPX

RSPX

Purpose

Used with the REMOTE.NLM, RSPX enables you to access the file server console from a workstation using the RCONSOLE utility program.

Syntax

```
LOAD RSPX
```

Rules and Considerations

To run a remote console, you must first load REMOTE and then RSPX.

Example

To load RSPX.NLM after REMOTE.NLM is loaded, enter the command:

```
LOAD RSPX
```

Note

Use the RCONSOLE menu utility to access the remote console using REMOTE.NLM and RSPX.NLM from any NetWare workstation on the LAN.

See also

REMOTE

RS232

SEARCH :3.11

Purpose

Sets a path at the file server to search for NLMs and network configuration (NCF) files.

Syntax

`SEARCH` *option*

Options

If the SEARCH command is entered by itself with no option, the current search paths display.

ADD *number* **searchpath**

Adds a new search path. The *number* variable is optional and refers to the desired position for inserting the new search path. The **searchpath** variable refers to the new search path.

DEL **number**

Deletes an existing search path. The **number** variable refers to an existing search path and must be included.

Rules and Considerations

Unless SEARCH is used, NetWare examines only the SYS:SYSTEM directory when looking for NLM and NCF files.

If you use the SEARCH ADD command without specifying a number, the new search path is appended to the end of the search paths.

Examples

To search the SYS:NLM and SYS:SYSTEM directories for NLM and NCF files, enter the following command:

`SEARCH ADD SYS:NLM`

To list the current search paths, enter the following command:

`SEARCH`

To delete the search path in the second position, enter the following command:

```
SEARCH DEL 2
```

Note

Use SEARCH if you keep NLMs in directories other than the SYS:SYSTEM directory. If you use SEARCH, you do not need to specify the path for the LOAD command every time you load these NLMs.

See also

LOAD

SECURE CONSOLE

SECURE CONSOLE   : 3.11

Purpose

Removes DOS from the file server and prevents the use of the OS debugger. SECURE CONSOLE also limits the loading of NLMs from only the SYS:SYSTEM directory, and SECURE CONSOLE permits only console operators to change the system date and time.

Syntax

```
SECURE CONSOLE
```

Example

To secure the file server console on a NetWare 386 file server, enter the following command:

```
SECURE CONSOLE
```

Note

The server must be rebooted to reverse the effects of SECURE CONSOLE.

See also

REMOVE DOS

SEARCH

SECURITY   F>

Purpose

Displays a list of possible security problems. This list can include users, passwords, login scripts, and access privileges.

Syntax

```
SECURITY /C
```

Option

/C   Optional switch that continuously lists potential security violations without pausing at the end of every screen page.

Rules and Considerations

To use the SECURITY program, you must log in as the SUPERVISOR or as a supervisor equivalent. The SECURITY program is run from the SYS:SYSTEM directory.

Important Messages

```
Usage: security [/Continuous]
```

If the preceding message appears after you enter the SECURITY command, then you ran the SECURITY program with incorrect syntax. Reenter the command again with the correct syntax.

The following sample output of the SECURITY program shows the types of violations you may encounter:

```
SECURITY EVALUATION UTILITY, Version 2.23

User BRANDON
    Has password expiration interval greater than 60 days
```

```
    Has no password assigned
    No Full Name specified

Group ADMIN
    No Full Name specified

User DANNY (Full Name: Danny R. Kusnierz)
    Is security equivalent to user SUPERVISOR
    Has password expiration interval greater than 60 days
    Has no password assigned

User DEDE (Full Name: Dede Kusnierz )
    Is security equivalent to user SUPERVISOR
    Has password expiration interval greater than 60 days

User GUEST
    Has no login script
    Has no LOGIN_CONTROL property
    No Full Name specified

Group EVERYONE
    No Full Name specified

User SUPERVISOR (Full Name: System Supervisor)
    Does not require a password
```

Example

To print a list of potential security violations on a printer at the LPT1 port, enter the following command:

```
SECURITY > LPT1:
```

Notes

Run SECURITY every time you modify the rights of a user or a group to ensure that you did not mistakenly introduce any security breaches into the system.

See also

GRANT
REVOKE
SETPASS

SEND (command-line utility) F>

Purpose

Enables you to send short messages from your workstation to any of the following: logged in users or groups, the file server console, a particular workstation, or a set of workstations.

Syntax

```
SEND "messagetext" TO destination
```

Options

messagetext	Specifies the message, which can be a maximum of 44 characters minus the length of the sending user's name.
destination	Specifies the user or group that will receive the message. Using any of the following formats, this variable can designate users, groups, the file server console, specific workstations, or all workstations.
USER *userlist*	Enables you to send messages to one or several users. The USER specifier is optional. The *userlist* variable is an optional file server name followed by the name of a user. Multiple users are separated by commas.
GROUP *grouplist*	Enables you to send messages to one or several groups. The GROUP specifier is optional. The *grouplist* variable consists of an optional file server name followed by the name of a group. Separate multiple groups with commas.
servername /CONSOLE	Enables you to send messages to the file server console. The optional *servername* variable specifies a file server; CONSOLE specifies the file server console.
servername/ EVERYBODY	Enables you to send messages to all workstations. The optional *servername* variable specifies a file server; EVERYBODY specifies all workstations.

STATION *servername* */stationlist*	Enables you to send messages to specific workstations. The STATION specifier is optional. The following variables are optional: *servername* defaults to the current server; *stationlist* consists of a station number. Additional station numbers are separated by commas.

Rules and Considerations

A SEND message can be up to 44 characters in length minus the length of your user name. The Supervisor, for example, can send a message only a maximum of 34 characters in length because the word Supervisor is 10 characters long.

If no file server name is specified, the default file server is used.

Users must be logged in to receive messages.

The workstation and login name of the sending user are displayed with the message text.

To send messages to users or groups on another server, you must be attached to that server.

Important Messages

```
User/Group FS1/ALL does not exist.
```

If the preceding message displays, the user or group you specified does not exist. Reenter the message with a valid user or group name.

```
Message sent to CSOS/SUPERVISOR (station 1).
```

In the preceding example, the message was sent successfully to user SUPERVISOR logged in on station 1.

```
Message not sent to CSOS/HEATHER (station 2)
```

According to the preceding example, your message was not sent to the user HEATHER. Either HEATHER used the CASTOFF utility so that her workstation cannot receive messages, or her workstation's incoming message buffer is full. To undo the effects of CASTOFF, HEATHER must use the CASTON utility to re-enable message receipt. If the cause is a full message buffer, HEATHER must read enough messages to make room in the buffer.

Examples

To send a note to all members of the group STAFF about the 4:00 staff meeting, enter the command:

```
SEND "Remember - Staff mtg at 4:00" TO GROUP STAFF
```

or the command:

```
SEND "Remember - Staff mtg at 4:00" TO STAFF
```

To send a note to the file server console to request that the console operator mount form 2 into printer 3 on the file server, enter the command:

```
SEND "Pls mount form 2 in printer 3" TO CONSOLE
```

To send a personal note to user JESSICA, enter the command:

```
SEND "How about dinner tonight @ 8:00" TO JESSICA
```

Notes

If you send a message to a user who is not currently logged in, the message will not be saved. To send messages that are longer than the maximum size allowed for your ID, you must purchase an electronic mail, or email, package. Email packages enable you to send messages to users who are not currently logged in.

Receiving a message stops all processing under DOS. For this reason, do not send messages to unattended workstations, unless you are ready to explain why you stopped the user's computer from completing its task while the user was away from his or her desk.

See also

BROADCAST	CASTON
CASTOFF	SEND (console command)

SEND (console command)   : 3.11

Purpose

Enables you to send short messages from the file server console to specific users, all users, or to workstations.

Syntax

```
SEND "messagetext"
```

or

    SEND "messagetext" TO userlist

or

    SEND "messagetext" TO stationlist

Options

messagetext	Specifies a message that can be up to 55 characters in length.
userlist	Specifies the user(s) who is to receive the message. Multiple users are separated by commas.
stationlist	Consists of a station number. Additional station numbers are followed by commas.

Rules and Considerations

A user must be logged in to receive a message from the console with the SEND command.

If a user list or station list is not specified, the message is sent to all workstations.

Examples

To remind all logged in users that the system will be shut down for maintenance this afternoon at 5:00, enter the command:

    SEND "Don't forget! Server shutdown today at 5:00"

To send a message from the console to the user MICHAEL, enter the command:

    SEND "Stop sending junk messages to the console!" TO   MICHAEL

To send a message from the console to workstations 14 and 17, enter the command:

    SEND "Please LOGOUT now!!!!" TO 14,17

Notes

NetWare 2.2 uses the BROADCAST command instead of the SEND command.

Workstations receiving messages halt all processing under DOS. Do not send messages to unattended workstations unless you are willing to explain why you interrupted the user's computer as it processed tasks while the user was away from his or her desk.

See also

BROADCAST	CASTON
CASTOFF	SEND (command-line utility)

SERVER

C> 3.11

Purpose

Installs or boots a NetWare 386 file server.

Syntax

```
SERVER
```

Rules and Considerations

After NetWare executes SERVER.EXE, it attempts to run the commands in STARTUP.NCF and AUTOEXEC.NCF if these files have been created.

Important Messages

```
*** This machine does not have an 80386 microprocessor ***
    NetWare 3.11 CANNOT BE RUN ON THIS MACHINE!!!
```

The preceding message informs you that NetWare 386 must be run on a system with an 80386 or higher processor. Install NetWare 386 on a file server with an 80386 or higher processor.

```
Insufficient memory to run NetWare 3.11
    (requires at least 1 megabyte of extended memory)
```

The preceding message informs you that NetWare 386 requires 1M of extended RAM (usually reported as 1640K) or 2M of RAM on most systems to load. Add memory to the file server and reload SERVER.EXE.

Examples

To begin the installation process on a new file server that has an 80386 or higher CPU, the required amount of extended RAM, and the network card or cards already installed, enter the command:

```
SERVER
```

To start the file server process on a NetWare 386 file server that has NetWare installed, enter the following command at the DOS prompt:

SERVER

Note

A few options are available with the SERVER command. Refer to the NetWare 386 installation manuals for more information on the available SERVER.EXE options.

See also

DOWN	REMOVE DOS
LOAD	SECURE CONSOLE

SET   : 3.11

Purpose

Enables you to display or change the values that tune the performance of the NetWare 386 operating system.

Syntax

SET *variable = value*

Options

The SET command entered without a variable displays the current parameter settings.

variable   Specifies a variable to change its setting.

value   Specifies a value to be assigned to the variable. Consult the *System Administration* manual for a list of variables and their allowed values.

Rules and Considerations

See Chapter 10 for more information on the SET commands.

Examples

To display at the console the current parameter settings on a NetWare 386 file server, enter the command:

    SET

To change the system parameter for NetWare 386 file servers that accept encrypted passwords and the parameter that forces older NetWare 286 file servers to accept passwords, enter the command:

    SET ALLOW UNENCRYPTED PASSWORDS=YES

Note

For a list of valid SET parameters, refer to the *NetWare System Administration* manual.

See also

SET TIME

SET TIME   :

Purpose

Enables you to set the time or date or both from the console on a NetWare file server.

Syntax

    SET TIME *mo/dy/yr hh:mm:ss*

SET TIME entered without any parameters displays the current system time.

Rules and Considerations

You can set the date and time independently or together.

To set the time, substitute the hour in 24-hour format for hh, the minutes for mm, and the seconds for ss.

Times entered greater than 24 hours will be changed to 24 hours. For example, 25:15:00 becomes 01:15:00.

Examples

To set the date and time to 1 minute before midnight on New Year's Eve, 1999, enter:

```
SET TIME 12/12/99 23:59:00
```

To set the time to 3:15 in the afternoon, enter:

```
SET TIME 15:15:00
```

To change the date to February 10th, 1993, enter:

```
SET TIME 2/10/93
```

Notes

Workstation dates and times will not correspond to the corrected file server date and time until the workstation shells are reloaded.

Time may also be entered in 12-hour format if it is followed by AM or PM.

Years entered prior to 1980 will be listed after the year 2000. You can change the date to some date up to but not including the year 2080.

See also

SET
TIME

SETPASS
F>

Purpose

Enables users to change their passwords if they have the rights to do so.

Syntax

```
SETPASS servername
```

Option

servername   Optional variable that is set to the name of the file server that
                stores the password you want to change.

Important Messages

```
You are not connected to file server ABRACADABRA.
```

In the preceding example, you entered **SETPASS ABRACADABRA** and thought that your current password would be changed to ABRACADABRA. To change your password correctly, enter **SETPASS** without any parameters and follow the prompts.

```
Access denied to NRP1/BRANDON, password not changed.
```

The preceding example message shows the current password for user BRANDON was entered incorrectly at the SETPASS prompt. Retry the command by entering your current password.

Example

In the following example, BRANDON changes his password using the SETPASS prompts. Note that the passwords he types are not displayed on screen when they are entered. BRANDON presses Enter after responding to the prompts.

```
F:\USERS\BRANDON>SETPASS

Enter old password for NRP/BRANDON:NCC1701

Enter new password for NRP/BRANDON:NCC1701A

Retype new password for NRP/BRANDON:NCC1701A

The password for NRP/BRANDON has been changed.
```

Note

NetWare security relies largely on users who must keep their passwords secret. Use SETPASS often to change your password, which helps to maintain a high level of security. You also can increase the security of your passwords by not using words associated with family, hobbies, friends, and so on. The best passwords are arbitrary combinations of letters and numbers.

See also

SECURE CONSOLE
SECURITY

SLIST

F>

Purpose

Lists file servers that are available for your workstation.

Syntax

SLIST *servername* /C

Options

servername   Specifies a file server. If you enter SLIST with a file server name, the file server displays if it is available.

/C   Specifies that SLIST continuously scroll the screens instead of pause at the end of every screen page.

Rules and Considerations

If you enter SLIST without a file server name, a list displays of every available file server.

Important Message

Server CSOS2 not found.

The preceding message shows the requested file server, CSOS2, is not available. In this case, the preceding command was **SLIST CSOS2**.

Example

The following is example output from the SLIST command:

Known NetWare File Servers	Network	Node Address	Status
CSOS	[19910001][	2608C0B39CA]	Default
Total of 1 file servers found			

See also

LOGIN

MAP

SMODE   F>

Purpose

Enables you to set or view the method a program uses to search for data files and overlays.

Syntax

```
SMODE filepath searchmode /SUB
```

Options

filepath Consists of an optional path and a file specification (wild cards are allowed).

searchmode Specifies the type of search method you want to use. Valid search modes include the following:

0 The shell default. Program follows instructions in SHELL.CFG.

1 If the program specifies a directory path, it will search only that path. If no path is specified, the search extends through all search drives.

2 If the program specifies a directory path, it searches only that path. If no path is specified, only the default directory is searched.

3 Similar to the preceding search mode. If, however, the search is Read Only, the search is extended to directories in the search drives.

4 (reserved, do not use)

5 If the program specifies a directory path, it searches that path followed by the search drives. If no path is specified, the default directory is searched, followed by the search drives.

6 (reserved, do not use)

7 If the program specifies a directory path, that path is searched first. Then, if the open request is Read Only, the program searches the search drives. If no directory path is given, the program searches the default directory. Then, if the open request is Read Only, the program searches the search drives.

If *searchmode* is not specified, the current search modes of the selected files display.

/SUB   Extends the effect of the commands to all subdirectories of the requested directory. A filepath must be used if /SUB is included.

Rules and Considerations

SMODE operates on executable files and ignores non-executable files.

Important Messages

```
No EXECUTABLE files could be found with pattern "*.*"
```

The preceding sample message displays when SMODE is executed in a directory that has no executable files. Change to a directory that contains executable files or specify the path to the desired files.

```
Mode 4 is reserved.
```

The preceding sample message displays when you attempt to set a reserved search mode. To correct this problem, assign a valid search mode.

Example

To set the program 123.EXE so that it does not search for data files on search drives, enter the command:

```
SMODE 123.EXE 2
```

Note

The default for most executable files is search mode 0 (shell default). You can set the default shell variable SEARCH MODE = searchmode in the NET.CFG file which should be located in the directory from which you load your DOS workstation shells.

See also

MAP

SPEED
: 3.11

Purpose

Displays a number that represents the relative speed of a NetWare 386 file server.

Syntax

```
SPEED
```

Example

To display the relative speed of a NetWare file server, enter the command:

```
SPEED
```

Note

The reported speed of a NetWare file server is relative. A speed of 300 compared to a speed of 150, for example, shows that the first file server is twice as fast as the second. For an accurate comparison of two file servers, both servers must run the same version of NetWare 386.

SPOOL
: 2.2

Purpose

Creates, maintains, and lists spooler mappings to print queues.

Syntax

```
SPOOL
```

or

```
SPOOL printernumber TO QUEUE queuename
```

Rules and Considerations

If you enter SPOOL without a printer number or a queue name, the current spooler mappings display.

Valid options for the *printernumber* variable range from 0 to 4.

Valid *queuename* options include any existing print queue name.

Important Message

```
Spooler 0 is directed into printer HPLASER
Spooler 1 is directed into printer MATRIX1
```

A SPOOL status message similar to this displays when the SPOOL command is entered with no options.

Examples

To spool printer 1 to a print queue named HPLASER3, enter the command:

```
SPOOL 1 TO QUEUE HPLASER3
```

To display a list of current spool mappings, enter:

```
SPOOL
```

Note

You can include SPOOL commands in the AUTOEXEC.SYS file to have these commands automatically load when a NetWare 2.2 file server is started.

See also

CAPTURE	PRINTER
NPRINT	QUEUE

SPXCONFG   :LOAD 3.11

Purpose

Configures NetWare 386 SPX parameters.

Syntax

```
LOAD SPXCONFG option...option
```

Options

`A=`	Sets SPX watchdog abort timeout in ticks (A *tick* is 1/18 of a second)
`V=`	Sets SPX watchdog verify timeout (in ticks)
`W=`	Sets SPX Ack wait timeout (in ticks)
`R=`	Sets SPX default retry count
`S=`	Maximum concurrent SPX sessions
`Q=1`	Quiet mode: suppresses display of the settings
`H`	Displays a help screen

Rules and Considerations

You must specify a path if SPXCONFIG.NLM is not installed in the SYS:SYSTEM directory.

Example

To load SPXCONFG, enter the command

```
LOAD SPXCONFG
```

and an SPXCONFG menu is displayed.

```
LOAD SPXCONFG A=500
```

SPXS :LOAD 3.11

Purpose

Used with NLMs that support the STREAMS-based IPX protocol services.

Syntax

```
LOAD SPXS
```

Rules and Considerations

To properly load STREAMS-based IPX/SPX protocol services for an NLM that requires these services, load these NLMs in the following order:

1. Load STREAMS.NLM first

2. Load CLIB.NLM second

3. Load TLI.NLM third

4. Load IPXS.NLM fourth

5. Load SPXS.NLM last

Example

To load SPXS, enter the command:

```
LOAD SPXS
```

See also

CLIB	STREAMS
IPXS	TLI

STREAMS :LOAD 3.11

Purpose

Provides an interface among NetWare and other transport protocols. STREAMS is loaded before CLIB or STREAMS-based protocol services.

Syntax

```
LOAD STREAMS
```

Rules and Considerations

STREAMS must be loaded before CLIB is loaded.

To properly load STREAMS-based IPX/SPX protocol services for an NLM that requires it, load these NLMs in the following order:

1. Load STREAMS.NLM first

2. Load CLIB.NLM second

3. Load TLI.NLM third

4. Load IPXS.NLM fourth

5. Load SPXS.NLM last

Example

To load STREAMS, enter the command:

```
LOAD STREAMS
```

Notes

For more complete information on the use of STREAMS and STREAMS-based protocol services, see Chapter 5.

See also

CLIB	SPXS
IPXS	TLI

SYSTIME   F>

Purpose

Enables you to view and change the date and time on your workstation to that of a file server.

Syntax

```
SYSTIME
```

or

```
SYSTIME fileserver
```

Option

fileserver   Specifies a file server that is to be used to set the date and time of a user's workstation.

Rules and Considerations

If a file server is not specified, SYSTIME configures your workstation's date and time to that of the default file server.

Important Messages

```
Current System Time:        Monday November 11, 1992  3:06 pm
```

The preceding example displays when the SYSTIME command is used without any parameters.

```
You are not attached to server HELP.
```

The preceding example displays when a nonattached file server is specified. Attach to the requested file server or reenter the command with a valid file server name.

Example

To set the workstation date and time to that of the default file server, enter the command:

```
SYSTIME
```

Notes

If you change the time on the file server with the SET TIME console command, you can synchronize the workstation clock with the file server clock by using SYSTIME.

See also

SET TIME
TIME

TIME
:

Purpose

Displays the date and time at the file server console.

Syntax

    TIME

Rules and Considerations

TIME displays only the system date and time. You must use SET TIME to change the date or time.

Example

To display the current system date and time at the file server console, enter:

    TIME

Note

See the NetWare manuals under menu utilities SYSCON and FCONSOLE for more information on checking and changing the file server system clock.

See also

    SET TIME
    SYSTIME

TLI
:LOAD 3.11

Purpose

Supports STREAMS and CLIB and enables them to use transport protocols such as SPXS and IPXS. *TLI* is a NetWare 386 NLM that stands for Transport Layer Protocol.

Syntax

```
LOAD TLI
```

Rules and Considerations

Both STREAMS and CLIB must be loaded before loading TLI because TLI supports STREAMS and CLIB.

One of the STREAMS protocol modules, such as SPXS or IPXS or both, must be loaded after TLI is loaded.

Example

To completely load STREAMS support with IPXS and SPXS at the file server console, enter these modules in the following order:

1. Load STREAMS.NLM first

2. Load CLIB.NLM second

3. Load TLI.NLM third

4. Load IPXS.NLM fourth

5. Load SPXS.NLM last

See also

CLIB   SPXS

IPXS   STREAMS

TLIST

F>

Purpose

Displays a list of trustees for the specified file or directory.

Syntax

```
TLIST dirpath option
```

or

```
TLIST filepath option
```

Options

dirpath | Specifies a NetWare directory on the currently logged file server.

filepath | Specifies a NetWare file path on the currently logged file server.

option | Lists group or user trustees or both, depending on the specified option. Leave *option* blank to list both group and user trustees. Specify GROUPS to list group trustees, or specify USERS to list to user trustees.

Rules and Considerations

Wild cards are supported for directory and file specifications.

If you do not specify USERS or GROUPS in the *option* parameter, both will be displayed.

Important Messages

```
NRP\PROGS:UTILITY
No trustees found.
```

The preceding example shows that the specified directory has no group or user trustees. Use GRANT or SYSCON to assign trustees.

```
Path does not exist.
```

The preceding message displays when a directory or file specification is entered that does not exist. Enter the correct directory or file specification.

Examples

To display the trustees of the SHAREDOC directory on volume DATA of file server NRP if you are currently logged into this file server, enter the command:

TLIST NRP/DATA:SHAREDOC

The previous command displays the following output:

```
NRP\DATA:SHAREDOC
User trustees:
        DEDE   [RWCEMFA] Dede Kusnierz
        FRED   [RWCEMFA] Fred Flinstone
        ──
```

```
Group trustees:
          SECS   [       ]
```

To list the user trustees of the PUBLIC directory on the default file server, enter the command:

TLIST SYS:PUBLIC USERS

To list the group trustees of the PUBLIC directory on the default file server, enter the command:

TLIST SYS:PUBLIC GROUPS

Note

To specify quickly the current directory or the parent directory, use the period (.) and double period (..) DOS specifications instead of typing the entire directory name.

See also

GRANT   REVOKE
REMOVE   RIGHTS

TOKENRPL   :LOAD 3.11

Purpose

Loads file server support enabling stations without floppy disk drives but with Token Ring network adapters to boot from the file server.

Syntax

LOAD TOKENRPL

Rules and Considerations

TOKENRPL supports remote program loading only on Token Ring network adapters.

The NetWork adapters in the workstations that do not have floppy disk drives must also support RPL (Remote Program Load).

Example

To enable Token Ring workstations that do not have floppy disk drives to attach to a NetWare 386 file server when they first boot, enter the following command at the file server console:

```
LOAD TOKENRPL
```

Note

Working with workstations that do not have floppy disk drives requires much planning. See the NetWare Administration manual for a complete explanation of TOKENRPL.

See also

DOSGEN

TRACK OFF :

Purpose

Turns off the display of router traffic from the file server console.

Syntax

```
TRACK OFF
```

Rules and Considerations

The TRACK OFF command is needed to turn off the display of router activity only after it has been turned on with TRACK ON.

Example

To disable the display of router activity from the file server console, type the following:

```
TRACK OFF
```

See also

ROUTER.EXE

TRACK ON

TRACK ON

Purpose

Displays router activity, including connection, network, and server requests, for troubleshooting or information.

Syntax

`TRACK ON`

Rules and Considerations

The TRACK ON command can be entered at the file server console or at the console prompt of a router running ROUTER.EXE.

TRACK ON displays connection, network, and server requests.

IN requests are those the file server or router is receiving. OUT requests are those the file server or router is sending.

Example

To enable display of the routing activity of the file server at the file server console, type the following:

`TRACK ON`

See also

ROUTER

TRACK OFF

UNBIND : 3.11

Purpose

Removes a communications protocol from a LAN driver for a network adapter card that was added to the LAN driver with BIND.

Syntax

```
UNBIND protocol FROM landriver
```

Options

protocol   The previously bound communications protocol, usually IPX

landriver   The name of the LAN driver from which to remove the communications protocol

Rules and Considerations

A protocol must have been added to a LAN driver with the BIND command in order for you to unbind it.

Currently supplied NetWare LAN drivers include NE1000, NE2, NE2000, NE232, RXNET, and TOKEN, although any vendor supplied LAN driver may be specified.

Example

To remove the IPX protocol from the NE232 LAN driver at the file server console, type the following:

```
UNBIND IPX FROM NE232
```

Note

When you unbind a protocol from an LAN driver, the LAN that was supported by that driver and all the workstations supported by that protocol can no longer communicate through the file server.

See also

BIND

UNLOAD
: 3.11

Purpose

Removes a NetWare Loadable Module (NLM) from file server memory.

Syntax

    UNLOAD nlmspec

Option

nlmspec   The name of the NLM to unload from memory

Example

    UNLOAD NE232

Notes

Use UNLOAD to remove unnecessary maintenance modules such as INSTALL that have been loaded for temporary use. After the NLM is unloaded, the memory it previously occupied returns to caching, which usually increases system performance.

Do not use UNLOAD to remove any NLMs necessary to the operation of your file server. This appears obvious, but the always "up" nature of a 386 file server might make you forget when you unload the particular NLM that some maintenance tasks require that you inform the users that the LAN will be unavailable, or a particular feature they expect to use will be unavailable.

See also

LOAD

UNMIRROR
: 2.2

Purpose

Manually shuts down mirroring on a dedicated file server.

Syntax

```
UNMIRROR drivenumber
```

Option

drivenumber   Substitute the drive number of one drive of a mirror pair

Rules and Considerations

After mirroring has been shut down on a particular drive, that drive no longer is updated with disk drive activity.

Hot fix remains in effect for the other drive in the mirror pair.

Important Messages

```
Invalid physical drive specified.
```

The preceding message indicates that you did not specify a drive number when entering the UNMIRROR command. Retry the command with the correct drive number specified.

```
Physical drive and its mirror do not exist or are totally shut
down.
```

This message indicates that you have specified a drive number that does not exist, or is not available. Retry UNMIRROR with the correct drive number specified.

Example

To turn off mirroring on drive 01, which you intend to replace with a new drive after you shut down the server, type the following:

```
UNMIRROR 01
```

Notes

The UNMIRROR command generally is useful only if: the mirroring feature is not working correctly; one of the drives in a drive pair keeps failing enough to slow performance but not enough for the operating system to disable mirroring; or if you intend to remove the specified drive after shutting down the file server.

Disabling mirroring leaves you with only hot-fix protection on the remaining drive.

If you accidentally unmirror a drive, be careful to specify the correct drive number when you invoke REMIRROR, or the newer information will be overwritten with the older information of the unmirrored drive.

See also

DISK

REMIRROR

UPS   :LOAD 3.11

Purpose

Loads hardware support for an uninterruptable power supply on a NetWare 386 file server.

Syntax

```
LOAD UPS upstype ioport discharge recharge
```

or

```
LOAD UPS
```

Options

upstype	The type of UPS (DCB, STANDALONE, MOUSE, EDCB, KEYCARD, OTHER)
ioport	The mouse port, communications port, or network card supporting the UPS, expressed in hexadecimal (consult the UPS documentation)
discharge	The estimated time required to discharge the UPS in minutes
recharge	The time to recharge the UPS in minutes

Rules and Considerations

If the **UPS** command is entered without parameters, you will be prompted to supply parameters.

The UPS must be one supported by the UPS.NLM, or you will have to use the NLM supplied with the UPS.

UPS.NLM must be loaded before UPS support is enabled.

Important Messages

```
WARNING: UPS hardware configuration error was detected. Check
for errors in your UPS hardware configuration settings.
```

If you receive the preceding message, the UPS NLM was not loaded because of a configuration error. LOAD the UPS NLM again, correcting the settings for the on-line and low battery configuration.

```
UPS is shutting down server GROUP1. Commercial power has failed
and the battery is too low.
```

This message indicates that file server GROUP1 has been automatically shut down by the UPS software because it recognized a power failure and the battery was too low or ran down because commercial power was out too long. To correct, wait until commercial power is restored and then restart the file server process.

Example

To install UPS hardware support and be prompted for the parameters, type the following:

```
LOAD UPS
```

Note

Use INSTALL.NLM to put the LOAD UPS parameters line into your AUTOEXEC.NCF to make sure that UPS support is loaded when the file server is booted.

See also

UPS STATUS
UPS TIME

UPS

: 2.2

Purpose

Displays the status of an uninterruptable power supply.

Syntax

```
UPS
```

Important Messages

```
UPS Monitoring Disabled
```

You receive this message if no UPS is attatched to your system, or if there is no SERVER.CFG file enabling the UPS.

```
UPS enabled on NPR3
```

This message displays at file server boot time to indicate that the SERVER.CFG contained proper information and UPS monitoring has been enabled.

Examples

To check the current status of a UPS attatched to the file server at the file server console, type the following:

```
UPS
```

To enable the UPS on a NetWare 286 file server to include the appropriate command lines, enter the command:

```
UPS TYPE=n
```

Replace *n* with one of the following numbers:

1   for stand-alone monitor boards

2   for Host bus adapter (e.g. DCB)

3   for SS keycard

4   for PS/2 mouse ports

To specify 10 minutes as the amount of time that users have to log out after a loss of commercial power, enter the command:

```
UPS DOWN=10
```

To specify 30 seconds as the amount of time in seconds that passes before users are notified that commercial power has been restored, enter the command:

```
UPS WAIT=30
```

Note

Refer to the manuals supplied with the UPS to find out the valid setting for the UPS DOWN= setting in the SERVER.CFG file. If the time you set for the server to shut down is longer than the battery will last, users will not be given ample notice to complete their work and the file server will be shut off by the UPS before the operating system has had a chance to down the file server.

See also

DOWN

UPS STATUS : 3.11

Purpose

Checks the status of the UPS attatched to the file server.

Syntax

```
UPS STATUS
```

Rules and Considerations

UPS must be loaded before UPS STATUS is a valid command.

Important Message

```
??? Unknown Command
```

The preceding message informs you that you have not loaded the UPS.NLM file for UPS support. You must LOAD UPS before UPS STATUS is available.

Example

To check the current status of the uninterruptable power supply attatched to the file server, type the following:

```
UPS STATUS
```

Note

When you invoke the UPS STATUS command, the times displaycd arc usually based on those entered with the UPS TIME command and are therefore not guaranteed. If UPS recognizes less power than was expected from one of the more intelligent UPS devices, or if battery power fails, the file server will be terminated regardless of the displayed status.

See also

UPS

UPS TIME

UPS TIME   : 3.11

Purpose

Sets or changes the estimates for UPS battery discharge and recharge times.

Syntax

```
UPS TIME dischargetime rechargetime
```

Options

dischargetime	The length of time the battery will keep the file server running after commercial power loss.
rechargetime	The length of time the UPS needs to recover after it has been used to run the file server after commercial power loss.

Rules and Considerations

The UPS loadable module must be loaded before UPS TIME is a valid command.

Example

To set the UPS battery backup time to 15 minutes and the recharge time to 30 minutes, type the following:

```
UPS TIME 15 30
```

Notes

Do not enter times that do not conform to the ratings for your UPS. Under certain conditions, your equipment can be severely damaged if a battery backup was run down to a complete loss of power before the file server and UPS were shut down.

Enter valid times for the discharge, as this will guarantee that the file server is not prematurely switched off by the UPS before the software shuts down the file server process.

See also

UPS

UPS STATUS

USERLIST   F>

Purpose

Displays a list of logged in users and some status information for those users.

Syntax

```
USERLIST userspec /C /Option
```

Options

userspec	An optional file server specification followed by a user name for which you are requesting status
/A	Display network address information with the user list display
/O	Display object type information with the user list display
/C	Display a continuous list without pausing at the end of each screen page for long lists

Important Messages

```
User Information for Server CSOS
Connection   User Name         Login Time
----------   ---------         ----------
No users named FS2.
```

This message shows that the requested user named with the USERLIST command was not found. In this case it appears as if the slash was not typed after the file server name. Type the slash after the file server name and try again.

```
You are not attached to server FS2.
```

This messages shows that you tried to check the user list on file server FS2, but that you are not attached to it. Log in to it or attach to it, and then retry the USERLIST command.

Example

If you type **USERLIST /A**, you receive output as follows:

```
User Information for Server NORTH386
Connection    User Name        Network   Node Address    Login Time
----------    ---------        -------   ------------    -----------------
1             * SUPERVISOR     [CDC]     [ 1B1EFDDB]     9-14-1992 9:10 am
2             *SU1             [  5]     [ 1B191D38]     9-14-1992 9:30 am
```

If you type **USERLIST /O**, you receive output as follows:

```
User Information for Server NORTH 386
Connection     User Name       Login Time             Object Type
----------     ---------       ------------------     -----------
1              * SUPERVISOR    9-14-1992  9:10 am     User
2              *SU1            9-14-1992 10:28 AM      User
```

Note

The asterisk in the user listing shows which entry shows the information for your workstation. Thus, if you are logged in on more than one workstation, you can determine which connection you are without having to use the WHOAMI command.

See also

> SLIST
> TLIST
> WHOAMI

VAP

: 2.2

Purpose

Displays a list of loaded value-added processes on a NetWare 286 file server.

Syntax

> `VAP`

Rules and Considerations

The VAP command displays not only a list of all loaded VAPs, but also the console commands the VAP will accept.

VAPs are loaded by copying them to the SYS:SYSTEM directory of the file server. The VAPs are loaded after the file server is booted.

Because VAPs also can be loaded on routers, the VAP command also works at the (:) prompt on routers.

Important Message

> `No Value Added Processes loaded.`

This message is displayed if you have not loaded any VAPS. To load VAPs, they must be copied into the SYS:SYSTEM directory. They are enabled after the server is booted.

Example

To view a list of all loaded VAPs and the command available to them, type the following:

`VAP`

See also

OFF

VER
: 2.2

Purpose

Checks the file server's NetWare operating system version, release, and user count information from the file server console.

Syntax

`VER`

Important Message

```
Dedicated Netware V2.2(100) Rev. A 2/11/91
```

This sample message displays operating system version, user count, revision, and release date.

Example

To check the version information, type the following:

`VER`

See also

NVER
VERSION

VERSION   F>

Purpose

Displays version information for NetWare EXE files containing version information.

Syntax

```
VERSION filespec
```

Option

filespec   Specifies the location of the file to check on the file server in-
               cluding the file server and directory name as well as the file
               name.

Rules and Considerations

Wild cards are supported.

If you invoke VERSION against a file without version information, the file's
checksum is calculated.

Important Message

```
NET$OS.EXE:
            Version Dedicated NetWare V2.2
            (C) Copyright 1983-1991 Novell Inc.
            Checksum is 61FD.
```

The preceding message displays example output from the VERSION command.

Example

To display the previous output, type the following:

```
VERSION SYS:SYSTEM/NET$OS.EXE
```

See also

NVER

VER

VERSION : 3.11

Purpose

Displays the NetWare 386 operating system version and copyright information at the file server console.

Syntax

    VERSION

Example

To display the NetWare 386 operating system version number and copyright information at the file server, type the following:

    VERSION

See also

    NVER

VOLUMES : 3.11

Purpose

Displays a list of available drive volumes from the file server console.

Syntax

    VOLUMES

Rules and Considerations

The VOLUMES command lists only volumes that are currently mounted.

Example

For a list of mounted volumes, type the following at the file server console:

`VOLUMES`

See also

DISMOUNT
MOUNT

VREPAIR   :LOAD 3.11

Purpose

Repairs problems with a NetWare hard drive recovering access to the data on the drive.

Syntax

`LOAD VREPAIR`

Rules and Considerations

Other volumes can be accessed while a defective volume is being repaired by VREPAIR.

The VREPAIR command should be invoked whenever file allocation table (FAT) errors, disk read errors, mirroring errors at boot time, or power failures have corrupted a volume.

Important Messages

```
Error reading in volume directory.
```
or
```
Invalid available entry.
```
or
```
Invalid deleted file block.
```
or

```
        Invalid directory number code.
or
        Invalid user restriction node...too many trustees.
or
        Invalid Maximum Space defined in Subdirectory.
or
        Invalid volume header / root directory entry.
```

The preceding messages indicate that NetWare 386 had trouble mounting a volume. Invoke VREPAIR to repair.

Example

To invoke the VREPAIR command on a damaged NetWare volume, type the following:

```
LOAD VREPAIR
```

Note

The VREPAIR command sometimes causes loss or damage to files. You should have a good backup and be prepared to replace some data after executing VREPAIR, although the command usually does not cause data loss.

WATCHDOG   : 2.2

Purpose

Monitors file server connections.

Syntax

```
WATCHDOG START=startsecs INTERVAL=intervalsecs
COUNT=intervalcount
```

Options

startsecs	Specify in seconds how long you want the file server to check a new connection. The time can be between 15 and 1200 seconds with 300 seconds as the default.
intervalsecs	Specify how long the interval between checks should be, in seconds. The *intervalsecs* variable ranges from 1 to 600, with a default of 60 seconds.
intervalcount	The number of intervals that must go by before clearing an active connection, ranging from 5 to 100 with a default of 10.

Examples

To enable WATCHDOG with the defaults, type the following:

```
WATCHDOG
```

To enable WATCHDOG with your own settings, type the following:

```
WATCHDOG START=10 INTERVAL=5 COUNT=20
```

Note

Place the WATCHDOG command in the AUTOEXEC.SYS to load it automatically when the file server is booted.

See also

MONITOR

WHOAMI   F>

Purpose

Displays connection, identification, and security information for the current user.

Syntax

```
WHOAMI [servername] option
```

Options

If you type **WHOAMI** and do not include parameters, you receive the user name, server name, workstation connection, NetWare version, and login time.

servername	Unless a file server is specified, information is provided for all attached servers.
/ALL	Displays group membership and security equivalence along with the basic WHOAMI information.
/G	Displays group information along with the basic WHOAMI information.
/O	Displays object supervisor information along with the basic WHOAMI information.
/R	Displays effective rights for each attached volume along with the basic WHOAMI information.
/S	Displays security equivalences along with the basic WHOAMI information.
/SY	Displays general system information along with the basic WHOAMI information.
/W	Displays workgroup manager information along with the basic WHOAMI information.

Rules and Considerations

You must be logged in to a file server to run WHOAMI.

If you type **WHOAMI** without any parameters, the user name, server name, workstation connection, NetWare version, and login time display.

Only one option at a time can be entered with WHOAMI.

Important Message

```
You are not attached to server DANNY.
```

This message indicates what happens if you enter **WHOAMI** followed by some text — in this case, **WHOAMI DANNY**. To correct, type **WHOAMI** without any options, or try one listed in the examples that follow:

Examples

If you type **WHOAMI**, you receive information similar to the following:

```
You are user DENISE attached to server NRP2, connection 7.
Server NRP2 is running Dedicated NetWare V2.2(100) Rev. A.
Login time: Tuesday  November  12, 1991  4:14 pm
```

If you type **WHOAMI /ALL**, you receive information similar to the following:

```
You are user BOB attached to server FINI, connection 1.
Server FINI is running Dedicated NetWare V2.2(50) Rev. B.
You are a workgroup manager.
Login time: Thursday  November  14, 1991  7:14 am
You are security equivalent to the following:
    EVERYONE (Group)
You are a member of the following groups:
    ACCOUNTING
    EVERYONE
    SHIPPING
[RWCEMFA]  SYS:
[RWCEMFA]  VOL1:
Server CSOS is not in a Domain.
```

See also

USERLIST

WSGEN   F>

Purpose

An installation utility that creates an IPX.COM file specific to a particular workstation's configuration.

Syntax

```
WSGEN
```

Rules and Considerations

The WSGEN command requires at a minimum a LAN driver disk for the network adapter card to complete execution.

WSGEN requires DOS 3.0 or higher to run.

    WSGEN

Note

Use IPX I after generating an IPX.COM file with WSGEN to check its version, suported LAN adapter, and configuration option.

See also

> DCONFIG
> IPX
> NETx

WSUPDATE   F>

Purpose

Updates NetWare shells on workstations with newer versions.

Syntax

    WSUPDATE source *dest*

or

    WSUPDATE /F=*scriptfile*

Options

source	Location and name of source file
dest	Location and name of file to be replaced with newer version
scriptfile	*scriptfile* is a file created to contain a list of source destination pairs for automatic execution

Rules and Considerations

WSUPDATE replaces files with newer versions only.

Examples

To update the workstation shells easily, copy the updated shells into one of the search drives on the network and type the following on a MS-DOS V5 workstation using the regular memory workstation shell:

```
WSUPDATE F:\PUBLIC\NET5.COM A:\NET5.COM
```

To update the workstation shells at login time, create a WSUPDATE configuration file for each user's workstation and execute the WSUPDATE program from the users login script. If the user's WSUPDATE script file was named WSUPDRK.CFG, you would type the following into the login script:

```
IF DAY_OF_WEEK = 2, RUN #WSUPDATE /F=WSUPDRK.CFG
```

Notes

A sample WSUPDATE script might resemble the following:

```
F:XMSNET5.COM A:XMSNET5.COM
F:IPX.COM A:IPX.COM
```

Do not accidentally replace the IPX.COM file on a workstation with an IPX.COM generation intended for another workstation. Although the NETx flavors are generic, the IPX.COM file must be generated for a particular workstation adapter card.

See also

EMSNETx	NETx
IPX	XMSNETx

XMSNETX   F>

Purpose

Loads the DOS NetWare shell program into extended memory on 286 and higher CPUs, with more than 1M of RAM conserving lower RAM for application software.

Syntax

```
XMSNETX option
```

Options

/C=filespec	Specify the directory location and the file name for the shell configuration file, usually NET.CFG for the default
/I	Displays version and configuration information without loading the workstation shell
/PS=fileserver	*fileserver* specifies the preferred default file server; the shell creates a connection with this file server even though another file server responds faster
/U	Unloads the XMSNETX workstation shell from the workstation memory
/?	Displays usage options for the XMSNETX command

Rules and Considerations

If you type XMSNETX with no option, the DOS workstation shell loads.

XMSNETX files can be found on the WSGEN disk and should be copied to the workstation boot disk.

The file server should be running before you attempt to connect to it or access it with the workstation shells.

IPX.COM must be loaded before XMSNETX to allow connection to a file server.

XMSNETX requires an XMA memory driver such as DOS 5's HIMEM.SYS before it can access extended memory for the NetWare DOS shells.

Important Message

```
NetWare V3.10 - XMS - Workstation Shell for PC DOS V5.x
(910307)
(C) Copyright 1990 Novell, Inc.  All Rights Reserved.
```

The preceding is an example output message from the /I option, showing the version and release date of the workstation shell along with the copyright information.

Examples

To load the workstation shell into workstation extended memory with HIMEM.SYS installed in the CONFIG.SYS file on a system running DOS 5, type the following:

```
XMSNET5
```

To unload the XMSNET4 workstation shell from a workstation's memory, type the following:

```
XMSNET4 /U
```

To check the configuration and version of an XMSNETx file on a DOS 5 version of XMSNETX.EXE, type the following:

```
XMSNETX /I
```

Note

Use the NET.CFG file to set several options for the IPX and XMSNETx flavors of the workstation shells. You can use the /C switch to make sure the configuration file is found when loading XMSNETX.

See also

EMSNETX
IPX
NETX

Index

Symbols

E

O

V

WANT MORE INFORMATION?

CHECK OUT THESE RELATED TITLES:

	QTY	PRICE	TOTAL

Inside Novell NetWare, Special Edition. This #1 selling tutorial/reference is perfect for beginning system administrators. Each network management task is thoroughly explained and potential trouble spots are noted. The book also includes a disk with an extremely easy to use workstation menu program, an MHS capable E-Mail program, and workgroup management tools. ISBN: 1-56205-096-6.

_____ $34.95   _____

NetWare 4: New Business Strategies. The ultimate guide to planning, installing, and managing a NetWare 4.0 network. This book explains how best to implement the new features of NetWare 4.0 and how to upgrade to NetWare 4.0 as easily and efficiently as possible. ISBN: 1-56205-159-8.

_____ $27.95   _____

Downsizing to NetWare. Get the real story on downsizing with *Downsizing to NetWare.* This book identifies applications that are suitable for use on LANs and shows how to implement downsizing projects. This book lists the strengths and weaknesses of NetWare—making it perfect for managers and system administrators. ISBN: 1-56205-071-0.

_____ $39.95   _____

LAN Operating Systems. Learn how to connect the most popular LAN operating systems. All major LAN operating systems are covered, including: NetWare 3.11, Appleshare 3.0, Banyan VINES 5.0, UNIX, LAN Manager 2.1, and popular peer-to-peer networks. The following client operating systems are covered as well: MS DOS, Windows, OS/2, Macintosh System 7, and UNIX. This book clears up the confusion associated with managing large networks with diverse client workstations and multiple LAN operating systems. ISBN: 1-56205-054-0.

_____ $39.95   _____

Name _____

Company _____

Address _____

City _____ State ____ Zip _____

Phone _____ Fax _____

☐ Check Enclosed   ☐ VISA   ☐ MasterCard

Card #_____Exp. Date _____

Signature _____

Prices are subject to change. Call for availability and pricing information on latest editions.

Subtotal   _____

Shipping   _____

$4.00 for the first book and $1.75 for each additional book.

Total   _____
Indiana Residents add 5% Sales Tax.

New Riders Publishing   11711 North College Avenue • P.O. Box 90 • Carmel, Indiana 46032 USA

Orders/Customer Service: 1-800-541-6789
Fax: 1-800-448-3804

NetWare: The Professional Reference
REGISTRATION CARD

NRP

Fill out this card to receive information about other New Riders titles!

Name _____ Title _____

Company _____

Address _____

City/State/Zip _____

I bought this book because _____

_____

I purchased this book from:

☐ A bookstore (Name _____)

☐ A software or electronics store (Name _____)

☐ A mail order (Name of Catalog _____)

I purchase this many computer books each year:

☐ 1-5   ☐ 5 or more

I currently use these applications: _____

_____

_____

_____

I found these chapters to be the most informative: _____

_____

I found these chapters to be the least informative: _____

_____

Additional comments: _____

_____

☐ I would like to see my name in print! You may use my name and quote me in future New Riders products and promotions. My daytime phone number is:_____

New Riders Publishing 11711 North College Avenue • P.O. Box 90 • Carmel, Indiana 46032 USA

Become a CNE
with Help from a Pro!

The NetWare Training Guides are specifically designed and authored to help you prepare for the **Certified NetWare Engineer** exam.

NetWare Training Guide: Managing NetWare Systems

This book clarifies the CNE testing process and provides hints on how best to prepare for the CNE examinations. NetWare Training Guide: Managing NetWare Systems covers the following sections of the CNE exams:

● NetWare v2.2 System Manager

● NetWare v2.2 Advanced System Manager

● NetWare v3.X System Manager

● NetWare v3.X Advanced System Manager

ISBN: 1-56205-069-9, **$59.95 USA**

NetWare Training Guide: Networking Technologies

This book covers more advanced topics and prepares you for the tough hardware and service/support exams. The following course materials are covered:

● MS-DOS

● Microcomputer Concepts

● Service and Support

● Networking Technologies

ISBN: 1-56205-145-8, **$59.95 USA**

NETWORKING TITLES

#1 Bestseller!

INSIDE NOVELL NETWARE, SPECIAL EDITION

DEBRA NIEDERMILLER-CHAFFINS &
BRIAN L. CHAFFINS

This best-selling tutorial and reference
has been updated and made even better!

NetWare 2.2 & 3.11
ISBN: 1-56205-096-6
$34.95 USA

MAXIMZING NOVELL NETWARE

JOHN JERNEY & ELNA TYMES

Complete coverage of Novell's
flagship product...for NetWare system
administrators!

NetWare 3.11
ISBN: 1-56205-095-8
$39.95 USA

NETWARE: THE PROFESSIONAL REFERENCE, SECOND EDITION

KARANJIT SIYAN

This updated version for professional
NetWare administrators and technicians
provides the most comprehensive
reference available for this phenomenal
network system.

NetWare 2.2 & 3.11
ISBN: 1-56205-158-X
$42.95 USA

Coming Soon

NETWARE 4: NEW BUSINESS STRATEGIES

SUNI PADIYAR

A guide to planning, installing, and
managing a NetWare 4.0 network that
serves the company's best objectives.

NetWare 4.0
ISBN: 1-56205-0159-8
$27.95 USA

To Order, Call: 1-800-428-5331